Communications in Computer and Information Science 2761

Rationale
The CCIS series is devoted to the publication of proceedings of computer science conferences. Its aim is to efficiently disseminate original research results in informatics in printed and electronic form. While the focus is on publication of peer-reviewed full papers presenting mature work, inclusion of reviewed short papers reporting on work in progress is welcome, too. Besides globally relevant meetings with internationally representative program committees guaranteeing a strict peer-reviewing and paper selection process, conferences run by societies or of high regional or national relevance are also considered for publication.

Topics
The topical scope of CCIS spans the entire spectrum of informatics ranging from foundational topics in the theory of computing to information and communications science and technology and a broad variety of interdisciplinary application fields.

Information for Volume Editors and Authors
Publication in CCIS is free of charge. No royalties are paid, however, we offer registered conference participants temporary free access to the online version of the conference proceedings on SpringerLink (http://link.springer.com) by means of an http referrer from the conference website and/or a number of complimentary printed copies, as specified in the official acceptance email of the event.

CCIS proceedings can be published in time for distribution at conferences or as post-proceedings, and delivered in the form of printed books and/or electronically as USBs and/or e-content licenses for accessing proceedings at SpringerLink. Furthermore, CCIS proceedings are included in the CCIS electronic book series hosted in the SpringerLink digital library at http://link.springer.com/bookseries/7899. Conferences publishing in CCIS are allowed to use our online conference service (Meteor) for managing the whole proceedings lifecycle (from submission and reviewing to preparing for publication) free of charge.

Publication process
The language of publication is exclusively English. Authors publishing in CCIS have to sign the Springer CCIS copyright transfer form, however, they are free to use their material published in CCIS for substantially changed, more elaborate subsequent publications elsewhere. For the preparation of the camera-ready papers/files, authors have to strictly adhere to the Springer CCIS Authors' Instructions and are strongly encouraged to use the CCIS LaTeX style files or templates.

Abstracting/Indexing
CCIS is abstracted/indexed in DBLP, Google Scholar, EI-Compendex, Mathematical Reviews, SCImago, Scopus. CCIS volumes are also submitted for the inclusion in ISI Proceedings.

How to start
To start the evaluation of your proposal for inclusion in the CCIS series, please send an e-mail to ccis@springer.com

Wenxing Hong · Binyue Cui · Yang Weng ·
Chao Li
Editors

Computer Science and Education

AI Shaping Education

19th International Conference, ICCSE 2025
Osaka & Fukui, Japan, August 19–24, 2025
Proceedings, Part II

Editors
Wenxing Hong
Xiamen University
Xiamen, China

Binyue Cui
Xiamen University
Xiamen, China

Yang Weng
Sichuan University
Chengdu, China

Chao Li
Tsinghua University
Beijing, China

ISSN 1865-0929 ISSN 1865-0937 (electronic)
Communications in Computer and Information Science
ISBN 978-981-95-7730-9 ISBN 978-981-95-7731-6 (eBook)
https://doi.org/10.1007/978-981-95-7731-6

This Springer imprint is published by the registered company Springer Nature Singapore Pte Ltd.
The registered company address is: 152 Beach Road, #21-01/04 Gateway East, Singapore 189721, Singapore

Preface

The theme of ICCSE 2025, "AI and Digital Literacy: Shaping the Future of Education", reflected the growing significance of integrating artificial intelligence and digital literacy into modern educational practices. The convergence of artificial intelligence, large-scale models, data science, and neurocognitive research opens new frontiers not only in how we educate, but also in how we understand human behaviors, cognition, and social interaction. ICCSE 2025 featured presentations that span educational technology, cognitive science, linguistic analytics, and intelligent healthcare—demonstrating how cross-disciplinary inquiry can generate solutions to the complex challenges facing today's digital society.

This conference proceedings constitutes selected papers presented at the 19th International Conference on Computer Science and Education, ICCSE 2025, held in Fukui, Japan, in August 2025. The 82 full papers and 2 short papers were thoroughly reviewed and selected from the 196 submissions. They focus on a wide range of computer science and education topics, especially AI, data science and engineering, and AI-based education practices, by addressing frontier technical and business issues essential to the applications of AI both in higher education and in advancing e-Society.

After the call for papers was announced, ICCSE 2025 attracted widespread attention from educators and researchers in computer science and education. The conference adopted a Single-Blind Review process, and reviewers did not evaluate papers that included their own names or created any conflict of interest. All submissions were managed through the EasyChair platform. After the submission period ended, the system administrator assigned papers to the program committee, with each paper independently reviewed by three reviewers. The system collected reviewers' comments and revision suggestions, and a paper was accepted only if at least two reviewers recommended acceptance. Authors were required to revise their papers based on the reviewers' feedback and submit the revised version. Only papers that passed the final review were officially accepted. Papers authored by committee members underwent the same rigorous process, with careful assignment to ensure they were not reviewed by their own authors. Through this strict peer-review process, all accepted papers were presented either in oral sessions online/offline or as poster presentations.

These conference proceedings are published in two volumes: *AI Technology Frontiers* and *AI Shaping Education*. The volume *AI Technology Frontiers* emphasizes cutting-edge advancements in Data Processing & Analysis, Visual Recognition, System Development, and Natural Language Processing, highlighting the interdisciplinary synergy between computational innovation and real-world applications. This volume showcases 36 rigorously selected papers (42.86% of total accepted submissions), reflecting the conference's thematic focus on integrating artificial intelligence and digital literacy into transformative educational and technological practices. Contributions in this volume address frontier challenges through diverse approaches, including CNN-Transformer hybrid models, student behavior analytics, and sign language recognition systems. The volume *AI Shaping Education* contains 48 papers, accounting for 57.14% of the total accepted contributions. The core research directions of this volume focus on innovations in teaching models, the practical applications of AI technologies in education (AI-driven development of intelligent teaching systems). In this volume, many reseachers address cutting-edge educational technology topics such as the BOPPPS teaching model, large language model (LLM)-assisted instruction, and computational thinking development, highlighting the trend of deep integration between AI technologies and traditional education. Both volumes reflect the rising momentum of interdisciplinary research at the intersection of computer science and education. Collectively, these scholarly contributions illuminate emerging trajectories in cross-disciplinary integration, advancements in AI technologies, and the profound transformations they are poised to bring to educational theory, instructional design, and teaching practices.

We extend our sincere gratitude to the authors, reviewers, program committee members, and editors for their invaluable contributions to advancing the fields of computer science and education. We hope that these proceedings will serve as a catalyst for future research at the intersection of AI, emerging technologies, and human-centric applications in the fields of computer science and education.

September 2025

Wenxing Hong
Hiroki Takada
Chao Li
Yang Weng
Binyue Cui

Organization

General Chairs

Hiroki Takada	University of Fukui, Japan
Wenxing Hong	Xiamen University, China

Program Committee Chairs

Xin Li	Texas A & M University, USA
Qing Wang	Tianjin University, China
Masumi Takada	Chubu Gakuin University, Japan

Publication Chairs

Yang Weng	Sichuan University, China
Chao Li	Tsinghua University, China
Yasuyuki Matsuura	University of Fukui, Japan

Steering Committee

Maoqing Li	Xiamen University, China
Jien Kato	Kochi University of Technology, Japan
Masaru Miyao	University of Fukui, Japan
Jonathan Li	University of Waterloo, Canada
Huiqiong Wang	Xiamen University Malaysia, Malaysia

Program Committee

Adam Saeid Pirasteh	Xiamen University Malaysia, Malaysia
Baojun Qiao	Henan University, China
Benmei Chen	Chinese University of Hong Kong, China
Binyue Cui	Xiamen University, China
Bo Sun	Beijing Normal University, China
Chao Li	BNRist, Tsinghua University, China

Renren Liu	Xiangtan University, China
Sena Seneviratne	University of Sydney, Australia
Shikui Wei	Beijing Jiaotong University, China
Shunzhi Zhu	Xiamen University of Technology, China
Taoshen Li	Nanning University, China
Teng Li	University of British Columbia, Canada
Tenghong Liu	Zhongnan University of Economics and Law, China
Tom Orthington	Australian National University, Australia
Tao Liu	Anhui University of Engineering, China
Wei Zhou	Beijing Jiaotong University, China
Wenxing Hong	Xiamen University, China
Xiajiong Shen	Henan University, China
Xianke Lin	Ontario Tech University, Canada
Xiangjian (Sean) He	University of Technology Sydney, Australia
Xiaohong Li	Tianjin University, China
Xin Li	Texas A & M University, USA
Xinda Wu	Neusoft Institute, Guangdong, China
Yang Li	Hubei Second Normal College, China
Yang Wang	Southwest Petroleum University, China
Yan Qiang	Taiyuan University of Technology, China
Yanling Li	Northeast Normal University, China
Ying Li	Beihang University, China
Ying Wang	Xiamen University, China
Yuanlong Yu	Fuzhou University, China
Yu Ding	Netease Fuxi AI Lab, China
Yunfei Zhang	ViwiStar Technologies Ltd, Canada
Yonghong Peng	Anglia Ruskin University, UK
Zhibo Chen	Beijing Forestry University, China
Zhicheng Dong	Xizang University, China
Zhigang Deng	University of Houston, USA
Zhiguo Chen	Henan University, China
Zidong Wang	Brunel University London, UK
Zhoubo Xu	Guilin University of Electronic Technology, China
Zongli Lin	University of Virginia, USA

Additional Reviewers

Baojun Qiao
Lingyu Yan
Ning Zhang

Contents

AI Applications in Education

AI Applications in Education

Towards Next-Generation Computer Network Education: AI-Driven Reform

Jigang Wen[1], Kun Xie[2](✉), Yuxiang Chen[1], and Wei Liang[1]

[1] Hunan University of Science and Technology, Xiangtan, China
{wenjigang,chenyuxiang,wliang}@hnust.edu.cn
[2] Hunan University, Changsha, China
xiekun@hnu.edu.cn

Abstract. This paper explores the reform of computer network course instruction in the context of rapid technological advancement and interdisciplinary integration. Traditional teaching models are constrained by outdated theoretical content, weak practical components, and limited responsiveness to emerging technologies such as AI, IoT, cloud computing, and edge computing. To address these issues, a collaborative model combining instructor-led design and large language model (LLM) support is proposed. LLMs are used to assist with dynamic content updates, interdisciplinary case generation, and intelligent teaching resource construction. The reform focuses on three major aspects: restructuring curriculum content with real-world applications, integrating interactive learning and hands-on tasks, and aligning theoretical instruction with cross-domain problem-solving. The curriculum reform introduces flexible course structures and AI-supported personalized learning paths, along with the establishment of an online teaching and experimentation platform to sustain continuous updates and student engagement. This framework provides a replicable model for cultivating high-quality network professionals with solid theoretical foundations, practical competencies, and innovative capabilities in the AI era.

Keywords: Computer Network Education · Artificial Intelligence in Education · Interdisciplinary Teaching

1 Introduction

In recent years, large language models have made remarkable progress [2,5] and become a core technology in the field of natural language processing. We are witnessing a transition from the era of big data to the era of artificial intelligence. Representative models such as GPT, BERT, and T5 demonstrate exceptional capabilities in language understanding and generation through massive pretraining and powerful deep learning algorithms. At the same time, the rapid development of emerging technologies—including edge computing, quantum computing,

W. Hong et al. (Eds.): ICCSE 2025, CCIS 2761, pp. 3–16, 2026.
https://doi.org/10.1007/978-981-95-7731-6_1

blockchain, 5G/6G networks, network function virtualization (NFV), software-defined networking (SDN), edge intelligence, network situational awareness, network slicing, and green computing—is driving the network domain toward higher efficiency, intelligence, and security [9].

In the context of rapid advances in artificial intelligence, these technologies are not only revolutionizing network infrastructure but also raising new demands for professional knowledge [7], practical skills, and innovative thinking among talent. The teaching of computer network courses must focus on cultivating application-oriented and innovative professionals. It is essential to strengthen the foundations of professional knowledge, broaden interdisciplinary understanding, and enhance practical competence to prepare students for future roles in product development and theoretical research.

Computer network courses are fundamental to disciplines such as computer science, information communication, and cybersecurity, and play an irreplaceable role in both teaching and practice within computer-related majors. With continuous technological advancement, computer networks are increasingly intertwined with large language models, artificial intelligence, software engineering, big data, and communication technologies, providing both theoretical underpinnings and technical support for emerging fields.

However, traditional teaching models face several challenges, including outdated knowledge structures, slow content updates, lack of focus on emerging technologies, and weak practical components [6]. To address these issues, our teaching and research group has conducted long-term curriculum development and instructional research. By thoroughly analyzing industry needs and technology trends, we have gradually developed a novel teaching system and methodology. This includes strengthening experimental teaching supported by large language models, incorporating cutting-edge technology cases powered by these models, integrating traditional theories with emerging technologies, and enhancing the synergy between theory and practice. Our goal is to cultivate students with a comprehensive understanding of networking, innovative thinking, and practical problem-solving capabilities, thereby laying a solid foundation for their ability to adapt to future technological transformations and challenges.

2 Problems in Traditional Computer Network Education

2.1 Lagging Curriculum Under Accelerated Network Technology Iteration

Currently, network technologies are experiencing exponential development, and the evolution cycle of global network architectures is becoming increasingly shorter. However, the traditional curriculum of network engineering fails to keep pace with the rapid iteration of technologies. This mismatch between technological evolution and educational supply has created a structural conflict that restricts the cultivation of innovative talent. The generational gap between current course content and modern technologies has led to systemic weaknesses in addressing emerging challenges brought by generative AI [8].

From the perspective of curriculum composition, existing teaching frameworks still heavily rely on classical network theory. Traditional topics such as the OSI model and TCP/IP protocol stack occupy a far larger proportion than modern technologies like Software-Defined Networking (SDN) and Network Function Virtualization (NFV). This imbalance is particularly evident in cloud and edge computing domains. Current textbooks lack sufficient content on dynamic network orchestration and distributed resource scheduling, and cannot effectively explain the principles of intent-based networking (IBN) in modern data centers.

This curriculum lag directly results in a disconnect between students' competency models and industry demands. In recent years, the need for skills in network automation and cloud-native security has increased rapidly, yet traditional courses still focus on static network configuration. Especially in the wake of generative AI's proliferation, cyberspace faces new security threats—such as increasing volumes of deepfake traffic generated by large language models—yet current courses offer little content on AI-generated traffic detection or defense. Consequently, students lack hands-on experience with AI-based DDoS attacks and fail to grasp how emerging technologies dynamically impact network bandwidth.

The updating mechanism for teaching resources also suffers from generational technological gaps. Comparative analysis reveals that mainstream network textbooks provide insufficient coverage of critical standards from the past five years—such as IPv6 transition mechanisms and the QUIC protocol—when compared with the latest white papers in the industry. Regarding AI-driven network transformations, the current curriculum rarely updates teaching cases involving zero trust security models and adaptive traffic scheduling, leading to weak understanding of network behavior prediction and QoS assurance in the era of models like GPT-4. This educational lag has already produced noticeable negative externalities. Industry surveys indicate that companies often need to retrain new hires for over six months, with the most significant skill gap appearing in network issues related to generative AI. Reform on the supply side of network education is urgently needed.

2.2 Disconnection Between Classroom Instruction and Engineering Practice

Computer network courses have long suffered from an overemphasis on theory at the expense of practical training—a problem particularly common in higher education [3]. Course designs are often centered on theoretical constructs such as the OSI seven-layer model, TCP/IP protocol stack, routing algorithms, and congestion control mechanisms [4]. While these theories form the foundation of networking science, instruction tends to prioritize conceptual explanation and formula derivation, with little attention paid to the connection between theory and real-world applications. As a result, students often have a top-heavy understanding—knowing how things work in theory but not why or how to apply them.

Many students can articulate the TCP three-way handshake and understand the principles of congestion control, but are completely lost when it comes to configuring actual devices, deploying services, or troubleshooting network issues. In addition, most universities still rely on simulation tools—such as Packet Tracer or basic Wireshark operations—for their lab components, lacking immersive, real-world training environments. These low-level, repetitive exercises fail to engage students and fall short of preparing them for understanding and operating complex network systems.

The disconnect between course content and practical application results in a significant gap in skill development. In the workplace, network engineers are expected to perform hands-on tasks such as configuring switches and routers, managing VLANs, deploying and optimizing routing protocols like OSPF and BGP, and building stable, efficient web service environments. However, due to inadequate training during their studies, many graduates are unprepared for these responsibilities, unable to even perform basic troubleshooting or configuration. Though theoretically strong, their lack of hands-on experience weakens their competitiveness in the job market and forces employers to invest significant time and resources in post-hire training. Over time, this misalignment between education and industry needs will worsen the imbalance in network talent development. Therefore, universities must urgently optimize their curriculum, enhance the role of practical instruction, and incorporate real-world projects, equipment configuration tasks, and enterprise case studies. By integrating theory and practice, students' comprehensive skills and job readiness can be greatly improved, truly realizing the goal of applying what they have learned.

2.3 Lack of Multidisciplinary Integration

With the rapid advancement of science and technology, computer networks have evolved from a relatively isolated discipline into a foundational technology deeply integrated with artificial intelligence, big data, the Internet of Things (IoT), cloud computing, and cybersecurity. However, current university-level computer network courses still exhibit a significant "island effect," lacking effective support for interdisciplinary integration and failing to meet the needs of cross-disciplinary development [1,10].

This is reflected in the overly narrow course structure, which remains focused on traditional topics such as network protocols, topology design, and routing algorithms, while neglecting the multiple roles networks play in complex real-world applications. For example, in IoT contexts, networks must support the connectivity of billions of devices while ensuring high concurrency, low latency, and high reliability. In AI or distributed machine learning tasks, the network infrastructure must enable large-scale data exchange and task scheduling, with performance directly impacting training efficiency and algorithm accuracy.

Nevertheless, most computer network courses fail to introduce such interdisciplinary scenarios or conduct systematic case analyses. Students therefore struggle to apply networking knowledge to real-world problems and lack both awareness and capability to handle interdisciplinary challenges. Experimental teaching is similarly limited to basic tasks such as static IP configuration, simple topology construction, and packet capture. It seldom includes practice modules relevant to emerging domains like IoT communication, cloud network scheduling, or distributed computing. This disconnection between theory and practice, and between single-discipline and multi-discipline instruction, significantly hinders the development of students' knowledge transfer and integrated application abilities.

The absence of multidisciplinary integration stems from several factors. First, course design often lacks a cross-disciplinary perspective. Most universities treat computer networking as a foundational subject for network engineering, primarily aimed at training traditional network professionals, without incorporating the network-related demands of other fields. For instance, in big data analytics, network throughput and latency directly affect processing efficiency, yet optimization techniques in this area are rarely covered.

Second, limitations in teaching resources and infrastructure pose significant barriers. Interdisciplinary applications often require integration of diverse hardware and software environments—such as sensor nodes, edge computing units, and communication platforms in IoT research—which traditional labs rarely support. Even when the necessary equipment exists, integration into the curriculum is often lacking.

Finally, a lack of diversity in faculty backgrounds is another underlying issue. Most instructors of networking courses have long focused on areas like network protocols and system architecture, with limited exposure to AI algorithms, distributed systems, or edge computing. This restricts content updates and leads to experimental designs that are out of touch with current demands. The imbalance in faculty expertise further entrenches disciplinary boundaries, leaving interdisciplinary integration as more of a concept than a practice.

To truly enhance students' adaptability and innovation capabilities in complex systems, computer network courses must break through disciplinary silos, enhance content renewal, integrate diverse resources, and broaden faculty expertise. Only then can interdisciplinary integration become a normalized and systematic part of education.

3 Theoretical Teaching Reform of Computer Network Courses Empowered by Large Language Models

To improve teaching quality and address the issues of outdated knowledge systems, disconnection between theory and practice, and monotonous instructional approaches in traditional courses, large language models (LLMs) offer powerful support. By leveraging their dynamic knowledge updating capabilities, course content can be quickly adapted to technological developments and cover emerging areas such as SDN, 5G, and cloud computing. LLMs enable personalized learning and interactive teaching, which stimulates students' interest, facilitates more efficient mastery of theoretical knowledge, and enhances their ability to solve real-world problems through integrated practical cases. The following reform measures have been adopted.

Course Content Reconstruction and Precision Teaching through Intelligent Tools

A key task in reforming computer network curricula is building a systematic, cutting-edge, and practically relevant teaching framework. Traditional curricula have focused on classical theories—such as the OSI model, TCP/IP protocol, routing algorithms, and network topologies. Although these form the foundational knowledge, they are insufficient to cover the increasingly integrated domains of SDN, 5G, cloud computing, IoT, and network security, which reflect rapid technological and industrial change.

To meet these challenges, instructors must shift their role from mere knowledge transmitters to curriculum designers and resource integrators. In this process, emerging AI tools such as large language models provide strong support for teaching innovation. Rather than replacing educators, these models serve as high-efficiency assistants in curriculum structuring and content organization. Instructors can use LLMs to retrieve technical literature, map knowledge structures, and distill key problems, thereby enabling a progressive course design based on a four-level structure: "TheoryMechanismCasePractice."

For instance, when teaching network security, instructors can employ LLMs to analyze the security features of the QUIC protocol, generate topic-specific handouts based on recent cyberattacks, and design classroom task sheets that guide students through a closed-loop learning process from technical principles to real-world issues.

To further align course content with practical realities and cutting-edge developments, educators should incorporate major cybersecurity events and industrial application cases from both domestic and international contexts. LLMs can assist instructors in quickly transforming such events into teachable material. For example, if a teacher wishes to create a case study based on the "3.2 Tbps DDoS attack on Deepseek in 2025", the model can help gather incident data, extract attack vectors, scheduling strategies, defense mechanisms, and generate visualized elements, forming a comprehensive classroom resource.

Other cases, such as the 2015 Ukrainian power grid hack, the 2019 Venezuelan blackout, and the 2025 cyberattack on Spain's national power system, can be compiled into thematic teaching units. With LLM assistance, instructors can systematically organize content related to ICS communication, SCADA systems, and nation-state cyberwarfare strategies, thus creating teaching modules with depth and critical insight.

At the same time, students can be guided to analyze industry threat intelligence and white papers from leading security vendors such as DBAPPSecurity, QiAnXin, and Antiy. LLMs can help students understand detection models, log analysis methods, and offensivedefensive strategies, achieving effective integration between classroom learning and real-world industrial practices.

In terms of teaching resource development and personalized support, LLMs can assist educators in efficiently creating diversified, tiered instructional materi-

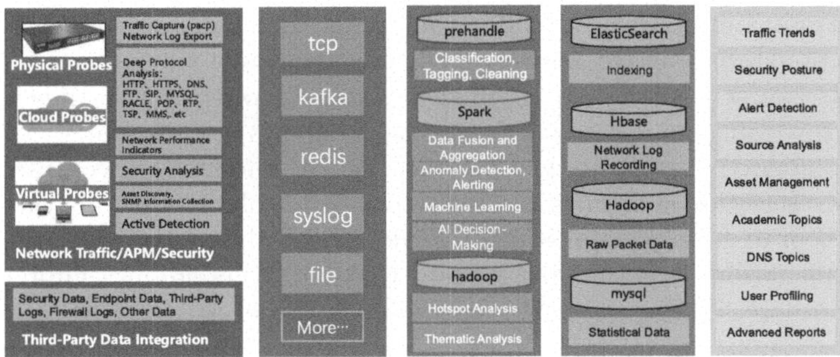

Fig. 1. Example Architecture of a Computer Network Teaching and Experimentation Platform.

als. Taking "Log Analysis and Attack Attribution" as an example, a three-level task structure can be designed: basic training in packet capture and log tagging using Wireshark, intermediate-level construction of attribution path graphs, and advanced-level development of anomaly detection scripts for real data.

During this process, LLMs can help generate experiment documents, code samples, and discussion prompts, reducing the workload of lesson preparation while improving teaching quality and responsiveness. Based on student feedback, instructors can further guide the model to generate supplemental materials tailored to different comprehension levels—for instance, flowcharts, analogies, and mini-quizzes for students struggling with protocol mechanisms, and challenging real-world scenarios such as traffic optimization in cloud data centers for advanced learners.

In addition, instructors can transform research data and cybersecurity competition content into educational resources, using LLMs to assist in format restructuring and experiment script generation. This promotes the internalization of scientific achievements into the classroom. By combining teacher guidance with model support, the efficiency of resource development is enhanced while offering students highly targeted, authentic, and exploratory learning experiences. Figure 1 illustrates the architecture of a computer network teaching and experimentation platform developed by our team for student use.

Interactive Teaching and the Integration of Theory and Practice

Large language models not only facilitate the updating of knowledge systems in computer network courses but also provide strong support for pedagogical transformation—particularly in promoting interactive teaching and integrating theory with practice. Traditional network instruction often adopts a unidirectional model of "teacher lectures, students listen," which tends to be abstract and dull, especially when covering complex theoretical topics such as the TCP/IP protocol or BGP routing mechanisms. This mode of teaching struggles to spark student engagement or exploratory interest.

By introducing LLMs as auxiliary tools, educators can more effectively build a bi-directional, interactive learning environment. Under the guidance of teachers, LLMs can act as "virtual teaching assistants," offering real-time explanations of key concepts, protocol flowcharts, comparative examples, and other forms of supportive content. For instance, when students are confused about BGP route selection strategies or OSPF link-state calculations, instructors can prompt them to pose questions to the model, which then returns layered, multimodal explanations—textual and visual—to enhance classroom comprehension.

Furthermore, educators can design in-class exercises that leverage model-based interaction. For example, they may guide students to explore a question such as "How can routing optimization be achieved in an SDN environment?" in structured dialogue with the model. The model can provide multiple solution strategies, which students then summarize, analyze, and discuss in groups. This interactive mechanism—led by instructors, supported by models, and centered on students—not only encourages active participation but also deepens theoretical absorption and intensifies cognitive training.

Fig. 2. Example of an Asset Identification and Vulnerability Scanning Competition.

More importantly, under the organization of instructors, LLMs can significantly enhance the connection between theoretical knowledge and hands-on application, driving the transformation of instruction from "theory-heavy, practice-light" to a model of "learning for application." One longstanding challenge in network education is the gap between understanding protocol mechanisms and applying them in real-world settings. Students may be able to recite the principles of network protocols yet struggle to configure or debug actual systems.

To bridge this gap, educators can use LLMs to help generate practice tasks and competition scenarios aligned with learning objectives. For example, in a themed module on "Asset Identification and Vulnerability Scanning," instructors can design a comprehensive task requiring students to identify device fingerprints, IP addresses, MAC addresses, operating systems, ports, and service types from a given dataset, assess vulnerabilities and risk levels, and propose remediation strategies. The model can assist in producing guiding documents, vulnerability description templates, and classification standards for security states, greatly improving instructional efficiency. Figure 2 presents a case module from our self-developed teaching platform, designed for asset identification and vulnerability scanning. It enables students to conduct device discovery, attribute analysis, and threat assessment using real or simulated datasets. By developing and validating detection strategies within this environment, students deepen their understanding of network protocols and communication principles. This scenario-based approach enhances both technical proficiency and conceptual comprehension under realistic cybersecurity conditions.

In more advanced scenarios, educators may design full attack-defense simulations based on real attack chains. A sample sequence might include: "Infection with cryptojacking malware (via vulnerability exploitation) → Command and control communication (model-assisted generation of covert channel detection rules such as DNS tunneling or TLS-obfuscated traffic) → Mining task retrieval (monitoring abnormal resource consumption) → Active response (dynamic blocking and attribution)." Students can then work on experimental platforms, incorporating threat intelligence to build attack path diagrams and defense strategies.

Such teaching designs allow students to deeply grasp the behavioral essence of network communication protocols through hands-on work and form knowledge chains linking protocol mechanisms, system behaviors, and security protections. These practical tasks can also naturally evolve into course-based competitions, reinforcing an integrated "teachingtrainingcompetition" model. This approach enhances student engagement and sense of achievement, while also strengthening their comprehensive ability to handle complex cybersecurity challenges.

In this framework, LLMs do not dictate the design or assessment of teaching content; instead, they function as multi-level support tools that provide "content generation + structural prompting + resource supplementation." This reduces the burden of instructional development and task organization, enabling instructors to focus more on curriculum design and student competency development—thus achieving meaningful, deeply integrated teaching.

Integration of Computer Network Courses with Interdisciplinary Research Empowered by Large Language Models

In the theoretical reform of computer network courses, the introduction of large language models (LLMs) has opened up new pathways for integrating interdisciplinary content. With the rapid development of technologies such as artificial intelligence, big data, the Internet of Things (IoT), cloud computing, and edge computing, computer networks have long transcended their role as an isolated discipline and evolved into a foundational platform that supports collaborative multi-disciplinary systems.

However, traditional network courses still center around classical knowledge such as network protocols, routing algorithms, and topology design. These courses tend to be closed in content and slow to update, making them insufficient to reflect the pivotal role that contemporary networking plays in interdisciplinary scenarios. For example, in IoT environments, networks must support massive device communications while accommodating low-power protocols and real-time processing at the edge. In big data platforms like Hadoop and Spark, network bandwidth and latency directly affect task scheduling and computational efficiency. These real-world challenges are rarely addressed in conventional curricula, resulting in students mastering theory but lacking the ability to transfer knowledge to complex application scenarios.

LLMs, through their ability to model technical connectivity across domains, can assist instructors in quickly extracting interdisciplinary cases relevant to course topics. For instance, when explaining the TCP/IP protocol, instructors can utilize the model to generate discussion-based tasks such as "How can edge nodes use TCP to optimize sensor data transmission efficiency?" This helps students understand the adaptability and limitations of protocols under different system architectures, thereby enhancing their skills in knowledge transfer and systems thinking. This integrated teaching model not only broadens the knowledge boundaries of the curriculum but also deepens students' understanding of the core role networking plays in collaborative multidisciplinary systems.

Beyond content integration, the adoption of LLMs also offers feasible mechanisms for pedagogical innovation, especially in enhancing interactivity and practicality. Interdisciplinary research emphasizes system integration and knowledge transfer, yet traditional theory-heavy, lecture-based instruction is ill-equipped to cultivate these compound competencies. Under teacher guidance, LLMs can be employed to generate structured practice tasks and contextual scenarios, helping students translate abstract networking concepts into concrete application problems.

For instance, based on scenarios involving the convergence of AI and networking, instructors can design a task such as "Optimizing communication efficiency in distributed deep learning," prompting students to explore how network configurations can enhance parameter synchronization. The model can assist by generating guided dialogues, architectural diagrams, and common bottleneck types. In IoT courses, instructors might present the goal of "Designing a low-latency, high-reliability communication system," while the model supplements task constraints, technology selection suggestions, and simulation scripts to support a full system design. In cloud computing environments, students can be supported by the model to analyze traffic scheduling mechanisms within data centers and experiment with AI-based resource allocation strategies.

Through these teacher-designed, model-supported, and student-driven learning activities, the curriculum achieves a genuine transition from theory to application and provides students with the foundation and tools to enter interdisciplinary research. The core role of LLMs is not to replace educators, but rather, under the instructor's direction, to support content generation and knowledge restructuring. This empowers the design of teaching tasks and case development, ultimately promoting the deep integration of computer network education with multidisciplinary talent cultivation.

4 Building a Systematic, Intelligent, and Scalable Teaching System for Computer Network Courses

As computer network education evolves from traditional theoretical instruction to a more integrated, multifaceted approach, the focus of teaching reform has gradually shifted from isolated innovations to systemic collaboration. Following stages of reform—such as content upgrading supported by large language models (LLMs), interactive classroom exploration, and the integration of theory with practice—the development of network courses is entering a new phase characterized by systematization and scientific structuring.

To further improve the quality of talent cultivation and the depth of knowledge guidance, it is necessary to systematically summarize and realign efforts across four dimensions: curriculum content, teaching management, knowledge maintenance, and educational dissemination.

In terms of curriculum content development, the teaching team has initially established a content framework centered around "theoretical foundations + application cases + practical tasks." With the assistance of LLMs in case analysis, the team continuously incorporates representative cutting-edge research and industrial applications in network security, such as traffic scheduling under edge intelligence, secure protocols in industrial IoT, and threat tracing in cloud platforms. This approach gradually forms a problem-driven instructional model based on the equation "top-tier research + industrial frontier = problem introduction," ensuring that students consistently learn within a cognitive framework connected to real-world challenges.

At the management level, the reform has explored a "flexible course mechanism" that balances diverse teaching models with multi-tiered talent development. This mechanism supports differentiated content and curriculum structures for undergraduate and graduate stages—ensuring systematic and comprehensive training at the undergraduate level, while offering thematic and exploratory space for graduate students. Course design also emphasizes a balance between broad knowledge delivery in large-class lectures and critical thinking training in small-group seminars. Supported by AI-driven learning behavior analysis systems, the course now enables intelligent resource delivery and personalized content matching. Some course modules have begun to experiment with custom learning path design, allowing students to choose supplementary content and tasks based on their learning goals and research interests, with LLMs assisting in learning plan generation. This "unified framework + flexible paths" management model provides scalable developmental space for students with diverse capabilities and trajectories.

Given the fast-paced updates and frequent technological iterations in the networking field, the teaching team is also advancing the scientific construction of a knowledge management system. A structured resource repository has been built on platforms such as "Learning Pass," encompassing core lecture notes, experiment materials, case libraries, references, and emerging trends. Regular events such as "Teaching Sharing Week" and "Monthly Knowledge Updates" are organized, using LLMs to curate the latest research and policy developments both domestically and internationally, ensuring that teaching resources remain aligned with technological progress. Moreover, student participation in content co-construction is actively encouraged. For instance, students can create learning cards consisting of "concept explanations + case analyses" that are shared on the platform, forming a preliminary loop of knowledge production supported by teacher guidance, student contributions, and intelligent assistance. This mechanism not only enhances resource utilization efficiency but also strengthens students' skills in knowledge organization and expression.

In terms of educational dissemination and ecosystem building, the course reform also strives to extend beyond campus boundaries. Through the optimization of teaching teams and the transformation of teaching outcomes, the vision and practices of network curriculum reform are being promoted on a broader scale. A cross-functional teaching team has been formed, comprising core instructors, researchers, and industry advisors, to develop course content focused on themes such as "IoT Cybersecurity" and "Intelligent Edge Network Operations." Outcomes of the reform have been shared with peer institutions within the province. One notable example is the derivative "IoT Cybersecurity Management System," featuring virtual simulation, traffic monitoring, and risk identification capabilities. This system is currently being piloted in the practical components of cybersecurity courses at multiple universities.

This path—"educational resource development → platform-based technical support → multi-institution joint adoption"—not only enhances the external influence of the curriculum but also establishes a replicable and scalable model for deepening network education reform in a sustainable manner.

5 Conclusion

To address the advanced demands of next-generation information technologies for network professionals, the reform of computer network courses has systematically restructured teaching content and methodologies through a collaborative model led by instructors and supported by Large Language Models (LLMs). Breaking free from traditional textbook constraints, the curriculum integrates cutting-edge technologies such as AI, IoT, and edge computing via dynamic knowledge updating mechanisms. With LLM-assisted generation of multi-tiered experimental tasks and real-time feedback, a closed-loop system of "theory-practice" integration is established. Personalized learning paths and flexible course structures accommodate the differentiated needs of undergraduates and graduate students. Simultaneously, leveraging a knowledge management platform, resources are standardized, shared, and co-created by teachers and students, effectively enhancing hands-on skills and interdisciplinary problem-solving abilities. This has preliminarily formed a practical paradigm of "teaching-research-industry" linkage.

Future reforms will deepen the integration of "top-tier research + industrial frontiers + instructional practice," using intelligent technologies as a bridge to further narrow the gap between education and real-world applications. The goal is to cultivate professionals equipped with systematic knowledge, engineering capabilities, and innovative thinking. Currently, a systematic evaluation is being conducted through cross-institutional collaboration, focusing on learning outcomes, platform effectiveness, and industry-academia alignment. This aims to validate the long-term sustainability of the reform, provide empirical support for building a high-quality, replicable cybersecurity education ecosystem, and drive educational model upgrades across regions and beyond.

Acknowledgment. The work was supported in part by the Ministry of Education Industry-University Collaborative Education Program under Grant 240805841311323 (August 2024 batch: Teaching Reform and Practice of Computer Network Courses), and by the Research Project on Undergraduate Teaching Reform of Hunan University of Science and Technology under Grant G32534 in 2025.

References

1. Allen, L., Kendeou, P.: Ed-ai lit: an interdisciplinary framework for ai literacy in education. Policy Insights Behav. Brain Sci. **11** (2023). https://doi.org/10.1177/23727322231220339
2. Bahrini, A., et al.: Chatgpt: applications, opportunities, and threats. In: 2023 Systems and Information Engineering Design Symposium (SIEDS), pp. 274–279 (2023). https://doi.org/10.1109/SIEDS58326.2023.10137850
3. Gurgel, P., Branco, L., Barbosa, E., Castelo Branco, K.: Development of a practical computer network course through netkit virtualization tool. Procedia Comput. Sci. **18**, 2583–2586 (2013). https://doi.org/10.1016/j.procs.2013.05.445
4. Hu, R., Cui, Y., Chen, L., Chen, Z.: Construction of the practical teaching system of computer network course for deep learning. Comput. Educ. (06), 113–117 (2022). https://doi.org/10.16512/j.cnki.jsjjy.2022.06.026
5. Kasneci, E., et al.: Chatgpt for good? on opportunities and challenges of large language models for education. Learn. Individ. Differ. **103**, 102274 (2023). https://doi.org/10.1016/j.lindif.2023.102274
6. Li, M.Z.X.Z.: Practice of teaching reform of computer network course under the background of emerging engineering education. Comput. Educ. (03), 154–160 (2024). https://doi.org/10.16512/j.cnki.jsjjy.2024.03.001
7. Luckin, R., Holmes, W.: Intelligence unleashed: an argument for ai in education (2016)
8. Song, Z., Shah, N., Guo, J., Zhu, Q.: Applying project-based learning to improve computer networks courses: an experience report. In: 2022 IEEE Global Engineering Education Conference (EDUCON), pp. 148–156 (2022). https://doi.org/10.1109/EDUCON52537.2022.9766750

9. Woolf, B.: Building Intelligent Interactive Tutors, Student-Centered Strategies for Revolutionizing E-Learning (2008)
10. Zhou, Z., Zhao, J.: Research on the path of deep integration of artificial intelligence and university education under the interdisciplinary background. High-Technol. Ind. **30**(10), 135–136 (2024)

Intelligent Teaching Assistant System of Computer Systems Course Based on Large Language Model

Kehua Yang, Huan Zhao(✉), Lida Huang, Xiongren Xiao, Guoqi Xie, and Yang Xu

Hunan University, Changsha 410082, China
huanz@hnu.edu.cn

Abstract. As a core course of computer science and technology, computer systems have the characteristics of strong theoretical foundation and high degree of abstraction. This paper focuses on the difficulties in the teaching process of computer systems courses, and designs and implements a teaching assistant system based on large language models. The system utilizes large model fine-tuning and multi-model collaboration technologies to improve the accuracy of question answering. Simultaneously, the system supports natural language question answering, teaching content retrieval, and other functions, which effectively enhance teaching efficiency and students' autonomous learning abilities. Experimental results demonstrate that the system exhibits good usability in actual question answering scenarios, providing practical references for the implementation of large models in educational settings.

Keywords: Large Language Model · Fine-Tuning · Multi-Model Collaboration · Teaching Assistant System

1 Introduction

The advent of large language model (LLM) technology marks a paradigm shift in human-computer interaction, offering unprecedented naturalness and contextual awareness. Trained on massive, diverse corpora of text and code, these models exhibit remarkable capabilities in natural language understanding (NLU), generation (NLG), reasoning, and even rudimentary problem-solving [1]. This technological leap unlocks immense potential within the educational domain, enabling intelligent support systems that transcend traditional boundaries. Applications such as personalized learning pathways tailored to individual cognitive styles, intelligent tutoring systems capable of nuanced question answering, automated grading with detailed feedback on complex assignments, and immersive simulation-based learning environments are rapidly evolving from concepts into practical realities. The integration of LLMs is not merely an incremental improvement; it fundamentally enhances pedagogical efficiency by automating labor-intensive tasks, freeing instructors to focus on higher-order pedagogical interventions and mentorship. Moreover, it presents novel avenues for optimizing the allocation and accessibility of educational resources, potentially democratizing access to high quality, adaptive instruction, particularly in resource-constrained settings or for complex subjects [2].

W. Hong et al. (Eds.): ICCSE 2025, CCIS 2761, pp. 17–28, 2026.
https://doi.org/10.1007/978-981-95-7731-6_2

Computer Systems, a cornerstone course in Computer Science and Technology curricula, delves into the intricate interplay between hardware and software that underpins modern computing. Its syllabus encompasses highly complex and abstract domains: computer architecture (processor design, memory hierarchies, I/O systems), the machine-level representation of data (binary encoding, integer/floating-point formats) and code (assembly language, instruction set architectures), the intricacies of program translation (compilation, assembly), linking (static vs. dynamic, symbol resolution, relocation), and performance optimization techniques. The inherently theoretical nature and high level of abstraction intrinsic to these topics pose significant cognitive hurdles for students. Learners frequently struggle to connect abstract concepts (e.g., virtual memory mechanisms)to concrete system behavior, grapple with the complexity of low level programming and debugging, and face difficulties in visualizing the multi-stage transformation from high-level code to executable binaries.

Compounding these inherent difficulties are limitations prevalent in traditional pedagogical approaches. The conventional lecture-lab model often fails to accommodate the diverse learning paces, prior knowledge bases, and preferred modalities of individual students. Critical bottlenecks emerge: students encounter limited avenues for seeking clarification – constrained by fixed office hours, potential hesitation to ask questions in large lectures, or the inability to articulate their confusion precisely. Furthermore, effective self-assessment proves exceptionally challenging. Without immediate, granular feedback on their understanding of intricate concepts (e.g., the precise effect of a compiler optimization flag or the state changes during a cache access), students struggle to gauge their mastery accurately and identify specific knowledge gaps before high-stakes assessments. This lack of timely, personalized feedback impedes metacognitive development and efficient learning progression.

Addressing these persistent challenges within the demanding context of Computer Systems education, this research undertakes the design and implementation of an advanced educational support system fundamentally powered by large language model technology. Using the Computer Systems course as a representative and demanding case study, the research integrates a synergistic suite of cutting-edge techniques:

(1) Domain-Specific Fine-Tuning [3]: Pre-trained foundational LLMs (e.g., models akin to GPT-4, LLaMA, etc.) undergo rigorous fine-tuning using meticulously cu-rated datasets encompassing core Computer Systems concepts. This includes authoritative textbooks, lecture notes, seminal research papers, carefully vetted Q&A pairs addressing common misconceptions, and crucially, authentic student assignment solutions (anonymized) and project artifacts. This process critically adapts the general linguistic prowess of the LLM to the precise technical lexicon, reasoning patterns, and problem-solving methodologies characteristic of systems-level computing.

(2) Structured Knowledge Base Construction: Beyond relying solely on the parametric knowledge of the fine-tuned LLM, a dedicated, retrievable knowledge base is engineered. This repository incorporates structured information such as formal definitions of architectural components (e.g., precise cache parameters, TLB structures), de- tailed specifications of instruction sets (x86–64, RISC-V), step-by-step algorithmic procedures (e.g., linking steps, page table walks), and curated collections

of common bugs and debugging strategies specific to systems programming (e.g., memory corruption patterns, concurrency errors). This knowledge base serves both as a grounding resource for the LLM to enhance factual accuracy and as a direct reference for students.

(3) Multi-Model Collaboration Framework: Recognizing that LLMs, while powerful, may exhibit limitations in deterministic reasoning, symbolic manipulation, or generating precise visual representations of system state, the architecture employs a collaborative approach. The core fine-tuned LLM acts as the primary interaction inter-face and reasoning engine. It intelligently delegates specific, well-defined subtasks to specialized modules: symbolic algebra systems for verifying arithmetic within bi-nary/hexadecimal conversions, formal verification tools for specific logic checks, code analysis engines for detecting common vulnerability patterns (e.g., buffer overflows), or dedicated visualization generators for illustrating concepts like pipeline stalls or memory hierarchy accesses. The LLM synthesizes outputs from these specialized components into coherent, natural language responses or visual explanations for the student.

This integrated system provides a comprehensive technical solution tailored to the unique demands of Computer Systems instruction. It offers 24/7 personalized tutoring, capable of engaging in Socratic dialogues to diagnose misunderstandings related to intricate topics like out-of-order execution or virtual memory management. It enables intelligent, context-aware Q&A, understanding queries phrased in natural language yet grounded in technical specifics (e.g., "Why did my loop cause a cache thrashing effect?"). It facilitates detailed automated feedback on programming assignments, pin-pointing logical errors in assembly code, inefficiencies in C programs, or misunderstandings revealed in written explanations. Furthermore, it supports dynamic learning assessment through tailored quizzes and concept explanations based on individual interaction history.

By successfully implementing this system within the challenging domain of Computer Systems, the research not only delivers a practical tool for enhancing pedagogy in this specific course but also establishes a replicable framework and valuable insights for the broader application of advanced LLM technology across diverse educational contexts in STEM and beyond. It charts a pathway towards truly adaptive, responsive, and resource-efficient intelligent learning environments.

2 Data Collection and Fine-Tuning of Large Language Models

2.1 Data Collection

The efficacy and reliability of a large language model (LLM) deployed within a specialized educational context are fundamentally contingent upon the quality, depth, and relevance of the underlying knowledge base data. This data directly governs the professionalism, factual accuracy, and contextual appropriateness of the model's generated responses. Substandard or superficial data sources inevitably lead to responses that are generic, technically flawed, or pedagogically misaligned—severely undermining the system's utility as a trusted learning aid. To construct a high-fidelity, domain-specific teaching corpus tailored for the rigorous demands of the Computer Systems course, this system implements a meticulous multi-source aggregation strategy, encompassing the following critical categories:

(1) Authoritative Textbook Materials: Serving as the foundational bedrock, core content is extracted from seminal, peer-reviewed textbooks such as "Computer Systems: A Programmer's Perspective" (CS:APP) and officially designated course texts from leading universities. These materials provide comprehensive, systematically structured coverage of essential topics including processor architecture, memory hierarchies, assembly programming, linking mechanisms (static/dynamic), process management, virtual memory, and system-level I/O. Their inherent rigor ensures conceptual depth and terminological precision vital for model training.
(2) Structured Pedagogical Resources: To bridge theoretical concepts with practical application, the corpus integrates curated teaching slides (PowerPoint presentations) and detailed laboratory/experimental guides sourced directly from the Computer Systems course offerings at Hunan University. These resources are particularly valuable as their pedagogical design and content sequencing are explicitly tailored to align with students' progressive learning trajectories and concrete operational requirements encountered in assignments and projects. They offer contextualized examples, illustrative diagrams, and step-by-step procedural guidance essential for grounding abstract concepts.
(3) Curated Open-Source Community Knowledge: Recognizing the dynamic nature of student queries and common debugging scenarios, the system harvests supplemental material from reputable open-source learning platforms like CSDN and Stack Overflow. Crucially, this involves rigorous filtering and validation processes. Only posts demonstrably marked as high-quality (e.g., through high user engagement, expert endorsements, or platform certification) and directly relevant to authentic student struggles(e.g. debugging inker errors, optimizing cache performance, understanding thread synchronization pitfalls) are incorporated. This enriches the corpus with pragmatic problem-solving patterns and diverse question-answer formulations encountered in real-world learning.
(4) Data Standardization and Preprocessing: To ensure uniformity and optimal processing by the LLM architecture, all collected materials—regardless of their original format (PDF, PPTX, DOCX, HTML)—undergo a rigorous conversion pipeline. They are transformed into standardized Markdown plain text. This format preserves essential structural elements (headings, lists, code blocks) while stripping away non-essential formatting that could introduce noise. Subsequently, the text undergoes intelligent seg-mentation, breaking down extensive documents into logically coherent chunks (e.g., by section, sub-topic, or example). This segmentation is crucial for efficient retrieval augmented generation (RAG) and fine-tuning processes, enabling the model to pinpoint and utilize the most relevant context for any given student query or pedagogical task.

2.2 Fine-Tuning of Large Language Models

ThisresearchstrategicallyleveragestheLLaMA3.23B model, released by Meta AI, as the foundational architecture for domain-specific adaptation. This model represents a significant achievement in efficient large language model design. Through Meta's profound architectural enhancements, LLaMA3.2 incorporates sophisticated structured pruning techniques and advanced knowledge distillation methodologies [4]. These innovations enable it to maintain a robust three-billion parameter scale – capturing substantial linguistic and reasoning capabilities – while simultaneously exhibiting exceptional computational efficiency and lightweight characteristics. Crucially, LLaMA3.2 demonstrates exceptional prowess in complex context comprehension and sustained, coherent multi-turn dialogue capabilities, attributes that are indispensable for effective educational interactions where students progressively build understanding through iterative questioning.

A salient operational advantage of LLaMA3.2 3B is its remarkable compatibility with edge computing environments. The model can execute inference efficiently on a consumer-grade GPU equipped with merely 3.4GB of VRAM. This represents a dramatically lower hardware barrier compared to many contemporary large models (e.g., those requiring 10GB + VRAM or specialized AI accelerators), making it eminently viable for deployment in common university computing labs, instructor work-stations, or even student laptops. This accessibility is paramount for ensuring wide adoption and practical utility within educational institutions lacking dedicated high-performance computing infrastructure.

The core adaptation process employs Supervised Fine-Tuning (SFT). To maximize the efficacy of this adaptation within resource constraints, the system integrates two complementary advanced techniques:

(1) Quantization-Aware Training (QAT): During fine-tuning, model weights and activations are constrained to lower precision data types (e.g., FP16 or even INT8 representations where feasible). This QAT process explicitly incorporates quantization effects into the optimization loop, ensuring the model learns robust representations inherently tolerant to the precision loss incurred during subsequent deployment quantization. This drastically reduces the final model footprint and accelerates inference speeds without significant accuracy degradation.
(2) Low-Rank Adaptation (LoRA) [5]: Instead of updating the entire vast parameter set (billions of weights), LoRA introduces small, trainable rank-decomposition matrices into specific layers. In this implementation, LoRA modules are seamlessly integrated into all 28 Transformer layers constituting the LLaMA3.2 architecture. Furthermore, fine-tuning capability is selectively activated only for critical sub-components within each layer: the Query (Q), Key (K), and Value (V) projection matrices of the attention mechanism, the output projection matrix, and the two dense layers within the MLP (Multi-Layer Perceptron) block. This targeted approach focuses adaptation capacity on layers most responsible for task-specific feature transformation.

The computational efficiency gains of this hybrid approach are profound. By freezing the original pre-trained weights and updating only the injected LoRA parameters (alongside potential quantization scaling factors), the total number of trainable parameters is reduced to a highly manageable 40,370,176. This figure is orders of magnitude lower than the multi-billion parameters requiring optimization in traditional full-parameter fine-tuning. Consequently, the strategy significantly alleviates VRAM pressure during training – enabling SFT on a single capable GPU – and simultaneously curtails computational costs and energy consumption. The resultant adapted model retains the core knowledge and reasoning power of LLaMA3.2 while acquiring deep expertise in the intricacies of computer systems education, all within a deployment-friendly efficient package.

3 Knowledge Base Construction and Semantic Retrieval

A core challenge in deploying large language models (LLMs) within specialized educational domains, such as computer systems, lies in ensuring the accuracy, consistency, and pedagogical appropriateness of generated responses, particularly concerning intricate terminology, nuanced conceptual relationships, and rapidly evolving technical standards. Standard LLMs, despite their impressive generative fluency, are inherently limited by the static nature of their parametric knowledge and potential factual hallucinations when encountering edge cases or deeply domain-specific queries. To decisively overcome these limitations and anchor responses firmly in authoritative course content, this system integrates a structured semantic knowledge base with a large language model, constructing a sophisticated Retriever-Augmented Generator (RAG) framework. This hybrid architecture directly addresses the critical issue of incomplete or superficial coverage of specialized course knowledge within the LLM's pre-trained parameters. The RAG mechanism operates through a tightly orchestrated sequence: upon receiving a user query, it first leverages semantic similarity retrieval to dynamically summon the most relevant contextual snippets from the verified knowledge repository; these retrieved passages are then concatenated with the original question, forming a rich, context-laden prompt that is fed into the generative LLM. This process decomposes into three fundamental, interconnected stages: Knowledge Base Construction, Semantic Indexing & Retrieval, and Context-Aware Language Generation, collectively ensuring responses are deeply rooted in vetted educational materials.

The foundation of the RAG system is a robust knowledge base meticulously constructed using the MaxKB [6] platform. MaxKB is not merely a vector database but a comprehensive, integrated knowledge management ecosystem designed for enterprise-grade AI applications. Its core strengths lie in its native support for the entire document lifecycle and seamless integration with LLM inference, underpinned by high scalability and exceptional flexibility. Key functionalities critical to our implementation include:

(1) Unified Document Management: Supports ingestion of diverse formats (PDF, DOCX, PPTX, Markdown, HTML) into a centralized repository. Documents retain metadata (source, authorship, timestamp) for provenance tracking.
(2) Automated Vectorization Pipeline: Upon upload, each document undergoes automatic chunking (based on semantic boundaries or fixed sizes) and transformation into high-dimensional vector embeddings using state-of-the-art models (e.g., OpenAI Embeddings, BGE, or custom models). This vector representation captures semantic meaning, enabling content-based retrieval beyond keyword matching.

(3) "Model Optimization" Hit Processing: A pivotal feature for educational ac-curacy. When creating the "Computer System Knowledge Base" instance within MaxKB, the retrieval process is explicitly bound to this method. It employs sophisticated algorithms during the semantic indexing stage—potentially involving re-ranking, cross-encoder refinement, or domain-specific synonym expansion—to ensure user queries are mapped with high precision to the correct and most pedagogically relevant document segments, minimizing irrelevant or misleading context retrieval.
(4) Dynamic Knowledge Agility: Supports real-time document updates with hot loading capability. New lecture notes, revised experiment guides, or emerging research summaries can be added or existing documents modified; the system automatically re-processes the changes (chunking, embedding) and makes the updated knowledge immediately quarriable without downtime. This is essential for keeping pace with curriculum evolution and addressing novel student inquiries.

The operational workflow of the RAG system demonstrates a sophisticated interplay between retrieval precision and generative adaptation:

(1) Query Vectorization & Retrieval: When a user submits a question (e.g., "Ex-plain the difference between write-back and write-through cache policies with an ex-ample"), the query is first converted into a dense vector embedding using the same model employed for indexing the knowledge base. This query vector is then compared against all stored document chunk vectors in the knowledge base using efficient Ap-proximate Nearest Neighbor (ANN) search algorithms (e.g., HNSW, IVF). The similarity metric is typically cosine similarity. The system retrieves the top k most semantically relevant chunks ($k = 3$ in our configuration, balancing relevance and context window limits).
(2) Prompt Engineering with Retrieved Context: The retrieved chunks (e.g., text-book definitions, diagram descriptions, relevant problem solutions) and the original user query are dynamically assembled into a structured prompt template. This template explicitly instructs the LLM to base its response primarily on the provided context. An example prompt structure might be:

[System Instruction] *You are an expert tutor for Computer Systems. Answer the user's question STRICTLY based ONLY on the following verified reference passages. If the answer cannot be conclusively derived from the passages, state "Based on the provided materials, I cannot confirm...".*

[Reference Passage 1]:*...text describing write-through policy...*

[Reference Passage 2]:*...text explaining write-back with coherence example... [Reference Passage 3]:...comparison table snippet...*

[User Question]: *Explain the difference between write-back and write-through cache policies with an example.*

(3) LLM Inference with Grounded Context: This context-rich prompt is sent to the Deepseek-R1:7b model deployed locally via Ollama. This model was chosen for its strong reasoning capability, efficiency, and compatibility with the Ollama inference stack. The LLM generates its response by attending heavily to the provided context passages, synthesizing the information, and formulating a coherent, pedagogically

sound answer. Crucially, the model integrates the retrieved facts into the logical flow of its response rather than merely copying text.

(4) OutputPresentationwithEnhancedInterpretability: Thefinalgeneratedan-swer is presented to the user. Significantly, adhering to principles of transparent AI in education, the system also displays the specific reference passages it retrieved and utilized. This dual output (answer + sources) achieves two vital goals:

- Accuracy Verification & Trust Building: Students (and instructors) can immediately cross-reference the answer against the original source material, verifying factual correctness and reducing reliance on "black box" outputs. This fosters trust in the system as a reliable learning aid.
- Contextual Learning & Deeper Exploration: Seeing the source excerpts allows students to understand the broader context from which the answer was derived, potentially stimulating deeper exploration of related concepts mentioned in the passages. It transforms the interaction from a simple Q&A into a guided learning moment.

This RAG architecture delivers profound improvements specifically targeted at the shortcomings of vanilla LLMs in specialized education:

(1) Mitigating Ambiguity & Hallucination: By grounding responses in retrieved passages, the system drastically reduces the generation of plausible-sounding but incorrect or speculative information ("hallucinations"), especially concerning precise terminology or complex mechanisms.
(2) Ensuring Logical Continuity & Conceptual Rigor: Responses are constrained by the logical structure and factual content present in the authoritative sources, promoting consistency and adherence to established pedagogical narratives within the course.
(3) Eliminating Factual Errors on Core Knowledge: Direct retrieval from vetted materials (textbooks, curated slides) guarantees that fundamental facts, definitions, and principles presented are accurate and aligned with course teaching.
(4) Enabling Continuous Knowledge Updates: The hot-load capability ensures the system's knowledge remains current, unlike static LLMs whose knowledge cutoff is fixed at training time.

By seamlessly integrating semantic retrieval, context-aware prompt engineering, grounded generation, and interpretable output, this RAG system transcended conventional chatbot limitations. It establishes a new paradigm for accurate, trustworthy, and pedagogically robust intelligent tutoring within the demanding field of computer systems education, setting a benchmark for applying LLM technology in specialized academic domains.

4 Multi-Model Collaboration

To further enhance the robustness and adaptability of the system's responses, a multi-model collaboration mechanism is introduced, where multiple large language models are simultaneously integrated at the backend [7], with dynamic selection, response fusion, and cross-validation occurring between the models. This mechanism not only improves the accuracy of responses but also provides technical assurance for the system's output quality control.

Building upon the previously described infrastructure, this system employs a sophisticated dual-model architecture to harness complementary strengths and address the multifaceted demands of computer systems education. The strategically selected models operate in concert:

- LLaMA3.2-3B: Serving as the domain cognition specialist, this model excelsin comprehending intricate computer systems terminology (e.g.,"TLB miss penalty," "speculative execution," "memory-mapped I/O") and navigating complex course-specific logical structures (sequential data flow in processors, concurrency primitives, virtual address translation pipelines). Its specialized fine-tuning via SFT, QAT, and LoRA ensures deep alignment with the pedagogical content and reasoning patterns unique to the discipline.
- DeepSeek-R1:7b: Functioning as the conversational engine and RAG integrator, this model provides robust general dialogue capabilities, fluent response generation, and crucially, excels at synthesizing responses grounded in the context retrieved by the RAG module from the MaxKB knowledge base. It handles broad conversational turns, clarifications, and the seamless integration of retrieved factual snippets into coherent explanations.

The collaboration mechanism coordinates the complementary abilities of the two models in context understanding, domain adaptation, fact retrieval, and response precision through weight adjustment, dynamic judgment, and fusion of outputs. The goal is to achieve a triple optimization of accuracy, response speed, and resource utilization efficiency under different types of tasks. The core of this mechanism is the Dynamic Weighted Fusion (DWF), which designed to extract multiple feature indicators at the onset of a user task and real-time evaluate which model is more suitable to dominate the generation for the current task, thereby assigning different response weights to each model.

We denote this weight as α, representing the relative dominance of the fine-tuned model LLaMA3.2 in the current task, while the other model, DeepSeek-r1, occupies the remaining proportion with 1-α. The final output response P_{final} is obtained by weightedly fusing the output probability distributions of the two models according to this ratio, as follows:

$$P_{final} = \alpha * (P_{llama}) + (1 - \alpha) * P_{deepseek} \tag{1}$$

Where α is not a fixed value, but rather dynamically calculated based on the task context and historical operating status, with its calculation formula being:

$$\alpha = \frac{\omega_1 \bullet M_d + \omega_2 \bullet A_h + \omega_3 \bullet C_r}{\omega_1 \bullet M_d + \omega_2 \bullet A_h + \omega_3 \bullet C_r + \omega_4 \bullet R_c} \tag{2}$$

The four factors in the above formula are: Domain Matching Degree (M_d), Historical Accuracy (A_h), Real-time Confidence (C_r), and Resource Consumption Penalty Factor (R_c). The Domain Matching Degree reflects whether the user's current question falls within the coverage domain of the fine-tuned LLaMA3.2 model's corpus, which can be determined through the similarity between question keywords and the model's training corpus or by a classifier. A higher value indicates that the task is more suitable for being led by the fine-tuned model. Historical Accuracy is based on the model's performance statistics in historical similar questions, obtained through a scoring mechanism or human feedback, and has a certain memory effect. If a model performs stably in similar tasks, its weight will increase. Real-time Confidence is reflected by the entropy of the model's output probability distribution and is an indication of the model's confidence in its own generated content for the current task. A lower entropy value indicates that the model is more "confident" in its output choices, so models with higher confidence should receive more weight. Finally, the Resource Consumption Factor is used to balance the cost of the model's use of system resources, mainly measuring the model's inference latency, GPU memory occupancy, etc., with the aim of controlling model selection according to GPU memory and reducing latency.

In terms of weight setting, we assign weights of 0.35, 0.25, and 0.30 to M_d, A_h, and C_r, respectively. This is because the Domain Matching Degree directly affects the relevance of the model's generated responses, playing a decisive role in semantic scene matching; Historical Accuracy reflects long-term learning effects, which is important but limited by the statistical sample size; Real-time Confidence represents the model's instantaneous self-assessment capability, often used in error correction and judgment mechanisms, thus occupying a significant weight. Resource Consumption, as a system-level factor, primarily serves as a penalty adjustment, so its weight R_c is set relatively lower at 0.10. When the system faces resource constraints or high real-time requirements, it tends to choose the lower-consumption model, automatically reducing the participation weight of complex models.

Depending on the value of α, the system adopts different collaboration strategies. If $\alpha \geq 0.87$, indicating that the fine-tuned model has a significant advantage, the system directly uses the LLaMA3.2's generation result as the final output. Conversely, if $\alpha \leq 0.2$, the system completely adopts the response from DeepSeek-r1. When the weight is in the middle range, i.e., $\alpha \in (0.2, 0.8)$, a soft-voting strategy is employed, where the top-k generation candidates from both models are fused through probability-weighted voting. This strategy effectively reduces the risk of misjudgment by a single model, enhancing the system's robustness.

Beyond the dynamic weighted fusion approach, the system incorporates a specialized fail-safe mechanism termed Candidate Voting (CV) to handle scenarios de-manding exceptionally high reliability. This mode is explicitly activated under two critical conditions: (1) during complex multi-turn dialogues where contextual dependencies accumulate and ambiguity risks escalate (e.g., debugging discussions spanning multiple system components), or (2) when confronting high-stakes decision-making queries where factual inaccuracy or logical flaws could lead to significant pedagogical consequences (e.g., explaining intricate hardware exceptions, validating student-de-signed memory safety solutions, or interpreting subtle concurrency race conditions).

In CV mode, the collaborative inference mechanism undergoes a strategic shift to a parallel evaluation paradigm. Upon receiving a query meeting the activation thresh-old, both the LLaMA3.2-3B and DeepSeek-R1:7b models are simultaneously invoked to generate independent, complete candidate responses based on their respective strengths and available context (including RAG-retrieved snippets for DeepSeek). This parallelism ensures maximum model capability is leveraged without premature bias.

The core intelligence resides in a dedicated Discriminator Module, which per-forms a rigorous, multi-dimension comparative assessment of the two candidate responses. This discriminator employs a tripartite scoring metric calibrated for academic rigor:

(1) Content Accuracy (Weight: 45%): Verifies factual alignment with authoritative course knowledge (textbooks, vetted slides), technical correctness of explanations, and precision of terminology usage. Employs cross-referencing with the knowledge base embeddings and pattern matching against predefined concept-relation graphs.
(2) Logical Consistency & Coherence (Weight: 35%): Evaluates clarity of argument flow, absence of contradictions, proper causal linkage between ideas, and structural soundness (introduction-body-conclusion suitability for complex topics). Lever-ages semantic role labeling and discourse relation parsing.
(3) ResponseC-onfidence&UncertaintyQuantification(Weight:20%):Assesses the model's intrinsic confidence scores associated with generated claims (e.g., token probabilities, calibration metrics) and flags excessive hedging or unwarranted assertions. Integrates model self-evaluation prompts where feasible.

Each candidate response receives a composite reliability score (0–100 scale) based on these weighted dimensions. Crucially, the discriminator isn't limited to simple score comparison. It employs heuristic rules (e.g., automatically rejecting responses containing unverified claims outside the RAG context) and can trigger a revote request if scores are statistically indistinguishable or both fall below a predefined reliability threshold. The highest-scoring candidate is then selected as the final output.

While this "parallel generation + discriminative selection" approach inherently increases computational overhead (roughly 2x inference cost) and latency compared to single-model pathways, the resultant enhancement in output reliability, factual robustness, and error resilience is substantial. The trade-off is strategically justified for application scenarios where task criticality is paramount – ensuring students receive consistently trustworthy guidance during pivotal learning moments, complex problem-solving sessions, or assessments. This mechanism exemplifies the system's commitment to pedagogical safety without sacrificing advanced AI capability.

5 Conclusion

The core objective of our system is to "apply large language model technology to the auxiliary teaching of specialized courses in universities," taking computer systems as an example to design and implement an instructional support system based on large language models [8]. The main work includes adapting an efficient few-shot fine-tuning scheme for the educational domain based on the open-source LLaMA3.2 model; integrating course materials with the RAG architecture to generate a knowledge base, effectively addressing the issues of "hallucination" and lack of domain knowledge in large language models, making the model's outputs more targeted; and designing a multi-model collaboration mechanism to achieve efficient and high-quality response control capabilities.

Acknowledgments. This study was funded by Foundation of Hunan Educational Committee Program (202502000227) 'Constructing a Practical Education System for Computer Majors Based on the Information Innovation Platform' and Regular Higher Educational Institutions Teaching Reform Project of Hunan Province, 2023JGSZ041.

References

1. Dong, B., Bai, J., Xu, T., Zhou, Y.: Large language models in education: a systematic review. In: 2024 6th International Conference on Computer Science and Technologies in Education (CSTE), Xi'an, China, pp. 131–134 (2024). https://doi.org/10.1109/CSTE62025.2024.00031
2. Küchemann, S., Avila, K.E., et al.: On opportunities and challenges of large multimodal foundation models in education. NPJ Sci. Learn. **10**(1), 11, 26 Feb 2025
3. Wang, D., Zheng, Y., Li, J., Chen, G.: Parameter-efficiently fine-tuning large language models for classroom dialogue analysis. IEEE Trans. Learn. Technol. https://doi.org/10.1109/TLT.2025.3567995
4. Ayesha, B., Thayasivam, U.: Multilingual student performance prediction using llama 3. In: 2024 IEEE International Conference on Big Data (BigData), Washington, DC, USA, pp. 5936–5945 (2024). https://doi.org/10.1109/BigData62323.2024.10825022
5. Hu, E.J., Shen, Y., Wallis, P., et al.: Lora: Low-rank adaptation of large language models. ICLR **1**(2), 3 (2022)
6. MaxKB Homepage. https://maxkb.cn/. Accessed 25 Apr 2025
7. Singh, A., Ehtesham, A., Kumar, S., Khoei, T.T.: Enhancing AI systems with agentic workflows patterns in large language model. In: 2024 IEEE World AI IoT Congress (AIIoT), Seattle, WA, USA, pp. 527–532 (2024). https://doi.org/10.1109/AIIoT61789.2024.10578990
8. Wang, R.E., Ribeiro, A.T., Robinson, C.D., et al.: Tutor CoPilot: A human-AI approach for scaling real-time expertise. arXiv preprint arXiv:2410.03017 (2024)

Integration of Computational Thinking and Artificial Intelligence in General Education: A Case Study of "Introduction to Computing and Artificial Intelligence" at Hunan University

Yuhui Cai and Juan Luo(✉)

Hunan University, ChangSha Hunan, China
rj_cyh@hnu.edu.com, juanluo@hnu.edu.cn

Abstract. This paper investigates the integration of computational thinking and artificial intelligence (AI) into general education, proposing a framework for cultivating AI-era talents. It analyzes the interdependence between AI literacy and computational thinking, advocating a pedagogical approach that extends AI education through computational thinking foundations. The study details Hunan University's "Introduction to Computing and Artificial Intelligence" course, which implements a tripartite teaching system focusing on knowledge construction, thinking cultivation, and ability development. This model effectively promotes synchronous growth in students' computational thinking and AI competencies. The course employs a four-dimensional operational framework combining objective guidance, interdisciplinary content, innovative methodologies, and comprehensive evaluation. Results show enhanced problem-solving abilities through computational methods, improved AI technology application skills, and strengthened innovative capacities. This practice provides a replicable paradigm for integrating computational thinking and AI education, offering practical insights for global higher education institutions. The research contributes to both theoretical understanding of computational thinking-AI synergies and pedagogical innovation in talent cultivation. Future work will optimize teaching content, explore advanced instructional methods, and expand real-world application scenarios to meet evolving societal demands. This study underscores the importance of integrating computational thinking into AI general education for developing future-ready talents.

Keywords: Computational Thinking · Artificial Intelligence · General Education · Teaching Reform

1 Introduction

Artificial Intelligence (AI) technology, with its unique advantages and vast application potential, is increasingly penetrating and profoundly transforming various sectors of society, triggering comprehensive changes. In the field of intelligent manufacturing, AI technology facilitates the automation and intelligent upgrading of production processes

W. Hong et al. (Eds.): ICCSE 2025, CCIS 2761, pp. 29–37, 2026.
https://doi.org/10.1007/978-981-95-7731-6_3

[1]; in the construction of smart cities, it promotes refined and efficient urban management [2]; in precise medical practices, AI provides robust support for disease diagnosis and treatment plan formulation [3]; and in smart education models, it optimizes the allocation of teaching resources and enables personalized learning [4]. AI technology has not only become the core driving force for industrial transformation and upgrading but also leads to disruptive changes in human lifestyles. With the rapid development of AI technology, how to deeply integrate it with higher education to cultivate high-quality talents with profound theoretical foundations and outstanding innovative practical abilities has become a critical issue to be addressed in the current educational domain.

Computational thinking, as a unique thinking paradigm, emphasizes transforming complex problems into computable models for solution [5]. It is not only the core literacy of computer science but also an important cornerstone for solving complex problems and driving technological innovation. Deepening the cultivation of AI literacy on the basis of computational thinking not only helps students comprehensively understand the principles and applications of AI technology but also stimulates their innovative thinking and interdisciplinary integration capabilities, laying a solid foundation for their future career development and social contributions. Therefore, integrating computational thinking into the AI general education system has become a key measure for cultivating innovative talents in the new era.

Taking the course "Introduction to Computing and Artificial Intelligence" at Hunan University as a typical case, this paper deeply analyzes its practical path and remarkable achievements in exploring the integration of computational thinking and AI in the field of AI general education. Rooted in general education, the course systematically advances the integrated teaching of computational thinking and AI literacy, bridging the technological frontier with professional domains for non-major students, and assisting them in growing into innovative and interdisciplinary talents in the intelligent era. By constructing a "knowledge, thinking, ability" trinity teaching system, the course effectively promotes the coordinated development of students' computational thinking and AI literacy, providing a practical paradigm for cultivating compound talents with both computational rationality and humanistic care. The research in this paper not only contributes to deepening the theoretical understanding of the integrated education of computational thinking and AI but also offers valuable experience and references for other universities to carry out relevant teaching practices.

2 The Integration of AI General Education and Computational Thinking

With the rapid development and widespread application of AI technology, the strategic position of AI general education in the higher education system has become increasingly prominent. How to scientifically and efficiently conduct AI general education, enabling it to not only widely popularize AI knowledge but also effectively cultivate students' innovative thinking and practical abilities, has become an important proposition that needs in-depth discussion in the current educational field. In this process, computational thinking, as a unique and critical thinking approach, opens up new perspectives and practical pathways for AI general education. This paper argues that AI general education should not exist in isolation but should closely rely on computational thinking training and achieve further expansion and deepening on its basis.

Computational thinking is a thinking paradigm that transforms complex problems into computable forms for solution, emphasizing the application of core concepts such as abstraction, logic, algorithms, and models. As the cornerstone ability of computer science, computational thinking not only helps students profoundly understand the essence and basic principles of computer science but also effectively cultivates their innovative thinking and problem-solving abilities. In the context of the current information and digital era, computational thinking has become an indispensable basic literacy, extensively permeating various disciplines and offering new possibilities for people's thinking styles and problem-solving strategies.

As a key pathway for popularizing AI knowledge and enhancing students' AI literacy, the core goal of AI general education is to enable students to comprehensively grasp the principles and applications of AI technology and flexibly apply it to solve practical problems. However, if we merely remain at the level of AI knowledge popularization and skill training while neglecting the cultivation of computational thinking, AI general education will fail to fulfill its true mission. Because the computational thinking inherent in AI technology is precisely the core driving force that propels its continuous innovation and development. Only through systematic computational thinking training can students truly comprehend the essence and principles of AI technology, thereby flexibly applying AI technology to solve practical problems and possessing the ability for continuous learning and innovation.

From the perspective of science and engineering, AI is essentially a deep extension of computational thinking in the field of problem-solving (as shown in Fig. 1). Building upon computational thinking, AI achieves a revolutionary breakthrough in traditional problem-solving paradigms by constructing self-optimizing algorithms and models. It no longer relies on manually preset rules or deterministic paths but employs data-driven approaches to automatically learn and optimize solution space search strategies, enabling exponential improvements in problem-solving efficiency. This intelligent method based on self-optimization not only inherits computational thinking's pursuit of formalization, abstraction, and automation but also propels the paradigm shift in problem-solving thinking from passive design to active evolution. Therefore, in AI general education, strengthening computational thinking training aids students in more deeply understanding and mastering the essence and principles of AI technology, laying a solid foundation for their subsequent learning and career development.

From the perspective of humanities and social sciences, AI serves as a paradigm for the fusion of data thinking and computational thinking (as shown in Fig. 2). In humanities and social sciences research, computational thinking emphasizes the identification, modeling, and deduction of data patterns, while AI, through advanced technologies such as deep learning, natural language processing, and large models, realizes intelligent mining and semantic parsing of large-scale unstructured data. This technological empowerment enables humanities and social sciences research to break through the limitations of traditional qualitative analysis and shift towards a new paradigm combining data-driven approaches with knowledge discovery. Therefore, in the AI general education of humanities and social sciences, equal importance should be attached to computational thinking

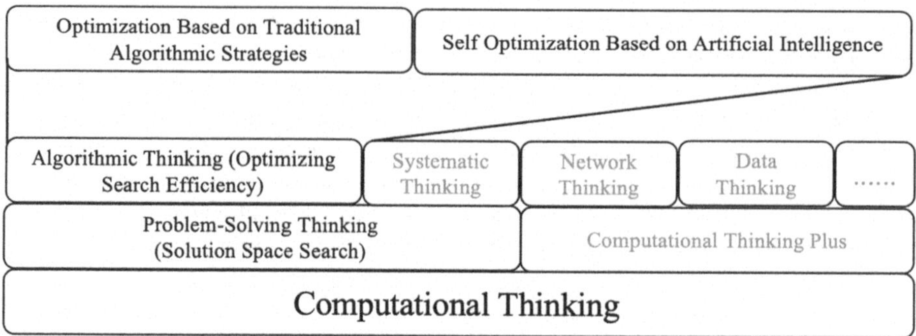

Fig. 1. Computational Thinking and Artificial Intelligence from the Perspective of Science and Engineering.

training. Through computational thinking training, students can more deeply understand and apply AI technology for data analysis and knowledge discovery, providing new perspectives and methods for humanities and social sciences research.

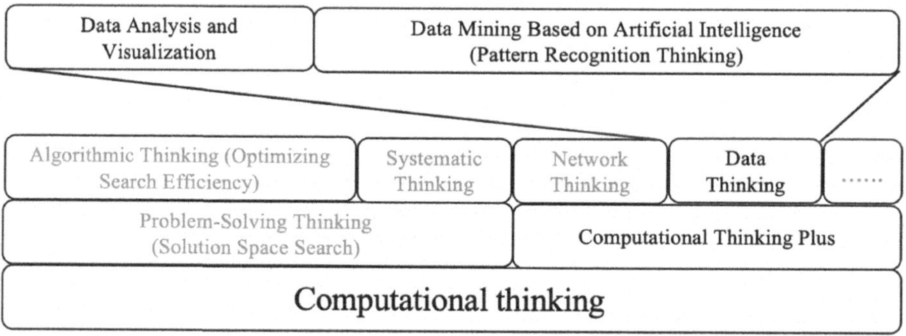

Fig. 2. Computational Thinking and Artificial Intelligence from the Perspective of Humanities and Social Sciences.

In summary, there is an inseparable and close relationship between AI general education and computational thinking. AI general education must be closely integrated with computational thinking training and achieve further expansion and deepening on its basis. Only in this way can students truly comprehend the essence and principles of AI technology, possess the ability for continuous learning and innovation, and lay a solid foundation for their future career development and social contributions.

3 The Integrated Practice of the Course "Introduction to Computing and Artificial Intelligence"

The course "Introduction to Computing and Artificial Intelligence" at Hunan University systematically carries out the integrated practice of computational thinking and AI literacy with general education as the carrier. Rooted in the core concept of "breaking barriers, strengthening foundations, and broadening horizons," the course forms a closed loop from top-level design to teaching implementation. By clarifying the course's positioning as a bridge in the general education system, it not only breaks down disciplinary and professional barriers to achieve knowledge inclusion but also anchors the "dual-core" goals of computational thinking and AI literacy. Through the construction of a three-horizontal and three-vertical course content system, coupled with a "knowledge, thinking, ability" trinity teaching paradigm, as well as a diversified and multi-dimensional evaluation system, it forms a four-dimensional linked operational framework led by the objective system, supported by the content system, underpinned by the methodological system, and guaranteed by the evaluation system (as shown in Fig. 3), promoting the organic integration of computational thinking and AI literacy in knowledge transmission, thinking training, and ability cultivation.

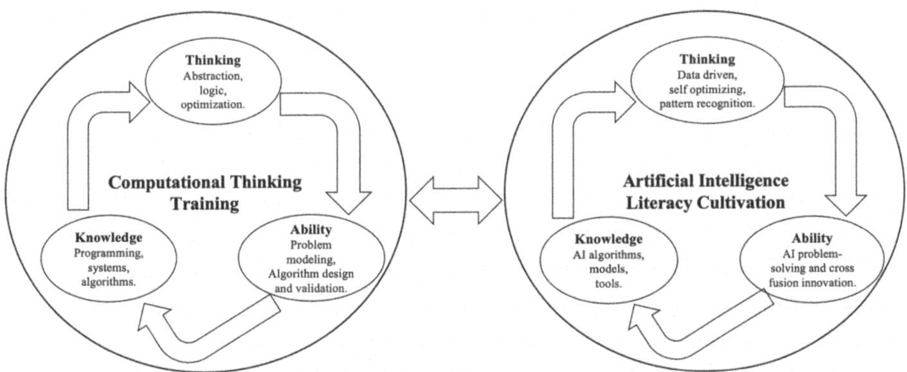

Fig. 3. Dual-Core Driven Course Objectives.

3.1 Course Background and Positioning

With the comprehensive penetration of AI technology from professional domains to various sectors of society, general education is facing the challenge of deep integration of "thinking, methods, and scenarios." Non-major students, while having access to AI tools, often struggle to apply computational thinking and AI technology to their professional practices due to a lack of methodological guidance.

Specifically, although science and engineering students can invoke AI tools, they often lack a deep understanding of the underlying principles and methodologies, limiting their ability to innovate and apply AI technology in depth. In contrast, humanities and social sciences students, while recognizing the value of AI technology, often face barriers in mastering its technical details and application methods, making it difficult to integrate AI technology into their research and practices. This dilemma not only hinders the effective popularization and application of AI technology but also restricts the cultivation of students' innovative thinking and practical abilities.

To address this issue, the course "Introduction to Computing and Artificial Intelligence" was designed with the goal of bridging this gap. It aims to cultivate students' computational thinking and AI literacy through a systematic and integrated teaching approach, enabling them to not only understand the principles and applications of AI technology but also possess the ability to apply computational thinking to solve complex problems and drive innovation.

3.2 Course Design and Implementation

Course Objective System. The course objective system is designed with a focus on "breaking barriers, strengthening foundations, and broadening horizons." It aims to cultivate students' computational thinking and AI literacy through a three-dimensional approach encompassing knowledge, thinking, and ability. Specifically, the course objectives include:

- *Knowledge Dimension.* Enabling students to systematically grasp the basic concepts, principles, and technologies of computing and AI, including algorithms, data structures, machine learning, and deep learning.
- *Thinking Dimension.* Cultivating students' computational thinking ability, enabling them to transform complex problems into computable models for solution and apply AI technology to analyze and solve practical problems.
- *Ability Dimension.* Enhancing students' practical abilities in programming, algorithm design, and AI application development, as well as their innovative thinking and interdisciplinary integration capabilities.

Course Content System. The course content system is constructed with a three-horizontal and three-vertical structure (as shown in Fig. 4). The three horizontal dimensions include basic knowledge, core technologies, and application scenarios, while the three vertical dimensions span science, engineering, and humanities and social sciences. This structure ensures the comprehensive coverage and progressive depth of the course content.

- *Basic Knowledge Dimension.* Covers the fundamental concepts and principles of computing and AI, including the history of computing, the essence of algorithms, and the basic principles of machine learning.
- *Core Technologies Dimension.* Focuses on the key technologies and methods of computing and AI, such as data structures, algorithms, neural networks, and natural language processing.
- *Application Scenarios Dimension.* Explores the practical applications of computing and AI in various fields, including intelligent manufacturing, smart cities, precise medicine, and smart education.

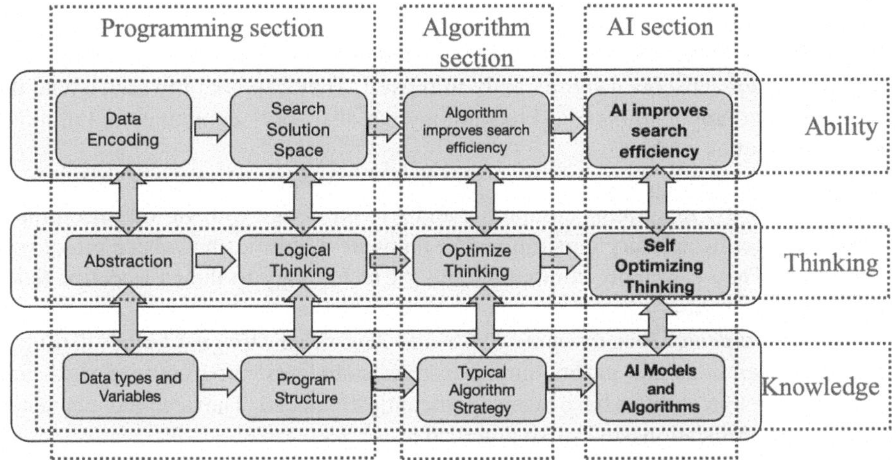

Fig. 4. The content structure of the three horizontal and three vertical courses

Course Teaching Paradigm. The course adopts a "knowledge, thinking, ability" trinity teaching paradigm, which integrates knowledge transmission, thinking training, and ability cultivation.

Knowledge Transmission. Through lectures, case studies, and practical operations, students systematically learn the basic concepts, principles, and technologies of computing and AI.
Thinking Training. By designing computational thinking training sessions and AI application projects, students' computational thinking ability and AI literacy are cultivated.
Ability Cultivation. Through programming exercises, algorithm design competitions, and AI application development projects, students' practical abilities and innovative thinking are enhanced.

Course Evaluation System. The course employs a diversified and multi-dimensional evaluation system that comprehensively assesses students' learning outcomes. The evaluation methods include:

- *Formative Evaluation.* Through regular quizzes, assignments, and class participation, students' learning process is continuously monitored and feedback is provided.
- *Summative Evaluation.* Through final exams and project presentations, students' comprehensive understanding and application abilities are evaluated.
- *Peer Evaluation.* Through group projects and peer reviews, students' collaborative abilities and communication skills are cultivated.

Course Implementation Effects. Since its implementation, the course "Introduction to Computing and Artificial Intelligence" has achieved remarkable results in cultivating students' computational thinking and AI literacy. The specific effects include:

- *Deepening the Cultivation of Students' Computational Thinking and AI Literacy.* Through systematic teaching and training, students' computational thinking ability and AI literacy have been significantly improved. They can not only understand the principles and applications of AI technology but also apply computational thinking to solve complex problems.
- *Promoting the Enhancement of Students' Interdisciplinary Integration and Innovation Abilities.* By integrating computing and AI knowledge with various disciplines, students' interdisciplinary integration and innovation abilities have been effectively cultivated. They can apply computing and AI technology to their respective fields and drive innovation.
- *Improving Students' Programming Skills and Algorithm Design Abilities.* Through practical operations and programming exercises, students' programming skills and algorithm design abilities have been significantly enhanced. They can independently develop AI applications and solve practical problems.
- *Cultivating Students' Understanding and Application Abilities of AI Technology.* By exploring the application scenarios of AI technology, students' understanding and application abilities of AI technology have been cultivated. They can recognize the value of AI technology and apply it to their respective fields.
- *Laying a Solid Foundation for Students' Future Career Development and Social Contributions.* By cultivating students' computational thinking and AI literacy, the course has laid a solid foundation for their future career development and social contributions. They can become innovative and interdisciplinary talents with both computational rationality and humanistic care.

4 Conclusion and Prospects

This paper takes the course "Introduction to Computing and Artificial Intelligence" at Hunan University as a case study to explore the practical path and effectiveness of integrating computational thinking and AI in general education. Through the construction of a "knowledge, thinking, ability" trinity teaching system, the course has achieved simultaneous improvement in students' computational thinking and AI literacy. The research not only contributes to deepening the theoretical understanding of the integrated education of computational thinking and AI but also provides valuable experience and references for other universities to carry out relevant teaching practices.

Looking ahead, we will continue to deepen the curriculum reform, optimize teaching content and methods, strengthen cooperation and exchanges with domestic and international universities and enterprises, explore more application scenarios adapted to the development of AI technology, and provide more diversified and personalized learning pathways for non-major students. We aim to assist them in becoming innovative and interdisciplinary talents with both computational rationality and humanistic care, thereby contributing to the development of AI technology and the progress of human society.

Acknowledgments. This study is funded by the Education Reform Project of Hunan Province, China in 2025.

Disclosure of Interests. The authors have no competing interests to declare that are relevant to the content of this article.

References

1. Lv, H.: The application of artificial intelligence in industrial automation. Inform. Record. Mater. **24**(8), 83–85 (2023)
2. Yu Zhou, Y., An, Q.L., Quan, Y., Han, X.: AI + Big Data" empowers smart cities and urban global digital transformation. Intell. Build. Smart Cit. **2025**(4), 6–10 (2025)
3. Tian, L., Ren, X., Zhengcheng, T.: Progress in the application of artificial intelligence, machine learning, and deep learning in medical diagnosis. Mod. Med. **52**(09), 1480–1484 (2024)
4. Li, W., Hei, X., Wang, L.: Exploration and practice of personalized teaching methods in the era of intelligent education plus. Comput. Educ. **2020**(10), 169–173 (2020)
5. Zhan, D., Wang, H.: The teaching content system of university computer courses oriented towards computational thinking. China Univ. Teach. **2014**(07), 59–66 (2014)

Construction and Practice of a Distinctive Science Popularization and Education Base for Artificial Intelligence and Future Transportation Technology—Taking Beijing Jiaotong University as an Example

Shouqiang Zhao[1,1(✉)], Ke Xiong[1], Wei Zhou[1,2], and Wenjuan Peng[1,2]

[1] School of Computer Science and Technology, Beijing Jiaotong University, Beijing, China
zhshq@bjtu.edu.cn

[2] Key Laboratory of Big Data and Artificial Intelligence in Transportation, Ministry of Education, Beijing, China

Abstract. In the era of deep integration between artificial intelligence and transportation technology, the establishment of specialized science popularization education bases has become a crucial pathway for enhancing public scientific literacy, promoting the spirit of science, and cultivating innovative thinking and capabilities. Beijing Jiaotong University Artificial Intelligence and Future Transportation Technology Science Popularization Education Base targets the cutting-edge technologies in the fields of artificial intelligence and intelligent transportation. It focuses on three key modules: facility and equipment construction, science popularization education courses development, and the establishment of science popularization volunteer teams and management systems, to build a distinctive and specialized science popularization education base. The successful implementation of science popularization activities such as "Science and Technology Activity Week" demonstrates the significant achievements of science popularization education bases in enhancing public awareness, cultivating talent, and fostering social collaboration. These initiatives have fostered a conducive learning atmosphere and academic environment, providing a replicable model for the development of distinctive science popularization platforms at higher education institutions.

Keywords: Artificial Intelligence · Future Transportation Technology · Science Popularization · Science Education Base

1 Introduction

In the context of the deep integration of artificial intelligence and transportation technology, the construction of specialized science education bases is an important means of promoting the integration of education, science and technology, and talent, and achieving the goal of becoming an education powerhouse. It is also an important path for enhancing public scientific literacy, promoting the spirit of science, and cultivating innovative

W. Hong et al. (Eds.): ICCSE 2025, CCIS 2761, pp. 38–51, 2026.
https://doi.org/10.1007/978-981-95-7731-6_4

thinking and abilities among young people. The Chinese government report [1] and State Council's "Outline of the National Plan for Improving Scientific Literacy (2021–2035)" [2] emphasize the need to vigorously strengthen the construction of science popularization bases, encourage and support all industries and departments to establish science popularization education and research bases, and improve science popularization service capabilities. With the advancement of this work, China's science popularization efforts have achieved remarkable results.

Science popularization activities have developed rapidly in fields such as artificial intelligence and intelligent transportation. In China, Southeast University Road Transportation Engineering Science Popularization Museum, through platforms such as a multi-degree-of-freedom driving simulation system and a road surface acceleration loading test system, receives over 10,000 visitors annually, establishing a typical path for "science popularization of research achievements." Baidu Apollo has established multiple Apollo Parks nationwide, integrating autonomous driving testing, science popularization education, and industrial incubation, driving the simultaneous advancement of technological implementation and public understanding [3]. Universities such as Tsinghua University and Sun Yat-sen University [4–8] have also achieved certain results in the popular science construction of artificial intelligence general education courses and interdisciplinary courses.

In other countries, science popularization work in artificial intelligence and intelligent transportation has shifted from single-technology demonstrations to a deep integration of "technology + ethics + education" [9, 10]. Leading companies and universities such as Toyota Motor Corporation in Japan, Stanford University in the United States, and Renault in France have enhanced public engagement through interactive games and scenario-based experiences, establishing best practices worth emulating (Table 1).

Universities are the convergence points of education, science and technology, and talent [11]. The School of Computer Science and Technology at Beijing Jiaotong University serves national strategic needs, leverages the disciplinary advantages of universities, and deeply integrates "education-research-practice" to establish Artificial Intelligence and Future Transportation Technology Science Popularization Education Base (hereinafter referred to as the "AITBase"). Focusing on three modules—facility and equipment construction, science popularization education courses construction, and science popularization volunteer team and management system construction—the AITBase transforms achievements and cutting-edge knowledge in the fields of artificial intelligence and intelligent transportation into engaging and interesting science popularization content, with the highlights of "in-depth integration of interdisciplinary disciplines, efficient transformation of industry, education, research and application, a well-structured educational system, and multi-dimensional science popularization approach",establishing a distinctive and professional science popularization brand and enhancing the public's understanding of the transportation industry. The successful hosting of a series of activities demonstrates the AITBase's significant achievements in promoting the coordinated development of science popularization and technological innovation, providing a replicable model for the construction of university-specific science popularization platforms.

Table 1. Comparison of implementation paths among different entities.

Entities	Implementation Paths
Tsinghua University	A comprehensive AI science popularization network covering the whole life cycle has been built through technology scenario-based approaches (such as laboratory openings and tool platforms), education stratification (from primary schools to vocational education), and diversified communication (live broadcasts, documentaries, and publications)
Sun Yat-sen University	A multi-level science popularization ecosystem has been constructed through open courses, laboratory experiences, interdisciplinary dialogues, and technology implementation cases
Toyota Motor Corporation	Automotive technologies, safety knowledge, and environmental protection concepts are disseminated to the public through diversified methods such as museums, educational programs, technical lectures, and school-enterprise cooperation, with a particular focus on children and adolescents' participation and practice
Stanford University	A multi-dimensional AI science popularization ecosystem covering all age groups and multiple fields has been established through various initiatives including open educational resources, interdisciplinary research transformation, community interaction projects, and media science popularization
Renault	With technology implementation scenarios at its core, AI technology is transformed into perceivable practical applications through school-enterprise cooperation, public experience, and industry collaboration

2 Development Strategy for the AITBase

2.1 Development Objectives

The AITBase at Beijing Jiaotong University leverages the research achievements and major engineering projects from the construction of the "Intelligent Transportation" first-class discipline. It also draws on platforms such as the national-level university computer teaching team, national- and municipal-level teaching achievements, national-level experimental teaching demonstration center, and national-level first-class undergraduate courses. The base aims to establish a leading science popularization benchmark for artificial intelligence and transportation technology with a domestic leading and international perspective.

The specific construction objectives of the AITBase are:

Social Objectives. Enhance the public's scientific understanding and safety consciousness of artificial intelligence and transportation technology;

Educational Objectives. Provide tiered science popularization education resources for teenagers, college students, and industry practitioners;

Research Objectives. Build a virtuous ecosystem of "research feeding back into science popularization and science popularization promoting innovation," promote the transformation of technological achievements, and drive "industry-academia-research and application" collaborative innovation.

2.2 Construction Framework

The construction approach for the AITBase is as follows: supported by first-class teaching and research achievements, with artificial intelligence thinking, computational thinking, future transportation, and rail transit as the core, the base will develop cutting-edge scientific and technological exhibition content, create high-quality science popularization resources and courses, and conduct diverse science popularization activities targeting teenagers, college students, the general public, and education volunteers, as shown in Fig. 1.

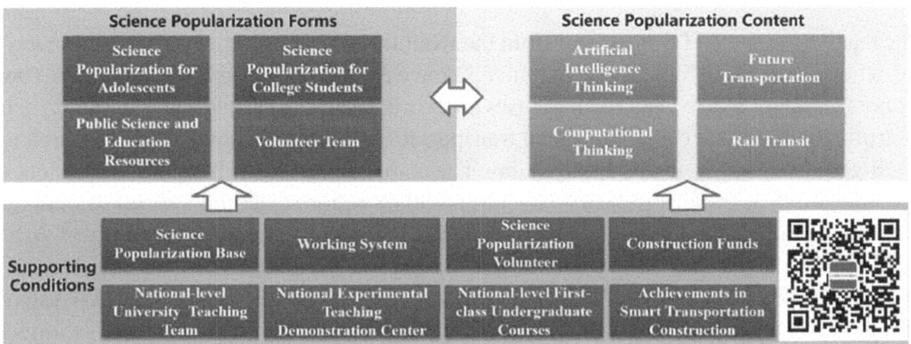

Fig. 1. Construction framework for the AITBase [12].

In-Depth Integration of Interdisciplinary Disciplines. Relying on the achievements of Beijing Jiaotong University in building the first-class discipline of "intelligent transportation", the AITBase has deeply integrated artificial intelligence with transportation technology, forming four core science popularization contents. this cross-disciplinary integration is not a simple superposition, but through resources such as virtual simulation platforms, it directly applies machine vision, large models, etc. to specific transportation scenarios such as high-speed rail operation and maintenance, and unmanned driving.

Efficient Transformation of Industry, Education, Research and Application. The AITBase directly transforms the scientific research and teaching achievements of colleges and universities into science popularization resources. The high-speed rail track inspection virtual simulation system and unmanned driving online courses developed by the base are all derived from scientific research projects and teaching courses, ensuring that the science popularization content always keeps up with cutting-edge technologies.

A Well-Structured Educational System. The AITBase has designed differentiated activities for four groups: teenagers, college students, the public, and educational volunteers, building a multi-dimensional educational system. Meanwhile, in the Course Construction, It Emphasizes Hierarchical Education Design. Taking "AI + Railway Maintenance" Virtual Experience and Exploration course as an example, it has built three levels: "cognitive experiments", "comprehensive experiments", and "innovative experiments", with the difficulty of experiments increasing from easy to difficult and the content progressing step by step.

Multi-Dimensional Science Popularization Approach. The AITBase pioneered a three-in-one science popularization model of "physical scenes + virtual simulation + online resources". It integrates the high-speed railway track condition comprehensive detection system, virtual simulation experiments, and study manuals, forming a closed loop of "experience - understanding - application".

2.3 Construction Content

The teachers at the AITBase are all from the front lines of teaching, research, and practical experiments at the School of Computer Science & Technology and the Jeme Tien Yow Honors College. The teacher team focuses on the cutting-edge technologies in fields such as artificial intelligence and intelligent transportation, conducting innovative research in intelligent technology and its applications. The team adheres to the integration of science and education, as well as industry-education collaboration, teaching a series of courses including "University Computer Fundamentals," "Principles and Applications of Artificial Intelligence," and "Comprehensive Training in Computational Thinking." Additionally, the team collaborates deeply with enterprises to build an educational ecosystem based on advanced enterprise technologies and platforms, forming a cooperative model of joint talent cultivation, platform co-construction, process co-management, and mutual benefit for all parties.

Based on the achievements of the AITBase teaching team in scientific research, teaching, and school-enterprise cooperation, as well as the need to establish a sound grassroots science popularization service system, the construction of the AITBase is divided into three major modules:

Facility and Equipment Construction. Traditional computer lab spaces are transformed into diverse demonstration areas focused on intelligent technology, while introducing cutting-edge scientific research projects and tangible achievements from school-enterprise collaborations for physical displays and interactive experiences, creating a professional, engaging, and highly interactive experimental and practical demonstration zone.

Science Popularization Education Courses Construction. The team's abundant teaching achievements will be transformed into engaging and interesting science popularization content suitable for students of different stages. teaching formats will be optimized, with learning content delivered through model building, virtual simulation, and practical experiments, enabling the public to more intuitively understand the practical applications of artificial intelligence in the transportation field [13].

Science Popularization Volunteer Team and Management System Construction. Mobilize more teachers, students, and enterprise technical personnel to join the science popularization volunteer service team, improve the science popularization volunteer service management system, and promote the professionalization, standardization, and normalization of science popularization activities.

3 Construction of the AITBase

The AITBase is primarily located in Room 101 of Yifu Building at Beijing Jiaotong University, featuring five core demonstration areas for regular equipment displays; one discussion area and one comprehensive activity area for small-scale discussions and lectures; and three large screens for course instruction and the playback of science popularization resources. The specific layout of the exhibition hall is shown in Fig. 2. The following sections provide an introduction to the five core demonstration areas.

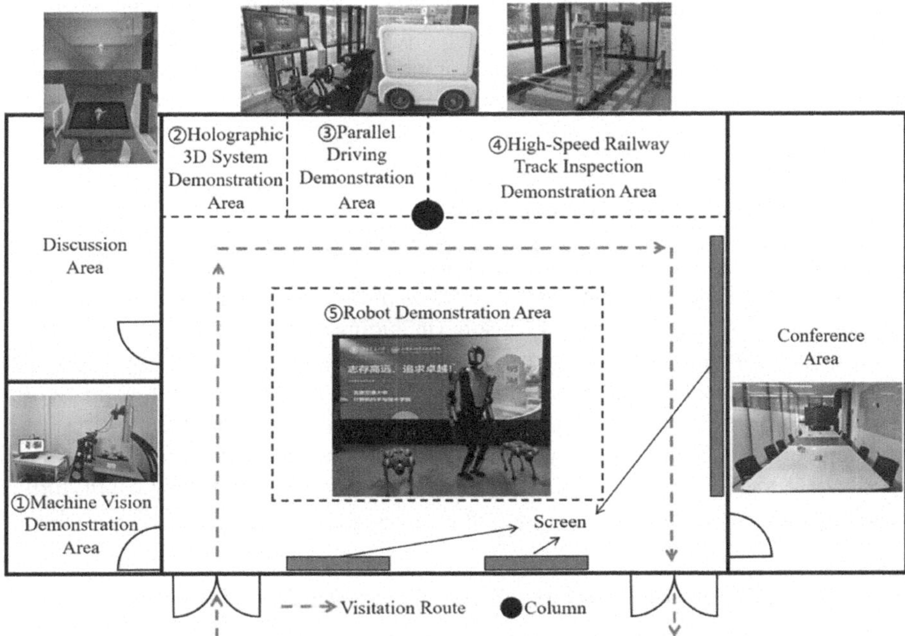

Fig. 2. Layout of Science Popularization Activity Areas.

3.1 Machine Vision Demonstration Area

The machine vision line scan experimental platform in the machine vision demonstration area features a mechanically adjustable structure that can be slid along tracks, enabling the line scan camera to be perfectly paired with various light sources. This maximizes the application advantages of the line scan camera, capturing clear and complete images, which is of significant importance for the selection of industrial cameras, light sources, and algorithm research. This platform focuses on surface inspection applications and has important applications in fields such as electronic/semiconductor products, printing, textiles, and track surface damage detection. The experimental platform is used for both science popularization demonstrations and equipment selection for track surface damage detection-related projects. Through this platform, teenagers can deepen their understanding of industrial vision inspection by learning about the selection and position adjustment of line scan cameras and light sources, as well as the matching of line frequency and movement speed.

3.2 Holographic 3D System Demonstration Area

The holographic 3D system consists of a cabinet, display equipment, holographic glass, and a video source. The cabinet provides support and protection, the display equipment plays content, the holographic glass is the key to imaging, and the video source provides the material. The core principle of the holographic 3D system is holographic refraction imaging, which enables 360-degree all-around display. Teenagers can use this system to learn about optical principles and holographic projection technology, spark creativity, and explore the application of holographic 3D technology integrated with artificial intelligence.

3.3 Parallel Driving Demonstration Area

The parallel driving system is an advanced driving solution that combines autonomous driving and remote control technology. It relies on high-speed communication networks, high-precision GPS, and a series of sensors (including cameras, lidar, etc.) to achieve remote control and autonomous driving of vehicles. The system covers key knowledge points and applications related to autonomous driving, including perception, prediction, planning, and control, to meet the needs of various scenarios such as education, research, and competitions. Through the parallel driving demonstration system, teenagers can experience vehicle driving in a safe environment via the parallel driving cabin, further deepening their understanding of autonomous driving and remote control technology.

3.4 High-Speed Railway Track Inspection Demonstration Area

The high-speed railway track condition comprehensive detection system integrates 2D line-scan and 3D cameras on a customized platform, enabling high-definition acquisition of 2D and 3D images with sub-millimeter precision, particularly in switch areas. Combined with intelligent defect detection models, it achieves rapid and precise identification of high-speed railway track defects, including switch detection, fastener damage detection, and rail surface scuffing detection, providing timely, accurate, and effective data analysis support for railway infrastructure maintenance and repair. This system also originates from practical needs and is a model of the integration of science and education. Through the high-speed rail track condition comprehensive inspection system, teenagers can understand the structural characteristics of high-speed rail track components and the working principles of typical track inspection sensors, fostering a sense of responsibility and mission to participate in national strategies such as "Transportation Powerhouse" and "High-Speed Rail Going Global."

3.5 Robot Demonstration Area

Robotics is a multidisciplinary technology that integrates mechanical engineering, electronics, computer science, artificial intelligence, sensor technology, control theory, and other fields. The Robot Demonstration Area showcases the most cutting-edge robotics technologies, from agile movement to precise sensing, showcasing the charm of science and technology. The AITBase has designed and implemented applications such as robot-guided tours, robot interaction, robot group dances, and robot dog dances through motion control and algorithm design, showcasing their rich functionality and intelligent interaction capabilities. Through the robot demonstration platform, students can observe, learn, and interact, fully experiencing the unique charm of robotics technology. Through practical experience, they can grasp the logic of robot programming and embark on their own journey of scientific exploration.

4 Science Popularization Education Courses Construction

In response to the needs of primary and secondary schools, youth palaces, communities, and other organizations, the AITBase has developed science popularization education courses for young people, leveraging our university's strengths in "intelligent transportation" and high-quality scientific research and educational resources in computer science and artificial intelligence. The five courses are divided into three levels—basic cognition, comprehensive experimentation, and innovative design—based on different age and skill levels. The content progresses from simple to complex, with experiments advancing step by step, and the knowledge is interconnected and builds upon one another. The basic cognition level aims to establish technical perception and interest initiation, focusing on "observation - experience - questioning" to ensure that the content conforms to the cognitive characteristics of young teenagers and avoids abstract theories. The comprehensive experimentation level is intended to deepen technical understanding and practical ability, adopting the "task driven + group cooperation" mode, equipped with experimental manuals and step - by - step guidance videos, so that teenagers can master the use of technical tools in practice. The innovative design level is to cultivate technical innovation and problem - solving thinking, guiding teenagers to be oriented by the needs of real scenarios, put forward personalized solutions and implement them by hand.

4.1 "AI + Railway Maintenance" Virtual Experience and Exploration Course

Teenagers visit the AITBase to view physical models and use our university's self-developed "Visual Perception Virtual Simulation Experiment for High-Speed Railway Track Inspection" on computers to experience the spirit of high-speed rail, learn about the composition of railway infrastructure, common inspection sensors, and inspection methods. They analyze typical track defects using AI technology, conduct virtual inspections of track health status, and explore the practical application and operational processes of artificial intelligence in railway transportation. The course encourages students to actively learn scientific knowledge, stimulates their curiosity, enriches their learning experience, and promotes the development of their scientific literacy.

4.2 "AI + Railway Inspection Vehicle" Model Course

A railway inspection vehicle is a tool for intelligent sensing, status analysis, and intelligent decision-making regarding the operational status of transportation infrastructure, involving technologies such as digital twin, the Internet of Things, big data, cloud/edge computing, and artificial intelligence. The AITBase has developed a cardboard model of the rail inspection vehicle based on the actual vehicle architecture. In the course, professional teachers explain the composition, working principles, and specific applications of the rail inspection vehicle, followed by students assembling the cardboard model. Finally, teachers connect the open-source hardware with the cardboard model to demonstrate the inspection process of the rail inspection vehicle, allowing teenagers to experience and familiarize themselves with the development process involving programming languages, modeling, coding, debugging, and execution.

4.3 Computational Thinking Exploration Course

The course starts with elementary and junior high school mathematics knowledge familiar to students, and through mathematical modeling, algorithm design, and problem-solving processes, it gradually leads students into the world of computer science. At the same time, university resources such as the ACM competition platform are opened to students to broaden their scientific horizons and improve their thinking and hands-on abilities.

4.4 Autonomous Driving Exploration Course

The course guides teenagers in exploring the various functions of autonomous driving, such as perception, planning, prediction, control, mapping, and road testing. Through watching the science popularization video "Exploring Autonomous Driving and Artificial Intelligence," utilizing laboratory software and virtual simulation tools, and using the textbook "Guidance on College Students' Innovative Experiments—Typical Applications of Autonomous Driving[ISBN 978-7-5121-5038-6],"teenagers are exposed to college students' experimental projects, learn new technologies and methods, and enhance their computational thinking, artificial intelligence thinking, and information processing abilities.

4.5 Digital Literacy and Competencies Course

In the digital age, countries around the world place great importance on improving the digital literacy and skills of their citizens. In this course, professional teachers interpret

"Introduction to Digital Literacy and Skills[ISBN 978-7-302-66645-5]" and "University Computer (7th Edition)[ISBN 978-7-04-059050-0]"and interact with teenagers through Q&A and discussion to explore the specific content of digital literacy and skills and the development direction of information technology.

5 Science Popularization Volunteer Team and Management System Construction

5.1 Science Popularization Volunteer Team Construction

Strengthening the construction of full-time and part-time science popularization teams is an important means to enhance the science popularization capabilities at the grassroots level [14]. The AITBase integrates the college's faculty, corporate technicians, and university student volunteers into the science popularization faculty team, forming a highly qualified science popularization force. The college's faculty, with their solid theoretical foundation, can inject professional depth into science popularization content; corporate technical personnel combine industrial and practical experience to make science popularization knowledge more closely aligned with real-world application scenarios; university student volunteers bring youthful vitality and innovative thinking to science popularization activities, introducing novel formats.

Expert Lectures and Professional Training. Invite authoritative experts and prominent figures in the science popularization field from both within and outside the college to deliver lectures, sharing cutting-edge developments, latest research findings, and advanced science popularization experiences in the field, while conducting systematic training to enhance the team's professional capabilities;

Corporate Partnership and Brand Building. The AITBase collaborates with well-known companies such as Baidu and VIA Technologies to invite corporate technical experts to introduce cutting-edge scientific knowledge and jointly build a science popularization brand;

Student Volunteer Program Development. Collaborate with the China Volunteer Service Foundation on the "Science and Technology Innovation Star Program" to form a college student science popularization volunteer service team and enhance students' science popularization work capabilities through practical experience.

5.2 Management System Construction

To ensure the safe, efficient, and orderly conduct of science popularization activities, the AITBase has established a science popularization work management system based on the school's laboratory safety work regulations, encompassing "safety and openness, activity reception, and emergency response plans." For equipment with potential operational risks, in addition to physical isolation and technical precautions, volunteers are also arranged to provide one-on-one management. Additionally, the AITBase has established a dynamic assessment mechanism to regularly evaluate the performance of science volunteers and the effectiveness of science popularization activities, rewarding those who perform exceptionally well.

The AITBase arranges teaching skills training courses, taught by senior teachers, to enhance team members' communication skills, classroom management abilities, and interaction capabilities with audiences. Furthermore, the AITBase organizes team members to visit outstanding science popularization bases for learning and exchange, promoting knowledge sharing and idea exchange among individuals with diverse backgrounds. This helps them continuously update their knowledge structures, broaden their science popularization horizons, and comprehensively enhance their professional competencies.

6 Science Popularization Achievements and Social Impact

6.1 Honors Achieved

Over the past decade, the AITBase has focused on the fields of artificial intelligence and intelligent transportation, consistently organizing a series of diverse activities aimed at fostering a spirit of scientific inquiry, disseminating scientific knowledge, and promoting scientific thinking among students of all ages. These include events such as "Science and Technology Activity Week," "National Science Popularization Day," and "National Youth University Science Camp." Each year, these initiatives reach over ten thousand participants both online and offline, fostering a conducive learning environment and academic atmosphere. The science popularization efforts have achieved significant results, been well-received by collaborating organizations, and have been recognized with multiple awards from higher-level authorities.

In 2023, the AITBase was recognized as a Beijing Science Popularization Base (2023–2025). In 2024, Beijing Jiaotong University was awarded the title of the first batch of Haidian District "Outstanding Innovative Talent Training Bases for Youth." In 2025, the AITBase was selected as one of the 15th batch of social classroom resource units for primary and secondary school students in Haidian District, Beijing. AITBase has become a leading science education base in China dedicated to disseminating scientific ideas, promoting the scientific spirit, cultivating innovative thinking and capabilities, and specializing in "artificial intelligence and future transportation." As shown in Fig. 3.

a)Designated as Beijing Municipal Science Popularization Base (2023-2025)

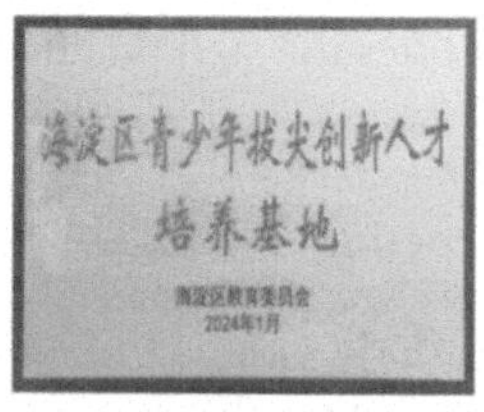

b)Selected as Haidian District Youth Elite Innovation Talent

c)Selected as Haidian District Primary and Secondary School Social Classroom Resource Unit

Fig. 3. Awarded to the AITBase.

6.2 Case and Impact

Taking a recent activity as an example, to celebrate the ninth National Science and Technology Workers' Day and promote scientific spirit and popularize scientific knowledge, the AITBase organized an "AI +" exploration and practice activities on May 25, 2025 [15]. The event was themed "Committed to Innovative Development and Building a Science and Technology Powerhouse." Through projects such as revealing the secrets of intelligent systems (robot interaction, robot dog performances, and unmanned vehicle experiences), taking "inspection vehicles" home (AI + track maintenance and model assembly), and college student science and technology project exhibitions, the event created an immersive AI science popularization feast for young people, allowing the general public to experience the charm of science and technology up close. The event was organized and implemented by six teachers from the AITBase and nearly 20 volunteers from the Science and Technology Innovation Star Program. Over 240 primary, secondary, and university students, as well as members of the public from various districts in Beijing, participated in the event, as shown in Fig. 4.

a) Robot performances and interactive activities

b) Explanation of the principles of the track inspection system

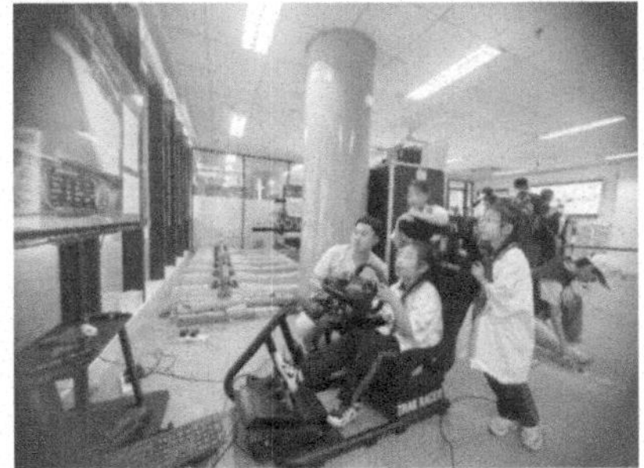

c) Parallel driving system experience

d) Model building activity

Fig. 4. 2025 Science and Technology Activities Week activity site.

The event was highly popular among teenagers and members of the public. Post-event surveys indicated that the activity achieved conducive results in terms of science knowledge dissemination and interest cultivation, with over 90% of participants stating that the content was innovative, rich in scientific elements and knowledge points, and expressing a desire to continue participating in AITBase activities. The event was reported by China Science News (ScienceNet) and the official website of Beijing Jiaotong University.

7 Conclusion

The establishment of the Beijing Jiaotong University Artificial Intelligence and Future Transportation Technology Science Popularization Education Base represents a successful practice of universities leveraging their disciplinary advantages to advance science popularization initiatives. The development of university-specific science popularization platforms must closely integrate disciplinary strengths, address public knowledge gaps, and employ diverse formats and tiered educational designs to achieve dual objectives of science popularization and talent cultivation. The AITBase integrates research achievements and educational resources from the fields of "artificial intelligence" and "intelligent transportation," establishing a virtuous ecosystem where "research supports science popularization, and science popularization promotes innovation." This has formed a complete science popularization chain encompassing "technology display—practical experience—knowledge dissemination—talent cultivation." In the future, the AITBase will continue to play a bridging role between industry, academia, research, and application, contributing to enhancing societal understanding of artificial intelligence and transportation technology, cultivating innovative talent, and serving national strategic needs. Its construction experience can serve as a replicable reference model for similar universities.

Acknowledgments. This study is funded by the National Computer Science Top Student Innovation Laboratory Equipment Update Project (Project No.: 269179529).

Disclosure of Interests. The authors have no competing interests to declare that are relevant to the content of this article.

References

1. Report of the 20th National Congress of the Communist Party of China. http://www.gov.cn/xinwen/2022-10/25/content_5721685.htm. Accessed 25 Dec 2024
2. State Council of the People's Republic of China: Outline of the National Plan for Scientific Literacy Literacy. http://www.gov.cn/zhengce/content/2021-06/25/content_5620813.htm. Accessed 25 Dec 2024
3. Baidu Builds World's Largest Autonomous Driving Test Base. https://www.apollo.auto/news/10544. Accessed 25 Dec 2024
4. Tsinghua University Department of Computer Science Artificial Intelligence General Education (AIGE) Research Center Officially Established. https://www.tsinghua.edu.cn/info/1182/118137.htm. Accessed 25 Dec 2024
5. Notice on the Publicity of the Recognition Results of the First Batch of Off-campus Science Education Bases for Primary and Secondary Schools in High-tech Zone, https://www.zhuhai-hitech.gov.cn/gxxw/tzgg/content/post_3755864.html. Accessed 25 Dec 2024
6. Jia, G.: Exploration on construction of universal science popularization innovation system in Nankai University. Tianjin Sci. Technol. **48**(6), 59–62 (2021). https://doi.org/10.14099/j.cnki.tjkj.2021.06.018

7. Lin, C., Li, Q., Yang, D., et al.: Construction and practice of science bases in universities under the background of "New Engineering". Sci. Popul. Res. **15**(6), 75–80+104 (2020). https://doi.org/10.19293/j.cnki.1673-8357.2020.06.010
8. Ling, H., Zhou, Y., Zhang, Y., et al.: Exploration and practice on work of popular science education base in Peking University. Exp. Technol. Manag. **33**(10), 241–244+248 (2016). https://doi.org/10.16791/j.cnki.sjg.2016.10.060
9. Fang, X.: UK and US strategic action of developing AI and the inspiration to China. Dev. Res. **4**, 23–30 (2018)
10. Zhao, Y., Ju, S., Guo, J., et al.: Analysis of science communication policies in developed countries and its enlightenment to China. Sci. Popul. Res. **17**(3), 72–82, 104, 109 (2022)
11. Li, C., Liu, L., Zhao, J., et al.: Exploration on promotion of popular science by laboratories in universities. Lab. Res. Explor. **38**(3), 214–217 (2019)
12. Zhou, W., Li, Q., Zhang, Y.: University information technology general courses assisting youth science education. Softw. Guide **23**(8), 32–36 (2024)
13. Dai, T., Huang, X.: Science popularization construction in the digital age: problems and paths. Sci. Educ. Prim. Second. Schools **2**(2), 35–40 (2025)
14. Li, W., Chen, J.: Exploration and practice of strengthening the work for science popularization in colleges and universities: a case of Jilin University. Association **1**, 49–53 (2020)
15. Science and Technology Week Collection: "AI+" Immersive Experience of Science and Technology Charm. https://cs.bjtu.edu.cn/kpjd/kphd/2a7bd676bb2646a3a4990ea5be1be2f1.htm. Accessed 25 Dec 2024

Design and Practice of Railway Track Visual Detection Science Popularization Teaching Aids for Youngsters

Wenjuan Peng[1,2](✉), Bohong Liu[3], Yixuan Zhou[4], Jiatu Yan[4], Wei Zhou[1,2], and Yueyang Cao[5]

[1] School of Computer Science and Technology, Beijing Jiaotong University, Beijing, China
wjpeng@bjtu.edu.cn

[2] Key Laboratory of Big Data and Artificial Intelligence in Transportation, Ministry of Education, Beijing Jiaotong University, Beijing, China

[3] School of Traffic and Transportation, Beijing Jiaotong University, Beijing, China

[4] School of Electronic and Information Engineering, Beijing Jiaotong University, Beijing 100044, China

[5] VIA Technologies (China) Co., Ltd. VIA Artificial Intelligence Research Institute, Beijing 100084, China

Abstract. Many science-education tools lag behind current computer-vision practice and offer limited interactivity. We introduce a simple, lightweight, and modular teaching aid for railway track detection that integrates low-cost hardware with on-device vision models to enable intuitive visualization and multi-dimensional interaction. The research includes: (1) Design of a compact electromechanical platform by integrating a detection vehicle and track modules with a power unit, enabling fast assembly and part replacement; (2) Implementation of a recognition algorithm based on the Maix-I development board, where a streamlined program for visual track detection was developed. At the algorithmic level, we fine-tuned a MobileNet_0.75 model and established a complete pipeline of training, evaluation, and local deployment through the nncase toolchain. This approach demonstrates extensibility across both software and hardware platforms. The resulting educational tool has been validated through multiple outreach activities and has received widespread acclaim from educators.

Keyword: Science Popularization Education · Teaching Aids Development · Railway Track Visual Detection

1 Introduction

Under the strategic background of building a strong science and technology country, China has issued the *Outline of the Plan for Action on the Scientific Quality of the Whole Nation* and a series of related policies to advance the popularization of science and technology [1–3]. These initiatives underscore the growing importance of science education for the public. However, current science popularization efforts, particularly

W. Hong et al. (Eds.): ICCSE 2025, CCIS 2761, pp. 52–63, 2026.
https://doi.org/10.1007/978-981-95-7731-6_5

regarding teaching aids, still suffer from limited interactivity and technological lag [4–6]. With the development of intelligent railway transportation, visual detection technology has become increasingly critical for railway operation and maintenance. However, as this technology requires interdisciplinary integration of optics, computing, mechanical control, and related fields, it remains highly specialized and abstract, posing significant challenges for effective introduction into youth-oriented science education. Existing teaching aids in this field are mostly based on static models [6], virtual experiments [7, 8] and explanatory videos [9]. These approaches dynamic simulation and interactive presentation of the detection process, making it difficult for young people to understand its principles. To address this challenge, this study proposes an innovative science popularization scheme of "technology simplification - layered practice". Specifically, we realizes the effective transformation of professional technology into science popularization teaching aids by simplifying the process of visual detection of tracks. We also developing low-threshold and highly interactive dynamic block model teaching aids. Furthermore, a step-by-step teaching contents is designed in combination with the Compulsory Education Science Curriculum Standards [10].

2 Design of Railway Visual Detection Teaching Aids

Railway visual detection technology is a cutting-edge approach that integrates machine vision, deep learning, and 3D reconstruction. It enables non-contact, all-weather, and high-precision monitoring of railway geometric parameters, surface defects, and the condition of key components. The core of the technology lies in combining industrial-grade optical equipment (such as line array cameras, surface array cameras, and LIDAR) with intelligent detection algorithms, thereby overcoming the limitations of inefficiency, strong subjectivity, high cost, and limited coverage of traditional manual detection. As a result, visual detection has become an indispensable component of the intelligent operation and maintenance of railway transportation.

The virtual simulation platform is one of the most important teaching tools. Our institution has independently developed the "Virtual Simulation Experimental System of Visual Perception for High-speed Railway Detection", which help students understand both the structural characteristics of high-speed rail track components and the working principle of typical track detection sensors. The system also enables them to acquire knowledge related to pattern recognition and large language model in the context of railway defect identification, along with essential data processing and analysis techniques. The goal is to train students in addressing the operational requirements of high-speed railway detection while familiarizing them with the forefront of Internet of Things (IoT) technology. The system strengthens the students' ability to analyze the structural features and technical parameters of different types of sensor components. Furthermore, it cultivates initial competencies in dismantling and assessing the influence of multifactorial, complex engineering issues.

To realize the science popularization transformation of railway visual detection technology, the core components of actual detection scenarios—including hardware, software, motion platforms, and railway infrastructure—must be simplified for teaching aids. By disassembling and organizing these elements, we established the overall architecture (Fig. 1) of the proposed teaching aid. The system consists of three parts: hardware, software, and electromechanical structure. In the hardware part, the Maix-I development board and camera are used to form the image acquisition and processing unit, replacing the high-performance server and industrial camera; at the software level, instead of complex models such as ResNet, a fine-tuned MobileNet_0.75 [11] network is employed to achieve fast and efficient detection; and the electromechanical structure contains the motion platform--detection vehicle, PLA material track, power unit, and other accessories. These three modules work together to form a compact visual detection system. The software and hardware collaborate to process visual information, while the electromechanical unit provides realistic motion and track representation. Combined, they create a complete railway detection scene that effectively supports defect detection tasks in an accessible and educational form.

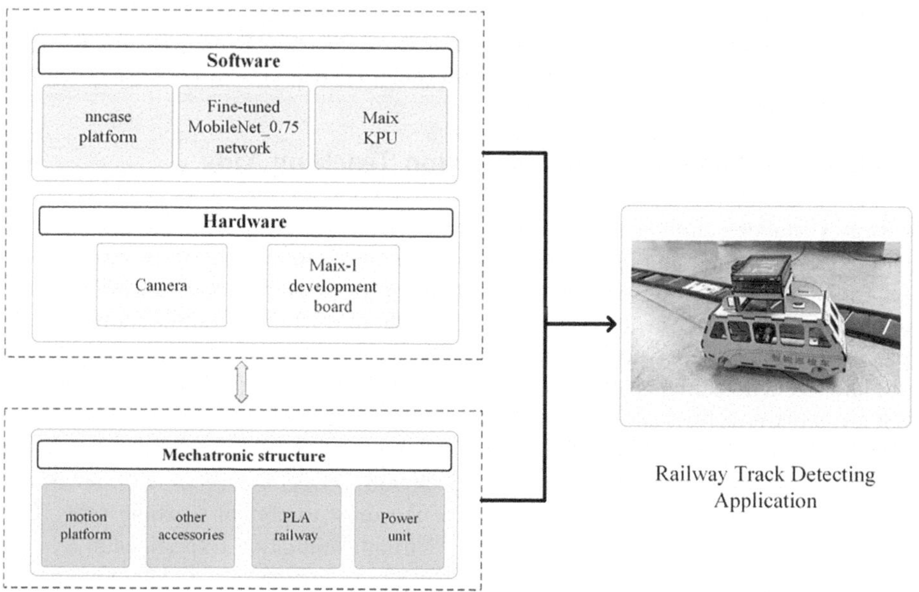

Fig. 1. Science Teaching Aids Design.

3 Design and Development of Electromechanical Structures of Teaching Aids

The electromechanical components of this system adopt the design principle of "functional visibility" to modularize and reconstruct the core components of the professional track detection equipment. As shown in Fig. 2, the system consists of three major functional units: (1) The detection apparatus, constructed from laser-cut wooden components in a modular block design to enable rapid assembly/disassembly; (2) The track infrastructure, manufactured through additive 3D printing technology with modular interlocking segments; (3) The drive mechanism, integrating a high-torque motor, precision gear assembly, and adjustable illumination system to ensure stable detection vehicle operation and optimal image capture quality. Together, these components form the hardware platform that supports the subsequent algorithm verification process.

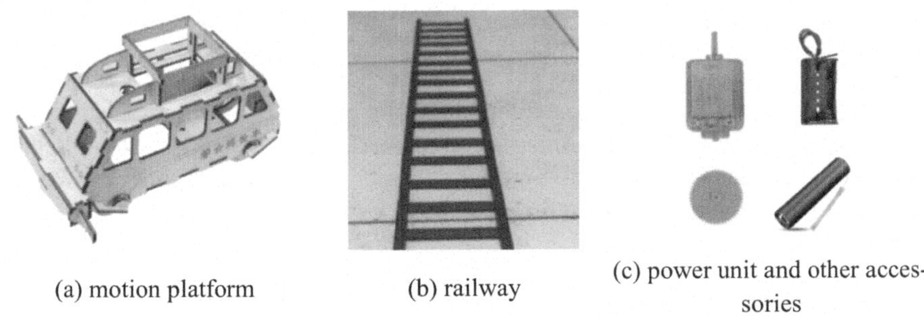

(a) motion platform (b) railway (c) power unit and other accessories

Fig. 2. Electromechanical Components.

To meet the practical needs of popularizing science education, we refer to the appearance of "Dr. Huang of the High Speed Railway (High-speed integrated detection vehicle)", and design a motion platform model of detection equipment based on the modular design concept - the building block detection vehicle. The shell of the vehicle is composed of laser-cut wooden boards, which can be quickly disassembled and assembled with bare hands through a plug-in structure, and the entire assembly can be completed without special tools. This design reduces production costs while offering students to understand the internal structure of the vehicle intuitively through the complete process of "hands-on assembly - functional debugging". The process is supported by detailed graphical tutorials that guide students on the installation positions of each component and their interface matching, allowing them to naturally grasp the hardware composition of track detection equipment.

The track model, produced through 3D printing, is designed with modular assembly of the sleeper and side rails is realized through parametric design. In many iterations of debugging, this paper optimizes the tolerance of the joint structure, so that the track can be firmly spliced and can be quickly disassembled, and at the same time to ensure that the detection vehicle in a straight line running smoothly. The track is simple, portable and suitable for mass production, making it suitable for subsequent participation in many science popularization activities. To address the issue of track damage in teaching scenarios, PLA material was finally used to print the tracks, which significantly improves durability while retaining the lightweight characteristics (weight of a single track is < 200g). The surface of the track image is matte-finished surface treatment and placed on the "sleeper", which provides a standardized experimental environment for the visual detection algorithm and avoids the interference of environmental factors on the recognition results.

In general, the track has the characteristics of simple, lightweight, easy to splice and so on. Due to resource constraints, only flat straight railway have been produced, and more rail scenes such as curved railway and railway on vertical curves can be expanded in the future, so as to facilitate the participants to understand more intuitively the actual situation of the railroad operation scene.

The drive mechanism employs a high-torque motor combined with a custom precision gear set to ensure the detection vehicle moves at a slow, uniform speed, enabling the camera to capture images accurately. The system features an adjustable light source that can be switched between two lighting modes via a physical switch, ensuring high-quality image acquisition in various environments. Safety is a key consideration in the mechanical design: all transmission components are enclosed within a sealed housing, and exposed interfaces use an asymmetric connector design (such as trapezoidal-shaped plugs) combined with anti-reverse circuitry. These physical and electrical safeguards prevent incorrect connections and eliminate the risk of misuse.

4 Development of Railway Detection Vehicle System

4.1 Hardware Design

In hardware selection, this study focuses on key criteria such as computational performance, size adaptability, and teaching friendliness. After careful consideration, we selects the Maix-I development board as the core processor. The board integrates a dual-core RISC-V processor and a 0.25 TOPS KPU accelerator, and realizes sufficient visual processing power in a compact size of $64 \times 64 \times 21$ mm, which is fully adapted to the top frame of the detection detection vehicle model. Maix-I supports the MicroPython programming environment, which significantly reduces the learning threshold for students, whereas the rich GPIO/UART/I2C interfaces provide sufficient flexibility for sensor expansion. The 8 MB of RAM and 16 MB of Flash storage in Maix-I meet the requirements of lightweight model deployment.

Maix-I achieves an impressive balance across several critical aspects. In terms of performance, it is fully capable of meeting the common requirements of science teaching, such as data collection, basic programming control, or simple sensor applications. Maix-I also operates stably, delivering accurate experimental results and a smooth user experience for students. In terms of size, its compact and well-designed structure makes it easy to carry and store, making it adaptable to a variety of environments, including classrooms, laboratories, or even outdoor teaching environments.

Moreover, Maix-I stands out for its cost-effectiveness, making it an ideal choice for bulk purchasing. This cost-effectiveness is a key advantage for educational institutions at all levels, from primary school science labs to university practical classrooms. Its low price point allows institution to acquire a sufficient number of units without exceeding their budgets, ensuring that every student has access to hands-on experience. This addresses the issue of limited equipment impeding the learning process, allowing each student to actively engage in practical experiments and projects.

4.2 Software Design

Data Preparation. In this study, the open-source railway surface injury dataset [12] was selected, and various types of railway injuries are listed in Table 1. The dataset primarily focuses on injury features such as cracks and spalling, which are prominent in real-world railway scenarios. All injury samples in the dataset are sourced from actual railway environments, ensuring the authenticity of the detection process and the reliability of model training. After many trials, considering the effect of the science demonstration, no defective, patches and scratches, which have a higher degree of mutual differentiation, were finally selected to train the final model.

Table 1. Schematic of various types of track injuries and data volume.

Label	No defective	Crazing	Inclusion	Patches	Scratches	Rolled-in scale
Example pictures						
Data volume	500	300	300	300	300	300

Model Construction. This system is based on the MaixHub online training platform to complete the development of algorithms, and selects the lightweight MobileNet_0.75 [11] as the backbone network for model fine-tuning. The specific parameters are shown in Table 2. A final kmodel file with a size of only 1.8mb was generated and burned into the Maix-I development board. while ensuring recognition accuracy, the inference delay was controlled within 120 ms to meet the real-time requirement.

Table 2. Training and testing configurations.

Configuration item	Parameter value
Core network	MobileNet_0.75 [11]
Epoch	100
Batch	32
Learning rate	0.001
Marker box restrictions	10
Deployment platforms	nncase

The change in each index in the training test with the number of iterations and the test confusion matrix are shown in Fig. 3. The results indicate stable model training, with the loss value continuously decreasing. A brief fluctuation at epoch 40 is observed, which is a common phenomenon in SGD optimization, where the optimizer temporarily explores flatter regions of the loss landscape before finding sharper descent directions [13]. However, the model quickly recovers and the loss approaches zero. The validation loss (val_loss) decreases synchronously, with only a slight fluctuation at epoch 50, indicating no overfitting. The training/validation accuracies are close to 100%, proving the effectiveness of the model in classification. Notably, ShuffleNet [14] achieved a perfect diagonal confusion matrix (i.e., 100% accuracy) on the well-separated dataset. The classification results showed that all three types of track samples were correctly identified without any misclassification, indicating strong generalization capability of the model and demonstrating. This indicates that the algorithm's reliability meets the requirements for educational applications. Taking into account both model size and hardware compatibility, the MobileNet_0.75-based model was ultimately selected for system deployment.

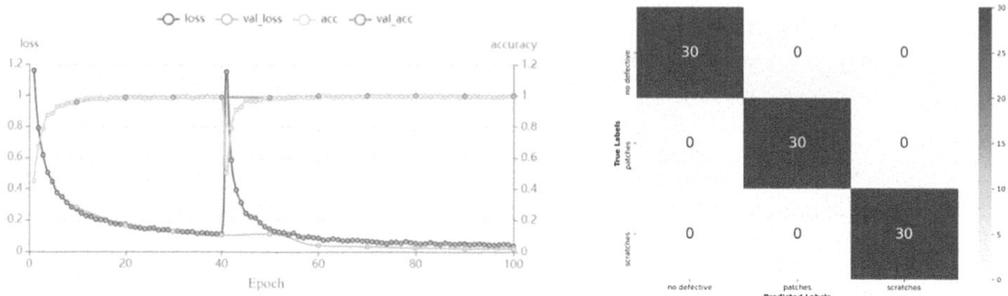

Fig. 3. Variation of the Metrics in the Training Test with the Number of Iterations and the Confusion Matrix.

System Integration. After completing the algorithm development and model training, this study deployed the optimized MobileNet [11] network to the Maix-I development board using the Nncase toolchain. The mechatronic structure was integrated to construct an end-to-end embedded visual detection system. This integrated solution realizes a completely closed loop from image acquisition and real-time reasoning to visualization alarms, which not only verifies the engineering applicability of the lightweight algorithm but also overcomes the problem of insufficient transparency of the embedded AI system through the error log display function and lays a reliable technical foundation for subsequent teaching applications.

The interaction logic and workflow of the detection system are systematically presented in Fig. 4. The system configuration consists of a fixed-view camera rigidly mounted on the detection vehicle, paired with the lightweight MobileNet [11] neural network for efficient onboard processing. Through precisely 147 lines of optimized Python code, the system implements a complete three-classification pipeline for identifying track injuries (normal, cracked, and peeled conditions). The classification process incorporates an adjustable confidence threshold parameter that can be modified during operation to adapt to different lighting or track conditions.

For user interaction and system monitoring, the interface combines real-time visualization with diagnostic functions. The primary display shows the camera feed with clear visual markers indicating detected defects, while the alarm interface provides immediate feedback when injuries are identified. During system operation, all operational anomalies are automatically recorded in a structured error log that displays on-screen, including error types and timestamps. This transparent design approach effectively addresses the "black box" challenges common in embedded systems by maintaining visibility into both the detection results and system status. The system runs efficiently on the Maix-I development board, maintaining a sub-0.5s response time required for real-time operation, while preserving the classification accuracy demonstrated in previous tests. All components are tightly integrated to ensure reliable performance during continuous track inspection tasks.

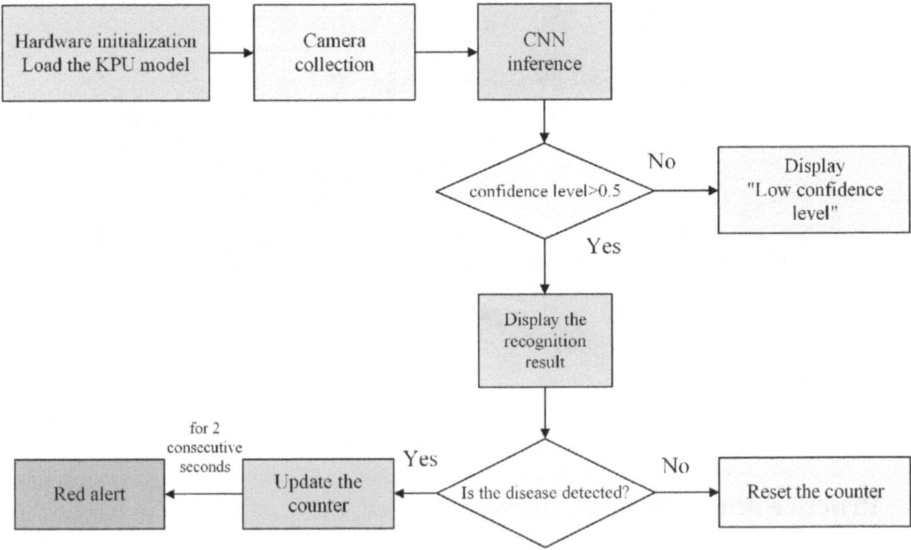

Fig. 4. Detection System Interaction Flowchart.

The detection system retains the core principles of detection technology while significantly reducing the cost of hardware. By allowing users to adjust parameters, the system provides intuitive insight into the algorithmic decision-making process, effectively transforming professional technology into accessible teaching aids.

4.3 Integration Verification and Validation

To ensure the reliability of the teaching aids, comprehensive running tests were conducted prior to practical application. By integrating the motion platform, modular railway segments, power unit, and supporting accessories in a systematic manner, we successfully assembled a complete detection vehicle prototype for comprehensive evaluation.

Tests were carried out on a flat surface to ensure proper alignment of the track modules and reliable mechanical interfacing. In accordance with the assembly instructions, the detection vehicle was assembled with the development board securely installed. System performance was monitored in real time via a computer running the CanMV IDE software.

The results confirmed the system's robust functionality. The detection vehicle moved smoothly along the track at consistent speeds, with the camera maintaining clear image capture throughout the operation. The defect recognition system responded reliably within 0.5 s, achieving immediate and accurate alarm triggering upon detection of anomalies. Throughout prolonged operation, the prototype demonstrated structural stability, compatible track-vehicle interaction, and consistent algorithm performance (Fig. 5).

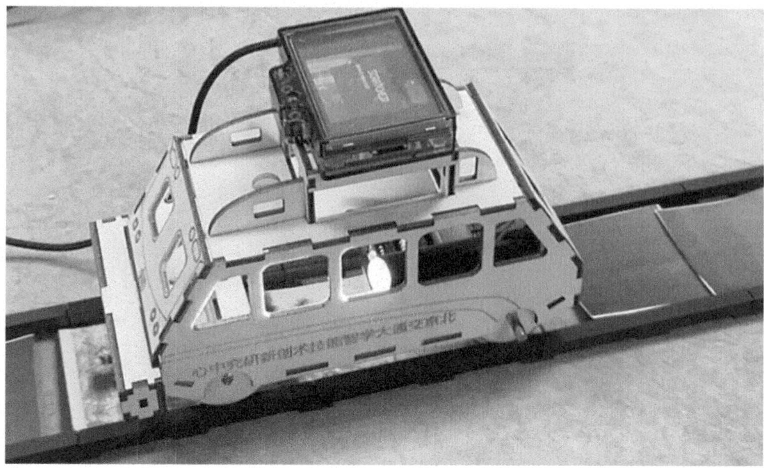

Fig. 5. Test Scene of the Application of Science Teaching Aids.

5 Practice and Feedback Integration

5.1 Implementing Activities

Teaching aids have been widely utilized in various science popularization events, such as the National Science and Technology Week and Science Popularization Day.

The activities include a broad spectrum of hands-on interactive modules, designed to engage and educate a variety of participant demographics, thereby enhancing public understanding and interest in science and technology. For elementary students, guided assembly activities help establish basic mechanical concepts through hands-on construction of modular components. Meanwhile, middle schoolers engage in threshold adjustment experiments to explore algorithmic impacts by modifying confidence parameters in real time.

The science popularization activities primarily comprise three key components: first, the technical principles session, where instructors and volunteers introduce participants to recent advancements in rail defect detection technologies and detection equipment applications. Second, the detection process demonstration, where educators showcase actual track detection vehicles operating on real tracks, allowing participants to closely observe the vehicle's hardware components and workflow. This visual presentation effectively stimulates participants' exploratory interest, establishing foundational knowledge for subsequent hands-on sessions. Third, the teaching aid assembly segment, where prefabricated modular components are used to construct detection vehicles and debug detection algorithms. As shown in Fig. 6, through this process, youth participants not only experience the enjoyment of assembling mechanical structures but also gain intuitive understanding of algorithm decision boundaries by adjusting parameters such as confidence thresholds, alarm conditions, and detection methods.

Fig. 6. Snapshots of Science Popularization Day Activities in Beijing Jiaotong University

5.2 Analyzing Feedback

Feedback analysis indicates the teaching aid's educational value through: elementary school parents praised its hands-on practicability, middle school students have reported a deepened understanding of AI technologies, and teen programmers focused on algorithm optimization potential. This tiered feedback validates the tool's professional design, maintaining technical authenticity while adapting difficulty levels to different cognitive stages. As a result, the teaching aid effectively presents railway track detection technology as both rigorous and engaging for science popularization.

6 Conclusion and Future Prospects

This study presents a systematic development framework for youth-oriented railway track visual detection teaching aids, addressing key limitations in technological authenticity and interactivity within current science popularization resources. By integrating industrial-grade computer vision technologies into accessible, hands-on educational tools, the proposed solution effectively bridges the gap between professional engineering applications and science education. The technical implementation leverages a lightweight MobileNet_0.75 [11] architecture to generate optimized.kmodel files, which were successfully deployed on energy-efficient Maix-I development boards. To ensure pedagogical suitability, detection algorithms were adapted to match the cognitive levels of primary and secondary school students, preserving technical accuracy while enhancing usability and engagement. The teaching aids have been extensively deployed in science outreach initiatives, such as the National Science and Technology Week. Educator feedback and field observations consistently confirm their effectiveness in illustrating real-world AI applications and fostering hands-on learning experiences. These results demonstrate the potential of integrating professional engineering methodologies into science education, providing valuable references for future research on science popularization teaching aids.

Future research directions will focus on enhancing the teaching aids' performance through two technical improvements. First, the interactive feedback mechanisms require optimization to provide more intuitive operational guidance, particularly in algorithm parameter adjustment and error debugging scenarios, with emphasis on improving error log interpretations. Second, the exploration of more robust yet lightweight network architectures could improve the system's demonstration capabilities under challenging conditions, such as operation on sloped or curved ground surfaces. These advancements aim to maintain the current sub-0.5s response time and classification accuracy while adapting to more complex physical environments.

Acknowledgements. This work was supported by the *Science and Innovation Starlight Program of Beijing Jiaotong University* (Grant No. K24L01420), and the *Undergraduate Innovation and Entrepreneurship Program of BJTU* (" Physical Model and System Development for Railway Visual Detection "). We also thank our research advisors, laboratory colleagues, and peer reviewers for their valuable contributions to this study.

References

1. State Council: Outline of the Plan for Action on the Scientific Quality of the Whole Population(2021–2035). https://www.gov.cn/gongbao/content/2021/content_5623051.htm
2. Central People's Government of the People's Republic of China: Law of the People's Republic of China on Popularization of Science and Technology. https://www.gov.cn/yaowen/liebiao/202412/content_6994555.htm
3. Ministry of Education, People's Republic of China: Ministry of Education Issues Guidelines on Strengthening AI Education in Primary and Secondary Schools. http://www.moe.gov.cn/jyb_xwfb/gzdt_gzdt/s5987/202412/t20241202_1165500.html
4. Kepupinghu: The Popularization of Science Act|From soft provisions to statutory obligations, what changes did the revision of the Popularization of Science Act bring? https://mp.weixin.qq.com/s?__biz=MzI5ODQ0MDQ0OQ%253D%253D&mid=224756211&idx=2&sn=92bdc98eefee6a7fc53e2f46b8e74a1d&chksm=ed161495dede0ecbf39c66e9d9b9522bb956d0a7848031b41d940de660ff6d62825f57fa30b1&scene=27
5. Guangming Daily: Insufficient course hours, disconnection between teaching materials and scientific and technological progress, few science laboratories - where does the source of science education come from. Guangming Daily (13), 23 Apr 2024
6. Huang, H., Liu, W., Ji, S.: A dynamic science equipment design based on AI image recognition technology. Equip. Manag. Mainten. **1**, 64–67 (2023)
7. National Virtual Reality Experimental Teaching Course Sharing Platform: Visual perception virtual simulation experiment for high-speed rail track Detection. https://www.ilab-x.com/details/page?id=12093
8. Peng, W., Li, Q., Zhou, W., et al.: Design and application of virtual simulation experiment for high-speed rail intelligent operation and maintenance. J. Comput. Technol. Educ. **10**(5), 49–56 (2022)
9. School of Computer Science, Beijing Jiaotong University: Understand autonomous driving; explore artificial intelligence. https://cs.bjtu.edu.cn/kpjd/kphd/2023145 61.htm
10. Ministry of Education: People's Republic of China: Compulsory Education Science Curriculum Standards, 2022nd edn. Beijing Normal University Press, Beijing (2022)
11. Howard, A.G., Zhu, M., Chen, B., et al.: Mobilenets: efficient convolutional neural networks for mobile vision applications. arXiv:1704.04861 (2017)

12. Zhang, D., Song, K., Niu, M., et al.: Fast detection of surface defects on cold heavy rails of production lines based on one-dimensional convolution. J. Northeastern Univ. (Natural Science Edition) **42**(2), 276–281 (2021)
13. Ruder, S.: An overview of gradient descent optimization algorithms. arXiv:1609.04747 (2016)
14. Zhang, X., Zhou, X., Lin, M., et al.: Shufflenet: an extremely efficient convolutional neural network for mobile devices. arXiv:1707.01083 (2017)

Paths and Strategies for Reshaping the Teaching Process of Software Engineering Courses Under the Background of AI

Gongzheng Lu(✉) and Yang Yang

Computing Science and Artificial Intelligence College, Suzhou City University, Suzhou 215104, Jiangsu, China
{lugz,yyang}@szcu.edu.cn

Abstract. In order to solve the impact of artificial intelligence technology on the teaching process of software engineering courses, paths and strategies for reshaping the teaching process are proposed. The teaching process is reshaped mainly from five aspects: teaching objectives, teaching content, teaching resources, teaching mode and teaching evaluation, providing a reference for the teaching reform and practical research of software engineering courses under the background of artificial intelligence.

Keywords: software engineering · artificial intelligence · teaching process · reshaping

1 Background

Wu Yan, Vice Minister of the Ministry of Education, stressed at the 2023 World Digital Education Conference: "Digital technologies represented by artificial intelligence are changing traditional higher education theories and paradigms and reshaping the form of higher education. This has become a global consensus and action" [1]. The current application of artificial intelligence (AI) in the field of education has shown great potential, and it is driving a fundamental change in education models and methods. By automating education management, building personalized learning experiences, and using game strategies to enhance the attractiveness of learning, artificial intelligence is not only optimizing the education process and affecting the traditional pattern of education. In addition, artificial intelligence also has the potential to identify knowledge blind spots, predict learning outcomes, and gain in-depth insights into the effectiveness of teaching strategies. This data-driven education approach enables educators to make informed decisions, adjust teaching methods, and ultimately improve the quality of education.

W. Hong et al. (Eds.): ICCSE 2025, CCIS 2761, pp. 64–73, 2026.
https://doi.org/10.1007/978-981-95-7731-6_6

2 The Main Innovations of This Paper

The main innovations of this paper includes:

(1) Take Job Impact Analysis as a Breakthrough to Reshape Teaching Goals. Starting from the impact of AI on software engineering-related positions, the new requirements of AI technology and the new risks brought by the application of AI technology are integrated into the existing teaching objectives to provide guidance for the entire teaching process.

(2) Reconstruct the Teaching Content Based on Knowledge Graph Technology. The knowledge graph technology in AI is used to construct the course knowledge graph and job ability map, analyze the requirements of the competition tasks, explore the close connection between the post-course-competition, realize the teaching closed loop of complementary theory and practice, improve the students' practical ability, innovation and entrepreneurship ability, and integrate the course content into AI to assist in completing tasks at all stages of software engineering.

(3) Experience Real-Time Interaction with Digital Intelligent Resources as the Carrier. With the help of virtual reality technology, virtual resources such as virtual teachers and virtual peers are generated, digital teaching materials are developed, and the learning experience is enhanced through real-time interaction with these digital and intelligent resources.

(4) Relying on Artificial Intelligence Technology, Realize Independent Exploration. Based on artificial intelligence technology, an intelligent question and answer system and an intelligent search system are built to realize the independent inquiry teaching mode and stimulate students' learning initiative and creativity.

(5) Improve the Quality of Teaching Based on Multiple Process Data. Through AI technology, we collect and analyze students' learning data and learning data, aggregate and analyze them, explore personalized learning and dynamic teaching mode oriented to learning conditions, and realize coherent teaching evaluation. In the teaching process, it stimulates students' interest in learning, grasps students' situation, enriches teaching evaluation methods, and takes improving teaching quality as the ultimate goal.

3 The Current Status of Software Engineering Course Teaching Reform Under the Background of Artificial Intelligence

At present, there is little research on the application of AI technology in higher education teaching reform, especially in software engineering courses. The research content mainly focuses on how artificial intelligence technology reshapes the form of higher education, how AI technology is used for learning evaluation and feedback, how AI assists in student situation analysis, and how AI empowers the teaching reform of program analysis courses.

In his paper, Liu [2] elaborated in detail how generative artificial intelligence reshapes the form of higher education from three aspects: educational scenarios, teaching processes, and thinking paradigms. He systematically sorted out typical practice cases and proposed coping strategies from four aspects. Zheng [3] proposed a technical architecture for designing a virtual scientific experiment autonomous inquiry learning platform using specific intelligent technologies to achieve evaluation and adaptive feedback of the autonomous inquiry learning process. Pu [4] used artificial intelligence technology to assist in the collection, analysis, feedback, and application of learning data, constructed a theoretical framework for learning analysis, and established a learning analysis system.

Gao [5] described the teaching transformation of AI-enabled programming courses in his paper and introduced the practical process of integrating large language models into the teaching process before, during, and after class. Zhang [6] proposed innovative strategies and methods for effectively integrating generative artificial intelligence into computer programming teaching, showing that it can better support personalized teaching.

The above studies either explored the reshaping of higher education by AI technology, the evaluation and feedback of the learning process, and the analysis of learning conditions using AI technology from a high level, or only studied the teaching reform of programming courses enabled by AI technology. However, software engineering, as a professional core course that combines theory and practice, has its own particularity, and the above studies cannot be directly applied to the teaching reform of software engineering. For this reason, some people have specifically studied the teaching reform of software engineering majors and courses based on artificial intelligence technology.

Wang [7] analyzed the obstacles and solutions to the use of AI technology in software engineering courses. Chen [8] used artificial intelligence technology to achieve a teaching environment that combines scale and personalization by sorting out the knowledge points and corresponding exercises of software engineering courses. Wang [9] integrated artificial intelligence with software requirements engineering throughout the project, carried out teaching reforms with hierarchical, directional and enhanced practice, and ensured the teaching quality and effect from four aspects: course content, teaching methods, textbook construction, and practical teaching.

Although the above work involves software engineering related content, it either only proposes high-level strategies and does not involve how to specifically solve the problems encountered in applying AI technology to software engineering professional courses; or it only studies the application of AI technology to reform a certain part of the software engineering course, such as personalized teaching and software requirements engineering.

This paper will mainly study the impact of AI technology on the teaching process of software engineering courses, analyze the reform trend of the teaching process, and provide specific paths and strategies for reshaping the teaching process.

4 Reform Trends in the Teaching Process of Software Engineering Courses

With the widespread application of AI technology in all walks of life, traditional software engineering education faces many challenges and transformation needs. The following mainly analyzes the reform trends in five aspects from the perspective of AI's impact on the teaching process of software engineering courses:

(1) Transformation of teaching objectives: In the context of artificial intelligence, the teaching objectives of the course need to be expanded to train students' interdisciplinary capabilities, especially to combine AI technology with software engineering practice, so that they can use AI technology to complete work in software engineering-related positions.

(2) Updating of teaching content: Software engineering focuses on cultivating engineering practice ability, and uses AI technology to explore the internal connections between course knowledge points and the correspondence between course knowledge points and job capabilities, to achieve the integration of theory and practice in teaching content.

(3) Enrichment and optimization of teaching resources: Use virtual reality technology and AI technology to realize virtual teachers and intelligent question and answering to achieve real-time interaction; use videos, simulation software, etc. Develop digital resources to improve students' understanding and interest in course content.

(4) Innovation in teaching model: hybrid teaching that combines online and offline teaching, using AI technology to analyze learning data on online student platforms and provide personalized learning paths, achieving real-time interaction with teaching resources to enhance learning flexibility and autonomy.

(5) Diversification of teaching evaluation: Use AI technology to analyze learning data from online learning platforms and conduct process-based and diversified evaluation; pay more attention to students' actual abilities, especially their abilities to solve complex problems and apply AI technology, and conduct ability-oriented evaluation.

5 Specific Paths and Strategies for Reshaping the Teaching Process of Software Engineering Courses

5.1 Research Methods of Reshaping Teaching Process

In this study we used the following research methods:

(1) Literature Research
By consulting relevant journals and books at home and abroad, we sorted and analyzed the theories, methods, and cases of teaching reform based on AI technology at home and abroad and formed a preliminary understanding of the research content. By consulting literature, we studied and practiced technologies such as knowledge graphs, large language models, data analysis,

intelligent question-answering systems, intelligent search, and virtual reality, providing theoretical and technical guarantees for the completion of the reshaping of the teaching process.

(2) Interview
By interviewing staff in relevant positions in computer companies, competition experts, etc., we analyzed the ability indicators and competition requirements of software engineering positions, laying the foundation for building a job capability map and reconstructing practical content.

(3) Survey Research
Through questionnaire surveys, we can understand the collection methods, dimensions, indicators of learning data and academic situation data, which will serve as the basis for personalized learning and academic situation analysis.

(4) Case analysis
By analyzing other cases of course teaching reform based on AI technology, typical case scenarios of the Ministry of Education's "Artificial Intelligence + Higher Education", etc., and drawing on the methods, ideas, and technologies therein, this paper provides theoretical and practical references for the reshaping of the software engineering course teaching process under the background of artificial intelligence.

5.2 Specific Path for Reshaping the Teaching Process

Through in-depth research on the impact of AI technology on the teaching objectives and teaching content of software engineering courses, as well as exploring the innovations brought by AI technology to the teaching mode, teaching resources and teaching evaluation of the course, a specific path for reshaping the teaching process of software engineering courses, as shown in Fig. 1:

5.3 The Main Goal of Reshaping the Teaching Process

The main goals of reshaping the software engineering course teaching process include the following five aspects:

(1) Reshaping Teaching Objectives: In-depth research on the impact of AI technology on software engineering course content and related job positions, and reshaping course objectives;

(2) Reshaping Teaching Content: By exploring the knowledge map of the course, the ability map of the job position, and the task requirements of the competition, the integration of the position, course, and competition can be achieved;

(3) Reshaping Teaching Resources: Using virtual reality technology to develop digital and intelligent resources and promote the construction of digital teaching materials;

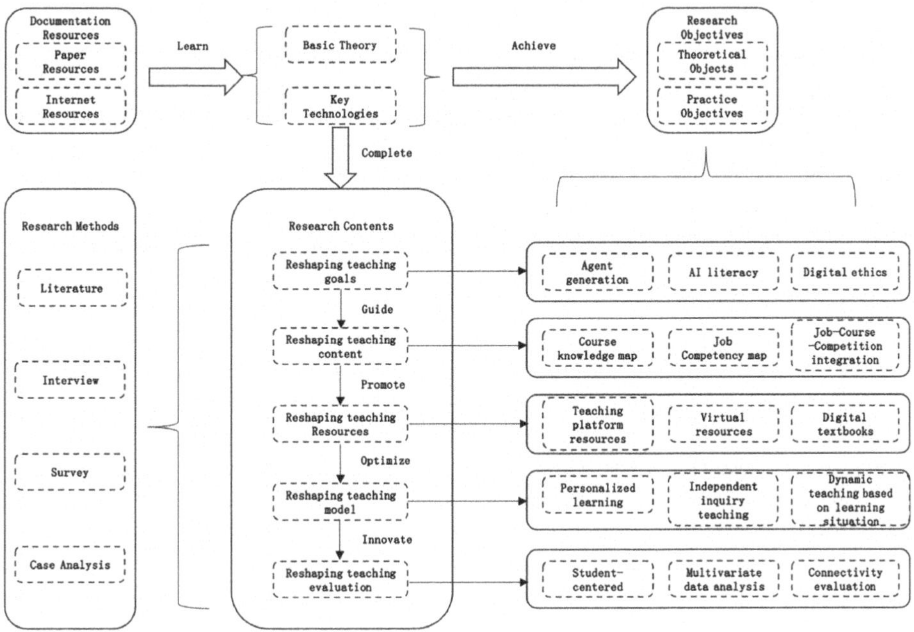

Fig. 1. Path for reshaping the teaching process of software engineering courses.

(4) Reshaping the Teaching Model: Make full use of AI technology to obtain student learning and academic situation data, explore personalized learning and dynamic teaching strategies, and explore autonomous inquiry-based teaching models by building an intelligent question and answering system and realizing intelligent search;

(5) Reshaping Teaching Evaluation: Using AI technology to build an intelligent evaluation system to achieve diversified, process-based and integrated evaluation centered on students.

5.4 Problems that Need to Be Solved in Reshaping the Teaching Process

In order to achieve the above goals, it is planned to solve the existing problems in the teaching objectives, teaching content, teaching resources, teaching mode and teaching evaluation of the "Software Engineering" course and reshape them with the help of artificial intelligence technology:

(1) Reshaping teaching objectives: Traditional course teaching objectives mainly include knowledge objectives, ability objectives, and emotional and value objectives. However, with the rapid development of artificial intelligence technology, a large number of industries that mainly rely on mental labor (such as software developers) may be replaced by it, so the course teaching objectives need to be repositioned. Secondly, students' mastery of the application of artificial intelligence technology is also one of the necessary skills. In the course teaching process, efforts should be made to cultivate students' artificial intelligence literacy. In addition, artificial intelligence technology has also raised a series of educational ethical issues. Students may use artificial intelligence technology to generate homework, etc. Therefore, it is also necessary to pay attention to students' digital ethics in course teaching.

(2) Reshaping teaching content: The current teaching content of software engineering focuses more on theory than practice, and there is a serious disconnect between theory and practice. Artificial intelligence technology has powerful analysis and mining capabilities, which can be used to discover the close connection between positions, courses, and competitions. On the one hand, artificial intelligence technology can be used to generate knowledge graphs of courses, mine the ability graphs of positions, and find the mapping relationship between the two graphs, so that theory and practice are closely connected, theory guides practice, and practice tests theory. On the other hand, competition-oriented curriculum reform is also a current hot topic. Artificial intelligence technology can be used to analyze competition requirements and tasks, reconstruct course practice content, and improve students' practical ability and innovation and entrepreneurship capabilities. In addition, in order to improve students' AI application capabilities, AI-assisted task completion in various aspects of software engineering can be integrated into the teaching content, such as the generation of requirement specifications and outline design specifications.

(3) Reshaping teaching resources: The "Software Engineering" course lacks digital and intelligent teaching resources. Artificial intelligence technology has the ability to generate multimodal content, which helps to generate multimodal resources. On the one hand, it can be used to generate emotional resources such as virtual teachers and virtual companions, so that students can interact with them in real time during the learning process to enhance the learning experience. On the other hand, teachers can use artificial intelligence to quickly retrieve teaching resources related to knowledge points or topics, build interdisciplinary knowledge graphs, break down disciplinary barriers, and accelerate the efficiency of digital teaching material development and construction.

(4) Reshaping the teaching model: The existing "online + offline" hybrid teaching model is still mainly based on teacher lectures, which is not conducive to stimulating students' learning interest and innovation ability. Artificial intelligence technology can be used to transform the traditional teaching model and actively explore teaching models oriented to personalized learning and autonomous exploration. On the one hand, combined with artificial intelligence technology, students' learning situation can be analyzed to generate personalized learning paths suitable for each student. On the other hand, with the help of artificial intelligence technology, an intelligent question-and-answer system can be built to answer questions in learning. Information in teaching videos can also be searched through artificial intelligence technology to answer questions. In addition, artificial intelligence technology can be used to analyze the learning situation, explore dynamic teaching models oriented to the learning situation, and continuously adjust and optimize teaching strategies and teaching content based on learning situation data.

(5) Reshaping teaching evaluation: For a long time, the teaching evaluation of the "Software Engineering" course has had problems such as focusing on "knowledge" and neglecting "ability", single evaluation indicators, and subjective evaluation methods. Artificial intelligence technology can be used to build an intelligent evaluation system. On the one hand, reshape the teaching evaluation concept. With students as the center, pay more attention to students' personalized and self-service learning ability. On the other hand, reshape the teaching evaluation method. Use artificial intelligence technology to gather multiple process and result learning data, conduct fusion analysis on the data, and realize the through-the-line evaluation of students' innovation.

5.5 Specific Strategies for Reshaping the Teaching Process

In order to achieve the above goals, this paper intends to solve the impact of AI technology on the teaching process of software engineering courses, analyze the problems and shortcomings in the five aspects of teaching objectives, teaching content, teaching resources, teaching mode, and teaching evaluation in the existing teaching process, and give specific strategies for reshaping them with the help of AI technology:

(1) Reshaping Teaching Objectives: Traditional course teaching objectives mainly include knowledge objectives, ability objectives, and emotional and value objectives. However, with the rapid development of artificial intelligence technology, a large number of industries that are mainly based on mental labor (such as software developers) may be replaced by it, so the course teaching objectives need to be repositioned. Secondly, students' mastery of the application of artificial intelligence technology is also one of the necessary skills. In the course teaching process, efforts should be made to cultivate students' artificial intelligence literacy. In addition, artificial intelligence technology has also raised a series of educational ethical issues. Students may use artificial intelligence technology to generate homework, etc. Therefore, it is also necessary to pay attention to students' digital ethics in course teaching.

(2) Reshaping of Teaching Content: The current teaching content of software engineering focuses more on theory than practice, and there is a serious disconnect between theory and practice. Artificial intelligence technology has powerful analysis and mining capabilities, which can be used to discover the close connection between job positions, courses, and competitions. On the one hand, artificial intelligence technology can be used to generate knowledge graphs of courses, mine the ability graphs of positions, and find the mapping relationship between the two graphs, so that theory and practice are closely connected, theory guides practice, and practice tests theory. On the other hand, competition-oriented curriculum reform is also a current hot topic. Artificial intelligence technology can be used to analyze competition requirements and tasks, reconstruct course practice content, and improve students' practical ability and innovation and entrepreneurship ability. In addition, in order to improve students'

AI application capabilities, AI-assisted task completion in various aspects of software engineering can be integrated into the teaching content, such as the generation of requirement specifications and outline design specifications.

(3) Reshaping Teaching Resources: Software engineering courses lack digital and intelligent teaching resources. Artificial intelligence technology has the ability to generate multimodal content, which helps to generate multimodal resources. On the one hand, it can be used to generate emotional resources such as virtual teachers and virtual companions, so that students can interact with them in real time during the learning process to enhance the learning experience. On the other hand, teachers can use artificial intelligence to quickly retrieve teaching resources related to knowledge points or topics, build interdisciplinary knowledge graphs, break down disciplinary barriers, and accelerate the efficiency of digital teaching material development and construction.

(4) Reshaping the Teaching Model: The existing "online + offline" hybrid teaching model is still mainly based on teacher lectures, which is not conducive to stimulating students' learning interest and innovation ability. Artificial intelligence technology can be used to transform the traditional teaching model and actively explore teaching models oriented to personalized learning and autonomous exploration. On the one hand, combined with artificial intelligence technology, students' learning situation can be analyzed to generate personalized learning paths suitable for each student. On the other hand, with the help of artificial intelligence technology, an intelligent question answering system can be built to answer questions in learning. Information in teaching videos can also be searched through artificial intelligence technology to complete question answering. In addition, artificial intelligence technology can be used to analyze the learning situation, explore dynamic teaching models oriented to the learning situation, and continuously adjust and optimize teaching strategies and teaching content based on learning situation data.

(5) Reshaping Teaching Evaluation: For a long time, the teaching evaluation of software engineering courses has been focusing on "knowledge" and neglecting "ability", with single evaluation indicators and subjective evaluation methods. Artificial intelligence technology can be used to build an intelligent evaluation system. On the one hand, it reshapes the teaching evaluation concept. It is student-centered and pays more attention to students' personalized and self-service learning ability. On the other hand, it reshapes the teaching evaluation method. It uses artificial intelligence technology to gather multiple process and result learning data, conduct fusion analysis on the data, and realize the through-the-line evaluation of students' innovation.

6 Conclusion

With the widespread application of artificial intelligence technology in all walks of life, traditional software engineering education faces many challenges and reform needs. This article proposes a specific path for reshaping the teaching process of software engineering courses under the background of artificial intelligence from five aspects: teaching objectives, teaching content, teaching resources, teaching mode, and teaching evaluation. In future work, AI technology will be specifically applied to reshape the above five aspects according to the ideas in this article, formulate new teaching objectives, integrate new teaching content, develop relevant teaching resources, and build a new evaluation system. In addition, the effects of the reshaping of the above five aspects will be tested in teaching practice.

Acknowledgements. This paper is supported by the Suzhou City University 2024 Higher Education Reform Research Project (No. 24JGJ18).

References

1. Wu, Y.: Speech by Wu Yan, Vice Minister of the Ministry of Education, at the Higher Education Parallel Forum of the World Digital Education Conference. https://www.163.com/dy/article/HTL0BTRH05366EUH.html. Accessed 13 Jan 2024
2. Liu, M., Guo, S., Wu, Z.M., et al.: Generative artificial intelligence reshapes the form of higher education: content, cases and paths. Educ. Digitalization **6**, 57–65 (2024)
3. Zheng, Y.F.: Research on evaluation and adaptive feedback of virtual science inquiry learning process enabled by intelligent technology. J. Audio-Vis. Educ. Res. (3), 99–103+105 (2024)
4. Pu, Q.P., Wang, X.T.: Theoretical framework and practical path of artificial intelligence-assisted learning situation analysis. Univ. Educ. Sci. **3**, 31–38 (2024)
5. Gao, H.H., Chen, Z.J.: Teaching reform of programming course empowered by artificial intelligence. Comput. Educ. (7), 41–43+48 (2024)
6. Zhang, H.Z., Zhou, X.B., Xu, Y.H., et al.: Generative artificial intelligence empowers computer programming course teaching innovation. Comput. Educ. **7**, 44–48 (2024)
7. Wang, H.Y.: Teaching of software engineering courses in colleges and universities based on artificial intelligence technology. In: Proceedings of the Seminar on Improving the Comprehensive Capabilities of Administrative Personnel on "AI Empowerment, Intelligent Office" , pp. 56–58. Metallurgical Industry Education Resource Development Center, Dalian (2024)
8. Chen, D.Q., Li, Y.M., Pang, G.L., et al.: Construction of a teaching environment combining scale and personalization based on artificial intelligence - taking software engineering course as an example. Univ. Educ. **4**, 84–87 (2024)
9. Wang, Y., Zhou, S.Y., Zhou, A.H.: Software requirements engineering teaching reform under the background of artificial intelligence. Fujian Comput. **39**(12), 116–120 (2023)

AI-Enhanced Production-Oriented Approach for Feedback and Assessment in EFL Writing

Wenhan Pan[1], Mingzhi Mao[2(✉)], and Niansheng Cheng[3]

[1] Guangzhou College of Commerce, Guangzhou 511363, China
[2] Sun Yat-Sen University, Zhuhai 519082, China
mcsmmz@mail.sysu.edu.cn
[3] Aisino Co., Ltd., Beijing 100195, China

Abstract. An AI-enhanced Production-Oriented Approach (POA) framework is proposed to improve English as a Foreign Language (EFL) writing instruction in higher education. By aligning POA's motivating–enabling–assessing cycle with large language models such as GPT-4, the framework facilitates task-based, feedback-driven, and adaptive learning experiences. Implemented through a design-based research methodology in a university writing course, the framework led to measurable improvements in students' writing performance, engagement with formative feedback, and learner autonomy. The results suggest that AI functions as an instructional augmentation rather than a replacement, offering scalable support for individualized scaffolding and functional feedback. The work contributes to smart language pedagogy by bridging pedagogical theory with AI capabilities and connecting human-led instruction with intelligent learning support.

Keywords: Production-Oriented Approach (POA) · Smart Learning · EFL Writing · AI Feedback · Automated Assessment

1 Introduction

The integration of artificial intelligence (AI) into the field of language education is gradually transforming how instruction is delivered. It is also reshaping how feedback is designed and how learners engage with language tasks. Recent advances in large language models (LLMs), such as GPT-4, have made it possible to provide adaptive support for a wide range of writing activities. These technologies can generate context-sensitive writing prompts and offer instant, personalized feedback. Such capabilities significantly enhance the individualization and scalability of language instruction. This is particularly valuable in large-class environments, where teachers may struggle to provide timely and differentiated feedback to every learner [1–3].

When embedded within clear pedagogical frameworks, AI tools have been shown to promote improvements in linguistic accuracy. They also support students in developing metacognitive skills, such as self-monitoring and reflective thinking. In doing so, AI systems help foster a greater sense of learner agency and autonomy [4, 5].

W. Hong et al. (Eds.): ICCSE 2025, CCIS 2761, pp. 74–87, 2026.
https://doi.org/10.1007/978-981-95-7731-6_7

Parallel to these technological developments, the Production-Oriented Approach (POA), developed by Wen Qiufang, has gained widespread adoption in Chinese higher education. It is especially influential in English as a Foreign Language (EFL) writing instruction. POA addresses the long-standing disconnect between language input and communicative output. It follows a structured three-phase cycle: motivating, enabling, and assessing. The approach emphasizes authentic tasks and performance-based learning, grounded in real-world communicative contexts [6, 7]. Based on principles from constructivist learning theory, POA encourages the integration of language learning and practical language use.

Despite their individual strengths, AI and POA are rarely integrated within a single instructional model. Traditional POA practice still depends heavily on teacher-led feedback. This model limits scalability and makes real-time support difficult. On the other hand, many AI applications operate without reference to theoretical principles. This often leads to fragmented or decontextualized feedback that may not meet students' instructional needs [8].

To address this gap, the present study proposes a new framework that integrates AI capabilities into the POA structure. The model uses LLMs to generate motivating tasks, deliver real-time scaffolding, and provide feedback aligned with the meta functions of Systemic Functional Linguistics (SFL) [9, 10]. This study investigates how the proposed AI-supported POA framework influences writing outcomes, feedback engagement, and learner autonomy in a university-level EFL writing course.

2 Related Work

The Production-Oriented Approach (POA) and artificial intelligence (AI) have emerged as two influential forces in the evolution of language education. POA, originally introduced by Wen Qiufang [6], was developed to address the long-standing gap between language input and communicative output. This disconnect remains a key challenge in foreign language classrooms, particularly in English as a Foreign Language (EFL) contexts.

POA centers on the idea that output drives learning. It emphasizes task-based activities that reflect authentic communicative situations. The approach follows a three-stage cycle: motivating, enabling, and assessing. Research has shown that this structure supports improvements in syntactic complexity, coherence, and pragmatic fluency. These benefits extend across different tasks, including writing, speaking, and translation [12, 13].

In recent years, POA has been applied to multiple instructional areas such as academic writing, business English, and English for Academic Purposes (EAP) [14]. Its focus on learner engagement and real-world communication makes it widely adaptable. However, most implementations still depend heavily on teacher-led instruction and manually delivered feedback. In large or mixed-ability classrooms, this reliance makes it difficult to offer timely and personalized support. As a result, the scalability of POA is limited, especially in digital, hybrid, or self-directed learning environments [15].

Meanwhile, rapid developments in AI—especially in large language models (LLMs) like GPT-3.5 and GPT-4—have introduced new tools for language learning. These technologies can generate prompts, provide individualized feedback, and evaluate learner writing with a high degree of accuracy [1, 2, 11]. When integrated into well-structured lesson plans, AI tools have been shown to enhance vocabulary range, grammatical precision, and revision quality. The effectiveness of these tools increases when the feedback is clearly aligned with instructional goals [8, 16].

Despite this potential, many AI applications still operate independently from pedagogical theory. As Zhao and Li [5] observe, this disconnect can result in fragmented learning experiences that lack depth and consistency.

Although some studies have explored AI-supported writing feedback [8] and POA-inspired intelligent systems [6], a systematic model that integrates AI into the full POA cycle is still missing. Specifically, there is a need for a framework that maps AI-generated prompts, scaffolding processes, and SFL-informed feedback onto the motivating–enabling–assessing structure.

This study responds to that need by proposing a theory-based, AI-enhanced POA framework. The model aims to deliver scalable, explainable, and feedback-driven writing instruction, particularly for academic English learners in university settings.

3 Theoretical Framework: Integrating POA with Artificial Intelligence

This study introduces a multi-layered instructional framework that systematically integrates artificial intelligence (AI) into the design of the Production-Oriented Approach (POA) for English language teaching. The framework aims to bridge the divide between AI-supported learning environments and task-based pedagogical design. It aligns the computational affordances of AI with the three foundational stages of POA: motivating, enabling, and assessing. As illustrated in Fig. 1, the model consists of three interconnected functional layers: (1) the Output-Oriented Design Layer, (2) the AI-Augmented Instructional Loop Layer, and (3) the Data-Driven Feedback Analytics Layer. Together, these layers promote individualized, feedback-rich, and output-driven instruction.

The first component, the Output-Oriented Design Layer, positions communicative output as the starting point of instruction. It defines the thematic focus, task type, language goals, and learning context for each instructional unit. This layer is informed by POA's emphasis on real-life language use and task completion. AI plays a supportive role in this stage by generating context-sensitive prompts, simulating role-play scenarios, and adapting tasks based on individual learner profiles. These functions operationalize the concept of "learning through doing," embedding meaningful output early in the instructional sequence.

The second layer, the AI-Augmented Instructional Loop Layer, serves as the operational core of the framework. It integrates large-scale language models such as GPT-4 into the POA instructional cycle. During the motivating phase, AI produces discourse prompts, rhetorical templates, and situational examples that engage students. In the enabling phase, AI provides real-time linguistic scaffolding. This includes lexical enhancement, grammatical correction, reference suggestions, and sentence restructuring to support drafting. In the assessing phase, the AI system generates formative feedback based on Systemic Functional Linguistics (SFL). This feedback addresses the ideational function (content and logic), the interpersonal function (stance and modality), and the textual function (cohesion and organization). Through this alignment, learners receive structured guidance that fosters self-regulation and raises linguistic awareness.

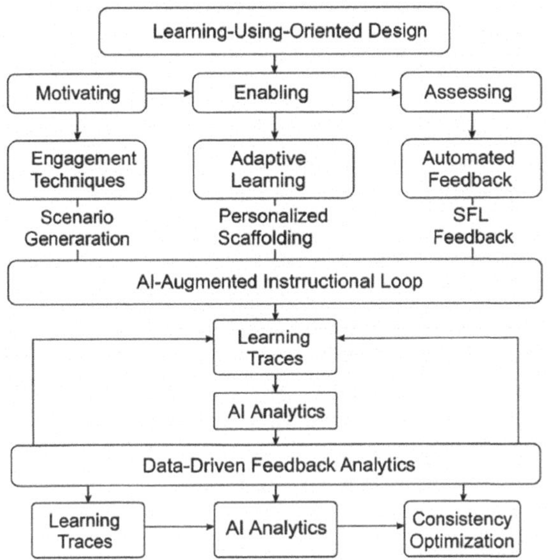

Fig. 1. AI-Enhanced POA Framework for Smart Language Instruction

The third component, the Data-Driven Feedback Analytics Layer, completes the instructional model by transforming feedback into actionable instructional insight. It collects and analyzes learner-AI interaction data, including prompt responses, revision histories, and performance progression. These data inform future task design, scaffold adjustments, and feedback calibration. Teachers can use this information to support differentiated instruction. Learners, in turn, are encouraged to reflect on their learning through accessible analytics.

In sum, the three interrelated layers provide a scalable and theoretically grounded model for intelligent English instruction. By embedding AI into each phase of POA, the framework supports adaptive teaching, personalized learning, and continuous feedback across digital, blended, and classroom-based contexts.

4 Methodology

This study employed a Design-Based Research (DBR) methodology to systematically examine the feasibility, instructional effectiveness, and educational value of an AI-supported framework based on the principles of the Production-Oriented Approach (POA). DBR was chosen for its ability to connect theoretical insights with iterative, practice-oriented interventions. This method is especially suitable for technology-enhanced learning environments, where ongoing refinement, contextual adaptability, and ecological validity are essential for sustainable instructional design. Given the complexity of incorporating large language models (LLMs) into process-based writing pedagogy,

DBR provided a structured yet flexible framework for guiding instructional development across multiple implementation phases.

The intervention was conducted over a six-week period in a second-year English writing course at a comprehensive university in China. A total of 80 undergraduates participated, all of whom were non-English majors. Their academic disciplines ranged from engineering to economics and environmental science. Although a portion of the students had passed the College English Test Band 4 (CET-4), most lacked formal training in genre-specific writing. They also had limited experience using AI-assisted writing platforms. This diverse student population created an authentic and transferable context for evaluating the proposed framework.

The instructional design followed the three sequential stages of POA: motivating, enabling, and assessing. Each stage was paired with a specific writing task and corresponding AI tool. During the motivating phase, GPT-4 was used to produce context-rich prompts for assignments such as personal narratives and argumentative essays. In the enabling phase, students engaged with AI tools like ChatGPT and Write & Improve. These platforms offered immediate support through grammar correction, lexical improvement, and sentence refinement. In the assessing phase, students received two types of feedback. Human instructors applied a four-dimensional analytic rubric, evaluating content, organization, language accuracy, and coherence. Meanwhile, AI-generated feedback was coded using the three metafunctions of Systemic Functional Linguistics (SFL): ideational, interpersonal, and textual.

To evaluate the impact of the framework, a mixed-methods research design was applied. Quantitative data came from pre- and post-intervention writing tasks, scored by three trained evaluators and cross-checked using GPT-4 and Grammarly. Statistical tests, including paired-sample t-tests and Quadratic Weighted Kappa (QWK), were conducted to assess improvement and reliability.

Qualitative data included AI feedback records, student revisions, reflective journals, and interviews. These materials were analyzed to identify trends in feedback use, revision strategies, emotional responses, and teacher facilitation. The next section reports these findings in detail.

5 Results and Discussion

This section reports key empirical findings from the application of the AI-enhanced Production-Oriented Approach (POA) in a college-level English writing course. The analysis is structured around three central themes. The first theme examines students' writing performance and the degree of alignment in scoring across evaluators. The second investigates the ways in which learners engaged with feedback and made revisions. The third analyzes student perceptions of AI-supported instruction. These three themes correspond to the foundational principles of the POA framework—output-driven learning, formative assessment practices, and functional alignment—and demonstrate how AI integration can enhance both instructional effectiveness and assessment consistency.

5.1 Learning Performance and AI-Human Scoring Alignment

The quantitative analysis revealed a consistent upward trend in students' writing performance during the implementation of the AI-enhanced Production-Oriented Approach (POA). Throughout the intervention, three experienced writing instructors assessed student essays using a detailed analytic rubric. This rubric evaluated several core dimensions of writing quality. These included the relevance and depth of content, the accuracy of language use, the coherence of discourse structure, and the overall communicative effectiveness of the text.

Over the course of the intervention, students' average scores improved significantly. The mean score increased from 62.4 in Task 1 to 72.7 in Task 3. This gain was not only statistically significant ($p < 0.01$), but also pedagogically meaningful. It indicated that students had made measurable progress in meeting both rhetorical and linguistic requirements embedded in the writing tasks. The results suggest that the structured, output-driven nature of the POA framework contributed to this improvement, especially when supported by AI-assisted feedback mechanisms.

In addition to the human ratings, automated evaluation tools were used to assess student writing. Specifically, GPT-4 and Grammarly served as AI-based scorers. These tools also reported positive performance trends. The average scores generated by AI systems rose from 61.9 to 72.1 across the three writing tasks. The close alignment between AI scores and those given by human instructors suggests a high level of consistency in the evaluation process. This finding highlights the potential of integrating AI tools into classroom assessment. When used alongside human judgment, these tools can provide timely and scalable feedback, especially in environments where instructional time and resources are limited.

To further assess the agreement between AI systems and human raters, the research team calculated the Quadratic Weighted Kappa (QWK) coefficient. This statistical measure evaluates inter-rater reliability while accounting for the extent of disagreement. As shown in Fig. 1, the QWK value increased from 0.61 in Task 1 to 0.73 in Task 3. This upward movement indicates a growing alignment between automated and human-generated scores. It also suggests that students were gradually adjusting their writing to better reflect the genre norms and rhetorical conventions emphasized throughout the course.

Figure 2 provides a visual representation of these patterns. The trajectories of average scores from both human raters and AI systems demonstrate a parallel upward trend. This convergence implies that both assessment methods captured similar aspects of student progress. The rising QWK values add further support to the reliability of automated scoring. From a methodological perspective, this consistency validates the integration of AI-based assessment tools within pedagogically informed frameworks such as POA.

Further analysis was conducted to identify which specific areas of writing showed the greatest improvement. The most noticeable gains were found in three key domains: ideational content, linguistic accuracy, and discourse organization. These dimensions align closely with the three metafunctions described in Systemic Functional Linguistics (SFL): ideational, interpersonal, and textual. SFL served as a guiding theory for both instructional design and the development of feedback strategies in this study.

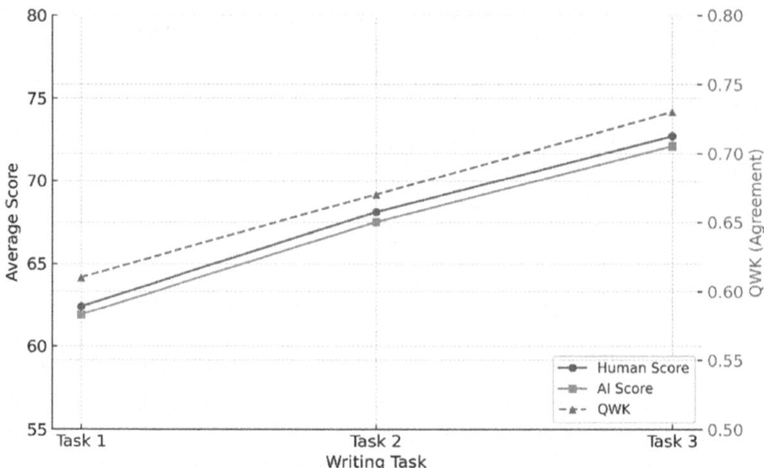

Fig. 2. Average Human and AI Scores with QWK Agreement across Writing Tasks

Students demonstrated enhanced ability to develop ideas and elaborate on topics. Their arguments became more relevant and clearly structured. Improvements in cohesion were also evident. Learners used more cohesive devices, better logical connectors, and clearer thematic progression. Over time, students showed increased control over interpersonal elements, such as tone, audience awareness, and modality choices. These changes reflect a deeper understanding of how language functions to create meaning in context.

In summary, the improvements observed were not superficial or mechanical. Rather, they represented meaningful development in students' rhetorical and linguistic skills. The AI-enhanced POA helped foster this growth by combining output-oriented tasks with timely, functionally grounded feedback. It also eased the workload on instructors without compromising the quality of assessment. These results lay the foundation for the next section, which explores how students interacted with the feedback they received and how these interactions influenced their writing revisions and development.

5.2 Feedback Utilization and Writing Improvement

To explore how students interacted with AI-generated feedback during the writing process, this study examined both their feedback uptake and related improvements in writing performance. The investigation focused on two sequential writing tasks designed under the Production-Oriented Approach (POA). The purpose was twofold: to measure how frequently learners incorporated the feedback and to assess how such engagement contributed to their writing development.

A total of 80 undergraduate students participated in this phase of the study. Feedback adoption was defined as the proportion of AI-generated suggestions that were visibly implemented in the students' revised drafts. These suggestions were produced by two widely used automated writing tools: GPT-4 and Grammarly. They included various types of input, such as lexical substitutions, syntactic rearrangements, elaboration of ideas, and enhancements to discourse organization. Revisions were identified through a built-in version comparison function provided by the writing platform, which enabled a side-by-side analysis of original and revised texts.

The results showed that, on average, students adopted 65.3% of the feedback suggestions in Task 1. In Task 2, this adoption rate increased slightly to 69.6%. Although the 4.3 percentage-point increase was not statistically significant ($p = 0.5893$), it pointed to a mild upward trend. This trend may indicate that learners became more comfortable with interpreting and applying AI feedback as the intervention progressed. While the change in adoption rate was modest, it offers initial evidence for growing engagement with automated assistance over time.

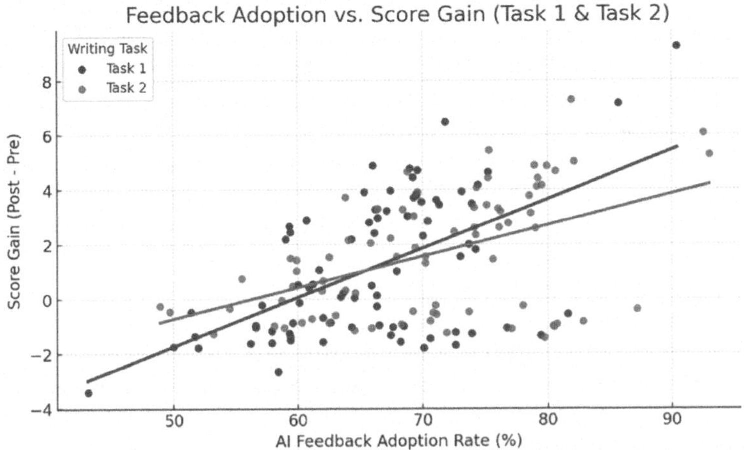

Fig. 3. Feedback Adoption vs. Score Gain across Task 1 and Task 2

Figure 3 illustrates the relationship between feedback usage and writing improvement. A Pearson correlation analysis was conducted to quantify this relationship. In Task 1, the correlation between feedback adoption and score gains was strong and statistically significant ($r = 0.604$, $p < 0.001$). In Task 2, the correlation remained positive, though weaker ($r = 0.389$, $p < 0.05$). The higher correlation in the earlier task suggests that initial exposure to AI feedback may have had a more pronounced influence. This effect could be attributed to the novelty of the tools or the motivational boost often associated with new learning technologies. Additionally, early feedback may have served a clarifying function, helping students understand the rhetorical and linguistic expectations of the task more effectively.

However, feedback adoption did not lead to uniform outcomes across all participants. Approximately 9% of students experienced minimal or even negative score gains, despite adopting a moderate to high number of suggestions. Closer qualitative analysis revealed that many of these students made surface-level edits. For example, they substituted vocabulary without considering context or altered sentence structure without addressing overall coherence. In such cases, the revisions lacked depth and were applied without critical evaluation, resulting in limited or counterproductive effects.

These observations highlight the central role of feedback literacy in maximizing the value of AI-generated suggestions. Learners must do more than accept feedback passively. They need to understand the function of each suggestion, assess its relevance, and integrate it meaningfully into their writing. Blind acceptance can undermine text quality, while informed use can promote genuine learning.

Within the POA framework, these findings emphasize the importance of the enabling and assessing phases, where learners receive structured guidance and revise their drafts. In this context, AI-generated feedback is not merely corrective. It also serves as a formative scaffold that supports students in refining meaning, clarifying purpose, and enhancing communicative intent.

Revisions that led to higher performance gains typically involved deeper textual improvements. These included more detailed ideational development, better paragraph structure, and stronger cohesion. Such enhancements correspond closely with the three meta functions of Systemic Functional Linguistics (SFL): ideational, interpersonal, and textual. Students who demonstrated these improvements appeared to be internalizing the functional principles of academic writing.

In addition to improving language accuracy, the AI-enhanced POA model also appeared to foster functional awareness. Some students used feedback as a springboard for broader rhetorical adjustments. These included adding clear topic sentences, strengthening logical flow, and employing evaluative language more effectively. These patterns indicate a shift from surface editing toward strategic composition.

In conclusion, while AI-generated feedback holds strong potential to enhance writing instruction, its effectiveness depends on how students process and apply the input. Simply providing feedback is not enough. Learners must be guided to interpret, evaluate, and transform feedback into meaningful revisions. These findings underline the importance of cultivating feedback literacy, particularly in technology-rich classrooms, to ensure that intelligent tools translate into real academic progress.

5.3 Learner Perceptions and Pedagogical Implications

In addition to tracking writing scores, we also collected student opinions about the AI-assisted instruction. All 80 participants completed a questionnaire after the intervention. The survey asked them to rate five aspects of the AI-generated feedback using a five-point Likert scale. These aspects included clarity, usefulness, trustworthiness, motivational impact, and preference compared to teacher feedback.

Overall, the responses were mostly positive. Students rated the clarity of AI feedback at an average of 4.2. Usefulness received a slightly higher average of 4.3. These scores suggest that learners generally found the feedback easy to understand and practically helpful. This aligns with findings from other studies, where students reported that automated feedback was clear and beneficial.

Trustworthiness received a mean rating of 3.9. Motivation was slightly lower at 3.8. These results indicate that students viewed the AI as moderately reliable and somewhat motivating. However, the lowest score was for preference over teacher feedback, which averaged just 3.1. This suggests that while students appreciated the AI, they still preferred human feedback when given a choice.

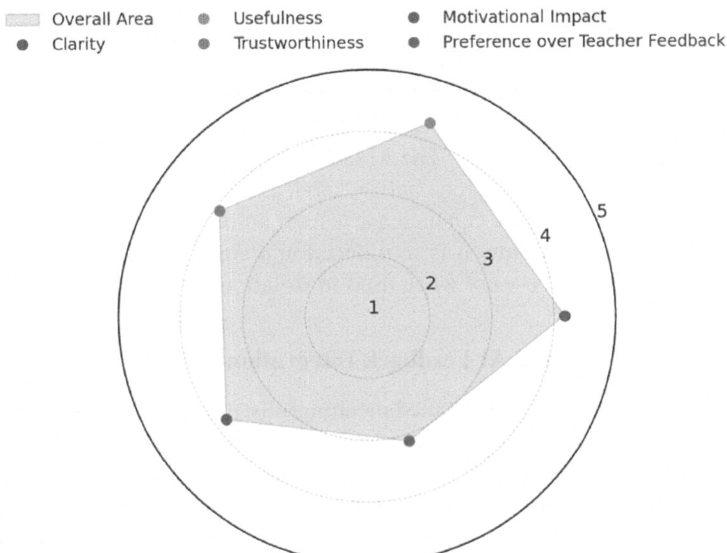

Fig. 4. Learner Perceptions of AI Feedback Across Five Dimensions (Radar Chart of Survey Results)

The radar chart in Fig. 4 highlights this pattern clearly. The axes for clarity and usefulness extend toward the edge, showing strong ratings. In contrast, the axis for preference remains closer to the center. This visual gap shows a key contrast. Students valued what the AI could do—mainly functional support like identifying errors and offering edits. But they were less confident in its ability to replace teacher guidance.

Many students described the AI as helpful for quick feedback. They used it to catch mistakes or improve word choice. However, when it came to complex issues—such as tone, argument logic, or content development—they turned to their teachers. The AI was useful for early-stage revision or surface-level editing. But for more nuanced guidance, students trusted human input.

Qualitative data from journals and interviews supported these trends. Students often described AI feedback as helpful but impersonal. The comments were sometimes too general. While learners did not always follow the AI's suggestions directly, they often used the feedback as a prompt to think more deeply about their writing. For example, a student might ignore the suggested wording but still decide to revise the sentence after considering the AI's comment. In this way, the AI helped foster metacognitive reflection.

These findings lead to two key takeaways for using AI feedback in English writing instruction. First, AI should serve as a supplement—not a replacement—for teacher feedback. Students still need the contextual insight that only teachers can provide. Second, students should be taught how to use AI feedback effectively. They need to understand when to apply it, when to ignore it, and how to evaluate its relevance.

Teachers can support this process by creating comparison tasks. For instance, during the assessing phase of POA, students could review both AI and teacher comments on the same draft. This activity helps them build critical reading skills. It teaches them to judge the quality of different feedback sources. It also encourages thoughtful revision rather than automatic acceptance of AI suggestions.

In summary, students found AI-generated feedback to be a helpful tool. It improved their editing process and supported clearer writing. However, they did not see it as a full substitute for human instruction. The AI lacked the ability to understand the broader context of student work or to offer personalized advice. When combined with a structured approach like POA, AI feedback can increase learner autonomy and revision awareness. Still, its impact depends on how it is introduced and supported. AI works best when paired with teacher guidance—not when used in isolation.

5.4 Teacher Mediation and AI Feedback Integration

While AI-generated feedback contributed meaningfully to student writing improvement and revision behavior, additional data pointed to another key factor. Evidence from classroom observations, instructor interviews, and student reflections underscored the essential role of teacher mediation. Teachers were not passive observers in this process. Rather, they acted as active facilitators who interpreted, filtered, and contextualized automated feedback in ways that supported instructional objectives and addressed learner needs.

To better understand this mediating role, semi-structured interviews were conducted with five writing instructors who participated in the intervention. All five instructors (100%) reported using AI-generated feedback—primarily from GPT-4 and Grammarly—as a diagnostic tool. They relied on these tools to identify recurring issues in student drafts. These included lexical repetition, sentence fragmentation, and weaknesses in textual cohesion. Four instructors (80%) also emphasized a critical limitation of AI feedback. In their view, AI tools often lacked awareness of academic discourse conventions. As a result, they found it necessary to supplement AI suggestions with explicit rhetorical guidance that aligned with genre-specific expectations.

Findings from classroom observations reinforced these perspectives. In eight out of ten POA assessing-phase sessions, teachers facilitated activities that required students to compare AI-generated feedback with teacher-provided comments. These comparative exercises aimed to enhance feedback literacy. They encouraged students to engage more critically with feedback from different sources. Instructors were also observed annotating AI suggestions in real-time. During these moments, they validated appropriate suggestions and flagged others as overly generic or misaligned with the learning objectives.

To illustrate how these mediating practices functioned together, Fig. 5 presents a co-occurrence network of core instructional strategies. This visualization is based on systematically coded classroom observation data. The network identifies five recurring types of mediation: Diagnostic Use of AI, Rhetorical Supplementing, Real-Time Annotation, Comparative Feedback Activities, and Promotion of Feedback Literacy. The connecting lines, or edges, indicate how often two practices appeared together during the same instructional session.

The strongest observed relationship was between Diagnostic Use of AI and Feedback Literacy Promotion (n = 19). This suggests that instructors frequently combined these two strategies—first using AI to detect problems, then guiding students in interpreting

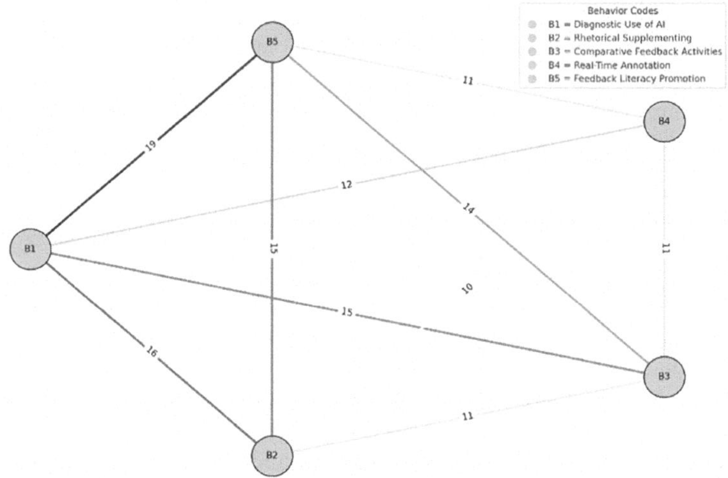

Fig. 5. Graph Representation of Mediation Behavior Co-occurrence

and applying feedback more effectively. The second most common co-occurrence was between Rhetorical Supplementing and Diagnostic Use of AI ($n = 16$). In these instances, teachers extended the diagnostic function of AI tools by providing rhetorical insights and genre-specific commentary.

Student reflections further confirmed these findings. According to survey data, 72.5% of students reported feeling more confident when teacher explanations accompanied AI feedback. Many students commented that teacher input helped them distinguish between surface-level corrections and deeper structural revisions. This distinction enabled more deliberate and effective rewriting.

These results suggest that AI-generated feedback is most impactful when integrated into teacher-led instructional routines. Teachers served as critical mediators. They helped students make sense of AI suggestions, aligned feedback with course goals, and promoted strategic engagement with revision tasks. The network displayed in Fig. 5 demonstrates that these practices functioned not in isolation, but as part of a cohesive instructional system.

In conclusion, teacher mediation remains a vital component of AI-supported writing pedagogy. Future implementations should include targeted professional development for educators. This training should cover interpretation of AI feedback, genre-sensitive prompt design, and the integration of multimodal feedback sources. Strengthening teacher capacity in these areas is essential for building sustainable and effective human–AI partnerships in writing instruction.

6 Conclusion and Future Work

This study introduced a pedagogical framework that integrates the Production-Oriented Approach (POA) with artificial intelligence (AI) to enhance English as a Foreign Language (EFL) writing instruction. The framework is grounded in constructivist learning theory and informed by Systemic Functional Linguistics (SFL). It connects the three core stages of the POA—motivating, enabling, and assessing—with AI-supported instructional strategies designed to scaffold learning at each stage.

The model incorporates state-of-the-art language technologies, including GPT-4 and the Write & Improve platform. These AI tools are employed to generate context-rich writing tasks, provide real-time linguistic support, and deliver formative feedback during the revision process. Importantly, the feedback is structured according to SFL's three meta functions: ideational (content and logic), interpersonal (stance and modality), and textual (cohesion and organization). By aligning feedback with these meta functions, the model facilitates a more functionally informed and learner-centered approach to writing instruction. These integrated components help construct a structured, output-driven learning cycle focused on authentic language use.

Empirical data from a classroom-based intervention confirmed the effectiveness of the framework. Students demonstrated measurable improvement in writing quality, as reflected in scores assigned by both trained human raters and automated scoring systems. Learners also showed deeper engagement with feedback and greater autonomy in the revision process. Notably, AI did not replace teacher input. Rather, it served as a supportive tool that reduced the teacher's feedback workload and reinforced consistent use of rubric-based evaluation.

One of the key insights from the study involves the role of teacher mediation. Interviews and classroom observations revealed that teachers played an active role in interpreting AI feedback, clarifying rhetorical choices, and guiding students to critically compare AI and human suggestions. These mediation strategies were often used in combination, reflecting a coordinated instructional approach.

Nonetheless, the study identified some limitations. In certain cases, AI feedback lacked genre sensitivity or failed to fully consider the contextual nuances of student writing. The reliance on generic prompts also limited the personalization of instruction. Therefore, effective integration will require targeted teacher training, particularly in designing prompts and managing AI-human feedback dynamics.

Future research should explore the extension of this framework to include spoken and multimodal communication tasks, particularly within English for Specific Purposes (ESP). Long-term studies are also needed to examine sustained learning effects, student perceptions of AI credibility, and the potential for explainable AI to support transparency and deeper learner understanding.

References

1. OpenAI. GPT-4 Technical Report (2023). https://cdn.openai.com/papers/gpt-4.pdf
2. Jiahui, H., Salmiza, S., Yufei, L.: A review on artificial intelligence in education. Acad. J. Interdisciplinary Stud. **10**(3), 206–212 (2021)
3. Feng, H., Li, K., Zhang, L.J.: What does AI bring to second language writing? a systematic review (2014–2024). Lang. Learn. Technol. **29**(1), 1–27 (2025)
4. Shi, H., Aryadoust, V.: A systematic review of AI-based automated written feedback research. J. EUROCALL **36**(2), 187–209 (2024)
5. Zhao, Y., Li, S.: Pedagogical gaps in AI applications for L2 writing: a critical review. J. Lang. Teach. Res. **15**(1), 23–35 (2024)

6. Wen, Q.: Developing a theoretical system of production-oriented approach in language teaching. Foreign Lang. Teach. Res. **47**(4), 547–558 (2015)
7. Pu, S.: Production-oriented approach in different cultural contexts: theory and practice. Chin. J. Appl. Linguist. **41**(2), 236–237 (2018)
8. Tsai, C.Y., Lin, Y.T., Brown, I.K.: Impacts of ChatGPT-assisted writing for EFL English majors: feasibility and challenges. Educ. Inf. Technol. **29**, 22427–22445 (2024)
9. Gleason, J.: Meaning-based scoring: a systemic functional linguistics model for automated test tasks. Hispania **97**(4), 666–688 (2014)
10. Kai, G., Mengru, P., Yuanke, L., Chun, L.: Effects of an AI-supported approach to peer feedback on university EFL students' feedback quality and writing ability. Int. High. Educ. **63**, 100962 (2024)
11. Yibin, H.: Reconstructing "Learning-Application Integration" practical training courses for English teacher trainees from the POA perspective. US-China Educ. Rev. **15**(4), 287–296 (2025)
12. Liu, J., Zhang, T.: Enhancing cohesion and coherence through POA in writing classes. Fore. Lang. World **5**, 89–97 (2021)
13. Lim, W.M., Gunasekara, A., Pallant, J.L., Pallant, J.I., Pechenkina, E.: Generative AI and the future of education: Ragnarök or reformation? a paradoxical perspective from management educators. Int. J. Manag. Educ. **21**(2), 100790 (2023)
14. Tossell, C.C., Tenhundfeld, N.L., Momen, A., Cooley, K., de Visser, E.J.: Student perceptions of ChatGPT use in a college essay assignment: implications for learning, grading, and trust in artificial intelligence. IEEE Trans. Learn. Technol. **17**, 1069–1081 (2024)
15. Ibrahim, K., Kirkpatrick, R.: Potentials and implications of ChatGPT for ESL writing instruction. Int. Rev. Res. Open Distrib. Learn. **25**(3), 394–409 (2024)
16. Rongrong, S., Yun, S.: Using Production-Oriented Approach (POA) to improve Chinese EFL writing. In: Proceedings of the 2021 International Conference on Information Technology, Education and Development, pp. 152–161. IATED, Ottawa (2021)

Large Language Model Helps the Teaching Reform of Programming

Zhan Tang, Xiaoli Peng(✉), Xiaoyu Lu, and Nian Yang

Sichuan University of Arts and Science, Dazhou 635000, China
93334586@qq.com

Abstract. In view of the problems existing in the current teaching of programming course, such as outdated teaching content, single teaching method, weak practice link, and weak innovation ability, this paper analyzes the application status of artificial intelligence and large language model in the field of education, and puts forward a teaching reform strategy based on AI model, which includes updating auxiliary teaching resources, enriching teaching mode, optimizing practice link, and improving auxiliary innovation ability. Through detailed course application case analysis, the actual effectiveness and operational process in updating teaching content, implementing personalized teaching paths, providing intelligent programming assistance, designing innovative project tasks, and stimulating student creativity are demonstrated. It also proposes targeted strategies to strengthen infrastructure construction and resource sharing, systematically enhance teacher AI capabilities, and guide students to adapt to AI assisted learning environments. The purpose of this study is to provide practical theoretical references and practical paths for the innovation and quality improvement of teaching modes in programming courses under the background of artificial intelligence era, and to promote the profound transformation of teaching from knowledge imparting to ability cultivation, from standardization to personalization, and from passive acceptance to active innovation.

Keywords: Artificial Intelligence · Large Language Model · Programming · Teaching Reform

1 Introduction

With the rapid development of artificial intelligence (AI) and large language model (LLM), significant progress has been made in many fields such as natural language processing [1]. LLM can not only generate high-quality text, but also provide intelligent assistance in a variety of application scenarios. In the era of artificial intelligence under this background, the program design course, as the core teaching content of computer science specialty, is facing new opportunities and challenges. The traditional teaching method of programming often focuses on the teaching of grammar and algorithm, but ignores the cultivation of students' innovative ability and problem-solving ability in actual programming. Therefore, the introduction of artificial intelligence and LLM into the teaching of programming course can not only enrich the teaching content, but also stimulate students' interest in learning and improve the teaching effect.

W. Hong et al. (Eds.): ICCSE 2025, CCIS 2761, pp. 88–99, 2026.
https://doi.org/10.1007/978-981-95-7731-6_8

The organic integration of LLM technology into various aspects of programming course teaching is not simply a combination of technology, but a key opportunity to promote profound changes in teaching paradigms. LLM can serve as powerful "intelligent assistants" and "knowledge engines", helping teachers break through the limitations of traditional teaching and providing students with unprecedented learning support and innovation space [2]. It can not only greatly enrich and update teaching content in real-time, keeping it close to the forefront of technology, but also effectively stimulate students' intrinsic learning motivation, improve learning efficiency and depth through personalized learning paths, intelligent practical assistance, and innovative task design, ultimately achieving a fundamental transformation from "teaching centered" to "learning centered", and from "knowledge imparting" to "ability cultivation". Exploring new forms of programming teaching empowered by LLM has important theoretical value and urgent practical significance.

2 Analysis

2.1 Problems in Current Programming Teaching

In the current programming course teaching, some teaching materials and teaching contents are not updated in time, and the latest programming technologies and tools are not covered; The teaching mode is mainly taught by teachers, which is lack of interactivity and practicality, and it is difficult to stimulate students' learning enthusiasm; The opportunities of experiment and project practice are limited, so it is difficult for students to combine theoretical knowledge with practical application; Students often rely on fixed models and examples in the process of programming, lacking innovative thinking. Therefore, at present, there are some problems in the teaching of program design course, such as outdated teaching content, single teaching method, weak practice link, weak innovation ability and so on.

(1) **Lagging and static teaching content.** Some textbooks and course content have long update cycles, making it difficult to cover rapidly changing technological ecosystems such as cloud computing, big data, AI frameworks (TensorFlow, PyTorch), new programming paradigms (functional, responsive), DevOps toolchains, etc. The teaching content often focuses on basic grammar and classic theories, lacking timely reflection on the latest industry practices, mainstream framework applications, and cutting-edge research trends, resulting in a significant gap between students' learned knowledge and actual work needs.

(2) **The singularity and indoctrination of teaching methods.** The mainstream teaching mode is still dominated by lecture based teaching, with insufficient teacher-student interaction and student collaboration. Students passively receive knowledge and lack opportunities for active exploration and deep participation. Although multimedia teaching is popular, it has not fundamentally changed the nature of one-way indoctrination, making it difficult to effectively mobilize learning enthusiasm and cultivate critical thinking.

(3) **Weakness and disconnect in practical aspects.** Experimental design is often limited to verifying syntax or simple algorithms, and project practice opportunities are scarce or small in scale, with low complexity, making it difficult to simulate real software development scenarios. Students lack systematic training in applying theoretical knowledge to solve comprehensive and open-ended engineering problems, resulting in a widespread phenomenon of "talking on paper" and poor effectiveness in cultivating practical and innovative abilities. The connection between practical activities and theoretical teaching is not tight enough, and the timeliness and pertinence of feedback and guidance are insufficient.

(4) **Lack and superficiality of innovation ability cultivation.** Excessive emphasis on standard answers and fixed patterns in the teaching process, insufficient design of exploratory and open-ended questions. Students are prone to developing a dependence on example code during programming exercises, and are accustomed to imitating rather than creating. They lack the awareness and ability to independently analyze problems, design novel solutions, and make technical selections. The evaluation system also tends to focus more on the correctness of results, with insufficient attention and motivation for innovative thinking processes.

A new way to solve these problems is to deeply integrate LLM into the core link of programming teaching, strengthen the combination with technological frontier and practical application, and stimulate students' learning interest and innovation ability.

2.2 Application Status of LLM in Teaching

In recent years, the application of LLM in the field of education has gradually increased, showing significant influence and innovative value [3], such as assisting the course content and the ideological and political design of the course [4]. Suggestions are put forward from three aspects: the AI intelligent setting of the course, the AI intelligent attempt of the teaching mode, and the AI intelligent evaluation of the teaching effect [5]. Artificial intelligence technology provides strong technical support for higher education and teaching innovation, making it more efficient, fair and personalized [6], and promoting students' learning initiative, enthusiasm and innovation [7].

LLM is profoundly influencing the field of education, with its core applications focused on personalized learning, improving teaching assistance efficiency, generating interactive content, and managing educational research [8]. At the level of personalized learning, LLM plays the role of an intelligent mentor, analyzing learning data to customize learning paths, recommend resources, and provide 24/7 Q&A (such as mathematical step analysis, essay ideas inspiration) and language learning support (such as dialogue exercises, grammar correction) for students. For teachers, LLM has become a powerful efficiency tool that can quickly generate lesson plans, practice questions, and test questions, assist in grading essays and programming assignments, provide initial feedback, and summarize key knowledge points for textbook generation, significantly saving preparation and evaluation time. In addition, LLM can simulate character dialogues, generate diverse learning materials (articles, stories, code examples), act as virtual learning partners, enhance learning interactivity and resource richness. In educational research management, it can analyze learning behavior data to identify difficulties or risks, and automate some administrative paperwork.

However, in the programming course, the application of artificial intelligence and LLM is still in the exploratory stage, and has not yet penetrated into the core link of the course teaching, nor has it formed a systematic teaching mode.

3 Teaching Reform Strategy Based on LLM

In order to improve the teaching effect of programming course, we propose the following teaching reform strategy based on LLM, as shown in Fig. 1.

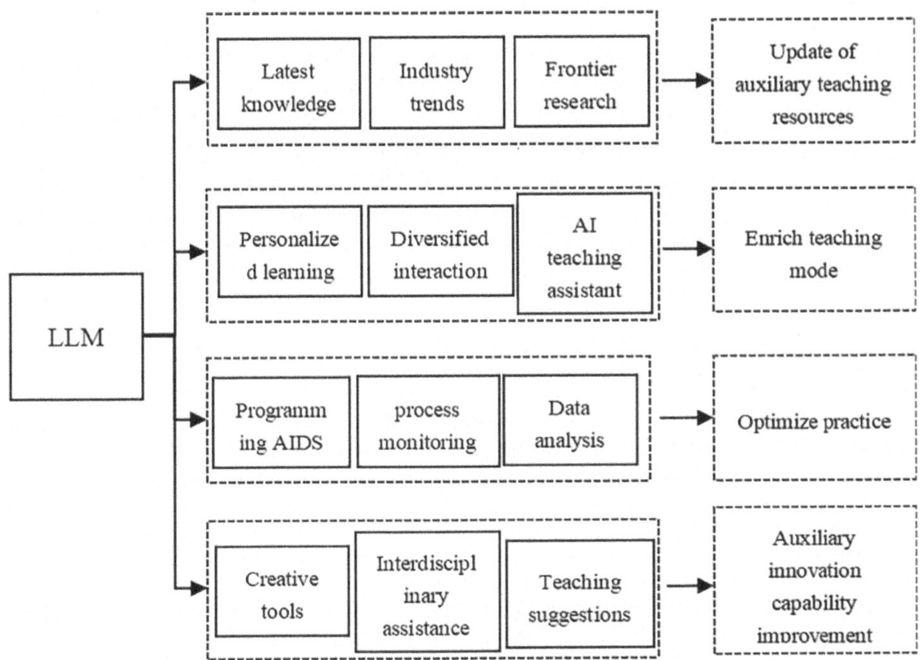

Fig. 1. Teaching reform strategy based on LLM

This figure shows the four pillar strategies and core supporting elements of program design teaching reform driven by LLM as the core engine. The update of auxiliary teaching resources relies on industry trends, the latest knowledge, and cutting-edge research; The "enriched teaching mode" is reflected in diversified interactions, personalized learning paths, and the participation of AI teaching assistants; The core of the "optimization practice phase" is programming assistance, process monitoring, and data analysis; The enhancement of auxiliary innovation capability is achieved through interdisciplinary assistance, creative tool support, and providing innovative teaching suggestions for teachers. The four major strategies collaborate with each other and jointly aim to improve teaching effectiveness and cultivate students' abilities.

Update of Auxiliary Teaching Resources. Using LLM to screen and integrate the latest knowledge and information from massive data, help teachers update teaching content in time, realize systematic, visual, interactive and convenient high-quality resource aggregation by matching the thematic resource database related to program design, and introduce the latest industry trends, research results and actual cases to update teaching content in real time.

Enrich Teaching Mode. According to different students' learning ability, personality characteristics and interest preferences, personalized learning paths and learning contents are designed. Assist teachers to design diversified classroom interaction links, such as group discussion, role play, interactive question and answer, etc., and also allow AI teaching assistants to participate in classroom discussion, so as to enhance the interactivity and interest of the classroom.

Optimize Practice. Using the powerful generation ability of AI model, develop intelligent auxiliary programming tools to provide students with code completion, error detection and repair, code optimization and other services to help students complete programming tasks more efficiently. Assist teachers in designing project-based learning tasks, guide students to improve their practical ability by solving practical problems, monitor students' performance in practice in real time, and provide detailed feedback and improvement suggestions. Teachers can analyze students' practice data through AI model, timely adjust the practice teaching content and methods, and improve the practice effect.

Auxiliary Innovation Capability Improvement. Provide students with creative tools to stimulate students' creativity through interesting learning tasks and open problem design. It can assist interdisciplinary teaching design, help students think from the perspective of different disciplines, cultivate comprehensive innovation ability, and provide teachers with suggestions and inspiration for innovative teaching methods, and help teachers break through the traditional teaching thinking.

4 Application Case

4.1 Python Language Programming Course

Taking *Python Language Programming* course in our school as an example, this paper discusses the specific application of AI model in teaching practice, which is shown in Fig. 2. The goal of this course is to systematically master the python grammar foundation, data structure application, algorithm design thinking and object-oriented programming method, and cultivate the ability to solve practical engineering problems. In the course of teaching, teachers introduced AI model to assist, and carried out in-depth teaching reform by updating teaching resources, enriching teaching mode, optimizing practice links and assisting in improving innovation ability.

Teachers use LLM to screen and integrate the latest python programming knowledge and information from massive data, as well as rich industry trends, research results and actual cases, so as to make the teaching content more timely and practical, including the latest Python framework and library application cases, such as the application of Django framework in Web development, the application of pandas Library in data analysis, etc. Then these cases are integrated into the teaching, so that students can understand the application and development trend of Python language in different fields.

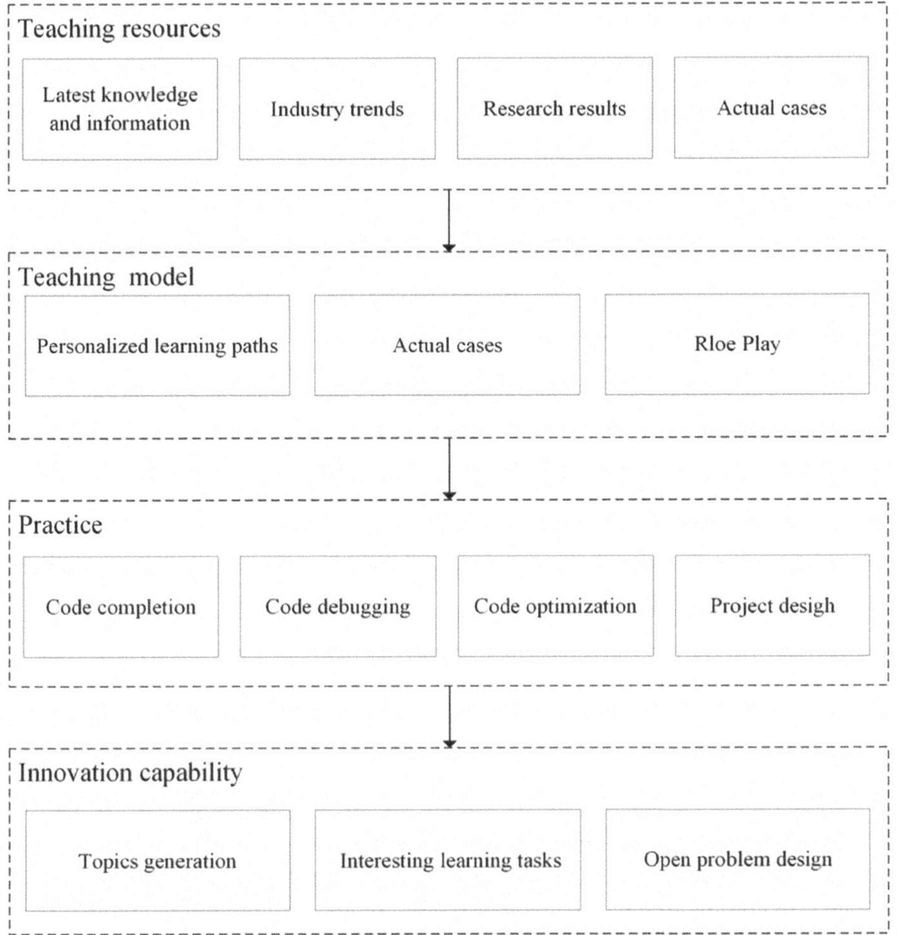

Fig. 2. Over view of Python Language Programming course

According to students' learning ability, personality characteristics and interest preferences, teachers use AI model to design personalized learning paths and teaching contents for different students. For students with weak programming foundation, LLM recommends the learning contents of basic grammar and simple algorithm, and provides corresponding exercises and case analysis; For students with strong programming ability, advanced algorithms, data structure optimization and project practice are recommended. This personalized learning path design meets the learning needs of different students, and improves the learning effect and satisfaction of students. Teachers also used AI teaching assistants to participate in classroom activities, which enhanced the interaction and interest of the classroom. In the group discussion, the AI teaching assistant assigns different discussion topics to each group and provides relevant background information and problem guidance; In role play, AI teaching assistants assign different roles to students and provide scenes and tasks for role play. These interactive links stimulate students' learning enthusiasm, cultivate students' teamwork ability and problem solving ability.

Using the powerful generation ability of AI model, teachers have developed intelligent auxiliary programming tools to provide students with code completion, code debugging, code optimization and other services to help students complete programming tasks more efficiently. When students encounter grammar errors or logic problems, intelligent auxiliary programming tools can prompt the error location and provide repair suggestions in time. Teachers also designed project-based python programming practice tasks with the help of AI model, providing detailed background information, needs analysis and step-by-step implementation guide for each project task. In the process of completing the project, students not only consolidate the programming knowledge they have learned, but also cultivate their comprehensive abilities such as teamwork, problem solving and innovative thinking. They can also record the data such as code writing progress, debugging process and problems encountered, and get real-time monitoring of the AI model, and get detailed feedback and improvement suggestions. Teachers also know the students' learning situation in time through these data, which helps to adjust the practice teaching content and methods and improve the practice effect.

In order to stimulate students' creativity, the teacher used the AI model to generate some inspiring and creative python programming topics. Through interesting learning tasks and open problem design, the teacher guided students to think creatively and let students freely exert their imagination and creativity in the process of solving problems.

Teachers and students have accumulated some valuable experience and lessons by introducing LLM to assist teaching in the course of Python language programming. In terms of updating teaching resources, teachers need to invest the necessary energy in screening and sorting out the massive information and materials produced by AI model, which should not only ensure the professional authority of the knowledge system, but also ensure the practical application value of teaching cases. In terms of enriching the teaching mode, teachers need to flexibly adjust the personalized learning path and teaching content according to the actual situation of students, avoid relying too much on the recommendation results of the AI model, and also need to give full play to their guiding role in the classroom interaction to ensure that students can actively participate in and benefit from it. In the aspect of practice optimization, teachers need to strengthen the guidance and supervision of students' practice process, ensure that students can correctly understand and apply the suggestions and feedback provided by intelligent auxiliary programming tools, and timely adjust the difficulty and requirements of project tasks according to students' practice performance, so as to meet the learning needs of different students. In terms of the auxiliary improvement of innovation ability, teachers need to encourage students' bold attempt and innovation, cultivate students' independent thinking ability and problem-solving ability, and constantly explore and innovate teaching methods to provide students with more innovation opportunities and platforms. These experiences provide a reusable implementation path for AI model enabling programming education, which can not only effectively improve the teaching effect, but also promote the collaborative development of students' engineering thinking and innovation ability.

4.2 C Language Programming Course

Another instance is the course of *C Language Programming*, in which the teacher reconstructed the traditional teaching mode based on LLM technology. In response to the difficulty in understanding abstract concepts such as pointers and memory management in C language teaching, teachers use LLM to dynamically integrate the latest industry application cases, such as IoT device driver development, real-time data processing of embedded systems, and other scenarios, combining dry grammar knowledge with cutting-edge technology. The course introduces real project cases based on Raspberry Pi hardware development, and uses AI generated interactive 3D memory model animations to visually display pointer operations and memory allocation processes, significantly reducing students' cognitive barriers. The overview is shown in Fig. 3.

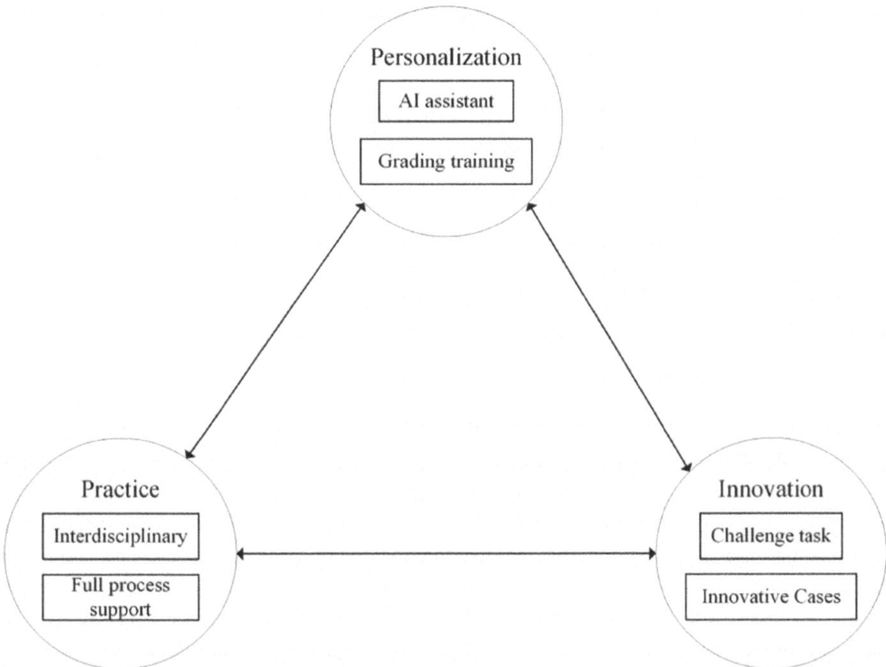

Fig. 3. Over view of C Language Programming course

During the teaching process, the LLM constructs personalized learning paths based on students' previous homework performance and online learning behavior. Push step-by-step pointer themed training to students with weak foundations, supplemented by dynamic debugging demonstrations; For students with outstanding abilities, it is recommended to perform Linux kernel source code fragment analysis tasks and match them with corresponding algorithm optimization challenges. Introduce an AI virtual teaching assistant system in the classroom to monitor student code in real-time during experimental sessions. When a null pointer or memory leak risk is detected, immediately locate the erroneous line and provide a repair plan reference. When developing the "Micro Operating System Scheduling Module" project in group collaboration, AI assistants provide customized development documents and test cases for groups with different roles (memory management, process scheduling, etc.).

To enhance engineering practical abilities, teachers utilize AI to generate interdisciplinary project task packages. For example, in the design of the "Intelligent Traffic Signal Control System" project, students are required to comprehensively apply structural, file I/O, and multi-threaded programming techniques. The AI toolchain provides full process support from requirement analysis to code refactoring: automatically completing commonly used data structure templates during the coding phase; During the debugging phase, explain the cause of paragraph errors through natural language interaction; Generate a visual performance analysis report during project review. Through the real-time heat map in the AI backend, teachers found that students generally have misunderstandings in the dynamic memory management module. They immediately adjusted the experimental course content and added practical training on memory pool design.

In terms of innovation cultivation, open challenge tasks for LLM design. For example, proposing an optimization competition for "implementing linked list inversion with minimal pointer operations", or designing an "embedded device energy-saving algorithm" based on hardware characteristics. In the final project of the course, a student was inspired by a computer graphics case recommended by AI and used C language to implement a simple ray tracing renderer, demonstrating innovative thinking that breaks through the course framework. Teachers can use AI assisted code similarity detection tools to ensure the efficiency of original review and accurately identify implementation solutions with innovative value.

During the implementation process, teachers need to continuously optimize the intervention boundaries of AI tools. For example, when explaining the underlying mechanism of pointers, deliberately reducing instant prompts and guiding students to think independently first; Manually review AI generated requirement documents during the project design phase to ensure compliance with teaching objectives. Student feedback indicates that AI assistance has significantly improved debugging efficiency, but it requires high hardware resources and some outdated devices may experience delays during operation. In response, the college provides centralized computing power support through cloud laboratories and establishes a localized model fine-tuning mechanism to make the generated content more in line with the course knowledge graph.

5 Existing Challenges and Improvement Strategies

5.1 Existing Problems and Challenges

AI model may have some errors and uncertainties in generating teaching content, providing personalized suggestions and feedback. When generating teaching resources and project tasks, it may be limited by data quality and training model, and cannot fully meet the teaching needs. In addition, the introduction of AI large-scale model to assist teaching requires certain technical infrastructure support, such as high-performance computing equipment, stable network environment and corresponding software tools, which requires high hardware equipment resources.

The introduction of LLM requires teachers not only to master traditional teaching methods and subject knowledge, but also to understand and master the basic principles and application methods of AI technology. Teachers need to learn how to effectively utilize the resources and tools provided by LLM and integrate them into the teaching process to improve teaching effectiveness. For example, teachers need to learn how to interpret the teaching suggestions generated by LLM, how to combine AI tools for personalized teaching design, and how to guide students to use intelligent auxiliary programming tools correctly. This requires teachers to constantly update their knowledge system, enhance their digital literacy and technological application abilities. Universities should provide relevant training and learning opportunities for teachers to help them adapt to the needs of teaching reform.

The application of LLM promotes the transformation of teachers from traditional knowledge transmitters to learning guides and facilitators. Teachers need to pay more attention to students' personalized learning needs, guide students to learn and explore independently, rather than relying solely on teachers' explanations. For example, in classroom interactive activities, teachers need to play a more guiding role, encouraging students to actively participate in discussions and practices, rather than directly giving answers. At the same time, teachers also need to learn how to use the data and feedback information provided by LLM to adjust teaching strategies and methods in a timely manner, in order to better meet students' learning needs. The adjustment of this teaching philosophy and method requires teachers to constantly explore and summarize their experience in practice.

Some students may feel unfamiliar or unadapted to the use of LLM assisted teaching tools, which will affect their learning effect. Students' acceptance of AI tools will also affect their learning enthusiasm and participation. Some students are accustomed to the traditional teaching mode and lack the motivation and ability of autonomous learning. When facing open problems and project tasks, they do not know how to start and lack the ability to think and solve problems independently.

Therefore, teachers need to focus on cultivating students' self-learning ability in the teaching process, guiding them to learn how to independently plan learning paths, search for learning resources, and solve problems encountered in learning. By setting challenging learning tasks and projects, students can be encouraged to explore and practice independently, cultivating their ability to think independently and solve problems innovatively.

5.2 Improvement Strategies

Strengthen the construction of technological infrastructure and resource sharing. Increase investment in technical infrastructure, including the purchase of high-performance computing equipment, the optimization of the network environment, the introduction of advanced software tools, etc., to provide good technical support for LLM assisted teaching. Establish a resource sharing mechanism with brother universities to share the teaching resources, data and experience related to the AI model, reduce the cost of resource acquisition and improve the efficiency of resource utilization.

Improve teachers' AI literacy and teaching ability. Provide teachers with systematic AI technology training and learning opportunities, and help teachers master the basic principles, application methods and teaching strategies of the AI model, including the application case analysis of AI technology in education, the operation and application of AI tools, AI based teaching design and implementation.

Guide students to adapt to AI assisted learning environment. Teachers should strengthen the training and guidance of students' use of AI tools in the teaching process, help students to be familiar with the functions and operation methods of AI tools through classroom demonstration and practical operation, and design interesting teaching activities and project tasks to stimulate students' interest and curiosity in AI tools and improve their willingness to use them. We should also pay attention to the cultivation of students' autonomous learning ability, guide students to learn to independently plan learning paths, find learning resources and solve problems encountered in learning, and cultivate their ability to think independently and solve problems innovatively, so as to adapt to the development of the era of artificial intelligence.

In order to ensure the effectiveness of LLM assisted teaching, universities should establish a scientific and reasonable teaching evaluation and feedback mechanism. The evaluation indicators should cover multiple aspects such as the quality of teaching resources, the innovation of teaching modes, the effectiveness of practical activities, and students' learning outcomes. At the same time, attention should be paid to collecting feedback from students and teachers, and timely understanding of their experiences and needs in using AI models to assist teaching processes. Through regular teaching evaluations and feedback, teachers can adjust teaching strategies and methods in a timely manner, optimize the application effectiveness of AI models, and improve teaching quality and student learning outcomes.

6 Conclusion

The application of artificial intelligence and LLM technology has become a new trend in the teaching of programming courses. The introduction of LLM assisted teaching has realized the dynamic updating of teaching resources, the diversification of teaching modes, the optimization of practice links and the auxiliary improvement of innovation ability. In the era of rapid development of artificial intelligence, teachers should constantly update teaching concepts and methods, actively learn new tools and technologies such as LLM, and pay attention to guiding students to change their learning concepts and improve their motivation and ability of active learning. Although this study has achieved certain results, there are still some limitations. Firstly, the research mainly focuses on the teaching reform of programming courses, and further verification is needed for their applicability to other courses or disciplines. Secondly, due to the limited research time and relatively small sample size, the universality of the research results may be affected to some extent. In addition, further tracking and research are needed to investigate the long-term effects and impacts of LLM application in teaching. In future work, one the one hand, It is important to expand the research scope, explore the application effects of LLM in other courses or disciplines, and verify its applicability and effectiveness in different teaching scenarios. On the other hand, it is necessary to increase the sample size and research time, and conduct long-term tracking studies to deeply analyze the long-term impact of LLM on teaching quality and student learning outcomes. Technology.

Acknowledgments. This study was funded by Sichuan Higher Education Quality and Teaching Reform Project (grant number JG2024-1129) and Applied Brand Course of Sichuan University of Arts and Sciences (grant number 2024YYXPPKC12 and 2024YYXPPKC02).

References

1. Alsafari, B., Atwell, E., Walker, A., et al.: Towards effective teaching assistants: from intent-based chatbots to LLM-powered teaching assistants. Microelec. J. (2024)
2. Velander, J., Otero, N., Dobslaw, F., Milrad, M.: Eliciting and empowering teachers' AI literacy: the devil is in the detail. In: Herodotou, C., et al. Methodologies and Intelligent Systems for Technology Enhanced Learning, 14th International Conference. MIS4TEL 2024. Lecture Notes in Networks and Systems, vol. 1171. Springer, Cham (2024). https://doi.org/10.1007/978-3-031-73538-7_13
3. Wang, F., Zhao, Z., Wang, Y., et al.: Exploration and practice of artificial intelligence in programming teaching. Comput. Educ. **2**(11), 45–50 (2023)
4. Qiang, N.: Research on the teaching reform of logistics management course from the perspective of new quality productivity: a case study of Logistics Information System. Exhib. Econ. **2**(24), 162–165 (2024)
5. Xu, W., Zhou, L.: Teaching reform and exploration of ship and ocean engineering based on AI technology. J. Higher Educ. **2**(04), 21–24 (2025)
6. Wang, H., Zhang, L.: Education and teaching reform in Colleges and Universities based on artificial intelligence technology. Res. Pract. Innov. Entrepreneurship **2**(24), 26–28 (2024)
7. Sui, X., Lu, X., Dong, Q., et al.: Exploration of AI tutor teaching mode in military colleges and universities based on large model. China Educ. Technol. Equip. **2**(22), 98–101 (2024)
8. Lan, Y., Chen, N.: Teachers' agency in the era of LLM and generative AI: designing pedagogical AI agents. Educ. Technol. Soc. **27**(1), 1–18 (2024)

AI-Assisted Discrete Mathematics Teaching Platform Based on Multimodal Learning Resources

Hulin Kuang, Hongdong Li(✉), Min Zeng, and Jianxin Wang

School of Computer Science and Engineering, Central South University, Changsha 410083, China
{hulinkuang,hongdong,zengmin,jxwang}@csu.edu.cn

Abstract. This paper proposes a discrete mathematics teaching platform based on a multimodal learning resource repository and the DeepSeek-RAG integration engine. The multimodal repository collects diverse data related to discrete mathematics, which undergoes preprocessing, annotation, and deep learning-based optimization (CNNs for images, RNNs for text or speech). Knowledge is stored using a dual-structure approach combining knowledge graphs and vector databases, enabling semantic association, intelligent retrieval, and inference of multimodal information. The DeepSeek-RAG integration engine combines retrieval-augmented generation (RAG) with the DeepSeek large language model to perform efficient sparse or dense retrieval, accurately locating relevant content within the multimodal repository. Through multimodal fusion, redundancy reduction, and enhanced relevance modeling, the engine generates results with improved contextual consistency, knowledge richness, and accuracy, effectively supporting retrieval, question answering, and assessment functionalities. Based on this platform, we propose a hybrid teaching model that integrates traditional instruction, intelligent platforms, and collaborative group learning, which has demonstrated significant effectiveness in practical teaching scenarios.

Keywords: Discrete Mathematics · Multimodal Learning Resource Repository · DeepSeek-RAG Fusion Engine · Hybrid Teaching Mode

1 Introduction

As a core component of the educational objectives of computer majors, discrete mathematics [1] occupies an indispensable position in the introductory courses of computer majors. Discrete mathematics can cultivate students' innovative consciousness, scientific thinking ability and practical problem-solving ability,

This work was supported by the Central South University Education and Teaching Reform Research Project (Grant No. 2024jy091, 2025jy126) and Hunan Province Graduate Education and Teaching Reform Research Project (No. 2023JGZD009).

W. Hong et al. (Eds.): ICCSE 2025, CCIS 2761, pp. 100–112, 2026.
https://doi.org/10.1007/978-981-95-7731-6_9

which is crucial for future research and work in computer-related fields. However, at present, the teaching of discrete mathematics mainly adopts the method of teaching theoretical knowledge offline. This teaching method is relatively simple and cannot meet the needs of various learning habits of students. It lacks flexibility and innovation. In addition, discrete mathematics is a strong theoretical and logical subject. Its content is relatively dull, the knowledge points are complicated, the concepts are relatively abstract, and it is difficult to understand. Therefore, mobilizing students' interest in learning is difficult, which dramatically increases the difficulty of learning the course.

With the development of the times, the way of knowledge dissemination and acquisition has changed, and many online education resources [2] have emerged, such as online education platforms such as MOOC and YuKeTang. These education platforms provide students with a large number of audio, video, picture, text and other resources for independent learning. However, the disadvantages of traditional teaching methods are becoming more and more evident in the digital age: teaching resources are limited, it is difficult to integrate the rich multimodal resources of online education platforms such as MOOC and YuKeTang, and there is a lack of real-time interactive functions; the teaching progress is fixed, students cannot adjust their learning pace according to their situation, and it is difficult to obtain expansion resources, which limits the cultivation of independent learning ability; traditional teaching emphasizes concentrated classroom teaching, lacks the flexibility and interactivity of online platforms, making it difficult for teachers to grasp the learning situation of each student promptly, affecting teaching efficiency and quality.

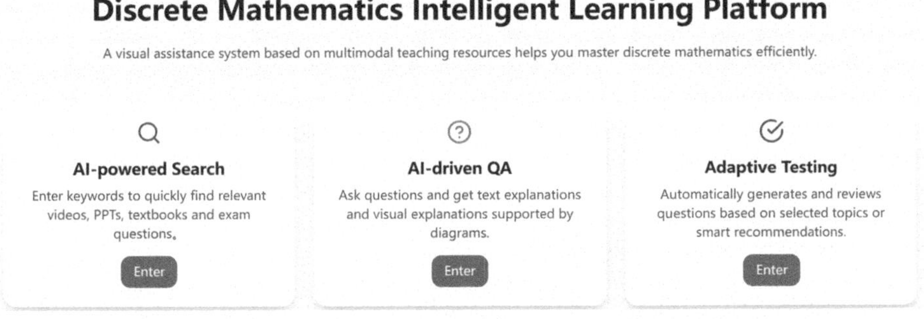

Fig. 1. The framework of the platform.

However, with the development of artificial intelligence technology and the introduction of large language models [3], generative AI and DeepSeek technologies have flourished rapidly. The development of this technology has made natural language interaction, intelligent question and answer, and image generation possible. The large language model combined with the multimodal knowledge repository can significantly improve teaching efficiency and learning experience in discrete mathematics teaching. It can intuitively present abstract concepts through intelligent teaching assistants, dynamically recommend learning resources based on students' personalized needs, automatically generate multimodal teaching [4] content that integrates formulas, charts and codes, and provide in-depth semantic analysis and multimodal feedback, thereby lowering the cognitive threshold while maintaining mathematical rigor, and realizing flexible, precise and interactive modern mathematics education. This paper will introduce a large language model to integrate multimodal educational resources to provide students with a more complete and intelligent discrete mathematics education and learning platform (Fig. 1).

2 Design and Construction of Platform

2.1 Design of Platform

Platform Framework. In order to customize personalized learning paths for students, automatically generate rich learning resources and dynamically adjust them, and support cross-modal interaction, we designed an AI-assisted discrete mathematics teaching platform based on multimodal learning resources. The framework of the platform (Fig. 2) mainly includes four main modules: the multimodal resource repository module builds a knowledge center with hierarchical storage to achieve semantic association and instant update of textbooks, videos and exercises; the user front-end module provides natural language interaction and a visual front-end interface to support data search, related knowledge questions and answers, and test operations; the back-end processing module uses the DeepSeek-RAG fusion engine combined with retrieval enhancement generation technology to extract content from structured knowledge graphs and video resources accurately, and generates personalized answers with examples and counterexamples through a large language model; the intelligent analysis module tracks learning behavior in real time, evaluates knowledge mastery through a Bayesian network, and dynamically adjusts the difficulty of questions and recommendation strategies.

2.2 Construction of Platform

The platform uses the DeepSeek-RAG fusion engine [5,6] as the intelligent center and builds a closed-loop learning environment of "questioning-retrieval-generation-verification". Its innovation lies in combining the reasoning ability of large language models with the precise retrieval of knowledge bases in discrete mathematics, while lowering the threshold for understanding abstract knowledge through multimodal interaction. The multimodal resource repository [7], user front-end module, back-end processing module, and intelligent analysis module form a closed loop of "questioning-retrieval-generation-feedback", transforming abstract discrete mathematics concepts into interactive, traceable and immersive learning experiences, improving teaching efficiency while ensuring academic rigor.

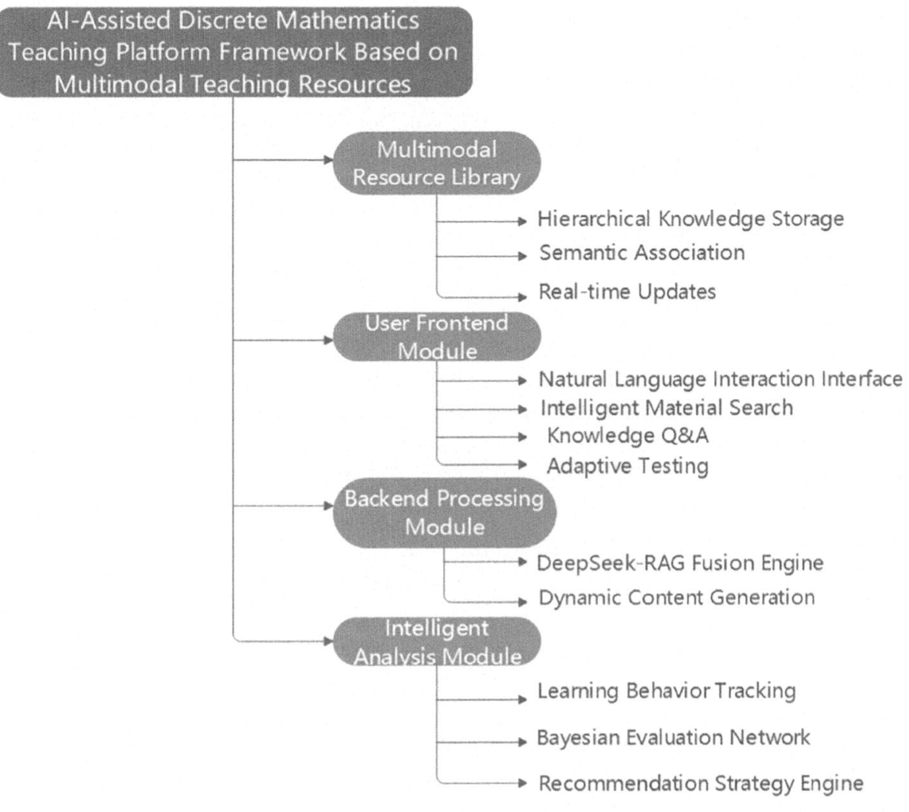

Fig. 2. The framework of the platform.

Multimodal Learning Resource Repository. The foundation for building a robust intelligent learning platform for discrete mathematics lies in the construction of a comprehensive and high-quality multimodal educational resource repository. We construct the multimodal knowledge base for discrete mathematics through three main stages: data collection and preprocessing, model training and optimization, and knowledge representation and storage. In the data collection and preprocessing stage, we gather multimodal data such as textual definitions and theorems, mathematical diagrams, and spoken explanations from textbooks, academic papers, instructional videos, and other sources. The collected data undergoes cleaning to remove noise, duplicates, and irrelevant information. We then annotate the data by assigning tags that indicate its content or characteristics, followed by formatting procedures that convert the data into structures suitable for subsequent processing and feature extraction. In the model training and optimization stage, we employ deep learning algorithms such as convolutional neural networks (CNNs) [8] for image data and recurrent neural networks (RNNs) [9] and their variants for text and speech data to train models on the preprocessed data. These neural network models are designed to understand and generate multimodal information. During training, model parameters (weights and biases) and structures (network depth, number of neurons) are iteratively adjusted to improve performance and accuracy, enhancing the model's ability to comprehend and process multimodal content. The objective of model training is to enable semantic understanding and expression of data; for example, interpreting the content of an image and generating a textual description is a form of knowledge representation that facilitates later storage in vectorized form. In the knowledge representation and storage stage, we employ structured formats such as graph-based representations (knowledge graphs [10]) and vector embeddings. Knowledge graphs organize information as entities and relations, making it easier to visualize and understand the connections among concepts. Vector representations transform knowledge into high-dimensional embeddings, enabling similarity-based retrieval and reasoning. Trained models are applied to convert multimodal data into structured knowledge representations, which are then stored to support subsequent retrieval and inference processes.

User Front-End Module Construction. The user front-end module of the platform has three core functional designs: retrieval, Q&A, and evaluation. The overall modern framework (such as React + Vite) [11] is adopted, with a simple interface and quick response. The homepage provides a function navigation entrance, and users can enter the search page to view multimodal learning resources (such as videos, PPTs, and textbooks) presented in the form of pictures and texts, supporting label classification and keyword screening, For example, if we want knowledge points related to Euler diagrams, we can enter Euler diagrams in the search box to return teaching materials, teaching videos, PPT and other resources related to Euler diagrams. (Fig. 3); the Q&A module supports the input of natural language questions and returns intuitive answers containing text and images by connecting to the DeepSeek large language model, For example, if we want to ask about Euler diagrams, we can enter "what is the Euler Graph" in the input box to return the answers to questions related to Euler diagrams. (Fig. 4); the evaluation module allows students to select knowledge points or system-intelligently recommended questions, and displays scores and detailed analysis after completion, For example, if we want to test the content of the graph chapter, we can select the graph-related chapter, and graph-related questions will appear, and the answers and analysis will be given after clicking Submit. (Fig. 5). The overall design emphasizes interactive friendliness and learning efficiency, which facilitates students' independent exploration and targeted training.

Backend Processing Module Construction. DeepSeek-RAG fusion engine. The DeepSeek-RAG fusion engine is the core of an intelligent system that combines retrieval-augmented generation (RAG) [6] technology and the DeepSeek large language model [5]. It uses an efficient sparse or dense retriever to find the documents or paragraphs most relevant to the user's question from the discrete mathematical multimodal knowledge base, and then inputs the

AI-powered Search

Euler Graph

Search

Teaching Materials

Discrete Mathematics Course (5th Edition)

Contains graph theory, sets, logic and other contents.

Teaching Materials | Graph Theory | Euler Graph

Video

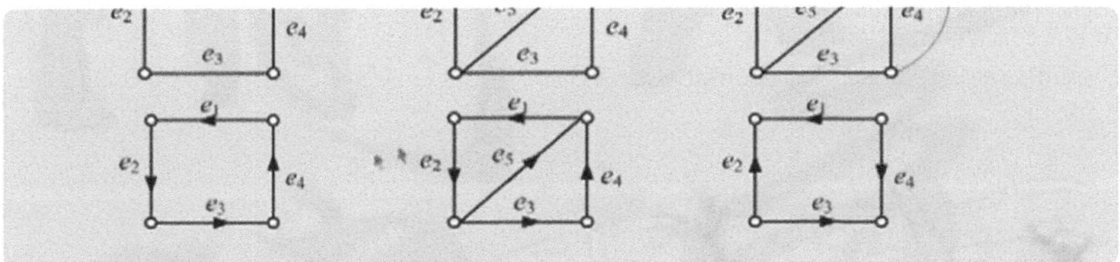

Euler diagram explanation video

Introducing the definition and determination method of Euler diagram in an easy-to-understand way.

Video | Euler Graph | Getting Started

PPT

具有欧拉回路的图称为**欧拉图**，具有欧拉通路而无欧拉回路的图称为**半欧拉图**。

规定：平凡图是欧拉图

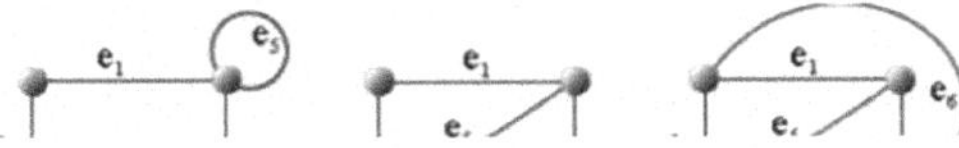

Euler Graph and Hamiltonian graph PPT

Clear illustrations, suitable for classroom teaching.

PPT | Graph Theory

Fig. 3. AI-powered Search. For example, when searching for Euler Graph, relevant learning resources for Euler Graph will appear.

AI-driven QA

what is the Euler Graph

Ask

? **what is Euler Graph**

Origin History:
- Graph theory originated in the 18th century. In 1736, Swiss mathematician Euler published the first graph theory paper "The Seven Bridges of Königsberg".
At that time, there was a Pregel River running through the city of Königsberg. The two islands in the river were connected to the two banks by seven bridges.
At that time, the residents there were keen on a difficult problem: how can a tourist walk through the seven bridges without repeating and finally return to the starting point.
In order to solve this problem, Euler used the four letters A, B, C, and D to replace the land as the four vertices, and represented the bridge connecting the two lands with the corresponding line segments. Then the Seven Bridges of Königsberg problem became a problem of whether there is a loop in the graph that passes through each edge once and only once and passes through all the vertices.
In his paper, Euler pointed out that such a loop does not exist.

Euler Graph is a graph in graph theory.:
- It is a connected graph;
- And the degree of each vertex in the graph is even.

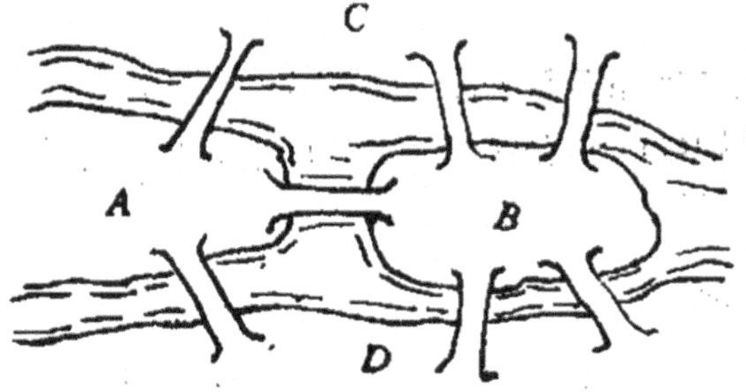

Fig. 4. AI-driven QA. Input what is the Euler Graph, and return the concept of the Euler Graph.

retrieved content together with the original question into the large language model for fusion-generated answers. Unlike traditional post-retrieval splicing answers, DeepSeek-RAG emphasizes multimodal fusion, content de-redundancy and enhanced relevance modeling, making the generated results more contextually consistent, knowledge-rich and accurate. This engine can not only effectively avoid the "hallucination" problem [12] common in large language models, but also automatically adjust the depth of the answer based on the student's learn-

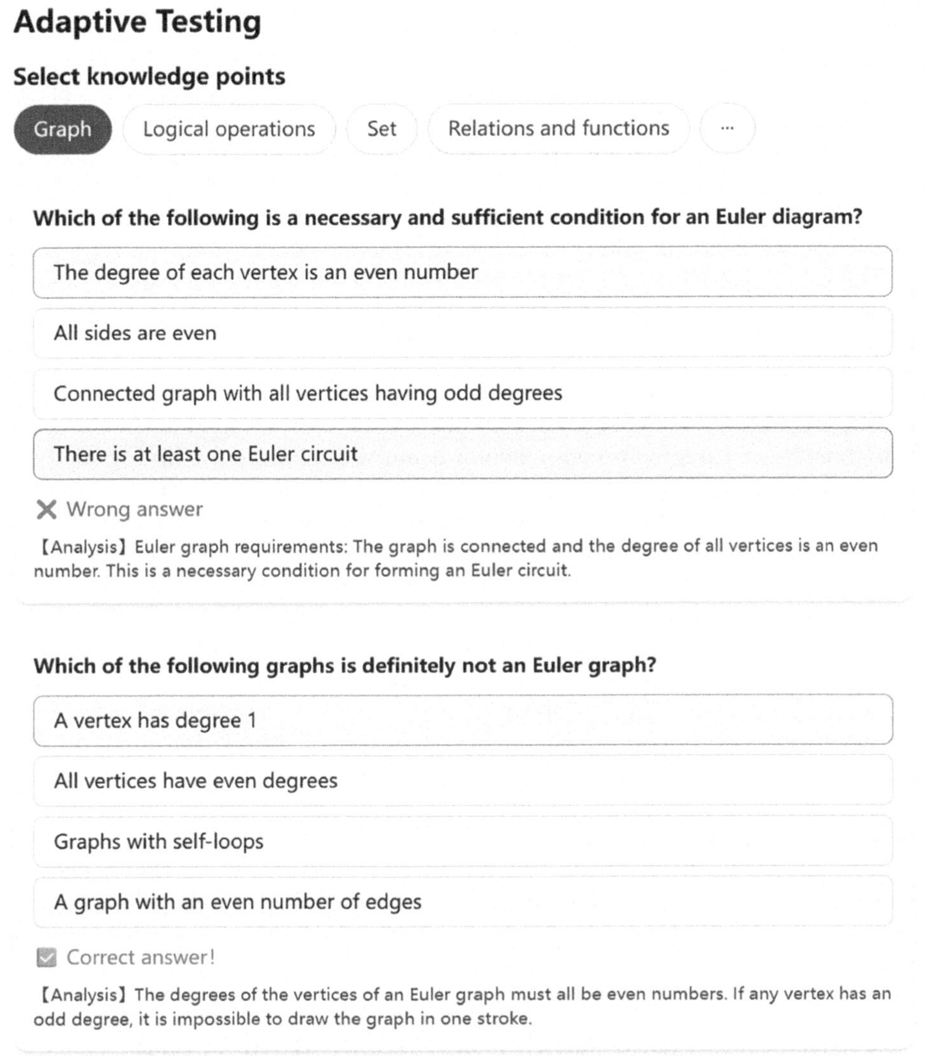

Fig. 5. Adaptive Testing. Select the chapter you want to test, automatically generate questions and give analysis to determine whether they are correct or not.

ing history, providing progressive guidance from basic definitions to advanced applications. In discrete mathematics teaching, it can not only strictly follow the mathematical logic to generate proof steps, but also associate multimodal resources (such as visual charts and teaching video clips) to make abstract concepts intuitive and operational, significantly improving the credibility of complex mathematical problem solving and teaching efficiency.

The multimodal resource repository establishes semantic associations between textbook concepts and video segments through a structured knowledge graph, and enables semantic retrieval by integrating the feature vectors of practice problems. When a user poses a question, the DeepSeek-RAG integration engine simultaneously retrieves relevant nodes from the knowledge graph and keyframes from video content, and leverages a large language model to fuse cross-modal information and generate explanatory answers accompanied by example problems (question answering). In the assessment phase, test sets related to specific knowledge points are dynamically assembled by the RAG framework based on the difficulty labels of practice problems in the repository and the user's historical data. Additionally, a counterexample library is used to automatically generate typical incorrect options, thereby providing accurate and personalized learning services.

Intelligent Analysis Module. The intelligent analysis module of the platform consists of three core components: a multi-dimensional learning analysis engine, real-time behavior tracking, and adaptive recommendation. It achieves accurate learning diagnosis by integrating educational data mining (EDM) [13] and machine learning technology. The module first uses a time series database to record the user's full-process interaction data (including answering time, error patterns, resource click heat maps, etc.), and constructs a dynamic knowledge mastery map through the Bayesian knowledge tracking (BKT) [14] model; secondly, it combines discrete mathematical ontology to analyze the attribution of errors (such as subdividing "propositional logic errors" into subcategories such as truth table confusion and misunderstanding of implied relationships); finally, based on the reinforcement learning recommendation engine, it generates personalized learning paths. The module is specially designed with a dual-channel feedback mechanism, which not only adjusts teaching strategies in real time (such as automatically reducing the difficulty of questions when three consecutive timeouts are detected), but also helps teachers and students optimize teaching through periodic cognitive diagnosis reports (including knowledge mastery radar charts and ability development curves).

3 Hybrid Teaching Model and Evaluation Based on Intelligent Platform and Traditional Teaching

Implementation of Teaching Strategies. Based on the AI-assisted multimodal learning resources teaching platform, we adopt a hybrid teaching model of "traditional teaching + intelligent platform + group collaboration". We have built a hierarchical and intelligent discrete mathematics teaching system by deeply integrating the advantages of offline systematic teaching and online personalized learning.

In the offline teaching session, teachers adopt the three-stage teaching method of "concept introduction-theorem derivation-example analysis". They ensure the systematic transmission of basic knowledge through carefully designed dynamic PPT demonstrations and blackboard deductions. Simultaneously, they introduce the "instant feedback system" and use the classroom transponder to detect students' mastery of key and difficult content in real time to achieve precise teaching. The online intelligent platform relies on the DeepSeek-RAG fusion engine to provide full-process support such as pre-class adaptive preview, real-time visual Q&A during class, and after-class targeted exercise generation. At the same time, based on the three-level framework of "foundation-extension-innovation", it intelligently matches multimodal resources for students of different levels. The purpose of student group cooperation reports is to deepen students' understanding and application of discrete mathematics through team collaboration. In group learning, students need to discuss course knowledge points together and break through the limitations of textbooks to conduct extended research. This not only cultivates their independent learning ability and knowledge exploration spirit, but more importantly, it promotes a deep understanding of abstract mathematical concepts through the exchange and collision of multiple perspectives.

Teaching Evaluation Methods. Due to changes in teaching models, traditional evaluation methods are no longer applicable. We have designed a multi-dimensional evaluation framework, whose evaluation factors include assessment results, questionnaires and teacher feedback.

Assessment results, as one of the most important evaluation factors, are a prominent feature of improved teaching quality and a reflection of the success of teaching reform. In addition to final exam results, they include in-class tests, homework, and online exercises. During the teaching process, the teaching mode can be dynamically adjusted through performance feedback, such as by adjusting the proportion of online and offline teaching. The questionnaire survey needs to be designed in stages. The content includes students' experience of the new teaching model, satisfaction with the teaching auxiliary platform, dissatisfaction, improvement hopes and needs, to serve as data support for the subsequent adjustment of the teaching model and the direction of optimization of the visual intelligent teaching platform. Teacher feedback is also one of the determining factors of teaching evaluation. It is necessary to follow up on the user experience of teachers teaching discrete mathematics courses in the school. On the one hand, statistics are collected on the satisfaction of different teachers with the educational resources and services provided by the visual intelligent teaching platform, as well as improvement suggestions, including whether the pushed resources are accurate and reliable, and whether the designated learning plan is feasible. On the other hand, the platform's positive role in improving the grades and abilities of students in different classes and possible problems are investigated.

Based on the feedback from the above evaluation factors, the visual intelligent teaching platform is continuously and dynamically optimized to provide students and teachers with more accurate, timely and high-quality learning resources and plans.

Comparison of Teaching Effects. Through preliminary implementation, our hybrid teaching model demonstrates a significant improvement in educational outcomes compared to traditional classroom instruction. In terms of academic performance, supported by the intelligent platform, students in the hybrid model performed better in routine assignments and in-class quizzes, with noticeable improvements in scores on questions involving abstract concepts. The average final grades are also expected to improve. Regarding learning engagement, the integration of the intelligent platform enabled real-time Q&A interactions during lessons, resulting in increased classroom interaction. Additionally, the average number of logins and the duration of platform usage per student were higher, indicating a substantial rise in student engagement. In terms of autonomous learning, unlike traditional instruction which often relies heavily on a uniform teaching pace, the platform offers AI-driven personalized learning paths that foster students' motivation and enhance their capacity for self-directed learning. From the perspective of resource allocation, AI-assisted grading and Q&A reduce the burden of lesson preparation and repetitive tasks for instructors. Meanwhile, the multimodal learning resource repository enables online resource sharing, thereby narrowing educational disparities among students and promoting equity in education.

4 Future Directions

With the continuous advancement of artificial intelligence and educational information technologies, AI-assisted discrete mathematics teaching platforms based on multimodal learning resources hold substantial potential for further development. Future research and practice may focus on the following aspects:

1. Generation and Expansion of Multimodal Resources: Leveraging the content generation capabilities of large-scale models to automatically construct richer repositories of instructional materials, including interactive graphical demonstrations, visualized reasoning processes, and spoken explanations, thereby enhancing the accessibility and interactivity of educational resources.
2. Deep Personalization of the Teaching Process: Integrating reinforcement learning and user modeling techniques to dynamically perceive students' learning states, adaptively adjust instructional strategies and content delivery, and optimize personalized learning pathways to achieve truly individualized instruction.
3. Integration with Cutting-Edge Educational Technologies: Exploring the combination of the platform with emerging interactive technologies such as AR/VR to enhance the visualization and immersive learning experiences of abstract concepts in discrete mathematics, thus reducing cognitive barriers to learning.
4. AI-Driven Collaborative Learning: Developing AI-powered modules for group collaboration that incorporate group projects and discussion tools, while analyzing communication patterns and participation levels in real time. The system can intelligently recommend collaboration strategies to improve group efficiency, thereby better supporting the proposed hybrid teaching model.

5 Conclusion

This study designs and constructs an AI-assisted discrete mathematics teaching platform based on multimodal learning resources. The platform operates through the coordinated integration of four core modules: multimodal resource repository, user interface, backend processing, and intelligent analytics. By incorporating multi-source data and hybrid knowledge representations, the system enables cross-modal semantic retrieval, personalized interaction, and dynamic instructional optimization, thereby creating an intelligent and individualized learning environment for discrete mathematics. In the instructional application, the platform supports a hybrid teaching model that combines traditional instruction, intelligent platforms, and collaborative group learning, forming a hierarchical teaching system. Multi-dimensional evaluations indicate that the platform significantly enhances academic performance, classroom engagement, and self-directed learning capabilities, demonstrating the transformative potential of AI in advancing discrete mathematics education.

References

1. Li, W.: Teaching reform and practice based on the course of "discrete mathematics". Int. J. Soc. Sci. Educ. Res. **8**(4), 359–362 (2025)
2. Nian, L.H., Wei, J., Yin, C.B.: The promotion role of mobile online education platform in students' self-learning. Int. J. Continuing Eng. Educ. Life Long Learn. **29**(1–2), 56–71 (2019)
3. Zhang, J., Huang, J., Jin, S., Lu, S.: Vision-language models for vision tasks: a survey. IEEE Trans. Pattern Anal. Mach. Intell. **46**(8), 5625–5644 (2024)
4. Philippe, S., et al.: Multimodal teaching, learning and training in virtual reality: a review and case study. Virtual Reality Intell. Hardw. **2**(5), 421–442 (2020)
5. Liao, H.: Deepseek large-scale model: technical analysis and development prospect. J. Comput. Sci. Electr. Eng. **7**(1), 33–37 (2025)
6. Siriwardhana, S., Weerasekera, R., Wen, E., Kaluarachchi, T., Rana, R., Nanayakkara, S.: Improving the domain adaptation of retrieval augmented generation (rag) models for open domain question answering. Trans. Assoc. Comput. Linguist. **11**, 1–17 (2023)
7. Meijer, D., et al.: Empowering natural product science with AI: leveraging multimodal data and knowledge graphs. Nat. Prod. Rep. **42**(4), 654–662 (2025)
8. Purwono, P., Ma'arif, A., Rahmaniar, W., Fathurrahman, H.I.K., Frisky, A.Z.K., ul Haq, Q.M.: Understanding of convolutional neural network (CNN): a review. Int. J. Robot. Control Syst. **2**(4), 739–748 (2022)
9. Dhruv, P., Naskar, S.: Image classification using convolutional neural network (CNN) and recurrent neural network (RNN): a review. Mach. Learn. Inf. Process. Proc. ICMLIP **2019**, 367–381 (2020)
10. Chaudhri, V., et al.: Knowledge graphs: introduction, history and perspectives. AI Mag. **43**(1), 17–29 (2022)
11. Lazuardy, M.F.S., Anggraini, D.: Modern front end web architectures with react. JS and next. JS. Res. J. Adv. Eng. Sci. **7**(1), 132–141 (2022)
12. Gunjal, A., Yin, J., Bas, E.: Detecting and preventing hallucinations in large vision language models. In: Proceedings of the AAAI Conference on Artificial Intelligence, vol. 38, pp. 18135–18143 (2024)

13. Batool, S., Rashid, J., Nisar, M.W., Kim, J., Kwon, H.Y., Hussain, A.: Educational data mining to predict students' academic performance: a survey study. Educ. Inf. Technol. **28**(1), 905–971 (2023)
14. Li, Z., Jiao, Y., Xu, J., Zhang, X.: Adaptive Bayesian knowledge tracing based on personalized characteristics. In: 2024 IEEE 7th International Conference on Information Systems and Computer Aided Education (ICISCAE), pp. 180–185. IEEE (2024)

GPE-DKT: An Enhanced Deep Knowledge Tracing Model Integrating Generalized Training and Personalized Fine-Tuning for Learning Assessment

Xin Dong[1], Qing Zhang[1(✉)], and Dapeng Qu[2]

[1] Computer Engineering College, Jimei University, Xiamen, China
a3167662732@163.com

[2] Faculty of Information, Liaoning University, Shenyang, China
dapengqu@lnu.edu.cn

Abstract. Knowledge tracing (KT) is a method used to evaluate learners' learning states in personalized learning environments. However, traditional KT faces several challenges, including the cold-start problem, inadequate modeling of individual differences, and noise in real-world learning data. To address these issues, we propose a generalized and personalized enhanced deep knowledge tracing (GPE-DKT) model. First, we extracted key behavioral features from student interaction data using decision tree analysis and Pearson correlation. We then combined these features, which include both static and dynamic features, and fed them into the model. Furthermore, we compressed the input and label spaces via dimensionality reduction to improve behavior pattern identification. To reduce data noise, we established an anomaly rate threshold and introduced a "Mini-Test Model" to identify untrustworthy records. The training process was innovatively decomposed into two sequential stages: generalized modeling to mitigate missing knowledge points in learning records, and personalized modeling to capture learner-specific behavioral patterns. Experiments on real-world learning data demonstrate the effectiveness of GPE-DKT in evaluating learning states and forecasting student performance, especially in data-limited scenarios, showcasing higher stability and accuracy. We further validate the proposed model through a system deployed for learning evaluation.

Keywords: Deep Knowledge Tracing · Behavioral Feature Extraction · Generalized Training · Personalized Fine-Tuning · Learning Assessment

1 Introduction

1.1 Research Background and Significance

The rapid development of information technology transforms the way students access educational content, facilitating anytime, anywhere learning via online platforms [1].

Yet, conventional assessment techniques, such as averaging or selecting peak exam scores, fail to adequately capture the multifaceted nature of student behavior in digital

W. Hong et al. (Eds.): ICCSE 2025, CCIS 2761, pp. 113–127, 2026.
https://doi.org/10.1007/978-981-95-7731-6_10

environments. Without sufficient interaction data, it is also difficult for learning platforms to accurately assess student progress and recommend appropriate exercises. Knowledge Tracing utilizes historical learning records to analyze and predict student performance, allowing educators to track concept mastery and provide personalized learning guidance [2].

1.2 Research Objectives and Contributions

Many KT models focus primarily on learning interaction sequences while neglecting crucial attributes such as learners' cognitive abilities and learning efforts. However, these factors significantly influence knowledge acquisition rates and performance on challenging tasks.

To address data sparsity, personalization, and noisy interactions, this study proposes an improved deep knowledge tracing model called GPE-DKT (Generalized and Personalized Enhanced Deep Knowledge Tracing), which integrates three key components:

Enhanced Feature Representation and Compression. Introducing features based on Pearson correlation and decision tree methods, selecting key features that significantly influence learning outcomes, and categorizing them into static and dynamic types for model input. An input–output compression mechanism is further designed to reduce model complexity and improve training stability under small-sample conditions.

Generalized Modeling. The generalized modeling phase allows the model to identify patterns across students by training on the full student dataset, thereby mitigating cold-start problems for students with scant interaction history.

Personalized Fine-Tuning. After completing the generalized modeling phase, personalized fine-tuning using each student's sequence of learning interactions continues to accommodate their personalized learning behaviors and trajectories.

2 Related Work

2.1 Knowledge Tracing

Knowledge Tracing is a task that aims to infer students' knowledge mastery based on their historical learning behaviors and predict their future performance. Early KT methods were based on statistical modeling, such as Bayesian Knowledge Tracing (BKT) [3] and decision tree models [4], but they struggled to capture complex learning behaviors. The introduction of deep learning techniques has significantly advanced the field of KT.

Deep Knowledge Tracing(DKT) involves applying deep learning to knowledge tracing tasks. Compared with traditional knowledge tracking models, DKT provides a high-dimensional continuous representation of the knowledge state, which can better simulate the complex human learning process. Long Short-Term Memory Networks (LSTMs) are initially employed to model students' response sequences in this context [5]. Subsequent research proposes numerous deep learning-based improvements. For instance, DKVMN

[6] incorporates a memory structure to enhance interpretability, while SAKT [7] and AKT [8] employ attention mechanisms to better capture learning behaviors. Similarly, GIKT [9] and SAKT-GCN [8] integrate structural graph information from exercises. However, most existing models still primarily address the binary classification task of predicting the next response based on historical sequences.

In the HELP-DKT model, researchers introduced program embeddings and error type mappings to dynamically construct a 'personalized knowledge mastery matrix' (P matrix) for each student. This provided interpretable outputs at the cognitive level for knowledge tracing models[10]. However, the model was only applicable to introductory programming courses, and its generalizability to other types of courses remained limited.

DKT still faces three major challenges: over-reliance on student data with rich interaction histories, weak cross-student generalization, and low interpretability of binary classification outputs. Recent work has explored cognitive diagnosis, graphs, and multi-task learning to address these issues [11–14]. Building on this, we incorporate more features, use all students' learning data for initialization, and reformulate the task as a regression problem to output fine-grained, interpretable scores for each knowledge point.

2.2 Cold Start and Generalized Modeling

Traditional DKT models rely heavily on extensive historical records from individual students for training purposes, which can limit their ability to capture long-term learning patterns. In real-life educational settings, students often only engage with a small number of problems, which can make it difficult to start learning effectively.

To overcome this problem, researchers have begun introducing general modeling ideas across students. For instance, the Deep-IRT model underwent continuous training on comprehensive student data to facilitate parameter sharing among students [15], yet it confined itself to behavior-based modeling and omitted explicit general transfer modeling. Similarly, dynamic memory networks (such as DKT + DKVMN) were also employed to enhance the model's generalization ability, and some studies proposed incorporating attention mechanisms to emphasize key historical information [6, 12]. These works established the groundwork for personalized modeling but failed to incorporate data from other students. The disconnect between new and existing students hindered the model's generalization to those with limited data.

To this end, the model proposed in this paper introduces a "general modeling–personalized fine-tuning" dual-stage strategy into the training process and adopts an input-output compression mechanism to reduce the model's parameter space, thereby alleviating training instability under small-sample conditions.

2.3 Feature Selection and Fusion

Traditional DKT models typically use only simple sequential inputs such as "question ID+ correctness", which makes it difficult to capture richer semantic and structural features in students' learning behaviors.

These features may include static attributes of students, item metadata, response time, and knowledge point tags, all of which help the model achieve better generalization in scenarios with sparse data or complex tasks [1, 11]. For example, the AKT model introduced multiple channels including question encoding, interaction embedding, and knowledge embedding to represent different dimensions of information [8]. SAINT+ integrated features such as timestamps and answering behaviors to enhance sequential modeling precision [16]. Similarly, Bi-CLKT established a contrastive learning framework within a graph structure and employed dual-channel representations to improve the combined modeling of behavioral and structural characteristics [17].

Different from existing methods that introduce features empirically, this study adopts the Pearson correlation coefficient to select features that are easily fitted, and then applies decision tree methods to further identify the most influential features with respect to learning outcomes from the candidate set.

3 Methods

3.1 Incorporating Richer Learning Features

Input structure of GPE-DKT is shown in Fig. 1.

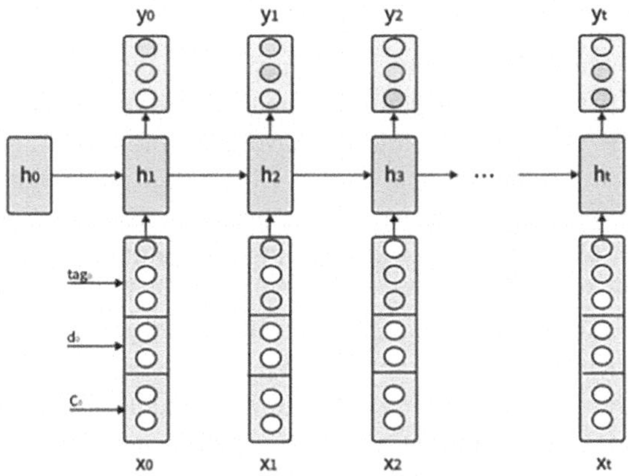

Fig. 1. The input structure of GPE-DKT, integrating static and dynamic features

The GPE-DKT model took as input the sequence of a student's learning interactions $\{x_0, x_1, \cdots, x_t\}$. The hidden layers represented the student's knowledge mastery state at each time step, while the output sequence corresponded to the predicted response outcomes at each time step. The model introduced additional learning features, enabling more historical information about the learner to be included in the model inputs. Here, d_t denoted the difficulty of the t-th question, tag_t represented its corresponding knowledge point, and c_t represented the cumulative number of exercises the student had completed that were tagged with the same knowledge point.

3.2 Compressing the Input and Output Dimensions

In general, learners often had limited historical interaction data, which made it difficult for the model to perform targeted analysis. The GPE-DKT model compressed and adjusted both the input and output data dimensions to better capture temporal features under small-data conditions. An example of the data compression method is shown in Fig. 2.

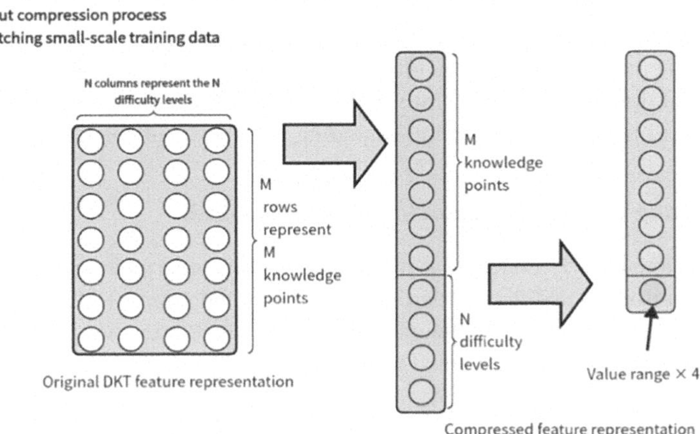

Fig. 2. Illustration of the data compression method

3.3 Introducing Element-wise Logical Multiplication

The structure of the input to the hidden layer, as illustrated in Fig. 3, comprised three large blocks, each representing the input states at distinct time steps. The small boxes labeled σ signified feedforward layers that employed sigmoid activation functions, while those labeled tanh indicated feedforward layers that utilized tanh activation functions [15].

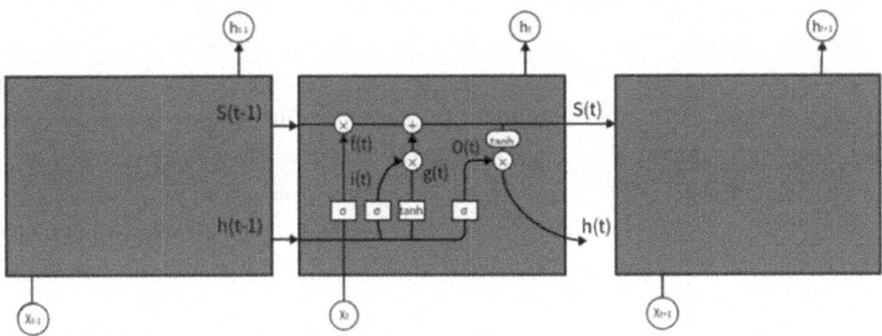

Fig. 3. Architecture of the hidden layer

Unlike the original DKT model, the GPE-DKT model introduced element-wise logical multiplication across outputs from multiple positions to enhance the integration of contextual information.

$$y_t = \sigma\left(y_{t1}{}^{tag} \cdot y_{t2}{}^{difficulty} \cdot y_{t3}{}^{repeat}\right) \quad (1)$$

The three prediction vectors corresponded to three selected dynamic features in this study—question difficulty, question tag, and repetition count. These features were determined through a feature selection process in this thesis. In practice, this structure was flexible and could adapt to other feature combinations based on different selection results.

Element-wise multiplication introduced a gating mechanism to model the joint influence of knowledge point, difficulty, and repetition. The prediction score increased only when all dimensions were jointly high—reflecting the pedagogical principle that successful learning required both understanding and sufficient challenge.

3.4 Modifying the Loss Function to a Regression Task

Unlike traditional DKT models that treated the task as binary classification, the GPE-DKT model reformulated it as a regression problem and adopted Mean Squared Error (MSE) as the loss function to better capture continuous score variations.

The MSE loss function is defined as follows:

$$MSE = \frac{1}{n}\sum_{i=1}^{n}\left(y_i - \widehat{y_i}\right)^2 \quad (2)$$

where y_i is the true score, and $\widehat{y_i}$ is the predicted score.

Joint Training for Generalized and Personalized DKT.

This study emphasized fine-grained personalized modeling by innovatively incorporating both static and dynamic features. A generalized model was first trained on data from all students, after which personalized models were fine-tuned for individual students. By learning from interaction records across the entire student population, the model captured relationships between knowledge points, which helped address knowledge gaps for students with limited records and enhanced the model's generalization capability.

To implement this approach, learning records from each student were organized into time-ordered sequences. Since each sequence could correspond to a different student, the model was designed to distinguish between individual learners by incorporating static features into the input. These included the Rasch ability [18] score (representing cognitive aptitude), total study duration (reflecting effort), and indicators of exercise rationality (e.g., whether the student avoided hard questions or engaged in excessive repetition).

```
Pseudocode: Training and Personalization Process of the
GPE-DKT Model:
// Phase 1: Train general model
Input:
    D = {D₁, D₂, ..., Dₙ} // Dynamic interaction sequences
    S = {s₁, s₂, ..., sₙ} // Static features
    T = {T₁, T₂, ..., Tₙ} // Knowledge point
Output:
    M_gen                 // Trained general model
    {M₁, M₂, ..., Mₙ}     // Personalized models
    {V₁, V₂, ..., Vₙ}     // Knowledge-point mastery
vectors (for GCN recommendation)

Step 1: Construct dataset
    For each student i:
        For each timestep t in Dᵢ:
            xₜ ← tagₜ ⊗ dynₜ ⊗ sᵢ
           // Merge static + dynamic + tag features
            yₜ ← true score at timestep t
            Add (xₜ, yₜ) to dataset D_all

Step 2: Train general model M_gen
    Shuffle D_all into batches B₁, B₂, ..., B_k
    for each batch B in D_all do:
        Perform forward pass through LSTM model
        Compute loss L ← MSE(ŷ, y)
        Update model weights via ∇L

Save trained general model M_gen

// Phase 2: Fine-tune for each student
for i = 1 to n do:
    Load M_gen → Mᵢ
    Fine-tune Mᵢ on (Dᵢ, Sᵢ, Tᵢ)
 // Fine-tuning on individual student records only.
    Mᵢ → per-tag knowledge scores Vᵢ
    if quiz data Qᵢ exists:
        Train M_quiz on Qᵢ
        if |Pred(Mᵢ) - Pred(M_quiz)| > δ:
            Mark student i as anomalous
```

4 Experiments and Results

4.1 Dataset

The dataset used in this study comes from the PTA platform, a programming assistance platform utilized by students in the C programming course at Jimei University (classes of 2022 and 2023). The platform records over 200,000 instances of students' problem-solving interactions, including exercise scores and program evaluation records, encompassing 1,897 practice problems across 79 problem sets.

4.2 Experiments

This study adopted a "Filter + Wrapper" strategy for feature selection. Initially, we utilized the Pearson Correlation Coefficient to screen out features displaying notable linear correlations with student performance, thereby efficiently eliminating unnecessary or duplicate variables [19]. However, localized nonlinear patterns still existed during actual modeling. To further capture these complex relationships, a decision tree model was employed on the filtered features to rank their importance. By leveraging information gain, decision trees automatically identified optimal split points, thus effectively modeling the nonlinear mappings between learner states and academic outcomes [4]. This approach achieved strong performance and interpretability in practical student performance modeling scenarios [3].

Correlation Analysis and Decision Tree-Based Feature Selection. To address potential data quality issues, especially among students exhibiting poor submission behaviors (e.g., copying, repeatedly submitting to guess the correct answer), an anomaly rate metric was introduced. This metric was computed based on the estimated minimum reading time required for a question of difficulty level d, below which the submission was flagged as suspicious.

$$g_d = 10 \times d \tag{3}$$

$$R_i = \frac{ERR_i}{SUM_i} \times 100\% \tag{4}$$

- ERR_i = number of anomalous submissions by student *i*
- SUM_i = total submissions by student *i*

This anomaly rate helped distinguish low-quality data from reliable records, enhancing the training signal for the model.

The study applied principles of cognitive science to analyze students' cognitive difficulties. The Rasch model [18] quantifies student ability by examining relationships between scores and question difficulty, while the Ebbinghaus forgetting curve illustrates predictable patterns of memory retention and loss. The research integrated key indicators, including total scores and correct answer counts, to evaluate students' basic competencies.

A modified Rasch model was adopted to estimate students' latent abilities, where continuous scores were normalized and interpreted as approximate response probabilities (e.g., a score of 50 was treated as a 0.5 probability of correctness).

$$ln\frac{P_{ni}}{1 - P_{ni}} = B_n - d_i \tag{5}$$

- P_{ni} = probability that student *n* correctly responds to item *i* correctly
- B_n = ability level of student *n*
- d_i = difficulty level of item *i*

$$P_{ni} = \frac{\exp(B_n - d_i)}{1 + \exp(B_n - d_i)} \tag{6}$$

To ensure model performance under limited data conditions, it was crucial to identify input features that were both relevant and predictive. Therefore, Pearson correlation was employed to filter out weakly associated features. Features with an r value greater than 0.5 were retained, as they exhibited clearer trends corresponding to learning outcomes and provided more valuable information for model training. This filtering step reduced dimensionality, highlighted key behavioral indicators, and improved generalization by eliminating noise from irrelevant variables. The Pearson Correlation Heatmap, as depicted in Fig. 4, illustrates the strength and direction of linear relationships between variables.

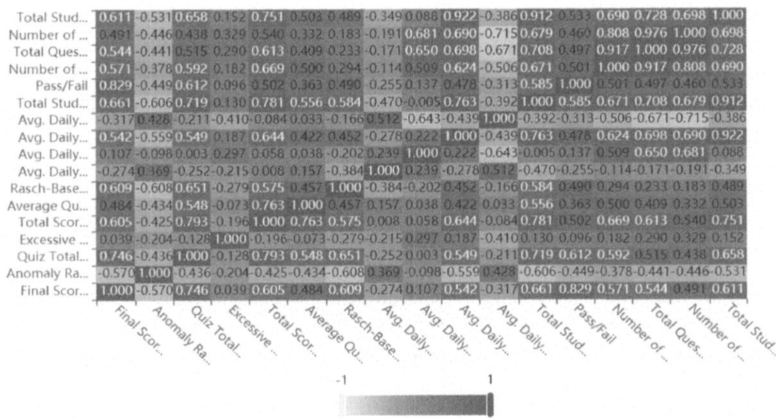

Fig. 4. Pearson Correlation Heatmap

To further reduce feature redundancy and capture non-linear relationships, a decision tree was applied as a classifier to rank and refine feature importance, as illustrated in Fig. 5. Gini impurity served as the metric to assess the discriminative power of each feature, based on its capacity to classify students into pass or fail categories. This step functioned as a wrapper-based refinement, subsequent to the initial Pearson-based filtering stage. Collectively, this dual-stage feature selection process enhanced model stability, reduced overfitting risk, and ensured that only the most representative features were retained for downstream modeling.

The Gini impurity at node a is defined as:

$$Gini(a) = 1 - \sum_{s=1}^{T} (q_s)^2 \tag{7}$$

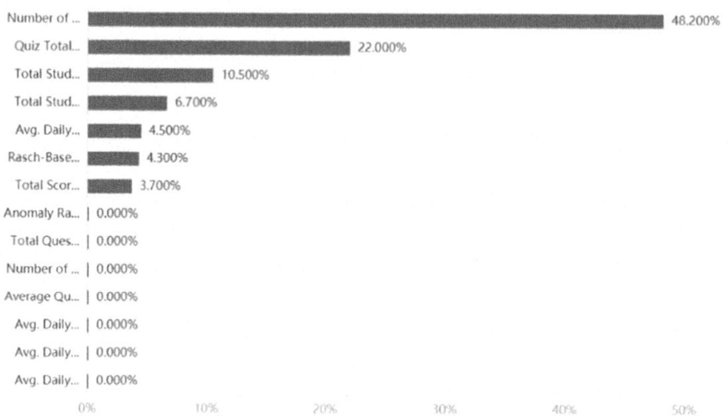

Fig. 5. Importance of Learning Features

Integration of Static Features. Based on the decision tree feature importance analysis, we observed that the number of hard questions solved and total study time significantly influenced students' final scores. As a result, two representative dynamic features were incorporated into the model input: question difficulty and repetition count, which reflected time-sensitive aspects of learning behavior.

Additionally, the model was fed a set of static features representing the stable learning profile of each student, including the Rasch ability to indicate cognitive aptitude, the number of hard and easy questions passed to reflect the balance and rationality of practice behavior, and the quiz score to capture actual test performance.

These static features were used during general model training to distinguish between different types of students, while the dynamic features captured time-series behavior, improving model personalization and robustness under sparse data scenarios.

Knowledge Point Analysis and Compression. To reduce overfitting and mitigate sparsity at the knowledge point level, related knowledge points were merged or compressed. Relationships among knowledge points included [15]:

Containment Relation: $\forall x_a,\ x_{beta} \in \Theta, \exists\ x_a \sqsubseteq x_{beta}$, which indicates a containment relationship between knowledge points. That is, if a learner has mastered knowledge point x_β, it is assumed that x_a, being a subset of x_β, has also been mastered.

Successor Relation: $\forall x_a,\ x_{beta} \in \Theta,\ \exists\, x_a \rightarrow_{next} x_{beta}$, indicating a prerequisite or successor relationship. In this case, x_a is a prerequisite for x_β. If a learner has not yet mastered x_a, it is inferred that they have not yet mastered x_β either.

Resolution Relation: $\forall x_a \in \Theta_1$, $x_{beta} \in \Theta_2$, $\exists x_a \rightarrow_{\text{solve}} x_{beta}$, which means knowledge point x_a can be used to solve problems related to x_β. Learners must first master x_a in order to be capable of solving problems associated with x_β. Hence, exercises targeting x_β should only be recommended once x_a has been sufficiently learned.

The compression rules are as follows:

If knowledge point A contains knowledge point B, then A is assigned as the label.

If knowledge point A is the successor of B (i.e., B is a prerequisite for A), A is used as the label.

If knowledge point A can be used to resolve B, then B is set as the label since the exercise primarily assesses B.

Anomaly Rate. In real-world educational environments, student exercise data often contained substantial noise. For example, a student might first submit a wrong answer scoring zero, but then swiftly correct it to achieve a perfect 100. Some students plagiarized by copying others' answers, achieving high practice scores but performing poorly in formal exams. In other cases, despite submitting correct answers, the excessive time spent on tasks suggested potential comprehension difficulties.

To identify such abnormal data and categorize students exhibiting irregular behavior, this study introduced the metric of an "anomaly rate". High-confidence data were integrated during the training process as reference points. Specifically, submission records from time-limited classroom quizzes were selected as reliable samples for training a separate "Mini-Test Model". The predictions of this model were compared to the predictions of the personalized model, and the resulting prediction errors form the anomaly rate values. Flagging students with high anomaly rates during teaching and, when necessary, excluded from general model training to enhance stability and generalization.

4.3 Results and Discussion

To validate the model's practical effectiveness, final exam scores were introduced as evaluation criteria. The model's predicted scores for each question were aggregated to compute a simulated total exam score, which was then compared with actual exam results to assess the model's applicability in real instructional settings.

Analysis of Model Performance. The impact of anomaly rate on average prediction error is illustrated in Fig. 6. When the anomaly rate exceeded 10%, prediction errors increased sharply, indicating that abnormal learning behaviors significantly degraded model performance. This confirmed that real-world student data contained considerable noise, which could negatively impact prediction accuracy. Therefore, a 10% threshold was adopted to mark unreliable records, ensuring that only higher-quality data were used for training and evaluation.

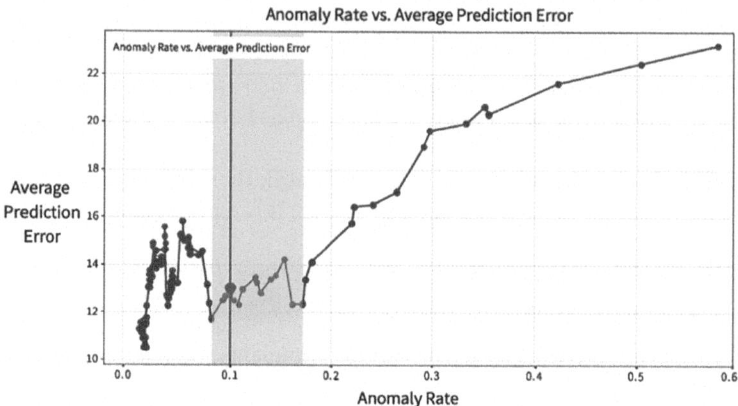

Fig. 6. Impact of Anomaly Rate on Prediction Error

Ablation Study of the General Model. Ablation experiments were performed to evaluate the contribution of the general model. As illustrated in Fig. 7, after the introduction of the general model (left figure), the correlation between the predicted score and the actual score was significantly enhanced.

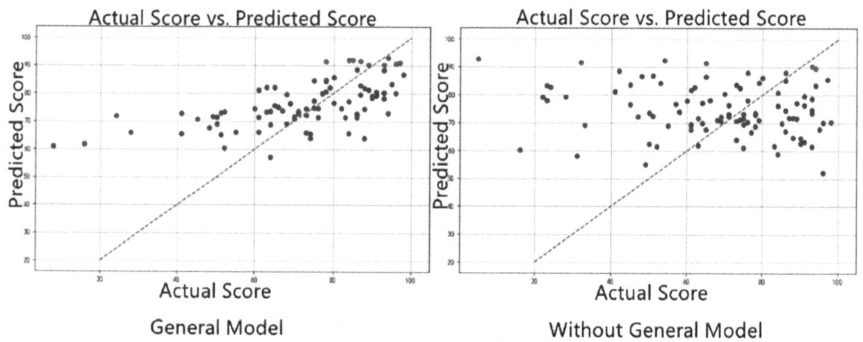

Fig. 7. Ablation Study on the Role of the General Model

For the 2023 cohort, incorporating the general model reduced MAE from 18.8 to 11.3, while in the 2022 cohort, it dropped from 25 to 14. The results demonstrated that the general model significantly improved prediction accuracy, particularly for students with limited historical data.

Model Comparison and Evaluation. Comparison of prediction models is shown in Table 1.

Table 1. Comparison of Prediction Models

Model Type	MAE	Description
Historical Average	17.7	Simple baseline method
Original DKT	18.0	Basic DKT without additional features
MLP (Non-Sequential NN)	16.5	Uses only static features
GPE-DKT (this study)	13.9	Includes difficulty, repetition, anomaly filtering
Linear Regression	11.7	Static features with a linear model

Linear regression yields a mean absolute error (MAE) of 11.7, demonstrating strong linear relationships between the selected static features and final scores. However, this approach lacked sequence modeling capabilities and interpretability. The GPE-DKT model proposed in this study attained an MAE of 13.9, outperforming traditional DKT and MLP baselines. While showing slightly higher overall error than linear regression, it successfully supported sequential prediction, knowledge points diagnosis, and cold-start adaptation, providing a superior balance between accuracy and educational interpretability. Furthermore, for reliable students in the 2023 cohort, the model achieved an MAE of 12.0 without utilizing prior exam scores. When excluding students flagged as anomalous, the model's performance further improved to an MAE of 11.2, establishing GPE-DKT as the best-performing model overall.

5 Application of GPE-DKT

The GPE-DKT was successfully implemented in a practical hybrid learning platform, enabling student performance prediction and intelligent recommendation capabilities. As shown in Fig. 8.

In this system, teachers defined a test outline that specified the percentage distribution of knowledge points. The GPE-DKT model generated predictions of students' mastery levels for each knowledge point, which were aggregated to compute the anticipated total test score. The system interface displayed comparative analyses between predicted and actual performance metrics. Through predictive performance analytics, the system identified students' competency gaps in specific knowledge domains and generated personalized learning recommendations. Furthermore, it enabled instructors to develop customized instructional strategies based on these insights.

Fig. 8. Data Analytics Page Display

6 Conclusion

This study proposes a GPE-DKT model for learning state assessment to address two challenges in educational AI: data scarcity and cold-start adaptation. Experimental results show that the model reduces the MAE from 18 (traditional DKT) to 13.9, and after excluding untrustworthy data through anomaly rate analysis, the MAE is further reduced to 11.2. These findings also suggest that hybrid generalized personalization modeling enhances the robustness of predictions by transferring patterns from the group level to individual cases, especially in data-limited scenarios. However, the framework's reliance on time-limited test validation may limit its application in informal learning environments. Future work should combine cognitive science and generative artificial intelligence to develop an intelligent cognitive-behavioral learning assessment framework, broadening its educational applications.

Acknowledgments. This study was funded by "The 13th Undergraduate Education And Teaching Research Projects of Jimei University" (number JY23029).

References

1. Zhang, Y.: Research on Student Knowledge Tracing Algorithm Based on Deep Learning. East China Normal University (2023)
2. Wang, Z., Xiong, S., Zuo, M., et al.: Knowledge tracing in the perspective of smart education: status, framework and trends. Distance Educ. J. **39**(5), 45–54 (2021)
3. Baker, R.S., Yacef, K.: The state of educational data mining in 2009: a review and future visions. J. Educ. Data Min. **1**(1), 3–17 (2009)

4. Quinlan, J.R.: Induction of decision trees. Mach. Learn. **1**(1), 81–106 (1986)
5. Piech, C., Bassen, J., Huang, J., et al.: Deep knowledge tracing. Adv. Neural Inf. Process. Syst. **28** (2015)
6. Zhang, J., Shi, X., King, I., Yeung, D.Y.: Dynamic key-value memory networks for knowledge tracing. In: Proceedings of the 26th International Conference on World Wide Web (WWW), pp. 765–774 (2017)
7. Pandey, S., Karypis, G.: A self-attentive model for knowledge tracing. arXiv preprint arXiv: 1907.06837 (2019)
8. Ghosh, S., et al.: AKT: Attentive knowledge tracing. In: Proceedings of the 30th ACM International Conference on Information & Knowledge Management (CIKM), pp. 1205–1214 (2020)
9. Yang, Y., Shen, J., Qu, Y., et al.: GIKT: a graph-based interaction model for knowledge tracing. In: Proceedings of the European Conference on Machine Learning and Principles and Practice of Knowledge Discovery in Databases (ECML PKDD), pp. 299–315 (2020)
10. Liang, Y., Peng, T., Pu, Y., Wu, W.: HELP-DKT: an interpretable cognitive model of how students learn programming based on deep knowledge tracing. Sci. Rep. **12**(1), 4012 (2022)
11. Liang, K., Ren, Y., Shang, Y., et al.: Review on knowledge tracing driven by deep learning. Comput. Eng. Appl. **57**(21), 41–58 (2021)
12. Shen, S., Liu, Q., Chen, E., et al.: Learning process-consistent knowledge tracing. In: Proceedings of the 27th ACM SIGKDD Conf. on Knowledge Discovery and Data Mining (KDD), pp. 1452–1460 (2021)
13. Sun, X., Zhao, X., Li, B., et al.: Dynamic key-value memory networks with rich features for knowledge tracing. IEEE Trans. Cybern. **52**(8), 8239–8245 (2021)
14. Abdelrahman, G., Wang, Q.: Knowledge tracing with sequential key-value memory networks. In: Proceedings of the 42nd International ACM SIGIR Conference on Research and Development in Information Retrieval, pp. 175–184 (2019)
15. Minn, S., Yu, Y., Desmarais, M.C., et al.: Deep knowledge tracing and dynamic student classification for knowledge tracing. In: IEEE International Conference on Data Mining (ICDM), pp. 1182–1187 (2018)
16. Shin, D., Shim, Y., Yu, H., et al.: Saint+: Integrating temporal features for EdNet correctness prediction. In: Proceedings of the 11th International Learning Analytics & Knowledge Conference (LAK), pp. 490–496 (2021)
17. Song, X., Li, J., Lei, Q., et al.: Bi-CLKT: Bi-graph contrastive learning based knowledge tracing. Knowl.-Based Syst. **241**, 108274 (2022)
18. Bond, T.G., Fox, C.M.: Applying the Rasch Model: Fundamental Measurement in the Human Sciences, 3rd edn. Routledge, New York (2015)
19. Zhang, Y., Wu, T.: Feature selection methods in educational data mining: a comparative study. Int. J. Emerg. Technol. Learn. (iJET) **15**(2), 124–134 (2020)

Research on the Growth Path of Network Practical Capacity Based on Tridimensional Pedagogical Model

Yongwei Wang, Yuchen Zhang, Pengcheng Liu(✉), and Mei Wang

Information Engineering University, Zhengzhou, Henan Province 450001, China
liupengcheng2016@163.com

Abstract. Information technology innovation characterized by digital intelligence has opened up a new track for economic and social development. How to cultivate innovative talents facing the digital intelligence era has become a modern higher education. As an interdisciplinary engineering specialty, network engineering specialty especially needs to cultivate innovative talents to adapt to the rapid development of digital intelligence technology and network security situation. Based on the construction of network engineering specialty, we constructs a path for the growth and training of innovative talents with "ability traction, system remodeling, and digital intelligence empowerment" by taking the cultivation of innovative ability as the goal, the reconstruction of curriculum system as the construction basis, the innovation of practice as the construction foothold, and the empowerment of teaching methods as the construction supplement, so as to promote the updating and adjustment of professional knowledge system structure, and test the effectiveness of the training mode through a new round of teaching implementation.

Keywords: Major Construction · Network Engineering · Tridimensional Pedagogical Model · Practical Capacity

1 Introduction

At present, digital intelligent technology is continuously promoting the development of social economy. The advent of the digital intelligence era has also had a profound impact on higher education. Network engineering majors need to adapt to the development of digital intelligence technology in terms of teaching philosophy, talent training mode, curriculum system and knowledge structure. The development of network engineering has also been iterative with the rise of big model, big data and other technologies. The object of network security has changed from electronic media to the application of big model, large-scale information and data analysis. Network engineering is an engineering specialty and ad hoc specialty integrating computer science, management, law and other disciplines. Under the background of the transformation of information security network engineering to digital intelligence, it has become an urgent requirement for network engineering major to cultivate talents who adapt to the network security situation, especially to cultivate their innovation ability for future technological development.

W. Hong et al. (Eds.): ICCSE 2025, CCIS 2761, pp. 128–139, 2026.
https://doi.org/10.1007/978-981-95-7731-6_11

2 Related Work

2.1 The Impact of Digital Intelligence on Education

AI governance has a bearing on the fate of all mankind and is a common issue facing all countries in the world [1]. While artificial intelligence, big data and other technologies have greatly improved people's quality of life, they have also brought new risks to social development. Especially in the field of network security, the security situation has become increasingly severe. The risks and challenges faced by network engineering mainly include the disclosure of open-source intelligence association brought about by big data analysis technology, the transformation of new protection methods brought about by artificial intelligence technology, and the network security risks brought about by the further popularization of mobile Internet. First, the application of big data technology and big language model makes the association and aggregation of open source intelligence more efficient and accurate. Secondly, artificial intelligence technology can realize automatic vulnerability identification and continuous attack on network threats, which requires the network security protection party to realize intelligent security management, situational awareness and dynamic response. Finally, with the further popularization of mobile Internet and network information system, network security protection needs to face more security threats from the network, such as malware, ferry attack, etc. the openness of the network also makes network security protection more complex and difficult. These risks and challenges require more rational governance planning and technology application of AI in the field of information security.

In the era of digital intelligence, the specialty construction in colleges and universities needs to be adjusted and reformed in combination with cutting-edge technology. Among them, the digital intelligence adjustment of engineering specialty teaching involves many aspects. First of all, in the path planning of talent cultivation, we need to face the integration of industry and education and discipline integration, improve the quality and ability of traditional industries with the help of emerging technologies such as artificial intelligence, and promote the transformation of education mode to multidisciplinary integration [2]. Secondly, in terms of teaching methods, the course content is changing from relying on Limited traditional high-quality resources to using globally shared intelligent resources, and the teaching methods are also changing from simple teacher-student interaction to in-depth interaction between teachers and students and machines. The research report issued by the American Association for higher education informatization in 2024 proposed that technologies such as intelligent learning tools, intelligent learning analysis, and hybrid learning mode will have an important impact on the development of higher education [3]. Finally, in terms of teaching philosophy, the application of digital intelligence technology has promoted education from the unified teaching mode in the traditional classroom to the personalized teaching that meets individual differences. At the same time, the focus of teaching has also shifted from one-way inculcation of knowledge to the all-round shaping of students' comprehensive ability. Starting from the new concept of knowledge in the digital intelligence era, it is necessary to implement the new quality education concept of transforming from school education to lifelong education, from knowledge transfer as the center to the realization of personalized learning, and cultivate talents who can cooperate with intelligent machines and are good at innovation and creation [4]. As the main position for the cultivation of network security technology talents, network engineering specialty also faces the requirements of the above-mentioned digital intelligence transformation in terms of teaching mode and ability training system.

2.2 Challenges of Network Engineering Education

Facing the impact of the wave of digital intelligence era, there is still room for optimization and adjustment in the construction of knowledge structure, the application of teaching methods and the cultivation of innovation ability in the talent training mode of traditional engineering majors. First of all, in the construction of knowledge structure, we should focus on the new engineering characteristics of teaching and research integration, inter hospital cooperation and curriculum intersection, and optimize the talent training path of new engineering education [5]. Secondly, in the application of teaching methods, we should face the impact and challenges of generative AI on higher education, and realize the transformation strategy of education in the digital era from knowledge learning to comprehensive application, from interpersonal collaboration to human technology collaboration, from knowledge-based to ability-based, from homogeneous development to unique growth [6]. Finally, in terms of innovation ability training, the reform of higher education innovation ability training needs to combine multi-dimensional innovation initiatives such as normal communication, knowledge foundation, system improvement, and competition practice to build a full stage talent training element for the frontier field of artificial intelligence [7]. The network engineering specialty has the characteristics of strong technical field and wide business scope, which requires students to meet the training requirements of talent innovation ability in multiple dimensions, such as the cross-border integration ability of information security network engineering of interdisciplinary intersection of computer, management, law, artificial intelligence and network security, the human-computer cooperation ability of network engineering comprehensive application of digital intelligence enabling network security, physical security and data security, and the innovation ability of network security protection technology of digital intelligence technology combined with engineering practice.

Building upon these multidimensional innovation imperatives, the network engineering curriculum must forge deep ontological integration across computer science, management systems, and legal governance—transcending superficial interdisciplinary touchpoints to embed regulatory compliance and ethical risk assessment directly within network architecture paradigms. This demands constructing cross-domain threat intelligence fabrics where machine-readable legal policies (e.g., GDPR article 17 automation) dynamically configure SDN security groups, while AI-audited operational workflows enforce ISO 27001 controls at the infrastructure-as-code layer. Simultaneously, human-machine collaboration evolves beyond tool-assisted workflows toward cognitive symbiosis frameworks: neural-symbolic AI systems now co-design zero-trust architectures with engineers, translating natural-language security policies into cryptographically enforced microsegmentation schemas, and autonomously optimizing physical-data-cyber security triads through federated reinforcement learning. Here, digital intelligence ceases to be merely assistive—it becomes an equal co-architect in securing hyper-converged edge-to-cloud environments. Crucially, innovation in protection technologies manifests as continuous adversarial evolution: quantum-resistant homomorphic encryption algorithms are stress-tested against AI-generated attack vectors in simulated critical infrastructure networks, while neuromorphic computing processors dynamically reconfigure threat detection logics based on live darknet telemetry. Such capabilities necessitate fundamentally reimagined pedagogical infrastructures—network cyber-ranges with genetically diverse attack surfaces that mutate via GANs during red team exercises, and digital twin federations mirroring cross-border cloud ecosystems where students deploy blockchain-anchored integrity proofs against supply chain compromises. Ultimately, this cultivates engineers who conceptualize security not as perimeter defense but as pervasive resilience metabolism, embedding self-regenerative capacities into 5G slicing profiles, IoT firmware streams, and satellite mesh protocols. The emergent paradigm shift lies in transitioning from technology-literate professionals to ecology-aware architects—visionaries who orchestrate organic growth of network intelligence ecosystems where cryptographic trust fabrics, ethical AI governance, and antifragile infrastructure co-evolve with human oversight, thereby materializing cybersecurity as the core circulatory system of digital civilization rather than its auxiliary safeguard.

2.3 Transforming Pedagogical Frameworks: Digital Intelligence in Curriculum Design

The integration of digital intelligence into curriculum design represents a paradigm shift from static, knowledge-transfer models to dynamic, competency-driven ecosystems. By leveraging data analytics, AI algorithms, and adaptive learning technologies, educational frameworks now dynamically reconfigure learning pathways in response to real-time student performance metrics. For instance, machine learning systems analyze engagement patterns and conceptual misunderstandings to autonomously adjust content sequencing—introducing reinforcement modules for struggling learners while accelerating advanced topics for proficient students. This transcends traditional "one-size-fits-all" approaches, fostering personalized mastery trajectories. Crucially, digital intelligence enables micro-credentialing architectures that fragment monolithic courses into skill-specific nano-modules. Each module correlates with industry-validated competencies (e.g., "SDN Configuration" or "Threat Mitigation Tactics"), allowing learners to assemble bespoke certification portfolios aligned with evolving job-market demands. Such granularity is operationalized through blockchain-verified digital badges, providing transparent, tamper-proof records of acquired capabilities. Furthermore, curriculum designers employ predictive simulation tools—such as network digital twins—to embed authentic problem-solving scenarios. Students interact with virtualized infrastructure replicating real-world anomalies (e.g., DDoS attacks or routing failures), developing diagnostic agility without operational risks. These simulations feed into AI-powered assessment engines that evaluate not only technical accuracy but meta-cognitive skills like troubleshooting strategy and collaborative decision-making. However, successful transformation necessitates overcoming inertial resistance. Faculty development programs must upskill educators in pedagogical data literacy—training them to interpret analytics dashboards and ethically deploy automation. Concurrently, institutions must redesign physical-digital hybrid spaces to support fluid transitions between AI-guided self-study and facilitated collaborative inquiry. The ultimate goal is a responsive, evidence-based curriculum that perpetually evolves through continuous data feedback loops, positioning network engineering education at the nexus of technological innovation and pedagogical excellence.

This evolutionary trajectory necessitates cognitive-technical-ethical tripartite scaffolding that transforms curricula into living organisms. Here, neuroplasticity-inspired learning architectures employ adaptive forgetting algorithms to strategically decay obsolete knowledge (e.g., IPv4 troubleshooting tactics) while reinforcing emerging paradigms like intent-based networking—mirroring the brain's synaptic pruning through educationally engineered digital neurodegeneration. Simultaneously, blockchain micro-credentials evolve into dynamic competency NFTs, where smart contracts autonomously void certifications when associated skills degrade below industry relevance thresholds, compelling continuous reskilling via just-in-time nano-modules on quantum-safe cryptography or AI-powered threat hunting. Crucially, digital twins transcend simulation to become pedagogical mutation engines: when students mitigate simulated zero-day attacks in SDN environments, their solution strategies are genetically recombined via GANs to generate next-generation training scenarios, creating an autonomous curriculum-evolution flywheel. However, such autonomy demands algorithmic accountability frameworks. Federated learning systems now train assessment AIs across decentralized educator nodes, preventing bias consolidation while enabling explainability interfaces that visualize grading decision trajectories—revealing how points were deducted for inadequate BGP hijacking mitigation not merely as technical failure, but as deficient systemic risk assessment. Faculty transformation correspondingly shifts from tool literacy to cognitive alliance engineering, training professors to co-orchestrate hybrid intelligence ensembles where human pedagogical intuition and AI's pattern recognition collaboratively redesign learning epigenetics. Physical spaces morph into neuro-adaptive laboratories with AR interfaces projecting personalized cognitive load heatmaps during packet analysis exercises, dynamically grouping students by complementary neurodiversity profiles to optimize collective problem-solving. Ultimately, this crystallizes education as perpetual beta ecosystems—self-optimizing through embedded data loops that convert assessment artifacts into training data for subsequent curricular generations, thereby achieving the first-principles redefinition of network engineering pedagogy: no longer knowledge transmission systems, but human-machine intelligence symbiosis incubators forging cognitive architectures inherently resilient to technological obsolescence.

3 Network Practical Capacity Based on Tridimensional Pedagogical Model

3.1 Building Capacity Model Based on Professional Demand

Network engineering is an ad hoc specialty to cultivate post talents for the cause of network security, which needs to have corresponding posts and professional abilities. Focusing on the professional needs of talent cultivation, the "four abilities" capacity model based on thinking and cognition, post competency, engineering practice and scientific research innovation is constructed.

Firstly, according to the adjustment requirements of the construction of network engineering specialty, the development of digital intelligence oriented to network engineering enables students to recognize the impact and role of generative artificial intelligence on network security, and then enhance the awareness of protection from both sides of network attack and defense, and build the cognitive ability of thinking. Secondly, according to the actual needs of the post, for typical business scenarios such as AI assisted office and data analysis in network security work, cultivate students' data security awareness, strengthen the ability of risk analysis and control, and build post competency. Thirdly, according to the development requirements of digital intelligence technology, based on the practice of host control, physical protection and digital forensics, combined with the application of big data analysis and generative artificial intelligence technology, students' hands-on ability based on traditional control and supplemented by intelligent control is cultivated and trained to build engineering practice ability. Finally, according to the training needs of innovative talents, facing the development trend of information network engineering, cultivate students' ability to adapt to and even promote the further popularization of digital intelligence technology in the field of network security protection, and build scientific research innovation.

This integrated framework necessitates deploying generative adversarial pedagogy where students co-create evolving cyber-threat scenarios with LLMs—prompt engineering becomes both offensive weaponry (designing polymorphic malware variants) and defensive strategy (automating intrusion detection rule synthesis)—thus crystallizing attack-defense consciousness through cognitive scaffolding. For AI-assisted workplace competencies, zero-trust data literacy is cultivated via blockchain-anchored office simulations: students configure GPT agents to redact sensitive network topology diagrams while preserving operational utility, mastering differential privacy mechanisms that enforce least-privilege data access during collaborative threat analysis. Engineering praxis further evolves through cyber-physical twin laboratories merging traditional controls with intelligent governance; digital forensics workflows now integrate multimodal AI—generating synthetic packet captures to train forensic models against novel attack vectors while physical security systems autonomously reconfigure access policies based on federated learning predictions from distributed honeypots. Ultimately, innovation cultivation transcends adaptation to drive paradigm invention: students architect neuro-symbolic security orchestrators that transform generative AI from productivity tools into sovereign technology incubators—designing quantum-key-distribution protocols via large language models constrained by cryptographic correctness theorems, and pioneering biologically inspired intrusion detection systems where spiking neural networks evolve defense mechanisms through Darwinian selection in simulated darknets. This manifests as engineers who don't merely implement digital intelligence but redefine its ontological boundaries, embedding China's cybersecurity sovereignty directly into the algorithmic fabric of next-generation network ecosystems.

3.2 Adjusting Subject Content and Reshaping Curriculum System

In the process of implementing the innovative talent cultivation ability model, the reconstruction of professional curriculum system based on interdisciplinary integration is the most important reform measure, mainly including the thick adjustment of professional basic courses, the renewal and optimization of professional core courses, and the addition and opening of digital intelligence and general education courses. In terms of the adjustment of the overall class hours, the class hours of professional basic courses were reduced, while the number and class hours of professional core courses and digital intelligence and general education courses were increased.

In terms of the adjustment of specific professional courses, first of all, enrich professional basic courses and add, delete or update knowledge points according to the development status of information network engineering. Add the content of big data analysis related technologies, including data aggregation, data association, etc., and focus on cultivating students' analysis ability for network security scenarios. Secondly, we should update the professional core courses and carry out the construction of interdisciplinary integrated teaching content in combination with multi-disciplinary knowledge, especially the frontier technology and reform situation of digital intelligence. For example, in the course of network security regulations, based on the existing laws and regulations related to network security, the generative AI management regulations and AI development initiatives issued by the United States and the European Union, as well as the legislation for the development of AI in the future, focus on how to improve the construction of relevant regulations of network security technology in the digital age, and cultivate students' legal literacy and interdisciplinary application ability. Finally, a general course of digital intelligence is added, that is, an "AI +" course is added, which mainly includes introduction to artificial intelligence, natural language processing, frontier of network security, introduction to big data, etc. In addition to achieving the goal of interdisciplinary knowledge learning, digital intelligence general education courses are cross cutting with the previous professional basic courses and professional core courses. For example, network security frontier courses integrate situational intelligence analysis, traffic data hiding, multi-agent confrontation technology, etc. based on the learning of access control, situational awareness, data hiding and other technologies in the pilot courses, so that students can understand the new applications of digital intelligence technology in network attack and defense and data hiding. Through the collaborative remodeling of the curriculum system in the three parts of professional foundation, professional core and digital intelligence general education, the convergence and integration of network engineering discipline and digital intelligence related disciplines, professional basic courses and digital intelligence higher-level courses are finally realized.

3.3 Constructing Digital Intelligence Environment and Empowering Teaching Methods

The application of digital intelligence technology has brought profound changes in the field of higher education, such as intelligent learning situation analysis, construction of subject knowledge map, intelligent question and answer, etc. [8]. As the implementation path of innovative talent training, teaching means plays an important role in the adjustment and optimization of talent training mode. Network engineering specialty realizes the whole process of enabling teaching means of digital intelligence technology through the construction of various digital intelligence environment.

The process of empowering teaching means with digital intelligence technology is divided into four stages. First, before class, based on the online teaching content of the course, teachers construct knowledge points and associated structures to generate the corresponding course knowledge map, and students preview the knowledge framework and report the progress through the knowledge map. Second, in the course, based on the traditional knowledge teaching, the generative artificial intelligence platform is used to transform the interaction between teachers and students to the three-way interaction between teachers and students, such as the simple code writing in the practice environment, the generation of the outline of the experimental report, etc., while allowing students to modify and refine the generated content. Third, after class, using the data of the educational administration information platform, combined with intelligent technology to realize the analysis of learning situation and auxiliary paper judgment, so as to realize the whole process of AI teaching assistant. Fourth, after class, actively cultivate students' interest in the frontier of network engineering, expand the content channels of Subject Competitions and subject clubs, participate in subject competitions such as information security and data mining, and achieve breakthroughs from classroom knowledge learning to engineering innovation and application.

4 Application of Tridimensional Pedagogical Model

4.1 Teaching of Network Engineering Knowledge

As an engineering specialty, the teaching of network engineering needs to be combined with the actual work field. On the one hand, in terms of network security technology, the OBE (Outcome Based Education) method is used in the teaching process of professional courses and advanced courses, focusing on the completion of students' tasks in the process of learning and practice, promoting the implementation of student-centered education concept, and effectively helping students realize the transformation from learning knowledge to strong ability. On the other hand, in the course of Ideological and political education, professional teaching needs to pay attention to the particularity of network security, which not only requires students to have good professional and technical ability, but also have excellent ideological and political quality, which requires teachers to establish correct teaching ideas and improve their ideological and Political Teaching ability [9]. In the increased content of digital intelligence general education, the influence and role of digital intelligence technology in network security work are analyzed in many aspects, so as to guide students to understand the importance and intrinsic value of network security technology in the digital intelligence era, and establish a firm belief in serving the country. On the basis of teaching students in accordance with their aptitude, comprehensively realize the cultivation of interdisciplinary and high-quality talents, and then provide basic support for the follow-up digital intelligence frontier teaching and the implementation of innovative digital intelligence projects.

This pedagogical integration necessitates deploying dynamic OBE frameworks where cybersecurity task completion metrics are continuously recalibrated through AI-driven competency mapping, transforming static learning objectives into adaptive skill trajectories aligned with real-world threat landscapes. Digital intelligence technologies here act as dual catalysts: machine learning algorithms analyze student performance in network penetration testing simulations to generate personalized upskilling paths, while blockchain-secured logs provide immutable evidence of hands-on competency for zero-trust enterprise environments. Concurrently, ideological-political education transcends conventional patriotism narratives by embedding sovereignty-by-design principles into technical workflows—students architecting encrypted DNS over HTTPS tunnels must simultaneously implement constitutional compliance modules that autonomously filter illegal content under Cybersecurity Law Article 12, thus fusing technical prowess with regulatory consciousness. The expanded digital intelligence literacy curriculum further engineers techno-ethical discernment through neuromorphic computing case studies where students debate algorithmic bias mitigation in 5G network slicing resource allocation, internalizing the geopolitical stakes of technological autonomy. Such synthesis achieves three-dimensional talent cultivation: network engineers who architect self-healing SD-WAN infrastructures using federated learning also develop critical civic epistemology—understanding firewall rule creation not merely as technical acts but as exercises in digital sovereignty preservation. Ultimately, this forms the foundation for frontier innovation: graduates initiate AI-Native security operations centers where large language models trained on cross-jurisdictional legal corpus automate compliance audits while preserving human ethical oversight, thereby actualizing the transition from talent training paradigms to ecosystemic intelligence co-creation. The core outcome manifests as engineers equipped with dual-code competency—mastering Python and cryptographic algorithms with equal fluency as constitutional articles and Marxist technological philosophy—ready to deploy 6G terahertz backhauls as both technical infrastructure and vectors of civilizational confidence.

4.2 Teaching of Digital Intelligence Frontier Professional Knowledge

Network engineering work needs the empowerment of digital intelligence emerging technology to realize the leap from traditional productivity to new quality productivity. Therefore, in addition to the adjustment and updating of the knowledge system, professional courses and digital intelligence general education courses, both course teaching and practice teaching, need to be based on the implementation means and teaching content combined with digital intelligent technology. For example, in the programming implementation of the big data analysis experiment, students carry out auxiliary programming through large commercial models such as DeepSeek and ChatGPT, and automatically generate small programs such as data format processing and file cleaning, which not only solves the repetitive work, but also exercises the students' ability to process data in the whole process, forming the teacher-student interaction of practical teaching. Finally, the training goal of enabling students to have a shared vision in the era of digital intelligence and to correctly use artificial intelligence technology is achieved.

The transformation of network engineering into a digitally intelligent discipline demands the seamless fusion of emerging AI technologies, propelling traditional methodologies toward new quality productivity. This evolution transcends mere curriculum updates—it necessitates reconstructing both specialized courses and interdisciplinary foundations around human-AI co-creation paradigms, where digital intelligence serves as the core engine for theoretical exploration and practical implementation. Within this framework, educators and learners collaboratively harness large language models to automate technical workflows, redirecting cognitive resources from repetitive coding to strategic innovation and ethical governance. The pedagogical shift redefines teacher-student dynamics, transforming instructors into orchestrators of augmented intelligence ecosystems while empowering students to architect self-optimizing network infrastructures through intent-driven design and autonomous orchestration. Critical competencies now prioritize precision in prompt engineering, rigorous validation of AI-generated outputs against security and fairness benchmarks, and systemic optimization of sustainability metrics across computational workflows. This cultivates a generation of digitally native network architects who intrinsically embed ethical AI deployment within neuromorphic computing frameworks and federated learning systems, ensuring that human oversight governs algorithmic autonomy. By converging technical mastery with symbiotic innovation, the discipline transcends conventional tool-based adaptation, instead fostering trust-centric network ecosystems capable of self-evolution amid volatile demands. Herein lies the essence of new quality productivity: networks that dynamically balance hyper-efficiency with resilience, privacy with transparency, and scalability with energy consciousness—all through the responsible integration of digital intelligence as a collaborative force multiplier. The future of network engineering thus emerges not as a human-AI dichotomy, but as a unified continuum where biological and synthetic intelligence co-evolve to pioneer infrastructures inherently aligned with both technological possibility and humanistic values.

4.3 Integrated Network-Digital Intelligence Application Practices

Integrated Network-Digital Intelligence Application Practices, bridges theoretical knowledge from network engineering and digital intelligence frontiers by immersing students in hands-on, real-world scenarios. This module focuses on designing, deploying, and optimizing converged systems where advanced networking (e.g., 5G/6G, IoT, SDN/NFV) synergizes with digital intelligence technologies (AI/ML, big data analytics, edge computing). Students engage in end-to-end projects—such as building smart industrial control networks, developing AI-driven network security solutions, or creating autonomous drone logistics systems—requiring holistic integration of hardware, software, and data layers.

Through collaborative labs and simulation platforms (e.g., NS-3, Mininet, Kubernetes clusters), learners simulate large-scale networked intelligence environments, tackling challenges like low-latency edge inference, intent-based networking automation, or cross-domain data federation. Emphasis is placed on DevOps/NetOps workflows, containerization (Docker), orchestration (Kubernetes), and infrastructure-as-code (IaC) tools to streamline deployment. Critical evaluation of ethical implications—algorithmic bias, privacy-preserving federated learning, and explainable AI in network operations—forms a core component, ensuring responsible innovation.

Industry-aligned case studies (e.g., smart grids, telemedicine networks, cloud gaming systems) contextualize learning, while hackathons or capstone projects foster agile problem-solving. Students master tools like TensorFlow Extended (TFX), PyTorch with ONNX, Prometheus for monitoring, and ELK stacks for log analysis. The curriculum culminates in performance benchmarking, resilience testing (chaos engineering), and cost-optimization exercises, preparing graduates to architect scalable, secure, and sustainable network-digital intelligence ecosystems for Industry 4.0 and beyond.

5 Conclusion

In view of the application prospect of digital intelligence technology in the field of network engineering education, we put forward the talent innovation ability training mode of "ability traction, system remodeling, digital intelligence empowerment", which takes the ability model construction and curriculum system remodeling as the main body, and the innovation and setting of practice links and digital intelligence empowerment teaching methods as the auxiliary. Through the adjustment and reconstruction of the curriculum system structure, the interdisciplinary and integrated teaching of network engineering discipline knowledge and cutting-edge digital intelligence discipline knowledge has been realized to a certain extent. Through the innovation of the practice teaching link setting, the whole process teaching means of digital intelligence empowerment and the implementation of innovative digital intelligence projects, the students' engineering ability and innovation ability have been improved, laying a good and solid foundation for students to engage in network engineering related jobs in the future. In the next step, we will continue to promote the reform and adjustment of the training mode of network engineering talents' innovative ability according to the era development and application needs of digital intelligence technology.

References

1. Arpaci, I., Emran, A.M., Qaysi, A.N.: What drives the use of generative artificial intelligence to promote educational sustainability? Evid. SEM-ANN Approach, 1–15 (2025). (prepublish). TechTrends
2. Zhao, F., Dai, Y.: Key technologies and development scenarios of digital transformation of Higher Education -- Interpretation of EDUCAUSE horizon report 2024 (Teaching and Learning Edition). China Educ. Informatization **30**(12), 44–57 (2024)
3. Wang, Q., Zhu, W.: Educational teaching design of health management course based on Constructivism. Educ. Teach. Summit Forum **1**(1), 38–41 (2025)
4. Zhang, J.: Practical exploration on the deep integration of PLC teaching and ideological and political education in the context of digital intelligence. forefront Educ. Times **7**(1) (2025)
5. Xie, Y.: The value implication and practical strategy of digital intelligence technology enabling ideological and political teaching in colleges and universities. Educ. Forum **6**(10) (2024)
6. Wei, L.: A strategic study on quality improvement of physical education teaching empowered by digital intelligence technology. Appl. Math. Nonlinear Sci. **9**(1) (2024)
7. Aldalur, I.: Introducing students to web engineering topics by teaching web augmentation. J. Web Eng. **23**(1), 1–26 (2024)

8. Expósito-Langa, M., Tomás-Miquel, J., Fotă, A.: Knowledge base and innovative practices: analysis of the moderating effect of network competence. An application in the Alicante wine industry. Int. J. Wine Bus. Res. **37**(1), 159–178 (2025)
9. Newman, L.J., Brook, Z., Cox, J.S.: Towards the automatic detection of activities of daily living using eye-movement and accelerometer data with neural networks. Comp. Biol. Med., 186109607–109607 (2025)

Design and Development of AIGC-Based Intelligent Teaching Assistance System

Lihan Jiang[2](✉), Gangyi Zhang[2], Xiangdong Li[1], Zhiqi Jin[2], and Yuefeng Cen[2]

[1] School of Economics, Zhejiang University of Science and Technology, Hangzhou 310023, China

[2] School of Computer Science and Technology, Zhejiang University of Science and Technology, Hangzhou 310023, China

1664284772@qq.com, cyf@zust.edu.cn

Abstract. As generative artificial intelligence (AIGC) becomes increasingly integrated into the education sector, Educational stakeholders are seeking more capable and intelligent assistance system. Traditional teaching assistance systems provide relatively limited support for after-class learning and lack systematicity and specificity. The content generated by AI-assisted tools tends to be fragmented, making it difficult to meet students' needs for personalized learning and continuous improvement. To address these issues, this paper designs and develops an intelligent educational assistance system based on AIGC. The system is centered around an AI Agent architecture, integrating user profile and local knowledge base technology to build a comprehensive system with adaptive learning capabilities and intelligent teaching support functions. The system consists of student, teacher, and management terminals, covering functions such as homework grading, exercise training, intelligent Q&A, and resource sharing. The system aims to improve students' after-class learning outcomes and provide personalized learning path guidance. At the same time, it helps teachers improve teaching efficiency, reduce repetitive workloads, and promote the intelligent transformation of the teaching process.

Keywords: AIGC · Agent · Smart education · Teaching assistant

1 Introduction

In recent years, the use of large-scale language models (LLMs) and generative AI in higher education has gained increasing attention. As a representative AIGC tool, ChatGPT has introduced transformative possibilities in education by enhancing pedagogy, personalization, and learning experiences [1]. Generative AI has a differential impact on students and teachers. Daniel Lee et al. surveyed Australian tertiary teachers' perceptions of AI and found that nearly half had experimented with AI tools in their teaching, but concerns about academic integrity persisted [2]. Aashish Ghimire's study showed that the majority

W. Hong et al. (Eds.): ICCSE 2025, CCIS 2761, pp. 140–153, 2026.
https://doi.org/10.1007/978-981-95-7731-6_12

of university faculty members have a positive attitude towards AI language models, with those with computer science backgrounds in particular showing higher levels of confidence in the technology. However, there is no significant difference in the ability of faculty members across all disciplines to recognize AI-generated content, suggesting the need to enhance the development and training of relevant detection mechanisms in the future [3]. From the students' perspective, a comparative study between Zayed University and King Abdulaziz University reveals that students generally believe that the use of generative AI tools can enhance learning efficiency and satisfaction [4]. Artificial Intelligence technology, while improving educational efficiency, also provides strong technical support for personalized education and resource sharing [5], the intelligence of student learning scenarios is expected to increase, and the popularization of tailored teaching and the equalization of high-quality education will be accelerated.

However, in the current educational practice, the after-class teaching training mechanism is still relatively weak, and it is difficult to effectively meet the diversified, personalized and continuous learning needs of students, and it is difficult to teach students in accordance of their aptitude [6]. Although artificial intelligence technologies have been increasingly applied in the field of education, AI education system is still unable to provide students with more systematic after-class tutoring [7].

In response to the above issues and technological opportunities, this study designed and developed an AIGC-based smart teaching assistance system. The system utilizes the natural language processing, logical reasoning, and multimodal generation capabilities of large models to empower smart education, optimize student adaptive learning services and experiences, and improve learning and teaching efficiency. Based on this, the system further integrates AI Agents technology. By combining student user profiles with learning behavior data, the system can provide intelligent services such as personalized answers to questions, learning path recommendations, and real-time guidance. This mechanism not only effectively improves students' knowledge mastery, but also enhances their independent learning abilities, thereby guiding them to form good learning habits. In addition, the system constructs a localized knowledge base through structured processing and semantic analysis of teaching resources, and leverages Retrieval-Augmented Generation (RAG) technology to enable efficient content retrieval and intelligent generation. This allows teachers and students to quickly access the information they need, thereby improving the efficiency and accuracy of teaching and learning.

2 Related Works

In recent years, researchers have explored a variety of approaches to better integrate artificial intelligence (AI) technologies into educational systems to enhance the teaching and learning experience. Zheyuan Zhang et al. verified the effectiveness of large language models (LLMs) in facilitating teacher-student interactions and student collaborations by constructing a multi-intelligent system,

SimClass, to simulate the classroom process [8]. Shi Yang et al. showed that the application of AIGC Big Models can significantly enhance student engagement and learning outcomes in terms of personalized learning path design, extension of teaching resources and automated assessment [9]. In the field of physical education, Quantao He et al. developed an interactive AI system based on visual analytics for optimizing the teaching process and interactions in university physical education courses [10]. This practice further expands the boundaries of AI applications in non-traditional teaching scenarios. Yuhao Dan and Zhikai Lei et al. proposed the EduChat system, a chatbot system that provides better support for intelligent education through personalized study guides and instant Q&A functions via natural language processing technology [11]. In addition, the P-Tuning v2 method proposed by Liu X et al. shows that cue tuning can be comparable to fine-tuning on different scales and tasks, a finding that provides new ideas for efficiently utilizing pre-trained language models [12]. The study by Ye C and Shi X demonstrates how instruction fine-tuning of ChatGLM3 can be optimized for news topic categorization, further demonstrating the strong adaptability of LLMs on specific tasks [13].

In summary, previous studies have explored the ways in which LLMs interact with humans in educational environments from a variety of perspectives, covering a wide range of aspects from classroom simulation to personalized learning path design to task-specific optimization. These studies provide an important theoretical foundation and technical support for the design and implementation of this project.

3 System Design

3.1 System Overview

This project develops a AIGC-based intelligent teaching assistance system, which is an adaptive learning and teaching assistance system. The system includes functional modules such as homework and intelligent correction, exercise training and intelligent Q&A and resource sharing, personal question bank and class management, user management (see Fig. 1).

The system consists of three types of users: teachers, students and administrators. Teachers carry out teaching activities through this system, including the maintenance and management of teaching resources and the statistical analysis of student data. Students carry out learning activities such as practicing, discussing, communicating and testing through the system. The administrator mainly carries out the maintenance of the system.

3.2 Detailed System Description

Exercise Training and Intelligent Q&A Module. In this module, students can choose their own topics for training according to subjects and knowledge points, and the system provides answer analysis and personalized Q&A based on

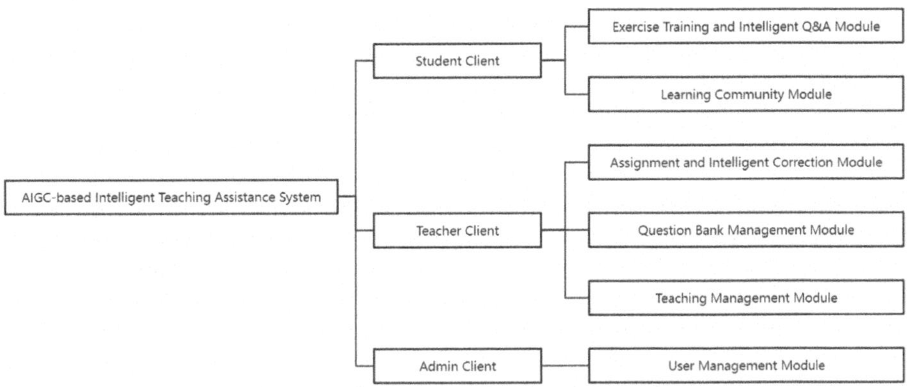

Fig. 1. Overall functional module diagram of the system

user profiles. The large model supports multiple rounds of conversational tutoring until the student thoroughly understands the knowledge points and problem solving ideas. At the same time, the module integrates stage-by-stage assessment and error recommendation functions, guiding the learning path through the user profile and realizing accurate leakage remediation. Students can automatically generate and organize their mistakes, favorites, and study notes, and can recommend similar questions or generate new questions from the big model based on their mistakes.

Learning Community Module. Through the open community structure, this module supports students to post and share learning materials, such as notes, problem solving, learning tips and experience summaries, to build a community learning ecology and promote the construction and sharing of high-quality resources. Students can also form study groups based on their interests and conduct seminars around specific topics to build a better learning environment.

Assignment and Intelligent Correction Module. This module provides a fully integrated online homework workflow and incorporates the large model's intelligent grading capability, enabling end-to-end automation of homework assignment, submission, and evaluation. Teachers assign homework on the teacher's end, students submit it after completion, the system carries out preliminary correction and analysis through the big model, and the teacher then reviews it, thus improving the efficiency of correction and providing personalized feedback for students.

Question Bank Management Module. This module supports teachers to build personalized question banks, review the contents of question banks and expand question banks, maintain the quality and timeliness of question banks, and serve the needs of teaching and testing. The module introduces AIGC technology, combining teaching objectives and student profiles to automatically generate diversified and targeted new questions, which provides strong support for scientific and accurate teaching evaluation.

Teaching Management Module. This module supports the management of courses and classes, learning statistics and analysis, analyzing reports and forming reports. Teachers can complete the whole process of course information release, teaching resources uploading, teaching task assignment, homework correction and quiz arrangement through this module, which is convenient for teachers to track the overall learning situation of the class and adjust the teaching strategy.

User Management Module. This module can accurately identify and categorize different types of users and provide basic support for subsequent personalized service recommendation and permission allocation. Administrators can carry out user authentication, authority control and platform data monitoring to manage platform data, which strengthens the platform's data security line of defense, improves the standardization of user operation and system management controllability, and ensures the safe and stable operation of the platform.

4 Technical Architecture and Core Technology

4.1 Technical Architecture

The system divides the technical architecture into four layers, including presentation layer, communication layer, business logic layer and data layer (see Fig. 2). Based on the front-end and back-end separation architecture, the front-end uses Next.js, Vue and other front-end frameworks to realize interactive and friendly user interface; the back-end uses Spring Boot, Spring Security, MyBatis-Plus framework to build a robust and efficient server architecture. The full process development of technical architecture utilizes MySQL database system to store user data, Redis as cache to pass system performance, and MyBatis-Plus framework to improve development efficiency.

Presentation Layer. The presentation layer is the interface for users to interact with the system, which is responsible for presenting information and receiving user inputs. The presentation layer is divided into student side, teacher side and administration side, which correspond to different user roles. The student side provides functions such as homepage, question bank, homework and error sets; the teacher side focuses on question bank and homework management; and the administration side covers background functions such as user management, permission management and data management.

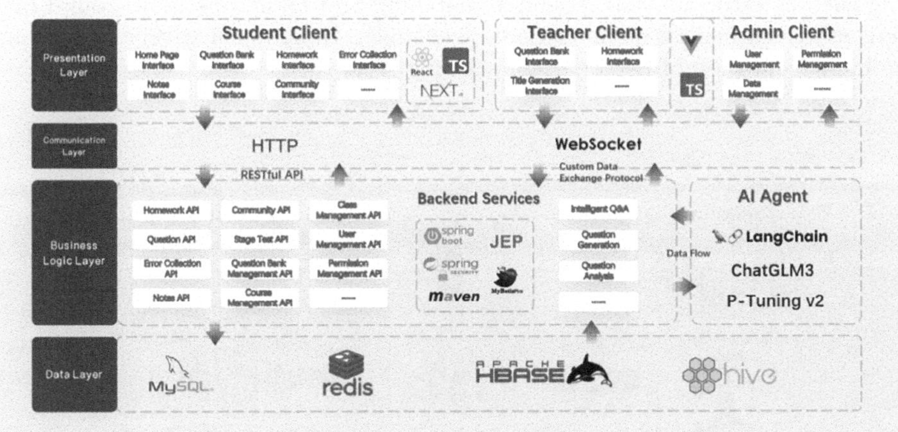

Fig. 2. Technical architecture of the system

Communication Layer. The communication layer is responsible for transmitting data between the client and the server. HTTP protocol realizes the data exchange between the client and the server through a RESTful API. Meanwhile, WebSocket protocol realizes real-time communication of large model generation data through a set of customized data exchange protocols.

Business Logic Layer. The business logic layer is the core part of the system, which contains various business rules and processing flow. The back-end service part provides various interfaces for the front-end, and at the same time establishes a connection with the big model, providing functions such as intelligent question answering, question generation, question parsing and wrong question analysis.

Data Layer. The data layer is responsible for storing and managing data.MySQL as a relational database is used to store structured data, such as user information and question content. Meanwhile, Redis, as a high-performance key-value pair storage system, is used as a caching database to improve data access speed and response time.

4.2 Core Technology

Agent. The Agent system uses a large language model (LLM) as its core controller, forming a perception-inference-execution closed loop (see Fig. 3). User input is parsed by the LLM to trigger dynamic decision-making: if external knowledge support is required, the system integrates user profiling systems, local knowledge bases, or search engines to fuse multi-source information. Simultaneously, based on the enhanced context, the LLM generates structured task planning such as error analysis, resource matching and maintains multi-round dialogue states through a memory pool mechanism, thereby effectively supporting the implementation of personalized learning services.

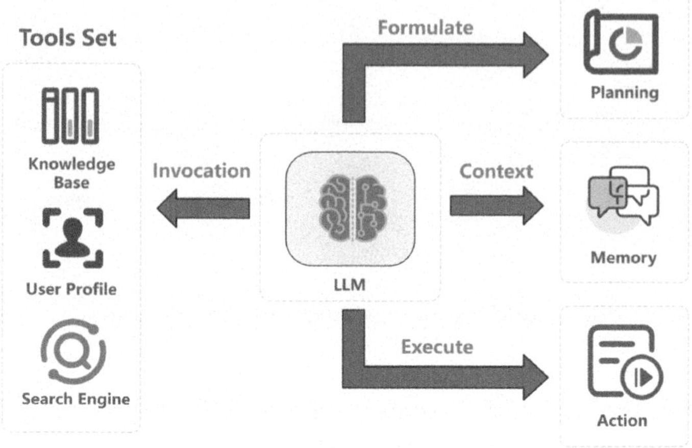

Fig. 3. Agent flow

User Profile. The system constructs a dynamic, multi-dimensional user profiling system. First, it uses mean imputation and IQR outlier detection techniques to clean raw behavioral data, and then converts text interactions into high-dimensional feature vectors through jieba word segmentation and BERT semantic encoding. The system further applies the K-means clustering algorithm ($k = 6$) to identify potential user group patterns, forming different types of user groups. In terms of data storage, the system implements a hierarchical storage strategy: short-term user profile data is stored in Redis, while medium- and long-term profiles are stored in HBase and Hive, respectively, to meet the needs of large-scale offline analysis and long-term behavior tracking. User profile tags cover learning trajectories, incorrect question features, community participation, and other tags, providing data support for personalized recommendations and learning path optimization.

Retrieval-Augmented Generation. In order to realize accurate Q&A support for domain knowledge, the system constructs a local knowledge base and implements a semantic search mechanism based on vector retrieval. When a user asks a question, the system vectorizes the question and retrieves the most similar text vector segments in the vector database. These matches are then used to construct prompts along with the original question, which are fed into the larger model to generate high-quality answers. The local knowledge base Q&A, realizing the complete knowledge chain from user question to intelligent response (see Fig. 4).

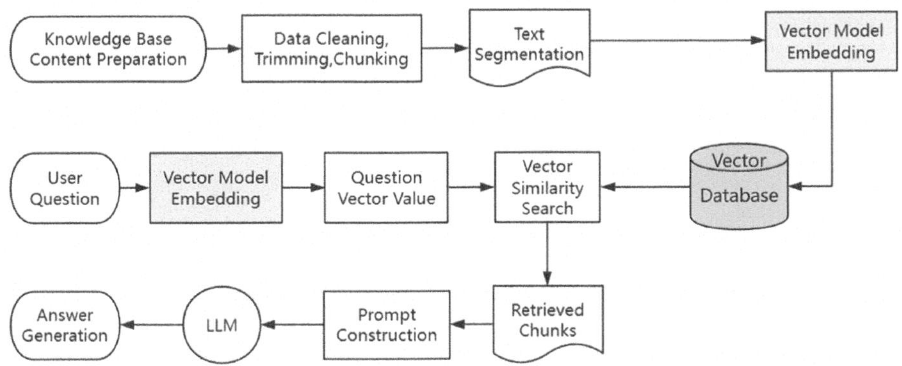

Fig. 4. The Process of Retrieval-Augmented Generation.

5 Experiment

5.1 Training Process of the Model

Data Collection and Processing. We adopted a two-phase data processing methodology: Taking computer networking as a representative course, we first employed Python scripts to extract knowledge point keywords based on curriculum standards for preliminary filtering, followed by manual verification of question quality and knowledge coverage to curate 5,000 core knowledge point seed entries from an initial pool of 100,000 data samples. Subsequently, we designed Chain-of-Thought (CoT) prompt templates to adapt to large language model input specifications, and ultimately leveraged the ERNIE-3.5-8K model to perform data augmentation through semantic paraphrasing and variant question generation, with confidence-based filtering yielding a high-quality training dataset.

Fine-Tuning Process. During the fine-tuning phase, we employed ERNIE-Speed-8K as the base model and implemented Low-Rank Adaptation (LoRA) for efficient parameter optimization. This approach preserves the original model parameters while training only the low-rank decomposition matrices, thereby enhancing task-specific performance without compromising the foundational knowledge. The dataset was partitioned into three distinct categories with a sampling ratio of $1:3:1$, resulting in approximate distribution percentages of 28.97%, 42.27%, and 28.76% across the subsets. Key training hyperparameters included: Epochs: 10, Learning rate: 2×10^{-4}, Maximum input sequence length: 4096 tokens.

Post-fine-tuning evaluation revealed favorable convergence characteristics, as evidenced by the perplexity and training loss trajectories depicted in Fig. 5. For generative task assessment, the model achieved competitive performance with BLEU-4, ROUGE-1, ROUGE-2, and ROUGE-L metrics all exceeding 50%, demonstrating robust text generation capabilities in educational contexts.

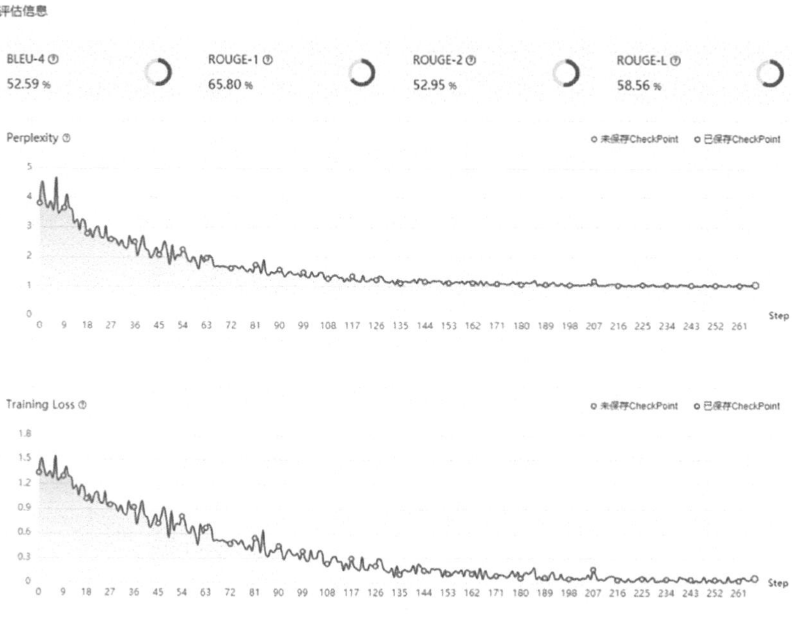

Fig. 5. Results of the automatic evaluation of the large model fine-tuning

5.2 Training Evaluation

Automatic Training Set Evaluation. ROUGE, BLEU and other metrics are used for regularized scoring to evaluate the model's performance in question-answering, question generation and parsing tasks. The results of the automatic rule-based evaluation of the training set are shown in Table 1, which shows that the model generates high quality in the question-answering and generation tasks, and the accuracy rate of the parsing task is slightly lower, but the indicators such as F1 and ROUGE are still of reference significance. The accuracy rate has limited applicability in long text scenarios, and some of the generation results are not exactly the same as the reference answer, but they perform better in terms of key point refinement and logical organization.

Table 1. Results of Automatic Rule Evaluation for Training Set

Metric	Question Answering	Question Generation	Question Analysis
Accuracy	77.05%	82.14%	35.64%
F1 Score	95.74%	91.86%	72.18%
BLEU-4	92.20%	86.56%	56.27%
ROUGE-1	95.49%	91.84%	72.76%
ROUGE-L	94.13%	89.60%	66.56%
ROUGE-2	93.09%	87.99%	61.44%

Automatic Test Set Evaluation. Test sets are generated through data enhancement and manual screening for evaluation. The results of the automatic rule evaluation of the test set are shown in Table 2. Although the accuracy of the test set is slightly lower, which is mainly limited by the consistency of the long text, it still maintains a better performance in key dimensions such as ROUGE and BLEU, indicating that the model fine-tuning training achieves the expected goal.

Table 2. Results of Automatic Rule Evaluation for Test Set

Metric	Question Answering	Question Generation	Question Analysis
Accuracy	61.63%	57.36%	44.79%
F1 Score	83.48%	74.65%	79.10%
BLEU-4	69.59%	57.67%	66.94%
ROUGE-1	82.14%	73.42%	79.40%
ROUGE-L	76.28%	66.05%	74.05%
ROUGE-2	72.76%	61.04%	70.36%

Manual Subjective Evaluation: Human subjective evaluations were conducted across four dimensions: usefulness, accuracy, satisfaction, and logical consistency, with results shown in Table 3. The results indicate that the model performs exceptionally well overall, particularly in question-answering and explanation tasks. In contrast, the question generation task relies more heavily on fine-tuned data, with generation outcomes being more sensitive to user prompts and creative inputs. In this process, fine-tuning operations are primarily used to optimize the generation direction and knowledge structure, thereby enhancing the relevance and educational value of the content.

Table 3. Results of Manual Assessment

Metric	Question Answering	Question Generation	Question Analysis
Average Score	1.99	1.71	1.98
Goodcase Ratio	98.77%	78.48%	98.01%
Usefulness	1.99	1.75	1.98
Accuracy	1.98	1.62	1.99
Logic	1.99	1.79	1.98
Satisfaction	1.98	1.67	1.96

5.3 Functional Verification and Effectiveness

Through front-end and back-end development, we implemented the core functions of both student and teacher terminals. We then tested key pages to evaluate system usability and assess the technical implementation's effectiveness. Through the front-end functional tuning and interface testing, the system has implement core modules including homework records, correction feedback, wrong notes, topic re-practice, similar topic recommendations, course materials and subject communities, which validate the practicability and completeness of the platform in terms of the support of students' learning paths (see Fig. 6 7 8).

Fig. 6. Study Notes. **Fig. 7.** Big Model Q&A. **Fig. 8.** Community.

The core function page of automatic question generation, the system supports automatic generation of test questions based on knowledge point settings, and links with individual teaching resource libraries to meet teachers' needs for personalized teaching resource construction (see Fig. 9). In short, the front-end and back-end of the system have been integrated through componentized design and technical framework to achieve the goal of closed-loop support for students' learning and teachers' teaching tools. The system has a clear functional structure and smooth interface response, laying a good foundation for further functional expansion and user experience optimization.

Fig. 9. Teacher-end Topic Generation

6 System Features

Big Model Assisted Education. The system integrates a large language model to enable homework grading, answering questions, and recommending similar questions. Students can ask questions at any time and receive immediate feedback.

AIGC Empowers Teachers to Teach. The system provides teachers with a question generation tool. By setting parameters based on teaching objectives, the large model can generate diverse questions, thereby reducing the burden of lesson preparation for teachers.

Community Interaction and Resource Sharing. The system builds an open, discipline-specific learning community that supports topic discussions, case studies, and learning notes, promoting student communication and collaboration and enhancing the social learning experience.

Full-Chain Education Service Architecture. The system construction includes a service system comprising student, teacher, and management ends, forming a closed-loop intelligent education service process to ensure that students can learn independently and efficiently, teachers can teach conveniently and accurately, and administrators can effectively maintain platform resources.

7 Conclusion

This study focuses on the key needs in educational scenarios and integrates a number of innovative features to construct a future-oriented intelligent education system. The large language model provides strong technical support for the teaching process and significantly improves the intelligence of education, while the AIGC technology plays an important role in assisting teachers in teaching and learning, and effectively enhances the ability of content generation and personalized adaptation. The system also stimulates collaboration and communication among students through community interaction and resource sharing mechanisms. Relying on the whole-chain education service architecture, the system realizes the comprehensive enhancement of the education process in the levels of intelligence, personalization and socialization. It not only significantly improves the learning efficiency of students and the teaching effectiveness of teachers, but also promotes the common construction and sharing of high-quality educational resources through the construction of an open learning community, which promotes the double improvement of education equity and education quality.

However, the model evaluation results did not meet the ideal requirements, and there is still room for improvement. In the long run, the system has a certain auxiliary effect on education with the help of artificial intelligence and other technologies, and it also predicts the development trend of education in the future - education will rely more and more on artificial intelligence, big data and other advanced technologies to achieve accurate teaching, personalized learning and deep interaction. The successful development and application of the system has certain value and significance for promoting the modernization process of education and cultivating talents who can adapt to the future society.

Acknowledgments. The project has been recognized by some of our peers and the system has been granted 3 software copyrights. This study was supported by national College Students' Innovation and Entrepreneurship Training Program (Project No. 202511057023) in 2025 and School Creation Program (Project No. 2024cxcy036).

References

1. Chen, X., Hu, Z., Wang, C.: Empowering education development through AIGC: a systematic literature review. Educ. Inf. Technol. **29**(6), 17485–17537 (2024)
2. Lee, D., et al.: The impact of generative AI on higher education learning and teaching: a study of educators' perspectives. Comput. Educ. Artif. Intell. **6**, 100221 (2024)

3. Ghimire, A., Prather, J., Edwards, J.: Generative AI in education: a study of educators' awareness, sentiments, and influencing factors. arXiv preprint arXiv:2403.15586 (2024)
4. Tbaishat, D., Amoudi, G., Elfadel, M.: Adapting teaching and learning with existing generative AI by higher education students: comparative study of Zayed University and King Abdulaziz University. Comput. Educ. Artif. Intell. **8**, 100421 (2025)
5. Xiong, F., Cen, Y.: Thoughts on the integration of ideological and political education of university science and engineering courses empowered by AI. Educ. J. **8**(2) (2024)
6. Holstein, K., Aleven, V., Rummel, N.: Key barriers to personalized learning in times of artificial intelligence: a literature review. Appl. Sci. **15**(6), 3103 (2023)
7. Arslan, B., et al.: Opportunities and challenges of using generative AI to personalize educational assessment. Front. Artif. Intell. **7**, 1460651 (2024)
8. Zhang, Z., et al.: Simulating classroom education with LLM-empowered agents. arXiv preprint arXiv:2406.19226 (2024)
9. Yang, S., Yang, S., Tong, C.: In-depth application of artificial intelligence-generated content AIGC large model in higher education. Adult High. Educ. **5**, 9–16 (2023)
10. He, Q., Chen, H., Mo, X.: Practical application of interactive AI technology based on visual analysis in professional system of physical education in universities. Heliyon **10**(3), e24627 (2024)
11. Dan, Y., Lei, Z., et al.: EduChat: a large-scale language model-based chatbot system for intelligent education. arXiv preprint arXiv:2308.02773 (2023)
12. Liu, X., Ji, K., Fu, Y., et al.: P-tuning V2: prompt tuning can be comparable to fine-tuning universally across scales and tasks. arXiv preprint arXiv:2110.07602 (2021)
13. Ye, C., Shi, X.: Optimizing news topic classification with instructional fine-tuning of ChatGLM3. In: Proceedings of the 3rd International Conference on Computer, Artificial Intelligence and Control Engineering, pp. 573–577 (2024)

Constructing a Transportation-Oriented Artificial Intelligence Curriculum System: A Core Competency Perspective

Hui Luo, Wei Zeng(✉), and Linjuan Wei

East China Jiaotong University, Nanchang 330013, Jiangxi, China
15307371@qq.com

Abstract. Amidst the intelligent transformation of the transportation industry, this research addresses the urgent demand for interdisciplinary talent in emerging fields such as smart transportation, autonomous driving, and transportation big data. By precisely defining the interdisciplinary convergence of Artificial Intelligence (AI) and transportation sciences, we establish a core competency framework for cultivating professionals in transportation-oriented Artificial Intelligence programs. Grounded in this framework, a dedicated transportation-oriented Artificial Intelligence curriculum system is developed. This initiative provides higher education institutions with a replicable "AI + Transportation" curriculum blueprint for Artificial Intelligence program development, advances industry-education integration for cultivating transportation-sector AI professionals, and supports China's national Transportation Powerhouse Strategy.

Keywords: Artificial Intelligence · Transportation-Oriented · Core Competencies · Curriculum System · Industry-Education Integration

1 Introduction

In 2017, "the Development Plan for the New Generation of Artificial Intelligence" issued by the State Council of China emphasized the need to promote deep integration of AI across industrial sectors. Regarding transportation, the plan specifically highlighted driving AI innovations in intelligent transportation systems and autonomous driving technologies to support the industry's intelligent transformation. In 2019, the "Outline for Building China's Strength in Transportation" released by the State Council further clarified the goal of essentially establishing China as a transportation powerhouse by 2035, stressing the deep integration of new technologies like AI with the transportation industry.

With the continuous advancement of AI technology, the demand for "new-era interdisciplinary talents with dynamic knowledge, grounded competencies, and deep-rooted qualities" in the transportation industry is experiencing explosive growth. However, the existing AI talent cultivation system with a transportation focus reveals three core challenges:

W. Hong et al. (Eds.): ICCSE 2025, CCIS 2761, pp. 154–166, 2026.
https://doi.org/10.1007/978-981-95-7731-6_13

Firstly, interdisciplinary integration remains superficial, lacking deep fusion between the fundamental logic of transportation technology and AI. This results in a "structural disjunction" in students' knowledge frameworks. Secondly, industry scenario integration is severely lagging. There exists a generational gap between course content and the actual demands of intelligent transportation. Students lack comprehensive practical training in the full process from algorithm design to real-world application deployment. Thirdly, ethical responsibility awareness is nebulous. When facing complex transportation problems, students struggle to develop solutions that integrate ethical responsibility with innovative approaches, falling short of the deeper requirements for engineering ethics practice and professional responsibility fulfillment demanded by the "Transportation Powerhouse" strategy. Therefore, the integration of AI across various industries has become an inevitable trend. As a critical application domain, the intelligent transformation of the transportation sector urgently requires the deep involvement of AI technology [1]. Simultaneously, the development of the AI industry exhibits characteristics of diversity, rapid change, and multidisciplinary breadth, necessitating comprehensive cross-disciplinary capabilities for support [2].

With the deepening integration of AI and industries, the interdisciplinary nature of knowledge systems and the complexity of engineering domains have become increasingly prominent [3, 4]. This places higher demands on talents' ability to integrate cross-disciplinary knowledge and apply technology in complex scenarios—precisely the core components of essential competencies.

Existing research indicates that the common foundational principle in curriculum system construction is to focus on interdisciplinary integration and competency-based orientation [5, 6]. Through structural optimization featuring "modularized foundational courses, scenario-based interdisciplinary courses, and systematized practical training", this approach promotes knowledge integration and skill transfer. There is also a widespread emphasis on breaking down disciplinary barriers, strengthening industry-education collaboration, and incorporating ethical awareness [7]. However, common challenges persist in areas such as deep curricular content coupling, quantifiable assessment standards, and coverage of emerging fields. There is an urgent need to establish a curriculum framework that demonstrates both industry relevance and measurable competency acquisition.

2 Conceptual Definitions

2.1 Definition of Core Competency

The intelligent transformation of the transportation industry urgently necessitates breaking down traditional disciplinary barriers and promoting deep integration of AI technologies throughout the full-chain transportation system. This transformation imposes new requirements for cultivating professionals in transportation-oriented Artificial Intelligence programs and compels us to redefine their core competencies. Explicitly defining these core competencies constitutes the cornerstone of talent cultivation, while constructing a tightly aligned curriculum system serves as the central hub for competency implementation. As the most direct and prominent vehicle for competency development, the quality of the curriculum system directly determines the efficacy of talent cultivation. Consequently, core competency-oriented curriculum construction represents the linchpin project for emerging engineering education talent development.

To systematically address the multidimensional, integrated, and advanced competency requirements of intelligent transformation, constructing a core competency framework for transportation-oriented AI professionals is paramount, wherein core competencies holistically integrate knowledge, capabilities, and dispositions [8, 9]. Specifically, knowledge encompasses Artificial Intelligence disciplinary expertise and transportation-related domain knowledge; capabilities include lifelong learning, interactive autonomy, innovation and entrepreneurship, leadership, AI and transportation engineering practice, computational thinking, design thinking, and human-system interaction mindset; dispositions comprise global perspectives, social responsibility, engineering ethics with professional standards, and proactive accountability. This framework not only defines precise talent development objectives but also provides targeted guidance for curriculum system design, with the fully constructed framework detailed in Fig. 1.

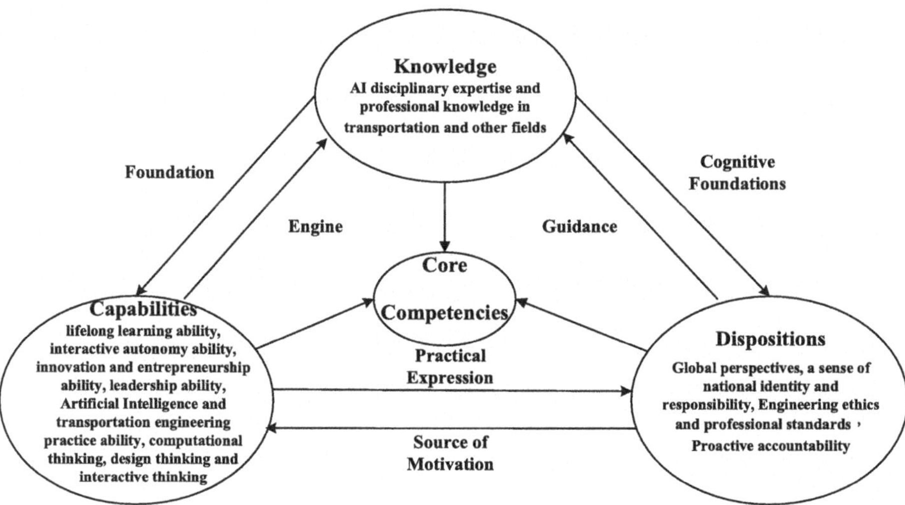

Fig. 1. Core Competencies Framework for Transportation-Focused AI Professionals

2.2 Educational Objectives

Core competencies exhibit dual attributes of being both outcome-oriented and process-oriented. As concrete manifestations of Artificial Intelligence program educational goals, they explicitly define the knowledge, capabilities, and dispositions graduates should possess. Simultaneously, they emphasize deep integration of pedagogical assessment with engineering practice, highlighting comprehensive quality monitoring and feedback mechanisms throughout the AI talent cultivation process. This dual orientation constitutes a unified objective system wherein educational objectives – as the system's core – crystallize program philosophies and talent development visions, permeating all stages of AI professional cultivation. Adopting a core competency theoretical lens, this study examines talent cultivation in transportation-oriented Artificial Intelligence programs, aiming to deepen understanding of AI professionals' essential characteristics and developmental trajectories, thereby addressing the urgent demand for interdisciplinary AI technical talent driven by the new wave of technological revolution and industrial transformation.

This study synthesizes the educational objectives for Artificial Intelligence program cultivation as follows: First, developing robust professional literacy to systematically master foundational theories, specialized knowledge, and technical competencies in Artificial Intelligence, enabling analysis and resolution of complex engineering problems. Second, cultivating innovation and entrepreneurship capabilities alongside AI and transportation engineering practice abilities, empowering leadership development and lifelong learning advancement through practical engagement. Third, fostering well-rounded character with strong social responsibility and expansive global perspectives, demonstrating proactive accountability in multicultural contexts while developing innovative solutions that integrate technical feasibility and social responsibility through theoretical and professional expertise.

2.3 Curriculum System

The curriculum system construction adopts curricular objectives as the foundational orientation, explicitly defining core competencies, capability standards, and dispositional benchmarks for AI talent cultivation to guide overall design. Curricular content serves as the core vehicle, selecting "AI + Transportation" knowledge modules, skill training, and practical projects to form a logically coherent and hierarchically clear architecture, ensuring systematic and targeted educational resources. Curricular implementation functions as the critical pathway, transforming content into instructional activities through scientifically designed pedagogical methods, organizational structures, and resource allocation, thereby guaranteeing effective objective and content delivery. Curricular evaluation operates as the optimization mechanism, establishing multi-dimensional assessment to comprehensively monitor objective attainment levels, content relevance, and implementation efficacy, driving continuous iterative upgrades. Ultimately, this forms a closed-loop curricular ecosystem characterized by objective orientation, content support, implementation assurance, and evaluation-driven refinement, with specific components detailed in Table 1.

Table 1. Curriculum System Framework for Transportation-Oriented Artificial Intelligence Programs

Component	AI Technology Integration Points	Objectives
Curricular Objectives	Cultivate students' mastery of interdisciplinary knowledge in AI and transportation fields; Enhance practical capabilities and innovation competencies for solving real-world transportation problems; Develop social responsibility and engineering ethics awareness	Centered on cultivating core competencies to ensure students' holistic development in knowledge, capabilities, and dispositions
Curricular Content	Constructing a multi-tiered knowledge system spanning foundational theories to cutting-edge applications, covering "AI + Transportation" fundamentals, applied technologies, and advanced seminars	
Curricular Practice	Providing students with full-cycle training from theory to practice through on-campus laboratories, industry fieldwork, and innovation competitions	
Curricular Practice	Implementing comprehensive assessment through knowledge evaluation, capability evaluation, dispositional evaluation, and application of digital assessment tools to ensure learning outcome quality and attainment of curricular objectives	

3 Talent Cultivation Pathways for Transportation-Oriented Artificial Intelligence Programs: A Core Competency Perspective

Confronting current challenges—where interdisciplinary integration in transportation-oriented talent cultivation remains superficial, lacking fundamental restructuring and innovative convergence of the "AI + Transportation" knowledge system; where industry scenario integration lags severely, causing disconnects between talent development and industrial needs; where students exhibit insufficient practical abilities to resolve authentic complex problems; and where technological application awareness and social responsibility cultivation require strengthening—this study addresses the urgent demand for interdisciplinary talent driven by the transportation industry's intelligent transformation. We propose a core competency-led approach with fundamental curriculum restructuring as the central engine for talent cultivation reform, committed to multi-dimensional, full-chain enhancement of students' comprehensive competencies and core competitiveness.

Innovatively constructing a three-dimensional cultivation model integrating knowledge, capabilities, and dispositions—which fundamentally responds to the core competency architecture of transportation-oriented AI professionals—this model directs curriculum systems toward defining "whom to cultivate", ensuring curricula master technological convergence, prioritize scenario implementation, and embody conceptual leadership. Simultaneously, the curriculum system provides "how to cultivate" pathways through systematic design of interdisciplinary courses, practice chains, and dispositional cultivation modules, transforming trinity educational objectives into actionable pedagogical practices.

On the knowledge dimension, an interdisciplinary "AI + Transportation" curriculum matrix is established, positioning AI technology as a methodological tool to solve core transportation problems, thereby achieving deep integration of transportation technology and AI technology. On the capability dimension, a three-stage chain of "campus labs - corporate projects - innovation competitions" is leveraged to strengthen comprehensive training from theory to real-world scenarios. Students apply learned AI and transportation knowledge to solve practical problems within authentic industry environments, using real-world data and under real constraints, thereby enhancing engineering practice abilities, leadership, and innovation/entrepreneurship skills. This progressively designed capability cultivation resonates with the systematic setup of practical components in the curriculum, providing clear curricular pathways for skill advancement. On the competency dimension, a three-step progressive cultivation path of "cognition - comprehension - application" is constructed. Combined with case-based teaching, it focuses on fostering students' self-confidence, global perspective, engineering ethics, professional standards, and social responsibility. Industry-education collaborative talent development is deepened, promoting students' knowledge transformation and competency reinforcement in authentic settings. The talent cultivation pathway for AI professionals with transportation characteristics, viewed through the lens of core competencies, is illustrated in Fig. 2.

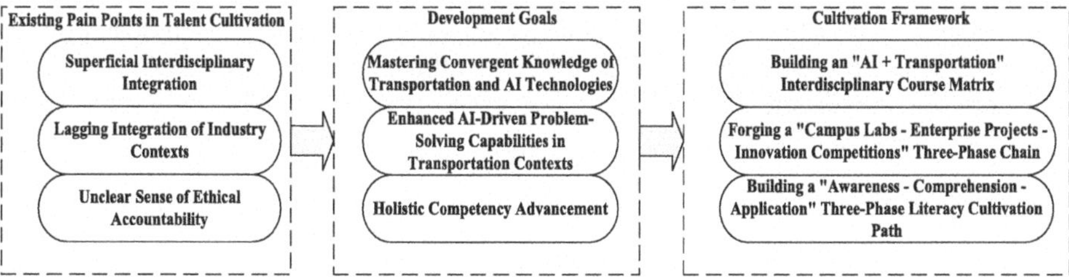

Fig. 2. Cultivation Pathway for Transportation-Focused Artificial Intelligence Professionals from a Core Competency Perspective

3.1 Establish an interdisciplinary curriculum matrix for Artificial Intelligence + Transportation

With the deep penetration and integrated application of new-generation information technologies, particularly AI, within the transportation sector, intelligent transformation is advancing at an unprecedented pace. This profound revolution imposes increasingly stringent demands on professionals' knowledge reserves and competency structures, requiring practitioners to possess not only specialized transportation engineering expertise but also mastery of core enabling technologies like AI, along with the capability to seamlessly integrate both domains for solving complex systems engineering challenges. Against this backdrop, traditional siloed curriculum systems have proven inadequate for cultivating high-quality interdisciplinary talents. Consequently, systematic reconstruction of the knowledge dimension has become imperative—establishing a curriculum architecture precisely aligned with industry's evolving needs and future trajectories constitutes the critical pathway for developing transportation-oriented AI professionals.

with core competencies. Focusing on cultivating industry-specific core competencies, this paper addresses superficial interdisciplinary integration through a knowledge-centered approach by constructing a three-tiered interdisciplinary curriculum matrix: Foundational Tier, Application Tier, and Extension Tier.

At the foundational tier, focused on interdisciplinary convergence of AI and transportation technologies, we first implement core transportation courses exemplified by Introduction to Transportation Systems B. Subsequently, we embed the fundamental logic of AI into essential engineering foundation courses such as Data Structures and Algorithms, introducing specialized modules on Algorithm Applications in Transportation Scenarios. This integration establishes cognitive connections between AI technologies and transportation challenges while dismantling disciplinary barriers. Progressing to the application tier, centered on domains including intelligent transportation and autonomous driving, we deploy elective courses like Vehicle-Infrastructure Cooperative Technologies and Transportation Big Data Analytics and Decision-Making. These incorporate authentic industry cases such as autonomous driving platforms and urban brain systems to enhance theory-to-scenario translation capabilities. The extension tier features frontier lectures and seminars conducted by academic and industrial experts analyzing emerging technologies. Through this exposure, we cultivate students' potential to track technological advancements, adapt to rapid industrial transformations, and develop cross-boundary thinking with systems integration competencies—ultimately expanding knowledge boundaries through engagement with cutting-edge industry trends and interdisciplinary convergence. The interdisciplinary curriculum matrix for AI + Transportation is presented in Table 2.

Table 2. The interdisciplinary curriculum matrix for Artificial Intelligence + Transportation

Course Tiers	AI Technology Integration Points	Objectives
Foundational Tier	Adding the "Algorithm Applications in Transportation Scenarios" module to Data Structures and Algorithms	Focus on interdisciplinary integration of AI and transportation technologies
Application Tier	Elective courses such as Vehicle-Infrastructure Cooperative Technologies and Transportation Big Data Analytics and Decision-Making	Strengthen theory-to-scenario implementation capacity
Extension Tier	Offering lecture series on international trends in intelligent transportation	Expose students to industry frontiers and interdisciplinary integration trends

3.2 Establishing a Three-Stage Chain of 'Campus Laboratories - Industry Projects - Innovation Competitions'

To meet the transportation industry's demands for AI talents with computational thinking, practical AI and transportation engineering capabilities, and innovation/entrepreneurship competencies: First, leveraging the intelligent cockpit HMI platform and transportation simulation laboratory, we implement scenario-based experimental modules such as Intelligent Traffic Signal Control Algorithm Verification. This strengthens foundational skills in algorithm debugging and simulation validation, ensuring students develop robust AI programming proficiency, model construction abilities, and preliminary simulation-based engineering literacy. Subsequently, through deepened industry-education integration with sector leaders, students engage in solving complex real-world problems. Guided by a dual-mentorship system, they participate end-to-end in authentic projects like AI Solutions for Traffic Congestion Management and Smart Urban Transportation System Design. This full-cycle practical experience—spanning requirement analysis, solution design, and algorithm development—enhances leadership, practical execution, and complex engineering problem-solving capabilities distinctive to transportation-oriented AI professionals. Ultimately, high-level competitions such as the Internet Plus Innovation Competition and Smart Transportation Innovation & Entrepreneurship Challenge serve as platforms for demand-driven innovation. These accelerate the transformation of theoretical knowledge into applied scenario capabilities, cultivating well-rounded applied talents equipped with design thinking, innovation/entrepreneurship competencies, and lifelong learning capacities.

3.3 Establishing a Three-Tier Progressive Cultivation Pathway: Cognition-Comprehension-Application

Within the cultivation framework for transportation-specialized AI professionals, holistically enhancing students' comprehensive competencies—particularly forging engineering ethics, robust social responsibility, and strategic global vision—constitutes the essential foundation for developing future industry leaders. To achieve this, we implement a tripartite cultivation pathway progressing through cognition, comprehension, and application dimensions, systematically embedding ethical education into transportation-contextualized Artificial Intelligence programs. Commencing at the cognition phase, educational philosophy integrates with intelligent transportation curricula via critical analysis of China's landmark infrastructure projects. This dual approach showcases national achievements while prompting profound reflection on technology's societal ramifications and inspiring commitment to critical national development initiatives. Advancing to the comprehension phase, sustainability principles including green transportation permeate specialized courses through instructional modules such as Low-Carbon Intelligent Transport Planning and Practice. Within this framework, students examine socio-environmental impacts of intelligent mobility systems, deepen their understanding of industry responsibilities and sustainable imperatives, and align technological innovation with social accountability. Culminating at the application phase, students proactively address societal challenges through innovation-driven solutions. This process achieves transformative evolution in ethical consciousness, advancing from cognitive awareness through internalized conviction toward proactive practice—ultimately cultivating multifaceted experts who demonstrate excellence in AI capabilities alongside principled social responsibility and global strategic perspective.

4 Practical Approaches and Safeguard Mechanisms for the Curriculum Framework

4.1 Implementation Pathways for the Curriculum System

Industry-Driven Continuous Optimization of the Curriculum
Guided by the practical demands of the transportation industry for AI talent, this initiative drives deep integration of domain-specific knowledge with AI technologies. It systematically structures core knowledge modules in transportation while enhancing curricula in transferable competencies—practical skills, leadership, and computational thinking. By identifying shared professional ethos between transportation and AI domains, we establish a specialized educational framework integrating global perspectives, social responsibility, and confident leadership. Through embedding value cultivation elements into case studies, project discussions, and industry trend analyses, we achieve synergistic alignment of knowledge delivery and principle-based guidance.

To ensure continuous alignment between the curriculum system and industry requirements, it is imperative to establish a collaborative academia-industry mechanism for content renewal. This involves systematically collecting talent demand reports from transportation enterprises at regular intervals, which must comprehensively document core position specifications, emerging technology trends, and evolving industry standards within the transportation AI sector. Building upon these insights, frontline enterprise technological needs should be pedagogically deconstructed into modular knowledge units suitable for curricular integration. Concurrently, authentic industry projects must be converted into course design challenges, requiring students to deliver implementable technical solutions during project execution. This practice-oriented approach cultivates AI and transportation engineering competencies through real-world problem-solving, thereby achieving dynamic synchronization between instructional content and industrial evolution while ensuring perpetual relevance amidst rapid technological iteration.

Through this academia-industry collaborative renewal mechanism, the curriculum system achieves real-time responsiveness to technological evolution and talent demand shifts within the transportation sector. This ensures teaching content maintains synchronized evolution with industry advancement. Whether addressing the extended application boundaries of AI algorithms in transportation scenarios or incorporating emerging requirements for technical ethics and data security, such developments are dynamically integrated into instruction. Ultimately, this cultivates interdisciplinary AI professionals who possess both robust theoretical foundations and practical problem-solving capabilities, while remaining agile amid the industry's intelligent transformation.

Innovating Instructional Models through Digital Tool Integration
Amidst digital transformation redefining educational paradigms, AI emerges as a pivotal enabler for optimizing pedagogy in transportation-specialized Artificial Intelligence programs. Harnessing robust data analytics and logical reasoning capabilities, AI technologies dynamically monitor evolving trends in educational planning, precisely identify core teaching-learning principles, and deliver intelligent implementation solutions for curricula [10, 11]. Consequently, three categories of digital tools require deep integration into the curriculum execution framework:

First, develop an "AI-Powered Learning Assistant for Transportation" based on large language models. This assistant will tailor reinforcement pathways for students' weak knowledge points according to their learning data, and regularly push customized learning resources focused on AI for transportation. Second, utilize knowledge graph technology to systematically integrate and structurally present the cutting-edge technologies, core concepts, and key technological pathways within the transportation industry. This constructs a knowledge system graph for the field of transportation AI, enabling the delivery of more diversified knowledge and advanced technologies to students. This facilitates the precise implementation of the teaching process and enables the sustainable improvement of educational quality. By embedding this graph into the teaching platform, instructors can organize cross-chapter teaching content more efficiently. Simultaneously, students can gain a clearer understanding of the logical relationships and developmental context between knowledge points. This achieves the goals of systematic mastery and deep comprehension of AI professional knowledge, realizing the leap from fragmented knowledge to systematic cognition. Furthermore, through functions like intelligent Q&A and knowledge recommendation, the interactivity and intelligence level of teaching are further enhanced. Third, deploy an "AI Virtual Simulation Platform" to simulate various high-difficulty and high-risk scenarios, incorporating decision-making checkpoints. This drives dual improvements in teaching and practical efficiency while cultivating students' technical application capabilities.

Through the synergistic effect of digital tools, this approach achieves a transition from traditional experience-dependent models to data-driven precision teaching and from one-way knowledge transmission to interactive scenario-based learning, while accelerating the transformation of theoretical knowledge into practical skills. The comprehensive implementation pathway of the curriculum system is shown in Fig. 3.

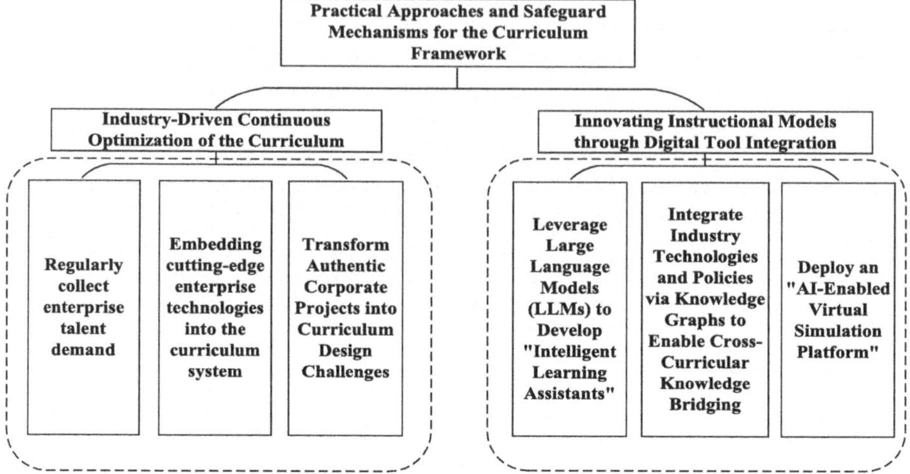

Fig. 3. Implementation Pathways for the Curriculum System

4.2 Quality Assurance and Evaluation Mechanism

The quality assurance system centers on core competency cultivation, establishing a full-chain, multi-stakeholder collaborative mechanism to provide robust support for curriculum implementation. Regarding faculty development, a "dual-mentor system" is implemented: university faculty deliver theoretical instruction and fundamental research guidance, while industry experts provide practical project support. University teachers must possess interdisciplinary knowledge and industry experience to enhance professional development. At the resource level, investments are increased in practical training platforms such as smart driving cockpits and traffic simulation laboratories. Virtual simulation scenario libraries and experimental datasets are regularly updated to ensure students access industry-synchronized technical tools and data environments, thereby providing hardware infrastructure for practical skills development.

The evaluation mechanism is designed to closely align with industry demands, establishing a multidimensional assessment framework encompassing knowledge, skills, and professional attributes. In the knowledge dimension, academic examinations evaluate students' comprehension and application of core professional knowledge through fundamental theories and industry-integrated problems, with enterprises validating test relevance to ensure practical competency alignment and accurately reflect technical mastery. In the skills dimension, industry practitioners assess project defenses based on practical value, technical feasibility, and collaboration effectiveness, while real-world project implementation outcomes serve as primary metrics with quantitative scoring; innovation competition achievements addressing industry challenges supplement these evaluations to holistically gauge practical execution, innovation, and problem-solving capabilities. In the professional attributes dimension, internship tracking mechanisms document workplace conduct through mentor observations, and joint academic-industry panels analyze critical decision-making cases to evaluate demonstrated professional ethics, holistic perspective, and risk awareness, cultivating industry-aligned professionalism. This integration of the dual-mentorship system with multidimensional evaluation achieves precise academia-industry alignment, enhancing graduates' competitiveness to produce professionals with rigorous theoretical foundations, demonstrated practical capabilities, and professionally sound attributes.

5 Conclusion

This study addresses talent demands arising from the intelligent transformation of the transportation industry. By analyzing the core competencies required for AI professionals in transportation, we construct a trinity curriculum system integrating knowledge, capabilities, and attributes. The study further explores implementation pathways and support mechanisms for this system. Designed with core competencies at its center, the curriculum achieves synergistic development through knowledge integration, capability forging, and attribute cultivation, meeting the industry's need for interdisciplinary professionals during its intelligent transition. This framework provides robust talent support for realizing China's strategic goal of building transportation power.

Acknowledgments. This study was supported by Jiangxi Provincial Education Science 14th Five-Year Plan Project (grant number 21ZD039).

Disclosure of Interests.
The authors have no competing interests to declare that are relevant to the content of this article.

References

1. Quan, L., Zhang, X.Q., Wu, C.W.: Curriculum construction for AI major in local universities oriented to core competency training. Res. High. Educ. Eng. **3**, 102–106 (2022)
2. Dai, R.T., Li, L.M.: Exploration of AI talent cultivation model in universities based on industry-education integration. Res. High. Educ. Eng. **3**, 19–25 (2024)
3. Wu, Z.F., Dai, R.T., Li, D.D., et al.: Innovative talent cultivation for AI frontier fields. Res. High. Educ. Eng. **5**, 48–53 (2023)
4. Shen, Y.X., Wang, M.H., Wu, F., et al.: Exploration of interdisciplinary curriculum development for AI: a case study of intelligent excavation course in intelligent mining engineering. J. Shanxi Inst. Energy **2**, 80–83 (2025)
5. Zhou, L., Fan, L.X., Fan, H.M., et al.: Current status of curriculum construction under emerging engineering education: an empirical study based on core literacy. J. Educ. Stud. Renmin Univ. China **3**, 52–77 (2021)

6. Hao, X.Y., Zhu, L.F., Qu, Y.: Teaching reform research and practice oriented to core literacy of emerging engineering talents: a case study of intelligent manufacturing equipment technology professional group. Pub. Relat. World **24**, 163–165 (2024)
7. Wu, F., Wu, C., Zhu, Q.: Integration of science-education and industry-education synergy for cultivating innovative AI talents. China Univ. Teach. **Z1**, 15–19 (2022)
8. Zhao, X.X., Zhu, M.C.: Exploration of intelligent construction talent cultivation model based on core literacy. High. Educ. Archit. Civ. Eng. **32**(04), 64–69 (2023)
9. Ma, Y.Q., Zhang, F.Y., Chen, X.M.: Enhancing core literacy of engineering students for cultivating excellent engineers. Theory Pract. Educ. **45**(15), 19–22 (2025)
10. Wang, J.R., Zhu, J., Wang, J., et al.: Role of data-driven knowledge graphs in informatization reform of undergraduate teaching. Res. High. Educ. Eng. **3**, 121–128 (2024)
11. Wang, Z.X.: Knowledge graphs and large language models for teaching resource construction in emerging engineering courses. Res. High. Educ. Eng. **1**, 40–46+110 (2025)

Cultivating Four-Dimensional Core Competencies of Undergraduate AI Talents Under the Emerging Engineering Education Framework

Hui Luo, Wei Zeng(✉), and Chongwei Huang

East China Jiaotong University, Nanchang 330013, Jiangxi, China
15307371@qq.com

Abstract. In response to the challenges faced by undergraduate artificial intelligence (AI) education under the emerging engineering education (EEE) framework-namely, fragmented knowledge acquisition, weak capability transfer, lack of systems thinking, and insufficient cultivation of core competencies-this study proposes a four-dimensional integrative model known as Knowledge-Ability-Thinking–Quality (K-A-T-Q). Building upon this model, a triadic, synergistic development pathway is constructed, encompassing curriculum system restructuring, pedagogical innovation, and assessment mechanism transformation. Practical implementation demonstrates that this integrated approach significantly enhances students' capacity for knowledge integration, technical adaptability, systems thinking, and overall quality development, thereby offering a replicable and scalable model for advancing AI undergraduate education.

Keywords: Emerging Engineering Education · Artificial Intelligence · Core Competencies · Undergraduate Talent Development

1 Introduction

The concept of EEE embodies a forward-looking development paradigm that responds to future transformations and actively shapes technological trajectories. It emphasizes the integration of inheritance and innovation, interdisciplinarity and convergence, as well as coordination and shared development, with the overarching goal of cultivating diversified and innovation-driven engineering talent [1, 2]. Such talent development extends beyond the traditional focus on knowledge transmission and skill acquisition; it requires the systematic enhancement of practical competencies, the cultivation of systems thinking, and the coordinated advancement of comprehensive qualities [3, 4]. These evolving demands impose higher expectations on conventional engineering disciplines and their educational models.

AI has become a key strategic domain within the development of EEE. AI technologies are rapidly accelerating in speed, expanding in scope, and deepening in impact—reshaping both industrial structures and the ecosystem of engineering education. According to McKinsey, China may face a shortage of up to 4 million AI professionals by 2030.

W. Hong et al. (Eds.): ICCSE 2025, CCIS 2761, pp. 167–180, 2026.
https://doi.org/10.1007/978-981-95-7731-6_14

In response, universities across the country have actively pursued innovations in curriculum design, university–industry integration, and practical teaching. However, these efforts often lack robust theoretical foundations and mechanisms for cross-dimensional coordination [5]. To address these challenges, Hao Xiuyun et al. proposed a core competency framework based on the KAPO model, through which they restructured the organizational architecture of discipline clusters and developed a four-tier progressive curriculum system. This approach fosters deep integration of course content, instructional methods, and industry demands, thereby effectively enhancing the core competencies of interdisciplinary engineering talent[6]. In the context of AI education reform, Hu Jingjing et al. advocated a case-based teaching approach grounded in the Outcome-Based Education (OBE) philosophy. Through curriculum redesign, case development, and diversified assessment, they successfully bridged theory with practice to improve the overall quality of talent development [7]. Similarly, Zong Xinlu et al. emphasized the enhancement of students' practical and innovative capabilities through course content optimization, pedagogical refinement, and the reconstruction of multidimensional assessment frameworks [8]. From the perspective of competency cultivation, Sun Qiuhong et al. adopted the IKAQ framework to incorporate non-technical elements into quality development. Through multi-party collaboration, they built a composite engineering talent development model tailored to the EEE context, offering viable strategies for fostering integrated competencies in next-generation engineers [9].

Despite significant progress achieved through various reform initiatives, the current undergraduate AI talent cultivation system under the EEE framework continues to suffer from a structural mismatch across four critical dimensions: knowledge, ability, thinking, and quality. As illustrated in Fig. 1, this misalignment poses a fundamental challenge to the development of well-rounded, future-oriented AI professionals.

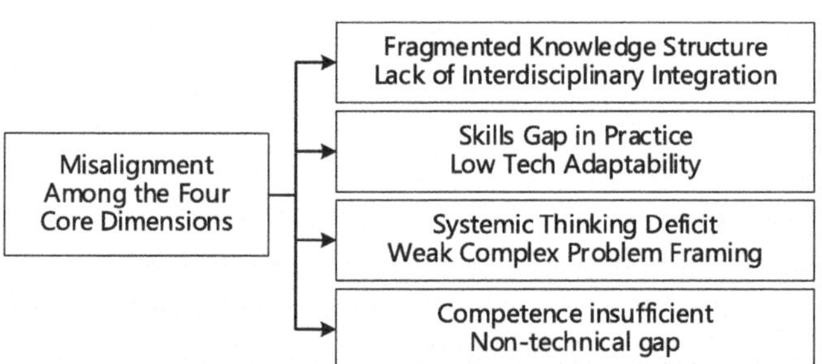

Fig. 1. Four-Dimensional Mismatch

To address the "four-dimensional mismatch" dilemma in undergraduate artificial intelligence education, this paper proposes the K-A-T-Q four-dimensional coupling model grounded in outcome-based education and complex adaptive systems theory. Based on this model, a trinity collaborative cultivation pathway—comprising curriculum system reconstruction, innovative teaching methodologies, and transformative evaluation mechanisms—is developed to foster innovative advancement in AI education. This approach aims to provide high-quality talent in alignment with national strategic priorities, ultimately establishing a distinctive new engineering education paradigm with Chinese characteristics that is competitive on the global stage.

2 Construction of a Four-Dimensional Core Competency Model for AI Talent in New Engineering Education

The K-A-T-Q four-dimensional coupling model is rooted in the interdisciplinary integration of educational theory, systems science, and practical demands, aiming to achieve theoretical innovation and practical breakthroughs in competency development from a systemic perspective. From the educational theory standpoint, the Outcome-Based Education (OBE) paradigm has gradually evolved from emphasizing "skill output" to focusing on "competency generation." This shift transcends the traditional engineering education's singular reliance on technical metrics, highlighting a comprehensive, integrative cultivation pathway that encompasses knowledge integration, capability advancement, cognitive development, and character formation. From the perspective of systems science, complex adaptive systems theory reveals the nonlinear and dynamic interactions among competency components. The shortening of technological iteration cycles alongside the cumulative effects of ethical risks necessitates a competency model with high adaptability and evolutionary capacity. Regarding practical demands, enterprises widely emphasize the holistic competencies of interdisciplinary talents, particularly the synergistic development of knowledge application, skill transferability, and engineering ethics awareness, thereby promoting an integrated talent standard centered on "knowledge transmission—ability cultivation—character development."

Based on this foundation, the K-A-T-Q model centers on knowledge, ability, thinking, and quality, establishing a four-dimensional synergistic framework for talent cultivation, as illustrated in Fig. 2.

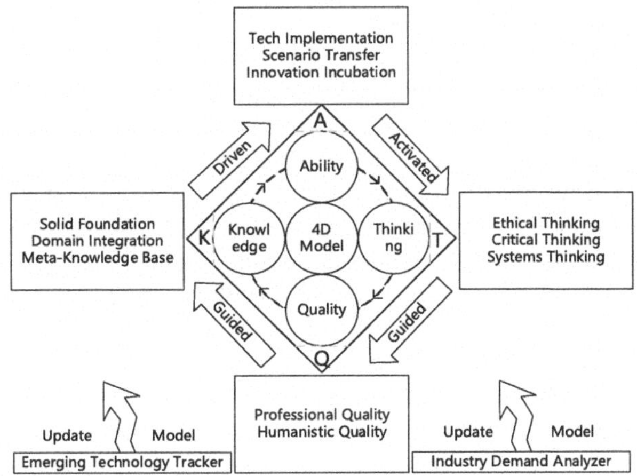

Fig. 2. The K-A-T-Q Four-Dimensional Coupling Model

In the knowledge dimension, grounded in the core principles of emerging engineering—namely interdisciplinary integration and iterative innovation—a three-tiered knowledge structure is constructed, encompassing foundational fundamentals, domain integration, and meta-knowledge reserves. This system not only emphasizes the consolidation of basic knowledge such as mathematical logic and computational foundations but also strengthens the interdisciplinary fusion of artificial intelligence with critical sectors like transportation and energy. Through the accumulation and reconstruction of meta-knowledge, it enhances students' comprehension, transferability, and regenerative capacity regarding the knowledge ontology. Consequently, this approach effectively addresses the current challenges of fragmented and outdated knowledge systems, promoting a knowledge structure that evolves dynamically and fosters self-enhancement.

In the competency dimension, a three-level capability chain—comprising technical implementation, scenario transfer, and innovation incubation—is established to emphasize the integrated cultivation of system design, engineering construction, and complex problem-solving skills. Particular attention is given to developing students' agility in responding to and devising solutions for practical engineering challenges such as distributed system deployment, heterogeneous data processing, and cross-scenario technology transfer. This approach aims to overcome the prevailing issues of narrow objectives and fragmented pathways in competency development, thereby achieving a systematic restructuring of the capability framework that aligns precisely with industry demands.

In the dimensions of thinking and quality, the synergistic educational philosophy of "thinking shapes character, and character guides thinking" is upheld. The thinking dimension establishes a triadic support system comprising systems thinking, critical thinking, and ethical reasoning, aimed at cultivating students' integrative cognitive abilities for holistic modeling, logical evaluation, and responsible judgment in complex environments. The character dimension focuses on two core indicators: the cultivation of professional qualities and the integration of humanistic literacy. By promoting the empowerment of character through knowledge and the shaping of character through thinking, it strengthens the coordinated development of students' professional competence and humanistic values in technical practice, thereby enhancing their vocational competence and social responsibility in technological applications. This "four-dimensional interactive" framework not only addresses emerging educational challenges related to engineering ethics and talent quality in the new era but also lays a solid foundation for nurturing interdisciplinary AI talents with a strong sense of mission, innovative spirit, and accountability. This framework aims to cultivate versatile AI talents endowed with a strong sense of responsibility, social commitment, and innovative mission, thereby underscoring the fundamental role of engineering ethics and social responsibility within the contemporary talent cultivation paradigm. Furthermore, to keep pace with technological advancements, the model innovatively integrates a technology hotspot tracker and an industry demand analyzer, ensuring the continuous alignment of competency content with cutting-edge industry developments.

Moreover, to precisely align with the rapid evolution of artificial intelligence technologies, the model innovatively integrates a Technology Hotspot Tracker and an Industry Demand Analyzer. The Technology Hotspot Tracker leverages big data mining and natural language processing techniques to capture cutting-edge developments in the global AI landscape in real time. By constructing a dynamically updated technical knowledge base, it ensures that the competency framework remains consistently synchronized with technological frontiers. Meanwhile, the Industry Demand Analyzer deeply interfaces with various industry ecosystems by collecting and analyzing multidimensional data—including corporate recruitment requirements, industrial policy orientations, and market feedback—to accurately identify specific demands for AI talent's capabilities, knowledge, and thinking across different sectors, thereby generating periodic industry demand profiles. The synergistic operation of these two innovative components establishes a closed-loop mechanism of "technology frontier capture—industry demand decoding—competency system iteration." This not only enables real-time alignment and upgrading of competency content with emerging industry trends but also proactively anticipates future industrial trajectories, integrating potentially mainstream technical skills and cognitive competencies into the training system ahead of time. As a result, the cultivated interdisciplinary AI talents are equipped not only to keep pace with current industry development but also to possess the potential to lead future technological and industrial advancements, thereby achieving true resonance between talent cultivation and industrial evolution.

3 Benchmarking the K-A-T-Q Model Against Mainstream Talent Development Frameworks

To verify the theoretical innovativeness and practical adaptability of the K-A-T-Q four-dimensional core competency model, this study conducts a systematic comparative analysis using the KAPO model and the Outcome-Based Education (OBE) framework as reference points. Both models hold substantial theoretical grounding and practical representativeness in the context of EEE reform, serving as key benchmarks in the development and positioning of the K-A-T-Q model.

The KAPO model, proposed by Jerome Bruner, emphasizes the dynamic generation and adjustment of competencies based on three core objectives—Knowledge and Skills (K), Attitudes and Values (A), and Process and Methods (P)—with a central focus on instructional events (O). It is particularly well-suited for the integrated design of curriculum structures and learning experiences. In contrast, the Outcome-Based Education (OBE) framework centers on student learning outcomes, emphasizing clearly defined learning objectives, closed-loop instructional feedback, and continuous improvement mechanisms. OBE has become a widely adopted standard in international engineering education accreditation.

In comparison, the K-A-T-Q model builds upon the foundational principles of the aforementioned frameworks while further integrating insights from systems science and the practical demands of AI education. Through the structural coupling of four dimensions—Knowledge, Ability, Thinking, and Quality—the model highlights the nonlinear interactions and dynamic evolution among core competency components. It emphasizes a holistic, process-oriented approach to development, spanning from knowledge internalization to character formation. This makes it particularly well-suited for talent cultivation in emerging engineering fields such as artificial intelligence, big data, and the digital economy.

As shown in Table 1, a comparative overview is provided between the K-A-T-Q model and the KAPO and OBE frameworks across several dimensions, including core components, structural characteristics, application orientation, and domain adaptability.

Table 1. Comparative Analysis of the K-A-T-Q Model and Mainstream Talent Development Frameworks

Comparison Dimension	KAPO	OBE	KATQ
Core Components	Knowledge & Skills Attitudes & Values Processes & Methods Instructional Events	Knowledge Ability Quality	Knowledge Ability Thinking Quality
Model Characteristics	"Three Dimensions with One Core" Dynamic Structure; Competency Development Driven by Instructional Events	Clear Learning Objectives; Strengthened Learning Outcome and Assessment Feedback Loop	Four-Dimensional Coupling Emphasizing Systemic Evolution and Quality-Driven Development
Application Orientation	Guides Curriculum Design and Dynamic Competency Adjustment	Enhance Measurability of Learning Objectives	Cultivating AI Talent's Four-Dimensional Competencies and Responsibility
Applicable Domains	Instructional Design Across Educational Stages	Engineering Accreditation Curriculum Reform	Emerging Engineering Disciplines in AI and Digital Technologies

In summary, by incorporating the two critical dimensions of "Thinking" and "Quality," the K-A-T-Q model addresses the limitations of traditional engineering education frameworks in expanding cognitive abilities and cultivating comprehensive competencies. It establishes a more adaptive, systematic, and interdisciplinary-transferable paradigm for competency development in engineering education. The model's practical application in undergraduate AI education further validates its tangible effectiveness and theoretical significance in promoting the "four-dimensional synergistic development" and fostering holistic student growth.

4 Design of the Triadic Integrated Training Pathway

Based on the element coupling mechanism of the K-A-T-Q model, this study systematically constructs an integrated cultivation paradigm that synergistically advances curriculum system, teaching methodologies, and evaluation mechanisms, following the developmental logic of "knowledge integration—ability advancement—thinking training—quality cultivation." Addressing the critical challenges within K-A-T-Q, three implementation pathways are designed accordingly: a tiered and progressive curriculum reconstruction, innovative blended teaching models, and dynamic, iterative evaluation systems. The curriculum system is systematically organized around the "four-dimensional core competencies," comprising four progressive modules—knowledge consolidation, skill training, cognitive expansion, and quality development. This is operationalized through a spiral advancement structure of "strengthening mathematical foundations—integrating software and hardware practice—infusing diverse thinking—empowering quality cultivation," effectively bridging disciplinary knowledge, engineering practice, and social responsibility. It facilitates students' progression from knowledge acquisition to competency internalization, ensuring a deep alignment between course content and competency objectives. The teaching model leverages a blended virtual-real platform and human–machine collaborative mechanisms to promote students' capability leapfrogging. The evaluation system integrates diverse assessment forms and functions to foster comprehensive development of core competencies while providing continuous feedback for teaching and learning. This element-driven design strategy not only preserves structural correspondence between each dimension's cultivation plan and the K-A-T-Q model but also fosters dynamic, balanced development of the four competencies through cross-module synergy, thus forming an orderly transformation channel from theoretical model to educational practice, as illustrated in Fig. 3.

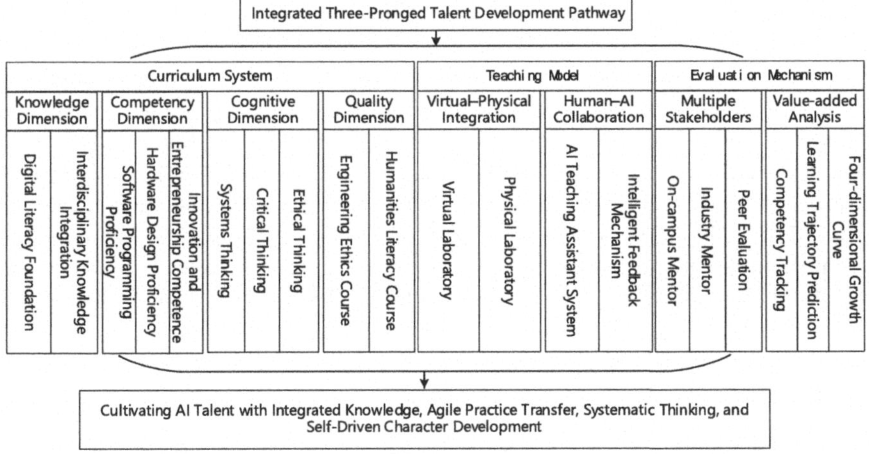

Fig. 3. Schematic Diagram of the Triadic Integrated Training Pathway

4.1 Curriculum System Reconstruction: A Hierarchical and Progressive Integration of Knowledge, Ability, Thinking, and Quality

The curriculum system is systematically restructured across four dimensions—knowledge, ability, thinking, and quality—guided by a spiral progression mechanism of "foundation consolidation, competency advancement, thinking expansion, and quality cultivation." This structure promotes the deep integration and internalization of core competencies required for AI talent development. Course selection follows a "core + integrative + practical" structure, with learning objectives designed based on the K-A-T-Q model to realign knowledge with skills and dismantle the traditional divide between core disciplinary and general education courses, ultimately forming an "AI + X" interdisciplinary curriculum architecture. In terms of integration pathways, a knowledge chain is established through foundational courses such as Fundamentals of Computer Science and Artificial Intelligence and Introduction to Artificial Intelligence, which are further enriched by technical modules like Python Programming and Embedded Linux, as well as application-oriented courses such as Human–Machine Interaction in Intelligent Transportation and Smart City System Design. Together, they form a cross-disciplinary, multi-dimensional curriculum system that supports collaborative learning and cultivates the comprehensive competencies required in emerging AI-driven fields.

Taking the course Fundamentals of Computer Science and Artificial Intelligence as an example, the curriculum is designed to align with the four dimensions of the K-A-T-Q model. In the knowledge dimension, the course emphasizes students' systematic mastery of logical foundations, mathematical modeling, and classical algorithms by integrating dedicated modules such as Mathematical Modeling Applications and Data Structures and Algorithm Practicum. In the ability dimension, modular programming tasks and hardware design exercises are incorporated to equip students with key skills in model training, code implementation, and performance optimization. For the thinking dimension, group discussions on Bias and Error Analysis in AI are embedded to foster systematic modeling approaches and critical reflection. In the quality dimension, a concluding public lecture themed AI Technology and Social Responsibility is conducted, combining keynote presentations and student-led reflections to enhance communication skills, teamwork, and a sense of social responsibility—ultimately reinforcing students' awareness of engineering ethics and strengthening their integrated humanistic qualities.

Another example is the course Human–Machine Interaction in Intelligent Transportation, which integrates intelligent transportation scenarios with the fundamentals of user interface design. In the knowledge dimension, it combines principles of human–computer interaction with the fundamentals of intelligent sensing systems in transportation. In the ability dimension, students are guided to develop interactive prototype systems based on real-world traffic data. For the thinking dimension, assignments such as seminars on User Experience and Data Feedback Loops are designed to cultivate students' critical analysis skills and iterative design thinking. In the quality dimension, a thematic field study titled Mobility Friendliness for Vulnerable Groups engages students in social research and human-centered practice within real transportation contexts. This enables students to refine their professional competencies through empathy-driven inquiry and to strengthen their career readiness and sense of social responsibility through data analysis and public communication. Ultimately, the course fosters a deep integration of technological rationality and humanistic values.

In terms of instructional approach, the course advances blended teaching reforms through problem-oriented learning, task-driven activities, and flipped classroom models, supported by AI-powered teaching assistants and intelligent feedback systems. These innovations enable full-process data support and competency tracking across teaching, learning, and assessment. During course implementation, emphasis is placed on interdisciplinary teamwork, real-world problem-solving, and staged outcome presentations. This facilitates a spiral progression of competency development—from cognitive understanding to behavioral application, and ultimately to comprehensive quality formation—promoting the integrated growth of both professional capabilities and humanistic literacy.

In summary, the reconstruction of the curriculum system involves not only the reorganization of course content, but more importantly, the structural coupling of cultivation mechanisms and the evolutionary refinement of development pathways. Through the anchoring role of core courses and the extension of integrative modules, a systematic curriculum framework is established to comprehensively address the four-dimensional competency goals. This provides robust support for cultivating interdisciplinary, responsibility-driven AI talent.

4.2 Innovation in Teaching Models: Bidirectional Empowerment Through Virtual-Physical Integration and Human-Machine Collaboration

Driven by the dual imperatives of EEE and the distinctive characteristics of AI disciplines, teaching models must transcend the traditional teacher-centered, didactic approach and shift toward a competency-oriented, integrative education pathway. This study proposes an innovative teaching model centered on virtual–physical integration and human–machine collaboration, aiming to reshape the instructional ecosystem by creating multi-dimensional, intelligently supported, and continuously responsive learning environments.

Leveraging the university's digital infrastructure, a collaborative practice system is established that integrates virtual simulation laboratories and physical laboratories, providing a deeply immersive "online + offline" and "virtual + real-world" experience. The simulation labs offer multi-scenario rapid rehearsal environments, supporting students in AI algorithm modeling, data simulation, and system emulation through pre-experimental exercises. Meanwhile, physical labs provide authentic equipment and real engineering contexts, enabling precise honing of students' hands-on skills and experimental design capabilities. Additionally, real-world industry projects are incorporated into the curriculum, where students engage in the full practice cycle of problem identification, solution design, engineering implementation, and outcome presentation. This approach emphasizes teamwork, task-driven learning, and phased deliverables, comprehensively enhancing students' ability to address complex engineering challenges with systematic problem-solving skills.

At the human–machine collaboration level, this framework emphasizes the deep integration of AI and education by establishing a teaching support architecture composed of an AI teaching assistant system and an intelligent feedback system. The AI assistant offers personalized Q&A, learning path recommendations, and knowledge graph navigation, effectively alleviating teachers' workload and providing individualized learning support for students. The intelligent feedback system dynamically analyzes student assignments, lab records, and classroom behaviors to generate a comprehensive "competency radar," furnishing educators with real-time data to inform instructional adjustments. Under the coordination of human instructors, AI tools and teachers operate within a closed-loop mechanism of precise diagnosis, intelligent delivery, and manual intervention, thereby enhancing classroom interaction efficiency and feedback responsiveness.

Furthermore, the curriculum integrates human–machine interaction experimental tasks—such as "algorithm fairness testing," "AI ethics dialogue simulation," and "human–machine adversarial experiments"—to guide students in critically exploring issues related to algorithmic bias, technological misuse, and privacy boundaries. This approach strengthens students' critical thinking, ethical awareness, and sense of social responsibility, fostering a reciprocal evolution of cognitive paradigms and technical competencies.

In summary, the dual drivers of virtual-physical integration and human–machine collaboration not only enrich the pedagogical modalities of AI-focused curricula but also establish a novel teaching paradigm finely attuned to the developmental trajectories of AI talent. This paradigm provides a robust foundation for the integrated cultivation of the four-dimensional competencies of knowledge, ability, thinking, and quality.

4.3 Iterative Evaluation Mechanism: Multidimensional and Dynamic Full-Cycle Competency Tracking

In the process of cultivating AI talent, a rigorous evaluation mechanism serves not only as a critical component for ensuring teaching quality but also as an intrinsic driver for the continuous generation and optimization of student competencies. To transcend the limitations of traditional static assessments that focus solely on knowledge acquisition, this study establishes a dynamic, comprehensive competency-tracking system. Comprising multiple evaluative agents and value-added analysis mechanisms, the system enables quantitative, full-cycle assessment and precise feedback on students' four-dimensional growth in knowledge, ability, thinking, and quality.

In terms of diversified evaluation agents, a triadic assessment structure is established, involving industry mentors, on-campus instructors, and peer evaluations. Industry mentors focus on the practicality of technical solutions, the feasibility of engineering outcomes, and job adaptability, reflecting alignment with industry demands. On-campus instructors emphasize depth of theoretical understanding, logical coherence in model construction, and academic rigor, highlighting control over foundational knowledge and professional competence. Peer evaluation is extensively applied in course projects and group tasks, stressing mutual assessment of teamwork, communication skills, and collective responsibility, thereby enhancing students' agency and engagement in the evaluation process. The synergy among these three evaluative dimensions disrupts the traditional teacher-dominated model, significantly improving the multidimensional comprehensiveness of assessment outcomes and the effectiveness of formative feedback.

Regarding the value-added analysis mechanism, this study incorporates student learning trajectory modeling based on Long Short-Term Memory neural networks. By leveraging multi-source data—including course assignments, laboratory performance, classroom interactions, and project participation—the system predicts students' growth trends at different stages. It dynamically generates personalized "competency radar charts" that visualize individual developmental trajectories and phase-specific changes across the four dimensions of knowledge, ability, thinking, and quality. This platform enables instructors to adapt teaching strategies in real time according to students' evolving competency profiles, facilitating precise content delivery and personalized academic interventions. Simultaneously, it provides students with insightful self-assessment tools for identifying competency gaps and optimizing learning plans.

Furthermore, the competency tracking system integrates a triadic assessment logic of "goals—process—outcomes," effectively linking initial learning objectives, key performance records during the process, and final project evaluations. This synergy fosters a comprehensive teaching–assessment–feedback–improvement cycle, enabling a truly student-centered continuous improvement mechanism.

In summary, this diversified and dynamic evaluation system not only expands traditional assessment dimensions but also empowers individualized developmental processes through intelligent technologies. By achieving breakthroughs in visualization, process orientation, and developmental tracking, it provides robust support and mechanistic assurance for the systematic cultivation of core competencies in AI talent.

5 Practical Outcomes

Based on the K-A-T-Q model and the integrated "three-in-one" collaborative pathway, East China Jiaotong University has actively advanced the reform of its AI education program, focusing on the development of a robust AI curriculum system. Over the past five years, students have secured 72 provincial-level and above innovation and entrepreneurship training projects, including 36 at the national level. They have contributed to 21 published papers, obtained 6 invention patents, 29 utility model patents, and nearly 100 software copyrights. Students have also won 4 national awards at the China International "Internet+" College Student Innovation and Entrepreneurship Competition, 1 national award in the "Challenge Cup" China College Student Entrepreneurship Competition, along with 45 other national and 283 provincial-level disciplinary competition prizes. More than 80% of these achievements are focused on the transportation sector. Collectively, these practical outcomes validate the effectiveness of the "AI+ scenario integration" pathway in enhancing students' technical application skills, engineering innovation capabilities, and cross-disciplinary competencies. The program has been recognized with 5 national-level first-class undergraduate courses and over 20 provincial-level first-class courses; published more than 30 textbooks, including one nationally planned textbook and one provincial outstanding textbook award; received over 10 provincial teaching achievement awards and 8 national and provincial teaching competition awards; and secured more than 70 teaching reform and planning projects at the provincial and ministerial levels or higher.

These achievements not only demonstrate the systematic advancement and multidimensional outcomes of AI curriculum reform but also indirectly validate the practicality and effectiveness of the K-A-T-Q model in real educational settings. To further elucidate the intrinsic relationship between the four-dimensional core competencies and tangible outcomes, this study conducts a systematic mapping and classification analysis of students' actual performance across multiple dimensions, including curriculum development, research projects, competition achievements, and intellectual property. By constructing a correspondence matrix between outcome types and competency dimensions (see Table 2), the analysis provides a clear illustration of the implementation efficacy and competency enhancement pathways facilitated by this collaborative cultivation model in knowledge integration, ability building, thinking expansion, and quality formation.

Table 2. Comparative Analysis of the K-A-T-Q Model and Mainstream Talent Development Frameworks

Achievement Category	Quantity	Knowledge	Ability	Thinking	Quality
National - level College Students' Innovation and Entrepreneurship Projects	36	✓	✓	✓	✓
National Awards of the "Challenge Cup"	1	✓	✓	✓	✓
National Awards of China's "Internet +" Innovation and Entrepreneurship Competition	4	✓	✓	✓	✓
Invention/Utility Model Patents	35	✓	✓	✓	✓
Software Copyrights	100+	✓	✓	✓	✓
Provincial and Ministerial - level Teaching Achievement Awards	10+	✓	✓	✓	✓

Each category of achievement can be effectively mapped to the dimensions of Knowledge, Ability, Thinking, and Quality, reflecting the integrated educational logic of the K-A-T-Q four-dimensional coupling model. Knowledge serves as the foundation, providing essential disciplinary grounding and enabling interdisciplinary integration. Ability acts as the implementation vehicle, driving the transformation of ideas into tangible outcomes through competencies such as software programming and hardware design.

Thinking functions as an empowering force, facilitating iterative innovation through systems thinking, critical reasoning, and ethical reflection. Quality plays a safeguarding role, ensuring the sustainability and social relevance of outcomes through professional resilience and humanistic collaboration. Together, this structure—knowledge as the base, ability as the vehicle, thinking as the driver, and quality as the compass—forms a complete talent development loop, validating the model's effectiveness in cultivating interdisciplinary AI talent and demonstrating that each achievement is a practical manifestation of four-dimensional synergy.

6 Conclusion

In response to the evolving demands of AI undergraduate education under the emerging engineering paradigm, this study proposes the K-A-T-Q four-dimensional coupling model and a corresponding "three-in-one" collaborative cultivation pathway. Practical outcomes demonstrate that the model and its implementation pathway significantly enhance students' capabilities in knowledge integration, technological transfer, systems thinking, and quality development. As such, it offers a replicable and scalable framework for advancing AI undergraduate education in a systematic and impactful manner.

Acknowledgments. This study was supported by Jiangxi Provincial Education Science 14th Five-Year Plan Project (grant number 21ZD039).

Disclosure of Interests. The authors have no competing interests to declare that are relevant to the content of this article.

References

1. He, B., Yang, G., Qin, L.Y., et al.: Collaborative cultivation of scientific thinking and practical innovation capabilities in New Engineering students. Mech. Des. **41**(11), 192–198 (2024)
2. Sun, R.X., Wang, Z.B., Liu, X.: Exploration of practical teaching reform in metal materials engineering under the New Engineering paradigm. Lab. Res. Explor. **44**(03), 170–173 (2025)
3. Qin, L.J., Wang, J.L.: How to cultivate the cognitive abilities of New Engineering talents: a case study of the transformation of engineering education at MIT. High. Educ. Explor. **05**, 70–76 (2023)
4. Liu, X.Q., Ge, W.Q., Li, B.: Reform and practice of New Engineering talent cultivation model based on competency-oriented education. Chin. Univ. Teach. **11**, 30–37 (2023)
5. Yang, Q., Liu, Z.J., Kong, G.Q., et al.: Research on strategies for higher engineering education in the context of interdisciplinary integration. High. Eng. Educ. Res., 1–5 (2025)
6. Hao, X.Y., Zhu, L.F., Qu, Y.: Research and practice of teaching reform oriented to the core competencies of New Engineering talents: a case study of intelligent manufacturing equipment technology program group. Pub. Relat. World **24**, 163–165 (2024)
7. Hu, J.J., Liu, Z.Y., Xue, J.F.: Teaching reform of fundamental AI courses under the OBE framework. Chin. J. Multimedia Netw. Teach. (First Issue) **2025**(05), 56–59 (2025)

8. Zong, X.L., Xu, H.: Teaching reform of basic artificial intelligence courses focusing on competency development. Comp. Educ. **05**, 133–137 (2025)
9. Sun, Q.H., Zhang, Y.X., Jin, H.B., et al.: Core competencies and cultivation of New Engineering interdisciplinary talents in the context of the "IKAQ" structure in the new development stage. J. High. Educ. **10**(23), 155–158 (2024)

The Design and Development of the AI Interviewer System

Xinzhou Ye[2], Zhehao Mou[1], Haonan Jiang[2], Yuefeng Cen[2](✉), and Gang Cen[2]

[1] School of Automation and Electrical Engineering, Zhejiang University of Science and Technology, Hangzhou 310023, China
[2] School of Computer Science and Technology, Zhejiang University of Science and Technology, Hangzhou 310023, China
3510163502@qq.com, cyf@zust.edu.cn

Abstract. The contemporary workplace demonstrates increasingly diversified and specialized requirements for candidates' professional competencies and qualifications. A substantial proportion of job seekers, particularly recent graduates, experience interview anxiety, demonstrate unfamiliarity with interview protocols and procedures, and exhibit insufficient understanding of position-specific competency requirements, thereby expressing considerable demand for interview skill enhancement. To address these challenges, an AI-powered virtual interviewer system has been conceptualized, designed, and implemented. The system's core functionalities encompass specialized competency training for job seekers, real-time multimodal dialogue capabilities during simulated interviews, and comprehensive visualization of candidate competency profiles. From a technical perspective, the system operates as an intelligent interview training platform that leverages WebRTC technology for real-time audiovisual communication and employs a fine-tuned, domain-specific Large Language Model (LLM) optimized for interview scenarios. Developed utilizing Vue3 and Spring Boot within a decoupled frontend-backend architecture, this AI interviewer system facilitates candidate acclimatization to professional interview environments, enhances familiarity with discipline-specific assessment methodologies, and enables identification of competency deficiencies through comprehensive diagnostic analytics.

Keywords: Mock Interview · Large Language Model · Real-time Voice Conversation · Competency Assessment

1 Introduction

As modern industries undergo development and transformation, the requirements for positional competencies and professional qualities have become increasingly diversified and refined. While enterprises demonstrate an urgent demand for talent acquisition, job seekers paradoxically encounter mounting difficulties

W. Hong et al. (Eds.): ICCSE 2025, CCIS 2761, pp. 181–193, 2026.
https://doi.org/10.1007/978-981-95-7731-6_15

in securing employment opportunities that align with their professional profiles. Certain individuals, who may lack proficiency in self-presentation, fail to effectively demonstrate their specialized expertise and professional attributes, consequently creating a disconnect between their capabilities and positional requirements—a challenge that underscores the necessity for an efficient evaluation system capable of assessing candidate competencies while providing strategic interview guidance [1]. Job seekers confront increasingly formidable self-presentation barriers: McKinsey's Asia-Pacific regional survey reveals that 63% of technical professionals lose over 40% of their competitive advantage scores during communication phases due to insufficient systematic interview training. The "2024 Borje Enterprise Recruitment Index Report" indicates that AI-powered interviews, as an emerging methodological approach, are experiencing rapid developmental momentum, with approximately 18.7% of surveyed companies exploring AI recruitment applications. Furthermore, LinkedIn's Economic Graph demonstrates that freelancers utilizing AI interview data exhibit a reduced hourly rate dispersion coefficient of 0.18 (compared to 0.37 in traditional markets), signaling the emergence of a novel value consensus based on digital twin technologies within labor markets [2].

The rapid development of next-generation information technologies has established a robust technological foundation for AI applications in talent assessment. Leveraging massive data support, AI achieves dynamic talent-position matching through scientific quantitative analysis, serving as a pivotal driving force for the transformation of human resource management systems.

AI-driven innovative talent evaluation systems are garnering widespread attention from both academia and industry. Gartner predicts that by 2025, 60% of enterprises will adopt multimodal AI interview tools. The core technology constructs high-dimensional capability representation spaces through heterogeneous data fusion (video streams, audio spectrograms, micro-expression temporal data), effectively overcoming the "signal deficiency" limitations of traditional assessment methods [3]. Nobel Prize laureate in Economics Christopher A. Pissarides emphasizes that AI-empowered talent selection will foster mutual achievement between talent and society, promoting high-quality development.

2 System Analysis

2.1 Operational Analysis

This study focuses on improving candidates' interview skills and helping them take the initiative in dynamic job-position matching. The system primarily implements simulated interviews and provides visualization analysis of individual competency maps [4].

This system is designed with the core objective of training users' interview skills through fine-tuning large language models to build an intelligent system specifically targeting the job interview domain. The system's development path encompasses two directions: first, continuously optimizing the large language model to achieve precise interview guidance and assessment while providing rich data support for the interview corpus; second, combining expert human coaching with large language model technical support to provide job seekers with personalized interview path planning and experience accumulation.

Based on the fine-tuned large language model [5], the system constructs an online simulated interview environment for users. Through video calls, it maximally replicates real online interview scenarios [6]. The system's built-in corpus uses the fine-tuned large language model as the primary data source and, combined with user resume information and job intentions, automatically generates personalized simulated interview content, including interview questions and expected performance standards. Meanwhile, the system integrates existing job position datasets to customize exclusive job-seeking corpora for each user and feeds user data back to the main system corpus for continuous optimization.

In the interview assessment phase, the system employs NLP technology and Word2Vec vector analysis to conduct semantic analysis and keyword extraction on users' interview responses, intelligently matching them with the corpus to provide a data foundation for subsequent scoring. Through the built-in "multi-dimensional scoring mechanism," the system can comprehensively analyze users' interview performance, providing detailed score assessments and personalized reviews, accurately identifying users' deficiencies during the interview process and offering targeted improvement suggestions. Additionally, the system generates capability analysis charts and ability maps to help users intuitively understand their strengths and weaknesses. Fig 1 illustrates the program's operational workflow.

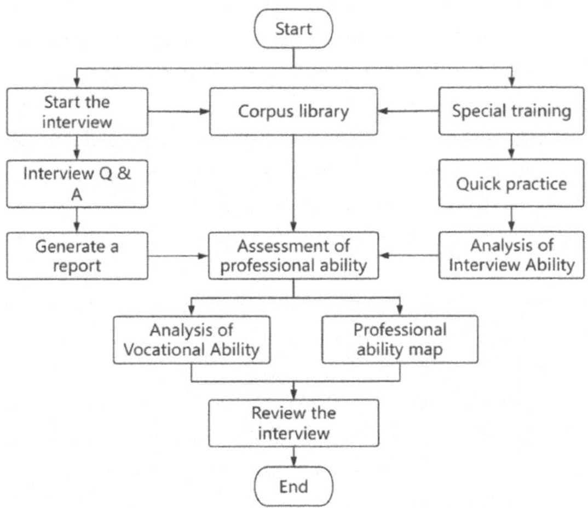

Fig. 1. Users use the platform to simulate the process of interview function.

To address the issues identified during mock interviews, the system provides specialized breakthrough training modules, enabling users to engage in targeted learning and intensive practice to continuously enhance their interview capabilities. The system also records users' learning progress and performance during specialized training, facilitating user review and reinforcement, thereby forming a complete learning loop. Fig 2 shows how to perform closed-loop training.

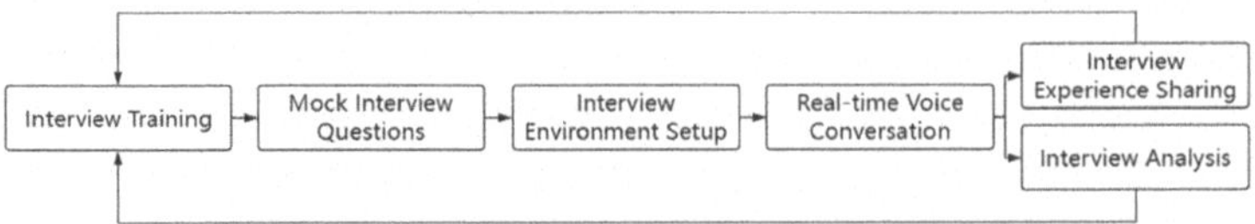

Fig. 2. User Closed-Loop Training Flowchart.

2.2 Interview Scoring System

The system's scoring criteria are based on rigorous human resource management theory and empirical research design. The technical ability weight of 0.4 derives from McKinsey's Global Skills Survey (2023), which shows a 0.68 correlation coefficient between hard skills and career success. Additionally, 85% of enterprises in LinkedIn's recruitment trend report list professional skills as the primary screening criterion [7]. Communication ability and logical thinking each account for 0.2 weight. This ratio comes from Harvard Business School's workplace success factors study, which found that effective communication ability is crucial for over 85% of management positions. Logical thinking receives equal importance in recruitment evaluations at technology giants such as Google and Microsoft. Problem-solving ability and professional knowledge each have a relatively low weight of 0.1, based on findings from the World Economic Forum's "Future of Work Skills Report." These abilities are often indirectly reflected through other dimensions and vary significantly across different positions [8]. The rating dimensions are summarized in Table 1.

Table 1. Interview Scoring Weight Summary Table

Dimensional	Weight	Evaluation content
technological capacity	0.4	Position-relevant hard skills proficiency
logical thinking	0.2	Clarity, orderliness and rigor in expressing opinions
communication ability	0.2	Speech fluency, answer clarity
problem-solving	0.1	Ability to identify problems, develop and implement solutions
professional knowledge	0.1	Industry-specific knowledge depth and professional competency assessment

Weight adjustment mechanism : According to the type of post, the weight is fine-tuned. For example, the sales post will increase the communication ability to 0.4, and the technical ability will be reduced to 0.2, Fig 3 illustrates the scoring rule triggering process.

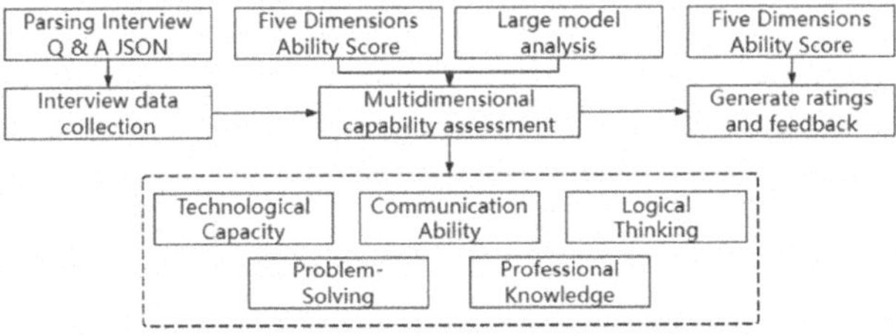

Fig. 3. The system simulates the interview scoring process for users.

Technological Capacity . Through NLP word segmentation and extraction technology, technical keywords are obtained from user answers and compared with annotated words in the cor-pus. The Sentence-BERT model encodes both user answers and standard answers as vectors [9]. Cosine similarity is then used to quantify the matching degree. Finally, based on the LLM-generated answer logic tree, the system identifies whether it contains the complete structure of "problem analysis - solution - result verification." The total technical ability score is calculated as shown in Formula 1:

$$S_1 = 0.4 \times K + 0.6 \times L \times C \tag{1}$$

where K represents the keyword matching degree, L represents logical integrity, and C represents the complexity coefficient. The complexity coefficient is dynamically adjusted based on question difficulty, ranging from 0.8 to 1.2.

Logical Thinking BERT is used for entity recognition on corporate culture description texts to construct a values dictionary. The Attention Mechanism calculates the weight distribution of keywords in user answers. This yields scoring Formula 2:

$$S_2 = 0.4 \times A + 0.4 \times F + 0.2 \times I \tag{2}$$

where A is structural integrity, F is coherence score, and I is argument clarity.

Communication Ability Audio is collected through WebRTC to calculate average speaking speed, measured as the number of full-width characters described per minute, along with pause intervals. The TextRank algorithm extracts core arguments from answers. Dependency Parsing detects the frequency of logical connectors such as "first" and "second". The total communication ability score is calculated as shown in Formula 3:

$$S_3 = 0.2(1 - T/10) + 0.8 \times N/D \tag{3}$$

where T is the number of pauses, N is the number of logical connectors, and D is the total number of sentences.

Problem-Solving The user's answer is compared with the case database using the TF-IDF algorithm to calculate text similarity. Three benchmark solutions are generated through LLM, and the Jaccard distance between the user's answer and the benchmark solutions is calculated [10]. The greater the distance, the higher the innovation, as shown in Formula 4 :

$$Jaccard = 1 - \frac{|A \cap B|}{|A \cup B|} \tag{4}$$

To get the problem solving ability as formula 5 :

$$S_4 = 0.4 \times H + 0.4 \times P + 0.2 \times E \tag{5}$$

where H is the degree of understanding, P is the feasibility of the scheme, and E is the depth of analysis.

Professional Knowledge Keyword matching and semantic similarity in technical ability, but more emphasis on non-pure technical content such as industry knowledge and job under-standing. Keywords or phrases that reflect learning willingness, reflection, adapt-ability, and growth mentality through NLP detection [11]. Get a professional knowledge score such as Formula 6 :

$$S_5 = 0.4 \times M + 0.4 \times U + 0.2 \times G \tag{6}$$

where M is knowledge relevance, U is learning attitude, and G is professional attitude.

Comprehensive Assessment The total score is weighted and summed by each dimension to obtain the following formula 7 :

$$S_m = \sum_{i=1}^{n} (S_i \times W_i) \tag{7}$$

where Si is the specific score of each dimension, and Wi is the weight of each dimension, as shown in Fig 4.

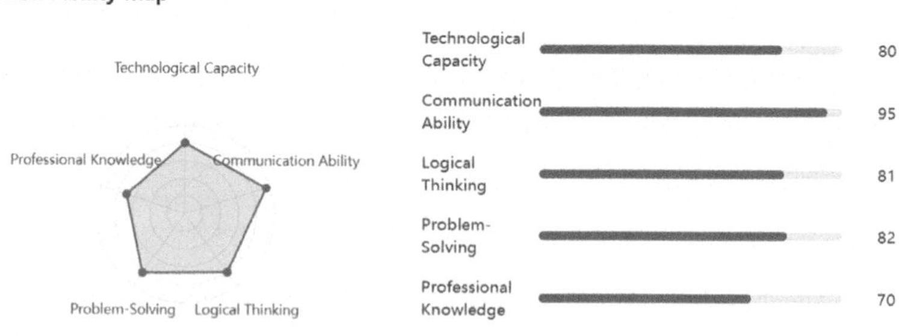

Fig. 4. User rating visualization implementation page.

3 System Design

3.1 Overall Design

The system adopts a modular architecture to ensure service flexibility and scalability while meeting the needs of various scenarios. Figure 5 shows the overall system design. The simulation interview modules and interview review module are the core of the system and will be discussed in detail below.

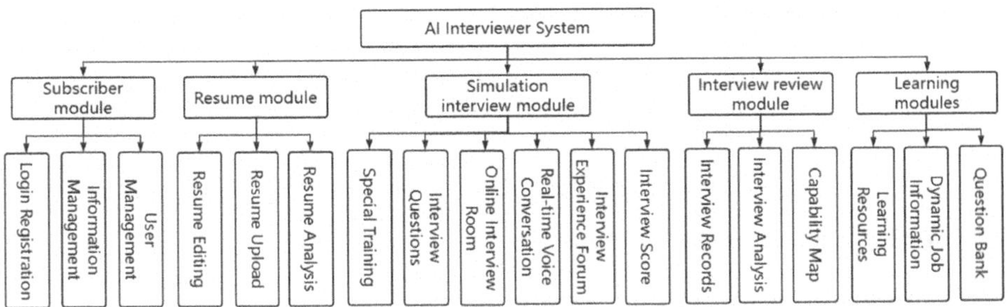

Fig. 5. System Function Module Diagram.

3.2 Simulation Interview Modules

The system utilizes an LLM to customize a targeted AI interview expert for users. Through training on preset topics such as self-introduction and project presentation, it helps users quickly master interview skills, prepare interview strategies and key points in advance, and improve their interview performance.

Additionally, based on common market interview questions and industry hot topics, the system provides simulated practice questions by leveraging the LLM, helping users adapt to potential interview questions in advance and providing reference answers for targeted preparation.

To help users quickly familiarize themselves with the interview process, the system uses WebRTC to build a virtual video interview system for online interview simulation [12]. This allows users to intuitively experience the interview atmosphere through realistic scenarios and engage in real-time voice dialogue via AI voice Q&A powered by voice LLMs, creating an authentic simulated interview environment [13]. After the simulated interview, users can share their interview experience and communicate with others about their interview process.

Furthermore, based on user responses in simulated interviews, the system quantitatively evaluates interview performance using the LLM and interview scoring system, providing comprehensive scores to help users understand their shortcomings and adjust interview strategies accordingly.

3.3 Interview Review Module

Users' mock interview records are stored in the system, allowing them to review their interview performance, including questions encountered and their responses. Leveraging the LLM combined with a multi-dimensional scoring system, the system comprehensively scores each answer and analyzes user performance in the simulated interview. Based on scores and performance, it identifies strengths and weaknesses exposed during the interview and provides corresponding improvement suggestions for user reference [14].

To help users intuitively understand their interview capabilities, the system generates quantified ability data through the scoring system and visualizes it as ability radar charts and histograms. This provides an intuitive display of ability distribution, helping users identify their strengths and weaknesses for targeted improvement.

4 Technical Route

4.1 Software Development Technology

This system adopts a distributed architecture pattern with front-end and back-end separation, constructing a comprehensive intelligent interview solution. At the front-end level, the system builds user interaction interfaces based on the Vue3 reactive framework and TypeScript strongly-typed language, implements full-duplex real-time communication mechanisms between client and server through WebSocket protocol, and integrates WebRTC peer-to-peer communication technology to support high-quality audio and video transmission capabilities. The interface design employs the TailwindCSS atomic CSS framework, achieving responsive adaptive layouts.

The back-end architecture adheres to the MVC design pattern, constructed on the Spring Boot microservice framework, integrating core components such as the Spring ecosystem and MyBatis-Plus persistence layer framework. The system adopts RESTful API design specifications, ensuring standardization and scalability of service interfaces. The data persistence layer utilizes the MySQL relational database management system, which, through optimized table structure design and indexing strategies, guarantees efficient storage and retrieval performance for core business data including user information management, interview process recording, and capability assessment analysis. Fig 6 shows the system technical architecture.

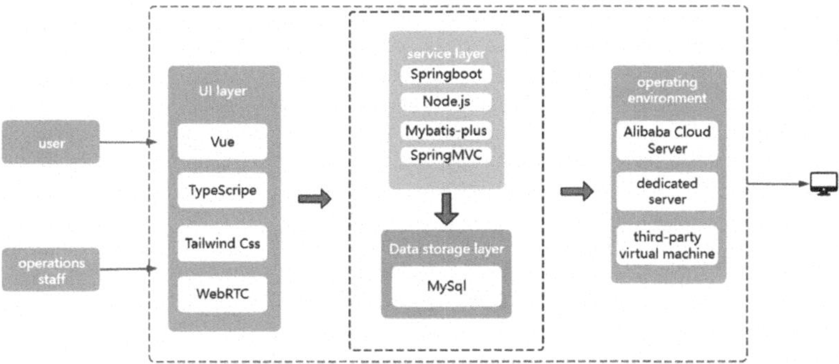

Fig. 6. System Technical Architecture Diagram.

4.2 Fine-Tuning The Large Model

For semantic understanding and generation tasks in the job-hunting field, the Deepseek-VL-7B open-source model is used as the foundation [15], with efficient domain adaptation achieved through Low-Rank Adaptation (LoRA). LoRA is a parameter-efficient fine-tuning technique that enables effective adaptation by adding low-rank decomposition matrices (BA) alongside the pretrained model weight matrices. It freezes the original pretraining weights, training only these low-rank matrices, which greatly reduces the number of trainable parameters while maintaining performance comparable to full-parameter fine-tuning. This method not only saves computing resources and storage space but also effectively prevents catastrophic forgetting, making model adaptation to specific domain tasks more efficient.

The LoRA training process first processes the original input through the Deepseek encoder, then extracts features via the LoRA branch, followed by low-rank matrix BA processing to reduce parameter count while preserving the model's professional capabilities in the interview domain. Domain task branch processing is then achieved by combining residual connections with domain-specific output heads, and model performance is optimized using multi-task loss functions [16]. Finally, BA parameters are updated through backpropagation, enabling the model to accurately understand interview questions, generate professional answers, and evaluate user responses across multiple dimensions, providing personalized interview guidance and feedback for job seekers. The training process is illustrated in Fig 7, and the implementation results are shown in Fig 8.

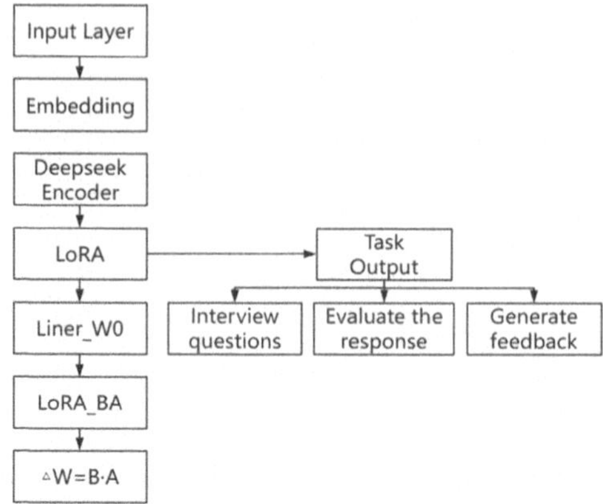

Fig. 7. LoRA training structure diagram.

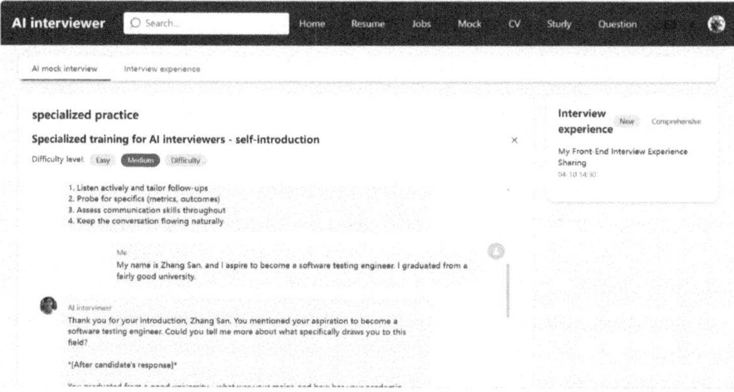

Fig. 8. Use of LLM in the system.

4.3 Real-Time Video Voice Dialogue

For real-time voice call functionality, the system integrates the Web Speech API to enable real-time voice interaction. Through speech recognition (STT), user responses are converted into text for LLM processing, then combined with speech synthesis (TTS) to generate AI interviewer feedback, creating a closed-loop real-time voice dialogue experience [17]. To ensure low-latency communication, the WebSocket protocol is used to transmit voice streams and model response data, while server-side asynchronous task queues decouple model inference from frontend interaction. This ultimately builds an end-to-end intelligent voice interview system that is both efficient and scalable, as shown in Fig 9.

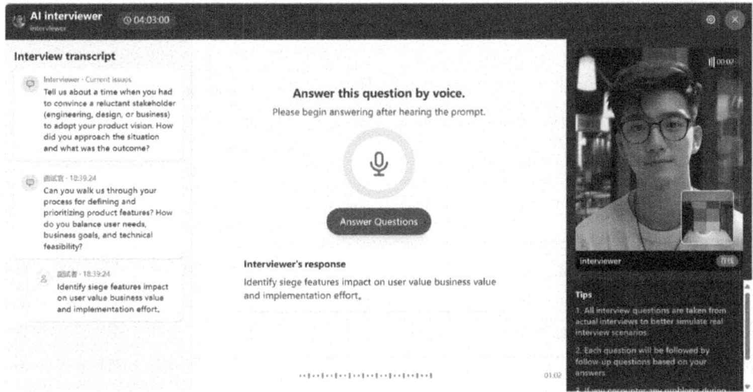

Fig. 9. Demonstration of real-time voice conversation process in the system.

5 System Feature

5.1 Multimodal Analysis of 'Voice + Text + Semantics

With high-precision ASR (automatic speech recognition) engine and deep neural network acoustic model, the accuracy of speech-to-text conversion reaches 98.2%. The intelligent voice simulation cabin supports millisecond-level response for multi-round dialogues, with voice endpoint detection accuracy con-trolled within 150ms, complemented by adaptive noise reduction algorithms.

5.2 Job Requirement Corpus Construction

The system simultaneously performs three levels of intelligent analysis—surface semantic analysis to extract keyword density and professional terminology matching; middle-level logic analysis to construct topic evolution maps and identify argument structure integrity; and deep reasoning modules that capture idea innovation and thinking coherence through attention mechanisms, forming multi-dimensional ability radar charts.

5.3 Training Closed Loop

Users initially upload their resumes and undergo preliminary interview training on the system. Subsequently, the system generates simulated interview questions based on the user's resume. The system then conducts statistical analysis of the user's simulated interview performance to generate a visualized capability report. Finally, users engage in targeted interview breakthrough training based on the visualized report from the simulated interview, initiating a new round of simulated interviews. This process encompasses a complete interview training workflow, forming a virtuous closed-loop training pathway.

6 System Practice

Part of the AI interviewer system's code has been open-sourced on GitHub. The link is https://github.com/1322135812yxz/AI_reviewer.git.

7 Conclusion

This paper describes the design and implementation of an AI-powered simulated interviewer system that integrates large language models, speech recognition, and WebRTC technology to construct a simulated interview environment. The system leverages AI technology to simulate corporate recruitment scenarios, assess interview performance, generate personal competency profiles and interview reports, helping job seekers identify deficiencies and providing improvement recommendations. The research encompasses the design and development of AI interviewers, workflow formulation, system analysis, and user capability visualization requirements, ensuring system compliance and user experience. It explores how to integrate AI applications in the field of user interview skill development. The ultimate goal is to help users improve their interview capabilities through training and achieve a continuously self-optimizing simulated interview system that promotes high-quality talent selection.

Acknowledgments. We gratefully acknowledge the support of the Ministry of Education's Humanities and Social Sciences Research Project (Grant No. 17YJA880004), titled "Re-search on the Construction of the Innovation and Entrepreneurship Environment for College Students under the Internet+ Background.

References

1. Chintalapati, P.V., Paluri, S.S., Nikhitha, S.S., et al.: A research model for automated prediction and analysis of job interview performance. In: 2024 Sixth International Conference on Computational Intelligence and Communication Technologies (CCICT), pp. 284–291. Sonepat, India (2024)
2. Chou, Y.C., Wongso, F.R., Chao, C.Y., et al.: An AI Mock-interview Platform for Interview Performance Analysis. In: 2022 10th International Conference on Information and Education Technology (ICIET), pp. 37–41. IEEE, Matsue (2022). https://doi.org/10.1109/ICIET55102.2022.9778999
3. Hirokazu, K., et al.: Group-Based Online Job Interview Training Program Using Virtual Robot for Individuals with Autism Spectrum Disorders. Front. Psychiatry **12** (2022)
4. Boudjani, N., Colas, V., Joubert, C., Amor, D.B.: AI Chatbot For Job Interview. In: 2023 46th MIPRO ICT and Electronics Convention (MIPRO), pp. 1155–1160. Opatija, Croatia (2023)
5. Mingzhe, L., Xiuying, C., Weiheng, L., Yang, S., Tao, Z., Dongyan, Z., Rui, Y., et al.: EZInterviewer: to Improve Job Interview Performance with Mock Interview Generator. WSDM, pp. 1102–1110 (2023)

6. Germanier, E., He, M., Rufai, A.M., et al.: Identifying storytelling in job interviews using deep learning. Comput. Human Behavior Rep. **1**, 100688 (2025). https://doi.org/10.1016/j.chbr.2025.100688
7. LinkedIn: 2024 Global Talent Trends Report: Data-driven insights into the evolving workplace (Europe - UK Edition). Technical report (2024). https://www.linkedin.com/content/dam/me/business/en-us/talent-solutions/global-talent-trends-report-2024-uk.pdf, last accessed 2025/01/01
8. World Economic Forum: The Future of Jobs Report 2025. Technical report, World Economic Forum, Switzerland, pp. 1–290 (2025). https://cn.weforum.org/publications/the-future-of-jobs-report-2025/digest/. Accessed 2025/05/29
9. Doshi, J.: Chatbot User Interface for Customer Relationship Management using NLP models. In: 2021 International Conference on Artificial Intelligence and Machine Vision (AIMV), pp. 1–4. Gandhinagar, India (2021)
10. Pandey, R., Chaudhari, D., Bhawani, S., Pawar, O., Barve, S.: Interview bot with automatic question generation and answer evaluation. In: 2023 9th International Conference on Advanced Computing and Communication Systems (ICACCS), pp. 1279–1286. Coimbatore, India (2023)
11. Koutsoumpis, A., Ghassemi, S., Oostrom, J.K., et al.: Beyond traditional interviews: psychometric analysis of asynchronous video interviews for personality and interview performance evaluation using machine learning. Comput. Human Behavior **154**, 108128 (2024). https://doi.org/10.1016/j.chb.2023.108128
12. Blum, N., Lachapelle, S., Alvestrand, H.: WebRTC - realtime communication for the open web platform. Commun. ACM **19**(1), 77–93 (2021)
13. Suen, H.-Y., Hung, K.-E., Lin, C.-L.: Intelligent Video Interview Agent Used to Predict Communication Skill and Perceived Personality Traits. Human-centric Comput. Inf. Sci. **10**(1) (2020)
14. Annareddy, G., Prasoona, K., Chinmai, S.: MOCK INTERVIEW PORTAL. Int. J. Innovative Eng. Manage. Res. 1209–1226 (2022)
15. Manuel, F.G., Weiwei, L., Lei, S., David, L.T., Carmen, E.L., Richard, J., Nicholas, R.M., et al.: Allying with AI? Reactions toward human-based, AI/ML-based, and augmented hiring processes. Comput. Hum. Behav. **130**, 107179–107179 (2022)
16. Hu, E., Shen, Y., Wallis, P., et al.: LoRA: Low-Rank Adaptation of Large Language Models. arXiv preprint arXiv:2106.09685v2 (2021https://doi.org/10.48550/arXiv.2106.09685
17. Fadya, A.H., Suaad, M.S., Shaymaa, M.A., Hassan, M.G., Ahmed, D.R., et al.: Design module for speech recognition graphical user interface browser to supports the web speech applications. Bull. Electr. Eng. Inform. **11**(6), 3392–3402 (2022)

A Human-AI Collaborative Strategy for Project-Based Learning Using Large Language Models

Yuan Fang[1](✉), Weizhen Wang[2], Shikai Guo[3], Mingjian Liu[4], and Xiang Li[5]

[1] School of Innovation and Entrepreneurship, Dalian Polytechnic University, Dalian, China
fangy@dlpu.edu.cn
[2] School of Fashion, Dalian Polytechnic University, Dalian, China
[3] School of Information Science and Technology, Dalian Maritime University, Dalian, China
[4] College of Information Engineering, Dalian Ocean University, Dalian, China
[5] Dalian University, Dalian, China

Abstract. The rapid advancement of Large Language Models (LLMs) has introduced novel opportunities for enhancing project-based learning (PBL), particularly in beginner-level Python courses for students from non-computer science backgrounds. These models offer a bridge between natural language and programming logic, allowing learners to concentrate on authentic problem-solving rather than syntactic complexities. However, most current applications of LLMs in education provide fragmented, short-term support and lack coherence across the full lifecycle of project development. To address these challenges, this study proposes a Human-AI Collaborative Strategy based on the Problem-Driven Cognition and Outcome-Based Education (PDC-OBE) framework. This strategy emphasizes structured learning progression, alignment with instructional objectives, and cognitive engagement. A case study involving a sentiment analysis project was conducted to evaluate the implementation of this model. The integration of LLMs across preparation, execution, reflection, and assessment phases demonstrated significant improvements in student engagement, computational thinking, and reflective learning. The proposed framework offers a scalable, pedagogically grounded approach for integrating AI into programming education and serves as a foundational model for future development of domain-specific educational agents.

Keywords: Human-AI collaboration · Problem-Driven Cognition · Outcome-Based Education · Project-Based Learning · Higher education

1 Introduction

The rapid development of LLMs has significantly expanded the possibilities for applying artificial intelligence (AI) in education, particularly in areas such as

W. Hong et al. (Eds.): ICCSE 2025, CCIS 2761, pp. 194–205, 2026.
https://doi.org/10.1007/978-981-95-7731-6_16

natural language processing and programming instruction [1]. As generative AI technologies continue to evolve, their integration into teaching and learning environments is accelerating. Models like ChatGPT, Bard, and Claude are being increasingly employed to support learners in understanding complex concepts, generating content, and solving domain-specific problems. Among various instructional approaches, project-based learning (PBL) presents a highly compatible setting for LLMs, as it emphasizes inquiry, problem-solving, and iterative learning—elements that LLMs can facilitate through language-level interaction and code generation capabilities. Especially for beginner-level programming courses designed for students from non-computer science backgrounds, the use of LLMs offers a means to bridge the gap between natural language understanding and formal programming languages, thereby reducing entry barriers and enabling learners to focus more on logical reasoning and problem-solving.

However, current applications of general-purpose LLMs in education often fall short in supporting the full process of project-based learning. While they are capable of providing immediate code suggestions or answering factual queries, their capacity to sustain coherent and contextually aware interactions over extended learning periods remains limited. This gap is particularly evident in educational settings that require support across pre-development planning, mid-development debugging, and post-development reflection. The lack of instructional alignment and contextual sensitivity in LLMs responses diminishes their ability to facilitate deeper cognitive engagement, scaffold learning progression, or adapt to individual learner needs. Moreover, in the context of foundational programming instruction, where learners are still constructing their understanding of computational thinking, reliance on such fragmented support may hinder rather than enhance learning.

To overcome these limitations, there is an urgent need to re-frame the integration of LLMs within pedagogically sound strategies that extend beyond tool-based assistance. This study responds to that need by proposing a human-AI collaborative education strategy grounded in the dual principles of Problem-Driven Cognition and Outcome-Based Education (PDC-OBE). The PDC-OBE framework emphasizes the alignment of learning activities with authentic problems that reflect real-world complexity while ensuring that instructional design remains anchored in clearly defined learning outcomes. It values learner initiative, emphasizes structured thinking, and promotes reflection—all essential for cultivating higher-order cognitive abilities. When combined with the capabilities of LLMs, this approach enables the design of learning environments in which AI agents do not replace instruction but rather participate in a collaborative ecosystem that involves students, teachers, and intelligent tools.

Based on this conceptual foundation, the study explores how LLMs can be pedagogically embedded into the design of project-based Python programming courses for non-CS majors. The proposed strategy outlines a structured pathway through which LLMs assist in problem formulation, task decomposition, code iteration, and post-task reflection. At the same time, it delineates the boundaries of human-AI collaboration, ensuring that learners are guided rather than passively dependent [2]. By aligning the use of LLMs with curriculum objectives, instructional scaffolds, and learner profiles, the framework aims to transform the role of AI from a reactive code generator to a proactive learning companion. Furthermore, this strategy is implemented and analyzed through classroom teaching practices, offering a foundation for future research and development of domain-specific educational LLMs.

Through this approach, the study contributes both theoretically and practically to the field of AI-enhanced education. It enriches the discourse on how human-AI collaboration can be operationalized in classroom contexts, advances the development of pedagogically aligned LLM applications, and provides insights into how intelligent systems can support deep learning within project-based instructional models. As such, the research offers a pathway for building intelligent, responsive, and educationally meaningful systems in the era of generative AI.

2 Literature Review

2.1 Outcome-Based Education

Outcome-Based Education (OBE) represents a fundamental shift in instructional philosophy, emphasizing the articulation and achievement of explicit learning outcomes [3]. Rather than focusing solely on the transmission of knowledge, OBE centers on the development of students' real-world competencies and their ability to apply what they have learned in complex, authentic contexts. This paradigm aligns closely with Bloom's Taxonomy [4], which outlines a hierarchy of cognitive goals—from remembering and understanding to analyzing, evaluating, and creating—providing a structured framework for designing instruction that promotes deep cognitive engagement and progression. In [5], an engineering academic information management system (CO-AIMS) based on the rapid application development (RAD) model is proposed to achieve intelligent evaluation and management of OBE through multi-level learning analysis. In [6]a standardized learning outcomes measurement model based on the direct achievement method was proposed. Through the grading and quantification of course learning outcomes (CLO) and the skill classification system, accurate course-level assessment of OBE was achieved in 7 majors of 11 universities.

In the context of AI-supported education, the OBE framework demands not only clarity in educational objectives but also intelligent systems capable of delivering adaptive support and timely feedback, thereby ensuring that each student's learning trajectory remains aligned with expected outcomes.

2.2 Project-Based Learning

Project-Based Learning (PBL) [7], as a practical expression of student-centered learning, plays a key role in the implementation of OBE. PBL organizes teaching activities around complex, real-world projects that require extended inquiry, interdisciplinary integration, and collaborative problem-solving. It enables students to experience learning as an active construction process, where knowledge and skills are acquired in the pursuit of meaningful outcomes. The alignment of project tasks with outcome goals reinforces the relevance of the learning process, while the tangible products of project work serve as authentic assessments of students' competencies. When integrated into an OBE framework, PBL promotes engagement, motivation, and the development of transferable skills, especially in practice-oriented disciplines such as programming.

The Gold Standard PBL seven-element framework was used to teach Python programming to 30 middle school students. Empirical evidence showed that this project-based learning significantly improved students' academic performance and enhanced the acquisition of programming skills [8]. Construct a deep learning-driven digital learning innovation capability training model, and use the Python programming course as an example to verify the role of the intelligent education platform in promoting this core literacy [9].

2.3 Problem-Driven Cognition

The Problem-Driven Cognition (PDC) approach further complements this model by introducing structured cognitive scaffolding rooted in problem exploration and resolution. PDC emphasizes learning as a process of progressively clarifying, analyzing, and solving domain-specific problems, fostering higher-order thinking such as abstraction, decomposition, and reflective evaluation. Unlike general problem-based learning approaches, PDC pays closer attention to the internal cognitive activities triggered by problem engagement, making it especially relevant to programming education, where logic, structure, and iteration are central. In a PDC-enhanced learning environment, problems are not only vehicles for contextual learning but also cognitive stimuli for metacognitive growth.

Based on Bloom's Taxonomy and the Cognitive Theory of Multimedia Learning (CTML), a hierarchical serious game design framework is proposed. Through interdisciplinary case studies of the Westminster research group, a mapping model between cognitive processes and game mechanisms is established to provide a theory-driven design guide for educational game development [10]. In [11], a P-S index based on the function-behavior-structure (FBS) ontology was proposed to classify 54 industrial design students into problem-driven and solution-driven types. Empirical results showed that problem-driven students were better at repeatedly reconstructing problem statements.

2.4 LLMs

With the advent of LLMs, education is entering a new phase of human-AI collaboration. LLMs exhibit powerful natural language understanding, code generation, and multi-modal reasoning capabilities, making them promising tools for enhancing both project-based and problem-driven learning. In programming education, LLMs have been adopted for debugging, concept explanation, real-time tutoring, and even design prototyping. Many univeristies have piloted the use of ChatGPT and similar tools to assist students with task decomposition, syntactic correction, and semantic clarification. Yet, despite their growing popularity, most implementations of LLMs remain functionally isolated from broader pedagogical frameworks such as OBE, PBL, or PDC. This disconnect limits their potential to support sustained, goal-aligned learning processes.

Indeed, current LLM-powered educational tools often serve as auxiliary assistants providing static feedback, template-based guidance, or factual retrieval rather than integrated learning agents within a pedagogically coherent system. These systems typically lack alignment with learning outcomes, ignore cognitive development stages, and fail to account for the dynamic roles of teachers and learners in knowledge construction. Furthermore, the absence of project-task alignment and cognitive scaffolding in many AI-driven platforms makes it difficult for students to engage meaningfully with content or develop transferable problem-solving strategies. As such, these tools tend to support surface learning rather than deep conceptual mastery.

The literature also reveals several gaps in the current practice of AI-enhanced education. First, many AI applications fail to align generated content with curriculum standards and instructional goals, leading to inconsistencies in learning progression. Second, they lack mechanisms to support structured problem engagement or cognitive task decomposition, which are essential in problem-driven learning. Third, there is often a disconnect between AI agents and human instructional roles, with limited support for teacher-mediated interaction, formative assessment, or collaborative feedback. Lastly, evaluations of AI usage tend to focus on outcome performance metrics while neglecting the quality of the learning process and student agency.

To address these challenges, this study proposes a PDC-OBE framework, which integrates the design logic of OBE, the project-based structure of PBL, and the cognitive scaffolding of PDC, augmented by large language models. Situated in the context of foundational programming courses for non-computer science majors, this framework emphasizes staged task decomposition, conceptual progression, and reflective iteration. It embeds intelligent agents—powered by LLMs—throughout the learning process, providing diagnostic feedback, just-in-time guidance, and adaptive prompts aligned with both cognitive states and instructional goals. Teachers, meanwhile, function not only as evaluators and content curators but also as co-designers of learning trajectories, working in collaboration with AI to guide students toward meaningful outcomes. This framework seeks to establish a new paradigm of human-AI co-teaching, grounded in pedagogical rigor and oriented toward the development of transferable, higher-order competencies.

3 Theoretical Framework and Model Construction

Traditionally, education has primarily focused on the transmission of knowledge and the training of skills, which can be conceptualized as the "knowledge cognition model." This model centers on students mastering existing concepts, formulas, principles, and cases, emphasizing understanding and memorization. However, this model often ignores the core mission of education, which is to cultivate students' ability to solve complex problems and engage in innovative cognition. Particularly in general education, the prevalence of score-driven evaluation systems encourages students to prioritize grades as the sole indicator of success, resulting in knowledge acquisition that rarely translates into practical problem-solving capacity.

Entering the digital-intelligent era, knowledge is increasingly depreciated due to the ubiquity of AI-enabled access to vast information repositories and ready-made solutions. Consequently, educational goals must evolve to emphasize "skills plus cognition," encompassing logical reasoning, problem-solving, teamwork, and innovative thinking. Cognitive development in this context involves a deeper understanding of problem essences, exploration of unknown domains, and the fostering of creativity. To meet the demands of future society, it is imperative to cultivate higher-order thinking skills and innovative cognitive models among learners.

This research addresses the widespread deficiency in problem-solving and innovation competencies among university students by advocating the adoption of the "problem cognition model" as a pivotal educational framework. Diverging from the traditional knowledge cognition model, the problem cognition model prioritizes problem-centered learning, guiding students to identify, analyze, and resolve authentic problems. Through integration with real-world scenarios, complex challenges, and innovative tasks, this model encourages students to construct logically rigorous and goal-directed learning pathways via task-driven, project-based, and problem-solving pedagogues. Such an approach not only bridges the gap between theoretical knowledge and practical application but also stimulates intrinsic motivation and innovation potential.

3.1 The PDC-OBE Model

In response to the pedagogical shifts necessitated by the digital-intelligent era, this study proposes the PDC-OBE model, which systematically integrates cognitive-driven learning design with outcome-based assessment strategies. By embedding problem discovery and cognitive development (PDC) at the heart of educational practice, this model reconfigures curriculum and instructional frameworks to align with emerging demands for higher-order thinking and AI-enhanced learning environments.

The PDC-OBE model is grounded in the transformation from content-centered knowledge transmission to learner-centered cognitive activation. It emphasizes the cultivation of problem-discovery capabilities, critical analysis, and innovative solution generation—competencies vital for navigating complex, real-world challenges. Furthermore, the model leverages large language models (LLMs) and other AI technologies to support personalized, adaptive, and context-aware learning, thus facilitating an intelligent transformation of teaching and learning practices. The overall structure of the PDC-OBE model is illustrated in Fig. 1.

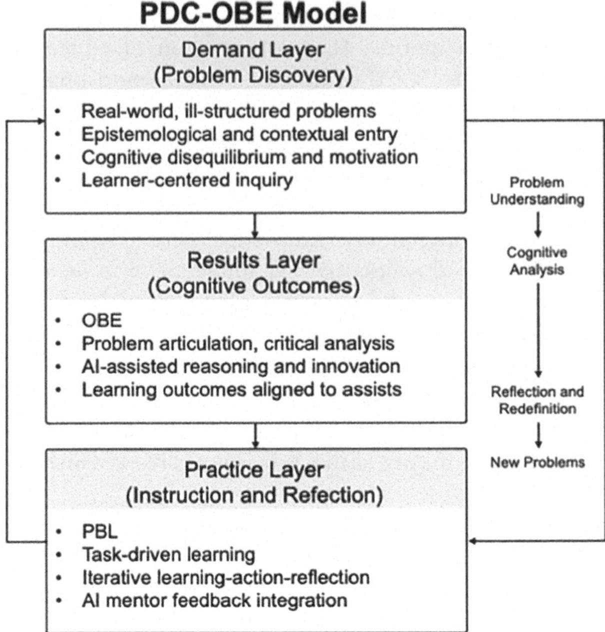

Fig. 1. PDC-OBE model.

3.2 Key Components of the PDC-OBE Model

The model comprises three interrelated layers: the Demand Layer, the Results Layer, and the Practice Layer. These layers collectively construct a dynamic and iterative system of teaching and learning that progresses from real-world complexity to actionable cognitive outcomes.

The Demand Layer The Demand Layer serves as the epistemological and contextual entry point of the PDC-OBE framework. Instead of initiating instruction with predefined content, this layer introduces learners to complex, ill-structured problems rooted in authentic professional, societal, or interdisciplinary contexts. These open-ended problems are intentionally designed to be uncertain and multifaceted, provoking cognitive disequilibrium and fostering intrinsic motivation for inquiry and exploration.

This paradigm marks a significant departure from conventional curriculum design. By front-loading real-world demands, learners are positioned as active agents who must interrogate, contextualize, and deconstruct the problem landscape. This process enhances both the perceived relevance of learning and the development of metacognitive engagement from the outset.

The Results Layer The Results Layer constitutes the outcome-driven core of the PDC-OBE model. Anchored in the principles of Outcome-Based Education (OBE), this layer focuses on observable and assessable outputs such as:

- The discovery and articulation of core problems
- Critical and systems-level analysis
- The development of creative and viable solutions

These outcomes are not limited to content reproduction but extend to knowledge transformation and methodological innovation. Throughout this process, AI technologies—particularly LLMs—function as intelligent collaborators, supporting learners in activities such as problem reframing, hypothesis generation, iterative evaluation, and solution optimization.

Moreover, the Results Layer aligns instructional strategies with performance indicators that are explicitly mapped to intended learning outcomes. This ensures transparency, accountability, and formative alignment across learning activities, assessments, and feedback mechanisms. In doing so, it operationalizes the OBE philosophy within an AI-supported, cognition-driven learning environment.

The Practice Layer. The Practice Layer provides the operational and pedagogical foundation of the model. It comprises a suite of instructional methods and strategies—including project-based learning (PBL), task-driven inquiry, and collaborative problem-solving—which enable students to iteratively engage with the challenges introduced in the Demand Layer.

This layer emphasizes iterative learning cycles that interleave action and reflection, facilitated by both human mentorship and AI-powered tools. Students are guided through staged learning processes, mirroring cognitive pathways from problem comprehension to solution execution. Activities in this layer are designed to foster interdisciplinary thinking, communication skills, team collaboration, and adaptive reasoning—all of which are critical for future-oriented professional development.

To ensure the efficacy and adaptability of learning, the Practice Layer integrates multiple forms of formative assessment, such as:

- Peer review and collaborative critique
- Reflective journaling and self-assessment
- AI-generated real-time feedback

Through these feedback-rich, iterative processes, learners refine both their disciplinary knowledge and cognitive strategies, thereby enhancing their capacity for lifelong learning and intelligent adaptation in uncertain environments.

4 Case Study and Empirical Practice

To validate the effectiveness of the PDC-OBE instructional model, a culminating project titled Sentiment Analysis on Product Reviews was implemented [12].

This task aligns with the three-layer architecture of the model by introducing a complex, real-world problem (Demand Layer), targeting cognitive outcomes such as analysis and innovation (Results Layer), and employing a staged, task-driven process (Practice Layer).

Students were required to build an end-to-end sentiment analysis pipeline for a specific product category (e.g., electronics, cosmetics, books) based on publicly available reviews. The project covered the complete data lifecycle: acquisition, preprocessing, sentiment classification, visualization, and reporting.

4.1 Project Structure and Learning Process

The implementation was divided into two phases: individual exploration and team collaboration.

- **Individual Tasks:** Each student completed two components: (1) a requirements analysis report identifying the task scope, data sources, and proposed workflow; (2) a module design report (e.g., text preprocessing, classification, or visualization), including flowcharts, pseudocode, and I/O specifications.
- **Team Collaboration:** Students formed groups of four to integrate individual modules into a complete system. Teams submitted consolidated codebases, technical documentation, and a project presentation.

This structure operationalized OBE through clear outcome alignment and embedded PDC by positioning learners within authentic, ill-structured tasks requiring problem identification, critical reasoning, and iterative refinement.

4.2 Integration of LLMs

Large Language Models (LLMs) were embedded as intelligent co-pilots throughout the four stages of instruction, forming a dynamic, responsive support system for both learners and instructors, as shown in Fig. 2.

Preparation Phase: Scaffolding Knowledge Activation. Instructors used LLMs to generate structured learning tasks and scenario-based prompts, such as data collection guidelines or tool-specific tutorials. These prompts helped activate prior knowledge and foreground domain-specific ethical considerations. Models also supplied sample code fragments, boosting early-stage understanding.

Execution Phase: Just-in-Time Assistance. During development, students accessed LLMs for troubleshooting, algorithm design, and documentation tasks. For example, the model provided debugging insights, improved regular expressions, and suggested modular architectures. Instructors also used agents to generate visual aids (e.g., flowcharts), accelerating knowledge externalization.

Reflection Phase: Iterative Refinement. Before submission, LLMs served as automated reviewers, analyzing technical documents and code for clarity, logic, and completeness. They assisted in summarizing results, generating captions, and preparing oral presentations—enhancing both coherence and communicative quality.

Assessment Phase: Analytics and Feedback. Interaction data—including model usage frequency, query topics, and revision patterns–was collected via the instructional platform to support diagnostic analytics. Combined with rubrics assessing modular integration, problem-solving depth, and presentation quality, these insights enabled outcome-oriented evaluation from multiple dimensions.

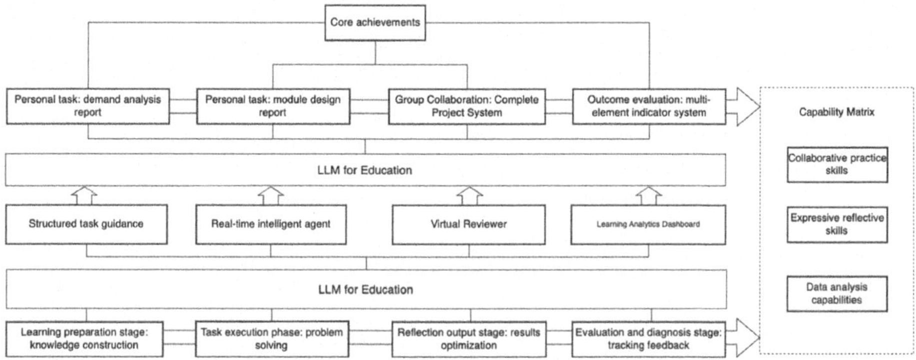

Fig. 2. Empirical framework for LLM-supported PDC-OBE implementation.

Preliminary observations reveal that the integration of LLMs into the PDC-OBE model significantly improves student engagement, promotes computational thinking, and facilitates reflective learning. The multi-modal assessment strategy—including analytics, peer review, and rubric-based scoring—confirms the model's effectiveness in supporting both cognitive development and measurable learning outcomes.

5 Conclusion and Future Work

This study proposes a human-AI collaborative teaching strategy for introductory programming, integrating the PDC-OBE model with LLMs to reshape teaching – learning dynamics. Grounded in demand-oriented problem scenarios, results-driven cognitive outcomes, and practice-centered task design, the model enables learners to engage in real-world, complex problem solving supported by intelligent agents.

Empirical implementation through a sentiment analysis project validates the effectiveness of this approach. The integration of LLMs throughout the learning cycle—scaffolding knowledge construction, supporting problem solving, enabling iterative reflection, and informing assessment—enhanced student engagement, fostered computational thinking, and improved the alignment between learning activities and intended outcomes. Multi-dimensional evaluation combining rubric-based scoring, peer feedback, and learning analytics confirmed both the feasibility and pedagogical value of the model.

Looking ahead, future work will focus on:

1. Model Generalization: Extending the PDC-OBE + LLM framework to other programming paradigms (e.g., object-oriented, data science) and interdisciplinary domains (e.g., intelligent manufacturing, business analytics);
2. Domain-Customized LLMs: Developing lightweight, pedagogically-informed LLMs tailored to specific curriculum content, learning goals, and student profiles;
3. Agent-Oriented Ecosystem: Building a fine-grained, multi-agent support system integrating role-specific agents (e.g., code tutor, ethics advisor, writing assistant) with adaptive feedback mechanisms;
4. Longitudinal Impact Studies: Conducting cross-semester evaluations to investigate sustained learning gains, knowledge transfer ability, and the evolution of learners' cognitive and metacognitive strategies.

This research contributes to the emerging field of human-AI co-teaching and offers practical insights into designing intelligent, scalable, and outcome-aligned instructional ecosystems in the age of AI-enhanced education.

Acknowledgments. The authors would like to acknowledge the help of the editor and anonymous reviewers. This research is supported by Key Research Projects in Higher Education of Dalian Polytechnic University (NO.2025021); Research Education Projects of Dalian Polytechnic University (NO.JGLX2025027);Project of Graduate Education in Liaoning Province (LiaoJiaoTong [2023] No.385-151); High-level Education Research Project Planning Topic (23LK0408); General Project of Liaoning Province 14th Five-Year Plan for Educational Science (JG22DB096); Undergraduate Education and Teaching Reform Research Project of Dalian Ocean University ([2023]No.39).

Disclosure of Interests. The authors have no competing interests to declare that are relevant to the content of this article.

References

1. Chang, Y., et al.: A survey on evaluation of large language models. ACM Trans. Intell. Syst. Technol. **15**(3), 1–45 (2024)
2. Wang, D., et al.: From human-human collaboration to human-AI collaboration: designing AI systems that can work together with people. In: Extended abstracts of the 2020 CHI conference on human factors in computing systems, pp. 1–6 (2020)
3. Spady, W.G.: Outcome-Based Education: Critical Issues and Answers. ERIC (1994)

4. Krathwohl, D.R.: A revision of bloom's taxonomy: an overview. Theory Practice **41**(4), 212–218 (2002)
5. Othman, N., Saat, E.H.M., Muhamad, N.A., Anuar, N.H.K., Majid, M.A.: The development an outcome base education (OBE) system for measuring student Programme attainment. J. Comput. Res. Innovation **9**(2), 177–187 (2024)
6. Tjandra, E., Ferdiana, R., Kusumawardani, S.S.: Strategic implementation of outcome-based education. Contemporary Educ. Res. J. **14**(2), 120–132 (2024)
7. Thomas, J.W.: A review of research on project-based learning (2000)
8. Jabbar, R.A., Abd Halim, N.D.: The impact of project-based learning through integrating the use of technology in computer science courses on students' acquisition of programming skills. Innovative Teach. Learn. J. **8**(1), 1–14 (2024)
9. Zou, L., Chen, D.: Construction of deep learning model based on digital learning and innovation literacy -take python programming teaching as an example. In: Proceedings of the 2024 International Symposium on Artificial Intelligence for Education. pp. 634–638. ISAIE '24, Association for Computing Machinery, New York, NY, USA (2024). https://doi.org/10.1145/3700297.3700406, https://doi.org/10.1145/3700297.3700406
10. Economou, D., Bouki, V.: Serious games design for higher education: aligning bloom's taxonomy, cognitive theory of multimedia learning, and gamification for effective learning. Springer International Publishing (2025)
11. Chen, G., Zhao, Q., Rong, P., Li, Z., Bei, K.: Comparing the design cognitive process between problem-driven and solution-driven industrial design students. Int. J. Technol. Des. Educ. **33**(2), 557–584 (2023)
12. Fang, Y., Wang, M.h., Xiu-yan, Z., Shao, L., Wei-zhen, W.: Research on project-based learning of python course for new liberal arts. Softw. Guide **22**(6), 80–84 (2023)

Research on the Practice of a Three-Dimensional Teaching Innovation System Empowered by AI in the Java Programming Course

Ze Yang(✉), Xuejuan Chen, and Yali Shao

Guangdong Technology College, ZhaoQing 526199, GuangDong, China
yangze@gdlgxy.edu.cn

Abstract. Against the backdrop of new engineering education construction, the teaching of the "Java Programming" course faces multiple challenges, including the disconnection between learning and application, the monotony of evaluation methods, and the obvious differences in students' ability levels. This study conducts an in-depth analysis of the problems existing in the traditional linear teaching model in terms of knowledge transmission, ability cultivation, and technological application. Based on constructivist learning theory and intelligent education paradigms, this research proposes an AI-empowered teaching innovation system named "Project Chain - Hierarchical Learning - Intelligent Assessment" to address the above challenges. Rooted in the "One Core, Seven Wings" teaching model, this innovative system aims to achieve the collaborative development of knowledge imparting, ability cultivation, and ideological and political education by comprehensively enhancing teaching quality. Guided by the "Six Dimensions, Three Realms" framework, the classroom reform plan meticulously designs the curriculum structure—from teaching objectives to specific content—to achieve the goals of knowledge transmission, ability cultivation, and value shaping for students. Meanwhile, by reconstructing the three-level capability stages of "Basic Grammar - Logical Modeling - System Implementation" and integrating real industrial cases with curriculum ideology and politics elements, the system enables personalized learning path planning, stratified teaching, and precise teaching intervention. The establishment of a multi-dimensional dynamic evaluation system comprehensively assesses students' knowledge, abilities, and qualities. Practical results demonstrate that this innovation system has significantly improved students' code debugging efficiency and project documentation standardization while enhancing the course's high-quality performance rate, providing a valuable exploration of intelligent pathways for curriculum reform in programming courses within the new engineering education framework.

Keywords: Java programming · AI empowerment · One core and seven wings · Six dimensions and three realms

W. Hong et al. (Eds.): ICCSE 2025, CCIS 2761, pp. 206–218, 2026.
https://doi.org/10.1007/978-981-95-7731-6_17

1 Background and Problem Analysis of Curriculum Reform

With the vigorous development of the information technology industry, the demand for software engineering professionals has surged, and the requirements for programming capabilities have become increasingly stringent. As a core course in software engineering, Java Programming shoulders the important task of cultivating students' programming thinking and engineering practice capabilities [1]. However, the traditional teaching model has frequently encountered problems in meeting modern industrial needs and urgently requires innovation.

Through nearly three years of follow-up research and teaching data analysis, the curriculum team has found that the learning conditions of freshmen in software engineering are complex. Most students have a weak programming foundation before enrollment and lack a deep understanding of key knowledge. Although some students show strong interest in the course, they develop feelings of fear and difficulty due to the abstract nature of grammar. There are significant differences in their learning habits: they have low enthusiasm for online pre-class preparation but high participation in puzzle-solving exercises on specific platforms [2]; they are prone to distraction during traditional lecture sessions in class but actively engage in PBL (problem-based learning) discussion sessions, while demonstrating insufficient initial project practice capabilities.

In response to this current situation, the curriculum team has proposed the "Project Chain - Hierarchical Learning - Intelligent Assessment" system. This system drives learning through projects, implements stratified teaching according to ability levels, and leverages AI-powered intelligent assessment to accurately identify students' weak areas, dynamically adjust teaching strategies, effectively enhance students' programming abilities and engineering practice literacy, and achieve precise alignment between teaching objectives and industrial needs. Through this system, students can not only master core programming skills but also cultivate the ability to solve complex engineering problems and develop good habits of autonomous learning and lifelong learning.

Practical evidence shows that this Teaching model has effectively ignited students' learning interest and enhanced course participation, laying a solid foundation for cultivating high-quality software engineering talents. The curriculum team will continuously optimize the "Project Chain - Hierarchical Learning - Intelligent Assessment" system, deepen the application of AI-empowered teaching, refine stratified teaching strategies, and strengthen project practice links to ensure that every student can achieve optimal growth through personalized learning paths [3]. Through continuous iteration and feedback, the team strives to maximize teaching effectiveness and contribute more wisdom and practical experience to software engineering education reform.

The curriculum team will further integrate cutting-edge industrial resources, optimize AI-assisted teaching tools, refine student capability profiles, and accurately position personalized needs to ensure that teaching strategies are updated in sync with industrial dynamics, comprehensively enhancing students' innovative and practical abilities to support the high-quality development of new engineering education. The team will continue to deepen industry-university-research cooperation, introduce real enterprise project cases, strengthen students' hands-on experience, build a teaching ecosystem seamlessly connected to industries, promote the deep integration of curriculum content with market demands, and achieve organic alignment among the education chain, talent chain, and industrial chain—injecting sustained momentum into new engineering education.

In the teaching of software engineering at application-oriented undergraduate institutions, Java Programming faces prominent contradictions [4]. The traditional teaching process fails to accommodate the needs of students at different proficiency levels, delayed learning situation diagnosis due to insufficient technical application makes it difficult to stimulate higher-order thinking, and the current assessment mechanism is disjointed from professional literacy cultivation. The single evaluation method overlooks core vocational competencies, experimental report feedback is untimely, and the curriculum does not align with industry standards—resulting in students with good in-school grades but poor job adaptation abilities, which runs counter to the educational mission [5]. Given these issues, introducing new teaching models and innovative classroom reform plans has become imperative to break through teaching bottlenecks and improve educational quality.

To address these teaching contradictions, urgent adoption of innovative teaching models and classroom reform plans is required to resolve bottlenecks and enhance educational quality. Through optimizing curriculum design, strengthening practical components, and improving evaluation systems, we aim to achieve effective integration of knowledge transmission and vocational capability cultivation, ensure that students' comprehensive qualities are highly aligned with job requirements, and return to the essence of education.

2 Construction of Three Dimensional Teaching Innovation System

2.1 Course Content Refactoring

The Java Programming course has undergone a systematic reconstruction of its teaching content, forming a three-level capability advancement system of "basic grammar - logical modeling - system implementation". Each stage integrates real industrial cases and curriculum ideology and politics elements to construct a trinity curriculum structure of "knowledge learning - ability cultivation - value shaping".

In the basic grammar stage, the course uses the "personal income tax calculator" project as a carrier, combined with Math class applications and formatted output exercises, to cultivate students' comprehensive application ability of basic grammar knowledge (e.g., data types) and strengthen the craftsmanship spirit of rigor and truth-seeking. In the logical modeling stage, teaching focuses on the "library management system", guiding students to improve object-oriented programming and data structure optimization capabilities through UML class diagram design and Lambda expression application, while integrating privacy protection education. In the system implementation stage, the course connects with real enterprise projects (e.g., smart home control systems), organizing full-process full-stack development practices to cultivate complex system design capabilities, with special emphasis on algorithm optimization, energy consumption control, and green computing concepts to foster students' ideals of serving the country through technology.

This progressive curriculum design helps students systematically build a programming knowledge system and enhance engineering thinking and patriotic sentiment. The course evaluation introduces a multi-dimensional feedback mechanism (student self-evaluation, peer review, and teacher comments), deepens industry-university-research cooperation, dynamically updates teaching content to ensure mastery of cutting-edge skills, and cultivates high-quality talents with innovative and practical abilities through diversified assessments (Fig. 1).

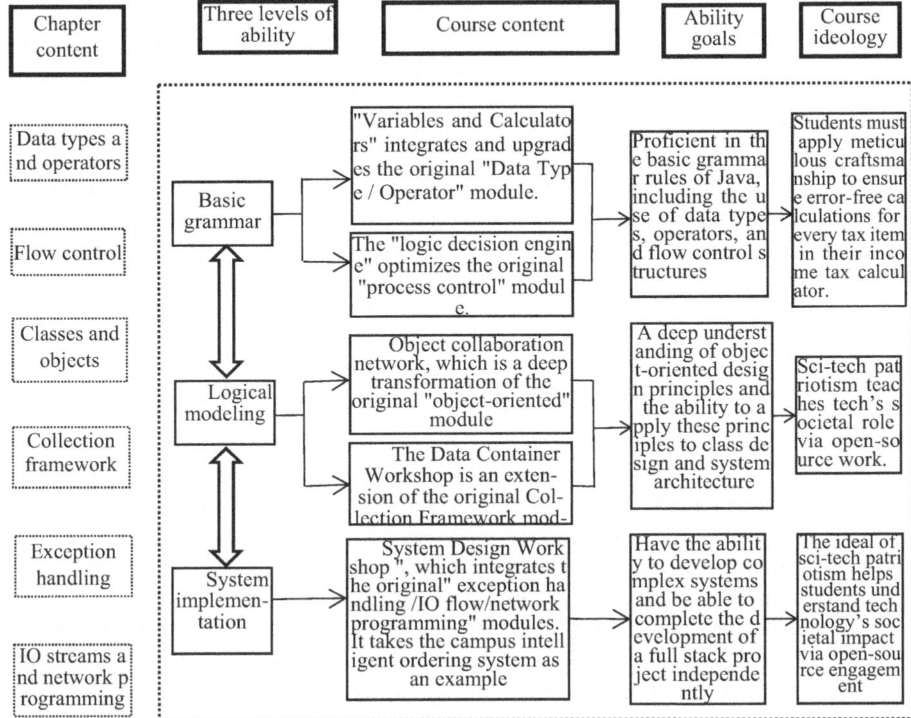

Fig. 1. Course content reconstruction

2.2 Reform of Teaching Methods

In the cutting-edge exploration of computer basic education reform, this study systematically addresses key issues in traditional teaching processes such as cognitive barriers, learning participation inertia, and delayed evaluation, focusing on the standards of "high-levelness, innovativeness, and challenge" in curriculum construction. Through five years of continuous iteration and practice, a reform framework centered on the main line of "three-dimensional goal reconstruction – multi-pattern innovation" has been gradually constructed, forming a teaching innovation system with demonstration significance as shown in Figs. 2 and 3. A blended teaching framework has been established with the core of "all-round optimization of teaching quality orientation and collaborative development of seven-dimensional capabilities," achieving the organic integration of knowledge imparting and ability cultivation. A classroom reform plan based on the "six-dimensional design elements and three-fold education realms" is proposed to deepen the integration of the learning process and value guidance, and promote the collaborative enhancement of interdisciplinary integration and students' innovative capabilities.

The "One Core, Seven Wings" teaching model takes the all-round optimization of teaching quality as its core guiding principle, dedicates to achieving the collaborative development of seven-dimensional capabilities, and constructs an organically integrated blended teaching system. Here, the "One Core" refers to the overall improvement of teaching quality, which runs through the entire teaching process and serves as the core goal of the model. The "Seven Wings" cover seven key domains: knowledge transmission, ability cultivation, ideological and political education, interesting experiments, teaching material development, online MOOCs, and process-oriented assessment.

In terms of knowledge transmission, the model helps students solidly master the core knowledge system of Java Programming through systematic combing and optimized integration of teaching content. The ability cultivation dimension focuses on nurturing students' programming thinking, practical operation skills, and problem-solving abilities, emphasizing the enhancement of comprehensive literacy through real-world project practices. The ideological and political education dimension organically integrates ideological and political elements into professional teaching—for example, when teaching code specifications, guiding students to establish a rigorous and responsible professional spirit and a sense of patriotism.

The interesting experiments dimension stimulates students' learning interest and autonomous exploration motivation by designing challenging and engaging experimental projects, enabling them to deepen their understanding of knowledge in a relaxed and pleasant environment. The teaching material development dimension emphasizes dynamic content updates and structural optimization to make teaching materials closer to industrial realities and student needs, effectively supporting teaching reforms. The online MOOCs dimension fully expands learning resources and channels to meet students' diverse and autonomous learning needs.

The process-oriented assessment dimension breaks through the traditional single summative evaluation model, focuses on comprehensive assessment of the entire learning process, covers multiple aspects such as classroom performance, homework completion, and project practice, and strives to comprehensively and accurately reflect students' learning outcomes, achieving the deep integration of knowledge and ability cultivation.

Fig. 2. The "One Core, Seven Wings" Teaching Model

The "Six Dimensions, Three Realms" classroom reform plan is based on multi-dimensional teaching design, pursuing three educational realms of knowledge transmission, ability cultivation, and value shaping. It aims to deepen the integration of the learning process and value guidance, and promote the collaborative development of interdisciplinary integration and innovative capabilities. The design of the six dimensions includes teaching objectives, teaching content, teaching methods, teaching evaluation, teaching resources, and teaching environment, striving to systematically and comprehensively improve classroom teaching quality. In terms of teaching objective design, the plan not only clarifies the cultivation requirements for knowledge and skills but also focuses on setting objectives for processes and methods, as well as emotional attitudes and values, ensuring that teaching objectives are systematic and targeted. Teaching content design emphasizes the close integration of theory and practice. By introducing real corporate cases and integrating cutting-edge industrial dynamics into classroom teaching, it enhances students' application awareness and practical capabilities. In teaching method design, it advocates the use of diverse approaches such as flipped classrooms and problem-based learning (PBL) to stimulate students' learning initiative and innovative thinking.

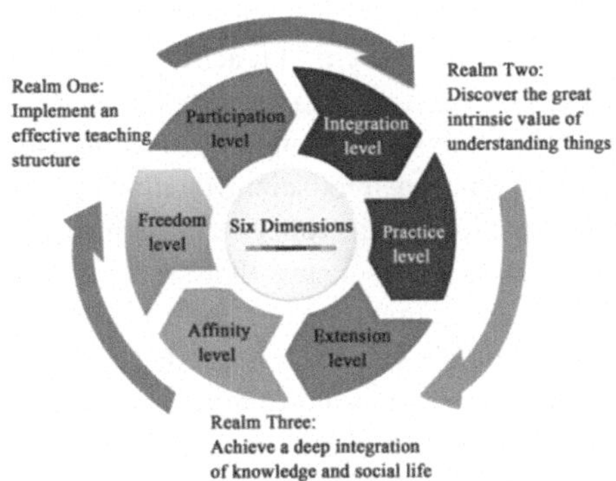

Fig. 3. The "Six Dimensions, Three Realms" Classroom

2.3 Reform of Curriculum Teaching Content and Organizational Implementation

The teaching content of this course systematically covers core modules such as the basic grammar of the Java language, object-oriented programming concepts, design and application of classes and objects, use of common class libraries and standard APIs, as well as exception handling and debugging techniques [6]. In the process of teaching organization and implementation, the course is closely integrated with the "One Core, Seven Wings" teaching model and the "Six Dimensions, Three Realms" classroom reform plan to promote the deep integration of teaching content and teaching methods, fully achieving the systematic optimization of the teaching system and the continuous improvement of teaching effects (Fig. 4).

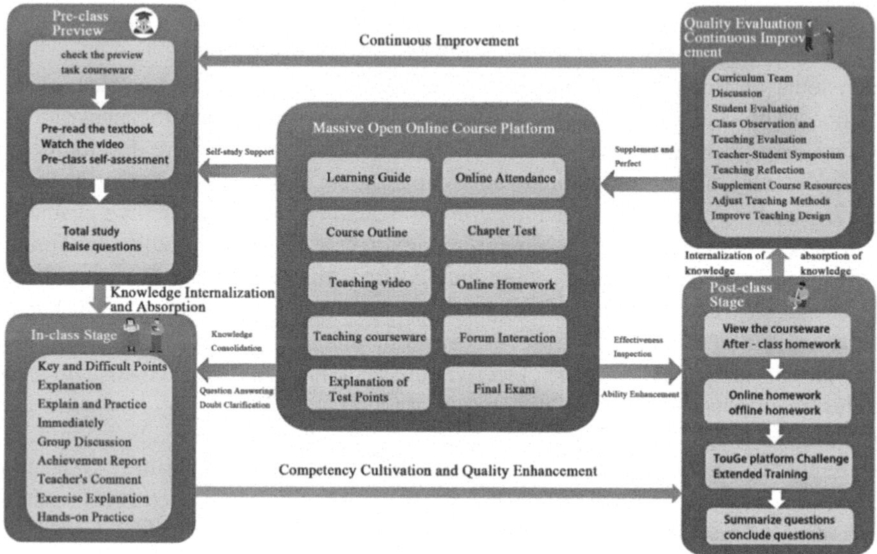

Fig. 4. Organizational Implementation of Teaching Content

Taking the comprehensive improvement of teaching quality as the core goal, namely the "One Core", this course gives full play to the synergistic role of the "Seven Wings" in all teaching links to construct a systematic and multi-dimensional teaching system. In terms of knowledge transmission, teachers scientifically reconstruct the teaching content according to the three-level ability advancement path of "basic grammar—logical modeling—system implementation" to ensure that students systematically master the core knowledge system of the Java language. For ability cultivation, relying on practical teaching platforms such as "TouGe", students are guided to exercise programming ability and problem-solving ability through real project-driven approaches. The course also emphasizes the integration of ideological and political education, organically incorporating content related to professional ethics and social responsibility into case teaching of system implementation to strengthen students' sense of mission and value identity (i.e., the ideological and political education dimension).

In the design of interesting experiments, challenging projects such as developing small games are used to enhance students' learning enthusiasm and programming interest (i.e., the interesting experiment dimension). To align with teaching content updates and industry requirements, the course team compiles supporting textbooks to timely supplement cutting-edge technical knowledge and typical engineering cases (i.e., the teaching material construction dimension). In teaching resource development, online MOOC systems are built using platforms such as "Rain Classroom" and "MOOC" to expand students' learning channels and meet personalized and diversified learning needs (i.e., the online MOOC dimension). In assessment, the course adopts a process-oriented evaluation mechanism, comprehensively considering students' classroom performance, homework completion, and project practice results to ensure comprehensive and dynamic feedback on their learning processes.

Through multi-dimensional teaching design and implementation, the course not only improves students' professional skills but also cultivates their comprehensive qualities, laying a solid foundation for future career development. The course also focuses on interdisciplinary integration, combining basic knowledge of mathematics, physics, etc., to deepen students' understanding of programming logic and enhance their cross-domain problem-solving abilities. Through interdisciplinary case analysis, students' ability to comprehensively apply knowledge is cultivated, and their innovative thinking and practical application abilities are strengthened. At the same time, the course emphasizes the cultivation of teamwork and communication skills, enhancing students' spirit of teamwork and communication skills through group project cooperation.

Based on the teaching practice of the "Six Dimensions, Three Realms" concept, systematic design is carried out from six aspects: teaching objectives, teaching content, teaching methods, teaching evaluation, teaching resources, and teaching environment, striving to achieve three educational goals of knowledge transmission, ability cultivation, and value shaping. At the teaching objectives level, specific requirements for students' knowledge mastery, ability development, and comprehensive literacy in each teaching stage are clarified. For example, in the logical modeling stage, while focusing on guiding students to master object-oriented design principles, their awareness of personal information protection is enhanced.

In terms of teaching content, emphasis is placed on the combination of theory and practice. Typical cases such as "library management systems" and "smart home control systems" are carefully selected to enhance the practical significance and application value of teaching. In teaching methods, diverse strategies such as flipped classrooms and problem-based learning (PBL) are flexibly used to stimulate students' learning initiative and spirit of inquiry. The teaching evaluation system adopts a multi-component approach, comprehensively examining students' comprehensive performance in knowledge mastery, programming practice, teamwork, etc., to ensure the comprehensiveness and scientificity of evaluation.

In teaching resources, high-quality online and offline resources are integrated to expand students' learning channels and provide multi-level learning support. Teaching environment construction focuses on creating an open and interactive classroom atmosphere to encourage active student participation and collaboration. Through the above teaching implementation paths, the course effectively guides students from mastering basic knowledge to gradually improving comprehensive abilities, and ultimately achieving the internalization and sublimation of values, helping them grow into high-quality applied talents with professional literacy and social responsibility.

Personalized Learning Path Planning and Intelligent Diagnosis. Knowledge Graph Construction: Based on curriculum standards and enterprise needs, a Java knowledge graph is established, incorporating multiple knowledge points and competency indicators. The Rain Classroom platform collects 23 dimensions of data, including pre-class preview behavior, video viewing duration, test question accuracy rate, in-class interaction (e.g., bullet chat keywords, question-answering time), post-class homework code submission frequency, and error type distribution. The LSTM algorithm is applied to predict learning outcomes. For 32% of students with weak foundations, personalized learning plans are automatically generated—for example, students struggling with polymorphism receive animated demonstrations of "inheritance chain memory allocation" and three micro-case tasks on the Touge Practice Platform for level-breaking practice. When students first log into the system, they complete a pre-test, and the AI system generates an initial knowledge graph based on the results, marking weak areas. After completing each learning unit, the system automatically updates the knowledge graph and dynamically adjusts recommended resources.

AI-Assisted Layered Progressive PBL Teaching. In today's education landscape, the application of artificial intelligence (AI) technology is gradually transforming traditional teaching models. The AI-empowered layered progressive project-based learning (PBL) teaching model represents an innovative educational approach that integrates the advantages of AI technology with PBL teaching concepts. This model aims to achieve personalized teaching content, intelligent teaching processes, and precise evaluation of teaching outcomes through intelligent means.

The AI-empowered layered progressive PBL teaching model achieves precise stratification of students' learning abilities through intelligent analysis of their learning data. Using machine learning algorithms, the system can identify students' strengths and weaknesses in different subjects and skills, thereby providing customized learning paths for each student. Such personalized learning plans ensure that students can progress at their own pace while engaging with learning materials at difficulty levels suitable for their capabilities.

Secondly, AI technology acts as a tutor and guide in the teaching process. Through natural language processing (NLP) and speech recognition technologies, AI can interact with students in real time, providing instant feedback and guidance. For example, an AI teaching assistant can answer students' questions, offer problem-solving approaches, and even adjust teaching strategies based on students' responses to ensure they fully understand the course content.

The AI-empowered layered progressive PBL teaching model also leverages big data analysis and predictive models to optimize teaching content and pacing. By analyzing large volumes of learning data, the AI system can predict potential difficulties students may encounter during learning and proactively prepare corresponding teaching resources and strategies to help them overcome obstacles. Additionally, the AI system can dynamically adjust teaching plans according to students' learning progress and comprehension levels, ensuring that teaching content always matches their abilities.

Finally, AI technology plays a critical role in evaluating students' learning outcomes. Through intelligent assessment systems, teachers can monitor students' progress in real time, identifying and addressing issues encountered during learning. AI assessment systems not only provide quantitative score evaluations but also offer qualitative feedback to help students understand their learning status and guide them on how to improve.

The AI-empowered layered progressive PBL teaching model creates a more efficient, interactive, and personalized learning environment through personalized learning paths, real-time interactive tutoring, dynamic adjustment of teaching content, and precise learning outcome evaluation. This model not only stimulates students' interest in learning but also significantly enhances teaching quality and learning efficiency. With the continuous development of AI technology, future education will become more intelligent and personalized, delivering higher-quality educational resources and learning experiences for students (Fig. 5).

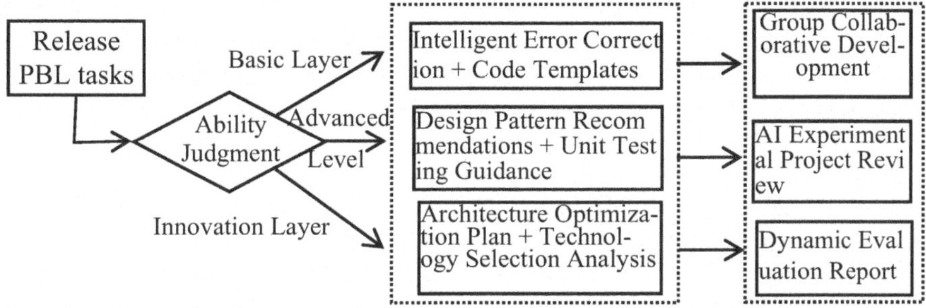

Fig. 5. Layered Progressive PBL Teaching Model

Intelligent Evaluation and Dynamic Feedback System. Multi-Dimensional Engineering Competency Assessent: Quantitative scoring is conducted across dimensions such as code standardization (naming conventions, comment rate), design quality (class coupling, cohesion), and exception handling (coverage, rationality). By recording behaviors like debugging breakpoint settings and variable monitoring operations, the effectiveness of debugging strategies is evaluated. Within 3 min of homework submission, a diagnostic report is generated, including a code heatmap (red areas indicate high-frequency errors), a list of refactoring suggestions, and links to weak knowledge points.

3 Teaching Evaluation Reform

3.1 Innovation of Evaluation Concepts

The learning outcomes of students are taken as the starting point and foothold of teaching evaluation, with a comprehensive focus on the comprehensive improvement of students in knowledge, ability, and quality. It not only pays attention to students' mastery of knowledge but also focuses on examining their ability to use knowledge to solve practical problems, as well as the professional literacy and values cultivated in the learning process. At the same time, the concept of "value-added evaluation" is introduced, emphasizing the extent of students' learning progress and development potential, rather than simply judging success or failure by final learning outcomes.

3.2 Construction of a Multi-Dimensional Evaluation Index System

To break through the limitations of traditional single-examination evaluation, the constructed multi-dimensional and hierarchical evaluation index system covers three dimensions:

Knowledge Dimension: Online tests and offline written exams are used to assess mastery of Java basic grammar, object-oriented programming concepts, data structures, and other knowledge. Meanwhile, Java programming tasks in enterprise business scenarios are set to evaluate knowledge transfer and application capabilities.

Ability Dimension: Relying on an intelligent evaluation system, programming practice capabilities are assessed from aspects such as code complexity, repetition rate, and exception handling. In PBL teaching, students' problem analysis and solving abilities are observed. Team collaboration and communication skills are evaluated through team peer review, teacher evaluation, and team project outcome assessment. Programming innovation is encouraged, with attention paid to students' dedication when facing complex problems.

Quality Dimension: Focus is placed on professional norms, examining the standardization of software development processes such as code comments and document writing. Students' innovative thinking is evaluated—such as whether they proactively propose novel solutions—along with their stress resistance and iterative capabilities when facing technical challenges. Sensitivity to Java technology trends and learning willingness are assessed through tasks like industry case analysis.

These three dimensions complement each other, forming a three-dimensional evaluation system of "underlying knowledge → mid-level skills → high-level values," which aligns with the needs of cultivating (composite talent.

3.3 Comprehensive Application of Multi-Dimensional Evaluation Methods

A variety of evaluation methods are comprehensively used to ensure the comprehensiveness, objectivity, and fairness of evaluation. The proportions of each evaluation item are shown in Table 1:

Table 1. Multi-Dimensional Evaluation Methods.

Evaluation type	proportion	Specific ways
formative evaluation	50%	Class performance evaluation (teacher's self-evaluation and mutual evaluation, 10%) Homework and experiment evaluation (automatic scoring by intelligent evaluation system and manual review by teacher, 20%) Project process evaluation (stage report, group discussion and teacher guidance, 20%)

(*continued*)

Table 1. (*continued*)

Evaluation type	proportion	Specific ways
summarized evaluation	30%	Final exam (closed, basic knowledge, 15%) Course project evaluation (inviting enterprise experts to participate, 15%)
Value-added evaluation	20%	Compare the learning outcomes at the beginning and end of the course, assess the level of knowledge, ability and quality before and after the test, and combine the data of the learning process

3.4 Establishing Timely and Effective Evaluation Feedback Mechanisms

In terms of teaching evaluation feedback, after each evaluation, students should receive detailed evaluation reports containing scores for each evaluation indicator, strengths and weaknesses, and targeted improvement suggestions. Students are organized to discuss evaluation results, enabling them to clarify their learning status, identify areas for improvement, and actively raise questions or suggestions to facilitate teacher-student communication.

Teac hers must analyze evaluation data to understand students' learning progress and teaching effectiveness, adjusting teaching content and methods promptly to optimize the teaching process in response to common issues. Regular teaching seminars are held to share teaching experiences and evaluation results with colleagues, collectively discussing challenges in teaching and exploring solutions.

Additionally, industry experts are invited to participate in course evaluation and teaching guidance to promptly grasp enterprises' needs and expectations for students. Curriculum content and teaching objectives are then adjusted based on corporate feedback, ensuring teaching aligns more closely with real-world industry requirements.

4 Conclusions and Prospects

This study focuses on addressing challenges in Java Programming curriculum teaching, such as the disconnect between learning and application, one-sided evaluation, and significant stratification of students' abilities. It introduces the "One Core, Seven Wings" teaching model and the "Six Dimensions, Three Realms" classroom reform plan, proposing an AI-empowered three-dimensional teaching innovation system of "project chain - stratified learning - intelligent evaluation." The "One Core, Seven Wings" teaching model takes the all-round optimization of teaching quality as its core, achieving collaborative development across seven dimensions including knowledge transmission, ability cultivation, and ideological and political education. Within the reconstructed three-level ability framework of "basic grammar - logical modeling - system implementation," real industrial cases and curriculum ideology elements are embedded to help students build knowledge systems and shape values. The "Six Dimensions, Three Realms" classroom reform plan meticulously designs classrooms across six dimensions to achieve the goals of knowledge transmission, ability cultivation, and value shaping. Combined with AI technology, it enables personalized learning path planning, dynamic grouping, and precise teaching intervention, constructing a multi-dimensional dynamic evaluation system. Practice has proven that this innovative system effectively improves students' code debugging efficiency, project document standardization, and significantly enhances the course's excellent performance rate, providing a practical intelligent solution for programming course reforms in the new engineering education context. Looking ahead, the study will further deepen the integration of AI technology and curriculum ideology, expand interdisciplinary project practices, optimize intelligent evaluation systems, and continuously improve teaching paradigms. By fully leveraging the advantages of the "One Core, Seven Wings" teaching model and the "Six Dimensions, Three Realms" classroom reform plan, it will provide more universal and forward-looking support for cultivating new engineering talents.

Acknowledgments. This study was funded by the Education and Teaching Reform Project of Guangdong Provincial Quality Engineering (2023–1106), The Demonstration Course Project of Curriculum Ideological and Political Reform of Guangdong Technology College Quality Engineering (SFKC202402) and Guangdong Technology College-Level Course Teaching and Research Section Construction Project (KCJYS202503).

References

1. Jiang, S.X.: Exploration and practice of curriculum reform for "Advanced Language Programming" through science-education integration and industry-education collaboration. Microcomputer (11), 274–276 (2024)
2. Yuan, J., Li, S.Q.: Research on teaching reform of "Java Advanced Programming" course in the context of artificial intelligence. Sci. Informatization **3**, 133–135 (2023)
3. Lv, J.B.: Promoting teaching reform of "Fundamentals of Programming" aimed at competency cultivation. Ind. Inf. Technol. Educ. **2024**(4)
4. Xu, Z.H., Lv, H., Ma, J.H., et al.: Teaching reform practice on engineering competency cultivation for C++ object-oriented programming. Comp. Educ. **2024**(4), 70–74
5. Pu, J.H., Shen, A.R., Wang, Y.H.: Data-driven teaching reform and practice of programming courses. Comp. Educ. **2024**(2), 128–135
6. Xie, G.F., Xie, J.Y.: Discussion on teaching reform of "C Language Programming" based on "Integration of Teaching, Learning and Practice." Ind. Inf. Technol. Educ. **1**, 55–57 (2023)

An Agent-Driven Programming Learning Support System Based on Proactive Insight Agent

Haojie Shi[1], Haoran Yang[3], Wenyi Xie[1], Ruobin Wang[1,2](✉), and Fengxia Li[4]

[1] School of Artificial Intelligence and Computer Science, North China University of Technology, Beijing, China
robin945@163.com

[2] Beijing Key Laboratory on Key Technologies for AI+ Domain Applications, Beijing 100144, China

[3] Brunel London School, North China University of Technology, Beijing, China

[4] School of Computer Science and Technology, Beijing Institute of Technology, Beijing, China

Abstract. Programming learning is of paramount importance for students in computer-related disciplines. However, conventional learning approaches often suffer from inefficiencies and delayed feedback. This paper designs and implements an intelligent programming learning support system based on a Proactive Insight Agent (PIA). Beyond providing fundamental features such as online code editing, execution, and testing, the system's core innovation lies in introducing a PIA-driven cognitive error correction mechanism and proactive dialogue intervention. The PIA can perceive learners' behavioral patterns in real-time, analyze their learning states, and, upon detecting potential learning impasses, proactively initiate context-aware dialogues by deeply integrating with Large Language Models (LLMs). These dialogues guide learners through cognitive reflection and error rectification. This paper elaborates on the system's design philosophy, architecture, and the implementation of its core functionalities. Furthermore, it demonstrates the system's potential in assisting learners to overcome programming obstacles and enhance learning efficiency through illustrative examples.

Keywords: Intelligent Tutoring Systems · Proactive Insight Agent · Personalized Learning · Programming Education · Large Language Model · Real-time Feedback

1 Introduction

Programming stands as a core competency within the discipline of Computer Science and Technology. However, beginners often encounter confusion and frustration during their programming learning journey due to the abstract nature of

H. Shi and H. Yang—Contributed equally.

W. Hong et al. (Eds.): ICCSE 2025, CCIS 2761, pp. 219–231, 2026.
https://doi.org/10.1007/978-981-95-7731-6_18

concepts, complex logic, and a lack of timely and effective personalized guidance [1]. While traditional online learning systems offer abundant learning resources, they predominantly function as static knowledge repositories [2]. They struggle to proactively discern individual learner differences and provide targeted, process-oriented guidance [3].

To address these challenges, researchers have begun exploring the application of artificial intelligence (AI) technologies, particularly Large Language Models (LLMs), to programming education [4,5]. LLMs demonstrate significant potential in code comprehension, generation, and dialogue, enabling the development of more intelligent learning support tools. Nevertheless, many existing LLM-based learning support tools remain predominantly"reactive". This reactive approach, while helpful, often fails to capture learners' difficulties at their nascent stages. Early Intelligent Tutoring Systems (ITS), built on expert systems and cognitive modeling, were often limited by the complexity of knowledge base construction and inflexible interaction, struggling to understand a learner's true intent or subtle cognitive shifts. Even with the advent of LLMs, many contemporary tools still function as passive assistants. They respond only when a student explicitly asks a question or submits code for evaluation. This model misses crucial opportunities for preemptive guidance, failing to intervene when a learner is merely hesitating, stuck in a loop of minor ineffective edits, or silently deviating from a viable solution path. Our work on the Proactive Insight Agent (PIA) is designed specifically to bridge this gap, shifting from a reactive paradigm to a proactive one that anticipates and addresses learning impasses before they lead to significant frustration.

This paper proposes and implements an intelligent programming learning support system based on a PIA. The core innovation of the system lies in its PIA architecture. The PIA aims to proactively perceive learners' programming behaviors and learning states. By leveraging the cognitive and generative capabilities of LLMs, it initiates guided dialogues at critical junctures to assist learners in "cognitive error correction," thereby enhancing the depth and efficiency of learning. The system incorporates a foundational online programming environment but places greater emphasis on deepening learners' understanding of programming concepts and problem-solving strategies through intelligent interaction.

The primary contributions of this system are:

- The proposal and preliminary implementation of a learning support framework driven by the Proactive Insight Agent (PIA).
- The design of an LLM-integrated **cognitive error correction mechanism** that guides student reflection through context-aware dialogues.
- The implementation of a **proactive dialogue intervention** function that provides timely assistance when learners encounter potential difficulties.

2 Related Work

Research on Intelligent Tutoring Systems (ITS) spans several decades, aiming to emulate human tutoring behaviors and provide learners with personalized support [6]. Early ITS implementations predominantly relied on expert systems and cognitive modeling [7], though they exhibited limitations in comprehending complex cognitive states and delivering adaptable instructional guidance.

Advancements in machine learning and natural language processing (NLP) catalyzed the emergence of data-driven ITS as a significant research focus. These systems leverage learner behavioral data—such as code submissions, error patterns, and debugging traces—to construct student models and refine pedagogical strategies [8], thereby enhancing the precision of instructional interventions [9].

The advent of Large Language Models (LLMs) has introduced transformative potential for ITS. LLMs demonstrate capabilities in natural language understanding, code generation, logical explanation, and preliminary error diagnosis [4]. Contemporary research explores conversational programming tutoring systems [10] powered by LLMs, simulating interactive dialogues between programming tutors and students [11]. Nevertheless, as noted previously, most existing systems remain fundamentally reactive, responding only to explicit user queries.

Proactivity represents an emerging paradigm in intelligent learning support systems. Proactive learning support systems seek to anticipate learner difficulties by analyzing behavioral data and inferred cognitive states, enabling preemptive intervention with contextually appropriate guidance [12]. The Proactive Insight Agent (PIA) framework proposed in this work builds upon this paradigm. By integrating LLM capabilities, PIA emphasizes deep insights into the learning process to deliver anticipatory, personalized guidance, with particular focus on advancing methodologies for cognitive error correction.

To synthesize our review of the field, Table 1 provides a comparative analysis of different programming learning support paradigms. This comparison highlights the key distinctions in intervention style, feedback focus, and ultimate pedagogical goals, positioning our Proactive Insight Agent (PIA) within the landscape of existing technologies.

This comparison underscores the novelty of our PIA-based system. By shifting from a reactive to a proactive stance and focusing on the learner's cognitive journey, our approach aims to address the fundamental limitations identified in prior systems, thereby fostering a more effective and empowering learning experience.

3 Design and Implementation

The system employs a frontend-backend decoupled architecture. The frontend handles user interaction and presentation, while the backend manages business logic, data persistence, and integration with external AI services (e.g., LLM APIs). Central to this architecture is the PIA, which permeates system layers to monitor learner behavior, perform analytical decision-making, and drive pedagogical interventions.

Table 1. Comparison of Learning Support System Paradigms.

Aspect	Traditional ITS	Reactive LLM Tutors	Our Proactive Insight Agent (PIA)
Intervention Style	Rule-based and pre-scripted. Triggered by specific, known errors.	Reactive and user-initiated. Responds to explicit questions or code submissions.	**Proactive and system-initiated.** Autonomously detects learning impasses from behavior.
Feedback Focus	Primarily on syntactic and logical errors against a known solution.	Code-level correction, explanation of concepts, and direct answers.	**Cognitive process and self-reflection.** Guides learners to identify their own misconceptions.
Context Awareness	Limited to predefined student models and problem states.	Session-based. Aware of the immediate conversation and submitted code.	**Deep and dynamic.** Analyzes real-time coding patterns, hesitation, and error iteration.
Pedagogical Goal	Mastery of specific concepts and successful problem completion.	Answering immediate queries and providing solutions or scaffolds.	**Development of metacognitive skills** ("learning to learn") and problem-solving proficiency.
Key Limitation	Rigid, difficult to scale, and often struggles with novel problems.	Lacks initiative; may not help a learner who does not know what to ask.	Relies on the quality of the LLM; potential for distraction if not carefully triggered.

The PIA framework is conceptualized through five hierarchical layers:

- **Perception Layer**: Collects multimodal behavioral data including code edits, execution results, error logs, AI dialogue history, and hint access patterns.
- **Memory & Knowledge Layer**: Maintains domain knowledge bases (programming concepts, canonical solution steps), dynamic learner models (historical performance, knowledge gaps) and pattern recognition repositories derived from interaction analytics.
- **Thinking & Decision Layer**: Performs real-time analytics on Perception Layer inputs against Knowledge Layer states. Generates intervention strategies upon detecting:
  1. Prolonged inactivity at specific problem-solving stages
  2. Recurrent error patterns in code iterations
  3. Significant deviations from expected solution trajectories
- **Action & Interaction Layer**: Executes guidance through UI prompts and dialogues.
- **Reflection & Learning Layer**: Optimizes strategies based on intervention outcomes.

The conceptual relationship and data flow between these layers are illustrated in Fig. 1.

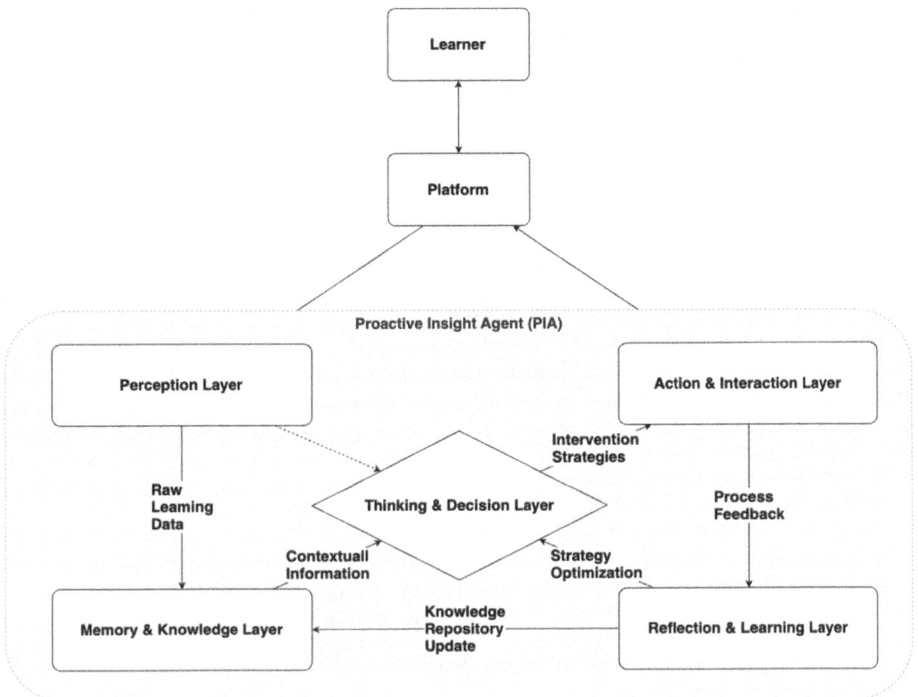

Fig. 1. High-level system architecture diagram illustrating components: Frontend, Backend, PIA Core, LLM Service, Database, and their interactions.

3.1 Programming Environment and Core Functionality

The system provides a fully functional online programming environment built upon Monaco Editor, offering essential capabilities including syntax highlighting and auto-completion for mainstream languages such as JavaScript and Python. Within this environment, learners can dynamically write, modify, and execute code. Problem descriptions and initial code templates are loaded upon topic selection, accompanied by optional step-by-step solution hints. Learners may validate implementations through custom test case execution or formal submission to predefined test suites, receiving immediate feedback on outcomes (pass/fail status, error diagnostics, and output comparisons). A dedicated progress navigation panel dynamically tracks advancement by mapping the learner's current code implementation against predefined problem-solving milestones, providing real-time contextual awareness of their developmental stage within the solution workflow.

3.2 Thought Error Correction Mechanism

Cognitive Error Correction serves as the cornerstone pedagogical strategy of this platform, designed to fundamentally address learners' conceptual misconceptions. When learners manifest potential cognitive impasses—whether through active help-seeking or system-monitored proactive interventions (detailed in Sect. 3.3)—the platform engages the following mechanisms to facilitate deep reflection. This approach transcends superficial code correction to foster comprehension of underlying cognitive biases:

LLM-Driven Scaffolded Dialogue. As the core methodology for cognitive refinement, the platform leverages deep integration with LLMs to enable context-aware, heuristic dialogues characterized by:

- **Socratic Questioning Techniques**: LLMs are engineered to withhold direct solutions, instead guiding learners through structured inquiries for self-discovery (e.g., "What functional purpose did you intend for this loop in your code?"; "Which segment of your code might correlate with the observed error message?").
- **Promotion of Self-Articulation**: Learners are encouraged to verbalize problems, explain code logic, and articulate solution approaches—enhancing conceptual organization while supplying diagnostic data to the LLM.
- **Granular, Stepwise Progression**: Dialogues commence with macro-level queries, progressively narrowing to specific code segments or logical nodes, thereby transitioning vague "cognitive blockages" into analyzable sub-problems.

Critical Phases of Cognitive Remediation.

- **Induction of Cognitive Dissonance**: Through targeted questioning, LLMs highlight inconsistencies between learners' reasoning and problem requirements or programming paradigms, stimulating conceptual conflict as a catalyst for knowledge reconstruction [13].
- **Guided Error Attribution**: Learners systematically categorize errors as conceptual misunderstandings, logical flaws, or implementation oversights, enabling precise corrective measures.
- **Conceptual Clarification & Knowledge Restructuring**: Upon detecting misconceptions about core programming concepts (e.g., recursion, data structure properties, algorithmic principles), LLMs deliver concise explanations, contextual examples, or curated learning resources to rebuild knowledge foundations.
- **Cultivation of Metacognitive Awareness**: By consistently guiding learners to evaluate their reasoning processes, monitor comprehension, and assess solution efficacy, the platform implicitly develops metacognitive competencies—equipping learners to "learn how to learn" and "think about thinking."

This entire workflow, from detection to metacognitive development, is depicted in Fig. 2.

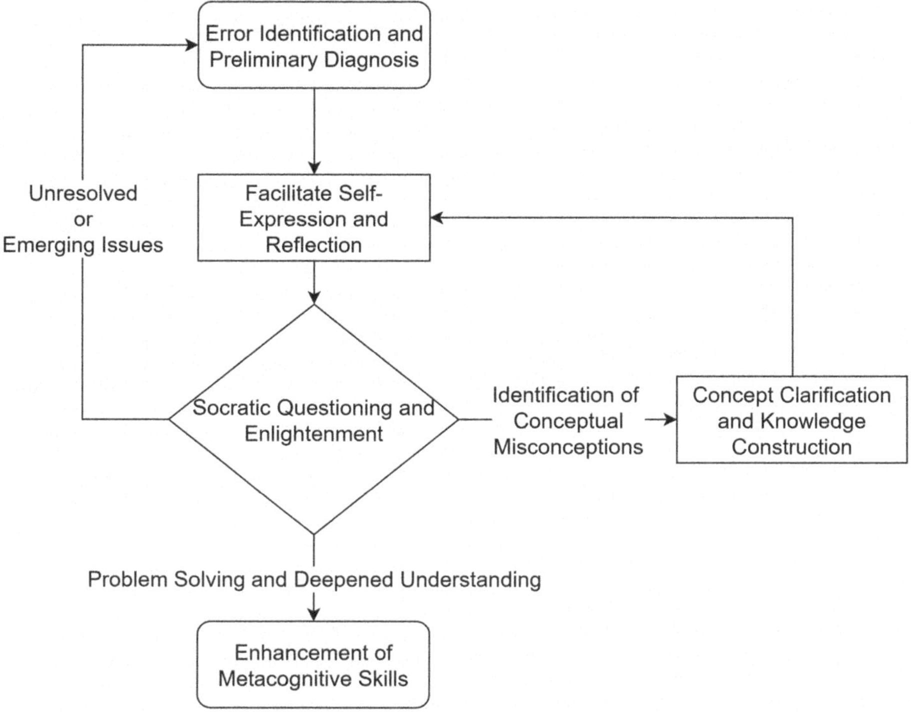

Fig. 2. Cognitive error correction workflow: Error Detection → Contextualization → Guided Reflection → Conceptual Reinforcement → Metacognitive Development.

The ultimate objective of this mechanism is to empower learners—not merely to solve immediate problems, but to master analytical and debugging methodologies that advance autonomous learning and problem-solving proficiency.

3.3 Proactive Dialogue and Intervention

Diverging from conventional tutoring tools reliant on learner-initiated requests, our platform's PIA autonomously initiates dialogues under predefined conditions. This capability enables earlier intervention in potential learning impasses, provides timely support, and may activate the cognitive error correction process detailed in Sect. 3.2.

Necessity of Proactive Intervention. Novice learners often struggle to self-diagnose assistance needs or hesitate to seek help. Proactive intervention delivers scaffolding support when confusion emerges before full frustration sets in, thereby sustaining learning motivation and flow states.

Behavior-Based Impasse Detection. PIA's perception layer continuously monitors programming behaviors and contextual data. Key indicators for identifying potential impasses include:

- **Persistent Error Duration/Frequency**: Recurring compilation/runtime errors unresolved beyond a threshold (e.g., 3 consecutive minutes).
- **Ineffective Code Iterations**:High-frequency minor modifications to the same code segment indicating trial-and-error guessing.
- **Significant Solution Path Deviation**:Real-time progress tracking shows prolonged misalignment with predefined solution milestones or core logic.
- **Extended Inactivity**:Abnormal pauses at critical phases (e.g., problem comprehension, algorithm design, debugging).

Intelligent Trigger Mechanism with State Machine. To ensure timely intervention while minimizing disruption, an internal state machine (Fig. 3) governs trigger logic (Table 2).

Table 2. State machine definitions for proactive intervention.

State	Condition
`Normal`	No significant impasse detected.
`ErrorDetected`	Initial detection of warning-triggering behavior.
`ErrorPersistent`	Error state persists >30 s with ongoing modification attempts.
`ChatTriggered`	Conditions met for dialogue initiation.
`Cooldown`	Post-intervention quiet period (>5min) preventing recurrence.

State transitions occur when behavioral patterns satisfy predefined rules (e.g., migration from `ErrorPersistent` to `ChatTriggered` requires cooldown expiration and no active system-initiated dialogue).

3.4 Context-Aware Dialogue Initiation

Upon transitioning to `ChatTriggered`, PIA executes:

1. **Context Aggregation**: Collects learning context (problem ID, current code, step diagnosis, impasse analysis).
2. **System Instruction**: Issues invisible LLM directive: `[SYSTEM] User struggles with [identified impasse]. Generate natural, encouraging opener to gently offer guidance.`
3. **LLM-Generated Opener**: Produces empathetic initiation: *"Hi! I notice you've been working on the bracket validation problem, particularly the closing-bracket logic. Would exploring this together help find a new approach?"*

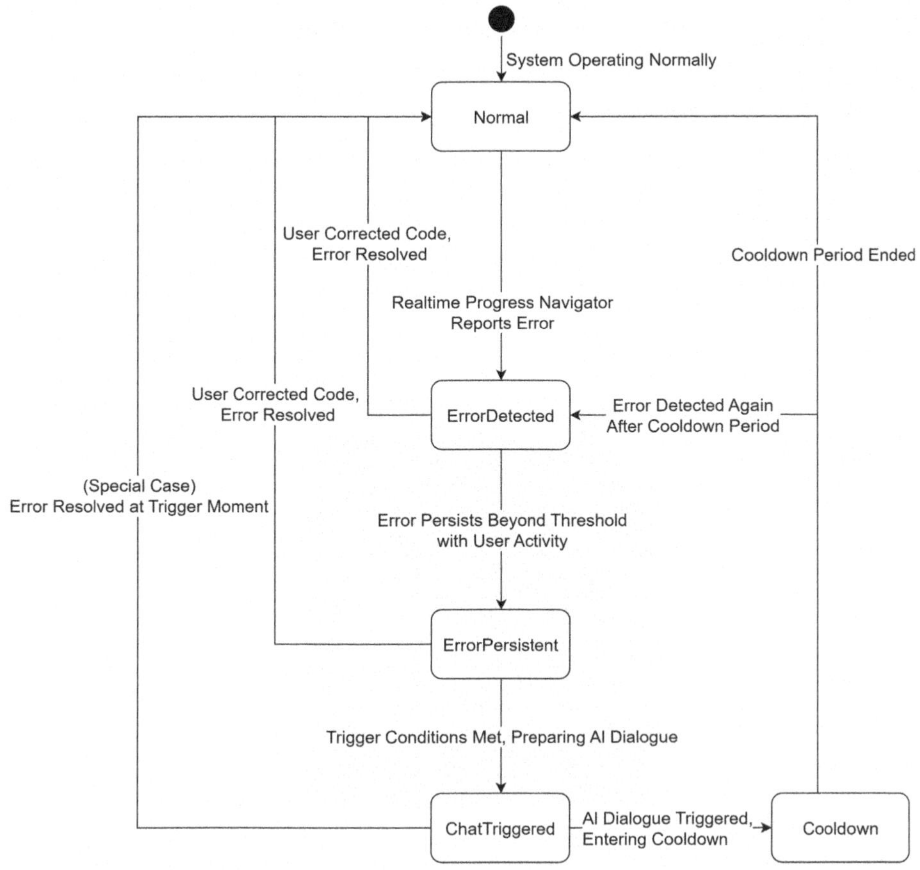

Fig. 3. State transition diagram for proactive intervention triggers.

4. **Guided Continuation**: Enables transition into cognitive error correction (Sect. 3.2).

This *contextually intelligent intervention* delivers support at optimal moments, minimizing disruption while maximizing pedagogical efficacy.

4 Application Example

To concretely demonstrate the system's core functionality, we present a learning scenario centered on the classic bracket matching problem. This example illustrates the learner's workflow within the system and elucidates how the PIA delivers assistance through its proactive dialogue and cognitive error correction mechanisms.

4.1 Core Code Editing and Progress Tracking

Upon selecting the bracket matching problem, the interface (Fig. 4) presents a tripartite layout comprising:

1. A left-hand pane containing the problem repository and detailed description.
2. A central workspace featuring the code editor with integrated development tools.
3. A right-hand panel consolidating the AI-assisted dialogue module, testing/execution controls, and real-time progress tracker.

Fig. 4. System interface architecture: Problem repository (left), code editor (center), and multifunctional workspace (right) containing AI dialogue and progress tracking components.

As the learner begins coding, the real-time progress tracker dynamically highlights the most relevant problem-solving milestones—such as "1. Initialize Stack" and "2. Traverse Input String"—based on the evolving implementation.

4.2 Proactive Intervention and Cognitive Error Correction Demo

Consider a scenario where the learner encounters difficulties implementing closing-bracket matching logic. Despite repeated code revisions, validation fails for test cases (e.g., '[()]') with errors indicating flawed stack operations. The PIA's monitoring subsystem detects this persistent error state and ineffective iteration pattern.

Upon meeting trigger conditions, the AI chat panel autonomously activates, displaying an LLM-generated conversational prompt as shown in Fig. 5.

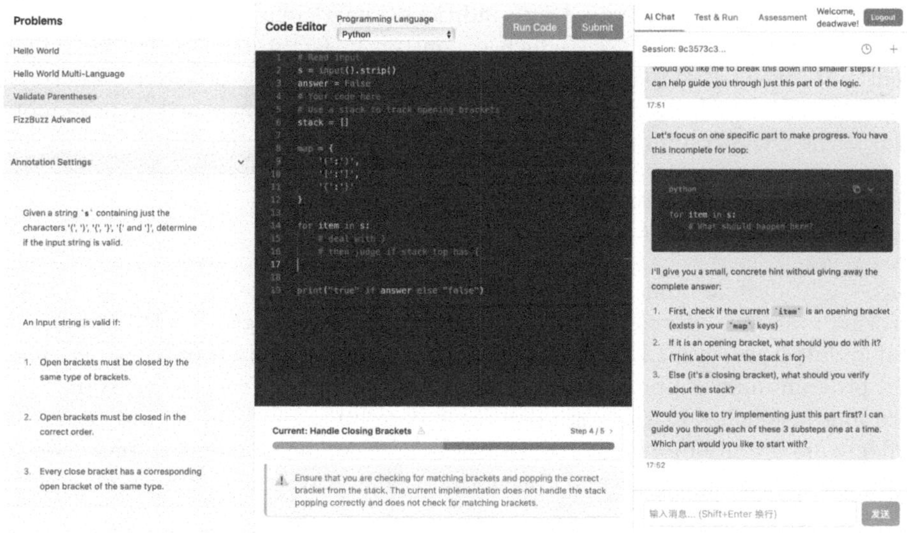

Fig. 5. AI-initiated dialogue: "I notice challenges with stack operations. Could you share your approach?"

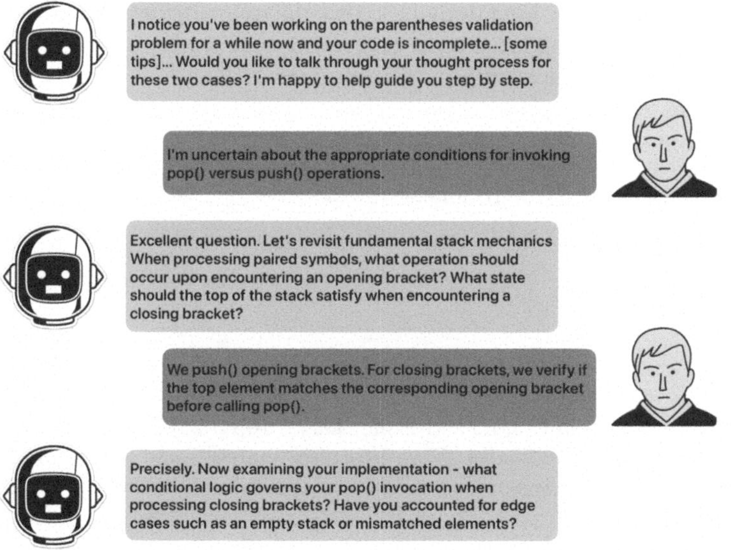

Fig. 6. A structured guidance dialogue between a learner and AI.

Following the learner's response, the system initiates a structured guidance dialogue. Through this scaffolded dialogue, the AI systematically guides the learner through critical examination of their implementation logic, enabling identification of unaddressed boundary conditions—particularly empty stack scenarios and element mismatches—which concurrently facilitates conceptual refinement and corrective implementation adjustments. A sample of such a structured guidance dialogue between the learner and the AI is shown in Fig. 6, demonstrating how the system guides the user from uncertainty to clarity.

5 Conclusion

This study designs and preliminarily implements an intelligent programming tutoring system centered on the PIA framework. By integrating PIA's conceptual architecture with LLM capabilities, the system delivers proactive, personalized programming support that transcends conventional reactive assistance. Its core innovation lies in the cognitive error correction mechanism and proactive dialogue intervention, which engage deeply with learners' cognitive processes to scaffold reflective thinking and conceptual refinement—moving beyond superficial solution provision.

Preliminary application scenarios demonstrate the system's efficacy in helping learners identify and overcome programming cognitive barriers, showing significant potential for enhancing both learning efficiency and educational experience. Future work will focus on: refining PIA's perceptual acuity and decision-making algorithms, enriching domain knowledge repositories [2] and pedagogical strategies [8], conducting large-scale user validation studies, and exploring granular personalization in learning path recommendations.

Acknowledgement. This work is supported by Beijing College Students Innovation and Entrepreneurship Training Project 2025 and Research Project on Party Building of North China University of Technology 2025.

References

1. Fan, G., Liu, D., Zhang, R., et al.: The impact of AI-assisted pair programming on student motivation, programming anxiety, collaborative learning, and programming performance. Int. J. STEM Educ. **12**(1), 16 (2025)
2. Papamitsiou, Z., Economides, A.A.: Learning analytics and educational data mining in practice: a systematic literature review. Educ. Technol. Soc. **17**(4), 49–64 (2014)
3. Denny, P., Prather, J., Becker, B.A., et al.: Computing education in the era of generative AI. Commun. ACM **67**(2), 56–67 (2024)
4. Jošt, G., Taneski, V., Karakatič, S.: The impact of large language models on programming education and student learning outcomes. Appl. Sci. **14**(10), 4115 (2024)
5. Kasneci, G., Sessler, K., Küchemann, S., et al.: ChatGPT for good? On opportunities and challenges of large language models for education. Learn. Individ. Differ. **103**, 102274 (2023)
6. Nwana, H.S.: Intelligent tutoring systems: an overview. Artif. Intell. Rev. **4**(4), 251–277 (1990)

7. Anderson, J.R., Corbett, A.T., Koedinger, K.R., Pelletier, R.: Cognitive tutors: lessons learned. J. Learn. Sci. **4**(2), 167–207 (1995)
8. Piech, C., Sahami, M., Koller, D., Cooper, S., Blikstein, P.: Modeling how students learn to program. In: Proceedings of the 46th ACM Technical Symposium on Computer Science Education, pp. 491–496. ACM, Kansas City (2015)
9. Loksa, D., Margulieux, L., Becker, B.A., et al.: Metacognition and self-regulation in programming education: theories and exemplars of use. ACM Trans. Comput. Educ. **22**(4), 1–31 (2022)
10. VanLehn, K.: The relative effectiveness of human tutoring, intelligent tutoring systems, and other tutoring systems. Educ. Psychol. **46**(4), 197–221 (2011)
11. Graesser, A.C., Chipman, P., Haynes, B.C., Olney, A.: AutoTutor: an intelligent tutoring system with mixed-initiative dialogue. IEEE Trans. Educ. **48**(4), 612–618 (2005)
12. Sheng, Y., Hu, H., Cheng, X., et al.: A web-based visual learning platform for data structure course. In: Proceedings of the 16th International Conference on Computer Science & Education (ICCSE 2021), pp. 86–91. IEEE, Lancaster (2021)
13. Yin, R.K.: Case Study Research and Applications: Design and Methods, 6th edn. Sage Publications, Thousand Oaks (2018)

Practice Teaching Reform of Software Engineering Specialty Under the Background of "AI + New Engineering"

Yunhua Wang(✉) and Shuguang Tao

Wuhan University of Technology, Wuhan 430070, China
yhwang@whut.edu.cn

Abstract. With the relentless advancement and continuous evolution of artificial intelligence (AI) technology, its integration and application within the realm of software engineering specialty have witnessed an exponential growth. This paper endeavors to undertake a comprehensive and in-depth exploration of the multifaceted applications of AI in the practical teaching methodologies of software engineering. It seeks to meticulously construct "one body, two wings" architectural framework, alongside a multi-tiered and holistic practical teaching system, specifically tailored for software engineering within the progressive context of the "New Engineering" paradigm. The paper proposes a versatile and dynamic practical teaching model that is characterized by its multi-subject engagement, multi-channel delivery, and multi-stage progression. This model is fundamentally grounded in the synergistic collaboration between academic institutions and industry partners, leveraging the benefits of internships, and embedding the principles of innovation and entrepreneurship education. By drawing upon the rich and diverse teaching practices inherent to this specialized major, the paper elucidates a series of strategic approaches, conceptual ideas, and practical methods that are pivotal for driving the reform of practical teaching. These insights are meticulously examined from various critical perspectives, including the reform of the practical teaching system, the integration of innovation and entrepreneurship into practical education, the fostering of school-enterprise cooperation within the new engineering landscape, and the strategic development and construction of a proficient dual-qualified teacher team. Through these comprehensive analyses, the paper aims to provide a road-map for enhancing the efficacy and relevance of practical teaching in software engineering specialty, thereby bridging the gap between theoretical knowledge and real-world application.

Keywords: Practical teaching · artificial intelligence · new engineering · software engineering

1 Background

In 2018, the Ministry of Education of China officially promulgated the "Action Plan for AI Innovation in Higher Education Institutions", marking the official launch of new engineering construction and AI innovation plans. In the current society, professionals

W. Hong et al. (Eds.): ICCSE 2025, CCIS 2761, pp. 232–242, 2026.
https://doi.org/10.1007/978-981-95-7731-6_19

in software engineering have always been highly sought after, with a persistent high demand for them [1]. At the same time, this major imposes strict requirements on the practical abilities of its talents. Under the new era of "AI + New Engineering", software engineering faces numerous new requirements. Facing these new requirements, how to transform and upgrade the traditional practical teaching and training models of software engineering has become an urgent issue to be addressed [2, 3].

In recent years, numerous experts and scholars have conducted extensive and fruitful explorations in this field. They have conducted multi-dimensional research on new engineering, with some delving deeply into its connotation and characteristics [4, 5], others proposing innovative suggestions for teaching model reforms based on the core competencies required by new engineering [6], and still others focusing on specific issues such as the reform of computer majors, software curriculum teaching models, and engineering management practical education under the background of new engineering [7–9]. Meanwhile, the rapid development of AI will undoubtedly bring profound changes to new engineering construction. Reference 10 suggests leveraging the power of AI to drive new engineering education reform practices [10]; Reference 11 emphasizes the need to deeply explore the intrinsic connections between AI development and new engineering construction, using AI development as an opportunity to propel new engineering construction to new heights [11]. Additionally, researchers have explored the "AI + New Engineering" innovation and development model from the unique perspective of innovation and entrepreneurship education [12, 13]. These diverse research findings provide valuable references and insights for our systematic study of practical teaching reform and talent training strategies in software engineering under the background of "AI + New Engineering" [13, 14].

2 Software Engineering Practical Teaching Architecture

Under the new perspective of "AI + New Engineering", the practical teaching system of software engineering can be constructed as a "one body, two wings" architecture (see Fig. 1). Here, "one body" represents the core content of practical teaching in software engineering, while "two wings" respectively embody the new requirements and characteristics brought about by the integration of new engineering and AI. Figure 1 visually displays the "new elements" covered by the practical teaching of software engineering under the background of "AI + New Engineering".

The integration of AI and new engineering has revolutionized the landscape of software engineering education. Traditional practical teaching methods, which primarily focused on coding and algorithm implementation, are now being augmented by AI technologies and new engineering paradigms. This transformation is not only a response to the rapid advancements in technology but also a strategic move to prepare future software engineers for the challenges and opportunities of the digital age.

The integration of AI into practical teaching has led to the development of intelligent tutoring systems and personalized learning platforms. These tools leverage AI algorithms to analyze students' learning behaviors and provide tailored learning resources and feedback, thereby enhancing learning efficiency and outcomes. Furthermore, AI technologies enable the simulation of complex software engineering scenarios, providing students with hands-on experience in solving real-world problems and fostering their practical abilities and innovative thinking.

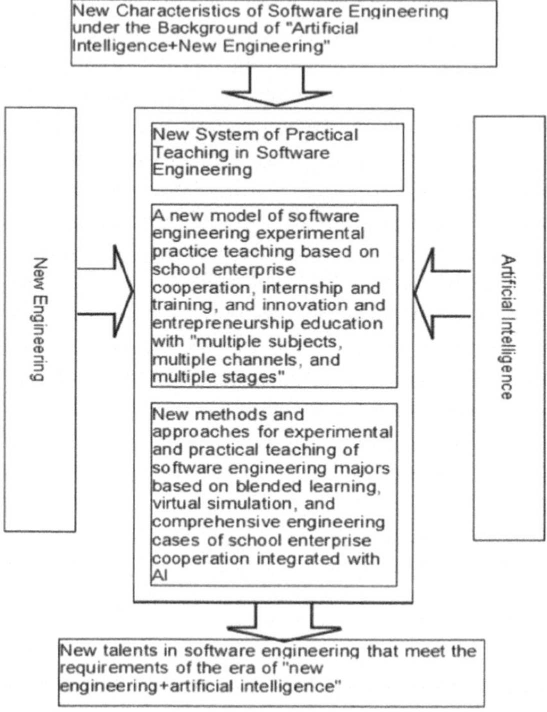

Fig. 1. Software Engineering Practical Teaching Architecture

2.1 Establishing New Concepts for Practical Teaching

The integration of new engineering and AI requires software engineering practical teaching to establish new concepts. This includes strengthening the abilities to analyze and solve complex software problems, data analysis, teamwork and communication, innovation, and lifelong learning. At the same time, attention should be paid to global vision and international exchange and cooperation, integrating new theories and knowledge of AI into practical teaching.

Furthermore, it is essential to continuously update and innovate practical teaching content to keep pace with the rapid development of technology and industry. By integrating the latest scientific research achievements and industrial demands into practical teaching, we can ensure that students are equipped with practical skills and knowledge that are relevant and in demand in the current job market. This approach not only enhances students' employability but also fosters their ability to innovate and solve real-world problems.

Specifically, the new concepts of practical teaching emphasize the following points: First, focus on the deep integration of theory and practice, enabling students to master theoretical knowledge through practical project operations and case analyses, thereby enhancing their ability to solve practical problems. Second, strengthen interdisciplinary cross-integration, encouraging students to explore the intersection points of software engineering with emerging technologies such as AI, big data, and cloud computing, broadening their technical horizons. Third, advocate a student-centered teaching model, stimulating students' learning interests and initiative, and cultivating their habits of autonomous learning and lifelong learning. Additionally, strengthen international exchange and cooperation, introducing advanced international practical teaching concepts and methods to enhance students' international competitiveness.

Moreover, the new concept of practical teaching emphasizes the close integration of practice and theory, encouraging students to deepen their understanding of theoretical knowledge through hands-on operations while continuously exploring and innovating in practice. It also focuses on cultivating students' critical thinking and problem-solving abilities, enabling them to quickly identify and implement solutions when faced with complex software issues. The establishment of this new concept has charted a clear direction for practical teaching in software engineering and laid a solid foundation for cultivating high-quality software engineering talents who can meet the demands of future society.

2.2 Establishing a New Practical Teaching System

Under the new perspective, innovative designs are needed for the content system of practical teaching. The new system should focus on exercising students' engineering qualities and enhancing their practical abilities, incorporating AI-related theoretical knowledge. Through cooperation with enterprises, the content of industry-university cooperation, internships, and other aspects should be improved, strengthening innovation and entrepreneurship practical education and engineering education, and constructing a multi-level and multi-dimensional practical teaching system.

The new system should encompass multiple components such as basic course experiments, specialized course design, corporate internship and training, as well as innovation and entrepreneurship projects. Each component should be closely aligned with the latest development trends in software engineering and artificial intelligence.

In basic course experiments, programming exercises related to AI fundamentals can be incorporated, enabling students to grasp programming skills while understanding the basic concepts and methodologies of artificial intelligence. For specialized course design, students are encouraged to apply AI technologies to solve practical problems in software engineering, such as intelligent requirements analysis and intelligent software testing. The corporate internship and training component involves deep collaboration with enterprises, allowing students to participate in real-world AI software development projects to enhance their practical skills and professional competence. The innovation and entrepreneurship projects encourage students to independently select topics and integrate AI technologies to innovate software products or services, fostering their innovative mindset and entrepreneurial capabilities.

Specifically, the construction of the new system can proceed from the following aspects: First, optimize curriculum settings, adding AI-related course content such as machine learning, deep learning, and natural language processing, enabling students to master the basic theories and key technologies of AI while learning software engineering professional knowledge. Second, strengthen laboratory construction, establishing laboratories that combine AI with software engineering, equipped with advanced experimental equipment and software tools to provide students with a good practical environment. Third, promote school-enterprise cooperation, jointly developing practical teaching projects with enterprises, enabling students to practice in real enterprise environments and enhance their ability to solve practical problems. Fourth, hold innovation and entrepreneurship competitions and practical activities, encouraging students to actively participate and cultivating their innovative consciousness and entrepreneurial abilities. Fifth, strengthen the construction of a dual-qualified teacher team, introducing teachers with enterprise practical experience, and sending existing teachers to enterprises for on-the-job training to enhance their practical teaching abilities.

3 Implementation Paths for the New Practical Teaching System

Under the perspective of "AI + New Engineering", strengthening practical teaching, enhancing engineering practical ability exercises, and cultivating outstanding engineering talents are required. The software engineering practical teaching system includes teaching links such as theoretical course experiments, curriculum designs, project trainings, enterprise internships, innovation and entrepreneurship education, and graduation designs. The modular division of the new system is shown in Fig. 2.

The implementation paths for the new practical teaching system should focus on several key areas. Firstly, it is crucial to update the teaching methodologies, incorporating more interactive and project-based learning approaches. This will allow students to actively engage with the material, apply theoretical knowledge in practical scenarios, and develop their problem-solving skills. Secondly, leveraging modern technology, such as online learning platforms and virtual simulation tools, can enhance the accessibility and flexibility of practical teaching. These tools can provide students with hands-on experience in a risk-free environment, facilitating their understanding and mastery of complex concepts. Moreover, establishing close collaborations with industry partners is essential for providing students with real-world experience and exposure to cutting-edge technologies. Through internships, guest lectures, and joint projects, students can gain insights into industry practices, strengthen their practical abilities, and develop a sense of professionalism and responsibility. Lastly, continuous evaluation and feedback mechanisms should be in place to monitor the effectiveness of the practical teaching system and make necessary adjustments to ensure it remains relevant and effective in nurturing future software engineers equipped with AI and new engineering competencies.

3.1 Hierarchical Progressive Practical Teaching for Software Development Abilities

This module aims to cultivate students' software development abilities and practical hands-on skills, focusing on inheritance and innovation, updating practical content

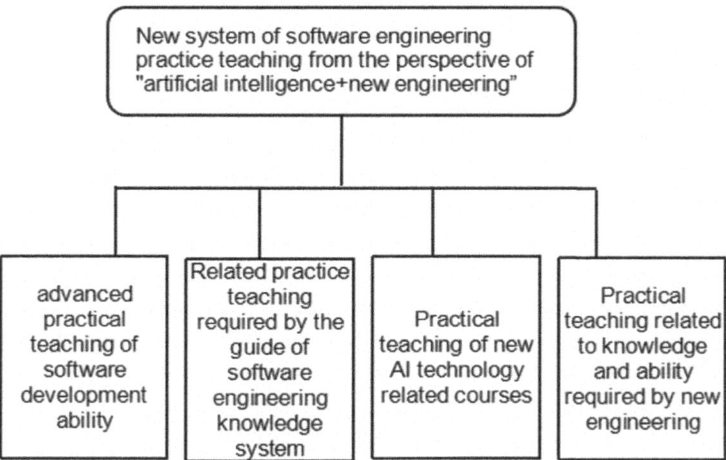

Fig. 2. New system of software engineering practice teaching

designs, and strengthening interdisciplinary cross-integration. With the development of AI, the experimental and practical parts of languages such as Python can be strengthened, and practical content in data analysis can be increased.

At the same time, practice projects of varying difficulty levels are designed for students of different grades and ability levels to ensure that every student can improve at a level suited to them. For example, lower-grade students can start with basic programming and algorithm practice, gradually transitioning to software engineering project development; higher-grade students can participate in more complex software engineering projects, or even engage in innovative practices incorporating artificial intelligence technologies. Additionally, through university-enterprise collaboration, real-world enterprise software development projects are introduced, allowing students to experience the complete software development lifecycle—from requirements analysis, design, and coding to testing, deployment, and maintenance—thereby comprehensively enhancing their software development capabilities.

Software Language Foundation Series Practical Teaching: The practical teaching of basic programming languages includes C language, object-oriented C++, Java, Python, and others. Learning these languages not only provides students with a solid programming foundation but also enables them to gradually grasp different programming paradigms and ideas through practice. In the series of practical teachings for software language fundamentals, we emphasize the integration of theory and practice. By designing a wealth of experimental cases and projects, we allow students to deepen their understanding of language characteristics while solving real-world problems. Meanwhile, we encourage students to attempt integrating AI-related technologies into their basic language practices, such as using Python for simple machine learning model training, thereby broadening their technical horizons and fostering innovative thinking. Through such practical teaching methods, we aspire to cultivate software engineering talents who possess both a solid programming foundation and the ability to apply AI technologies.

Professional Foundation Course Series Practical Teaching: The practical teaching of professional foundational courses includes data structures, operating systems, database principles, compiler principles, and others. Through course design practices, students' understanding and application abilities of theoretical knowledge are deepened.

In the series of practical teachings for professional foundational courses, we also place great emphasis on the tight integration of theory and practice. For example, in the data structures course, various algorithm practice projects are designed to enable students to gain an in-depth understanding of the essence and application scenarios of data structures through hands-on operations. In the operating systems course, students are guided to simulate the design and implementation of operating systems, thereby mastering the core principles and design methodologies of operating systems. In the database principles course, students construct actual database systems to become familiar with database design, management, and optimization techniques. In the compiler principles course, students write simple compilers to gain an in-depth understanding of the working principles and implementation methods of compilers. These practice projects aim to cultivate students' hands-on abilities and problem-solving skills, laying a solid foundation for their subsequent professional studies and career development.

3.2 Practical Teaching According to the Software Engineering Knowledge System Guidelines

This module aims to cultivate students' professional abilities in software engineering and enhance their professional qualities. Through practical exercises based on real enterprise cases, students gain an in-depth understanding of professional course knowledge such as software requirements engineering, software testing, software project management, software processes, and software architectures.

The practical exercises are designed to simulate real-world software engineering projects, allowing students to experience the entire software development lifecycle, from requirements analysis and design to coding, testing, and maintenance. By working on these projects, students can apply the theoretical knowledge they have learned in class to practical situations, deepening their understanding and enhancing their practical abilities. Additionally, these practical exercises emphasize teamwork and communication skills, preparing students for collaboration in future software engineering projects.

Furthermore, practical teaching through virtual simulation not only bridges the gap between theory and practice but also offers a risk-free environment for students to explore and experiment. It allows them to make mistakes in a controlled setting, learn from them, and refine their skills without incurring actual costs or risks associated with real-world projects. This approach fosters creativity and innovation among students, encouraging them to think outside the box and develop unique solutions to complex problems.

3.3 Practical Teaching Related to New AI Technologies

This module focuses on interdisciplinary cross-integration, cultivating students' knowledge literacy in AI through practice. It includes practical exercises for courses such as machine learning, computer vision, big data technology, data mining, natural language processing, and large model principles and applications.

In these practical exercises, students are introduced to cutting-edge AI technologies and encouraged to apply them to solve practical problems. For instance, in machine learning courses, students engage in projects that involve training and evaluating machine learning models using real datasets. In computer vision courses, they develop algorithms for image recognition and object detection. In big data technology courses, students learn to process and analyze large datasets efficiently. Through these hands-on activities, students not only gain a deeper understanding of AI technologies but also develop the skills necessary to integrate them into their future software engineering projects. The practical exercises in this module are designed to challenge students, pushing them to explore new territories and innovate within the realm of AI.

3.4 Engineering Practical Education Required by New Engineering

This module focuses on cultivating engineering practical abilities required by new engineering, including enterprise internships and innovation and entrepreneurship education. Through enterprise internships, students gain an in-depth understanding of industry dynamics and technological development trends; through innovation and entrepreneurship education, students' innovation and entrepreneurship abilities are cultivated.

In recent years, with the rapid development of new engineering fields such as artificial intelligence, big data, and cloud computing, the demand for engineering talents with innovative and practical abilities has increased significantly. Traditional engineering education, which focuses more on theoretical knowledge imparting, has gradually shown its limitations in cultivating talents who can meet the needs of new engineering development. Therefore, it is urgent to reform and innovate the practical teaching mode of engineering education to better adapt to the development trend of new engineering.

4 New Methods and Approaches for Practical Teaching

4.1 Online-Offline Hybrid Practical Teaching

Cloud-based online practical teaching methods can enhance the flexibility and interactivity of the teaching process. For software engineering majors, practical exercises for courses such as software programming and software engineering can all be completed through online practice.

However, purely online practical teaching has its limitations, particularly in terms of hands-on experience and practical skills development. To address these limitations, Online-Offline Hybrid Practical Teaching has emerged as an effective solution. This approach combines the convenience and accessibility of online teaching with the tangible and immersive experience of offline practical sessions. It aims to provide students with a comprehensive learning environment that fosters both theoretical understanding and practical proficiency.

4.2 Virtual Simulation Practical Teaching

Establishing virtual simulation practical environments for certain courses can effectively improve teaching effects. For example, virtual simulation practical projects can be constructed for courses such as algorithm analysis and dynamic demonstration, as well as professional foundation courses like computer composition principles and operating systems.

Through these virtual environments, students can engage in hands-on practice without the limitations of physical resources or space. This approach allows for a more flexible and personalized learning experience. Additionally, virtual simulation can simulate complex scenarios and edge cases that may be difficult or dangerous to replicate in real-world settings, providing students with a comprehensive understanding of the subject matter. Furthermore, by integrating assessment and feedback mechanisms within the virtual environment, teachers can monitor students' progress and provide timely guidance and support.

4.3 Open-Source Software Project Practical Teaching

Utilizing resources from open-source software platforms such as Github, TensorFlow, and OpenCV to carry out software engineering project practical teaching is an excellent teaching method.

In this approach, students engage in hands-on activities by collaborating on real-world software projects. This not only enhances their coding skills but also exposes them to the nuances of teamwork, project management, and version control systems. By working with popular open-source platforms, students gain access to a vast pool of knowledge and community support, facilitating their learning process. Furthermore, the transparency and openness of these platforms encourage students to contribute back to the community, fostering a sense of responsibility and ownership in their learning journey.

4.4 Multi-subject Collaborative Education Comprehensive Practical Teaching

We systematically organize from the perspectives of domain knowledge, curriculum system, and practice projects to design several complex and comprehensive engineering problem cases in software engineering, effectively supporting the practical teaching of the software engineering major. We adopt a multi-participant "new engineering" model suitable for software engineering majors in higher education institutions, integrating industry and education through mechanisms such as the Ministry of Education's industry-university cooperation collaborative education projects, strengthening the construction of practical conditions, and establishing off-campus practice bases. We utilize AI large models throughout the software development lifecycle, from requirements analysis, system design to coding implementation, testing, and maintenance, comprehensively enhancing students' engineering practical abilities. Meanwhile, we encourage deep cooperation between enterprises and universities to jointly develop practical teaching cases, introducing real enterprise projects into the classroom. This enables students to deepen their understanding and application of software engineering knowledge while solving real-world problems.

4.5 Practical Teaching Achievements

Driven by the reform of practical teaching, students actively participate in innovation and entrepreneurship activities such as discipline competitions, such as the ACM International Collegiate Programming Contest, the China College Students Service Outsourcing Innovation and Entrepreneurship Competition, and the China College Students "Internet + " Innovation and Entrepreneurship Competition. Through innovation and entrepreneurship practices, students' practical abilities are exercised, and their employment competitiveness is enhanced.

In the construction of software engineering majors, emphasis is placed on in-depth cooperation with enterprises. Through co-constructing laboratories, internship and training bases, and carrying out joint project research and development, the actual needs and technological frontiers of enterprises are introduced into the teaching process. At the same time, enterprises can also select outstanding talents from the cooperation, achieving a win-win situation for both schools and enterprises.

Professional teachers, in addition to theoretical research, should also consider how to cultivate students' practical abilities in combination with frontier ideas and technologies of AI during the teaching process. More than half of the teachers in our software engineering department should actively cooperate with enterprises, seeking new ways to enhance their professional abilities, such as participating in teacher training programs for the Ministry of Education's industry-university cooperation collaborative education projects.

5 Conclusion

The software engineering major is a highly practical-oriented discipline, deeply rooted in the application of theoretical knowledge to real-world scenarios. Under the innovative perspective of "AI + New Engineering," the practical teaching of software engineering confronts a myriad of new concepts, objectives, and challenges that demand fresh approaches and solutions. In the realm of teaching practices, it is imperative to enhance and refine the existing educational framework, while simultaneously exploring novel teaching models, methodologies, and strategies that align with the evolving landscape of technology and industry demands.

Although this paper has undertaken certain practical explorations within the context of practical teaching under the new paradigm of "AI + New Engineering," and has indeed achieved notable results, there remains a considerable gap when measured against the rigorous construction requirements of the new engineering discipline. This gap underscores the need for ongoing efforts to bridge the divide between current practices and the aspirational standards set by the new engineering framework.

Looking ahead, we are committed to continuing our diligent explorations, striving to continuously improve and perfect the practical teaching system. Our aim is to ensure that the educational experience remains relevant, dynamic, and effective, thereby contributing significantly to the cultivation of more outstanding talents in the field of software engineering. By fostering a robust and innovative educational environment, we aspire to equip future software engineers with the skills, knowledge, and adaptability necessary to thrive in an ever-evolving technological landscape.

Acknowledgments. This study was funded by Teaching Research Project of Wuhan University of Technology (grant number W2023112).

Disclosure of Interests. The authors have no competing interests to declare that are relevant to the content of this article.

References

1. Zhong, D.: The connotation and actions of new engineering construction. High. Eng. Educ. Res. **44**(3), 1–6 (2023). (in Chinese)
2. KaifaZhou, Y.Z.: Exploration of core competencies and teaching models in new engineering. Chongqing High. Educ. Res. **5**(3), 22–35 (2017). (in Chinese)
3. Wang, T., Liu, R.: Talent training program for computer majors under the construction situation of new engineering. Comp. Educ. **90**(2), 10–13 (2022). (in Chinese)
4. Jiang, Z.: Reform of computer majors under the background of new engineering construction. China Univ. Teach. **56**(8), 34–39 (2019). (in Chinese)
5. Leiyang, F., Rao, Y.: Research on software curriculum teaching models under the background of new engineering: Taking Anhui Agricultural University as an example. J. Chongqing Univ. Sci. Technol. (Soc. Sci. Ed.) **22**(10), 116–117 (2022). (in Chinese)
6. Dai, X., Liu, C.: Practical teaching reform of engineering management majors in newly established undergraduate colleges under the orientation of new engineering. Lab. Res. Explor. **38**(12), 221–224 (2019). (in Chinese)
7. Li, D., Ma, N.: New engineering in the intelligent era: AI-driven education reform practices. High. Eng. Educ. Res. **45**(5), 8–12 (2024). (in Chinese)
8. Chen, J., Lv, W.: AI and new engineering talent training: a major turn. High. Eng. Educ. Res. **38**(6), 18–23 (2017). (in Chinese)
9. Tao, X., Yan, L., Yin, J., et al.: Research on the development mode and path of "AI + New Engineering" from the perspective of innovation and entrepreneurship education. Distance Educ. Mag. **16**(1), 80–88 (2018). (in Chinese)
10. Zhang, N., Zhao, Y., Lan, K., et al.: Several thoughts and suggestions on virtual simulation experiments under the background of "New Engineering." Exp. Technol. Manage. **37**(3), 185–188 (2020). (in Chinese)
11. Liang, H., Yang, G., Jian, H., et al.: Construction of a composite laboratory system for AI teaching and research under the orientation of new engineering. Exp. Technol. Manage. **36**(7), 266–269 (2022). (in Chinese)
12. Ye, H., Ni, X., Zhu, Y.: Exploration and practice of engineering training teaching: design and implementation of engineering science frontiers and practice courses. Lab. Res. Explor. **39**(5), 237–239 (2020). (in Chinese)
13. Dai, Y., Li, H., Yangbo, W., et al.: Reform of the "learning-practicing-researching-creating" four-in-one practical teaching system under the background of new engineering. Exp. Technol. Manage. **34**(12), 189–195 (2017). (in Chinese)
14. Wei, W., Yan, D., Song, H., et al.: Innovative practical teaching in software engineering majors at ethnic colleges. Lab. Res. Explor. **36**(2), 226–230 (2017). (in Chinese)

On the Design of AI Teaching Assistants for Algorithm Courses with Integrated Teaching, Learning, Assessment and Practice

Chao Peng, Kecheng Cai(✉), Yaying Guo, and Chenyang Xu

Software Engineering Institute, East China Normal University, Shanghai, China
cpeng@sei.ecnu.edu.cn, 51265902069@stu.ecnu.edu.cn

Abstract. Algorithm courses are fundamental in undergraduate majors related to information technology. However, with the rapid advancement of artificial intelligence, traditional instructional approaches are encountering both new opportunities and challenges. This study investigates the integration of large language model-based teaching assistants into undergraduate algorithm courses, aiming to establish a new instructional framework that combines teaching, learning, assessment, and practice. By designing intelligent teaching processes and developing an AI assistant system capable of providing personalized guidance, real-time feedback, and adaptive learning support, we seek to promote synergy between algorithm education and AI technology. The proposed model is expected to improve students' learning efficiency and foster stronger algorithmic thinking and practical problem-solving skills in the context of AI applications. This work offers theoretical perspectives and practical experience on the transformation of algorithm teaching in higher education.

Keywords: AI teaching assistants · Algorithm courses · Large language models · Intelligent education

1 Introduction

In the era of digital transformation, algorithms play an increasingly important role in the training of professionals across information-related disciplines such as computer science, software engineering, and artificial intelligence. However, traditional approaches to teaching algorithms often reveal limitations, including a gap between theoretical concepts and practical application, limited student engagement, and insufficient personalized support. Recent developments in artificial intelligence, especially large language models, have opened up new possibilities for addressing these challenges [1]. Advanced AI systems such as ChatGPT and DeepSeek demonstrate strong capabilities in natural language processing, providing technical foundations for building intelligent educational tools [2]. Integrating AI into algorithm education holds promise for enhancing teaching quality, promoting equitable access to learning resources, and improving students' practical and innovative abilities [3].

W. Hong et al. (Eds.): ICCSE 2025, CCIS 2761, pp. 243–256, 2026.
https://doi.org/10.1007/978-981-95-7731-6_20

This study explores the deep integration of AI technologies into algorithm course instruction by combining content delivery, learning assessment, and hands-on practice within a unified framework. We focus on designing an AI-assisted instructional model that provides personalized guidance, real-time feedback, and adaptive support to students. The goal is to improve both the effectiveness and efficiency of algorithm teaching while fostering students' algorithmic thinking and practical problem-solving skills. By embedding AI into the teaching process, we aim to support the development of students' foundational skills for further studies in AI-related fields, while also advancing the pedagogical practice of algorithm education in higher education.

2 Mutual Influence of AI and Education

2.1 Research on AI-Empowered Education and Teaching

In recent years, research on the theme of "AI empowerment in education and teaching" has surged significantly. Scholars have systematically and scientifically investigated the integration of AI and big data technologies from various perspectives. Based on the CNKI extended database in Chinese and English, we analyzed trends in research on "AI empowerment in education." As depicted in Fig. 1, research combining AI and education has noticeably increased since 2018, particularly between 2022 and 2025, corresponding precisely with the wave of large language models exemplified by ChatGPT. (The first five months of 2025 alone recorded 1,220 publications, projecting approximately 2,928 publications for the entire year.)

Fig. 1. The number of references related to AI empowerment in education and teaching, from 2016 to 2025, based on data retrieved from CNKI extended database in Chinese and English.

Numerous studies suggest that the most significant value of AI in education lies in its ability to tailor learning experiences based on individual needs [1, 4]. AI technology can analyze extensive data concerning students' performance, preferences, and learning styles to craft customized educational paths that suit their unique needs. For instance, researchers in [5] emphasized that AI can adapt educational materials and methods automatically to various learning conditions, significantly improving students' comprehension and application skills in diverse contexts. This transformation challenges traditional "one-size-fits-all" education, allowing educators to deliver more precise and impactful teaching [6]. Additionally, AI systems can detect students' strengths and weaknesses, enabling educators to provide more targeted support and accurate predictions [1, 3].

In addition to supporting personalized instruction, AI-based virtual assistants have the potential to enhance student engagement by facilitating more interactive learning experiences. Through the incorporation of adaptive feedback and elements such as gamified tasks, AI systems can help increase students' attention and participation. As noted in [7], the use of human-like instructional strategies enabled by AI may improve interactivity and learner satisfaction, which in turn contributes to higher engagement levels. These developments allow instructors to shift their focus from unidirectional content delivery toward creating more collaborative and student-centered learning environments.

Furthermore, AI technology optimizes educational efficiency by streamlining administrative tasks, providing educators with additional time for student interactions and support. For example, automated assessment systems quickly evaluate assignments and offer immediate feedback, critically optimizing learning processes [8]. This efficiency reduces teachers' workloads, allowing them to build deeper interpersonal relationships with students.

Some researchers have examined the integration of artificial intelligence into education, with particular attention to its effectiveness, ethical implications, and the potential challenges it poses [9]. These studies emphasize the importance of responsible AI application and its role in supporting educational equity. While existing literature recognizes the increasing relevance of AI in formal educational settings and identifies it as a key area of development [1, 3, 9], relatively little attention has been paid to its application in the teaching of algorithm courses, thus this study seeks to address this gap.

2.2 Education as a Driver of AI Advancement

Education is not merely a passive recipient of AI technology; it actively drives the evolution of AI itself. In particular, education scenarios demand that models represent knowledge more accurately, understand contextual information more effectively, and respond to prompts in a more refined manner to support interaction with different types of learners [18, 19]. These have promoted progress in model expressiveness, alignment with human instructions, and adaptation to domain-specific knowledge [20].

In addition, the application of AI in education goes beyond solving short-term tasks. Teachers and students increasingly expect AI systems to provide real-time tutoring, continuous feedback, and long-term learning support [21]. To meet these expectations, AI systems need to enhance their capabilities in real-time observation, process analysis, and formative assessment. There is also a growing need to implement mechanisms such as long-term memory and personalized learning plans in practical educational scenarios [22]. These requirements from educational practice are influencing the development of the next generation of AI systems, making them more focused on human needs and specific contexts.

However, several aspects of AI-assisted education remain underexplored. Most current evaluation methods rely on text or dialogue [23], typically analyzing students' written answers or interactions in conversation. This leaves out other important parts of the learning process, such as reading, comprehension, and hands-on practice. To provide a more complete understanding of student learning, there is a need for more systematic research and evaluation frameworks. In this study, we propose an evaluation system for programming education, aimed at capturing a broader range of student behaviors and learning interactions.

3 Theoretical and Technological Foundations of AI-Empowered Algorithm Course Teaching

3.1 Current Status and Challenges of Algorithm Course Teaching

Algorithm courses are fundamental components of curricula in information technology-related disciplines. The quality of instruction in these courses has a direct impact on students' professional abilities and future academic development. However, several challenges persist in the current teaching practices of algorithm courses.

First, there is a notable disconnect between theoretical instruction and practical application. Traditional teaching often places heavy emphasis on theoretical content, such as time complexity analysis and correctness proofs, while giving less attention to implementation and problem-solving in real programming contexts. This is partly due to the assumption that students have already acquired sufficient programming skills from prerequisite courses such as data structures and programming fundamentals. As a result, although students may understand the basic ideas of algorithms, they often face difficulties applying this knowledge to real-world problems, particularly in complex topics such as dynamic programming, network flow and etc.

Second, learning feedback mechanisms remain inadequate. In many cases, feedback is provided primarily through homework and final exams, which leads to delayed and often generalized responses to students' learning problems. With the growing enrollment in computer-related majors in Chinese universities, algorithm classes typically contain more than 60 students, making it difficult for instructors to maintain effective classroom interactions or provide individual feedbacks after class. This situation often leads to unresolved learning issues, which may accumulate over time and affect students' understanding of subsequent content. For abstract topics such as algorithm complexity analysis or the distinction between P and NP problems, timely and personalized feedback is especially important.

Third, personalized instruction remains difficult to implement in large-class environments. Faculty resources are limited, and usually only one teaching assistant is available per class. Students vary significantly in terms of mathematical background, programming experience, and logical thinking ability. As a result, a uniform teaching schedule and standardized content cannot meet the needs of all learners. This often leads to a polarized distribution of learning outcomes: students with strong foundations may feel unchallenged, while those with weaker backgrounds struggle to keep up.

3.2 Application of AI Technology in Education

Over the past decade, the integration between education and information technology has advanced significantly with the continuous development of new-generation technologies like big data, cloud computing, and artificial intelligence, propelling the education sector into a new developmental phase. Since the release of ChatGPT 3.0 at the end of 2022, the application of AI technology in education has emerged as the predominant trend in educational technology. With the launch of DeepSeek in early 2025, which swiftly became one of the fastest-growing AI tools globally, a wave of efficiency improvements and cost reductions emerged across large language model-based technological services, demonstrating immense potential in educational applications.

In recent years, intelligent tutoring systems based on large-scale language models have significantly evolved, offering novel solutions for personalized instruction. These intelligent systems integrate machine learning modules that dynamically adapt educational content and instructional strategies according to students' learning behaviors and performance. Research indicates students using intelligent tutoring systems experience markedly improved learning outcomes compared to traditional teaching approaches [11]. These systems can identify students' weak points by analyzing response patterns, study habits, and error types, subsequently providing targeted recommendations for improvement [12].

Advancements in natural language processing (NLP) enable AI systems to better understand and respond to students' inquiries. Modern large language models such as the GPT series and BERT demonstrate near-human levels in text comprehension and generation, forming the technical foundation for AI tutoring systems capable of natural language interactions [13]. Consequently, students can pose questions using everyday language to AI assistants and receive accurate, detailed responses, significantly lowering barriers to effective human-computer interaction [3].

The maturation of code generation and analysis technologies introduces new possibilities for programming education. AI systems can generate executable code from natural language descriptions and analyze code correctness, efficiency, and coding style. Such capabilities are particularly valuable in algorithm instruction, assisting students in grasping algorithmic implementation details and offering optimization suggestions for their code.

3.3 Theoretical Basis of Integrated Teaching, Learning, Assessment, and Practice

The concept of integrating teaching, assessment, and practice originates from constructivist learning theory and competency-based education theory. Constructivism posits that learning involves learners actively constructing knowledge, emphasizing the learner's initiative and situational learning contexts [14]. Within algorithm courses, students need continuous practical engagement and reflective practices to construct deeper conceptual understanding of algorithms.

Competency-based education emphasizes developing students' practical skills, advocating the comprehensive growth of knowledge, skills, and attitudes [15]. In algorithm teaching, this means that beyond merely imparting theoretical knowledge, educators should cultivate students' capacities to utilize algorithms in solving practical problems.

The integration of teaching, assessment, and practice embodies precisely this principle, combining knowledge transmission, capability assessment, and skill training in a cohesive manner.

Formative assessment theory provides evaluative support for the integrated approach to teaching, assessment, and practice [16, 17]. This theory stresses continuous assessment and feedback throughout the learning process, aimed at facilitating learning rather than merely measuring outcomes. Within AI tutoring systems, formative evaluation can be realized by monitoring students' real-time learning behaviors and performance, thus offering immediate and individualized learning guidance.

4 Design and Development of the Intelligent Assistant "Huashi Xueban"

Based on the survey analyses mentioned above and our extensive teaching experience accumulated over many years, we independently developed "Huashi Xueban"—an integrated virtual coding assistant combining teaching, learning, practice, and evaluation. Rooted in artificial intelligence and supported by big data, this platform delivers educational support to frontend devices. By accurately identifying students' learning habits and knowledge gaps through data analytics, the system provides customized learning plans, effectively achieving personalized instruction. Furthermore, "Huashi Xueban" assists teachers in generating teaching syllabi and course materials, significantly easing lesson preparation and reducing teaching burdens. This innovative approach not only enhances students' learning interests but also moderately reduces teachers' workload, ensuring equitable distribution of educational resources and the widespread delivery of quality education. The system supports both PC-based operations and mobile usage, enabling flexible, convenient access to education anytime and anywhere, further enhancing user experiences and instructional outcomes.

4.1 Core Modules and Technological Elements

(1) LLM-Agent.

In traditional software agent designs, agents typically have capabilities such as environmental perception, decision-making, execution, and autonomous learning. With the integration of Large Language Models (LLM), an LLM-Agent surpasses the conventional rule-based engine, leveraging natural language understanding and generation capabilities acquired from massive pre-training data to drive decisions and interactions. Its core components include perception capabilities, reasoning and decision-making, execution interfaces, and feedback-driven learning.

(2) Multi-Agent Collaborative Architecture.

A single agent can effectively handle simple tasks but tends to encounter cognitive blind spots or resource bottlenecks in complex scenarios involving cross-domain knowledge or extensive collaborative processes. A multi-agent architecture addresses these issues through role specialization and collaboration, enhancing overall capabilities. Core elements of this architecture include role division, communication protocols, coordination strategies, and conflict resolution among agents.

(3) Workflow.

Workflow provides a formalized description of business processes or task flows, emphasizing ordered execution and automation from inputs to outcomes. In scenarios involving large language models or intelligent agents, workflows facilitate orchestrating interactions among agents or modules. Key elements include tasks, transitions, control flows, and state management.

(4) MCP (Model Context Protocol).

In scenarios involving multi-system and multi-component collaboration to invoke large language models (LLMs), the lack of standardized context formats and transfer protocols often results in high integration costs, fragmented protocols, and redundant developments. MCP establishes a unified context protocol and development standard, making the integration and interaction of different services, languages, and vendor models more standardized and reusable. Its core components include standard message structures and community tool integration.

(5) RAG (Retrieval-Augmented Generation).

While pure generative models like LLMs are powerful, their knowledge remains static, confined to their training period. RAG compensates for this limitation by retrieving external knowledge sources such as documents, databases, and webpages, thus enhancing the accuracy and timeliness of responses. Key elements include a Retriever, an Augmenter, and a Generator.

(6) UGC (User-Generated Content).

Within educational platforms, UGC encompasses not only student-generated materials like study notes, coding examples, and problem-solving records but also content contributed by teachers and advanced users, such as instructional blueprints, exercise templates, and knowledge guides. High-quality UGC significantly enriches platform content and promotes collaborative sharing among users.

(7) Cross-Origin Issues, Load Balancing, and Nginx Reverse Proxy.

Cross-origin issues arise due to the browser's Same-Origin Policy, which restricts webpages from accessing resources differing in protocol (HTTP/HTTPS), domain, or port to prevent malicious data theft. Nginx resolves these issues through reverse proxying, unifying access points for all services under the same domain and port, thereby bypassing cross-origin restrictions. Additionally, Nginx supports cross-origin requests through configured HTTP headers. When user traffic increases, Nginx can scale to function as a load balancer, distributing requests across multiple Flask instances to enhance system throughput and fault tolerance.

4.2 Framework and Key Technologies of "Huashi Xueban" Platform

(1) Platform Framework Design.

The core service provided by "Huashi Xueban" to students is an integrated desktop combining teaching, practice, and evaluation. It incorporates instructional blueprints, an online Integrated Development Environment (IDE), and an intelligent agent. The high-level block diagram illustrating this one-stop learning desktop is shown in Fig. 2. Students engage with instructional blueprints as textbooks, use the IDE and chat window for practical exercises and questions, and all actions (including real-time code editing), commands, and queries are managed by the "Huashi" multi-agent system.

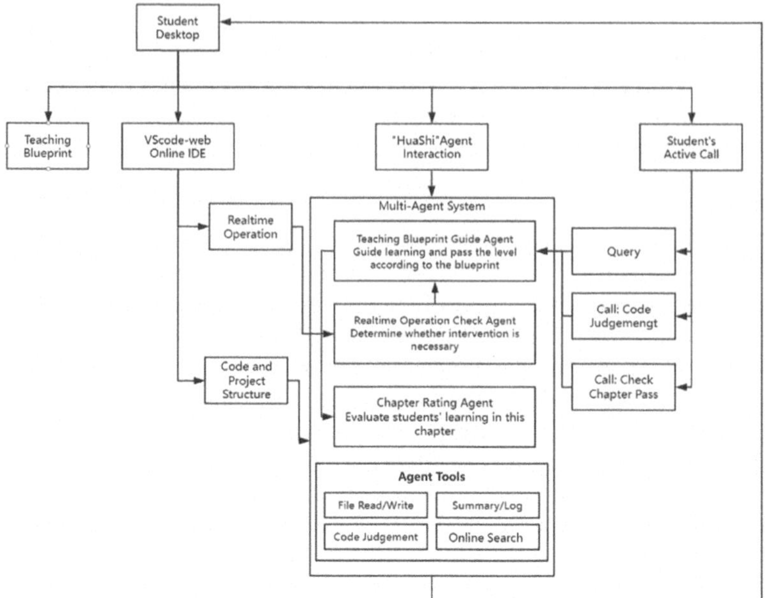

Fig. 2. Functional Block Diagram of the One-Stop Learning Desktop.

Although student and teacher accounts diverge post-login, the platform provides unified communication channels to enhance UGC experiences, allowing students to contribute instructional content beneficial to peers. Moreover, due to the cloud-based VSCode-web development environment, an anticipated major feature update involves users uploading personalized coding environments, including source code repositories, to cloud servers, combined with instructional blueprints and agent guidance, facilitating faster learning or community-driven open-source collaborations.

(2) Implementation Architecture and Key Technologies.

① Browser/Server (B/S) Service Architecture.

Our product, built primarily on a web platform, provides a cloud-based, one-stop service requiring no client installation or environmental setup, thus eliminating entry barriers and enabling students to focus purely on coding knowledge.

Figure 3 illustrates our primary learning platform: instructional blueprints detailing the content and progress are on the left, a VSCode-web-based online code editor in the center, and the large model-based agent "Huashi" on the right. Our B/S service implementation primarily utilizes Python's Flask framework.

② Agent Interaction via WebSocket.

WebSocket establishes a bidirectional communication channel between the web server and users. Unlike other model-based conversational solutions, this two-way communication allows the agent to proactively analyze teaching content and student progress even without explicit user-initiated interactions.

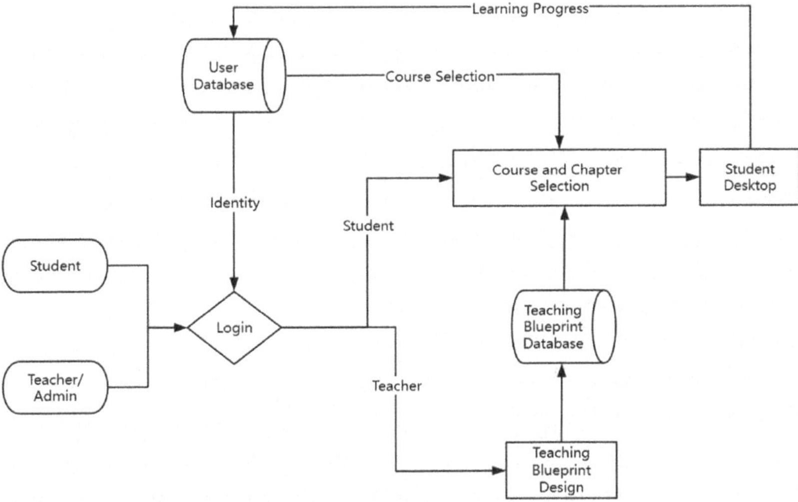

Fig. 3. Student Learning Progress and Teacher Instructional Blueprint Management.

An essential scenario is "anti-cheating," wherein the agent proactively questions students suspected of copying or directly pasting code, thereby verifying genuine comprehension of instructional content. Our WebSocket implementation utilizes the flask-socket library, with the multi-agent cluster implemented via AgentScope.

③ Voice Agent Interaction Based on RTC.

Real-Time Communication (RTC) enables low-latency, bidirectional data transfer over networks, facilitating instant voice, video, and message exchanges. To enhance natural agent interactions and reduce cognitive load from typing, we integrate voice-based RTC tools from third-party providers. Advantages include:•Faster and more immediate voice communication enhancing user experience.•Reduced screen attention switching, fostering greater student focus.•Planned integration of voice and agent-based toolchains to enable "keyboard-free" code editing solutions.

- Faster and more immediate voice communication enhancing user experience.
- Reduced screen attention switching, fostering greater student focus.
- Planned integration of voice and agent-based toolchains to enable "keyboard-free" code editing solutions.

5 Technological Innovations

Integrating practical experiences in teaching computer programming and algorithms, we have introduced agent technologies into teaching, learning, evaluation, and practice, resulting in distinctive technological innovations.

(1) Teaching: Instructional Blueprint System.

We innovatively merged the traditional hierarchical teaching structure—course plans, lesson plans, and chapters—with large language model prompt engineering to design an instructional blueprint system. In this system, professional educators guide the agents' instructional paths using standardized blueprints, enabling agents to carry out individualized student tutoring effectively.

(2) Learning: Interactive, Level-based Learning.

Students engage in a purpose-driven and interactive learning experience directed by the instructional blueprint-driven agent. Through a "gamified" interaction approach integrated within each lesson plan chapter, this methodology ensures student focus and significantly enhances learning engagement.

(3) Practice: One-stop Online Practice Platform.

The online practice platform combines an integrated development environment (IDE), instructional blueprints, and an agent communication window into a unified, web-based platform. Leveraging VSCode-web, it provides students with cloud-based coding environments, thus lowering barriers related to language installation and coding environment management. The IDE-Agent communication channel, established via plugins, enables agents to monitor and analyze students' coding progress automatically, without explicit student prompts. Additionally, an innovative design supports mobile coding on smaller screens, liberating productivity even away from conventional computers and facilitating coding and project development anytime and anywhere.

(4) Evaluation: Personalized Teaching at its Core.

Student evaluation constitutes a critical component of the system and forms the cornerstone of personalized instruction, focusing on diverse and multifaceted assessments. Specifically, the instructional blueprint includes chapter-based assessment standards reflecting students' mastery of the corresponding chapters. The system logs historical operational data from students' learning and coding activities, analyzed by agents to provide multidimensional evaluation metrics, including syntax accuracy, semantic understanding, and coding proficiency per chapter. These evaluations inform subsequent personalized instructional recommendations and learning plans.

6 Further Research Design and Implementation Plan

6.1 Research Subjects and Experimental Design

Undergraduate students from two classes majoring in Software Engineering at a university will constitute the research subjects. Employing a quasi-experimental design, one class will serve as the experimental group (using the AI-assisted teaching model), and another class will serve as the control group (using traditional teaching methods). Both classes, randomly assigned, will consist of approximately 60 students each (designated as Class A for the experimental group and Class B for the control group). The absence of significant differences in entrance scores and academic backgrounds between groups ensures the comparability of the experiment.

The experiment will span an entire semester of 18 weeks, including 16 instructional weeks, covering primary content from the "Introduction to Algorithms," such as sorting algorithms, searching algorithms, dynamic programming, greedy algorithms, divide-and-conquer methods, graph algorithms, and complexity classes.

6.2 Research Objectives

The principal objective of this study is to establish and verify the effectiveness of an AI-assisted "integrated teaching, learning, assessment, and practice" model for algorithm course instruction. Specific objectives include:

1. Designing and developing an AI tutoring system suitable for algorithm courses, achieving personalized instructional guidance.
2. Establishing a curriculum framework that integrates teaching, learning, assessment, and practice to optimize instructional processes in algorithm courses.
3. Evaluating the effects of the new teaching model on students' learning outcomes and skills development.
4. Exploring reciprocal empowerment pathways between algorithm instruction and AI technologies.

6.3 Validation Experiment

To validate the reliability and consistency of AI-based scoring in algorithm teaching, we designed a controlled validation experiment. We prepared 15 short-answer questions across five categories (computer fundamentals, programming syntax, basic algorithms, intermediate algorithms, and advanced algorithms) and responses from three types of students (beginner, intermediate, advanced), we do not list these questions here due to space limitations. Each student's answer was independently evaluated using an AI-based scoring model from three different perspectives to assess scoring stability and differentiation ability. Several prompts used in the system are provided in the appendix. The average scores for each question at varying student levels are depicted in Fig. 4, which indicate that our system is able to provide relatively appropriate evaluations based on students' responses during the interaction process.

Furthermore, an additional observation was made for higher-difficulty questions: due to the inherently abstract nature of these problems, which require conceptual articulation and interpretation, lower-level students were sometimes able to produce superficially plausible but incorrect responses. These "fishing-in-the-dark" answers, despite reflecting little actual understanding, occasionally received relatively favorable scores. This suggests a need for further research into refining the scoring mechanisms to more effectively distinguish between genuinely informed answers and vague or approximate language that merely resembles correctness.

Larger-scale student validation and experiments, as well as further investigation into the aforementioned issues, will be addressed in future research. The planned experimental framework for these follow-up studies is outlined in the subsequent section.

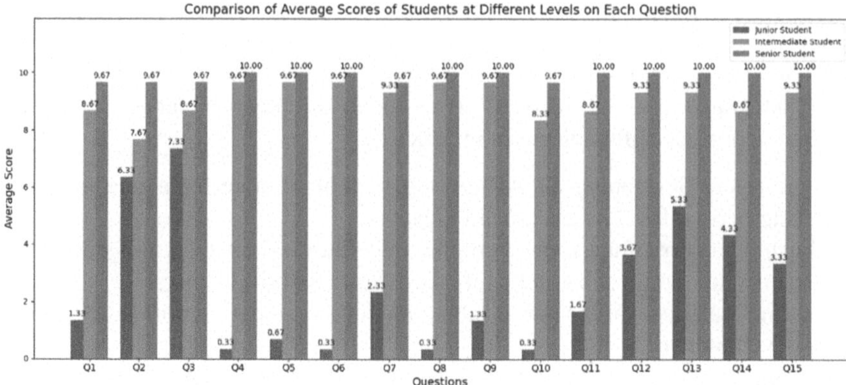

Fig. 4. Illustrates the average AI-generated scores across different levels of student performance for each question, demonstrating distinct scoring differentiation.

6.4 Teaching Experiment Implementation Plan

The experimental instruction is scheduled to commence in September 2025 and continue for 16 weeks. Throughout the implementation, we will regularly collect feedback from both students and teachers to iteratively refine instructional strategies.

To comprehensively evaluate the new instructional model's effectiveness, multiple assessment methodologies, including standardized tests, online programming evaluations, and questionnaires, will be utilized. Primary areas of evaluation will encompass theoretical knowledge comprehension, programming practice abilities, and algorithmic thinking skills.

7 Conclusions and Future Perspectives

In this paper, we proposed a theoretical framework for an "integrated teaching, assessment, and practice" model in algorithm instruction, offering a novel theoretical perspective on algorithm teaching reforms. We established a theoretical model of mutual empowerment between algorithm instruction and AI technologies and explored their intrinsic mechanisms of reciprocal enhancement. The tutoring system introduced herein creates personalized profiles for each student to guide their learning journey, inherently merging instructional and evaluative processes to minimize interference in assessments and to achieve personalized education at scale. A brief validation experiment confirmed the feasibility of the proposed approach while also highlighting several open questions that warrant further investigation. Future research will empirically validate the system's effectiveness through instructional practice and data analysis, further exploring methods to enhance real-time classroom interactions using the AI tutoring system.

Acknowledgement. This research was partially supported by the Shanghai Municipal Key Curriculum Project of Shanghai Colleges and Universities, Shanghai Municipal Education Commission.

Appendix

Prompts Used by AI Expert for Scoring (0–10 points)

The scoring AI was instructed with three different prompts to test the consistency and robustness of the ratings. The prompts used were as follows:

Prompt 1 (Accuracy-oriented):

"Evaluate the student's answer for correctness and accuracy relative to the standard definition or commonly accepted explanation. Assign a score from 0 (completely incorrect) to 10 (fully accurate and comprehensive)."

Prompt 2 (Understanding-oriented):

"Evaluate how well the student's answer demonstrates understanding of the underlying concept or algorithm. Give a score from 0 (no understanding demonstrated) to 10 (full, clear, and insightful understanding demonstrated)."

Prompt 3 (Relevance and Completeness-oriented):

"Evaluate whether the student's answer is relevant, sufficiently detailed, and covers the essential aspects of the concept or algorithm asked. Provide a score from 0 (irrelevant or incomplete) to 10 (completely relevant and adequately complete)."

References

1. Merino Campos, C.: The impact of artificial intelligence on personalized learning in higher education: a systematic review. Trends High. Educ. **4**(2), 17 (2025)
2. DeepSeek-AI et al.: DeepSeek-R1: incentivizing reasoning capability in LLMs via reinforcement learning. arXiv:2501.12948 (2025)
3. Minjing, N.: The impact of ChatGPT/AIGC on learning from the perspective of learning evolution. J. East China Normal Univ. (Educ. Sci.) **41**(7), 151–161 (2023)
4. Schroeder, K.T., Hubertz, M., Van Campenhout, R., Johnson, B.G.: Teaching and learning with AI generated courseware: lessons from the classroom. Online Learn. **26**(3), 73–87 (2022)
5. Sunayna, I., Pratibha, G., Sridhar, A., Pratima, M., Mihirkumar, B.S., Priya, C.: AI in personalized learning and educational assessment. J. Inf. Educ. Res. **5**(2) (2025)
6. Klarisa, I.V., Svetlana, B., Natalia, V.S., Lyudmila, M.S., Svetlana, A.N., Sergei, P.Z.: Personalized learning through AI: pedagogical approaches and critical insights. Contemp. Educ. Technol. **17**(2), ep574 (2025)
7. Kersten, T.S., Martha, H., Rachel, V.C., Benny, G.J.: Teaching and learning with AI-generated courseware: lessons from the classroom. Online Learn. **26**(3) (2022)
8. Eileen du, P., Daleen, C., Denise, F.: Personalized adaptive learning in higher education: a scoping review of key characteristics and impact on academic performance and engagement. Heliyon **10**(21) (2024)
9. Isolda, M., Daniel, F.B., Daniel, F., Sonia, M.G., Victor, O.V.: AI in higher education: a systematic literature review. Front. Educ. **9** (2024)
10. Monica, F.C., Maribell, R., Patricia, V., Jorge, M.: Using an adaptive learning tool to improve student performance and satisfaction in online and face-to-face education for a more personalized approach. Smart Learn. Environ. **11**, Article number: 6 (2024)
11. Sajja, R., et al.: Artificial intelligence-enabled intelligent assistant for personalized and adaptive learning in higher education. arXiv:2309.10892 (2023)

12. Haochen, L., et al.: Personalized multimodal feedback generation in education. arXiv:2011.00192 (2020)
13. Maity, S., Deroy, A.: Generative AI and its impact on personalized intelligent tutoring systems. arXiv:2410.10650 (2020)
14. Youqun, R.: An epistemological view on constructivism. Glob. Educ. **35**(5) (2006)
15. Guoqing, X.: Contemporary significance and development of competence-based curriculum model. Vocat. Tech. Educ. Forum **38**(1), 57–64 (2022)
16. Royce Sadler, D.: Formative assessment and the design of instructional systems. Instr. Sci. **18**(2), 119–144 (1989)
17. Lin, Z., Wenye, Z.: Formative assessment: promoting the cultivation of students' self-regulated learning ability. Shanghai Res. Educ. **2020**(2), 53–57 (2020)
18. Wang, S.: LongMem: augmenting language models with long-term memory. arXiv:2306.07174 (2023)
19. Razafinirina, L.: Pedagogical alignment of large language models for personalized learning: a survey. arXiv:2404.12345 (2024)
20. Li, Y., TutorLLM: customizing learning recommendations with knowledge tracing and RAG. arXiv:2502.15709 (2025)
21. Dong, Z.: How to build an adaptive AI tutor for any course using knowledge graph-enhanced RAG. arXiv:2311.17696 (2023)
22. Sanyal, S.: Investigating pedagogical teacher and student LLM agents: genetic adaptation meets RAG. arXiv:2505.19173 (2025)
23. Long, Y., Luo, H., Zhang, Y.: Evaluating large language models in analysing classroom dialogue. Sci. Learn. **9**, 60 (2024)

A Unified Digital Twin Platform for the Experiment Education of "The 101 Plans" Hardware Courses

Yu Huang, Zonghui Li(✉), Ke Xiong, and Ziyao Shen

School of Computer Science and Technology, Beijing Jiaotong University, Beijing, China
{lizonghui,kxiong,ketted,23331192}@bjtu.edu.cn

Abstract. This paper presents a Digital Twin-based teaching platform that supports the main hardware courses for undergraduate education. It is part of "The 101 Plans" initiative, which aims to unify and improve computer hardware experimental courses. We develop a Digital Twin platform and a series of RISC-V-based courses on computer organization and system architecture. The platform supports hybrid teaching with physical experiment board and a Digital Twin client when the physical boards are not in hands. This setup overcomes equipment constraints, allowing for centralized hardware management and improved maintenance and efficiency. The platform can support hardware courses from digital circuits to CPU design and CPU performance optimization and finally covers System-on-Chip (SoC) development and operation system booting. We have written a series of detailed experimental guides for these courses. It combines clear instructional guidance with carefully designed problems. Some engineering challenges are intentionally required to encourage independent problem-solving and deeper hands-on engagement. The platform has been granted three patents and serves as the official competition platform for the RISC-V Cup track of the 2025 China College IC Competition. A pilot run of the Computer Organization course at Beijing Jiaotong University this year received positive student feedback and demonstrated effective learning outcomes.

Keywords: Hardware Education · RISC-V · Digital Twin · Online-Offline Hybrid Teaching · Computer Organization

1 Introduction

"The 101 Plans" [1] is a pilot initiative launched by the Chinese Ministry of Education to reform undergraduate computer science education. As part of efforts to develop first-class core courses that are advanced, innovative, and challenging, experimental teaching plays a vital role in strengthening students' practical abilities in computer systems. However, compared to software-focused courses, hardware experiments often present greater challenges, from complex curriculum design to the high cost of hardware. Therefore, hardware courses have long

W. Hong et al. (Eds.): ICCSE 2025, CCIS 2761, pp. 257–268, 2026.
https://doi.org/10.1007/978-981-95-7731-6_21

been regarded as a weak area in the cultivation of system-level capabilities in undergraduate computer education.

In recent years, the open-source RISC-V instruction set architecture has emerged as a game-changer in computer architecture education and research. As an open standard, anyone can use RISC-V as a building block in their open or proprietary solutions and services [2]. With its modular design, high scalability, and open-access nature, RISC-V offers an ideal foundation for hardware experiment design.

In response to current challenges in experimental teaching, we have developed both a Digital Twin platform and a corresponding series of courses on computer organization and system architecture based on the RISC-V architecture.

To support both in-person and remote teaching, the platform combines real hardware boards for offline use with Digital Twin software that collects hardware data and presents hardware behavior. Even when students do not have access to physical devices, they can still complete experiments in a nearly identical environment. This setup helps reduce equipment limitations and makes it easier to manage and maintain the hardware centrally.

A structured and progressive practice pathway is embedded throughout the curriculum, beginning with digital logic and hardware programming in Digital Circuit, moving to CPU architecture design in Computer Organization, exploring performance optimization in Computer Architecture, and culminating in operating system-level experiments in SoC Design with OS Integration. This integrated approach enables students to understand the principles of hardware-software co-design and enhances their practical skills in hardware development and system implementation.

Recognizing the critical role of the Computer Organization course, we piloted its reformed version at our institution in the 2025 spring semester. During the process, the course and platform were well adopted by students.

The rest of the paper is organized as follows. Section 2 presents motivation and related works. Section 3 presents an overview of the proposed teaching platform and course system. Section 4 presents the design and implementation of the platform, including its architecture and core systems. Section 5 introduces the structure and content of our proposed hardware experimental curriculum. The computer organization course is used as a representative case study to demonstrate the course design in practice. Section 6 introduces platform deployment and educational impact. Finally, we conclude our work in Sect. 7.

2 Motivation and Related Work

Although engineering-oriented education and hands-on learning are gaining more attention in China, several long-standing issues remain in the teaching of computer system courses. These challenges can be broadly grouped into three areas:

1) Lack of integration: Many courses are taught separately, without a clear link between them. Students often struggle to see the connection between the content of one course and another.

2) Overemphasis on theory: Teaching often focuses too much on theory and explaining fundamental concepts but not enough on completing real projects [3,7]. Students typically learn through slides, equations, and simple examples rather than working with real hardware or writing programs for actual systems.
3) Weak self-research: In many courses, students follow instructions to complete small lab tasks on pre-made platforms. While many labs help them understand basic ideas, they do not give students the chance to design and build a system from scratch. There are a few open-ended tasks where students can try their ideas, explore different solutions, and learn how to solve real problems [4].

To better understand and address these issues, we reviewed recent efforts by researchers from leading Chinese universities. Yuan et al. [5] proposed a project-based curriculum on high-performance processor design with I/O and exception handling, but its complexity challenges students with weaker foundations. Qin et al. [8] proposed using a unified FPGA platform to connect multiple courses, though specific implementation practices and results were not well documented. Zhang et al. [6] proposed MIPS-based experiments and developed an intelligent evaluation platform, though details on implementation and outcomes were limited.

Building on insights from previous work, we identified three key requirements for a more effective teaching model. First, the curriculum should be well-integrated across related courses, guiding students progressively from basic digital logic to complete system design. Second, we must consider the cost and complexity of managing hardware resources, which often make it challenging to ensure that every student has access to hands-on use of physical circuit boards [9]. Third, the courses should emphasize meaningful, engineering-driven tasks that go beyond step-by-step instructions and encourage students to tackle real-world design problems.

To address these challenges, we developed a Digital Twin platform that lowers hardware costs by reducing the need for physical FPGA boards. Students can complete hardware programming in a virtual environment with behavior close to real devices. Based on this, we designed a series of structured courses focused on computer organization and system architecture, combining guided tasks with open-ended problems to strengthen practical skills and independent thinking.

3 Overview of the Platform and Courses

We developed four hardware-focused courses namely, Digital Circuit, Computer Organization, Computer Architecture, and SoC Design with OS Integration, that follow the full hardware practice path of "The 101 Plans". These courses guide students from basic logic to CPU design and building a SoC system with RT-Thread OS. To support flexible learning, we provide a hybrid environment that includes a physical FPGA board and a Digital Twin client software. Digital

Twin platform is composed of four main modules: the Client, the Remote Control System (RCS), the Data Communication System (DCS), and the Student Experiment System (SES). Figure 1 illustrates the overall structure, featuring the progression through four courses alongside the hybrid hardware course Platform. Technical details are provided in Sects. 4 and 5.

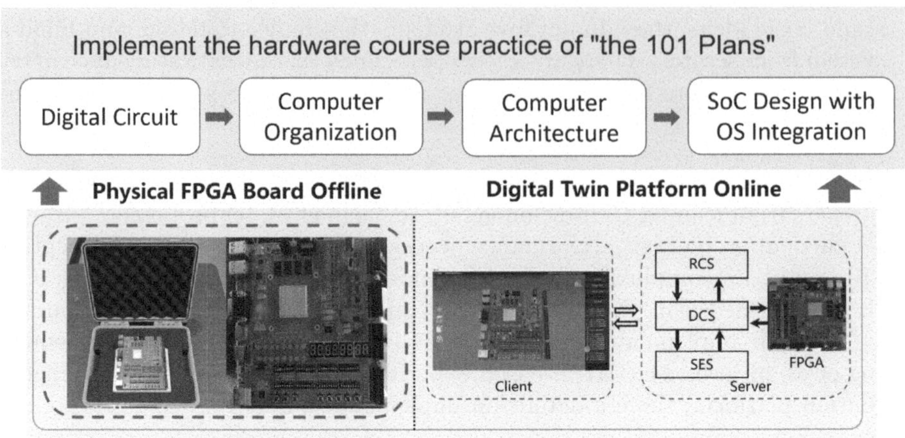

Fig. 1. Overview of the Hybrid Hardware Course Platform for "The 101 Plans".

4 Architecture of Digital Twin Platform

The Digital Twin platform enables students without physical FPGA access to complete experiments remotely while maintaining familiar interaction patterns. It includes four modules: Client, RCS, DCS, and SES, as previously mentioned above. The Client provides an interface similar to a physical FPGA board and connects to the RCS via the internet to retrieve FPGA status. Students write hardware description language (HDL) code in the SES, which, together with the DCS, is used to program the FPGA. The DCS communicates with the RCS through a serial connection to keep the FPGA synchronized. By operating the Client, students can remotely control and interact with the FPGA in real-time. Figure 2 illustrates the overall architecture of the Digital Twin platform, highlighting the interactions among three subsystems, the Client and the FPGA.

4.1 Design of Remote Control System

RCS sends control commands to DCS programmed into the FPGA via serial. To maintain stable control and synchronize data, the system employs periodic scheduling to manage the sending of commands and the receipt of responses. This timing prevents response errors and resource conflicts. Meanwhile, a status

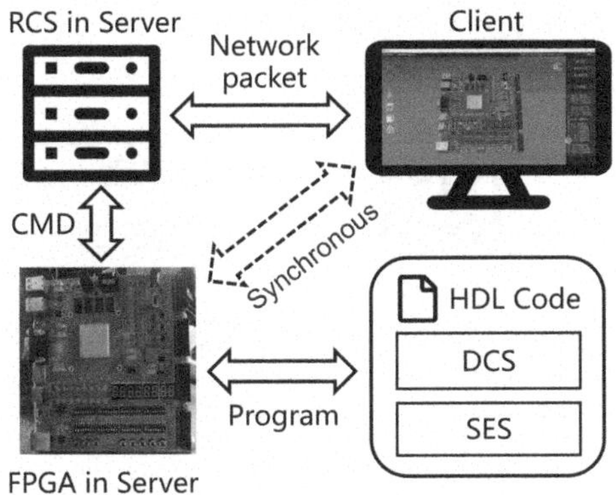

Fig. 2. Architecture of Digital Twin Platform.

check automatically identifies and resolves any discrepancies between the client and FPGA in the server, ensuring accurate operations and consistent platform behavior.

4.2 Design of Data Communication System

DCS uses UART (8N1) and a simple command set to exchange control and status data with the RCS, ensuring stable transmission through dejittering and timed sampling.

To unify the board's complex pin layout, all 144 I/O pins are mapped into four peripheral groups: 64 DIP switches, 8 buttons, 32 LEDs, and 8 seven-segment displays. Switches and buttons are virtualized as writable inputs, while LEDs and seven-segment displays are mapped to real FPGA outputs and updated in real-time.

Two commands suffice. READ (opcode 0×80) returns all peripheral states in 18-byte. WRITE uses 1 byte to set a virtual input: the MSB indicates value, and the lower 7-bit selects one of 72 input addresses (0×01–0×40 for switches, 0×41–0×48 for buttons). As shown in Fig. 3, both commands fit in a single UART frame with no handshaking, and invalid opcodes are ignored.

4.3 Design of Student Experiment System

SES provides a standardized programming interface for students to complete their designs, which includes several internal modules, as shown in Fig. 4. Students can only interact with the student module, which encapsulates internal complexity and streamlines the process of development.

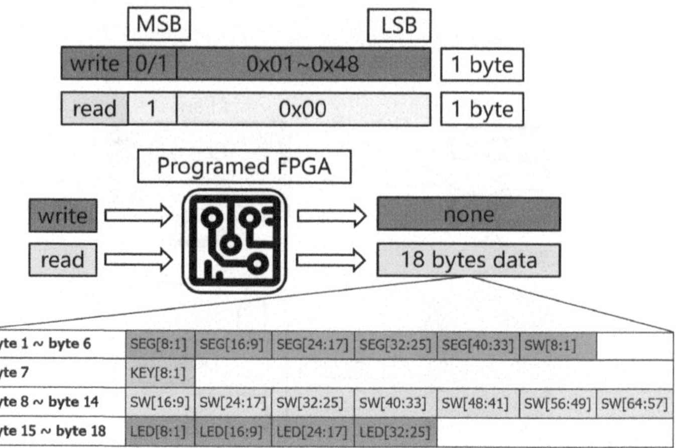

Fig. 3. WRITE & READ Command Structure in DCS.

The student module provides a unified interface with clock, reset, and standard I/O ports (LEDs, displays, switches, buttons), using consistent signal naming to simplify development. Inputs are virtualized for remote use, while outputs remain connected to the FPGA for real-time feedback. Students integrate their designs into Student_top.sv to complete their design.

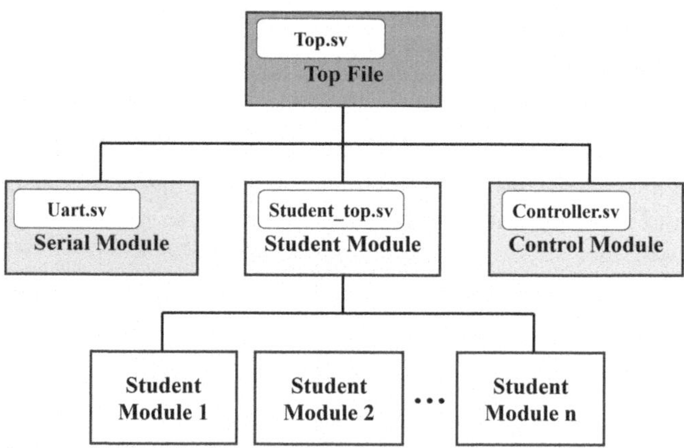

Fig. 4. Module Hierarchy of SES.

5 A Case Study of Computer Organization in Four Integrated Hardware Courses

To address the problems of fragmented courses, overemphasis on theory, and weak independent research, we designed a clear, step-by-step practical course framework that connects separate course units into a closed teaching loop.

The curriculum guides students from digital circuit basics to advanced system-level design. It begins with foundational hardware programming, followed by designing a single-cycle CPU implementing the RV32I instruction set verified on hardware. Next, students enhance performance with pipelining, branch prediction, and caching. Finally, they integrate a floating-point unit, interrupt handling, AXI bus, and DMA to build a complete SoC and run an OS on their custom processor. This approach emphasizes hands-on engineering over traditional textbook methods. Table 1 summarizes all experimental designs and details of the four courses.

As an important example among these courses, the Computer Organization course was newly launched at Beijing Jiaotong University in the 2025 spring semester and serves as a case study in the paper. The experimental component of the course is divided into three stages.

Stage 1: Learning hardware basics and RISC-V ISA;

Stage 2: Implementing a CPU with a minimal 7-instruction RISC-V subset;

Stage 3: Expanding to a 24-instruction subset of RV32I (MiniRV) validated by Trace testing and hardware deployment.

5.1 Stage 1: Basic Knowledge

Stage 1 aims to equip students with the fundamental knowledge and tools of hardware design. The "Hardware Programming Basics" module introduces SystemVerilog, Vivado 2023.2, and FPGA usage. Student learning is assessed through quizzes and programming exercises. (e.g., Fig. 5). Before designing the CPU, students complete a "RISC-V Assembly Programming" lab to understand the instruction set, preparing them for software hardware co-debugging. Experiments provide clear guidance with questions to stimulate thinking. Lab reports are managed via the Feishu platform (similar to GitBook) with step-by-step instructions. Some engineering details are omitted intentionally to encourage independent project building and skill development.

5.2 Stage 2: Design and Verification of a Core Instruction Set

After completing the foundational modules, students move on to designing a simplified RISC-V CPU based on a minimal set of seven core instructions. This stage emphasizes a bottom-up approach to building essential CPU components, including:

1. **Arithmetic unit design:** Modeling basic operations and extending to components like multipliers;

Table 1. Table of Four Integrated Hierarchical Hardware Courses

Course	Lecture Topic	Main Experiment
Digital Circuit	Basics of Hardware Description Languages	Basic Syntax of SystemVerilog
		Vivado Usage
		FPGA Development Kit
	Digital Systems Experiment	Logic Gate
		Combinational Logic Circuits
		Sequential Logic Circuits
	Comprehensive Experiment	Intelligent Quiz Buzzer
		Digital Clock
Computer Organization	Arithmetic Logic Unit(ALU)	Two's Complement Arithmetic
		ALU Implementation
	Memory	Usage of Block RAM in Vivado
		Bit/Word Extension
	Datapath in RV32I CPU	Instruction Analysis
		Datapath Component Design
	CPU Controller	μ-operation Analysis
		Controller Design
	Validate Design On FPGA	Bus and I/O Implementation
		RV32I Assembly Verification
Computer Architecture	Single-Cycle RV32I CPU	ISA Introduction
		Experimental Environment Setup
		Implementation of RV32I CPU
	Pipeline Experiment	Classic Five-Stage Pipeline
		Hazard Handling
		FPGA On-Board Verification
	Optimization Techniques	Branch Prediction
		Out-of-Order(Optional)
		FPGA On-Board Verification
	Design of Cache	Mapping Rules
		Replacement Policies
		Performance Evaluation
SoC Design with OS Integration	RISC-V ISA	Basic Concepts of ISA
		Basic Concepts of Architecture
		Evaluation Methods
	Floating-Point Unit(FPU)	Fixed-Point Addition
		Floating-Point Addition
		FPU Implementation
	Interrupt	CSR Register
		Core Local Interruptor System
		Implementation
	AXI Bus and DMA	AXI Protocol Overview
		an AXI-Based DMA Controller
		Connection to DDR Memory
	OS Integration	Cross-Compilation Environment
		Compilation of RT-Thread Nano
		On-Board Verification

4 FPGA Description

Please read carefully Appendix 4 FPGA Board Information , which is very important for you to understand our development board.

Then read the Twin Platform and Physical Board User Guide .

After reading the above, you should have some basic understanding of FPGA and HDL. In order to test whether you have read carefully, we have set several questions. If you have a clear understanding of these questions, you can proceed to the next step of reading. Otherwise, please search for them or read them again.

1. What is the relationship between FPGA, Vivado and System Verilog?
2. What is the CPU chip model of the JYD development board? (This question is very important. You may need to activate it with a license. Otherwise, the chip may report an error during synthesis.)
3. What is the main frequency of the system clock of the development board?
4. How to simulate and test the implemented hardware module?
5. How to bind pins? (We have developed a script for binding the pins of JYD peripherals. Colleagues who want to use it please refer to Appendix 5: Using Vivado XDC Files)
6. What is the difference between combinational logic and sequential logic?
7. What is the difference between the circuits formed by using blocking and non-blocking assignments in sequential logic?
8. What is the difference between a latch and a flip - flop?

When you are confident to answer these questions, please try to run the FPGA development board test case and complete the experiment we require.

Fig. 5. Some Guiding Questions in Stage 1.

2. **Data path design:** Learn the interconnections and data flow control between different modules to build a simplified but functional CPU;
3. **Memory module expansion:** Use horizontal expansion and vertical expansion to achieve larger storage capacity;
4. **Controller design:** Implementing the controller based on instruction analysis;
5. **Single-cycle CPU integration test:** Integrate the above modules to build a complete processor system and pass the basic integration test code.

5.3 Stage 3: Implementation of MiniRV and on-Board Verification

In this stage, students expand their CPU to support the 24-instruction MiniRV subset, encountering more complex datapath and control requirements. They learn to adjust the processor structure to accommodate extended instruction semantics.

For verification, a trace test system is employed to compare key signals of the tested module against a golden reference at each clock cycle, enabling precise error detection. Upon passing the test, students deploy their CPU to an FPGA board, analyze the I/O address space, and correctly place the test program in memory to complete on-board execution.

Figure 6 illustrates the overall setup: the left half depicts the architecture of the trace test system. In contrast, the right half shows the Digital Twin client interfacing with the physical FPGA board during program execution.

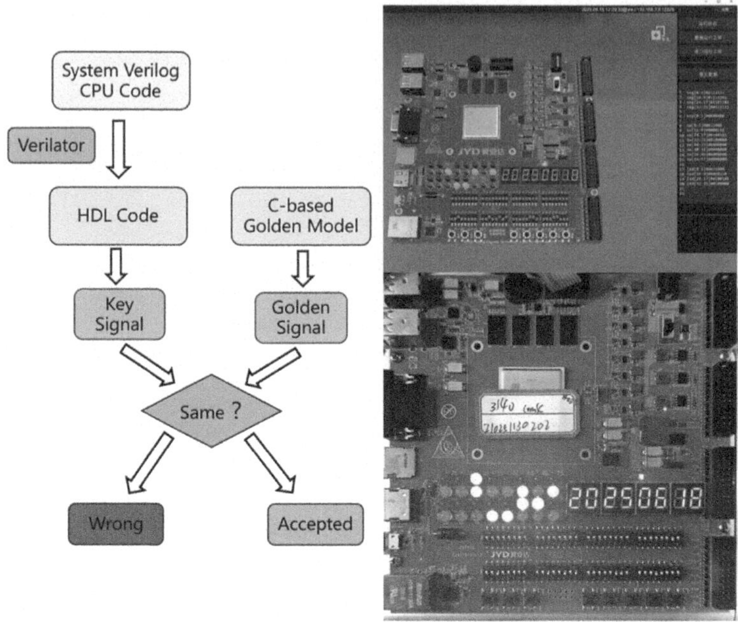

Fig. 6. Trace Test and Digital Twin System Overview.

6 Platform Deployment and Educational Impact

The proposed experimental platform has demonstrated both technical and educational value. It has been granted three educational patents [10–12], and was exhibited at the 33rd Beijing Education Equipment Expo and the 61st China Higher Education Expo. In collaboration with JinYeda Corporation, the platform has been commercialized and adopted as the official platform in the RISC-V Cup track of the 2025 China College IC Competition [13]. With the support of this platform and curriculum system, Beijing Jiaotong University also participated in drafting the RVEI Committee's talent development framework [14].

As part of the pilot implementation, the Computer Organization course was launched in the "Zhan Tianyou Class" (70 students) this year. Students completed the whole design and implementation of a 32-bit RISC-V CPU. According to the final assessment results shown in Table 2, the average scores across all key experiments exceeded the preset target scores, with achievement ratio of 1.23 (equivalent to 85.75 out of 100). The course outcomes met the expected targets, demonstrating the effectiveness of the proposed approach.

Table 2. Course Experiment Evaluation Table

Experiment	Target Score	Average Score	Achievement Ratio
Arithmetic Logic Unit	14/20	18.07/20	1.29
Memory	14/20	17.77/20	1.26
Datapath in RV32I CPU	14/20	16.94/20	1.21
CPU Controller	14/20	16.79/20	1.20
Validate Design On FPGA	14/20	16.20/20	1.16
Total Score	70/100	85.75/100	1.23

7 Conclusions

The paper presents an integrated solution to challenges in hardware-oriented computer system education, such as course fragmentation, limited hands-on experience, and insufficient opportunities for independent design. A significant contribution is the construction of a layered and unified experimental curriculum, which connects four core hardware courses —Digital Circuit, Computer Organization, Computer Architecture, and SoC Design—with OS Integration through the platform. This structure enables a smooth progression from digital logic fundamentals to complete SoC design, including OS booting, addressing the fragmentation common in traditional curricula.

The platform is powered by a Digital Twin system that extends traditional offline labs to support real-time remote interaction with FPGA-based hardware. This approach provides flexible, scalable, and location-independent access to experimental resources while enabling centralized hardware management for enhanced reliability and maintenance.

As a representative plot, the newly restructured Computer Organization course demonstrated the effectiveness of this approach. Students completed a 32-bit RISC-V CPU, exceeding the expected learning goals. The platform has been granted three educational patents, has been adopted in national competitions, and has contributed to the RVEI Committee's talent development framework.

Acknowledgments. This work was supported in part by the Undergraduate Teaching Reform Project under Grant LX20250081, the Postgraduate Teaching Reform Project under Grant YJSSQ20250095.

References

1. MOE. MOE holds meeting to review progress on "The 101 Plans" (2024). http://en.moe.gov.cn/news/press_releases/202404/t20240422_1127028.html, Accessed 17 June 2025
2. RISC-V International. About RISC-V. https://riscv.org/about/, Accessed 18 June 2025

3. Kojmane, J., Aboutajeddine, A.: Enjoyeering junior: a hands-on activity to enhance technological learning in an engineering dynamics course. In: 2016 International Conference on Information Technology for Organizations Development (IT4OD), pp. 1–6, Fez, Morocco(2016). https://doi.org/10.1109/IT4OD.2016.7479267
4. Lopez-Rosenfeld, M.: Tell me and i forget, teach me and i may remember, involve me and i learn: changing the approach of teaching computer organization. In: IEEE/ACM 1st International Workshop on Software Engineering Curricula for Millennials (SECM), pp 68-71, Rio de Janeiro (2017). https://doi.org/10.1109/SECM.2017.9
5. Yuan, C.F., Tao, X.P., Wang, L., Gu, R., Li, J.:Construction on curriculum experiment system for ability training of computer system. Experimental Technology and Management **35**(06), 12–16 (2018). https://doi.org/10.16791/j.cnki.sjg.2018.06.004
6. Qin, G.F., Ding, Z.J., Wang, L.S., Wei, Z.H., Zhang, D.D.:Focusing on capacity building and continuously promoting experimental linkage. Exper. Technol. Manag. **37**(05), 142–145 (2020). https://doi.org/10.16791/j.cnki.sjg.2020.05.030
7. Lee, S.J., Jung, A., Park, J., Yun, M.: Cost-efficient hands-on learning design for computer organization course. In: 2020 15th International Conference on Computer Science & Education (ICCSE), Delft, Netherlands, pp. 150–155 (2020). https://doi.org/10.1109/ICCSE49874.2020.9201854
8. Zhang, L., Wang, J.P., Zheng, R., He, J., Qi, Y.: Through experiment model of "Computer organization" course based on VerilogHDL intelligent evaluation platform. Exper. Technol. Manag. **38**(03), 236–241 (2021). https://doi.org/10.16791/j.cnki.sjg.2021.03.048
9. Papazoglou, P.P.: Hardware oriented microprocessor simulator. In: 2024 IEEE Global Engineering Education Conference (EDUCON), pp. 1–5, Kos Island (2024). https://doi.org/10.1109/EDUCON60312.2024.10578582
10. Li, Z., et al.: A computer hardware teaching platform for talent cultivation in universities. Chinese Patent CN202410450390.6 (2024)
11. Li, Z., et al.: A computer hardware experimental box for talent cultivation in universities. Chinese Patent CN202420773756.9 (2024)
12. Li, Z., et al.: An IoT teaching experimental platform for universities. Chinese Patent CN202410450411.4 (2024)
13. CICIEC. The topic of the 9th JiChuang Cup Competition - Jingyeda Cup. http://univ.ciciec.com/nd.jsp?id=879#_jcp=1, Accessed 18 June 2025
14. RVEI Committee. Notice on Public Solicitation of Participating Units for the Drafting of the "RISC-V Talent Training Standard". https://mp.weixin.qq.com/s/0rNhrGCGUDhzqut7Q_cdTw, Accessed 18 June 2025

Coding of Classroom Dialogues and Mining of Learning Paths Based on Large Language Models

Tengda Qi[1], Wang Ruan[2], Guomin Zheng[1], Bo Sun[2], Jun He[2(✉)], and Yongkang Xiao[2]

[1] Beijing Normal University, Beijing 100875, China
[2] Beijing Normal University, Zhuhai 519000, China
hejun@bnu.edu.cn

Abstract. Existing studies have achieved automatic coding of classroom dialogue and the mining of learning patterns based on the results of automatic coding. However, they have failed to focus on conducting automatic coding research and data mining analysis on classroom dialogue in native language education. In view of the technological advantages of large language models, this study proposes a strategy that combines the construction of training data and model fine-tuning to achieve automatic coding of classroom dialogue in the field of Chinese native language education. Through large-scale coding, data analysis is carried out to extract learning patterns, and then educational experiments are conducted to verify the effectiveness of these learning patterns. The empirical results show that this study has improved the efficiency of automatic coding of classroom dialogue in Chinese native language education, achieved in-depth mining of subject teaching patterns, and effectively contributed to the improvement of learning outcomes in the classroom.

Keywords: Classroom dialogue · Automatic coding · Lag sequence analysis · Learning path mining

1 Introduction

Classroom dialogue is the main carrier for carrying out interactive teaching and an important means to help students explore knowledge and inspire thinking [1]. Effective classroom dialogue has unique value in promoting students' deep learning, the advancement of thinking and the improvement of competencies [2]. However, traditional methods for analyzing classroom dialogue face two major bottlenecks: (1) Relying solely on experts for subjective evaluation or only on manual coding of classroom dialogue leads to strong subjectivity and relatively low efficiency, making it difficult to efficiently and accurately process large-scale classroom teaching data; (2) There is a lack of subject specificity. The existing label systems for classroom dialogue mostly refer to the content of general classroom dialogue in the dimension of dialogue content and lack effective subject focus. The scale of classroom dialogue coding data and the accuracy

W. Hong et al. (Eds.): ICCSE 2025, CCIS 2761, pp. 269–287, 2026.
https://doi.org/10.1007/978-981-95-7731-6_22

of classroom dialogue data coding are crucial for conducting classroom dialogue analysis and mining the effective learning paths implied in classroom dialogue that promote students' knowledge construction and thinking development. Mother tongue education is the core curriculum of basic education in various countries and undertakes the core mission of integrating four aspects: strengthening the foundation of students' language application ability, promoting the development of high-order thinking, cultivating cultural identity and a sense of responsibility, and inheriting the excellent cultural heritage of the nation. Its teaching content takes the cultivation of language ability as the axis and deeply integrates the four dimensions of language construction, thinking development, aesthetic appreciation and cultural inheritance, forming the cognitive basis for interdisciplinary learning. Against this background, accurately identifying effective classroom dialogue patterns, such as dialogue structures and the transition paths of cognitive levels, is of key significance for optimizing students' language acquisition efficiency and the development of comprehensive competencies.

To break through the efficiency bottleneck of traditional manual coding, this study introduces the automatic coding technology driven by large language models. Based on the scenarios of Chinese mother tongue education, a label system for classroom dialogues in Chinese mother tongue education with three dimensions and multiple subjects is constructed. Through the combined use of training corpus construction and model fine-tuning techniques, automatic coding for classroom dialogues in Chinese mother tongue education is achieved. On this basis, educational data mining and educational experiment verification are carried out to form a closed loop of the research.

The contributions of this paper can be summarized as follows:

Construction of high-quality pre-training corpora: 60 lesson cases annotated by experts (with 7,868 dialogues) provide the benchmark for disciplinary annotation pre-training and automatic coding evaluation.

Achievement of model fine-tuning and optimization: By adopting the LLaMA-7B architecture, an 87.2% coding accuracy rate is achieved.

Mining of classroom dialogue laws: Based on the automatic coding results of 300 lesson cases, the key focuses of effective teaching in classroom dialogues are extracted.

Verification through teaching experiments: Randomized controlled experiments are conducted for 60 classes. By feeding back the automatic coding results of classroom dialogues, the positive promoting effect of following the extracted key focuses of classroom dialogues on improving students' reading ability is verified.

Meanwhile, this technological path provides teachers with quantifiable and operable teaching decision-making support, promoting classroom dialogues to shift from being experience-oriented to being data-driven.

2 Related Work

Existing studies have explored the laws of classroom dialogue through the paradigm of "manual/automatic coding - data analysis", but there are three major bottlenecks, namely coarse technical granularity, weak subject adaptability, and the absence of experimental verification. This study focuses on conducting a review regarding the construction of the classroom dialogue coding label system and the automatic coding technology for classroom dialogue.

2.1 Construction of the Classroom Dialogue Label System: From the General Framework to Subject Deepening

Sinclair (J.M. Sinclair) and Coulthard (R.M. Coulthard) described the classic pattern of classroom dialogue as Initiation—Response—Feedback or Follow-up, abbreviated as IRF [3]. It pointed out the typical form of classroom dialogue. Zheng Tainian constructed a learner-centered classroom dialogue analysis framework. On the basis of focusing on the subjects and forms of classroom dialogue, he further concentrated on the content of classroom dialogue that was more closely related to students' knowledge construction and ability cultivation [4]. Cui Yunhuo took student learning, teacher teaching, curriculum nature and classroom culture as four elements and put forward 20 perspectives and 68 observation points for classroom observation and analysis [5]. This study integrated the learning theory of constructivism and paid attention to the interactive relationship between classroom dialogue content and factors such as teaching objectives and learning methods. The above studies have clarified the classroom dialogue analysis framework with dialogue form, dialogue subject and dialogue content as the core, but still showed the defect of lacking labels pointing to specific subject content. Cao Yiming et al., based on the general evaluation system of Coding Instrument for Productive Classroom Dialogue (CI-PCD) constructed by the Cambridge University Classroom Dialogue Team, focused on the subject of mathematics and emphasized evaluating classroom dialogue from aspects such as dialogue content and quality [2]. It showed obvious progress. To sum up, the classroom dialogue label system is generally composed of elements such as dialogue subject, dialogue form, dialogue purpose and dialogue content, and the dialogue content is refined from subject teaching content.

2.2 Automatic Coding of Classroom Dialogue: From Traditional Machine Learning to Large Language Models

Sun Zhong et al. noticed the connection between the quantitative structure and effective meaning in classroom dialogue. Taking teaching practice as a unit, they combined machine learning technology to conduct automatic coding and theoretical analysis on classroom dialogue [6].

Song Yu et al., based on the work of the Cambridge University Classroom Dialogue Team, created a classroom teaching analysis and evaluation system named Coding Instrument for Productive Classroom Dialogue (CI-PCD), which embodies complex information processing and cognitive processes such as basic knowledge, analysis and interpretation, summary and induction, and transfer and innovation. They also adopted a method combining manual coding and machine learning to achieve automatic coding of classroom dialogue and improve the efficiency of data processing [7].

Yang Xiaozhe et al. utilized the neural network analysis model to conduct automatic coding on questions, answers, and feedback in the classroom, realizing the quality assessment of classroom dialogue based on semantics. It can achieve the level-based assessment of the IRE model in classroom teacher-student dialogue within a short period of time, that is, to evaluate and classify the levels of questions, answers, and feedback, thus constructing a comprehensive, rapid, and accurate way of classroom dialogue assessment. It has become a key link in understanding the process of learning occurrence in the classroom and laid an important foundation for large-scale intelligent analysis of the classroom [8].

Existing studies have carried out preliminary explorations of the laws of thinking development in classroom dialogue based on automatically coded data. However, the coding systems they used are mostly general classroom dialogue indicators, which fail to effectively focus on the content of specific subject classroom dialogue and conduct in-depth mining of the subject learning paths contained in classroom dialogue. Therefore, this study focuses on the field of Chinese mother tongue education. Based on educational experiments and large-scale automatic coding, it conducts in-depth research on the improvement of students' learning abilities by automatic coding, the hierarchical division of the level of classroom dialogue in Chinese mother tongue education, typical characteristics, and the effective learning paths contained in classroom dialogue.

3 Method

Focusing on the field of Chinese mother tongue education, this study constructs a classroom dialogue label system and an automatically coded pre-training corpus, and uses the fine-tuning technology of large language models to carry out deep learning training, providing technical support for the automatic coding of classroom dialogue; it conducts teaching experiments and automatic coding of 300 classroom dialogues, providing empirical verification for the improvement of classroom teaching by automatic coding technology. Based on the above description, this study constructs the following research framework to guide the smooth progress of this study (Fig. 1).

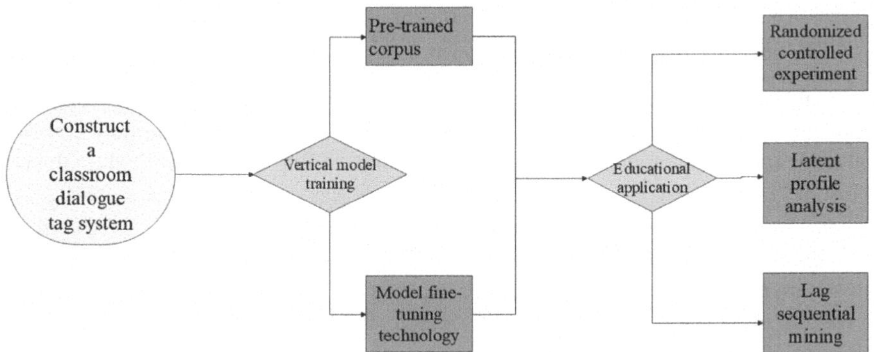

Fig. 1. Research Framework

3.1 Construction of the Classroom Dialogue Label System for Chinese Mother Tongue Education

Based on a comprehensive analysis of existing research results and in combination with the characteristics of the research content and the research purposes of this study, this study constructs a classroom dialogue label system composed of dialogue subjects, dialogue forms, dialogue purposes and dialogue contents. Among them, language construction, thinking development, aesthetic appreciation and cultural inheritance are the secondary indicators that constitute the content of classroom dialogue. Meanwhile, this study further splits each secondary indicator of the classroom dialogue content to form 13 tertiary indicators. Based on the construction of literature and through two rounds of expert consultations for modification, the classroom dialogue label system for Chinese mother tongue education is formed. The specific contents are shown in the following table (Table 1).

Table 1. Chinese L1 Classroom Dialogue Labeling System [9]

Dimension	Interpret
Perceptual Accumulation	Perceive and accumulate linguistic materials and verbal experience by comprehending textual characteristics and connotations
Organization & Integration	Systematically organize and integrate linguistic materials using notes, mind maps, or annotations to structure language knowledge
Comprehension & Analysis	Analyze the meaning and expressive features of specific words or sentences
Expression & Communication	Select and organize language materials for purposeful communication in contextualized situations
Association & Imagination	Engage in associative or imaginative thinking to gain intuitive understanding of textual content/form
Summarization & Comparison	Extract key information, draw conclusions, or compare differences in perspectives/materials
Inference & Deduction	Hypothesize and logically justify implicit or unknown information to solve problems
Insight & Reflection	Critically evaluate information using disciplinary/cross-disciplinary knowledge
Aesthetic Experience	Gain personal aesthetic/emotional engagement through activities like reading aloud or role-play
Appreciation & Evaluation	Analyze textual/linguistic artistry and evaluate characters, events, or rhetorical techniques
Creative Expression	Express original aesthetic perspectives or recreate idealized representations
Awareness & Understanding	Identify cultural elements in texts and connect them to daily life/global heritage
Interpretation & Internalization	Contextualize and critically examine cultural characteristics across traditions
Teacher	Dialogue initiated by the teacher
Student	Dialogue initiated by the student

(continued)

Table 1. *(continued)*

Dimension	Interpret
I	Posing questions/instructions to stimulate discussion
R	Replying to questions/topics
F	Evaluating or summarizing responses
Expand	Expanding perspectives/solutions
Deepen	Advancing in-depth analysis

3.2 Automatic Coding of Classroom Dialogues in Chinese Mother Tongue Education

Based on the classroom dialogue label system for Chinese mother tongue education, work such as recording and transcribing classroom dialogues and cleaning the transcribed texts is carried out to form the construction path of the automatic coding vertical model for classroom dialogues. The specific contents are shown in the following figure (Fig. 2).

Fig. 2. Construction Path of the Automatic Coding Vertical Model for Classroom Dialogues in Chinese Mother Tongue Education

Preparation of Training Data. In this study, 120 classroom dialogues in Chinese mother tongue education were recorded in schools at high-level, medium-level and low-level respectively by means of random sampling. These were then transcribed into texts and manually cleaned, resulting in a total of 360 texts of classroom dialogues in Chinese mother tongue education. Twenty texts of classroom dialogues at different levels were selected from each group, and expert manual coding was carried out. The coding results were used as pre-training corpora.

To ensure the coding quality of the classroom dialogue texts, this study formed an expert team composed of professors of Chinese curriculum and teaching theory, doctoral students and special-class teachers, as well as a coding team consisting of master's students majoring in Chinese subject teaching and normal students majoring in Chinese language and literature. The expert team wrote a coding manual on the basis of full discussions and trained the coders according to the coding manual. Subsequently, the coders were grouped in pairs, and the coders were required to conduct independent and repeated coding on the classroom dialogue texts in accordance with the requirements of the coding manual. Then, the consistency test of the intraclass correlation coefficient was carried out on the coding data of each coder. The test results are shown in the following table (Table 2).

Table 2. Intraclass Correlation Coefficient Consistency Test for Coders

Screening stage	Number of coders	Mean range of ICC	Pass rate	Kendall's W
Initial training	48	0.72 (0.58–0.85)	41.7%	0.69
The first round of screening	38	0.81 (0.75–0.89)	86.8%	0.83
The final team	32	0.88 (0.82–0.94)	100%	0.91

After two rounds of screening, a total of 32 team members with an average Intraclass Correlation Coefficient (ICC) above 0.800 were recruited to form a formal coding team and carry out formal coding and manual proofreading work. Meanwhile, the researcher took the examples written by experts as anchors and compared the degree of overlap between the results of expert coding and those of the coders as a detection method for the coding quality of the coders. After testing, the degree of overlap between the coding results of all coders and the expert anchor coding results was above 95%. The specific contents are shown in the following table (Table 3).

Table 3. Consistency detection of manual coding for classroom dialogues

Professional background	Number	Mean value of ICC	Degree of coincidence with expert anchor points
Master of Subject Teaching	12	0.85 ± 0.03	$94.1\% \pm 2.1\%$
Normal School Students	20	0.83 ± 0.02	$93.6\% \pm 2.3\%$
The whole team	32	0.88	$95.4\% \pm 1.8\%$

As can be seen from the content in the above table, the results of manual coding have high accuracy and high consistency. Through manual coding, a total of 60 coded texts of classroom dialogues were formed, with a total of 7,868 coded dialogue texts. In this study, 40 of these coded texts of classroom dialogues were selected as the pre-training corpora for the automatic coding of classroom dialogues, and deep learning training was carried out based on the model fine-tuning technology.

Model Technical Preparation. This study employs the Chain of Thought (CoT) technique, which involves designing a dataset format where each entry includes the "content" of the utterance and its corresponding "coding explanation" as the CoT. By integrating manually constructed coding explanations, the reasoning process in real human classroom dialogues is revealed and simulated, enabling more precise understanding and classification of classroom dialogue content. This approach enhances the model's semantic understanding ability and automatic coding accuracy in the domain of mother tongue education classroom dialogues. The specific technical architecture is shown in the following figure (Fig. 3).

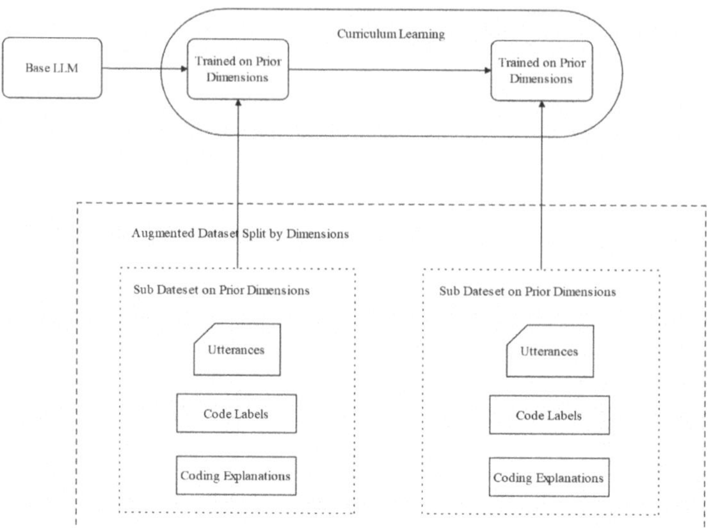

Fig. 3. The training framework

4 Experiment Setup

For the base model, this study uses LoRA (Learning Rate Adjuster) for fine-tuning. The parameters are set as follows: rank = 8, alpha = 16, dropout = 0.5. The fine-tuning is carried out on a single NVIDIA Tesla A100 (80G) GPU, and the batch size is set to 8 to make full use of the GPU memory. Meanwhile, this study uses cross-entropy as the loss function and AdamW as the optimizer to conduct fine-tuning on the LLM for 15 epochs, with the learning rate set to 3e−4. After the training is completed, the final checkpoint is used for evaluation [10].

After the deep learning training of the model, this study takes the remaining 20 manually annotated classroom dialogue coding texts as the test corpus to detect the accuracy, recall rate, F1-score and consistency of the automatic coding [8]. The specific contents are shown in the following table (Table 4).

Table 4. Detection Results of Automatic Coding for Classroom Dialogues.

Label Category	Accuracy	Recall	F1-score	Consistency
Language Construction	95.10%	94.80%	0.949	96.30%
1. Perceptual Accumulation	96.20%	95.70%	0.959	97.10%
2. Systematic Integration	94.80%	93.50%	0.941	95.90%
3. Comprehension & Analysis	95.30%	94.10%	0.947	96.50%
4. Expression & Communication	94.50%	94.20%	0.943	96.00%

(continued)

Table 4. *(continued)*

Label Category	Accuracy	Recall	F1-score	Consistency
Cognitive Development	91.70%	90.20%	0.909	95.80%
5. Association & Imagination	92.80%	91.50%	0.921	96.30%
6. Induction & Comparison	92.10%	90.80%	0.914	95.70%
7. Deductive Reasoning	90.30%	89.10%	0.897	94.60%
8. Critical Reflection	92.50%	91.40%	0.919	96.20%
Aesthetic Appreciation	92.60%	91.80%	0.922	96.00%
9. Aesthetic Experience	93.10%	92.40%	0.927	96.80%
10. Artistic Evaluation	91.50%	90.70%	0.911	95.20%
11. Creative Expression	93.20%	92.30%	0.927	96.10%
Cultural Heritage	90.30%	88.60%	0.894	95.10%
12. Cultural Awareness	91.00%	89.20%	0.901	95.50%
13. Contextual Comprehension	89.60%	88.00%	0.887	94.70%
Teacher (T)	98.50%	98.10%	0.983	99.20%
Student (S)	97.90%	97.70%	0.978	98.80%
I. Initiation	97.30%	96.50%	0.969	98.10%
R. Response	96.80%	96.00%	0.964	97.80%
F. Feedback	96.10%	95.20%	0.956	97.00%
E. Extension	92.10%	91.20%	0.916	95.70%
D. Deepening	91.80%	90.50%	0.911	95.30%

As can be seen from the content in the above table, the accuracy and recall rates of the automatic coding results for each indicator are both above 88%, the F1-score is above 0.88, and the consistency between the automatic coding and expert manual coding is above 94%. Thus, an intelligent agent capable of real-time coding of classroom dialogues was formed, and automatic coding was carried out on 300 classroom dialogue texts.

5 Data Mining and Analysis

The mining and analysis of the automatic coding data of classroom dialogues consist of latent profile analysis, lag sequence mining and educational experiments on the automatic coding data of 300 classroom dialogues. In this study, through latent profile analysis, descriptive statistics and lag sequence analysis methods, the typical types contained in classroom dialogues at different levels, the typical characteristics presented by different types of classroom dialogues, and the educational laws implied in high-level classroom dialogues were mined. Through the implementation of a 2×2 factorial randomized controlled trial (RCT), the positive promoting effect of the application of automatic coding of classroom dialogues on classroom teaching was verified.

5.1 Latent Profile Analysis

Latent Profile Analysis usually employs fit indices (such as AIC, BIC, and LMR) to evaluate the model. The smaller the fit indices are, the better the model fit is. The analysis reveals that as the number of categories increases, the values of AIC and BIC keep decreasing. Starting from Model 3, the rate of decrease in the values begins to slow down, and the value of LMR is always less than 0.05, indicating that the accuracy of classification is constantly improving [11] (Table 5).

Table 5. Fit Indices for LPA of Chinese L1 Classroom Dialogues

Model	AIC	BIC	LMR
2	3250.42	3289.67	0.032
3	3018.15	3072.83	0.021
4	2954.08	3024.19	0.018
5	2912.37	2997.91	0.016

Taking into comprehensive consideration both the accuracy and simplicity of the model, this study finally selects the model that contains three subgroups. Through a comprehensive analysis of the typical characteristics of dialogue subjects, dialogue forms, dialogue purposes and dialogue contents, and based on the characteristics of the coding scale scores of 300 classroom dialogues, this study names the three subgroups of Chinese mother tongue education classroom dialogues as the high-level classroom dialogue group, the medium-level classroom dialogue group and the low-level classroom dialogue group in sequence.

Typical Characteristics of Classroom Dialogues at Different Levels. By describing and statistically analyzing the dialogue behaviors of teachers and students in 300 lesson cases with automatic coding, the occupancy rate of teachers' behaviors in classroom dialogues at different levels can be calculated. Meanwhile, through a comprehensive analysis of the frequencies of dialogue forms, the number of turns and the dialogue subjects, the conversion rate of teacher-student behaviors in classroom dialogues at different levels can be calculated [12]. The specific contents are shown in the following table (Table 6).

Table 6. Statistical Results of Teacher Behavior Dominance and Teacher-Student Transition Rates in Coded Classroom Dialogue

	Number of Lessons	Mean Teacher Behavior Dominance	Mean Teacher-Student Transition Rate
Low-proficiency classroom dialogue	300	37%	71%

(*continued*)

Table 6. (*continued*)

	Number of Lessons	Mean Teacher Behavior Dominance	Mean Teacher-Student Transition Rate
Medium-proficiency classroom dialogue	300	58%	46%
High-proficiency classroom dialogue	300	86%	25%

As can be seen from the above table, in Chinese mother tongue education, from high-level to low-level classroom dialogues, the occupancy rate of teachers' behaviors in classroom dialogues shows a significant upward trend, while the occupancy rate of students' behaviors in classroom dialogues shows a significant downward trend. Meanwhile, the average conversion rate of teacher-student behaviors also shows a continuous downward trend. Classroom dialogue is a process that promotes students' autonomous and cooperative learning, a process that unifies students' cognitive development and emotional cultivation, and a process that promotes students' mutual understanding and self-understanding. Although the frequency of classroom dialogue cannot fully predict the quality of classroom dialogue, the occupancy rates of teachers and students in classroom dialogue can still effectively predict whether the classroom dialogue is learner-centered and whether the dominant position of students as the main body of classroom learning has been effectively established. Meanwhile, there is a significant negative correlation between the conversion rate of teacher-student behaviors and the occupancy rate of teachers' behaviors. The higher the conversion rate of teacher-student behaviors is, the more frequent the conversion of dialogue behaviors between teachers and students and among students in classroom dialogue will be, and the richer the classroom dialogue activities will be.

By describing and statistically analyzing the data of classroom dialogues at different levels in dimensions such as dialogue frequency, dialogue content, dialogue purpose and dialogue subject, the typical characteristics of Chinese mother tongue classroom dialogues at three levels can be found. The differences in the coding distribution of classroom dialogues at different levels are relatively significant, showing the characteristics of differences in the overall cognitive level. In this study, the frequency proportions of the coding of classroom dialogues at three levels in the dimension of dialogue content are extracted. For the convenience of table presentation, in this study, "A", "B" and "C" are used to represent low-level, medium-level and high-level classroom dialogues respectively, and "1" - "14" are used to represent each sub-dimension of the dialogue content respectively. The specific contents are shown in the following table (Table 7).

Table 7. Distribution Table of the Proportion of Classroom Dialogue Coding and Dialogue Content

	1	2	3	4	5	6	7	8	9	10	11	12	13	14
A	16%	12%	37%	4%	3%	7%	12%	1%	3%	3%	1%	1%	0	0
B	11%	11%	28%	8%	6%	9%	13%	3%	3%	3%	2%	2%	1%	0
C	4%	5%	15%	17%	7%	15%	10%	8%	4%	4%	3%	4%	2%	2%

By comparing and analyzing the above table, it can be seen that both low-level and medium-level classroom dialogues in the field of Chinese mother tongue education pay relatively little attention to the cultural education contained in the mother tongue, while high-level classroom dialogues maintain appropriate attention to the cultural education contained in the mother tongue. In low-level and medium-level classroom dialogues, the proportion of classroom dialogues with language accumulation and application as the dialogue content is both above 50%. While this kind of classroom dialogue helps to consolidate the foundation of students' language learning, it neglects the cultivation of students' thinking development, aesthetic appreciation ability and cultural understanding ability to varying degrees.

Based on the proportion distribution of the coded dialogue content in classroom dialogues and the calculation formula of DQI (Dialogue Quality Index) DQI = (100 × Proportion of Cognitive Dialogue) × (100 × Teacher-Student Turn Transition Rate) × 100, this study calculates the DQI values of classroom dialogues at low, medium and high levels respectively [13]. The specific contents are shown in the following table (Table 8).

Table 8. Cognitive Dialogue Proportion, Turn Transition Rates, and DQI by Classroom Performance Level

Classroom Level	Cognitive Dialogue Proportion	Turn Transition Rate	DQI
Low-Performing	23%	25%	5.75
Mid-Performing	31%	46%	14.26
High-Performing	40%	71%	28.4

When the proportion of teachers' behaviors is less than or equal to 0.3, it is the practice-oriented classroom teaching mode. When the proportion of teachers' behaviors is greater than or equal to 0.7, it is the lecture-oriented classroom teaching mode. When the teacher-student behavior conversion rate is greater than or equal to 0.4, it is the dialogue-oriented classroom teaching mode. When the teacher-student behavior conversion rate is less than 0.4 and the proportion of teachers' behaviors is between 0.3 and 0.7, it is the mixed classroom teaching mode [14]. Through a comprehensive analysis of the content in the above table, it can be known that in this study, the DQI of high-level classroom dialogues is significantly higher than that of other groups ($F = 210.3$, $p < 0.001$), which verifies the effectiveness of "the teacher-student behavior conversion rate

≥ 0.4" as the core criterion for dialogue-oriented classrooms. A DQI greater than 20 is the threshold for high-quality classrooms [15], and only the high-level group meets this standard in this study. Low-level classrooms (DQI = 5.75) are mainly dominated by teachers' lectures (T% = 86%), with very little thinking interaction (23%), which conforms to the characteristics of the lecture-oriented mode. The classroom dialogues at the medium-level belong to the mixed classroom teaching mode, that is, the teaching of this class includes practice behaviors, dialogue behaviors and typical lecture behaviors, and the teaching effect of dialogue-oriented classroom dialogues is significantly better than that of mixed classroom dialogues. Therefore, classroom dialogues at the medium level need to increase student-student interactions, and low-level classroom dialogues need to reduce the proportion of teachers' behaviors.

5.2 Results of Lag Sequence Analysis

Automatically code the classroom dialogues at the three levels, and based on the automatic coding results, use the GSEQ software to conduct lag sequence analysis. Mine the teaching evolution paths contained in the low-level and high-level classroom dialogues, and then, through comparative analysis, explore the effective teaching laws contained in high-level classroom dialogues. The specific contents are shown in the following figure (Figs. 4 and 5).

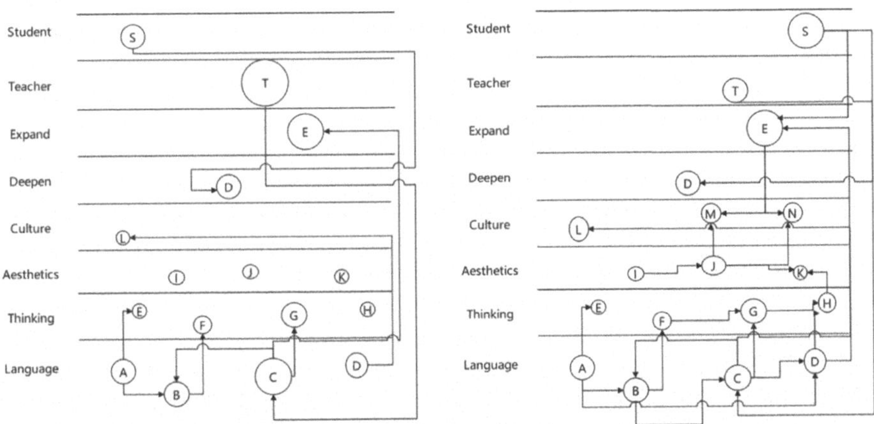

Fig. 4. Sequential Pattern Map of Low-Proficiency Classroom Dialogue

Fig. 5. Sequential Pattern Map of High-Proficiency Classroom Dialogue

As can be seen from the content in the above figure, in the classroom dialogues at the low-level, key dialogue contents such as "insight and reflection", "aesthetic experience", "appreciation and evaluation", and "performance and creation" are in a state of fragmentation and isolation, indicating that in classroom dialogues, the above-mentioned dialogue contents fail to form a reasonable and organic connection with the dialogue contents focusing on dimensions such as language and thinking. Meanwhile, in the low-level classroom dialogues, the dialogue purposes of "expansion" and "deepening" fail to form a reasonable echo with the dialogue contents in dimensions such as thinking development, aesthetic appreciation and cultural understanding. That is to say, there is a serious misalignment among dialogue contents, dialogue behaviors and dialogue purposes, which restricts the teaching effect of classroom dialogues.

In the classroom dialogues at the high-level, there are extensive connection relationships among different dimensions of dialogue contents, within the same dimension of dialogue contents, between dialogue purposes and dialogue contents, and between dialogue subjects and dialogue contents, making the classroom dialogue contents become a comprehensive learning field that effectively promotes students' language accumulation, thinking development, cultivation of aesthetic appreciation ability and cultural understanding. This study further extracts the evolution path of dialogue contents in high-level classroom dialogues. The specific contents are shown in the following figure (Fig. 6).

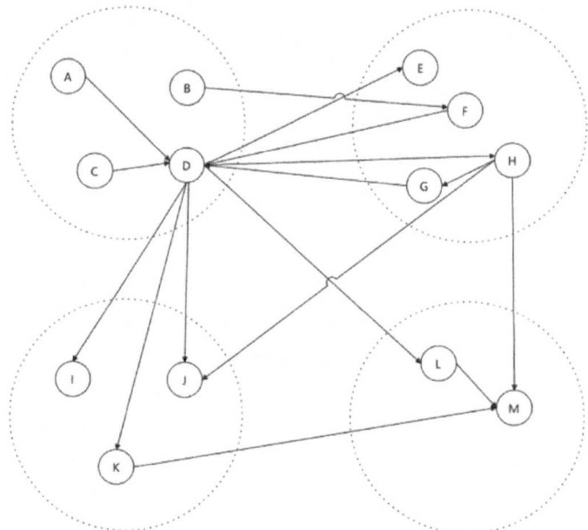

Fig. 6. Evolution Path of High-level Classroom Learning

As can be seen from the content in the above figure, in high-level Chinese mother tongue classroom dialogues, "expression and communication" occupies the core node position in the content evolution path, and its core role is specifically manifested in the following key dimensions:

Firstly, expression and communication is the cornerstone of language construction. Students' effective accumulation and construction of personalized language materials and speech practice experience rely on their ability to clearly express their feelings and understandings of the overall connotations of texts. Meanwhile, the in-depth process of language expression and communication itself is an effective way for students to deepen their understanding of the expressive features of words and sentence patterns as well as their inherent implications.

Secondly, expression and communication is the carrier of thinking development. Effective language practice significantly promotes the cultivation of students' abilities of association and imagination. Adequate communication can activate and deepen students' intuitive experience abilities regarding language and literary images. More importantly, students can truly cultivate key thinking abilities such as induction and generalization only by clearly elaborating on the reasoning processes and conclusions. The process of critically examining existing information and viewpoints and forming reflective insights not only improves deductive reasoning abilities but also enriches and optimizes the content and effect of their expression and communication in return.

Thirdly, expression and communication runs through the whole process of aesthetic appreciation cultivation. Fully expressing oneself in language practice activities such as role-playing and conducting in-depth communication in the appreciation of the expressive effects of texts, words, phrases and sentences - the core link in classroom dialogues aiming at the development of aesthetic appreciation abilities is precisely the typical language practice activity of expression and communication. It can be said that sufficient and in-depth language expression and communication is an indispensable core path for cultivating and improving students' aesthetic appreciation abilities.

Finally, expression and communication drives cultural understanding and comprehension. Adequate expression and communication in classroom dialogues can effectively guide students to pay attention to and explore the cultural elements in language materials. Through dialogues and discussions, students can understand and comprehend more deeply the typical characteristics and spiritual cores contained in outstanding cultures both at home and abroad throughout history.

To sum up, in Chinese mother tongue education, guiding students to conduct "expression and communication" independently and adequately is the core dynamic mechanism by which classroom dialogues promote students' language accumulation and construction, thinking development and improvement, cultivation of aesthetic appreciation abilities as well as cultural understanding and inheritance. It constitutes the key evolution path for the coordinated development of students' language abilities and core competencies.

6 Educational Experimental Research

By focusing on the key behaviors in classroom dialogues at different levels, it can be found that in the classroom dialogues at medium and low levels, the proportion of "expression and communication" is relatively low, which is consistent with the higher occupancy rate of teachers' behaviors and the lower conversion rate of teacher-student behaviors in these two types of classroom dialogues. That is to say, both types of classroom dialogues present the teaching characteristics centered on teachers' lectures, which restricts the space for students to freely express and communicate in classroom dialogues. Meanwhile, in the classroom dialogues at medium and low levels, "comprehension and analysis" is the dialogue content indicator with the highest proportion. Through a comprehensive analysis of the occupancy rate of teachers' behaviors and the conversion rate of teacher-student behaviors in these two types of classrooms, it can be known that in these two types of classroom dialogues, the main body of "comprehension and analysis" is teachers rather than students. The large amount of teachers' lectures in the classroom is the main reason for the highest proportion of this indicator. In the classroom dialogues at the high level, "expression and communication" becomes the dialogue content indicator with the highest proportion. Combining the lower occupancy rate of teachers' behaviors and the higher conversion rate of teacher-student behaviors in classroom dialogues at this level, it can be found that students are the main body of "expression and communication". It can be seen from this that whether students are regarded as the main body of "expression and communication" in the classroom and whether the content of classroom dialogues focuses on the "development and improvement of students' thinking" are important factors that determine the level of classroom dialogues.

Based on the above research findings, this study designed a randomized controlled experiment. Twelve classes were selected and randomly divided into a control group and an experimental group to conduct a one-month quasi-experimental research. In the experimental group, this study adopted measures such as setting up a mandatory speaking mechanism, group cooperative learning, and classroom debates to increase students' participation in classroom dialogues and raise the proportion of student-student dialogues and teacher-student dialogues in classroom dialogues.

This study conducted classroom observations on the two groups of classes and recorded the following data: the occupancy rate of teachers' behaviors, the conversion rate of teacher-student behaviors, the proportion of thinking-oriented dialogues, and the proportion of "expression and communication". Meanwhile, Chinese reading comprehension tests (with a full score of 100 points) and critical thinking tests (using the CTT scale, with a full score of 50 points) were conducted on students in both groups before and after the experiment. After one-month teaching experiment intervention, this study collected data and analyzed them. The specific contents are shown in the following table (Table 9).

Table 9. Significantly Enhanced Dialogue Quality and Student Engagement in Experimental Group Post-Intervention

Indicator	Experimental Group (n = 6 classes)	Control Group (n = 6 classes)	Difference	Effect Size (d)
DQI	36.7 ± 4.1	28.4 ± 3.8	8.3	1.37
Student-Student Dialogue Ratio	41% → 58%	40% → 42%	16%	1.82
Expression/Interaction (D) Frequency per Class	12.3 → 24.5	11.7 → 13.2	11.3	1.94
Teacher-Student Behavior Transition Rate (S/R)	51% → 73%	47% → 52%	21%	1.65
Reading Comprehension Score Gain	+8.7 points	+2.1 points	6.6	1.28

Based on a comprehensive analysis of the content in the above table, it can be known that increasing the frequency of "expression and communication" in classroom dialogues and raising the proportion of "student-student dialogues" in classroom dialogues can effectively improve the conversion rate of teacher-student behaviors and further enhance students' reading ability performance. Meanwhile, the improvement of students' participation promotes the redistribution of the right to speak in classroom dialogues, increases the depth of dialogues and promotes the development of high-order thinking, which has a positive promoting effect on improving the quality of classroom dialogues.

7 Conclusion

This study achieved highly accurate automatic coding of classroom dialogues by constructing a coding label system for Chinese mother tongue education classroom dialogues, creating an automatic coding dataset for classroom dialogues, and carrying out pre-training for automatic coding of classroom dialogues based on large language models (LLMs). Based on the automatic coding results of 300 teaching cases, we conducted descriptive statistical analysis and lag sequential analysis (LSA), thus clarifying the typical characteristics of classroom dialogues at different proficiency levels in the field of Chinese mother tongue education and revealing the effective learning laws contained in high-level classroom dialogues. Finally, relying on the automatic coding of diachronic classroom dialogues and in-depth data mining, this study designed educational experiments and verified the significant promoting effect of increasing the frequency of students' "expression and communication" and the proportion of students' dialogues in classroom dialogues on the development of students' learning abilities.

The results of this study can provide important implications for the research on automatic coding and analysis of classroom dialogues in other disciplines:

Firstly, the construction idea of the coding system for Chinese mother tongue education classroom dialogues can be borrowed. Combined with the core learning contents of the discipline, a classroom dialogue coding system targeting the key abilities of the discipline can be developed to lay a tool foundation for automatic coding.

Secondly, by referring to the constituent elements and structural design of the pre-training corpus for Chinese mother tongue education, systematically collecting, sorting out and annotating classroom dialogue texts at different levels of the discipline, supplemented by detailed annotation explanations, an automatic coding pre-training corpus for classroom dialogues specific to the discipline can be effectively constructed. On this basis, using the model fine-tuning technology to conduct automatic coding generation experiments for classroom dialogues can form a high-efficiency vertical model applicable to the discipline.

Thirdly, by drawing on the main framework and methodology of this study (such as the combination of automatic coding and LSA analysis), the typical characteristics of classroom dialogues at different proficiency levels within the discipline can be effectively explored, and then the key characteristics and effective teaching paths of high-level classroom dialogues can be extracted, providing a powerful quantitative basis for the improvement of discipline classroom teaching.

Finally, by referring to the design and implementation process of the educational experiment adopted in this study, quasi-experimental studies on classroom dialogues can be carried out within the discipline to verify the actual effectiveness of the extracted high-level classroom dialogue teaching paths on improving students' learning abilities.

The results of this study have important reference value for the practice of mother tongue classroom teaching:

Firstly, mother tongue classroom teaching should fully establish the dominant position of students in dialogues and focus on promoting the effective development of student-student dialogues and teacher-student dialogues. By significantly increasing the proportion of students' dialogues in the total amount of classroom dialogues and stimulating students' enthusiasm to actively participate in dialogues, more sufficient opportunities for students' expression and communication can be created.

Secondly, dialogue tasks and scaffolds aiming at in-depth language construction, high-order thinking development, meticulous aesthetic appreciation and profound cultural understanding should be carefully designed to guide students to conduct in-depth and high-quality expression and communication around the core learning contents. This requires teachers to focus on the core role of "expression and communication" and provide clear goal guidance and necessary thinking tools for students in activities such as role-playing, text appreciation and opinion debate.

Finally, teachers need to pay attention to the depth and quality of dialogues, go beyond the simple question-and-answer form, and guide students to carry out high-order cognitive activities such as explanation, reasoning, reflection and evaluation. Through timely and specific feedback, students can be helped to continuously optimize the logic, accuracy and richness of their expressions, so that classroom dialogues can truly become the core engine driving the coordinated development of students' language abilities and core competencies.

References

1. Yu, S.: Research hotspots and frontier trends in the field of classroom dialogue. Global Educ. Outlook **49**(12), 27–40 (2020)
2. Cao, Y., Yu, S., Zhao, W., et al.: Research on the construction of an artificial intelligence evaluation system for mathematical classroom dialogue oriented to education 2030. J. Math. Educ. **31**(01), 7–12 (2022)
3. Yan, W., Song, L.: From in-depth dialogue to high-order thinking: classroom dialogue teaching in high school mathematics based on the IRF theory. Jiangsu Educ. **16**, 46–49 (2023)
4. Zheng, T.: Learner-centered classroom dialogue: theoretical framework and case analysis. Open Educ. Res. **25**(04), 59–65 (2019)
5. Cui, Y.: On the LICC paradigm of classroom observation: a professional way of classroom observation and evaluation. Educ. Res. **33**(05), 79–83 (2012)
6. Sun, Z., Lü, K., Shi, Z., et al.: TESTII framework: the development trend of artificial intelligence supporting classroom teaching analysis. E-Educ. Res. **42**(02), 33–39 + 77 (2021)
7. Yu, S., Xu, C., Zhu, J., et al.: Oriented to thinking cultivation: intelligent classroom teaching analysis and application based on precise annotation technology. J. East China Normal Univ. (Educ. Sci.) **41**(08), 79–89 (2023)
8. Yang, X., Wang, Q., Jiang, J.: Analysis of classroom teacher-student dialogue based on artificial intelligence: automatic classification and level-based construction of IRE. E-Educ. Res. **44**(10), 79–86 (2023)
9. Formulated by the Ministry of Education of the People's Republic of China. Chinese Curriculum Standards for General High Schools (2017 Edition), vol. 7. People's Education Press, Beijing (2018)
10. Yue, M., et al.: Automated coding utterances toward chinese course core competence with large language models. In: Proceedings of the International Conference on Intelligent Computing (2025). Unpublished

11. Wen, Z., Xie, J., Wang, H.: Principles, steps and procedures of latent class models. J. East China Normal Univ. (Educ. Sci.) **41**(01), 1–15 (2023)
12. Jia, L., Sun, H., Jiang, J., Yang, X.: High-quality classroom dialogue automatic analysis system. Appl. Sci. **15**(3), 1613 (2025)
13. Zhang, Z.: Research on teacher-student interactive behaviors in effective classroom teaching. Shanghai Normal University (2015)
14. Wang, X.: Research on the development of teachers' teaching abilities from the perspective of curriculum reform. East China Normal University (2006)
15. Zhong, Z.: Research on the construction and application of the intelligent learning model supported by artificial intelligence. Northeast Normal University (2023)

Exploration and Practice of Aesthetic Education in College Computer Courses from the Perspective of AI

Niefang Yu[1,2,3](✉), Xiaomei Li[1,2,3], and Xiaoning Peng[1,2,3]

[1] School of Computer Science and Artificial Intelligence (Software College), Huaihua University, Huaihua 418000, Hunan, People's Republic of China
Ziseyu1006@163.com

[2] Key Laboratory of Wuling-Mountain Health Big Data Intelligent Processing and Application in Hunan Province Universities, Huaihua 418000, Hunan, People's Republic of China

[3] Key Laboratory of Intelligent Control Technology for Wuling-Mountain Ecological Agriculture in Hunan Province, Huaihua 418000, Hunan, People's Republic of China

Abstract. In the new era where Artificial Intelligence profoundly empowers educational transformation, the traditional "technology-first" teaching paradigm in university computer science curricula can no longer meet the contemporary demand to "cultivate well-rounded socialist builders and successors excelling in moral, intellectual, physical, aesthetic, and labor education". Guided by the Opinions on Comprehensively Strengthening and Improving Aesthetic Education in Schools in the New Era, this study systematically examines the theoretical foundations and practical challenges of integrating aesthetic education into computer science curricula. By establishing a trinity teaching framework encompassing technical cognition, aesthetic experience, and value guidance—supported by AI empowerment, interdisciplinary integration, faculty development, and a multi-dimensional evaluation mechanism—we explore innovative pathways for deep convergence between technological education and aesthetic education. Through restructured content, pedagogical innovation, AI-enabled applications, and assessment reform, the research significantly enhances students' computational thinking and aesthetic literacy. The integration of AI not only optimizes aesthetic education efficiency but also stimulates students' creative potential through intelligent feedback and immersive experiences. Meanwhile, interdisciplinary collaboration and value guidance facilitate students' transition from technical executors to digital civilization architects.

Keyword: Artificial Intelligence · University Computer Courses · Aesthetic Education

1 Introduction

With the promulgation of the Opinions on Comprehensively Strengthening and Improving Aesthetic Education in Schools in the New Era [1], China's higher education has formally entered a new developmental phase of "technology-humanities synergy" [2].

W. Hong et al. (Eds.): ICCSE 2025, CCIS 2761, pp. 288–300, 2026.
https://doi.org/10.1007/978-981-95-7731-6_23

Against this backdrop, the field of university computer science education has undergone profound transformations. The traditional teaching model centered on technical application" has gradually been replaced by a new pedagogical system framed through the lens of aesthetic empowerment." This shift requires students not only to master computer operation skills and programming abilities but also to develop keen aesthetic judgment, thereby becoming well-rounded "digital civilization builders."

The single principle of "Prioritizing Functional Realization" in traditional teaching has been completely subverted, replaced by a three-dimensional comprehensive teaching system of "Technical Cognition - Aesthetic Experience - Value Guidance". As artificial intelligence technology is fully integrated into all fields of social production, it provides a new opportunity for the teaching reform of university computer courses. With the power of AI technology, we can more efficiently achieve the in-depth integration of aesthetic education concepts with computer course teaching, thereby cultivating students' aesthetic taste and innovative ability. This is not only an important measure to respond to policy calls, but also an inevitable requirement for contributing to the cultivation of socialist builders and successors with all-round development of morality, intelligence, physical fitness, aesthetics and labor.

2 Current Challenges in Aesthetic Education Within University Computer Courses

In the current teaching of college computer courses, we generally attach importance to the cultivation of technical skills, but to a certain extent, overlook the importance of aesthetic education. As an essential part of quality-oriented education, aesthetic education aims to cultivate students' aesthetic awareness, aesthetic taste, and ability to create beauty. However, in the current computer teaching, aesthetic education has not received due attention.

First, curriculum learning often focuses on computer application capabilities, leading students to invest their main energy in technical learning and practice. This tendency makes students only pay attention to the practicality of computers during the learning process, while ignoring the aesthetic value contained in this course. With the rapid development of computer technology, we should not only teach students how to use these technologies but also guide them to discover the aesthetic charm behind the technology.

Secondly, in the selection of teaching materials and the organization of classroom content, there is also a lack of cultivation and guidance for students' aesthetic abilities. Traditional teaching materials often focus on the infusion of theoretical knowledge and the explanation of technical operations, while ignoring the cultivation of students' aesthetic literacy. This makes it difficult for students to form a deep understanding and perception of beauty during the learning process.

Furthermore, the traditional teaching model hardly stimulates students' interest in and pursuit of beauty. In college computer courses, teachers often adopt teaching methods of lecturing and demonstration, lacking interactivity and innovation. Such teaching methods make it difficult to trigger students' thinking and perception of beauty, and cannot meet their pursuit and yearning for beauty. In addition, aesthetic education teaching resources and methods are relatively scarce. On the one hand, there is a lack of specialized aesthetic education teaching materials and resources; on the other hand, the existing teaching methods and means have not fully utilized the advantages of modern information technology, failing to provide students with rich and diverse aesthetic experiences.

In summary, the current situation of aesthetic education in college computer courses is not optimistic, facing many challenges. To cultivate students' comprehensive qualities and improve their aesthetic and creative abilities, we need to re-examine the teaching objectives and content of computer courses, and strengthen the infiltration and integration of aesthetic education in them.

3 Teaching Reform Ideas and Practices

Under the backdrop of the AI era reshaping the educational ecosystem, the aesthetic education reform in university computer science courses is not only a crucial measure in response to the national strategy of "coordinated development of technology and humanities," but also an inevitable choice for cultivating innovative and versatile talents equipped with both technical expertise and humanistic literacy. Confronted with the current reality of the lack of aesthetic education in traditional teaching, we adopt a problem-oriented approach and implement systematic reform focusing on key aspects: the teaching system, curriculum content, teaching methodologies, teaching practice, and teaching evaluation. By integrating AI technology with aesthetic education resources, we construct an innovative teaching model that combines theory and practice, aiming to break down the barriers between technology and the humanities, and ultimately achieve the organic unity of knowledge impartation, skill cultivation, and value shaping.

3.1 Integrating Technology and Aesthetic Education to Construct a New Teaching System

To integrate the concept of aesthetic education into the teaching of university computer courses, we have constructed a trinity teaching system of "Technical Cognition - Aesthetic Experience - Value Guidance" [3]. As shown in Fig. 1: Framework of the Trinity Teaching System, this system aims to strengthen students' understanding and application of computer technology through the technical cognition link; cultivate students' aesthetic taste and appreciation ability through the aesthetic experience link; and foster students' cultural sense of responsibility and ethical commitment through the value guidance link.

In the technical cognition link, we focus on cultivating students' innovative thinking and practical ability. By guiding students to explore new methods and ideas, we stimulate their desire for exploration and creative potential. At the same time, we also encourage students to participate in scientific research projects and practical activities, allowing them to continuously exercise and improve their technical capabilities in the process of solving problems.

In the aesthetic experience link, we cultivate students' aesthetic taste and appreciation ability through classic case analysis and practical operations. The definition of beauty has been endowed with new connotations in the new AI era. In the field of computer science, beauty is not only reflected in aspects such as algorithm optimization, user-friendly interfaces, and data visualization, but more importantly, in how to realize the harmonious coexistence between humans and machines through technical means, and create works that both meet human aesthetic needs and have practical value. Meanwhile, students are encouraged to participate in creation, integrating their personal emotions and aesthetic concepts into their works, thereby enhancing their ability of aesthetic expression.

In the value guidance link, we integrate humanistic elements into university computer courses, such as historical background, ethics and morality, and social responsibility. By broadening students' horizons and enhancing their sense of social responsibility, we enable them to become well-rounded builders of digital civilization. In addition, we also attach importance to cultivating students' teamwork spirit and innovative ability, laying a solid foundation for their future career development.

The logical relationship among the three is as follows: Technical cognition serves as the foundation, providing tools and methods for aesthetic creation; Aesthetic experience is the core, realizing the transformation of technical learning into aesthetic education; Value guidance is the elevation, endowing technical application with humanistic warmth. AI technology, through intelligent tools, immersive experiences, dynamic evaluation and other means, provides a supporting engine for the integration of these three dimensions.

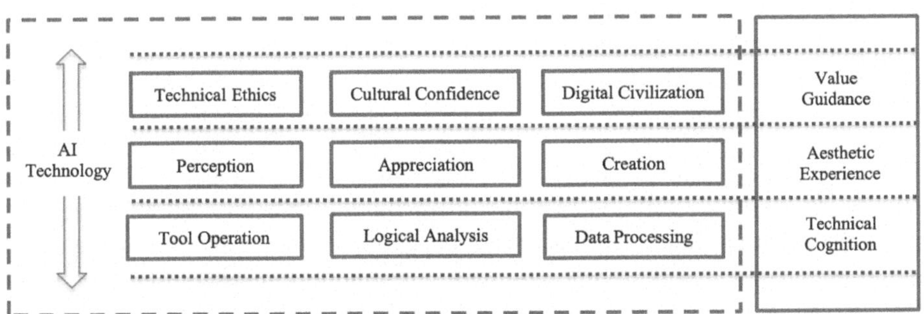

Fig. 1. Framework of the Trinity Teaching System

3.2 Optimizing Teaching Content to Enhance Aesthetic Perception

When teaching data structures, we not only require students to understand the logical and physical structures of various data types, but also guide them to appreciate the symmetry and simplicity within data structures [4]. In algorithm design, while emphasizing correctness, we equally encourage students to pursue concise and efficient algorithms [5]. During computer hardware instruction, we not only ensure students master the construction and functions of components, but also help them perceive the aesthetic qualities in hardware design. By incorporating aesthetics into knowledge delivery, students not only acquire professional expertise but also discover beauty within the realm of computing.

In university computer course teaching practices, we focus on cultivating students' creative abilities. By encouraging students to apply acquired knowledge in original projects and guiding them to emphasize aesthetic design elements such as composition, layout, color, and shape, we help students progressively enhance their aesthetic sensibility and creativity. Simultaneously, we implement peer review mechanisms requiring students to exercise aesthetic judgment when evaluating peers' work, thereby further advancing their aesthetic literacy.

To elevate faculty members' aesthetic proficiency and pedagogical capabilities, we have intensified teacher training. Through organizing specialized workshops and seminars on aesthetic education, we equip instructors with effective methodologies and techniques for integrating aesthetic concepts into teaching, ensuring successful implementation of aesthetic education principles.

In summary, by integrating aesthetic principles, leveraging multimedia resources, strengthening in-class creative projects with peer evaluation systems, and enhancing faculty development initiatives, we have optimized aesthetic education content in university computer curricula and significantly elevated students' aesthetic capabilities.

3.3 Improving Teaching Methods to Enhance Aesthetic Education

In the current wave of educational reform, innovating teaching methods is particularly important, especially for enhancing students' aesthetic experience. We should actively seek changes and introduce new teaching models such as project-based learning and inquiry-based learning. These methods can not only enhance classroom interaction but also stimulate students' initiative and creativity.

Project-Based Learning (PBL) is a student-centered teaching method. It cultivates students' critical thinking, cooperation ability, and problem-solving skills by involving them in the process of solving real-world problems [6]. In computer graphics design courses, teachers can design a project related to urban planning, allowing students to work in groups to plan the layout of a virtual city using computer graphics design software. Students need to consider the aesthetics, functionality, and environmental protection of the city, and experience the process of creating beauty through practical operations, thereby deeply understanding the connotation and value of beauty. In this process, students can not only develop critical thinking, cooperation ability, and problem-solving skills but also improve their aesthetic literacy.

Inquiry-Based Learning (IBL) focuses on cultivating students' spirit of inquiry and autonomous learning ability [7]. By putting forward challenging questions and guiding students to actively explore, research, and discover, students can not only acquire knowledge but also experience the joy of discovering beauty in this process. In computer programming courses, we encourage students to explore the aesthetic characteristics of different programming languages, such as the conciseness, readability, and efficiency of code. By comparing and analyzing the advantages and disadvantages of different programming languages, students can gain a deeper understanding of the logic and principles behind programming, thus experiencing the joy of discovering beauty. In addition, we also guide students to explore the artistry of computer algorithms to further improve their aesthetic appreciation.

In addition to new teaching models like PBL and IBL, we have also tried to introduce gamified learning into university computer courses. By designing challenging game tasks, we stimulate students' learning interest and participation. In the process of playing games, students need to use the computer knowledge and skills they have learned to solve problems, thereby continuously improving their technical ability and aesthetic taste.

3.4 AI-Assisted Aesthetic Education Teaching Practices

With the continuous development of artificial intelligence technology, its application in the field of education has become increasingly widespread. In the aesthetic education of university computer courses, we have fully utilized the advantages of AI technology to carry out a series of innovative teaching practices.

Case 1: AI-Assisted Graphic Design Teaching. Driven by AI technology, graphic design teaching has undergone a transformative revolution. By using AI graphic design software, teachers can more efficiently impart design principles, while students can more intuitively understand and master core knowledge such as color matching, composition, and other design elements, ultimately creating independent and creative design works [8].

During the teaching process, instructors first introduce the basic functions and interface of AI graphic design software. Subsequently, through the software's built-in intelligent tutorials and example demonstrations, students are guided step-by-step to learn the principles of color matching, composition techniques, and the application of design elements. Students can freely experiment with different design schemes in the software's virtual environment, with the software providing real-time feedback and suggestions to help them continuously optimize and refine their works.

The AI graphic design software also features intelligent analysis capabilities, conducting in-depth evaluations of students' design works, identifying shortcomings, and offering targeted improvement suggestions. This not only significantly enhances students' design efficiency but also helps them gradually develop their own design style and thinking through continuous experimentation and refinement.

Through AI-assisted graphic design teaching, students can quickly grasp design principles and practical skills while continuously stimulating their innovative thinking and aesthetic abilities. Ultimately, with the help of the software, they independently complete creative and visually appealing design works, laying a solid foundation for their future career development.

Case 2: Project Practice Combining Programming and Art. In an innovative educational project, students explored the perfect integration of programming and artistic creation. The project aimed to allow students to create unique digital artworks through coding, deeply experiencing the creativity and artistry of programming.

At the beginning of the project, students first learned the basics of programming, including variables, loops, and conditional statements. Subsequently, they were introduced to graphical programming environments such as Scratch or Processing, which enabled them to draw shapes, colors, and animations through code. After mastering basic programming skills, students began creating their own digital artworks. They used code to control color variations, shape combinations, and animations, transforming programming logic into visual artistic expression. Throughout this process, students not only honed their programming skills but also unleashed their artistic creativity.

Through this project, students deeply experienced the infinite possibilities of combining programming with artistic creation. They not only learned how to create beauty through code but also developed a strong interest in interdisciplinary learning and innovation.

Case 3: Application of Virtual Reality Technology in Aesthetic Education. As a cutting-edge technology, virtual reality (VR) has introduced new teaching models and experiences to the field of aesthetic education [9]. In simulating artistic creation environments, VR technology demonstrates unique advantages. Through VR, students can immerse themselves in virtual museums, recreate historical scenes, and more. This immersive experience greatly enriches students' artistic perspectives and inspires their creative ideas.

The application of VR technology has significantly enhanced students' learning interest. They are no longer satisfied with traditional textbooks and images but instead seek to explore and discover the charm of art through firsthand experiences. This proactive learning attitude not only improves their learning outcomes but also lays a solid foundation for their artistic journey [10].

In summary, the application of VR technology in aesthetic education holds broad prospects and profound significance. It not only provides students with richer and more diverse learning resources but also stimulates their creative inspiration and learning enthusiasm, injecting new vitality and momentum into aesthetic education.

3.5 Interdisciplinary Integration: Breaking the Boundaries Between Technology and Art

In university basic computer courses, interdisciplinary integration can break the boundaries between technology and art, providing students with a more comprehensive and innovative learning experience. Here are several carefully designed interdisciplinary teaching cases.

The "Drawing Artistic Charts with Python" case is aimed at students majoring in science and engineering. As a powerful programming language, Python has significant advantages in data processing and visualization. Students can use Python's plotting libraries such as Matplotlib and Seaborn to transform experimental data from science and engineering majors into artistic charts. For example, in physics experiments, students can plot the changing data of physical quantities obtained from experiments into line graphs. By adjusting line colors, styles, and marker shapes, and combining knowledge of color psychology, warm colors can be used to represent positive changes and cool colors to represent negative changes, making the charts not only accurately convey data information but also possess artistic beauty. Meanwhile, in terms of chart layout, referring to the composition principles of graphic design, the positions of coordinate axes, titles, and legends are reasonably arranged to make the charts clearer and more attractive.

The "Achieving Data Visualization Aesthetics with PS" case is more suitable for students majoring in liberal arts. Adobe Photoshop is a powerful image processing software, with which liberal arts students can integrate text, pictures, and data to realize visual expression of data. For example, in sociological research, students can insert survey data into PS in the form of charts, and use PS functions such as color adjustment and filter effects to beautify and artistically process the charts. They can also combine text descriptions and picture elements to create narrative and appealing data visualization posters, presenting sociological research results in a more attractive way.

Take the algorithmic art work Fractal Trees of Four Seasons as an example:

Technical Implementation: Students use Python's turtle library to generate four distinct fractal trees by adjusting the branch angles of recursive functions (45° for spring, 60° for summer, 30° for autumn, and 15° for winter) and dynamically changing line colors (RGB values).

Aesthetic Expression: It integrates the concept of "coloring according to categories" in traditional Chinese landscape painting (green for spring, red for summer, yellow for autumn, and white for winter) and embeds Morse code of school motto keywords into the trunk texture, achieving the triple expression of "technical logic-visual beauty-cultural symbols".

Teacher's Evaluation: "The work not only demonstrates a profound understanding of recursive algorithms but also conveys the Eastern philosophy of 'the cycle of four seasons' through parametric design, reflecting the high-level integration of computational thinking and aesthetic thinking."

These interdisciplinary teaching cases have a close collaborative mechanism with art courses and humanities courses. In collaboration with basic design courses, the technologies learned by students in basic computer courses can be applied to design practice, while the aesthetic principles and design methods in basic design courses can guide the creation of works in computer courses. For example, in the "Drawing Artistic Charts with Python" case, students can draw on the color matching and composition knowledge learned in basic design courses to improve the aesthetics of charts. In collaboration with art history courses, students can draw inspiration from art history and integrate different artistic styles into digital works. For instance, in the "Achieving Data Visualization Aesthetics with PS" case, students can imitate artistic styles such as Impressionism and Cubism to endow data visualization works with unique artistic charm. Through interdisciplinary integration, students can break the boundaries between technology and art, and cultivate comprehensive literacy and innovative ability.

3.6 Methodology for AI-Enhanced Aesthetic Education

First, direct feedback was collected from students and teachers through questionnaires. The survey covered multiple dimensions including teaching satisfaction, AI tool usability, and perceived learning outcomes, helping us understand participants' overall perspectives and specific suggestions regarding AI-assisted aesthetic education.

Second, in-depth evaluations of student works were conducted. We focused on students' creative processes under AI assistance, work originality, technical application, and artistic expression to assess the actual impact of AI technology on enhancing students' aesthetic capabilities.

Simultaneously, classroom observations served as an essential component. By monitoring teachers' usage of AI tools, student interactions, and classroom dynamics, we gained direct insights into the practical effectiveness of AI in aesthetic education and identified potential areas for improvement.

Based on these evaluation results, we implemented timely teaching strategy adjustments: optimizing AI tools' functionality and design according to survey feedback;

modifying instructional content and methods based on work evaluations to better stimulate students' creative potential; and refining teaching processes through observation findings to enhance AI-aesthetic education integration.

Ultimately, this scientific evaluation and feedback mechanism enables continuous optimization of AI-assisted aesthetic education models, delivering richer, more efficient, and personalized learning experiences.

4 Empirical Analysis: Teaching Experiment Based on Non-computer Majors in Our University

4.1 Experimental Design

1) Sample Selection and Grouping

Four natural classes (100 students in total) of the 2024-grade Biological Science major in our university were selected as the research subjects. The pre-test results of the computer basic test (full score 100, $t = 0.82$, $P = 0.41 > 0.05$) and the aesthetic literacy scale (using the College Students' Aesthetic Literacy Assessment Scale, pre-test results $t = 0.63$, $P = 0.53 > 0.05$) verified that there was no significant difference in technical foundation and aesthetic ability between the two groups, indicating comparability. The specific grouping is as follows:

Experimental group (50 students): Adopting the "Technical Cognition-Aesthetic Experience-Value Guidance" trinity teaching system, integrated with the AI aesthetic education toolkit;

Control group (50 students): Adopting the traditional teaching model, focusing on software operation and theoretical knowledge impartation, without introducing AI tools or aesthetic education content.

2) Control of Experimental Variables

Independent variable: Teaching system (the Trinity Teaching System vs. the Traditional Teaching System);

Dependent variables: Including three aspects: computational thinking ability, aesthetic literacy, and course satisfaction. Computational thinking ability is assessed using the National Computer Rank Examination Level 2 Python question bank (with a reliability of $\alpha = 0.87$), covering 5 dimensions such as algorithm design and data processing. Aesthetic literacy is evaluated through the College Students' Aesthetic Literacy Assessment Scale (including 3 dimensions: aesthetic perception, aesthetic creation, and aesthetic evaluation, with a reliability of $\alpha = 0.89$) and work scoring (blindly rated by 3 computer teachers and 2 art teachers, with an intraclass correlation coefficient ICC = 0.85).Course satisfaction is measured using a self-designed questionnaire (covering 3 dimensions: teaching content, methods, and tools, with a reliability of $\alpha = 0.91$).

Extraneous variables: Both groups are taught by the same teacher, with 4 class hours per week for a total of 12 weeks. The same textbook is used, but the experimental group is supplemented with the AI Aesthetic Education Case Manual.

3) Data Collection and Analysis Methods

Data Collection: Pre-tests and post-tests on computational thinking and aesthetic literacy were conducted before and after the experiment. Satisfaction questionnaires were collected after the course concluded. Meanwhile, semi-structured interviews were conducted with 10 students from the experimental group (each interview lasted 20–30 min, with transcribed texts totaling approximately 30,000 words).

Analysis Methods: SPSS 26.0 was used for independent samples t-test and paired samples t-test. Nvivo 12 was applied for coding analysis of interview texts (Kappa value = 0.82, indicating good consistency).

4.2 Quantitative Results Analysis

1) Improvement in Computational Thinking Ability

Table 1. Comparison of Pre-test and Post-test Results of Computational Thinking Ability between Experimental Group and Control Group (x ± s, full score 100)

Dimension	Group	Pre-test	Post-test	Difference	t-value	P-value
Algorithm Design	Experimental	58.2 ± 8.3	76.5 ± 7.2	18.3 ± 5.6	19.24	<0.001
	Control	57.8 ± 7.9	65.3 ± 6.8	7.5 ± 4.2	9.87	<0.001
Data Processing	Experimental	62.5 ± 9.1	81.3 ± 6.5	18.8 ± 5.1	22.31	<0.001
	Control	63.1 ± 8.7	70.2 ± 7.3	7.1 ± 4.5	8.92	<0.001
Problem Decomposition	Experimental	56.3 ± 8.5	78.6 ± 6.9	22.3 ± 4.8	28.45	<0.001
	Control	55.9 ± 8.2	64.7 ± 7.1	8.8 ± 3.9	12.53	<0.001
Overall Ability	Experimental	59.7 ± 7.8	79.2 ± 6.3	19.5 ± 4.3	27.68	<0.001
	Control	59.2 ± 7.5	66.8 ± 6.7	7.6 ± 3.8	11.26	<0.001

As shown in Table 1, both groups demonstrated significant improvement in post-test scores compared to pre-test ($P < 0.001$). However, the experimental group showed significantly greater progress in all dimensions (18.3–22.3 points) than the control group (7.1–8.8 points), with the largest gap in the "Problem Decomposition" dimension (13.5-point difference). This indicates that the trinity teaching system effectively cultivated students' computational thinking through tasks such as "algorithmic art creation" and "aesthetic transformation of data visualization." As one student noted in an interview: "When drawing fractal trees with Python, I had to decompose the recursive logic of 'trunk-branch-leaf' first. This 'technology + aesthetics' task deepened my understanding of algorithms."

Analysis Methods: SPSS 26.0 was used for independent samples t-test and paired samples t-test. Nvivo 12 was applied for coding analysis of interview texts (Kappa value = 0.82, indicating good consistency).

2) Improvement in Aesthetic Literacy

Table 2 shows that the experimental group's overall aesthetic literacy score (75.4 points) was significantly higher than that of the control group (58.9 points), with a large effect size (d = 2.77), indicating a significant impact of the teaching intervention. The largest gap appeared in "Aesthetic Creation" (18.6 points), confirming the empowering role of AI tools in enhancing creative abilities. The experimental group's "24 Solar Terms" posters, created using Stable Diffusion, scored significantly higher than the control group's traditional hand-drawn works in "cultural element integration" (e.g., combining paper-cut patterns with solar term customs) and "visual expressiveness" (e.g., color harmony, compositional balance) ($t = 8.76$, $P < 0.001$).

Table 2. Comparison of Aesthetic Literacy Post-test Results between Experimental Group and Control Group (x ± s, full score 100)

Dimension	Experimental Group	Control Group	t-value	P-value	Effect Size d
Aesthetic Perception	75.6 ± 6.8	62.3 ± 7.5	9.23	<0.001	1.85
Aesthetic Creation	72.4 ± 7.1	53.8 ± 8.2	12.65	<0.001	2.53
Aesthetic Evaluation	78.3 ± 6.5	60.5 ± 7.8	11.42	<0.001	2.28
Overall Literacy	75.4 ± 6.2	58.9 ± 7.1	13.87	<0.001	2.77

4.3 In-Depth Feedback from Students and Teachers

1) Student Feedback: New Experiences in Aesthetics and Creation

Student interviews revealed multiple positive outcomes demonstrating the significant impact of the new teaching system and methodologies. Regarding aesthetic experiences, many students reported that AI tools provided them with completely new understandings of beauty. One student commented: "The AI color-matching tool gave me the confidence to explore artistic expression. I used to know nothing about color coordination and was always afraid of using wrong colors. Now with this tool, I can boldly experiment with different color combinations, which has significantly improved the aesthetic quality of my work."

Another student shared: "The AI image generation tool opened up new creative possibilities for me. When I have an idea but don't know how to execute it, the tool can quickly generate relevant images that inspire me and help me better transform my creative concepts into actual works."

2) Teacher Reflections: Achievements and Challenges in Teaching Innovation

In their teaching reflections, educators have both affirmed the effectiveness of the new teaching strategies and identified existing challenges.

Regarding teaching outcomes, teachers generally agree that the new teaching system and methods have stimulated students' learning interest and engagement. One instructor noted: "The interdisciplinary cases have sparked students' learning enthusiasm. Previously, students showed little interest in basic computer courses, but now through these engaging cases, their active participation has significantly increased."

However, teachers have also encountered certain challenges. In terms of value guidance, some teachers reported: "During discussions on 'the social impact of digital works,' some students demonstrated insufficient understanding of technology ethics and aesthetic responsibility, requiring further guidance." Regarding the use of AI tools, despite having received training, some teachers expressed: "The rapid technological updates of certain AI tools necessitate continuous learning to better guide students, which places higher demands on our professional development as educators."

The in-depth feedback from both students and teachers demonstrates that the trinity teaching system of "Technical Cognition - Aesthetic Experience - Value Guidance" and its innovative implementation strategies have achieved remarkable results in enhancing students' aesthetic abilities and stimulating creative potential. However, continuous improvement and refinement in practice remain necessary to better adapt to students' evolving needs and the advancement of education.

5 Conclusions and Prospects

5.1 Summary of Research Findings

The "Technical Cognition - Aesthetic Experience - Value Guidance" trinity system provides a systematic framework for aesthetic education in fundamental computer courses. The Technical Cognition module integrates aesthetic elements into teaching content, enabling students across disciplines to enhance both technical proficiency and aesthetic literacy, thereby laying groundwork for digital era development. The Aesthetic Experience module employs AI technologies like intelligent color-matching systems and virtual art platforms to stimulate creative potential through immersive artistic experiences. The Value Guidance module facilitates students' transformation from technical executors to digital civilization builders by emphasizing social values in creative works, achieving alignment with socialist core values.

5.2 Future Development Directions

Sample Expansion: While achieving preliminary results, this study's sample size remains limited. Future research should incorporate broader participant pools across more institutions and disciplines to comprehensively validate the pedagogy system's effectiveness and enhance findings' generalizability.

Specialized AI Tool Development: Current AI tools predominantly serve general purposes. Future work should develop dedicated aesthetic education tools for computer fundamentals, such as discipline-specific intelligent aesthetic evaluation systems and personalized creative assistance platforms, to better address pedagogical needs.

Interdisciplinary Integration: Existing cross-disciplinary cases require deeper implementation. Enhanced collaboration with fields like philosophy and psychology should explore technology-aesthetics and techno-ethical relationships, providing more comprehensive learning experiences.

Teacher Training Enhancement: Evolving technologies demand continuous faculty upskilling. Future efforts should optimize training systems through increased frequency and depth, enabling better mastery of both AI applications and aesthetic education theories.

In conclusion, integrating aesthetic education into computer fundamentals through AI represents an ongoing, long-term endeavor. Through persistent refinement, we anticipate achieving optimal fusion between technical and aesthetic education, cultivating high-caliber talens with computational thinking and aesthetic competence to contribute to socialist modernization.

Acknowledgments. University-level Project "Exploration of Aesthetic Education in University Computer Fundamentals Curriculum in the Social Media Era".

References

1. Ministry of Education of the People's Republic of China: Opinions on Comprehensively Strengthening and Improving Aesthetic Education in Schools in the New Era (2020)
2. Li, L.: Exploration of challenges and transformation strategies for higher education art education in the digital age. Art Sci. Technol. **37**(18), 218–220 (2024)
3. Cao, Y.: Construction of a three-dimensional evaluation system for aesthetic education project-based learning. Gansu Educ. **11**, 34–41 (2023)
4. Reshitdin, A., ·Mamat, P.: Research on integrating ideological education into computer majors at vocational colleges in the AI era. China New Telecommun. **26**(16), 77–79 (2024)
5. Wang, W., Chen, X., Qiu, D.: Teaching reform of java programming based on "Ideological Education + Blended Learning." Indust. Technol. Vocat. Educ. **22**(6), 80–85 (2024)
6. Wang, Y., Guo, Y.: Research on computational thinking cultivation model based on project-based learning. Teach. Admin. **7**, 115–118 (2020)
7. Wang, C.: Application of inquiry-based teaching in computer programming instruction. Technol. Innov. Herald **17**(5), 184–186 (2020)
8. Liu, Y.: Aesthetic education immersion in digital-intelligence convergence: AI-art driven innovative thinking model and practice. China Univ. Teach. **8**, 60–68 (2024)
9. Cai, X., Chen, Q., Zhang, J.: Design and implementation of a VR experience system for classical chinese poetry culture via AI co-creation. Publish. J. **31**(4), 80–83 (2023)
10. Sun, L.: Redefining the "Cloud" Era: technological transition and emotional logic of virtual reality. Theory Monthly **4**, 146–152 (2024)

High-Speed Reading Aloud as a Pedagogical Strategy for Enhancing Cognitive and Expressive Language Skills in Non-kanji Background Learners

Kenichiro Kutsuna[1(✉)], Kunaj Somchanakit[1], Yoko Honda[2], and Hiroki Takada[3]

[1] Thaksin University, Songkhla 90000, Thailand
kenichiro.k@tsu.ac.th
[2] Kamakura Women's University, Kanagawa 247-8512, Japan
[3] University of Fukui, Fukui 910-8507, Japan
takada@u-fukui.ac.jp

Abstract. This study explores the nonlinear relationship between text length and oral reading speed among Japanese language learners from non-kanji backgrounds. Over four years, 126 university students read texts ranging from 50 to 700 characters. Reading speed (characters per second) showed a distinctive non-monotonic pattern: it decreased up to approximately 300 characters, increased between 300 and 600 characters, and declined again beyond 600. These findings suggest that moderately long texts facilitate fluent reading by supporting contextual prediction and rhythm formation, whereas very short or overly long texts disrupt processing due to fragmentation or cognitive overload. A comparison between two reading formats—whole-text reading (Condition A) and paragraph-segmented reading (Condition B)—revealed that Condition A generally led to faster reading speeds in the 300–600 characters range, highlighting the importance of cohesive rhythm and uninterrupted flow. Crucially, the nonlinear trend observed may reflect not only surface-level behavior but also deeper neurocognitive dynamics. Studies in cognitive neuroscience suggest that oral reading engages distributed brain regions and that reading rhythm and fluency are associated with synchronized brain activity. Therefore, this study proposes the need for future research using EEG to investigate real-time neural processing during oral reading. The findings have pedagogical implications for optimizing reading materials and training methods. They also open new directions for evidence-based language education supported by neuroscience, particularly in identifying optimal reading conditions that enhance both performance and cognitive efficiency.

Keywords: Oral Reading Fluency · Text Length and Processing Speed · Nonlinear Cognitive Dynamics · Neurocognitive Approach in Language Learning · Instructional Design for Second Language Reading

W. Hong et al. (Eds.): ICCSE 2025, CCIS 2761, pp. 301–314, 2026.
https://doi.org/10.1007/978-981-95-7731-6_24

1 Introduction

1.1 Background and Rationale

Reading aloud is widely recognized as a fundamental activity in Japanese language education. It contributes not only to vocabulary acquisition and grammar reinforcement but also to the development of pronunciation, rhythm, and reading comprehension skills [1, 2]. In particular, for learners from non-kanji backgrounds, reading aloud serves as a bridge that integrates visual decoding with auditory processing, supporting comprehension and reducing cognitive burden [3].

However, the effectiveness of reading aloud is influenced not only by learners' proficiency levels and the complexity of texts but also by the length of the reading material itself. Despite the general assumption that longer texts naturally require more time to read, recent research has suggested that reading speed does not always decrease proportionally with increased text length [4, 5].

1.2 Significance from a Cognitive Neuroscience Perspective

Recent studies exploring the relationship between language processing and brain activity have demonstrated that the sequence of processes involved in reading aloud—visual recognition, semantic interpretation, and vocal articulation—is executed through the coordinated activation of multiple brain regions, including Broca's area, Wernicke's area, the supplementary motor area, and the prefrontal cortex.

It has been suggested that performing reading aloud at high speed can repeatedly reinforce the neural coordination among these regions, thereby promoting automatization of the reading process.

Furthermore, research utilizing electroencephalography (EEG) has shown that when learners read syntactically well-structured texts rapidly, there is a notable increase in attentional focus, as reflected by frontal midline theta activity, as well as elevated activation in the speech-motor network [6, 7]. These findings suggest that increasing oral reading speed is not merely a matter of articulation training but also contributes to improved neural processing efficiency.

Based on these insights, the present study hypothesizes that high-speed reading aloud promotes advanced language processing, such as the transition from word-level to sentence-level accentuation, faster semantic integration, and the internalization of reading rhythm. These effects are empirically examined in relation to both reading performance and speed.

1.3 Purpose of the Study

The present study investigates how varying text lengths affect oral reading speed in Japanese among learners from non-kanji language backgrounds. Specifically, it examines whether moderately long texts (approximately 400–600 characters) facilitate faster reading than either shorter or significantly longer texts. Furthermore, it compares two types of reading formats: whole texts (Condition A) and segmented texts by paragraph (Condition B), to determine how text segmentation affects fluency.

This investigation is motivated by the hypothesis that high-speed reading aloud enhances not only reading efficiency but also the natural acquisition of Japanese sentence-level intonation. In Japanese, lexical accent (word-level pitch) and phrasal or international accent (sentence-level pitch) often conflict, making it difficult for learners to replicate natural prosody [8]. Fast-paced reading is considered to simulate natural spoken rhythm and may therefore aid in acquiring native-like intonation patterns.

1.4 Significance and Novelty

This study contributes to the field of Japanese language education by identifying the optimal text length for promoting reading fluency through speed-oriented reading aloud. By combining insights from pedagogy, cognitive linguistics, and neurocognitive science, it provides a foundation for designing effective reading materials tailored to learners' processing capacities. Moreover, it lays the groundwork for future empirical validation using EEG (electroencephalogram) to analyze real-time cognitive load and attention during oral reading tasks.

2 Literature Review

2.1 Educational Functions of Reading Aloud

Reading aloud plays multiple roles in Japanese language education. Mozumi and Adachi [7] categorized its pedagogical purposes as follows: (1) drawing learners' attention to form and meaning, (2) enhancing comprehension, (3) providing opportunities for teacher evaluation, (4) supporting classroom management, (5) enabling embodied language learning, and (6) boosting learners' confidence and motivation. Especially in reading instruction, reading aloud encourages learners to notice errors in their pronunciation and become more conscious of new vocabulary items.

2.2 Development of Reading Fluency

Kobayashi [8] emphasized that fluent reading results from the accumulation of learning time, vocabulary expansion, pattern recognition, and reading experience. These elements, once internalized, allow learners to read without conscious decoding, thus achieving high-speed reading. Furthermore, Taguchi & Gorsuch & Sasamoto [5] noted that repeated oral reading of coherent passages can foster automatization of the reading process, especially when learners benefit from contextual support that allows for prediction of upcoming words or structures.

Reading fluency, therefore, is not merely a matter of decoding speed but also involves the integration of prosody, comprehension, and rhythm, especially in reading aloud. These components work together to improve learners' overall processing efficiency.

2.3 Text Length and Cognitive Load

Reading aloud is an activity that requires multiple cognitive processes (character recognition, meaning processing, and vocalization) simultaneously, and therefore has a close relationship with cognitive resources (working memory and attention). According to Sweller [9] Cognitive Load Theory, as the amount of information increases, it is possible to exceed the capacity of working memory, resulting in a decrease in learning efficiency and processing speed.

Reading speed is influenced not only by vocabulary difficulty and syntactic complexity but also by the number of characters in the text. Breznitz [4] noted that as reading materials become longer, working memory load increases, often leading to slower performance. However, when texts are moderately long, they may provide enough semantic cohesion to allow for more efficient top-down processing, thereby supporting faster reading.

Taguchi [2] observed that learners tend to read more fluently when passages are long enough to support rhythm and chunking, but not so long that they overwhelm cognitive resources. In other words, there may exist an optimal text length that maximizes fluency by balancing predictability and load.

2.4 Prosody, Intonation, and Speed

Japanese pitch accent operates at two levels: lexical accent, which differentiates words, and phrasal or sentence-level intonation, which determines natural rhythm and meaning in context. These two levels sometimes conflict in actual speech. Sadanobu [10] proposed the "conflictive model," which explains how pitch realization in spoken Japanese results from the interaction between lexical and phrasal accents. For learners unfamiliar with this prosodic system, sentence-level intonation is often difficult to acquire.

One hypothesis of the present study is that reading aloud at higher speeds can induce prosodic adjustments more naturally. This approach simulates the rhythm of spontaneous speech, potentially facilitating the internalization of native-like intonation.

3 Method

3.1 Purpose

This study aims to investigate how variations in text length influence the oral reading speed of Japanese language learners from non-kanji backgrounds. Specifically, it analyzes whether moderately long texts (approximately 400–600 characters) yield faster reading than both shorter and longer texts. Additionally, it compares two text formats: whole-text reading (Condition A) and paragraph-separated reading (Condition B), to evaluate their impact on fluency.

3.2 Participants

The participants were second-year students majoring in Japanese at the Faculty of Humanities and Social Sciences, Thaksin University, Thailand. The experiment was conducted over four academic years. The number of participants by year was as follows:

2018: 37 students
2019: 31 students
2020: 23 students
2021: 35 students

All participants were native speakers of Thai and had Japanese proficiency equivalent to JLPT N5–N3. Prior informed consent was obtained from each participant.

3.3 Materials

Reading materials were taken from two different textbooks:

2018–2019: *GENKI II: An Integrated Course in Elementary Japanese II* (2nd ed.) by Banno et al. [11].

2020–2021: *Dekiru Nihongo: Beginner to Intermediate* (1st ed.) by Shimada [12].

Each textbook included about 10 lessons. Texts ranged from 50 to 700 characters per passage. In 2018 and 2021, each lesson was read as a whole passage (Condition A). In 2019 and 2020, the same texts were segmented into two or three paragraphs (Condition B) for separate reading to reduce time loss and cognitive load.

3.4 Procedure

The reading tasks were conducted individually in a face-to-face setting. Students were allowed to attempt the task multiple times. If they made pronunciation or accent errors, the trial was canceled, and they were instructed to retry. The number of characters read per second (characters/second) was calculated as a performance score, and students were permitted to continue until they achieved a satisfactory result.

In 2018, long texts were used in their entirety. While motivated students repeated the task to improve, the need to restart after a single error led to time inefficiencies. In 2019 and 2020, texts were divided into shorter segments to reduce fatigue and enhance focus. In 2021, due to COVID-19 restrictions, the segmented format was discontinued, and long texts were used again.

3.5 Data Collection and Analysis

Three metrics were collected:

Reading Time (seconds): Time required to complete each reading task

Character Count: Total number of characters in each passage

Reading Speed (characters/second): Calculated by dividing the character count by the reading time

Text lengths were categorized into ranges (e.g., $\leq$100, 101–200, … $\geq$600 characters), and mean reading speeds were computed. A paired t-test was used to compare Conditions A and B. In addition, qualitative analysis of the voice recordings was conducted, focusing on hesitations and restarts, particularly in texts exceeding 600 characters.

4 Results

4.1 Relationship Between Text Length and Reading Time

The aggregated data from 126 participants revealed a clear but nonlinear relationship between text length and reading time (Fig. 1). As expected, reading time generally increased as text length increased up to approximately 300 characters. However, for texts between 300 and 600 characters, the increase in reading time was disproportionately small, resulting in a temporary increase in reading speed.

In contrast, for texts exceeding 600 characters, reading time increased again and reading speed declined, suggesting a drop in efficiency for longer texts.

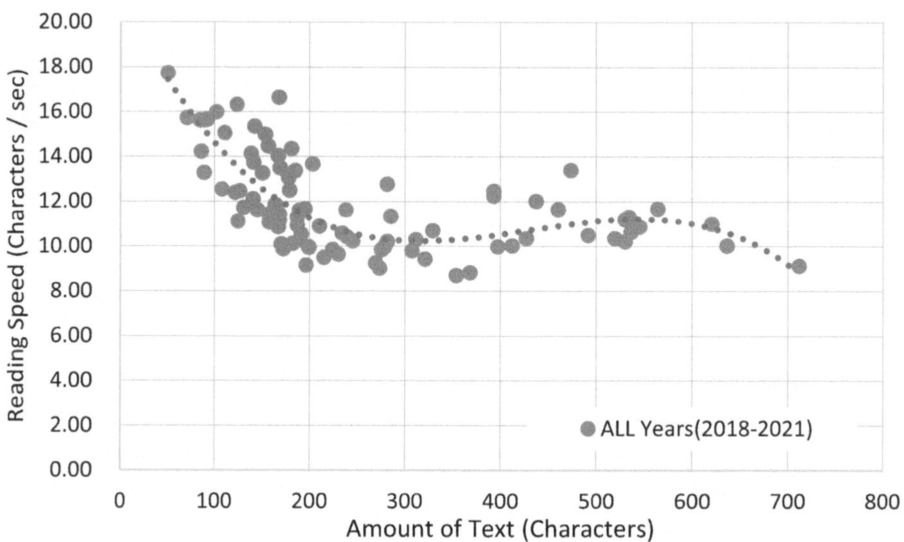

Fig. 1. Average Reading Time by Character Count. (Reading time increased steadily until 400 characters, then leveled off between 400–600 characters, and rose again beyond 600.)

4.2 Average Reading Speed (Characters per Second)

Reading speed was calculated using the formula:

Reading Speed = Character Count ÷ Reading Time (seconds)

The following trends were observed:

≤100 characters: ~14 characters/sec

101–200 characters: ~12.8 characters/sec

201–400 characters: ~10.5 characters/sec

401–600 characters: ~11.3 characters/sec (a slight increase)

≥601 characters: ~10.1 characters/sec

This pattern suggests that moderately long texts (300–600 characters) allow learners to leverage context, prediction, and rhythm to read more efficiently (Fig. 2). Conversely, very short texts result in fragmented processing, while very long texts impose increased cognitive and physical demands.

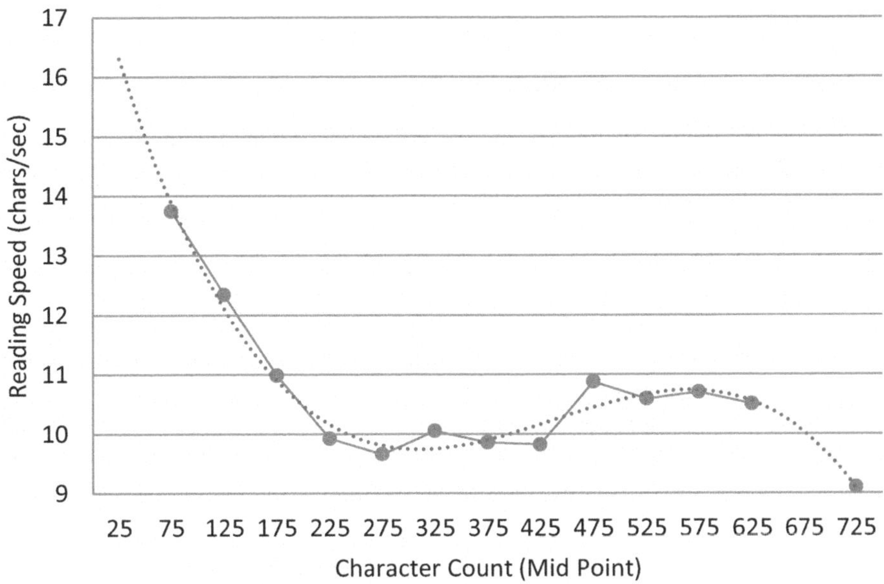

Fig. 2. Average Reading Speed by Character Count Range (50-char bin avg speed)

4.3 Comparison Between Conditions A and B

A paired t-test was conducted to compare the reading speeds between:

Condition A: Reading the entire text as one passage

Condition B: Reading segmented texts (by paragraph)

Key findings include:

For 300–600 character texts, Condition A resulted in significantly faster reading than Condition B ($p < .05$).

For 200–300 character texts, no significant difference was observed.

For texts over 600 characters, both conditions showed decreased speed, although Condition A had a slightly smaller decline.

These findings suggest that cohesive, continuous texts facilitate better rhythm and processing efficiency than segmented texts of similar length. However, when texts are too long, the benefits of context are outweighed by fatigue and attentional limits.

4.4 Qualitative Observations: Hesitations and Repetitions

Audio recordings revealed that texts longer than 600 characters frequently caused hesitation, false starts, and restarts. Learners paused more often to breathe, rephrase, or correct pronunciation. These behaviors indicate increased cognitive and articulatory load, which negatively impacted fluency.

5 Discussion

5.1 Nonlinear Changes in Reading Speed

This study revealed that reading speed does not decrease linearly with increasing text length. While shorter texts (≤300 characters) exhibited a typical pattern where longer passages took more time to read, a notable acceleration in reading speed was observed in the 300–600 characters range. Beyond 600 characters, however, reading speed declined again.

These results suggest that moderately long texts allow learners to establish a reading rhythm and benefit from top-down contextual processing, which increases fluency. This supports previous findings that coherent context enables learners to anticipate upcoming content and process language more efficiently [5].

The temporary acceleration indicates that a certain level of text length may activate fluency-enhancing mechanisms, such as phrase chunking, rhythm formation, and prosodic grouping, which are less effective in overly short or overly long texts.

5.2 Factors Contributing to Decreased Speed Beyond 600 Characters

The decline in reading speed for passages exceeding 600 characters can be attributed to multiple interacting factors:

Increased cognitive load: Longer texts require more working memory to retain context, leading to processing slowdown [10].

Sustained attention difficulty: Maintaining focus across extended passages can be challenging, particularly in second-language reading.

Articulatory fatigue: Reading aloud for extended periods imposes physical demands on the learner's vocal apparatus, resulting in hesitations and breakdowns [4].

These results align with the voice recording analysis, which revealed increased pausing, misreading, and repetitions in longer texts, especially beyond 600 characters.

5.3 Effects of Text Segmentation

Comparing Condition A (whole-text reading) and Condition B (segmented reading), the results show that moderately long continuous texts foster more fluent reading than shorter, segmented texts. This suggests that segmentation interrupts rhythm and requires learners to re-establish context for each new segment, imposing a switching cost.

However, for very short texts (≤200 characters), there was no significant difference between the two conditions, likely because these passages do not allow rhythm or prediction to develop, regardless of format.

5.4 Repeated Practice and Learner Motivation

In this study, students were allowed to repeat the reading test as many times as necessary until they achieved their desired performance score. This format encouraged highly motivated learners to engage in multiple attempts, through which they were able to internalize reading rhythm and improve processing speed. These findings suggest that repeated practice promotes automatization, and this approach can be considered an effective instructional strategy in reading fluency training.

However, in a previous study conducted by the authors (see Fig. 3), it was observed that although linking performance to academic grades enhanced learner motivation initially, over time, some students began to experience a decline in motivation due to feelings of security or resignation about their grades [13]. In particular, students who ultimately received a grade of C showed a notable drop in engagement during the second half of the course.

Interestingly, students who achieved an A-grade appeared to slow down in the final task—presumably because they were already confident that their score would remain high after achieving an A by Lesson 19. Nevertheless, even in the final assignment, their overall performance did not fall below that of the B-grade group, indicating that the fluency and intonation skills acquired through repeated high-speed reading continued to support their competence (Fig. 3).

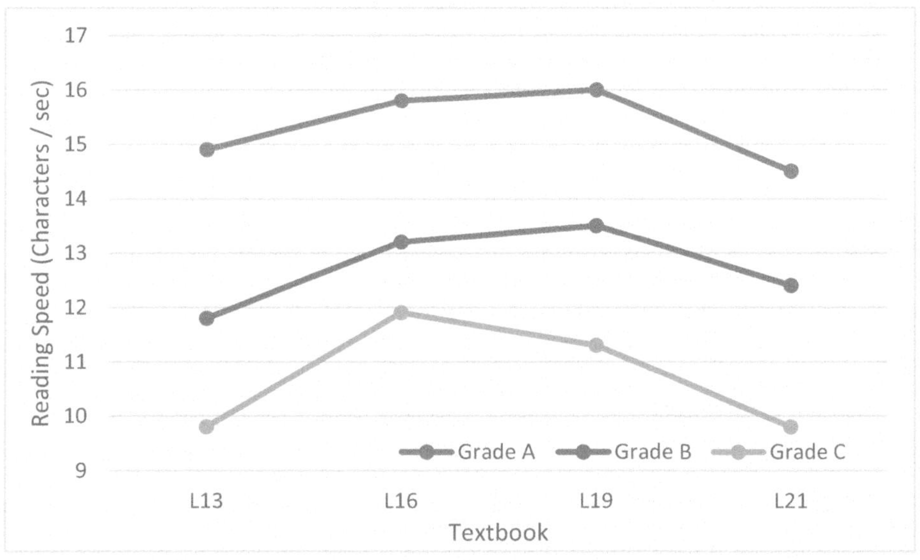

Fig. 3. Changes in Reading Speed Across Lessons

5.5 Variations Due to Instructional Materials

This study was conducted within the framework of a university curriculum that used designated textbooks for each academic year. As a result, two different textbooks were used: Textbook A for 2018 and 2019, and Textbook B for 2020 and 2021. This change introduced a degree of variation across years. The average values for each year are summarized in Table 1.

Table 1. Summary of Yearly Data

	Reading Speed (Characters / sec)	SD.	Amount of Text (Characters)	Text Style	Textbook	Sample Size
2018	11.40	1.06	452.45	A (Long Text)	a: GENKI	11
2019	13.45	2.10	161.61	B (Short Text)	a: GENKI	28
2020	11.13	1.75	204.14	B (Short Text)+Mask	b: DEKIRU	43
2021	10.43	0.64	579.00	A (Long Text)+Mask	b: DEKIRU	8

This variation can be quantified in terms of characters per second. Under Condition A (long texts), the average reading speed was 0.97 characters/sec, while under Condition B (short texts), it was 2.32 characters/sec.

A Welch's t-test (assuming unequal variances) was performed to compare the two data sets for Condition A. The results were:

$t = 2.36$, p (two-tailed) $= 0.0309$.

Since the p-value is below the 5% significance level ($p < .05$), there is a statistically significant difference in reading speed between 2018 and 2021.

A similar Welch's t-test was applied to the data for Condition B. The results were:

$t = 4.79$, p (two-tailed) $= 0.0000154$.

This value is far below the 5% threshold, confirming a highly significant difference between the short-text reading speeds of 2019 and 2020. Therefore, it can be concluded that learners in 2019 read significantly faster than those in 2020.

These two comparisons indicate that the difference in textbooks—Textbook A (used in 2018 and 2019) and Textbook B (used in 2020 and 2021)—had a statistically significant impact on reading speed for both long and short texts. In particular, the materials in Textbook B appear to have contributed to slower reading performance. Two possible explanations are proposed:

(1) Reduced Reading Speed Due to Face Mask Usage

In Thailand, the academic year begins in June and ends the following March. In June 2020, the COVID-19 pandemic had reached Thailand, and face masks were mandatory during all public activities, including classroom experiments. Participants wore masks during the reading tasks, which may have restricted oral movement, reduced oxygen intake, and made breathing during reading more difficult. Additionally, because masks reduce vocal volume, students were instructed to speak louder for clearer pronunciation, which may have inadvertently increased physical strain and slowed down their performance. This hypothesis should be verified in future controlled experiments.

(2) Increased Text Difficulty in Textbook B

As shown in Table 1, Textbook B contains longer passages compared to Textbook A—on average, 126.5 more characters for long texts and 42.5 more characters for short texts. This suggests a higher cognitive load and processing difficulty in reading, which likely contributed to slower reading speeds.

Taking these discrepancies into account, a corrected data visualization is presented in Fig. 4.

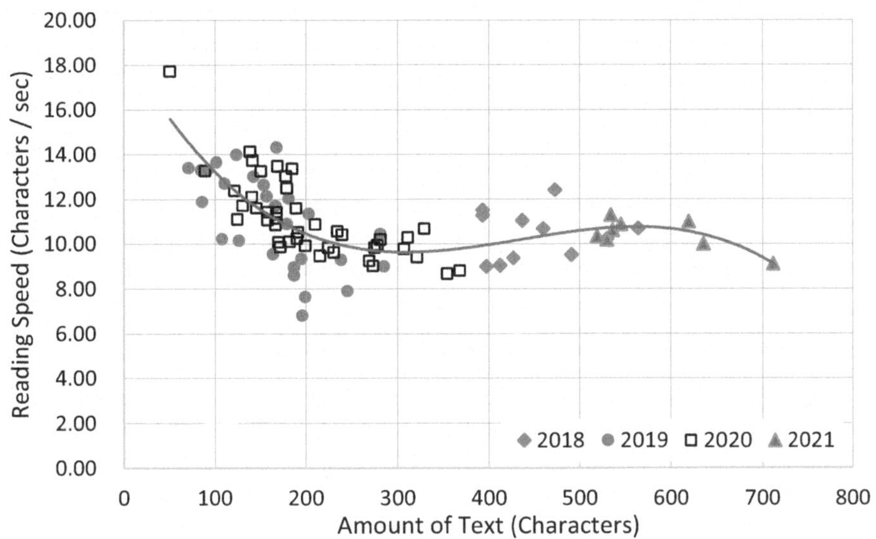

Fig. 4. Adjusted Reading Speed Data

When compared with Fig. 1, Fig. 4 shows no major changes in the overall trend. Even after correction, reading speed continues to increase gradually for texts between 300 and 600 characters and drop sharply for texts longer than 600 characters. These results confirm that the nonlinear change in reading speed is consistent, regardless of variations in textbook content or mask usage.

5.6 Summary of Discussion

This study identifies the 300–600 characters range as a potential "sweet spot" for oral reading practice, balancing contextual richness with manageable cognitive demands. Extremely short or long texts may hinder fluency by disrupting rhythm or overloading working memory. Additionally, segmentation can interfere with processing efficiency if overused.

These findings have implications for designing reading materials and instructional methods that promote efficient, fluent oral reading in second-language learners.

6 Pedagogical Implications and Future Directions

6.1 Optimal Text Length for Reading-Aloud Practice

The primary pedagogical implication of this study is the importance of selecting reading materials with an appropriate length. The results demonstrate that texts of moderate length (approximately 400–600 characters) optimize reading fluency, allowing learners to take advantage of contextual cues and rhythm while avoiding cognitive overload.

This finding challenges the common assumption that shorter texts are always easier for learners and suggests that educators should consider text cohesion and processing demands when designing or selecting materials for reading-aloud activities.

When using longer passages, it may be helpful to incorporate planned pauses or paragraph-level comprehension checks to support learners' cognitive processing.

6.2 Open Practice and Performance-Based Feedback

The study employed an open practice format in which learners could repeat the reading task as many times as they wished until achieving a satisfactory performance score based on characters per second. This design not only supported skill acquisition through repetition but also enhanced learner motivation by allowing self-paced progression.

Quantitative feedback using reading speed scores served as a clear and motivating benchmark for learners, providing a tangible goal for improvement. Such data-driven feedback systems can be incorporated into computer-assisted learning environments or mobile applications for self-directed study.

6.3 Application to Material and Curriculum Design

The findings offer concrete guidance for curriculum developers and teachers. Instructors should consider:

- Selecting or creating texts within the optimal character range for reading fluency training
- Avoiding excessive segmentation of texts that could disrupt rhythm and comprehension
- Incorporating repetition opportunities and speed-based assessment criteria into classroom routines

This approach is particularly beneficial for non-kanji background learners, who often struggle with the integration of form, meaning, and sound in Japanese.

6.4 Future Research: A Neurocognitive Approach Using EEG

With regard to learning and the structural recognition of character forms in the writing process, we have already undertaken experimental investigations employing neuroscientific techniques such as electroencephalography (EEG) [14]. Future research is expected to adopt similar neuroscientific methodologies to analyze real-time fluctuations in attention, working memory load, and cognitive engagement during oral reading.

By correlating EEG data with text length, reading speed, and accuracy, researchers can gain a deeper understanding of the neural mechanisms that support or hinder reading fluency. Such insights may lead to the development of personalized reading instruction tailored to each learner's cognitive profile.

This interdisciplinary approach will strengthen the scientific foundation of oral reading pedagogy and promote innovation in language learning technologies.

7 Conclusion

This study investigated how the length of Japanese reading materials affects oral reading speed among learners from non-kanji language backgrounds. Over a four-year period, participants read texts ranging from 50 to 700 characters, and their reading speed was quantitatively analyzed. The results revealed a nonlinear pattern: reading speed decreased up to 300 characters, increased in the 300–600 characters range, and declined again beyond 600 characters.

This suggests that moderately long texts enable more efficient reading, likely due to the facilitation of contextual prediction, rhythm formation, and prosodic chunking. In contrast, excessively long texts may place greater demands on working memory, attention, and articulation, leading to slower reading. Furthermore, the comparison between whole-text reading and paragraph-segmented reading indicated that continuity and rhythm are key contributors to reading fluency.

The instructional design, which allowed for repeated, self-paced practice with performance-based scoring, successfully promoted learner motivation and fluency development. This approach demonstrates the educational value of integrating quantitative fluency metrics into classroom practice.

Future research should explore the use of neurocognitive tools such as EEG to investigate the real-time cognitive load and attention patterns during oral reading. Such interdisciplinary studies will enhance our understanding of the mechanisms underlying fluent reading and contribute to the design of scientifically grounded, personalized learning systems.

Overall, the findings of this study provide a pedagogical and theoretical foundation for optimizing reading-aloud practices in Japanese language education, especially for learners with limited exposure to kanji and Japanese prosody.

Acknowledgements. The authors gratefully acknowledge the support of JSPS KAKENHI (Grant-in-Aid for Scientific Research (B), No. 23K28367), the White Rock Foundation, and the Hakuhodo Foundation.

References

1. Koda, K.: Insights into second language reading: A cross-linguistic approach. Cambridge University Press (2005)
2. Taguchi, E.: Teaching reading fluency in a foreign language. Read. Foreign Lang. **24**(1), 1–14 (2012)

3. Leong, C.K., Joshi, R.M. (eds.).: Cross-language studies of learning to read and spell: phonologic and orthographic processing. Springer, New York (2007). https://doi.org/10.1007/978-0-387-47668-1
4. Breznitz, Z.: Fluency in reading: synchronization of processes. Lawrence Erlbaum Associates (2006)
5. Taguchi, E., Gorsuch, G.J., Sasamoto, E.: Developing reading fluency in EFL: how assisted repeated reading and extensive reading affect fluency development. Read. Foreign Lang. **16**(2), 70–96 (2004)
6. Pope, A.T., Bogart, E.H., Bartolome, D.S.: Biocybernetic system evaluates indices of operator engagement in automated task. Biol. Psychol. **40**(1–2), 187–195 (1995). https://doi.org/10.1016/0301-0511(95)05116-3
7. Mozumi, K., Adachi, N.: Teachers' reasoning towards the use of students' 'reading aloud' in class -based upon an investigation using questionnaires directed to japanese language teachers. Bull. Tokyo Univ. Inform. Sci. **8**(1), 35–44 (2004)
8. Kobayashi, S.: A teaching approach for intermediate japanese: aiming at speed reading. Bull. Japan. Lang. School **18**, 107–115. Tokyo University of Foreign Studies, Japanese Language School (1992)
9. Sweller, J.: Cognitive load theory, learning difficulty, and instructional design. Learn. Instr. **4**(4), 295–312 (1994). https://doi.org/10.1016/0959-4752(94)90003-5
10. Sadanobu, T.: Competition and realization of pitch accent: Accentual behavior in Japanese sentences. Onsei Kenkyū [J. Phonetic Soc. Japan] **9**(1), 22–32 (2005)
11. Banno, E., Ohno, Y., Sakane, Y., Shinagawa, C., Tokashiki, K.: GENKI: an integrated course in elementary Japanese II, 2nd edn. The Japan Times, Ltd., Tokyo (2011)
12. Shimada, K.: Dekiru Nihongo: beginner to intermediate. Alc Corporation, Tokyo (2012)
13. Kutsuna, K., Somchanakit, K., Honda, Y., Takada, H.: The effects of high-speed reading-aloud practice on language learning and development. Proc. Symp. Soc. Sci. Form, Japan **4**(1), 33–34 (2019). ISSN 2433-6165 (Print), 2433-6173 (Online)
14. Kutsuna, K., Somchanakit, K., Teppradit, C., Nilaubol, P., Rongdech, C., Takada, H.: Development of Kanji learning materials for dysgraphia and EEG measurement. Computer Science and Education. Computer Science and Technology: 18th International Conference, ICCSE 2023, Proceedings, vol. 2023, pp. 466–477. Communications in Computer and Information Science. Springer Singapore (2024) https://doi.org/10.1007/978-981-97-0730-0_41

Teaching Models and Educational Reform

GAI-Empowered BOPPPS Teaching Model and Teaching Practice in Classroom Teaching Scenarios

Qingzheng Xu(✉), Yufeng Ma, Na Wang, Weihu Zhao, and Peilei Liu

College of Information and Communication, Information Support Force Engineering University, Wuhan 430035, China
xuqingzheng@hotmail.com

Abstract. Aiming at the teaching realities of traditional classroom teaching scenarios in the era of digital intelligence, a GAI-empowered teaching model is proposed in this study. Taking "heuristic search" as an example of teaching content, it elaborates in detail on the interactive processes of both teachers and students at each stage of this teaching model, as well as the effectiveness of applying this model to course teaching practice.

Keywords: Generative Artificial Intelligence · BOPPPS Teaching Model · Classroom Teaching Scenarios · Participatory Learning · Teacher Activities · Student Activities

1 Introduction

The report of the 20th National Congress of the Communist Party of China explicitly called for advancing the digital transformation of education, further integrating information technology with teaching practices, and accelerating educational modernization. General Secretary Xi Jinping has consistently emphasized that educational digitalization represents a pivotal breakthrough in charting new pathways and cultivating competitive advantages in China's educational development. In February 2023, the Central Committee of the Communist Party of China and the State Council issued the *Overall Layout Plan for Building a Digital China*, which outlines a national strategy for educational digitalization and promotes innovative applications of digital technologies within the field of education. Furthermore, in January 2025, they released the *Outline of the Planning Framework for Constructing an Education Power (2024–2035)*, reinforcing the implementation of the national educational digitalization strategy and emphasizing the supportive role of Artificial Intelligence (AI) in educational reform.

Huai Jinpeng, Minister of Education, highlighted at the 2024 World Digital Education Conference the importance of AI-driven initiatives to deepen the integration of intelligent technologies across education ("AI for Education"), scientific research ("AI for Science"), and society ("AI for Society"). He underscored the need to support teaching, learning, and academic inquiry through intelligent tools and platforms. Aligning

W. Hong et al. (Eds.): ICCSE 2025, CCIS 2761, pp. 317–331, 2026.
https://doi.org/10.1007/978-981-95-7731-6_25

with global trends and responding to the evolving technological landscape, the digital transformation of education has emerged as a shared international priority, holding profound implications for the modernization of education systems and the realization of an educationally strong nation.

In late 2022, OpenAI in the USA launched ChatGPT, a natural language processing tool based on the Transformer neural network architecture. By leveraging extensive corpora for training, ChatGPT achieves near-human performance in language comprehension and text generation. It has demonstrated capabilities such as passing Google's Level L3 software engineer examination and the USA Medical Licensing Examination. Consequently, it attracted over one million users within five days and surpassed 100 million users within three months - a record adoption rate among consumer applications - sparking widespread attention across industries. This advancement has catalyzed the transition from weak artificial intelligence to strong artificial intelligence.

In July 2023, DeepSeek emerged from MixQuant, a prominent Chinese hedge fund firm, focusing on developing large-scale language models and continuously pushing the boundaries of AI innovation. In January 2025, DeepSeek introduced the DeepSeek-R1 model, achieving performance comparable to that of OpenAI's leading models at only one-tenth of the cost, marking a significant technological milestone. Built upon the Transformer framework, DeepSeek incorporates sparse attention mechanisms and a mixture-of-experts architecture, enabling efficient processing of large datasets. The model utilizes Multi-head Latent Attention (MLA) to optimize cache usage, enhancing inference speed, while employing multi-token prediction and lossless load balancing strategies to significantly improve efficiency and overall performance in generative tasks.

The emergence of DeepSeek-R1 model has narrowed the technological gap between China and the USA in the field of AI, challenging traditional dominance and even influencing tech stock markets of USA. DeepSeek's open-source approach accelerates the development and diffusion of AI technologies, fostering a thriving global developer ecosystem and reshaping international competition dynamics.

Currently, Generative Artificial Intelligence (GAI), exemplified by models such as ChatGPT and DeepSeek-R1, is increasingly serving as a novel instrument for innovation, communication, and learning. Within this transformative wave, higher education faces both unprecedented opportunities and complex challenges, prompting a reimagining of educational forms and ecosystems [1–3]. In April 2023, UNESCO published *ChatGPT and Artificial Intelligence in Higher Education: Quick Start Guide*, which underscores the vast potential of GAI in higher education amid global digital trends and provides actionable recommendations for institutions to ensure that digital technologies enhance educational quality and drive meaningful innovation [4].

The BOPPPS teaching model, grounded in constructivist and cognitive learning theories, is guided by clearly defined educational objectives and recognized for its effectiveness in teaching design. As a closed-loop teaching framework, it emphasizes student engagement and feedback throughout the learning process [5]. The acronym BOPPPS derives from six English terms representing its core stages: Bridge-in, Objective, Pre-assessment, Participatory Learning, Post-assessment, and Summary. Recently, some scholars have explored the integration of GAI technologies into the BOPPPS model to enhance teaching efficacy.

For instance, Xu applied the BOPPPS model in blended teaching practices using the Chaoxing Learning platform, tailored to the characteristics of vocational students and the content of *Introduction of AI* courses [6]. Each stage was carefully interlinked, resulting in improved classroom management and positive learning outcomes. Ji incorporated Zhipu AI agents into *Systematic Anatomy Laboratory* course, enabling their use across multiple phases of the BOPPPS process, thereby optimizing teaching strategies and enhancing both learning efficiency and quality [7]. Hatwalne proposed a flipped classroom model combining BOPPPS with AI technologies to achieve advanced teaching goals, demonstrating benefits such as increased student motivation, enhanced teaching quality, and more dynamic classroom interactions [8]. Ou aimed to develop a hybrid teaching framework based on the BOPPPS model by integrating Bayesian knowledge-tracing models and reinforcement learning algorithms, examining the factors influencing its effectiveness [9]. Research findings revealed a positive correlation between the success of this integrated model and students' cognitive abilities, skill sets, and emotional attitudes, indicating its potential to significantly elevate educational outcomes. However, most researches remain at the theoretical level, lacking concrete, practice-oriented case studies.

Jiang used a *Comprehensive Business English* course for vocational students as a case study to illustrate how AI can be effectively integrated into all six phases of the BOPPPS model to foster active and deep student engagement [10]. Xue also employed the BOPPPS model as a structural framework, introducing ChatGPT into high school *Geography* classrooms as a teaching assistant or virtual instructor [11]. Through human-machine interaction, an application framework was developed for GAI in geography education, focusing on topics such as the transformation of resource-exhausted cities. This approach helped cultivate critical thinking, deepen geographic competencies, and stimulate creativity. Zhu explored the integration of Artificial Intelligence Generated Content (AIGC) into personalized instruction, using a *Video Surveillance* course as an example to examine AIGC's application across the entire BOPPPS teaching cycle [12]. AI agents were utilized as intermediaries between students and large language models, facilitating individualized assessments and generating customized test materials to provide targeted feedback. Despite these promising developments, many studies continue to focus primarily on teacher-led activities, often overlooking the central role of students in the learning process.

2 Basic Concepts

2.1 Higher Education Scenarios

Grounded in ecological principles, educational ecology investigates the underlying rules and mechanisms that govern various educational phenomena, as well as the complex interactions between education and its surrounding environment. From the perspective of educational ecology, teaching can be conceptualized as an ecosystem in which teachers and students form a collaborative and interdependent community. This community coexists symbiotically with the teaching environment, contributing to a dynamic equilibrium within the entire educational system. In such a balanced setting, learning transcends basic knowledge acquisition and becomes a higher-order, value-laden process. To facilitate this enriched learning experience, teachers are encouraged to cultivate a more diverse and vibrant learning ecosystem. By doing so, students can engage in a wide range of educational contexts, gaining varied learning experiences and progressively developing the skills and qualities necessary for personal and professional growth.

Higher education settings are inherently dynamic and extensible, blending the real and virtual dimensions of time and space with the certainty and uncertainty inherent in social life. These characteristics give rise to multidimensional educational scenarios. Specifically, they include fixed time-space scenario such as traditional "physical classrooms," semi-fixed time-space scenario such as "extracurricular practices," and indefinite time-space scenario represented by "online learning." Building upon the theoretical foundation of educational ecology, Liu classifies higher education scenarios into three primary types: (1) classroom teaching scenarios (offline instructional settings), (2) extracurricular practice scenarios (blended online-offline experiential settings), and (3) online learning scenarios (student-directed digital learning environments) [13].

This paper primarily focuses on teaching research and practical exploration centered on the first type - traditional classroom teaching scenario. Its aim is to examine how ecological principles can inform and enhance teaching design and practice within this foundational educational context.

2.2 BOPPPS Teaching Model

The BOPPPS teaching model structures the teaching process into six sequential phases: Bridge-in, Objective, Pre-assessment, Participatory Learning, Post-assessment, and Summary. These interlinked modules form a cohesive, closed-loop teaching cycle that facilitates structured and effective teaching and learning. Grounded in constructivist theory, the BOPPPS model emphasizes the active engagement of both instructors and learners throughout the entire pedagogical process. By integrating teaching design with learner-centered strategies, it ensures alignment between learning objectives, student participation, and performance assessment. A detailed overview of each phase is provided in Table 1.

Table 1. BOPPPS Teaching Model.

Teaching phase	Teaching activities or strategies		Teaching task
	Teacher	Student	
Bridge-in	Tell an engaging story related to the theme; broadcast live news or show an animated comic of the relevant event; present striking data or reveal a rare phenomenon	Reflect on "Why do I need to learn this?"; connect the topic to previously learned knowledge	Engage students' attention, enhance their interest and motivation, and clarify the significance of the course content in order to start a new learning cycle

(continued)

Table 1. (*continued*)

Teaching phase	Teaching activities or strategies		Teaching task
	Teacher	Student	
Objective	Learning outcomes should adhere to the SMART principle, which stands for Specific, Measurable, Achievable, Relevant, and Time-bound	Be mindful of the knowledge and skills you are expected to acquire	Outline the purpose of the learning and specify the knowledge, critical thinking skills, evaluative abilities, or practical skills that students should achieve at the end of the course
Pre-assessment	Pose an open-ended question; carry out a short online survey; lead students in experiencing the fundamental operations	Respond to the question, fill out the questionnaire, and attempt to carry out the basic tasks	Gather, either formally or informally, an understanding of students' prior knowledge regarding the lesson's topic and intended learning outcomes

(*continued*)

Table 1. (*continued*)

Teaching phase	Teaching activities or strategies		Teaching task
	Teacher	Student	
Participatory Learning	The teacher serves as a guide who facilitates students' active engagement through thoughtful teaching design. Potential methods include: (1) facilitating group discussions centered around inquiry-based questions related to the subject matter; (2) encouraging reflective thinking through written assignments, class discussions, or guided questioning; (3) engaging students in problem-solving activities followed by peer review; (4) implementing role-play scenarios; (5) analyzing real-life case studies; and (6) participating in simulated environments, among others	Actively participate in learning tasks or establish connections with learning materials to build a personal knowledge framework	Facilitate students' active engagement in the learning process through carefully designed teaching activities that support the attainment of predefined learning outcomes
Post-assessment	Create a series of multiple-choice or fill-in-the-blank questions; administer a short online questionnaire; assess students' capability to carry out the relevant skills independently	Respond to the questions, fill out the questionnaire, and try to carry out the skill-related tasks on your own	Conduct a formal or informal evaluation to verify whether students have successfully met the intended learning outcomes

(*continued*)

Table 1. (*continued*)

Teaching phase	Teaching activities or strategies		Teaching task
	Teacher	Student	
Summary	Summarize the main content and key points of the course; recognize and commend students' dedication and accomplishments; re-examine the learning objectives and evaluate how well students have achieved them	Provide a brief overview of the course material and main points; engage in reflection on the group cooperation process and exchange personal reflections	At the end of the lesson, give students a chance to briefly reflect on their learning and make connections with prior knowledge

3 GAI-Empowered BOPPPS Teaching Model

This section explores the technological advantages of GAI, exemplified by models such as DeepSeek and ChatGPT, and integrates GAI into each phase of the BOPPPS teaching model in a systematic and meaningful way. By embedding GAI capabilities throughout the teaching process, a GAI-empowered BOPPPS teaching model is proposed, as illustrated in Table 2. This integration aims to address the transformative changes in the structure and ecosystem of higher education brought about by the digital and intelligent revolution, fostering more adaptive, interactive, and learner-centered educational environments.

Table 2. GAI-Empowered BOPPPS Teaching Model.

Teaching phase	Teacher activities or strategies	Student activities or strategies
Bridge-in	Teachers can leverage GAI to create engaging content such as brief narratives, practical life scenarios, teaching animations, or thought-provoking questions to draw students' attention, facilitate classroom engagement, and deepen their immersion into the learning context	Students are expected to attentively listen to the case study, observe the demonstration, and engage in critical thinking. When they have any questions, they are encouraged to proactively consult the AI, whose responses will help them quickly understand the background and context of the lesson

(*continued*)

Table 2. *(continued)*

Teaching phase	Teacher activities or strategies	Student activities or strategies
Objective	Teachers can utilize GAI by providing inputs such as the lesson topic, course outline, or core knowledge points, allowing the system to assist in formulating well-structured learning objectives. Furthermore, GAI can be instructed to generate objectives aligned with different levels of Bloom's Taxonomy - covering cognitive, psychomotor, and affective domains. It is important to note that the objectives produced by AI are initial and general in nature, requiring further review, adaptation, and refinement by teachers to align with the specific teaching context and students' needs	Students can inquire with GAI about course objectives to gain a thorough understanding of the specific content and the steps required to achieve them. This promotes more purposeful and self-directed learning, while helping students stay aligned with the intended learning trajectory
Pre-assessment	Teaching can leverage GAI to create assessment items that rapidly evaluate students' prior knowledge, thereby informing the adaptation and enhancement of teaching materials. The format of these assessments can vary widely, including multiple-choice, fill-in-the-blank, short-answer questions, and questionnaires. Furthermore, GAI is capable of generating differentiated pre-test questions tailored to students' disciplinary backgrounds and previous coursework, enabling more effective and customized diagnostic assessment	Students can engage with GAI tools to conduct self-assessments, including the generation of customized questions and access to explanatory feedback. This process enables a clearer understanding of their knowledge proficiency and individual learning requirements. Additionally, students can request GAI to analyze the underlying causes of their mistakes and offer targeted recommendations for academic growth

(*continued*)

Table 2. (*continued*)

Teaching phase	Teacher activities or strategies	Student activities or strategies
Participatory Learning	Teachers can use GAI to design specific interactive activity plans or provide original materials for case analysis, which students can study before class and discuss during lessons. To better meet students' needs, GAI should take into account students' backgrounds and prior assessment results when customizing interactive activities - such as role-playing, group discussions, and problem-solving tasks. These activities encourage students to think from multiple perspectives and foster teamwork, ensuring that every student is actively engaged and benefits from the experience. In addition, GAI can draw on large volumes of real-world industry data and social phenomena to generate representative and realistic cases for students to analyze. Moreover, it can also provide detailed analytical frameworks and step-by-step guidance for each case, helping students systematically examine the cases, broaden their perspectives, and deepen their understanding	Students can leverage GAI to rapidly access resources, develop innovative ideas, and support the completion of teaching tasks, thus improving both the quality of their learning experience and academic outcomes. Nevertheless, it is crucial to approach the information provided by GAI with a critical mindset, carefully assessing its accuracy and applicability. Where appropriate, students are encouraged to consult additional sources to validate the information from multiple perspectives

(*continued*)

Table 2. (*continued*)

Teaching phase	Teacher activities or strategies	Student activities or strategies
Post-assessment	Teachers can leverage GAI to create customized assessment items aligned with the teaching material, ensuring that each question accurately measures students' comprehension and ability to apply knowledge. Furthermore, GAI is capable of conducting statistical analysis on student responses and generating detailed reports that illustrate both class-wide performance trends and individual learning gaps. This data empowers teachers to make informed, real-time adjustments to the difficulty level of future assessments	Students may utilize GAI tools to conduct self-assessments through automatically generated test items accompanied by comprehensive feedback. Following the post-assessment, students can request GAI to analyze their performance and pinpoint specific knowledge deficiencies or conceptual misunderstandings, thereby enhancing their awareness of personal learning achievements and areas requiring further development
Summary	Teachers can leverage GAI to create course summaries and review resources, thereby enhancing both teaching efficiency and learning outcomes. Beyond written summaries, GAI is also capable of generating visual aids such as infographics, slide presentations, and concept maps, catering to diverse learning styles and supporting more effective revision and knowledge retention	Students can leverage GAI tools to revisit course materials, efficiently identify central concepts and critical knowledge points, and compile them into clear and structured summaries. These summaries can be further categorized according to the significance and complexity of each topic, facilitating deeper comprehension and more effective memorization

4 Teaching Practice

The course *Fundamentals of Artificial Intelligence* is a general elective offered to engineering majors, such as Communication Engineering, at the Information Support Force Engineering University. The course spans a total of 48 teaching hours, comprising 38 h of lectures and 10 h of practical training sessions. It is designed with three primary teaching objectives: (1) to provide students with a comprehensive understanding of the research domains, application areas, and developmental trends in AI; (2) to equip them with foundational knowledge of key AI concepts, principles, and methodologies; and (3) to cultivate their ability to apply AI techniques to solve real-world problems, thereby establishing a solid foundation for further theoretical study and advanced interdisciplinary practice in intelligent systems.

The curriculum is structured into five thematic modules [14]. The first module serves as an introduction (Chapter 1 of Textbook [15]), offering an overview of core concepts, research paradigms, historical evolution, and major technical paradigms within the field of AI. The second module focuses on reasoning (Chapters 2 and 3 of Textbook [15]), addressing fundamental principles and methods of classical AI, including state space search, game theory, predicate logic representation, and associated reasoning techniques. The third module centers on knowledge (Chapter 4 of Textbook [15]), exploring commonly used approaches to knowledge representation and reasoning. The fourth module emphasizes learning (Chapters 5–7 of Textbook [15]), introducing key paradigms such as machine learning, artificial neural networks, and intelligent agent technologies - representing learning mechanisms based on data, network architectures, and environmental perception and response, respectively. The final module addresses the frontier topics (Chapter 8 of Textbook [15]), presenting cutting-edge applications of AI and facilitating student-led discussions on contemporary issues and emerging trends in this field.

4.1 Teaching Practice Case

This section takes the topic of "heuristic search" from Section 3, Chapter 2 of Textbook [15] as an example to elaborate in detail on how both teachers and students engage in the stages of the GAI-empowered BOPPPS teaching model within traditional classroom teaching scenarios.

Bridge-in Phase. Teacher Activities: (1) Before the formal class, the teacher utilizes GAI tools to identify appropriate teaching videos. For example, the teacher may input the following prompt into a GAI system: "I am teaching an undergraduate course titled *Fundamentals of Artificial Intelligence*. The topic today is 'heuristic search'. I need a video showing a mouse navigating a maze. Please provide specific URLs." In response, the GAI generates a list of relevant URLs, provides brief descriptions for each video, and offers teaching suggestions. (2) The teacher reviews and selects the most suitable video based on the class level and student characteristics. In this semester's teaching practice, the teaching team selected the following link: https://www.163.com/v/video/VFMN4DR8I.html. This video effectively illustrates various search strategies, including edge-following search, depth-first search, breadth-first search, and flood fill search. (3) During the bridge-in phase of the BOPPPS teaching model, the teacher plays the selected video to capture students' attention and generate interest in the topic.

Student Activities: (1) Students watch the video attentively, developing an intuitive understanding of different search strategies and recognizing how these approaches significantly influence search efficiency. (2) Advanced students are able to differentiate between blind search and heuristic search methods depicted in the video, and attempt to summarize their similarities and differences.

Objective Phase. Teacher Activities: (1) Before the formal class, the teacher uploads the course syllabus and lesson plan and prompts GAI with: "Today's topic is 'heuristic search'. Based on the syllabus and lesson plan, please generate a set of learning objectives using Bloom's taxonomy of educational objectives." The GAI tool will automatically generate a comprehensive set of objectives covering all six cognitive levels of Bloom's taxonomy. Examples include: Remember: List the common heuristic search algorithms. Understand: Explain in your own words how heuristics improve search efficiency. Apply: Implement a simple heuristic search algorithm using pseudocode or programming language. Analyze: Evaluate the suitability of heuristic search in specific problems. Evaluate: Critically discuss limitations of heuristic search (e.g., sub-optimal solutions due to poor heuristic design). Create: Develop a project demonstrating the application of heuristic search in real-world scenarios (e.g., robot path planning, mouse maze navigation). (2) The teacher further refines the generated objectives according to teaching standards and student needs. (3) In the objective phase of the BOPPPS model, the teacher clearly presents the teaching objectives to guide students' expectations and focus.

Student Activities: If teaching objectives are unclear, students can proactively consult GAI to ensure they remain aligned with the intended learning outcomes.

Pre-assessment Phase. Teacher Activities: (1) Before the formal class, the teacher uses GAI to generate diagnostic test questions to gauge students' prior knowledge. Sample questions include: Q1: What is the main difference between Breadth-First Search (BFS) and Depth-First Search (DFS)? (A) BFS uses a queue; DFS uses a stack. (B) BFS uses a stack; DFS uses a queue. (C) BFS is always faster than DFS. (D) BFS and DFS have the same space complexity. Q2: Which blind search algorithm is best suited for finding the shortest path? (A) Depth-First Search (DFS). (B) Breadth-First Search (BFS). (C) Iterative Deepening Search. (D) Bidirectional BFS. Q3: In a real-time strategy game (RTS), units must quickly calculate the shortest path from start to end on a grid-based map with dynamic obstacles. Analyze BFS from both theoretical feasibility and engineering optimization perspectives. (2) In the pre-assessment phase of BOPPPS model, the teacher selects 1–2 questions via the Rain Classroom platform for students to complete. By analyzing performance statistics and randomly calling on students, the teacher adjusts the pace and content of teaching accordingly.

Student Activities: (1) Students respond promptly using mobile phones, computers, tablets, etc. (2) If unsure about any question, students may seek help from peers or use GAI tools.

Participatory Learning Phase. Teacher Activities: (1) Before the formal class, the teacher asks GAI for interactive activity suggestions. While GAI often recommends role-playing, coding practice, and case studies, which require strong foundational skills, the teaching team instead chooses an alternative suitable for the traditional classroom: Revisiting classic papers. (2) With GAI assistance, three interactive activities are designed. Activity 1: Encounter the classics -- Dialogue with masters. Students read the original paper of A* algorithm (Reference [16]) and are grouped accordingly. In the formal class, each group explains a specific section of the paper (e.g., heuristic function design, time complexity) to the whole class. Other groups are encouraged to ask questions or add insights, creating a dynamic and engaging discussion environment. Activity 2: Role-play - Imagine you are a node in A* algorithm. Review definitions of open and closed sets. Ask the students: "Why do nodes move between these two sets?" Then simulate the process physically: Mark two zones on the floor as open set and closed set. Students act as nodes holding cards with coordinates and heuristic values. The teacher acts as the algorithm controller, selecting random start and end points. Students move according to algorithm rules. To deepen critical thinking, two students intentionally claim equal

$f(n)$ values, prompting discussion on how to handle tie-breaking and priority conflicts. Activity 3: Academic salon - If the authors of A* algorithm were present. From a modern perspective of intelligent science, each group prepares three questions for the inventors of A* algorithm, fostering deeper reflection on its limitations. Additionally, students write short essays titled "A letter to the inventors of A* algorithm", offering improvement suggestions based on current AI research and the paper's limitations.

Student Activities: (1) Actively participate in the three interactive activities and complete assigned tasks. (2) Use GAI tools during activities for quick reference and task support.

Post-assessment Phase. Teacher Activities: (1) Before the formal class, the teacher uses GAI to generate post-class assessment questions. Sample questions include: Q1: In A* search, if the heuristic function $h(n)$ is admissible, then: (A) $h(n)$ must be greater than actual cost. (B) $h(n)$ must be less than or equal to actual cost. (C) $h(n)$ must be exactly equal to actual cost. (D) $h(n)$ can be any value. Q2: Which of the following heuristics in the 8-puzzle problem satisfies both admissibility and consistency? (A) Misplaced tiles. (B) Manhattan distance. (C) Euclidean distance. (D) Randomly generated heuristic. Q3: In A* algorithm, which method is most effective to avoid re-expanding nodes? (A) Use an open list for unexpanded nodes. (B) Use a closed list for expanded nodes. (C) Use a priority queue for expansion order. (D) Use a hash table to track minimum path costs. (2) In the post-assessment phase of BOPPPS model, the teacher selects 2–3 questions via Rain Classroom flatform. Based on the results, the teacher conducts reflective adjustments to better achieve teaching goals.

Student Activities: (1) Answer post-assessment questions via electronic devices. (2) Seek help from GAI or the teacher when encountering difficulties.

Summary Phase. Teacher Activities: (1) Before the formal class, the teacher uploads the lesson plan and requests GAI to generate a summary: "Please generate a teaching summary for today's topic 'heuristic search'." (2) In the summary phase of BOPPPS model, the teacher builds upon the auto-generated summary, integrating reflections and feedback from the three interactive activities. The teacher reiterates key objectives and highlights important knowledge points.

Student Activities: Using GAI tools, students create personalized mind maps or knowledge graphs based on core concepts and key points, building their own structured understanding of the material.

4.2 Teaching Outcomes

During the fall semester of 2024, the teaching team successfully delivered the *Fundamentals of Artificial Intelligence* course to two undergraduate classes majoring in Communication Engineering. Throughout the semester, the GAI-empowered BOPPPS teaching model was fully implemented. The teaching outcomes were highly encouraging: the course achieved a 100% pass rate for the first time, with the excellence rate increasing by 5% compared to previous academic years.

Students reported that the course provided rich and life-relevant learning resources, and featured innovative, engaging, and teaching targeted activities that facilitated their understanding of complex AI theories and algorithms. Supervisory experts noted positively on the integration of advanced technologies into teaching practice, stating: "The course team has effectively incorporated GAI tools into teaching reforms, making the approach exemplary and worthy of wider adoption."

As a result, the course received the "Outstanding" rating in the university's classroom teaching quality evaluation. Furthermore, the teaching team developed a teaching case titled *A* Algorithm*, which was awarded the National Third Prize in the Teaching Case Competition at the 2024 China Computer Education Conference.

5 Conclusion

In recent years, the countries around the world have intensified efforts to integrate artificial intelligence into higher education, leveraging intelligent technologies to drive pedagogical innovation, reshape traditional teaching models, and reconstruct educational ecosystems. This article integrates GAI with the BOPPPS teaching model to propose a GAI-empowered BOPPPS teaching model. Taking the topic of "heuristic search" as a case study, this paper elaborates on the roles of both instructors and students at each phase of the model, highlighting the transformative potential and educational value of GAI in contemporary learning environments.

Through multiple rounds of in-depth interaction with GAI tools, the teaching team transformed static academic papers into dynamic objects of exploration. Building on this, our team creatively designed a participatory learning model centered on the concept of "deep deconstruction + scenario reconstruction + temporal and spatial exploration". This activity plan can enable students to engage with the A* algorithm technically and contextually, and understand its core principles and implementation details within their historical and applied frameworks.

Next, the research team will attempt to apply the GAI-empowered BOPPPS Teaching Model to more disciplines and courses to validate the universality of this instructional model and amplify the impact of the research outcomes. Additionally, we will analyze the effects of different GAI tools used (e.g., DeepSeek-R1, ChatGPT versions) on the teaching practice process, providing practitioners with fundamental principles and recommendations for tool selection.

Acknowledgments. This study was funded by the Education Science Planning Project of Hubei Province (grant number 2024GB424), and the Undergraduate and Professional Education Teaching Research Project of National University of Defense Technology (grant number U202320).

Disclosure of Interests. The authors have no competing interests to declare that are relevant to the content of this article.

References

1. Royer, C.: Outsourcing humanity? ChatGPT, critical thinking, and the crisis in higher education. Stud. Philos. Educ. **43**(5), 479–497 (2024)

2. Naz Ansari, A., Ahmad, S., Muzaffar Bhutta, S.: Mapping the global evidence around the use of ChatGPT in higher education: a systematic scoping review. Educ. Inf. Technol. **29**(9), 11281–11321 (2024)
3. Jensen, L.X., Buhl, A., Sharma, A., Bearman, M.: Generative AI and higher education: a review of claims from the first months of ChatGPT. Higher Education. (OnlineFirst)
4. Liu, Y., Xu, J.H., Dong, Y.W., Su, F.G.: How to apply ChatGPT-based generative artificial intelligence in higher education – an interpretation of ChatGPT and artificial intelligence in higher education: Quick start guide by UNESCO. Chin. J. ICT Educ. **30**(2), 71–80 (2024). (in Chinese)
5. Instructional Skills Workshop Network. ISW Handbook. https://www.iswnetwork.ca/resources/isw-and-fdw-handbooks/
6. Xu, Y.C.: Research on blended learning of Introduction to Artificial Intelligence based on "Chaoxing Xuexitong + BOPPPS." J. Hunan Post Telecommun. College **21**(3), 32–35 (2022). (in Chinese)
7. Ji, S.L., Zhang, Q., Luo, H.X.: Application and considerations of Zhipu Qingyan AI agent in anatomy laboratory courses. Basic Med. Educ. **26**(12), 1080–1083 (2024). (in Chinese)
8. Hatwalne, P.A., Chaudhary, S.S., Prayagi, S.V., Adkane, R.V., Vairagade, S.: Comparative investigation of BOPPPS-AI integrated flipped classroom method and conventional teaching method in mechanical engineering education. In: 2nd DMIHER International Conference on Artificial Intelligence in Healthcare, Education and Industry, pp. 1–5. November 29–30, 2024, Wardha, India (2024)
9. Ou, Y.: Strategies for applying BOPPPS model supported by intelligent algorithms in blended teaching of College English. Appl. Math. Nonlinear Sci. **9**(1), Article ID: 20241719 (2024)
10. Jiang, J.H., Tang, H.: AI+BOPPPS model in design of participatory learning mode in business English teaching in higher vocational education – case study of "Integrated Business English" course. J. Hubei Indust. Polytechn. **37**(5), 81–84 (2024). (in Chinese)
11. Xue, S.Y., et al.: Digital empowerment: logical construction and reflective practice of integrating ChatGPT into geography teaching under the BOPPPS model. Geography Teach. **15**, 26–31 (2024). (in Chinese)
12. Zhu, G.B., Zhao, B., Tang, J.B.: A study of the AIGC-Enabled BOPPPS smart teaching model. In: International Symposium on Artificial Intelligence for Education, pp. 166–170, September 6–8, 2024, Xi'an, China (2024)
13. Liu, M., Guo, S., Wu, Z.M., Liao, J.: Generative artificial intelligence reshaping the higher education: contents, cases and pathways. E-educ. Res. **6**, 57–65 (2024). (in Chinese)
14. Liu, W., Li, M., Xie, H.B.: Course reform and practice of Artificial Intelligence Foundation. J. Electric. Electron. Educ. **45**(1), 7–10 (2023). (in Chinese)
15. Liu, W., Li, M., Chen, S.F., Xie, H.B.: Fundamentals of Artificial Intelligence. Science Press, Beijing (2025). (in Chinese)
16. Hart, P.E., Nilsson, N.J., Raphael, B.: A formal basis for heuristic determination of minimum cost paths. IEEE Trans. Syst. Sci. Cybern. **4**(2), 100–107 (1968)

A Study on Teaching Models for Embedded Systems Courses Under the Guidance of Intelligent Educational Robots

Xiaochun Xu, Haibo Luo(✉), and Ping Fan

School of Computer and Big Data, Minjiang University, Fuzhou 350108, China
robhappy@mju.edu.cn

Abstract. Amid the ongoing wave of the artificial intelligence revolution and industrial transformation, emerging industries are imposing increasingly stringent demands on the engineering design and innovation capabilities of computer science students. Despite having completed a broad spectrum of foundational courses—including C programming, Python programming, digital systems, and deep learning—many undergraduates continue to face difficulties in effectively integrating knowledge acquired from these diverse disciplines. To address this challenge, we propose the integration of intelligent educational robots into the junior-level Embedded Systems course. This initiative aims to enhance students' practical skills and foster innovative thinking through AI-driven instructional design, the development of innovative experimental projects, and the implementation of multi-dimensional achievement assessments. Additionally, it facilitates the seamless integration of foundational course knowledge. The course adopts a novel blended teaching model that combines "intelligent guidance" with "engineering practice", striving to overcome the limitations of conventional pedagogical approaches. This model seeks to establish a new AI-enhanced educational ecosystem and holistically advance students' comprehensive competencies and interdisciplinary proficiencies.

Keywords: Intelligent Educational Robot · Embedded Systems Course · Instructional Design · Intelligent Guidance · Engineering Practice

1 Introduction

Currently, the world is undergoing the Fourth Industrial Revolution, driven by emerging technologies such as artificial intelligence (AI), big data, the Internet of Things (IoT), and intelligent manufacturing. This technological revolution is profoundly reshaping production models, business paradigms, and technological ecosystems across various industries, posing unprecedented challenges to the cultivation of talent in computer science and related disciplines [1, 2]. On the one hand, there is a growing demand from industry for interdisciplinary professionals equipped with innovative thinking and strong engineering practice capabilities [3]. On the other hand, mastery of isolated technical skills is no longer sufficient to meet the complex requirements of system integration and

W. Hong et al. (Eds.): ICCSE 2025, CCIS 2761, pp. 332–346, 2026.
https://doi.org/10.1007/978-981-95-7731-6_26

innovative design in real-world engineering projects. For example, fields such as intelligent hardware development, autonomous driving systems, and robotics not only require solid programming proficiency but also demand comprehensive knowledge in digital systems, deep learning, and hardware design, along with the ability to apply this knowledge flexibly in complex engineering environments. Moreover, the rapid and iterative nature of industrial transformation has rendered traditional "knowledge transmission" teaching models [4] increasingly inadequate in keeping pace with technological advancements. Therefore, cultivating students with lifelong learning capabilities, independent innovation skills, and the ability to solve complex engineering problems has become a critical objective in higher education. Please note that the first paragraph of a section or subsection is not indented. The first paragraphs that follows a table, figure, equation etc. does not have an indent, either.

Engineering design and innovation capabilities are not only essential competitive advantages for students' future career development but also serve as key drivers of technological advancement and industrial innovation. In the face of complex and rapidly evolving real-world engineering challenges, isolated theoretical knowledge and programming skills are far from sufficient [5]. Students must develop thc ability to translate theory into practice, encompassing the full spectrum of engineering competencies, including problem analysis, system design, algorithm implementation, hardware debugging, and teamwork. However, many computer science curricula at universities currently suffer from knowledge fragmentation, with a lack of organic connections between courses. This often leads to the formation of "knowledge silos," preventing students from building a coherent knowledge framework and cultivating an engineering mindset [6]. Moreover, some courses place excessive emphasis on theoretical instruction while neglecting the development of innovative practices. As a result, students frequently lack hands-on experience and the ability to address real-world engineering scenarios. Therefore, starting with the Embedded Systems course, it is imperative to implement scientifically grounded instructional designs that dismantle disciplinary barriers, effectively integrate multidisciplinary knowledge—including programming, digital logic, and artificial intelligence—and prioritize engineering design and innovative practice. This comprehensive approach represents a key focus for curriculum reform aimed at enhancing students' holistic competencies.

To address the issues of knowledge fragmentation and insufficient innovation and practical abilities prevalent in current computer science education, this study proposes an innovative teaching model based on intelligent educational robots. Serving as a comprehensive instructional platform that integrates programming control, hardware interaction, sensor applications, and artificial intelligence algorithms, intelligent educational robots not only provide students with authentic engineering practice environments but also effectively promote the organic integration of multidisciplinary knowledge. By reforming the instructional model of the Embedded Systems course and adopting project-driven and task-oriented teaching strategies, students are guided to apply and synthesize their knowledge of programming, digital logic, embedded systems, and artificial intelligence while solving real-world problems. Additionally, an intelligent guidance mechanism is introduced, incorporating robot feedback, automated assessment, and personalized learning path design. This approach enhances the interactivity and adaptability of instruction, thereby stimulating students' learning interest and fostering their motivation for innovation.

2 Course Design Philosophy and Objectives

2.1 Teaching Philosophy

As shown in Fig. 1, this study proposes an instructional philosophy for the Embedded Systems course centered on the fusion of intelligent guidance and engineering practice, aiming to overcome the limitations of traditional teaching models and to enhance students' comprehensive competencies and innovative capacities. Intelligent educational robots [7, 8] are employed as the primary instructional platform, leveraging their integration of programming control, hardware interaction, sensor applications, and artificial intelligence algorithms to create an authentic and open engineering practice environment. Furthermore, the course places a strong emphasis on engineering practice. Theoretical learning is no longer conducted in isolation but is closely integrated with real-world project experiences. Students are required to apply theoretical knowledge to the analysis and resolution of authentic engineering problems, thereby fostering solid engineering thinking and hands-on skills. This practice-oriented instructional model effectively enhances students' ability to translate theoretical knowledge into practical engineering solutions, laying a robust foundation for their future professional development.

Specifically, the course adopts a project-driven instructional strategy, designing innovative teaching projects centered around real engineering challenges. Throughout project execution, students are encouraged to integrate multidisciplinary knowledge across programming, digital logic, embedded systems, and artificial intelligence. The projects encompass the entire engineering process, including requirements analysis, system design, algorithm development, hardware debugging, and teamwork, comprehensively strengthening students' system design and innovation capabilities. This instructional philosophy helps dismantle the traditional knowledge silos among courses, promotes the cross-disciplinary integration of knowledge, and facilitates the construction of a coherent and systematic knowledge framework. Ultimately, it equips students with the interdisciplinary thinking and comprehensive problem-solving abilities required to tackle complex engineering challenges and to meet the evolving demands of technological advancement and industrial transformation.

2.2 Teaching Objectives

The Embedded Systems course establishes three primary instructional objectives aimed at comprehensively enhancing students' engineering practice skills, innovative thinking, and interdisciplinary literacy, as shown in Fig. 1.

First, the course incorporates innovative experimental projects and real-world engineering challenges to cultivate students' hands-on abilities and problem-solving skills in practical engineering environments. During project implementation, students are expected to confront complex design challenges, engage in independent thinking, and propose innovative solutions. This practice-oriented instructional approach not only strengthens students' self-directed learning and creativity but also improves their capacity to apply theoretical knowledge to real-world engineering projects, thereby laying a solid foundation for future research and industry practice.

Second, the course content spans multiple disciplines, including programming, digital logic, artificial intelligence, and hardware design, with the goal of helping students build an interdisciplinary knowledge framework. Through project-driven learning, students are encouraged to organically integrate knowledge from various domains, fostering systematic thinking and multidimensional problem analysis skills. This objective equips students with the ability to synthesize diverse technological resources when addressing complex engineering tasks, thereby enhancing both the depth and breadth of their engineering design capabilities.

Third, in the development and application of intelligent educational robots, students are required to master both software algorithm design and hardware system development, thereby significantly advancing their software-hardware collaborative design skills. The course emphasizes a complete design process encompassing system architecture, functional implementation, and performance optimization, enabling students to understand the interdependencies between software and hardware. This competency is crucial for meeting the engineering demands of contemporary fields such as artificial intelligence and intelligent hardware.

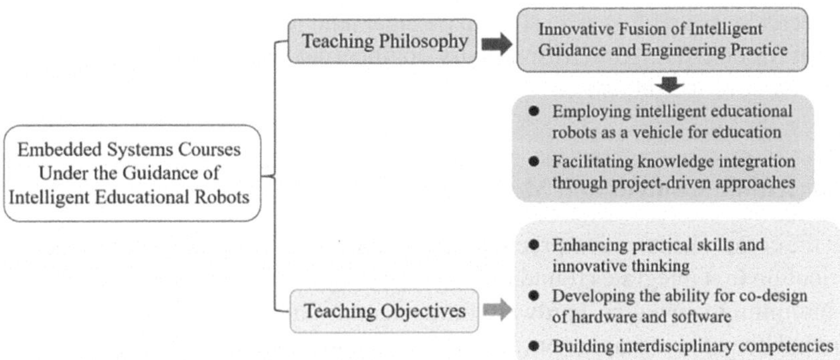

Fig. 1. The illustration diagram of course design philosophy and objectives

3 Instructional Implementation Plan

3.1 Introduction and Functions of Intelligent Educational Robots

To achieve the instructional reform objectives of the Embedded Systems course guided by intelligent educational robots, the course incorporates a Jetson Nano-based intelligent robot as the central instructional tool. The robot's functional design and applications span teaching assistance, classroom interaction, and serving as a platform for experimental projects, thereby comprehensively supporting all instructional activities.

Teaching Assistance and Classroom Interaction. The Jetson Nano-based intelligent robot is equipped with programming control, sensor data acquisition, and human-machine interaction capabilities, enabling it to function as an auxiliary teaching tool.

Through predefined tasks and feedback mechanisms, the robot can dynamically respond to students' programming inputs and hardware operations, enhancing classroom interactivity and engagement. Additionally, instructors can leverage the robot's data collection and feedback capabilities to monitor students' learning progress and operational performance in real time, providing timely guidance and adjustments. This approach increases the level of instructional personalization and accommodates the learning needs of students with varying skill levels.

Platform for Experimental and Project Design. Beyond its role in classroom assistance, the Jetson Nano-based intelligent robot serves as the core platform for experimental and project-based learning. Students engage in multidisciplinary experimental and project development focused on the implementation and optimization of the robot's functions. These projects encompass programming, digital logic control, hardware debugging, and artificial intelligence algorithm applications. Throughout the project lifecycle—spanning requirement analysis, system design, coding implementation, and testing—students complete a comprehensive engineering practice process. This structure effectively enhances students' system integration capabilities and innovation skills, enabling them to apply knowledge holistically when addressing complex engineering challenges.

By integrating the Jetson Nano-based intelligent robot, the course successfully bridges theoretical learning with practical application, significantly improving instructional effectiveness and fostering student engagement. Moreover, it establishes a robust foundation for cultivating interdisciplinary engineering professionals equipped to meet the demands of future industries.

3.2 Curriculum Content and Module Design

To meet the comprehensive and practical requirements of the Embedded Systems course, the curriculum first integrates foundational knowledge from multiple disciplines, including programming languages, hardware fundamentals, and AI algorithms, thereby forming a unified knowledge framework. C, as the core language for embedded development, covers syntax structures, pointer operations, and hardware interface programming, laying the groundwork for subsequent embedded control tasks. Python is employed for data processing, AI algorithm implementation, and advanced hardware interaction control, fostering students' scripting proficiency and rapid prototyping skills. The Digital Systems component encompasses logic gates, sequential logic, and fundamentals of digital communication, aiding students in understanding the underlying hardware principles and programming interfaces of digital circuits. The Deep Learning module introduces the basic principles of neural networks, model training, and the concept of edge AI, equipping students with the ability to embed AI algorithms into practical systems. Through interdisciplinary knowledge integration, students develop a systems-oriented mindset for hardware-software co-development and enhance their capability to address complex engineering challenges.

The Embedded Systems course is structured around the Jetson Nano-based intelligent robot and features a modular instructional design covering the following key technologies. First, the Sensor Control Module focuses on data acquisition and processing from ultrasonic sensors, infrared sensors, vision cameras, and gyroscopes, fostering students' proficiency in hardware programming and environmental perception. Second, the Path Planning Module introduces relevant path planning algorithms, such as SLAM, and their implementation within embedded systems to enable autonomous navigation. Third, the AI Algorithm Application Module covers object detection (based on YOLO, SSD, and similar algorithms), facial recognition, speech recognition, and basic behavior decision-making using state machines or deep reinforcement learning, emphasizing their deployment and realization in embedded systems. The course emphasizes a combination of theoretical instruction and hands-on practice, enabling students to understand the application of artificial intelligence in robotic control and to master the implementation of essential technologies.

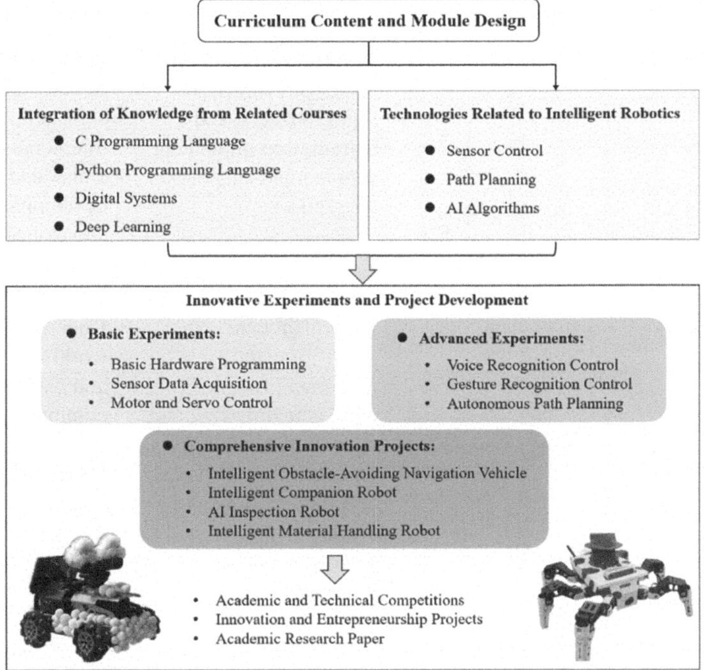

Fig. 2. The illustration diagram of curriculum content and module design

The Embedded Systems course adopts a three-tier progressive instructional framework—"Fundamentals-Advanced-Innovation"—that systematically integrates multidisciplinary knowledge throughout the curriculum. Figure 2 presents the overall arrangement of the course content and module design. As shown in Fig. 2, the course systematically organizes the instructional content to effectively integrate relevant knowledge from multiple foundational courses. Aligned with current technological demands, the curriculum incorporates intelligent robotics technologies to cultivate students' competencies in hardware-software co-design, embedded AI algorithm applications, and engineering innovation and practice. This approach addresses common challenges found in traditional embedded systems courses, such as the disconnect between theory and practice, the gap between classroom learning and market requirements, and the insufficient development of students' innovative capabilities.

Table 1. Experimental Plan for Embedded Systems.

Experiment Types	Experimental Content	Content Overview	Learning Objectives and Skills
Basic Experiments (Mandatory) (40%)	Basic Hardware Programming	Learn and practice GPIO (General Purpose Input/Output) control, master basic programming operations for LED lights, buzzers, and buttons, and implement simple input-output interactions	• Acquire proficiency in basic C language hardware programming • Understand hardware pin configuration and signal control of microcontrollers or embedded development boards • Develop skills in hardware debugging and trouble shooting
	Sensor Data Acquisition	Implement data acquisition and processing for ultrasonic, infrared, and temperature-humidity sensors, and achieve real-time reading and display of environmental information	• Understand the working principles and data communication methods (e.g., I^2C, UART) of different types of sensors • Be able to write programs to perform data acquisition, filtering, and basic data visualization • Develop skills in hardware-software integration for sensor systems

(*continued*)

Table 1. (*continued*)

Experiment Types	Experimental Content	Content Overview	Learning Objectives and Skills
	Motor and Servo Control	Learn the generation and modulation of PWM (Pulse Width Modulation) signals, and implement speed control and direction adjustment for DC motors and servos	• Master the fundamentals of motion control algorithms • Implement precise control of motors and servos, and understand feedback control mechanisms • Develop skills in debugging and optimizing robotic drive systems
Advanced Experiments (Mandatory) (40%)	Voice Recognition Control	Utilize Python or edge AI modules to invoke speech recognition APIs, enabling the recognition and response to voice commands for controlling robot actions	• Understand the basic principles of speech recognition • Master the application of AI algorithms in voice interaction • Achieve seamless integration between hardware and voice input
	Gesture Recognition Control	Utilize a camera or IMU (Inertial Measurement Unit) sensors to recognize user gestures and implement interaction control based on visual or motion data	• Understand the application of gesture recognition algorithms, such as OpenCV or deep learning models • Master preprocessing and feature extraction of image or sensor data • Develop skills in designing natural human-computer interaction systems

(*continued*)

Table 1. (*continued*)

Experiment Types	Experimental Content	Content Overview	Learning Objectives and Skills
	Autonomous Path Planning	Implement environment-aware path planning, enabling autonomous navigation and obstacle avoidance for the robot	• Understand path planning algorithms and their application in real-world robotic control • Be able to convert sensor inputs into path decision information • Develop skills in designing and implementing control logic for autonomous systems
Innovation Projects (Optional: Choose one experiment.) (20%)	Intelligent Obstacle-Avoiding Navigation Vehicle Intelligent Companion Robot AI Inspection Robot Intelligent Material Handling Robot	Consolidate foundational knowledge, engage in hands-on practice and innovative design, and enhance teamwork and engineering implementation skills	• Hardware-software integrated design capability • Implementation of multi-sensor fusion algorithms • Real-time control and autonomous decision-making • Human-computer interaction design and user experience optimization • System integration and complex project management skills

Table 1 presents the detailed experimental plan for the Embedded Systems course guided by intelligent robotics. The initial phase of the course focuses on fundamental knowledge modules, including the hardware architecture of embedded systems, software structure, mainstream processing cores, input/output interfaces, and communication protocols. A blended instructional approach combining theoretical lectures, robot demonstrations, and small-scale foundational experiments is employed to establish hardware and software fundamentals while fostering programming skills and hardware logic thinking. During the technical skill development phase, theoretical instruction on embedded system topics is integrated with specialized training in sensor control, path planning, and AI algorithm applications. Project-based assignments are organized through group discussions, enabling students to translate theoretical knowledge into hands-on practice while cultivating skills in system integration and hardware-software debugging. In the advanced application and capability enhancement phase, students are trained to deeply integrate AI algorithms with hardware control to achieve complex human-computer interaction and autonomous decision-making functions. A guided experimental methodology, combined with team-based development and periodic reviews, supports students in independently selecting and executing comprehensive innovation projects. This approach fosters independent design, engineering implementation, and innovation capabilities, while also strengthening teamwork and project management skills.

3.3 Multi-dimensional Achievement Assessment System

To comprehensively assess students' learning outcomes in the Embedded Systems course, a three-dimensional competency evaluation framework has been developed. This framework centers on knowledge mastery, practical skills combined with innovative thinking, and teamwork coupled with project management abilities, as shown in Fig. 3. Additionally, it is supported by a teaching feedback and continuous improvement mechanism to ensure the sustained enhancement of instructional quality.

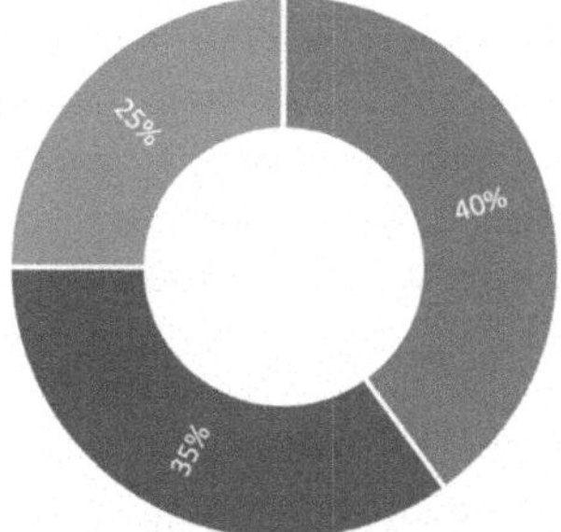

Fig. 3. The score distribution of the three-dimensional competency evaluation framework.

Specifically, the knowledge mastery assessment includes formative evaluations—such as in-class quizzes, homework assignments, and spontaneous classroom questioning—and summative evaluations, including midterm/final examinations and open-ended problem assessments conducted via online platforms. The assessment of practical skills and innovative thinking focuses on evaluating students' ability to apply theoretical knowledge to real-world problem solving, system design, and innovative development. Both process-based assessments (e.g., laboratory reports, project execution logs) and outcome-based assessments (e.g., physical demonstrations, pitch presentations) are employed. Students are encouraged to engage in interdisciplinary design and participate in relevant technological competitions and innovation and entrepreneurship projects. For the evaluation of teamwork and project management skills, milestone checkpoints and outcome presentation sessions are established to simulate real-world engineering management processes. The evaluation emphasizes students' communication, collaboration, role allocation, and project management capabilities within team settings. Specific components include team role distribution, communication and writing, project management, peer evaluation, and instructor assessment. The detailed score distribution is illustrated in Fig. 4.

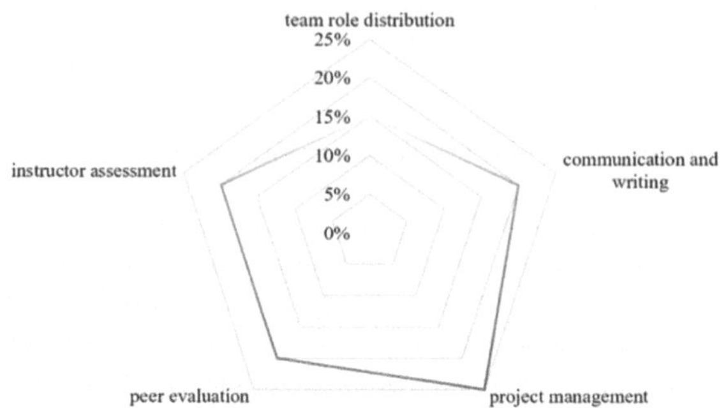

Fig. 4. The score distribution for the evaluation of teamwork and project management skills.

In summary, the proposed multi-dimensional achievement assessment framework emphasizes the integration of theory and practice, balances individual and team contributions, and gives equal weight to both process and outcomes. This approach enables a comprehensive and objective reflection of students' achievements in knowledge, skills, and overall competencies, while the continuous improvement mechanism ensures the ongoing enhancement of course quality and instructional effectiveness.

3.4 Teaching Effectiveness Evaluation

To comprehensively evaluate the effectiveness of the instructional reform in the Embedded Systems course guided by Jetson Nano-based intelligent robots, this study conducts a systematic assessment from three key perspectives: the enhancement of student competencies, comparative analysis between the experimental and control groups, and the identification of implementation challenges along with corresponding mitigation strategies. The detailed evaluation is presented as follows.

In terms of changes in students' knowledge mastery, hands-on skills, and self-directed learning ability before and after instruction, comparative assessments conducted at the beginning and end of the course indicate significant improvement in both theoretical understanding and practical competence. First, the average accuracy of students' responses to key concepts—such as embedded system architecture, GPIO control, and AI algorithm deployment—increased from 62.5% to 89.1%, with particularly notable gains in sensor communication and deep learning model integration. Second, leveraging the Jetson Nano-based intelligent robot platform, students were able to independently complete full system implementations by the end of the course, ranging from sensor integration to AI-based recognition tasks. The experimental task completion rate reached 92.6%, reflecting strong capabilities in hardware-software co-development and debugging. Third, in optional innovation projects, nearly half of the students proactively explored advanced topics by reviewing relevant literature and applying the technologies in extended implementations. The average duration of after-class self-study increased by approximately 40% compared to the beginning of the course, demonstrating enhanced initiative and improved capacity for cross-domain knowledge transfer.

reform, the teaching team established two parallel groups: an experimental group, which adopted the Jetson Nano-based intelligent robot platform and project-driven teaching model, and a control group, which followed a traditional experimental curriculum. Quantitative comparisons were conducted based on students' final comprehensive scores, project task completion rates, and subjective learning satisfaction. The results are summarized in Table 2.

Table 2. Comparison of Academic Performance and Learning Satisfaction Between the Experimental and Control Groups

Indicators	Experimental Group (N = 32)	Control Group (N = 30)	Improvement Margin
Final Comprehensive Score (Average)	86.4 points	78.2 points	10.5%
Project Task Completion Rate	92.6%	73.3%	19.3%
Course Satisfaction (4-Point Scale)	3.76	3.12	20.5%
Percentage of Students Who Agree That "Teaching Is Closely Integrated with Real-World Applications"	90.6%	63.7%	26.9%
Percentage of Students Who Believe the Course "Enhanced Practical Interest and Engineering Understanding"	92.3%	61.8%	49.4%

The data above clearly demonstrate that the experimental group outperformed the control group across multiple dimensions, including academic performance, task completion quality, and perceived learning experience. Notably, the project task completion rate and course satisfaction showed significant improvements, highlighting the distinct advantages of integrating an intelligent robot platform in stimulating students' practical interest, enhancing engineering comprehension, and promoting deep learning. Moreover, over 90% of students in the experimental group agreed that the course was "closely integrated with real-world applications" and that it "enhanced their practical interest and engineering understanding." This reflects a strong perception among students that the course content was highly relevant to engineering practice and that the instructional approach was both effective and engaging. These quantitative findings provide compelling evidence for the effectiveness of the "intelligent robot + project-driven" instructional model in significantly improving learning outcomes in embedded systems education.

In the practice of reforming the Embedded Systems course using Jetson Nano-based intelligent robots as the instructional core, notable improvements in teaching effectiveness have been achieved. However, several practical challenges have arisen during implementation, primarily in the following three areas. First, high equipment costs. The intelligent robot platform integrates components such as vision sensors and embedded computing units, leading to significantly higher procurement and maintenance costs compared to traditional experimental setups. To address this issue, the teaching team adopted a "shared platform + group rotation" approach to optimize resource usage. In parallel, industry-academia collaborations and extracurricular innovation project funding were leveraged to secure targeted support, thereby enhancing the sustainability and scalability of equipment utilization. Second, a steep technical learning curve. Due to the complexity of the platform, particularly for students new to embedded AI systems, instructors restructured the course content into modular and hierarchical segments. A "step-by-step + task-driven" strategy was employed to help students progressively master essential technical skills. Additionally, video demonstrations, user guides, and supplementary learning materials were developed to reduce the entry barrier and support independent learning. Third, ongoing pressure on teacher training and technology updates. With the rapid advancement of AI technologies, instructors face constant demands to update teaching content, learn new platforms, and deploy emerging algorithms. To mitigate this, the university has supported faculty participation in technical training programs, instructional reform workshops, and enterprise-led practical courses. Internally, the teaching team has fostered a collaborative teaching ecosystem, regularly engaging in resource sharing and experience exchange to build collective instructional capacity. By implementing these strategies, the reform initiative has not only delivered strong outcomes in its current phase but also laid a solid foundation for broader dissemination and long-term sustainability in embedded systems education.

In this course, an AI-driven formative assessment mechanism was introduced through the integration of the intelligent robot platform, enabling automated feedback and behavioral data collection to support instructional decision-making and periodic learning evaluations. However, while AI-enhanced educational assessment can significantly improve teaching efficiency, it also raises important ethical concerns that must be carefully addressed and properly regulated. Regarding data privacy and compliance, students' rights to informed consent must be respected. Prior to any data collection, explicit authorization is obtained through course documentation and informed briefing sessions. All data storage and analysis strictly adhere to the university's data security policies, ensuring that collected information is used solely for instructional improvement and not for high-stakes purposes such as ranking or punitive evaluation. To mitigate risks of bias and ensure fairness in assessment, the teaching team employs a multi-dimensional evaluation framework, integrating AI-generated insights with human judgment to provide a more holistic assessment of student performance. AI is not treated as the sole arbiter of student ability. Additionally, model decision-making processes are designed with interpretability in mind, helping students understand how the system operates and enhancing their trust and engagement in AI-supported evaluation. Moreover, the course emphasizes a "human-AI collaboration" philosophy, positioning AI as a supportive tool rather than a replacement for educators. Critical evaluations—such as project assessments and the appraisal of innovation capacity—are conducted under the guidance of instructors to ensure ethical integrity and maintain the humanistic dimension of education. In summary, while AI technologies hold great promise for enhancing instructional quality and assessment efficiency, their implementation must be accompanied by strong ethical oversight and transparent governance. Only through the alignment of technological advancement with principles of educational fairness can a trustworthy, explainable, and sustainable assessment system be established.

4 Conclusion

This study proposes an innovative instructional model that integrates intelligent educational robots into the Embedded Systems course, addressing common challenges in traditional curricula such as fragmented knowledge, insufficient practical experience, and a lack of interdisciplinary integration. By adopting a blended teaching approach that combines intelligent guidance with engineering practice, the course effectively bridges the gap between theoretical knowledge and real-world applications. Through modular course design, a tiered set of experimental projects has been introduced, ranging from basic hardware programming to comprehensive innovation projects. This structure ensures the progressive development of students' skills, fostering problem-solving abilities, system design proficiency, and innovative thinking. To objectively evaluate learning outcomes, a comprehensive multi-dimensional achievement assessment system has been implemented. This study provides a replicable model for engineering education reform and offers valuable insights for other disciplines seeking to align teaching strategies with the evolving technological landscape and industry demands.

Acknowledgments. This work is supported by 2023 Minjiang University Teaching Research and Development Project: Research on Integrating Scientific Research Achievements into the Construction of Microcomputer and Microcontroller Principles Laboratory Courses (No.: MJUJG2023A033), Reform and Practice of General Computer Courses in the Context of Emerging Engineering Education (MJUJG 2023A010), and Application-Driven Smart Teaching Innovation Team (Team Leader: Haibo Luo).

References

1. Ruiz-Rojas, L.I., Acosta-Vargas, P., De-Moreta-Llovet, J., Gonzalez-Rodriguez, M.: Empowering education with generative artificial intelligence tools: approach with an instructional design matrix. Sustainability **15**(15), 11524 (2023)
2. Weng, X., Chiu, T.K.: Instructional design and learning outcomes of intelligent computer assisted language learning: systematic review in the field. Comput. Educ.: Artific. Intell. **4**, 100117 (2023)
3. Stefaniak, J.E., Cha, E.E., Yang, F., Gilstrap, S., Yang, L.: A comprehensive review of instructional designer research and approaches in learning design. Educ. Technol. Res. Develop. 1–23 (2025)

4. Chen, J., Brown, G.T.: Tensions between knowledge transmission and student-focused teaching approaches to assessment purposes: helping students improve through transmission. Teach. Teach. **22**(3), 350–367 (2016)
5. Zhao, D., Muntean, C.H., Chis, A.E., Rozinaj, G., Muntean, G.M.: Game-based learning: enhancing student experience, knowledge gain, and usability in higher education programming courses. IEEE Trans. Educ. **65**(4), 502–513 (2022)
6. Baabdullah, A., Alajlan, H., Alebaikan, R.: The perceptions and experiences of in-service teachers in a computer science professional development program. Sustainability **16**(4), 1473 (2024)
7. Chen, X., Cheng, G., Zou, D., Zhong, B., Xie, H.: Artificial intelligent robots for precision education. Educ. Technol. Soc. **26**(1), 171–186 (2023)
8. Yang, D., Oh, E.S., Wang, Y.: Hybrid physical education teaching and curriculum design based on a voice interactive artificial intelligence educational robot. Sustainability **12**(19), 8000 (2020)

Cultivating Computational and Mathematical Thinking by Solving Programming Contest Problems

Yonghui Wu[1,2](✉) and Juan Zhou[3]

[1] Fudan University, Shanghai 200433, China
yhwu@fudan.edu.cn
[2] Quanzhou University of Information Engineering, Fujian 362000, China
[3] East China Jiaotong University, Jiangxi 330013, China

Abstract. Now all professions and works reliant on tool-based skills, including most programmers' work, are being displaced by AI technologies. Cultivating students' computational and mathematical thinking by solving programming contest problems can be as a breakthrough point for the reform of computer education in the AI era. It is implemented by constructions of teaching materials, curricula and a cross-institutional and cross-regional programming training system. And innovations and effects are introduced.

Keywords: Computational Thinking · Mathematical Thinking · Programming Contest Problem · Solving Problems by Programming · AI

1 Introduction

Programming technology has become a foundational technology for the information society. Generative AI models, such as ChatGPT, DeepSeek, and so on, are advancing at a remarkable pace; and excel particularly in performing repetitive and rule-based tasks. All professions and works reliant on tool-based skills, including most programmers' work, are being displaced by AI technologies [1]. However, AI models still lack creativity and innovative thinking—a critical limitation in their current state of development [2, 3].

Programming teaching materials and curricula have been developed since the late 1950s, covering programming languages, data structures, algorithm design and analysis, along with their mathematical foundations including set theory and graph theory. In the AI era, however, these existing educational resources often exhibit deficiencies in several aspects: programming practice integration, effective combination of computational and mathematical thinking in pedagogy, and systematic curriculum interconnectivity.

Programming contests are contests solving problems by programming. These contests have grown rapidly because the problem-solving skills they cultivate align closely with the core competencies required of computer professionals. Since the late 1980s,

W. Hong et al. (Eds.): ICCSE 2025, CCIS 2761, pp. 347–358, 2026.
https://doi.org/10.1007/978-981-95-7731-6_27

a substantial collection of programming contest problems has been accumulated, contributed by problem setters worldwide. These problems serve not only as training materials for programming competitors, but also as valuable resources for programming curricula and laboratory experiments. Through systematic training solving programming contest problems, students can significantly enhance their computational and mathematical thinking abilities. Such abilities represent the core requirements for computer professionals in the AI era.

Now there are some successful cases for cultivating computational thinking in courses [4]. And these courses typically feature: (1) Interdisciplinary integration: Elements of computational thinking, such as decomposition, pattern recognition, abstraction, and algorithms, integrated into different disciplines like data science, engineering, medicine, social science, and so on; (2) Real-world problem-driven: analyzing practical issues in different fields; (3) Technology tool support to facilitate learning. However, these efforts focus on integrating computational thinking training in individual courses rather than systematically and comprehensively cultivating students' computational thinking abilities.

2 Cultivating Computational and Mathematical Thinking by Solving Programming Contest Problems

2.1 Cultivating Computational and Mathematical Thinking by Solving Programming Contest Problems

Computational thinking is a problem-solving methodology that involves decomposition, pattern recognition, abstraction, algorithm design, and so on. Decomposition is breaking down complex problems into manageable components. Pattern recognition is discovering patterns in data or problems. Abstraction is focusing on essential information while ignoring irrelevant details. Algorithm design is creating clear, efficient step-by-step solutions by programming. That is, computational thinking is the process of solving problems like a computer scientist, using logic, patterns, and structured steps.

Computational thinking is not only widely applied in computer science, but also extends to other disciplines, fostering logical reasoning and systematic approaches. It is a meta-skill in the AI era.

Cultivating students' computational thinking by solving programming contest problems can be structured into three progressive levels:

(1) Cultivation of fundamental abilities:

Using programming languages, data structures, and algorithms to solve practical problems, and initially establishing computational thinking;

(2) Methodology and Skill Enhancement:

Building upon foundational abilities, further mastery includes:

- Programming paradigms: Such as mechanism analysis (designing algorithms/models based on problem descriptions) and statistical analysis (deriving global solutions by analyzing partial solutions);

- Programming techniques: Such as time and memory optimization, simulation, recursion, offline processing, binary search, real number precision handling, and structured programming, and so on;
- Mathematical tools: Including the addition principle, multiplication principle, and more;
- Cross-Disciplinary knowledge: Integrating domain-specific expertise to deepen problem-solving capabilities.

(3) Comprehensive application and optimization:

Integrate programming knowledge, adapt problem-solving strategies dynamically, and resolve issues efficiently with advanced data structures and optimized algorithms.

Mathematical thinking is the ability to analyze problems logically, abstract patterns, and justify solutions using mathematical principles. Its key characteristics involves logical reasoning, abstraction, generalization, problem-solving, and quantitative modeling.

There are two aspects for cultivating mathematical thinking by solving programming contest problems.

(1) Mathematical formalization training:

By solving mathematical programming contest problems, such as set theory, graph theory, number theory, combinatorics, computational geometry, game theory, and probability theory, students become proficient in using mathematical language to rigorously analyze and express problems, and compute and deduce solutions.

(2) Modeling-Proof-Optimization training:

By solving mathematical programming contest problems, students formulate mathematical models for given problems, prove algorithms' correctness along with time/space complexity analysis, and identify optimal solutions under specified constraints.

2.2 Cultivating Students' Computational and Mathematical Thinking by Solving Programming Contest Problems: A Breakthrough Point for the Reform of Computer Education

Cultivating students' computational and mathematical thinking by solving programming contest problems can be as a breakthrough point for the reform of computer education in the AI era.

(1) Requirements for computer professionals in the AI era:

- Computational thinking as the core competency.

In the AI era, computational thinking serves as the fundamental mindset. AI technologies—ranging from algorithm design to data modeling and optimization—demand strong computational thinking skills. This approach enables professionals to systematically break down complex problems into computable components and develop efficient solutions.

- Mathematical thinking as the theoretical foundation.

Mathematical thinking underpins AI development. Modern AI models rely on advanced mathematical theories, including linear algebra, probability, calculus, and optimization. Proficiency in mathematical reasoning allows developers to understand model mechanics deeply and drive innovations in AI technology.

- Programming as an essential skill and implementation tool.

Programming is not only a critical literacy in today's digital society but also the primary means of implementing AI solutions. Mastery of programming ensures that theoretical designs can be effectively translated into functional systems.

(2) Computer education in the AI era:

With AI being widely adopted across diverse fields—including healthcare, finance, and education, computer education must shift toward a "knowledge + competency" pedagogical paradigm.

- Computational thinking as a universal skill.

The universality of computational thinking extends its relevance beyond computer science, equipping students with a systematic approach to solving interdisciplinary problems.

- Mathematical Thinking as a Foundational Framework.

By emphasizing logical reasoning and abstraction, mathematical thinking provides the necessary foundation for comprehending complex systems and designing efficient algorithms in AI development.

- Growing demand for advanced competencies

The rapid expansion of AI applications will dramatically increase the need for skilled developers who possess strong computational and mathematical thinking—essential capabilities for cross-domain adaptability and effective real-world problem-solving.

(3) The feasibility of the training for "solving programming contest problems":

Inherently, programming is a technology. Years of practice demonstrate that structured training for solving programming contest problems can systematically and efficiently cultivate students' computational and mathematical thinking. This approach transforms contest-driven problem-solving into a scalable methodology for building future-proof competencies.

3 The Implementation of Cultivating Computational and Mathematical Thinking

Cultivating computational and mathematical thinking utilizes on programming contest problems and their analysis and solutions, emphasizes students' solving problems by programming, transcends the limitations of traditional programming syllabi, and establishes systematic connections across programming curricula. It deeply integrates computational and mathematical thinking training into programming education. It involves:

- Developing teaching materials and curricula based on programming contest problems and their analysis and solutions, to deeply integrate computational and mathematical training into programming education;
- Constructing cross-institutional and cross-regional programming teaching systems.

By doing so, it promotes the adaptation of programming education to meet the requirements for computer professionals in the AI era.

3.1 Teaching Materials for Collegiate Programming Contests and Education

The series "Collegiate Programming Contests and Education" [5–10] is built upon the core paradigm that "algorithms + data structures = programs." Through systematic analysis and organization of a vast collection of programming contest problems, this series establishes a dual-purpose textbook system that serves both course instruction and contest training.

In the series, there are 825 carefully selected classic programming contest problems. The 825 problems in this curriculum were systematically selected through a two-tiered filtering model to ensure pedagogical rigor, diversity, and alignment with competitive programming standards:

(1) Selection Criteria:

- Difficulty Spectrum: Stratified by contest tiers: ICPC regional-level, ICPC world finals-level, invitation contest, university local contest, and other contest. All problems tagged with empirical solve rates (30–70% for optimal learning friction).
- Knowledge Coverage: programming language, data structures, algorithms, mathematics, programming strategies, and so on;
- Problem Types: implementation-heavy (emphasizing debug resilience), theoretical/proof-based (e.g., complexity analysis), insight-driven, and so on;

(2) Pedagogical Adaptation and Chapter Integration

- Minimum 3 problems per subtopic;
- Progressive sequencing: introductory, intermediate, and mastery (multi-concept synthesis).

Key characteristics of the series are as follows:

- Cultivates computational and mathematical thinking through hands-on programming problem-solving;
- Breaks through the constraints of traditional syllabi while seamlessly bridging programming courses with mathematics;
- Introduces original teaching materials on problem-solving strategies, covering advanced data structures and optimized algorithms beyond standard curricula.

This series builds a bridge between conventional coursework and contest skill development, enabling mutual reinforcement of theoretical foundations and practical training while presenting a comprehensive programming knowledge framework.

The series adopts programming contest problems and their analyses as experiments, employing a four-stage progressive teaching framework:

(1) Knowledge instruction: Explains key concepts of relevant algorithms and data structures, clarifying learning objectives;
(2) Problem presentation: Selects representative contest problems as experimental cases;
(3) Analytical thinking training: Provides analyses to problems integrating computational and mathematical thinking, including problem modeling, algorithm design, and complexity optimization strategies;
(4) Program: Delivers program with detailed annotations.

Such a closed-loop "theory-problem-thinking-implementation" ensures students simultaneously acquire knowledge while enhancing problem-solving skills and programming proficiency.

Taking the organization of minimum spanning trees and their extensions in "Data Structure Practice" [6] and "Data Structure Strategies Solving Problems" [5], as well as the experiment for combinatorial counting in "Algorithm Design Practice" [7] as cases, to demonstrate the organization of series and experiments based on programming contest problems and their analysis and solutions.

"Data Structure Practice" covers both syllabus algorithms (Kruskal algorithm and Prim algorithm) and maximum spanning tree, while "Data Structure Strategies Solving Problems" includes advanced applications and variants like ratio-optimal and degree-constrained spanning trees. The following Table 1 shows the organization of minimum spanning trees and their extensions.

The experiment combinatorial counting in "Algorithm Design Practice" is organized as follows:

(1) Experiment Objectives: $C(n, r)$ is denoted as the number of r-combination of an n-element set. $C(n, r) = \frac{n\times(n-1)\times......\times(n-r+1)}{r\times(r-1)\times......\times 1}$. Master the mathematical principles and optimized algorithm for combinatorial counting, to cultivate computational and mathematical thinking, while enhancing awareness of algorithm optimization.
(2) Experiment Content:

   - Mathematical theory: The formula derivation and proofs for combinatorial counting C(n, r); and binomial coefficient formulas and their proofs.

Theorem 1. $C(n, r) = \frac{n\times(n-1)\times......\times(n-r+1)}{r\times(r-1)\times......\times 1}$.

Proof. $C(n, r)$ denotes the number of ways to choose r elements from n elements. Since there are $r!$ permutations for any selected r elements, the multiplication principle implies that the number of permutations of r elements chosen from n is given by P(n, r) $= C(n, r) \times r!$. Thus, solving for $C(n, r)$:

$C(n, r) = \frac{n\times(n-1)\times......\times(n-r+1)}{r\times(r-1)\times......\times 1}$. ■

Theorem 2. For any k, $1 \le k \le n$, $C(n + 1, k) = C(n, k) + C(n, k\text{-}1)$.

Proof. Let X be a set with n elements, and $a \notin$ X. Then, $C(n + 1, k)$ is the number of k-element subsets of $Y = X \cup \{a\}$.

Table 1. The organization of minimum spanning trees and their extensions.

Teaching Stage	Content	Ability Development
Fundamental experiment 1: Algorithm implementation and comparison	Implementation, proof, and comparison of Kruskal's algorithm and Prim's algorithm (sparse graph vs. dense graph). Solving programming contest problems (POJ 2421, POJ 1258)	Implementation and proof of algorithms
Fundamental experiment 2: Concept extension	Implementation and proof of Maximum Spanning Tree. Solving a programming contest problem (POJ 2377)	Implementation and proof of the algorithm
Strategy enhancement 1	Formulate the problem into a graph model and apply a minimum spanning tree solution. Solving programming contest problems (UVA 10368, HDOJ 4081)	Graph Modeling
Strategy enhancement 2	Optimal Ratio Spanning Tree, Minimum k-Degree Constrained Spanning Tree. Solving programming contest problems (POJ 2728, POJ 1639)	Mathematical modeling and derivation that motivates the algorithm
Strategy enhancement 3	Second Minimum Spanning Tree. Solving programming contest problems (UVA 10600, POJ 1679, HDU 4126)	Mathematical modeling and derivation that motivates the algorithm

The k-element subsets of Y can be partitioned into two classes:

1. Subsets not containing a:
   These are exactly the k-element subsets of X, totaling $C(n, k)$.
2. Subsets containing a:
   Such subsets consist of a along with k-1 elements chosen from X, yielding $C(n, k\text{-}1)$ possibilities.

By the addition principle, the total number of k-element subsets of Y is the sum of the two cases: $C(n + 1, k) = C(n, k) + C(n, k\text{-}1)$. ■

– Optimized algorithm:

- Successive multiplication of r integer quotients, to avoid factorial overflow. That is, for $C(n, r)$, in the sequence of r consecutive natural numbers $(n - r + 1)$, $(n - r + 2)$,..., n, there must exist: One number divisible by r, and one number divisible by $r - 1$, ..., and so on. Thus, during computation, divide the numerator by the denominator in descending order (largest denominator first) at each step, then multiply the r resulting integer quotients together.
- Binomial coefficient formula, based on two-dimensional array, utilizing recurrence relations. That is, $C(i, j) = C(i\text{-}1, j) + C(i\text{-}1, j\text{-}1)$; can be calculate based on two-dimensional array c, where $c[i][j] = c[i\text{-}1][j] + c[i\text{-}1][j\text{-}1]$, and $c[i][0] = 1$.

- Related programming contest problems, and analysis and solutions.

The experiment is designed to integrate training in computational and mathematical thinking.

3.2 Curricula for Solving Programming Contest Problems

Curricula are based on teaching materials. In curricula, the teaching model follows case-based teaching. And online judge systems are utilized as supporting information technologies.

The case-based teaching method in an experiment proceeds as follows:

- Introduction: After a knowledge point is introduced, students read a related programming contest problem, and consider how to solve it using the newly learned knowledge and design an appropriate data structure and algorithm.
- Analysis: Teachers present the analysis to the problem, and students compare it with their own reasoning.
- Implementation: Students implement, debug, and optimize their programs to pass all test cases within the given time and memory limits.

Such case-based teaching helps students integrate theory with practice while fostering strong interest and a deep desire for knowledge.

Online judge systems are automated platforms that evaluate the correctness of submitted programs. In curricula:

- For students, they serve as a tool to refine programming skills through practice;
- For teachers, they provide an efficient way to manage homework and examinations.

Their integration represents an informatization strategy for programming-based problem-solving in education.

The guiding principle of curricula is that programming is a practical skill. Students' problem-solving abilities are honed through structured practice. Curricula incorporate programming contest problems, requiring students to solve them through coding. Students practice within a structured programming knowledge framework, and they solve problems based on systematic analysis and solution strategies. Homework and exams are designed as mock programming contests on online judge systems, pushing students to improve their skills efficiently under time constraints.

The chapter "minimum spanning tree (MST)" is used as a teaching case:

(1) The implementation and the proof of correctness for Kruskal's algorithm is showed. Students are required to solve a programming contest problem (POJ 2421) by applying Kruskal's algorithm.
(2) The implementation of Prim's algorithm is introduced, with emphasis on comparing it to Kruskal's, allowing students to understand their respective applications (sparse vs. dense graphs). Then students independently prove the correctness of Prim's algorithm (by analogy with Kruskal's proof) and apply it to solve another programming contest problem (POJ 1258).
(3) An open discussion is held: modifying Kruskal's/Prim's algorithms to select maximum-weight edges instead, requiring students to independently analyze and justify their reasoning. They then implement this variation to solve a programming contest problem (POJ 2377).

From Kruskal's algorithm to Prim's algorithm, and then to the maximum spanning tree, students progressively develop their understanding—first proving Prim's correctness by analogy, then independently analyzing and proving the properties of the maximum spanning tree. This step-by-step approach strengthens mathematical reasoning and encourages deep thinking. Each stage is paired with programming contest problems to bridge theory and practical coding skills.

The proof of Kruskal's algorithm is the foundation for the chapter "minimum spanning tree (MST)".

Theorem 3. The graph T obtained by Kruskal's algorithm is a minimum spanning tree for a connected Graph $G(V, E)$, where $|V|=n$.

Proof. First, T is a spanning tree of a Graph G with n-1 edges, based on the definition of a tree.

Second, we prove that T is a minimum spanning tree. Assume T is not a minimum spanning tree of G, and let S be a minimum spanning tree of G such that $W(S) < W(T)$. The edges in T are ordered by weight in non-decreasing sequence: $e_1, e_2, \ldots, e_k, \ldots, e_{n-1}$. Let e_k be the first edge in T that does not belong to S. That is, means $e_1, e_2, \ldots, e_{k-1}$ are common edges in both S and T.

A perform a fundamental transformation on S: Add e_k to S, creating a fundamental cycle C. Since C is a cycle, there must exist an edge $e' \in S$ such that $e' \notin T$ (otherwise, T would contain a cycle, leading to a contradiction). Remove e' from $S \cup \{e_k\}$, resulting in a new spanning tree S'. Because $w(e_k) \leq w(e')$, it follows that $W(S') \leq W(S)$. Moreover, S' shares one more common edge with T than S does.

By repeating this process, each transformation reduces the total weight and increases the number of common edges between the intermediate spanning tree and T. Eventually, S transforms into T, with $W(T) \leq W(S)$. This contradicts the initial assumption that $W(S) < W(T)$. Therefore, T must be a minimum spanning tree. ■

3.3 The Cross-Institutional and Cross-Regional Teaching System

The cross-institutional and cross-regional teaching system now operates as a "$1 + M + N$" teaching and experimental framework:

- 1: A unified online programming course series for problem-solving;
- M: various kinds of M universities participating in the system;

- *N*: *N* students from diverse institutions honing their programming skills.

Key components of the system are as follows.

(1) Integrated programming curricula.

- The system provides online programming curricula for problem-solving, integrating computational and mathematical thinking into university programming education;
- The system aims to improve students' programming skills while meeting the demand for computer professionals in the AI era.

(2) Intensive training camps.

- Online and offline programming camps are held during vacations to prepare students for programming contests;
- These camps offer advanced training beyond standard university syllabi, ensuring systematic skill development.

The course "Programming Practice for Problem Solving", based on books "Algorithm Design Practice"[9] and "Data Structure Practice"[10], serves as a representative case of the Cross-Institutional and Cross-Regional teaching system. This course has been repeatedly taught in international programming training camps. Through the Academic Exchange Program between Fudan University and University of Buenos Aires, it is also a course at the University of Buenos Aires. Additionally, it has been offered as an international summer course at Fudan University and Shanghai Jiao Tong University, respectively. This case exemplifies how one practical training course can be shared by *M* universities domestically and abroad, enhancing problem-solving skills of *N* students with diverse learning needs.

For the "1 + M + N" teaching and experimental system, AI technology is also employed to manage learning process data.

(1) The systematic analysis is conducted on both common and individual programming challenges faced by students from diverse institutions:

- Common Issues: Identifying and extracting recurring problems in problem-solving processes, particularly high-error-rate segments in code or test data, enabling instructors to address them with targeted interventions.
- Personalized Support: Leveraging online testing platforms and virtual contests, individual student performance, such as solution time and submission frequency, is analyzed to provide tailored guidance for improvement.

(2) The learning process is managed through:

- Code Similarity Checks: Automated plagiarism detection.
- Automated Reporting: Generation of individualized student performance reports and class-wide analytics.

4 Innovations

First, unlike traditional programming pedagogy, this approach cultivates computational and mathematical thinking through programming contest problems. By requiring students to synthesize knowledge and implement solutions in code, it deepens their understanding of programming concepts and their underlying relationships. This paradigm shifts programming education from passive "knowledge acquisition" to active "knowledge application + ability development".

Second, programming education is tightly coupled with contest training, creating a mutually reinforcing cycle. Contest-driven learning not only strengthens conceptual mastery but also fosters a scalable, cross-institutional training framework. Such a system elevates problem-solving abilities across universities of varying tiers and geographic regions, promoting equitable skill development.

5 Effects

The teaching materials and curricula for solving programming contest problems, and the cross-institutional and cross-regional teaching system have been implemented in practice for an extended period. Online programming curricula designed for problem-solving cover a comprehensive range of subjects, including programming language, data structure, algorithm design and analysis, and more. Since 2022, a total of 22,002 participants (person-time) have enrolled in five online programming training camps across China, while 16 programming training camps have been conducted internationally. The author has delivered lectures at over 30 universities worldwide and presented more than 20 keynote speeches at various conferences and workshops [11]. These works have been adopted by more than 400 universities and have gained widespread recognition from educators and students globally.

It has been proven in practice that cultivating computational and mathematical thinking by solving programming contest problems effectively enhance students' problem-solving skills and are adaptable to various types of universities and students. According to "China College Graduate Employment Reports", graduates with programming contest experience earn 30–50% higher starting salaries than their peers in the same field. LinkedIn data analysis reveals that 82% of new hires in R&D teams at top-tier IT companies in the past two years had programming contest experience, compared to just 15% among general computer science graduates [12]. Research from ICPC (International Collegiate Programming Contest) further indicates that "ICPC alumni published 1.67 AI papers per PhD year vs. 1.0 for controls" [13].

6 Conclusion

Cultivating computational and mathematical thinking by solving programming contest problems enables students to achieve both competitive success and professional readiness for the AI era's demands.

In the future, we will focus on two key improvements: enhancing and globally disseminating the teaching materials and curricula; and perfecting cross-institutional and cross-regional programming teaching system.

Acknowledgments. The work is financially supported by following projects: Office of Global Partnerships (Key Projects Development Fund), Fudan University (IDH6282016); Research projects for Computer Education from Association of Fundamental Computing Education in Chinese Universities(2024-AFCEC-027); Ministry of education – Touge collaborative education project (230901311065830); and University Computer Curriculum Teaching Advisory Committee of the Ministry of Education - Empowerment-Oriented University Computer First-Class Curriculum Development and Teaching Reform Project (Phase IV) (FNJY-2024-19).

References

1. Human Centered Artificial Intelligence. Introduction to the AI Index Report 2024. https://aiindex.stanford.edu/wp-content/uploads/2024/04/HAI_AI-Index-Report-2024.pdf. Accessed 15 April 2024
2. Wu, Y., Zhou, J.: Constructions of teaching materials, curriculums, and the teaching system cross-region for "Solving Problems by Programming". In: Chen, Y., et al.: Proceedings of The 30th International Computing and Combinatorics Conference (COCOON 2024), Springer in Lecture Notes in Computer Science (LNCS 15163), pp. 24–29 (2025)
3. Wu, Y.: Promoting students' programming skills in constructions for teaching materials and curriculums: experiments for comprehensive application of programming methods. In: Proceedings of 2022 Global Conference on Robotics, Artificial Intelligence and Information Technology (GCRAIT), pp. 770–773. IEEE CPS (2022)
4. Google for Education: "Exploring Computational Thinking" (2023). https://edu.google.com/resources/programs/exploring-computational-thinking/
5. Wu, Y., Wang, J.: Data structure strategies solving problems: for collegiate programming contest and education. 1st edn. China Machine Press, Beijing (2023)
6. Wu, Y., Wang, J.: Data structure practice: for collegiate programming contest and education. 3rd edn. China Machine Press, Beijing (2021)
7. Wu, Y., Wang, J.: Algorithm design practice: for collegiate programming contest and education. 2nd edn. China Machine Press, Beijing (2020)
8. Zhou, J., Wu, Y.: Preliminary programming practice: for collegiate programming contest and education. 1st edn. China Machine Press, Beijing (2021)
9. Wu, Y., Wang, J.: Algorithm design practice: for collegiate programming contest and education. 1st edn. CRC Press, Orlando (2018)
10. Wu, Y., Wang, J.: Data structure practice: for collegiate programming contests and education. 1st edn. CRC Press, Orlando (2016)
11. Wu, Y.: Promoting Students' programming skills in constructions for teaching materials and curriculums: experiments for comprehensive application of programming methods. In: Proceedings of 2022 Global Conference on Robotics, Artificial Intelligence and Information Technology (GCRAIT), pp770–773. IEEE CPS
12. LinkedIn. Global Tech Talent Trends 2022. [EB/OL] (2022). https://linkedin.com/business/talent-solutions/tech-talent-report
13. Lee, H., Zhang, Y.: Competitive programming and AI research output: evidence from ICPC and Topcoder. IEEE Trans. Educ. **2022**(65(4)), 567–576

Construction and Optimization Path of Digital Literacy Index System for Securities Practitioners

Yifeng Yan[1] and Ning Wang[2(✉)]

[1] Xiamen Huaxia University, Xiamen 361024, Fujian, China
[2] Ningde Normal University, Ningde 352100, Fujian, China
nwang97@163.com

Abstract. The cultivation of digital literacy among securities practitioners plays a significant role in enhancing work efficiency, preventing financial risks, promoting business innovation, and elevating brand value. In constructing the indicator system, we adopted UNESCO's digital literacy framework as the theoretical foundation and incorporated specific guidance on digital literacy and skills from the Cyberspace Administration of China. This integration resulted in 28 indicators and a tailored digital literacy assessment framework for the securities industry. To evaluate the relative importance of these indicators, we explored the application of the entropy method for determining indicator weights. Leveraging the inherent characteristics and information content of the data itself, the entropy method enables objective and equitable weight allocation, thereby enhancing the accuracy and credibility of assessments. This study proposes optimization strategies for improving digital literacy among securities practitioners, including: formulating detailed training plans, implementing targeted digital literacy programs, conducting regular effectiveness evaluations, establishing incentive mechanisms and support systems, and refining the digital literacy framework.

Keywords: Securities · Digital Literacy · Indicator System

1 Introduction

The report of *the 19th National Congress of the Communist Party of China* put forward the policy of deepening financial system reform and enhancing the ability of financial services to serve the real economy, which has planned the development path for the financial construction of the socialist market economy with Chinese characteristics in the new era.

In November 2021, the Central Cybersecurity and Information Technology Commission released the *Action Plan for Enhancing the Digital Literacy and Skills of the Whole People*, which pointed out that enhancing the digital literacy and skills of the entire population is a necessary path to achieve the transition from a large network country to a strong network country. In 2021, the China Securities Regulatory Commission released the *14th Five Year Plan* for the technological development of the securities and futures

W. Hong et al. (Eds.): ICCSE 2025, CCIS 2761, pp. 359–378, 2026.
https://doi.org/10.1007/978-981-95-7731-6_28

industry, which clarified the basic direction of digital transformation in the securities and futures industry. At the same time, the People's Bank of China issued the Financial Science and Technology Development Plan (2022–2025) to guide financial institutions to give full play to the role of "Digital Technology+Data Elements" and promote the cultivation of digital capabilities.

In March 2023, the Central Committee of the Communist Party of China and the State Council issued the Overall Layout Plan for the Construction of Digital China. Building a digital China is an important engine to promote Chinese path to modernization in the digital era and a powerful support to build a new competitive advantage of the country. In April 2024, the Ministry of Human Resources and Social Security issued the *Action Plan for Accelerating the Cultivation of Digital Talents to Support the Development of the Digital Economy* (2024–2026), which clearly stated the fundamental role of digital talents in supporting the digital economy and promoting the formation of new quality productive forces.

As an important pillar of the financial industry, the securities industry shoulders the mission of serving the real economy. The application of digital technology in the securities industry is changing the securities business model in unprecedented ways, with the widespread use of digital technologies such as big data, artificial intelligence, and blockchain being particularly significant. The application of digital technology has improved industry operational efficiency and promoted the upgrading of business models. Under the new situation, new requirements have been put forward for the digital literacy of securities practitioners.

2 Research Status of Digital Literacy Indicator System

The EU's research in the field of digital literacy plays an important role, and specific requirements for digital competence are described in documents such as the *Digital Education Action Plan* (2021–2027) and the *European Framework for Digital Competence of Education Workers*. The Digital Capability Framework released by the UK Joint Information Systems Committee includes five key elements: digital tool operation, information data management, digital content innovation, digital engagement, and self-development. The Norwegian Centre for Information and Communication Technology Education has released the *Teacher Professional Digital Competence Framework*, which constructs a framework for teacher professional digital competence.

Domestic scholars' research on the digital literacy indicator system focuses on groups such as citizens, college students, teachers, leaders, and rural residents.

In terms of research on citizen digital literacy indicators, Cui Binyue and Hong Wenxing (2024) [1] have constructed certification standards and evaluation systems for citizen digital literacy and skills, and launched the Digital Capability Level Certification - Talent Digital Competence (DCLC-DCI) Digital Literacy Certification, which provides a typical demonstration for China to improve citizen digital literacy and skills. Chen Mingming and Chen Yu (2024) [2] drew on the European Union's digital skills measurement method and used CGSS data to analyze the level and structural characteristics of digital literacy among Chinese residents. YAN Yifeng,WANG Ning,CHEN Tingting (2024) [3] analyzes the connection and difference between digital literacy and other literacy, and elaborates on the definition and framework of digital literacy that is commonly used in the context of digital China's construction, based on the actual situation in the current industry, propose methods for improving digital literacy in China to promote the adaptation of the general public to the learning, work and living needs of the digital age. Zhang Rongxu, Liu Xiaojuan, and Pan Yinrong (2024) [4] explored the connotation framework of Citizen Digital Literacy suitable for the Chinese context based on social constructivism, extracted 12 constituent elements of the citizen digital literacy framework in the Chinese context, and elaborated in detail from three dimensions: knowledge, skills, and attitudes.

In terms of research on digital literacy indicators for college students, Peng Wei (2024) [5] constructed an evaluation system for college students' digital literacy consisting of four dimensions: digital knowledge, digital awareness, digital ability, and digital responsibility, and 19 specific elements. The research results showed that the overall level of digital literacy among college students in Shandong Province was average, with varying degrees of differences in six aspects including gender, education level, and school type. Li Wenhuan (2024) [6] used the Delphi method and network analytic hierarchy process to construct an evaluation index system for the digital literacy of applied undergraduate students. Based on empirical analysis of undergraduate students in Shanxi Province, the digital literacy level of applied undergraduate students was evaluated. Wang Nan, Li Baohong, and Wang Zhiguo (2023) [7] used finance and accounting students as research subjects, adopted a questionnaire survey method, and organically embedded primary and secondary indicators into the items of the college students' digital literacy evaluation questionnaire, and sorted out the evaluation index system of finance and accounting college students' digital literacy. Chen Lu, Jia Jing, and Xiao Manling (2023) [8] used qualitative literature research and analytic hierarchy process to construct an evaluation index system for college students' digital literacy. Li Chaofeng, Yu Li, Li Tanyu et al. (2023) [9] constructed a preliminary evaluation model for college students' digital literacy, and verified the feasibility of the model using the Delphi method. After two rounds of Delphi consultation, the evaluation model was determined to have 5 primary indicators and 24 secondary elements, and empirical research was conducted among college students. Yao Zheng and Song Hongyan (2022) [10] constructed a digital literacy evaluation index system consisting of 5 primary competency domains and 10 secondary indicators based on the experience of media university students and UNESCO.

Regarding the research on teacher digital literacy indicators, Fang Zifan and Xu Juan (2023) [11] focus on the study of the international Chinese teacher digital literacy indicator system. Cheng Yaling and Tan Aiping (2024) [12] constructed a digital literacy assessment model that integrates "Qualitative Analysis+Quantitative Evaluation". The model organically integrates objective data generated dynamically by teachers during the teaching process with questionnaire evaluation data, achieving continuous monitoring and tracking evaluation of teachers' digital literacy levels.

In the study of digital literacy indicators for rural residents, Zhou Lijuan and Cai Anwen (2024) [13] used the Delphi method and Analytic Hierarchy Process to screen the core indicators of digital literacy for new professional farmers and determine their weights, constructing a new digital literacy system for professional farmers. Du Jiahui

(2023) [14] studied a digital literacy indicator system applicable to rural areas. The Delphi method was used to improve the indicators after two rounds of expert consultation, and the weights of each evaluation indicator were determined using Yaanalytic hierarchy process software, forming a weighted digital literacy indicator system.

Wei Peipei (2024) [15] constructed the Digital Leadership Index for Primary and Secondary School Principals, which includes 8 primary indicators, 17 secondary indicators, and 50 tertiary indicators. The Analytic Hierarchy Process was used to assign weight values to the indicators and determine the index calculation method. Li Fage (2023) [16] constructed a digital competency system framework for leaders based on the EU Citizen Digital Competency Framework and the UNESCO Global Digital Literacy Skills Reference Framework. The digital competencies of leaders are divided into 6 competency domains and 23 specific competencies.

Domestic and foreign scholars have conducted relatively comprehensive research on the index system of digital literacy, but there is a relative lack of research on digital literacy in the field of securities practitioners. There is an urgent need to establish a scientific and reasonable indicator system for the digital literacy of securities practitioners.

3 The Role of Enhancing Digital Literacy Among Securities Practitioners

With the development of financial technology, digitization has penetrated into every aspect of the securities industry, from transaction execution, risk management, customer service, investment advisory to market research, all of which are deeply influenced by digitization. Improving the digital literacy of securities practitioners is not only related to the future of personal career development, but also the key to promoting industry innovation, enhancing competitiveness, and achieving sustainable development.

3.1 Improvement of Work Efficiency

With the support of digital tools, securities practitioners efficiently process data, retrieve information, and conduct market analysis, using advanced algorithms and models to quickly and accurately identify market trends and trading opportunities, providing more scientific basis for investment decisions. The improvement of digital literacy means that securities practitioners are more flexible in using various digital tools. Intelligent customer management systems enable securities practitioners to better understand customer needs and provide diversified, personalized, and precise securities services to customers.

3.2 Financial Risk Prevention

In the digital age, the dissemination of financial risks has undergone profound changes. Traditional financial risk control methods are no longer able to adapt to the increasingly complex and ever-changing financial market environment. Securities practitioners need to continuously improve their digital literacy and use cutting-edge digital technologies such as big data and artificial intelligence to identify, assess, manage, and control financial risks. Through data analysis and model prediction, securities practitioners can accurately predict the market, timely identify potential risks, and take corresponding risk prevention measures.

3.3 Business Innovation

The securities industry is facing unprecedented opportunities and challenges. Securities practitioners need to constantly learn and master new digital technologies to better understand market demand, grasp trends in the securities industry, and promote business innovation. By utilizing digital technologies such as big data, cloud computing, and blockchain, securities companies develop competitive financial products and services that meet market demands. These new products and services help securities firms gain market share and increase profits.

3.4 Brand Value Shaping

The core competitiveness of securities companies is increasingly reflected in their digital transformation and innovation capabilities. A securities company that gathers high-quality digital talents can not only flexibly respond to market changes, but also demonstrate professionalism and efficiency. High quality digital talents represent securities companies to participate in financial industry seminars and exchange meetings, showcasing the company's innovative spirit. Securities practitioners actively use social media to interact and communicate with the public, effectively enhancing the company's visibility and reputation, and shaping the company's brand value.

4 Construction of Digital Literacy Indicator System

4.1 Source and Reconstruction of Digital Literacy Indicators

Currently, the international general standards fail to specifically cover the securities industry, while domestic relevant guidelines also lack systematic support in terms of literacy dimensions. The combination of the two fills the research gap in the field of digital literacy in the securities industry and is innovative. At the theoretical level, it provides practical cases in industry-specific areas for the localization of the digital literacy framework. At the practical level, it is the first to construct a digital literacy indicator system for the securities industry that meets both general standards and industry regulatory requirements. This is something that existing general indicator systems or single regulatory documents have failed to achieve.

The digital literacy framework formulated by UNESCO provides theoretical support. This framework is divided into seven dimensions in detail, including operation of devices and software, information and data, communication and collaboration, creation of digital content, security, problem-solving, and career-related literacies. Under these seven dimensions, it is further refined into 26 basic elements, comprehensively and systematically covering all aspects of digital literacy. The digital literacy framework released by UNESCO has wide international recognition and authority, providing an important reference for countries to formulate digital literacy policies and digital literacy evaluations. By drawing on this framework, it is ensured that the digital literacy index system for securities practitioners is in line with international standards.

The Cyberspace Administration of China has clarified the definition of digital literacy and skills in the Action Plan for Enhancing Digital Literacy and Skills for All, providing specific guidance for building a digital literacy indicator system. Digital literacy and skills not only include basic digital literacy, skills such as digital acquisition, production, use, evaluation, interaction, and sharing, but also encompass advanced literacy such as innovation, security, and ethics. These abilities and qualities play an important role in the comprehensive development of digital society citizens in learning, work, and life. The Action Plan for Enhancing National Digital Literacy and Skills issued by the Cyberspace Administration of China provides macro guidance and strategic direction for the improvement of digital literacy and skills at the national level. Taking this outline as an important basis for constructing an indicator system, ensuring that the direction of digital literacy improvement for securities practitioners is in line with national strategies.

When constructing the digital literacy index system for securities practitioners, the digital literacy framework of UNESCO is used as a support, combined with the guidance of the Cyberspace Administration of China on the connotation of digital literacy and skills, to reconstruct the digital literacy index framework for securities practitioners. During the reconstruction process, integrate international advanced experience with the actual situation of the securities industry to form a digital literacy index system for securities practitioners with Chinese characteristics. Considering the uniqueness of the securities industry and the actual needs of practitioners, the framework should be appropriately adjusted and supplemented to strengthen the practical application value of the indicator system and ensure that it can meet the actual needs of securities companies. Focus on the digital operation ability, data usage ability, information security awareness, teamwork ability, innovation ability, and professional ethics of securities practitioners in the securities business.

When reconstructing the digital literacy index system for securities practitioners, it is explained in three levels.

The first level is the target layer, which corresponds to the core concept of Digital Literacy of Securities Practitioners.

The digital literacy of securities practitioners refers to a series of qualities and abilities related to digital acquisition, production, use, evaluation, communication, sharing, innovation, security, and ethics that securities practitioners need to possess in the context of the digital age.

The second level is the connotation level, which corresponds to the first level indicators. Under the core concept of Digital Literacy of Securities Practitioners, it is refined into seven first level indicators. Each primary indicator is refined into 4 secondary indicators, and 7 primary indicators are refined into 28 operable and measurable secondary indicators.

The third level is the operational level, which corresponds to the secondary indicators. The 28 secondary indicators cover the basic competencies that securities practitioners should possess in the digital environment. These basic competencies provide specific standards for evaluating the digital literacy of securities practitioners.

The digital literacy index system for securities practitioners is shown in Table 1:

Table 1. Digital Literacy Index System for Securities Practitioners

Target layer	Primary indicator	Secondary indicator
Digital literacy of securities practitioners	Equipment and software operation literacy	Equipment usage, software usage, exclusive equipment and software usage, equipment protection
	Acquiring, utilizing, and evaluating literacy	Digital content browsing, searching, filtering, digital content usage, digital content evaluation, digital content interpretation
	Communication and Collaboration Literacy	Digital technology interaction, digital technology sharing, digital technology collaboration, database management
	Innovation and Creativity Literacy	Digital content development, digital content integration, programming applications, and new technology innovation practices
	Safety compliance literacy	Data privacy protection, copyright and licensing, business compliance management, information security awareness
	Problem solving literacy	Technical problem handling, regulatory communication, identification of gaps, and application of computational thinking
	Ethical and moral literacy	Network etiquette, algorithmic fairness, ethical judgment, customer right to know

Source: UNESCO Global Framework for Digital Literacy, Central Cybersecurity and Informatization Committee Action Plan for Enhancing Digital Literacy and Skills for All

4.2 Explanation of Digital Literacy Indicators for Securities Practitioners

Equipment and Software Operation Literacy

Equipment and software operation literacy refers to the ability of securities practitioners to proficiently operate general office equipment such as computers and printers, master general office software such as Word and Excel, proficiently use securities specific equipment and software such as trading terminals and quantitative analysis software, and regularly maintain and upkeep the aforementioned equipment and software (Table 2).

Table 2. Explanation of Equipment and Software Operation Literacy Indicators

ID	Secondary indicator	Explanation
1	Equipment usage	Proficient in operating basic office equipment such as computers, printers, scanners, etc., to meet the daily office needs of securities companies
2	Software usage	Proficient in using basic office software such as Word document editing, Excel data processing and analysis, and PPT presentation production
3	Exclusive equipment and software usage	Use equipment and software specifically designed for the securities industry, including trading terminals, market servers, analysis software, quantitative trading software, etc
4	Equipment protection	Standardize the use of various equipment, ensure that their operating environment meets standards, avoid physical damage, and regularly carry out equipment maintenance and upkeep work

Source: Compilation of materials from securities company interviews and internal documents

Acquiring, Utilizing, and Evaluating Literacy

In the era of knowledge explosion, acquiring, using, and evaluating literacy requires securities practitioners to have the ability to accurately acquire and efficiently utilize information, objectively evaluate and deeply interpret digital content, and through information screening, tool application, multi-dimensional evaluation, and data analysis (Table 3).

Table 3. Explanation of Obtaining, Using, and Evaluating Literacy Indicators

ID	Secondary indicator	Explanation
1	Digital content browsing, searching, and filtering	Regularly browse digital content such as financial news, market reports, and company announcements to stay up-to-date with market trends and industry information; Using search engines and professional financial databases to accurately retrieve specific company, industry, or market information; With the ability to filter information, extract valuable information from massive amounts of data

(*continued*)

Table 3. *(continued)*

ID	Secondary indicator	Explanation
2	Digital content usage	Proactively acquire, analyze, and apply various digital information and data in the work environment, complete information access and organization through securities professional software or platforms, and improve information utilization efficiency
3	Digital content evaluation	Conduct quality assessment on the obtained digital content, verify its authenticity and reliability, and consider key factors such as the source, accuracy, timeliness, and relevance of the digital content
4	Digital content interpretation	Deeply interpret digital content, transform it into insights and strategic solutions that can guide business through data comparison, market trend analysis, predictive model application, and other methods

Source: Compilation of materials from securities company interviews and internal documents

Communication and Collaboration Literacy

Digital communication and collaboration literacy refers to the ability of securities practitioners to rely on digital platforms and comprehensively use digital technology to achieve efficient communication and collaborative operations, covering aspects such as digital technology interaction, sharing, collaboration, and database management (Table 4).

Table 4. Explanation of Communication and Collaboration Literacy Indicators

ID	Secondary indicator	Explanation
1	Digital technology interaction	Utilize digital technologies such as email, instant messaging tools, video conferencing software, etc. for real-time or asynchronous communication and exchange abilities, and use these technological tools to send information, receive feedback, conduct discussions, etc. in the work
2	Digital technology sharing	Master the usage methods of cloud storage, file sharing platforms, and collaboration tools, possess the ability to share documents, reports, presentations, and other materials, and achieve digital distribution of information, data, and resources

(continued)

Table 4. (*continued*)

ID	Secondary indicator	Explanation
3	Digital technology collaboration	Using digital technologies such as project management software, online collaboration tools, and shared calendars, coordinate team members' work, complete task allocation, progress tracking, and resource allocation, and achieve collaborative work goals
4	Database management	Capable of database management and maintenance, covering tasks such as database creation, data entry, information retrieval, and data updates

Source: Compilation of materials from securities company interviews and internal documents

Innovation and Creativity Literacy.
Innovation and creativity literacy require securities practitioners to fully utilize innovative thinking in the digital environment, explore and construct new business models through digital content development, integration, programming applications, and new technology innovation practices (Table 5).

Table 5. Explanation of Innovation and Creativity Literacy Indicators

ID	Secondary indicator	Explanation
1	Digital content development	Using text editors, image processing software, presentation production tools, etc., create securities digital marketing materials, investment strategy presentation documents, and develop online education course resources for the securities industry
2	Digital content integration	Utilize innovative thinking and creativity to sort, analyze, refine, and recreate diverse digital content, forming logically clear and practical comprehensive information or knowledge products
3	Programming applications	Write computer programs using one or more programming languages to meet the practical needs of securities business and promote business innovation
4	New technology innovation practices	Introduce and apply emerging technologies to optimize, upgrade, or innovate existing securities products, services, business processes, and business models

Source: Compilation of materials from securities company interviews and internal documents

Safety Compliance Literacy

Security compliance literacy is the comprehensive ability that securities practitioners need to possess in their business activities to ensure data, information, and business security, maintain legal compliance order, including strict protection of data privacy, avoidance of copyright infringement risks, compliance with securities regulations, strengthening information security protection, and ensuring business compliance and asset security (Table 6).

Table 6. Explanation of Safety Compliance Literacy Indicators

ID	Secondary indicator	Explanation
1	Data privacy protection	In the processing and storage of customer data, company data, and other sensitive information, relevant principles and norms must be strictly followed, and technical and management measures must be taken to prevent data from being illegally obtained, abused, or leaked
2	Copyright and licensing	When using digital content such as software, data resources, research reports, etc., securities practitioners should be familiar with copyright regulations, ensure that their behavior complies with copyright requirements, and avoid violating relevant license agreements and infringing on others' intellectual property rights
3	Business compliance management	During the period of conducting securities business, strictly abide by relevant laws and regulations of the securities industry and financial regulatory provisions, and establish and improve compliance management mechanisms
4	Information security awareness	Proficient in basic information security knowledge such as password management and identifying phishing attacks, implementing various protective measures to ensure the security of information assets

Source: Compilation of materials from securities company interviews and internal documents

Problem Solving Literacy

Problem solving literacy refers to the use of technological tools by securities practitioners in digital business to troubleshoot, proactively respond to regulatory oversight, identify business gaps, and optimize, and solve complex problems through computational thinking modelling (Table 7).

Table 7. Explanation of Problem Solving Literacy Indicators

ID	Secondary indicator	Explanation
1	Technical problem handling	In the digital work environment, use digital technology and tools to troubleshoot, debug, and repair technical failures, and seek professional support when necessary to ensure stable operation of systems and equipment
2	Regulatory communication	In the face of financial regulatory requirements, understand regulatory logic and intentions, maintain close communication with regulatory agencies, provide timely feedback on issues, and ensure that business meets regulatory standards
3	Identification of gaps	In the process of digital operation, identify the gap between business operation, technology application, process design and expected goals, and propose targeted improvement plans
4	Application of computational thinking	Using computer science concepts and methods to solve complex securities problems, abstracting actual problems into mathematical models or algorithm problems, and achieving effective solutions through logical deduction

Source: Compilation of materials from securities company interviews and internal documents

Ethical and Moral Literacy

Ethical and moral literacy refers to the high level of professional ethics and ethical standards that securities practitioners need to maintain in the digital environment, ensuring fairness and transparency in business activities, involving network etiquette, algorithmic fairness, ethical judgment, and customer informed rights (Table 8).

Table 8. Explanation of Ethical and Moral Literacy Indicators

ID	Secondary indicator	Explanation
1	Network etiquette	When carrying out work communication, information release and customer service through the Internet, it is necessary to follow the corresponding etiquette rules and ethics. Whether using email, instant messaging tools or social media, it is necessary to maintain a formal and professional communication style and avoid using casual and inappropriate language
2	Algorithmic fairness	In the process of designing and implementing securities business algorithms, ensure that they treat different groups and individuals equally, and avoid discriminatory or biased results based on specific attributes of individuals or groups

(continued)

Table 8. (*continued*)

ID	Secondary indicator	Explanation
3	E thical judgment	When facing ethical choices in the securities industry, it is necessary to rely on professional knowledge and moral cognition, carefully judge the legitimacy and legality of behavior or decisions, always adhere to the moral bottom line, maintain market order, and effectively protect the legitimate rights and interests of investors
4	Customer right to know	In the process of providing securities services to clients, it is necessary to fully and comprehensively disclose business-related information to ensure that clients have a clear understanding of the risks and benefits of the purchased securities products or services, so as to make rational decisions

Source: Compilation of materials from securities company interviews and internal documents

5 Determination of Indicator Weights

5.1 Principle for Determining Indicator Weights

Accurately and reasonably determining the weights of various indicators is crucial in building a digital literacy index system for securities practitioners, which directly affects the fairness, effectiveness, and practicality of the final evaluation results.

5.2 Principle of Scientificity

The principle of scientificity emphasizes that weight allocation must have a solid theoretical foundation and be combined with rich practical experience in the securities industry. When determining weights, relevant research results at home and abroad should be fully referred to, and theoretical methods in the fields of statistics and decision science should be applied to ensure the scientificity of the evaluation model. By analyzing and verifying the effectiveness of weights, ensure the accuracy and reliability of the evaluation results.

Principle of Comprehensiveness
The principle of comprehensiveness requires that weight allocation should cover all key digital literacy indicators, without omitting important aspects, and should not overly emphasize certain non core factors. This requires a profound understanding of the connotation, extension, and application of digital literacy in the securities field, and the allocation of weights should comprehensively reflect the overall level of digital literacy of securities companies.

Principle of Operability
The principle of operability emphasizes that weight allocation should be easy to operate and calculate, reducing human errors and computational complexity. This requires

the use of simple, clear, and easily understandable weight allocation methods when designing evaluation indicator systems, reducing tedious calculation steps and complex models. Detailed operation guidelines and calculation tools should also be provided to quickly and accurately complete weight allocation.

Principle of Dynamic Adjustment
With the development of digital technology and the continuous changes in the industry environment, the requirements for digital literacy are also constantly evolving. The weight allocation should be dynamically adjusted and optimized according to the actual situation. This requires evaluators to closely monitor industry trends and technological developments, collect feedback information in a timely manner, and revise and improve the evaluation system. Establish a regular evaluation mechanism to monitor and evaluate the effectiveness of weight allocation, ensuring the forward-looking nature of the evaluation system.

5.3 Method for Determining Indicator Weights

Expert Consultation Method
Expert consultation method is a method of assigning weights to evaluation indicators based on expert professional knowledge and practical experience. This method usually adopts various forms such as seminars, questionnaire surveys, one-on-one interviews, etc., to widely collect expert evaluation opinions on the importance of various indicators. Subsequently, statistical methods will be used to systematically organize, summarize, and deeply analyze the expert rating results, in order to determine the weight coefficients of each indicator.

The expert consultation method can fully leverage the professional accumulation and experience advantages of experts in specific fields, and the weight system determined often has high authority and credibility, which is widely used in the determination of indicator weights in many fields. Due to its reliance on subjective judgments from experts, there are individual cognitive differences, personal preferences, knowledge limitations, and other factors that interfere, resulting in a certain degree of subjective bias affecting the weight allocation results.

Questionnaire Survey Method
The questionnaire survey method is a research method that collects opinions and feedback from the target group through a structured questionnaire system. In the implementation process, the first step is to anchor the survey purpose, clearly define the survey scope, design logically clear and targeted questionnaire content based on this, reasonably set closed and open-ended question options, and scientifically formulate scoring standards to ensure that the question expression is concise, easy to understand, and unambiguous.

After completing the questionnaire design, the target audience will be reached through online platform publishing and offline on-site distribution. After collecting the raw questionnaire data, professional statistical software is used to clean, denoise, classify and organize the data, and statistical methods are used to explore the value of the data and determine the weights of each indicator.

The questionnaire survey method can cover a wide range of survey subjects with different backgrounds, fully reflecting the overall opinions and preferences of the target group. However, due to factors such as sample selection strategy, respondent cooperation, and question guidance, there may be sample selection bias and answer distortion. Therefore, careful consideration should be given when interpreting data and deriving conclusions to avoid result errors.

Analytic Hierarchy Process (AHP)
Analytic Hierarchy Process is a systematic analysis method that breaks down complex decision-making problems into multi-level structures. When allocating weights, first decompose the decision factors and construct a hierarchical structure, determine the relative importance of the factors through pairwise comparisons, and form a judgment matrix; Utilize mathematical algorithms to calculate the matrix eigenvectors and maximum eigenvalue, and determine the weight ranking of each factor. The Analytic Hierarchy Process can effectively organize complex relationships, but it is still influenced by subjective judgments of evaluators.

Entropy Value Method
The entropy value method is an objective weight determination method based on the concept of entropy in information theory. In information theory, entropy is used to measure the uncertainty of information. In the entropy value method, the importance of indicators is evaluated by analyzing the degree of data dispersion (i.e. uncertainty) - the higher the data dispersion, the greater the amount of information carried by the indicators, and the higher the weight.

This method does not rely on subjective judgment and can effectively avoid human interference, improving the objectivity and accuracy of weight allocation. However, the results are highly dependent on data quality, and if there are missing data, outliers, or insufficient sample size, it will significantly affect the reliability of weight calculation.

5.4 Determining Weights Using Entropy Value Method

When constructing a digital literacy indicator system for securities practitioners, traditional subjective judgments are difficult to accurately measure the relative importance of each indicator. The entropy value method stands out due to its objectivity. This method only calculates based on the characteristics of the data itself, without introducing additional parameters or assumptions. By analyzing the degree of data dispersion and trends, it automatically generates indicator weights, improving the accuracy of weight allocation.

In the data-driven decision-making securities industry, entropy value method can deeply explore the value of existing data resources, analyze the key information behind the data, and provide solid data support for determining the weight of digital literacy indicators. The entropy value method has dynamic adaptability and can flexibly adjust weights based on real-time changes in data to ensure that weight allocation meets the actual needs of the industry. If a certain indicator shows significant differences between samples, it means that it contains rich information and has a significant impact on the evaluation results,the entropy value method assigns higher weights to it to enhance the effectiveness of the evaluation system.

Using the entropy value method to determine the weight of digital literacy indicators for securities practitioners, the specific steps are as follows:

(1) Data collection and preprocessing

Before applying the entropy value method, it is necessary to comprehensively and accurately collect data covering 28 digital literacy indicators of securities practitioners. After data collection is completed, preprocessing is used to ensure the reliability and comparability of the data: identifying and removing outliers caused by input errors or special circumstances; For missing values, mean or median filling can be used, or records containing missing values can be directly deleted; Finally, through normalization processing, the interference of different indicator dimensions and numerical ranges on subsequent analysis is eliminated.

(2) Calculate the specific gravity

For each preprocessed indicator, calculate the proportion of each sample value in the total sum of the indicator to quantify the relative importance of the sample value in the corresponding indicator. The specific operation is to sum up all sample values under each indicator, and then divide each sample value by the total to obtain the proportion of each sample value. This step expands the analysis based on relative values, improving the universality and interpretability of the results.

(3) Calculate information entropy

Based on the obtained proportion values, use the information entropy formula to calculate the information entropy of each indicator. Information entropy is used to measure the uncertainty or randomness of information, and in the entropy value method, it can reflect the degree of dispersion of indicator values. When calculating, special treatment is required for zero probability or extremely low probability situations.

(4) Calculate the coefficient of difference

The coefficient of difference, as a supplementary indicator of information entropy, can intuitively reflect the degree of dispersion of indicator values. The larger the coefficient of difference, the more dispersed and uncertain the distribution of indicator values, and the richer the evaluation information they carry. This step converts the indirect measure of information entropy into a more intuitive difference coefficient, laying the foundation for subsequent weight calculations.

(5) Determine weights

Calculate the weight of each indicator based on the coefficient of difference, that is, the proportion of the coefficient of difference of each indicator in the total coefficient of difference of all indicators. This weight reflects the importance of the indicator in the overall evaluation system. The higher the weight, the greater the impact of the indicator on the digital literacy assessment of securities practitioners.

5.5 Python Code Framework

A simplified Python code framework to illustrate the core steps of using entropy value method to calculate the weight of digital literacy indicators for securities practitioners:

```
import numpy as np
#Assuming that the data is a normalized matrix of 28 indicators with a shape of
(n_samples, 28)
#Calculate the specific gravity
p = data / data.sum(axis=0)
#Calculate information entropy
EPS=1e-12 # Avoid log (0)
e = -np.sum(p * np.log(p + eps), axis=0) / np.log(data.shape[0])
#Calculate the coefficient of difference
d = 1 - e
#Determine weights
w = d / d.sum()
Print ("The weights of each indicator are:", w)
```

The entropy value method focuses on considering the degree of data dispersion when determining weights. The weights obtained by this method are applied to the digital literacy evaluation of securities practitioners, and the digital literacy score is calculated by weighted summation, which is then used for ranking or classification evaluation.

6 Optimization Path for Digital Literacy of Securities Practitioners

In the context of accelerating the digital and intelligent transformation of the securities industry, enhancing the digital literacy of securities practitioners is not only an inevitable requirement to comply with market changes, but also a core driving force for high-quality development of the industry.

6.1 Develop a Detailed Training Plan

Based on the evaluation index system of digital literacy, develop a training plan, clarify training objectives, content, methods, and schedule. Before formulating the plan, use methods such as questionnaire surveys and in-depth interviews to understand the current status and learning needs of digital literacy among employees in different positions and job levels.

Integrate online and offline resources, innovate training forms. Through diversified teaching methods such as online courses, offline lectures, and case studies, real securities business scenarios are integrated into the training, allowing employees to use digital tools in simulated environments to solve practical problems and strengthen the combination of theory and practice. By utilizing flexible forms such as micro courses and online communities, we can meet employees' personalized learning habits and time arrangements, and improve training effectiveness.

Implement a hierarchical and classified training strategy based on the job characteristics and business needs of the securities industry. Customize differentiated course content according to the three job levels of junior, junior, and senior, as well as the positions of front desk, middle desk, and back-end, to ensure that training accurately matches the actual work needs of employees.

6.2 Implementation of Digital Literacy Training

According to the training plan, a three in one teaching mode of theoretical teaching, practical operation, and case study will be adopted. In the theoretical teaching process, relying on online courses, special lectures and other forms, the core concepts and cutting-edge trends of digital literacy are systematically taught to enhance the theoretical foundation of practitioners; In the practical operation stage, organize practical activities such as data analysis software application, financial technology tool operation, network security attack and defense drills, etc., to promote the transfer of knowledge to work scenarios; In the case analysis stage, select typical cases in the securities industry to conduct group discussions, guide employees to analyze problems, summarize experiences, and deepen their understanding of the value of digital literacy.

Build a hierarchical and progressive digital literacy training system, covering three core modules: popularization of basic knowledge, strengthening of professional skills, and exploration of cutting-edge technologies. By combining industry experts with internal lecturers, we aim to create a knowledge transfer model that combines external theoretical empowerment with internal experience sharing, and foster a learning atmosphere for all staff.

6.3 Regular Evaluation of Training Effectiveness

Establish a sound mechanism for evaluating the training effectiveness of securities practitioners, monitor the effectiveness of digital literacy improvement through quantitative and qualitative assessments, and construct a multidimensional evaluation system that includes knowledge testing, skill implementation, project achievement acceptance, and peer evaluation. The training effectiveness is comprehensively measured from multiple dimensions such as theoretical mastery, practical application, and team collaboration.

Using digital tools to collect real-time data during the training process, optimizing teaching strategies and adjusting course content based on student learning dynamics and course evaluations, ensuring that the training program meets actual needs. Based on the evaluation results and feedback, iteratively improve the digital literacy evaluation index system.

6.4 Establishing Incentive and Guarantee Mechanisms

Build a comprehensive incentive system that combines material rewards with spiritual recognition to stimulate employees' enthusiasm for improving their digital literacy. Establish special honors such as the Digital Pioneer Award and the Digital Transformation Innovation Award to commend employees who have performed outstandingly in improving their digital skills and implementing digital business practices; Incorporate digital literacy achievements into performance evaluation indicators as a basis for promotion and salary adjustment.

Strengthen resource and technological support, establish a special fund for digital literacy training, which will be used to purchase advanced teaching equipment, professional software tools, and build an intelligent online learning platform; Establish a technical support team to provide response services to employees' problems encountered in the application of new technologies.

Cultivate a digital corporate culture, advocate an innovative atmosphere of open collaboration, and promote knowledge sharing and technology collaboration across departments and fields. Regularly hold digital literacy themed forums, technology salons, and innovation competitions to integrate digital transformation concepts into corporate values and stimulate employees' innovative thinking through diverse activities.

6.5 Improve the Digital Literacy System

Systematically track the policies and regulations, technological innovation, and business model transformation trends of the securities industry both domestically and internationally, collect cutting-edge industry information through market research, expert consultation, and other channels, and provide data support for the iteration of the indicator system. Based on the latest developments in digital transformation and the results of employee digital literacy assessments, we will dynamically adjust the content, weight, and assessment standards of indicators to address common weaknesses and individual differences, ensuring that the system is adapted to market demand and business development.

Establish a closed-loop management model of Evaluation Feedback Improvement Re-evaluation, and help employees clarify the advantages, disadvantages, and improvement directions of digital literacy through one-on-one communication, group discussions, and other forms. In response to the weak links exposed in the assessment, allocate training resources, customize learning plans based on personalized needs, and promote continuous improvement of employees' abilities.

7 Conclusion

This article focuses on the construction and improvement path of the digital literacy index system for securities practitioners, and demonstrates the significance of digital literacy for the development of the securities industry. Research has shown that digital literacy is not only a core element in improving work efficiency, service quality, and risk management capabilities, but also a key driving force for driving business innovation and shaping corporate brand value. The constructed digital literacy index system covers the core competencies and qualities required by securities practitioners, providing an evaluation framework for the industry and proposing specific implementation paths including training plan formulation, incentive mechanism establishment, dynamic evaluation optimization, etc. It provides a practical solution for securities companies to enhance employees' digital literacy.

With the rapid iteration of digital technology, the securities industry needs to continuously optimize its digital literacy indicator system, closely align with industry development trends and market demands, and dynamically adjust evaluation indicators to achieve iterative upgrades of the evaluation system.

Acknowledgments. This study was funded by Fujian Provincial Education Science Collaborative Innovation Project(No.: Fjxczx22-470, Fjxczx23-302), Research Projects of Ningde Normal University(No.:2024Y17).

Disclosure of Interests. The authors have no competing interests to declare that are relevant to the content of this article.

References

1. Cui, B., Hong, W.: Research and practice of citizen digital literacy and skill assessment dystem. Software Guide **05**, 175–185 (2024)
2. Chen, M., Chen, H.: The basic connotation, level measurement, and structural characteristics of digital literacy of chinese residents. E-Government (09), 91–101 (2024)
3. Yan, Y., Wang, N., Chen, T.: Research on the concept, framework, and enhancement path of digital literacy. Software Guide **23**(08), 145–150 (2024)
4. Zhang, R., Liu, X., Pan, Y.: Construction and implementation suggestions for citizen digital literacy framework in the chinese context. China Elec-tron. Educ. (06), 78–86 (2024)
5. Peng, W.: Research on the evaluation and improvement strategies of digi-tal literacy of college students in shandong province. Shandong Normal University (2024)
6. Li, W.: The current situation and improvement path of digital literacy among application-oriented undergraduate students: an empirical analysis based on 1452 application-oriented undergraduate students in Shanxi Province. Digital Library Forum (07), 72-82 (2024)
7. Wang, N., Li, B., Wang, Z.: Research on the construction of evaluation index system for digital literacy of college students. Statist. Consult. (05), 23–27 (2023)
8. Chen, L., Jia, J., Xiao, M.: Research on the construction of evaluation index system for digital literacy of college students in the digital age. Jiangsu Sci. Technol. Inform. (10), 45 (2023)
9. Li, C., Yu, L., Li, T., et al.: Research on the construction of digital litera-cy model and evaluation index system for college students. Educ. In-form. Technol. (Z1), 70–74 (2023)
10. Yao, Z., Song, H.: Development and measurement of evaluation index system for chinese public digital literacy: a study of media college stu-dents. Chin. J. Radio Telev. (08), 26–31 (2022)
11. Fang, Z., Xu, J.: Research on the construction of digital literacy indicator system for international chinese teachers. J. Tianjin Normal Univ. (Soc. Sci. Edn.) (06), 25–33 (2023)
12. Chen, Y., Tan, A.: Evaluation and enhancement of digital literacy of vo-cational college teachers under the background of education digital trans-formation. J. Hunan Post. Telecommun. Vocat. Techn. College **23**(02), 53–58 (2024)
13. Zhou, L., Cai, A.: Research on the construction of evaluation index sys-tem for digital literacy of new professional farmers. Agric. Technol. **44**(13): 137–142 (2024).
14. Du, J.: Research on the evaluation index system of digital literacy for rural resi-dents in China . Nankai University (2023)
15. Wei, P.: Research on the construction of digital leadership index for pri-mary and secondary school principals in the intelligent era. Shandong Normal University (2024)
16. Li, F.: Beyond citizens' digital literacy skills: construction of digital com-petence and indicator system for leading cadres. J Sichuan Univ. Admin-ist. (03), 52–63 (2023)

Innovation and Practice of the Full-Process Management Framework for Postgraduate Education

Zhe Wang[1], Huiying Lv[1], Yuhong Zhong[1], Xiaohua Liu[1], and Rui Zhang[1,2](✉)

[1] CCST, Jilin University, Str. Qianjin 2699, Changchun, Jilin, China
rui@jlu.edu.cn
[2] Key Lab of International Collaboration on Big Data and Intelligent Computing, Changchun, Jilin, China

Abstract. The Era of Artificial Intelligence places great emphasis on the high-quality development of postgraduate education, and improving the quality of cultivation has become a key focus in degree program work. This paper revolves around the construction and practice of a full-process framework on postgraduate education in natural science major – computer science and technology, with a particular focus on the practical experiences of colleges to enhance the postgraduate cultivation quality It is accomplished through the formulation of various management policies and the implementation of a diversified evaluation indicator system.

Keywords: Postgraduate Education · Full-process Management · Graduate Training Mechanism · Evaluation Indicator System

1 Introduction

In the context of global trends, the wave of transformation in postgraduate education is sweeping across. With the advancement of the Third Industrial Revolution, technologies such as artificial intelligence, the Internet, and big data have been deeply integrated. The global demand for highly qualified laborers and innovative talents is extremely urgent. In this situation, postgraduate education, as a crucial link in cultivating high-level intellectual talents, is increasingly showing development trends of diversification, flexibility, specialization, high quality, innovation, rule of law, informatization, internationalization, and openness. For example, the education management systems in the UK and the US have enabled the training objectives of their postgraduate education to develop towards a balance between cultivating traditional academic talents and applied talents [1]. Taught postgraduate education, part-time postgraduate education, and professional degree postgraduate education have emerged in an endless stream.

Socialism with Chinese characteristics has entered a new era. China is also at a critical juncture in the great changes unseen in a century in the world and the strategic overall situation of the great rejuvenation of the Chinese nation. Domestically, economic and

W. Hong et al. (Eds.): ICCSE 2025, CCIS 2761, pp. 379–389, 2026.
https://doi.org/10.1007/978-981-95-7731-6_29

social development faces challenges such as transformation and upscore and the pursuit of high-quality development. All industries are eager for high-level innovative talents, and the public's demand for postgraduate education is becoming increasingly diverse. Internationally, competition among major powers is becoming increasingly fierce, and the strategic importance of postgraduate education in enhancing national competitiveness has become more and more prominent.

Facing such domestic and international situations, China has actively introduced relevant policies to promote the transformation of postgraduate education [2]. On September 4, 2020, the Ministry of Education, the National Development and Reform Commission, and the Ministry of Finance jointly issued the *Opinions on Accelerating the Reform and Development of Postgraduate Education in the New Era*, clearly stating that it is necessary to take Xi Jinping Thought on Socialism with Chinese Characteristics for a New Era as the guide, comprehensively implement the Party's education policy, firmly take the path of connotative development, and take moral cultivation, serving demands, improving quality, and pursuing excellence as the main line. We are now facing the forefront of global scientific and technological competition, the main battlefield of economic and social development, the new demands of the people, and the major strategies of national governance. In response, several actions are required. First, we need to deeply promote the adjustment of disciplines and specialties. Second, it is essential to improve the level of the supervisor team. Third, we should enhance the talent training system. Fourth, efforts should be made to promote the modernization of the postgraduate education governance system and governance capabilities. The ultimate goal of these measures is to accelerate the construction of a strong country in postgraduate education. By doing so, we can provide solid talent and intellectual support for national development. The introduction of these policies demonstrates China's determination and positive attitude towards postgraduate education reform in the context of global trends. Attempts are made to enhance this full-process education system. Chai et al. proposes a graduate education quality evaluation system based on value added evaluation [3]. Chen et al. list the reform experiences on world-class university talent cultivation index [4]. Yang et al. notice the generative ai equipped postgraduate education [5] and Wang et al. even propose a data-driven data-based model for assessing the quality of graduate quality education [6]. Liu et al. have done some research [7] on the model and method of postgraduate education evaluation based on bp neural network. Lu et al. study a mixed methods study of fellowship program directors [8]. Chen et al. study the executives' postgraduate education and corporate ambidextrous innovation [9]. Razak, et al. proscribe the acceptance of artificial intelligence in education among postgraduate students in Malaysia [10]. But the state of the art research reported are not systematic nor good enough practical in real-word scenarios.

The paper analyzes the problems exist in postgraduate education such as separation of duties in the full-process, shortage of global training view and static supervision qualification assessment mechanisms. With a top-down design on the full-process postgraduate training, the college proposes a set of revolution regulations. The active participation of post-graduates and the increasing top publications illustrate the effectiveness of the framework.

2 Problem Statement

The postgraduate training process encompasses a series of pivotal links that form the core framework of academic development, primarily including curriculum study, literature review reports, thesis proposal, intermediate inspection, pre-defense certification, thesis submission for review, and final defense as is shown in Fig. 1.

- **Curriculum study**, the cornerstone of this process, is meticulously designed to provide students with a comprehensive foundation in both theoretical knowledge and advanced research methodologies. Through a combination of specialized courses and interdisciplinary seminars, students are not only exposed to the latest academic frontiers but also encouraged to develop the analytical and problem-solving skills essential for independent research.
- **Literature review** reports serve as a crucible for cultivating critical thinking. By delving deep into existing scholarship, students are challenged to analyze, synthesize, and evaluate research findings from diverse perspectives. This process not only broadens their understanding of the research field but also helps identify research gaps and formulate innovative research questions.
- **Thesis proposal** marks the transition from theoretical study to independent research, with the topic selection as the intermediate outcome. It requires students to clearly articulate their research objectives, hypotheses, methodologies, and expected outcomes, thereby demonstrating their ability to design and execute a research project. The mid-term assessment, on the other hand, acts as a checkpoint to evaluate the progress of the research, ensuring that students are on track and making necessary adjustments in a timely manner.
- **Intermediate inspection** provides a milestone for both the student and the supervisor. It inspects whether the process is smooth and clear goals are achieved such as article drafting and publication, or system design and implementation.
- **Pre-defense** provides a platform for students to present their research to a panel of experts, receiving constructive feedback and suggestions for improvement. Thesis submission for review subjects the research to external scrutiny, where the work is rigorously evaluated by peers in the field.
- **Final defense** is the culmination of the entire training process, where students must defend their research findings in front of a committee, demonstrating their mastery of the subject matter and the validity of their research. Each of these components plays a unique and indispensable role in shaping a well-rounded postgraduate researcher.
- **Supervision quality** is controlled by the monitoring mechanism in the college level. The details will be describe in Sect. 3.2.

However, the traditional postgraduate training model harbors systemic challenges. The curriculum study relies on the duty of teachers in class education, the literature review reports, thesis proposals, and mid-term assessments are typically managed at the supervisor level, the pre-defense and final defense are organized on department level or college level. This process lacks centralized oversight. This decentralized approach creates information silos, preventing academic programs from obtaining real-time and holistic insights into students' research trajectories. Without standardized monitoring mechanisms, variations in assessment rigor among supervisors are inevitable. Some

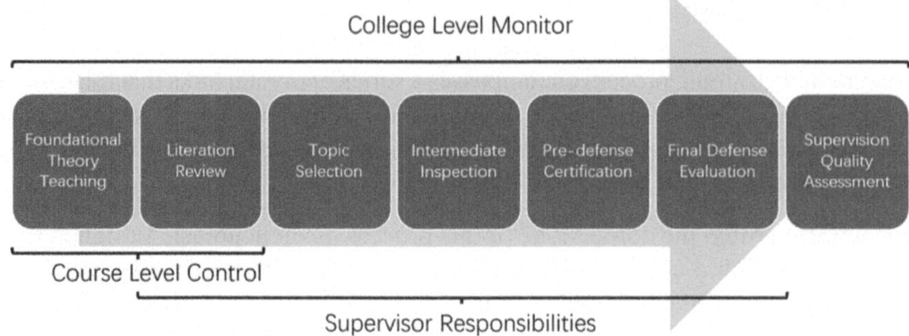

Fig. 1. Classical Postgraduate Training and Management Process

students may pass evaluations with minimal effort due to lenient supervision, allowing underlying issues—such as insufficient data collection, flawed theoretical frameworks, or unclear research directions—to persist undetected until the final year of study. By this stage, rectifying these problems becomes arduous, often resulting in rushed research, compromised thesis quality, and delayed graduation. This latent crisis undermines the integrity of the entire postgraduate training system and impedes the achievement of overarching quality improvement goals.

To achieve high-quality postgraduate training, it is necessary to strengthen the full-process management of training links, establish and improve an effective connection mechanism among various links, timely identify and solve problems, and shift the quality inspection threshold forward. Combining practical work, this paper deeply explores how to integrate the concept of full-process management into all stages of postgraduate training, and constructs a college-level postgraduate training mechanism with full-process management as the core, so as to effectively improve the quality of postgraduate training and ensure the full realization of training objectives.

3 Full-Process Management Framework

Through in-depth research and benchmarking against high-level domestic and international institutions, the college has launched the postgraduate training framework consisting of program dynamic optimization, dynamic adjustment of enrollment eligibility,

close loop monitoring of the training quality, standardization of the defense and review, academic training matrix and the integration of ideological and political education.

3.1 Dynamic Optimization Mechanism on Training Programs

The college has comprehensively revised *Postgraduate Training Program* and *Regulations on Postgraduate Teaching Management* in order to standardize the teaching part in the full-process of postgraduate training. The revision has clearly standardized all the phases including curriculum setting requirements, teaching organization and implementation, assessment and score, grade evaluation, as well as the evaluation and feedback of teaching quality. The specific key points are as follows:

- **Doctoral postgraduates** are required to accumulate at least 16 credits in their course studies, with no less than 12 credits from compulsory courses. After directly enrolled doctoral postgraduates select their supervisors upon admission, they should formulate their individual course study plans under the guidance of their supervisors. These plans, after being signed and confirmed by the supervisors, should be submitted to the training units for record - keeping. In addition to the public compulsory courses, public elective courses, professional compulsory courses, and compulsory components offered uniformly by the Graduate School, each doctoral postgraduate must choose two courses from the specialized courses of their disciplines. If any adjustments are needed during the implementation of the course study plan, they should be modified only after prior consent from the supervisors and then reported to the college for record - keeping.
- **Master postgraduates'** courses are divided into two categories: compulsory courses and elective courses. The compulsory courses include public courses, basic theoretical courses, restricted professional courses, and specialized courses. Meanwhile, scientific ethics and academic norms, literature reviews, and thesis proposals are set as compulsory components, and the corresponding credits will be calculated as required. Master's postgraduates should obtain no less than 32 credits in total. The training program and teaching management regulations effectively ensure the teaching quality of postgraduates.

3.2 Dynamic Adjustment of Enrollment Eligibility

Postgraduate supervisors play a crucial role in the postgraduate training process, with their responsibilities extending beyond academic guidance to encompass multiple dimensions such as scientific research capability development, career development guidance, and psychological support. Effective supervision by supervisors is of great significance for enhancing postgraduates' academic literacy, strengthening academic ethical norms, and improving the quality of their thesis. To further enhance the quality of postgraduate training, the college has formulated documents such as the *Doctoral Supervisor Enrollment Eligibility Review Criteria, Doctoral Enrollment Quota Allocation Plan,* and *Standards for Defining Relevant Scientific Research Achievements of Postgraduate Supervisors,* setting strict requirements for supervisors' enrollment eligibility. Such policies reconstruct the supervisor responsibilities with the specific requirements.

- **Postgraduate supervisors should have well-defined and cutting-edge research directions.** Their research work must hold significant theoretical and practical value, with academic standards ranking among the top in the domestic discipline. Supervisors are required to keenly grasp the development trends of their disciplines, accurately identify innovative and forward-looking research topics, and provide clear academic guidance for postgraduate students. In theoretical research, their work should contribute to the improvement and expansion of the disciplinary theoretical system, offering new perspectives and methods for academic progress. In applied research, supervisors should actively align with national strategic needs and industrial development directions, focusing on solving practical problems and promoting the transformation of scientific and technological achievements. Moreover, supervisors should have a high academic influence in their respective fields, enhancing the discipline's visibility through participation in domestic and international academic exchanges and serving in academic organizations, thereby creating a favorable academic atmosphere for postgraduate students.

- **Supervisors are expected to have undertaken high-level research projects and secured sufficient research funding in the past three years.** High-level research projects serve as crucial platforms for cultivating postgraduate students' innovation and practical abilities. By leading national or provincial key research projects or significant horizontal cooperation projects with enterprises, supervisors can provide students with opportunities to engage in real-world research. Adequate research funding is the foundation for ensuring the smooth progress of scientific research, supporting students in purchasing experimental equipment, conducting investigations, and participating in academic conferences. Meanwhile, the rational management and utilization of research funds also reflect a supervisor's research competence. Supervisors should establish sound fund management systems to ensure transparent and standardized fund usage, thereby improving the efficiency of fund utilization.
- **Supervisors should have achieved a certain number of high-quality academic outputs in the past three years.** Academic achievements directly reflect a supervisor's academic level and research capabilities and are also important indicators for evaluating postgraduate training quality. These achievements may include high-impact publications in authoritative domestic and international journals, academic monographs, invention patents, or software copyrights. High-quality academic outputs not only provide examples for students to learn from but also boost their confidence and competitiveness in the academic community. Additionally, supervisors should emphasize the transformation and application of academic achievements, promoting the integration of research with practical needs and contributing to social development. By achieving outstanding academic results, supervisors can establish a strong academic reputation in their fields, attracting more excellent students to engage in related research.

To ensure the above regulations, the college has taken the following actions.

- Establish a mechanism for the full-process cultivation of postgraduates with the participation of a supervisory committee consisting of more than three supervisors. Such a committee are personalized for each postgraduate student, led by her/his supervisor. The supervisor may not only take responsibility in one of the 16-credit curriculum but also drive the courses that the student is supposed to take.
- Implement a thesis review based score system to enforce the supervisors' responsibilities in the thesis quality control process.

The specific score rules are based on the double-blind review results of the (doctoral) thesis into the quality supervision and management system for postgraduate theses. At the beginning of the academic year, each qualified supervisor will be granted 12 points each score cycle, without accumulation. Based on the review outcomes of submitted thesis, one review result of C (minimum qualified) will cost her/his supervisor 2 points; one review result of D (not qualified) will cost 6 points.

The scoring cycle is one year, with a total score of 12 points, calculated from the first review of the doctoral dissertation supervised. At the end of a scoring cycle, if the accumulated score remain positive, the scores within that cycle will be cleared and not carried forward to the next cycle.

During the doctoral supervisor enrollment eligibility qualification, the college will calculate the scores of all teachers participating in the review. For doctoral supervisors whose scores reach 12 points, their eligibility to participate in the doctoral enrollment review will be suspended once (Table 1).

Table 1. Supervision Quality Control Score System

Initial Score	Topic Selection		Intermediate Inspection		Pre-defense Certification		Final Defense		Eligibility Assessment
	C	D	C	D	C	D	C	D	
12	−2	−6	−2	−6	−2	−6	−2	−6	>=0
	−2	−6	−2	−6	−2	−6	−2	−6	

Through these mechanisms, the college has effectively eliminated the lifetime supervisor system, to ensure that supervisors have adequate research funding and academic activity, thus providing a solid guarantee for the quality of postgraduate training.

3.3 Closed-Loop Monitoring of Training Quality

Full-process oriented management of postgraduates focuses on the major outputs of all the phases before the final defense in Fig. 1 including literature review reports, thesis proposal, mid-term assessment, and pre-defense, effectively shifting quality inspection forward. The college has formulated a complete set of whole-process training documents, including five regulations such as the *Measures for Thesis Proposal and Mid-term Management of Postgraduates*, *Measures for Pre-defense Management of Postgraduate Theses*, and *Measures for Handling Thesis Review Results*. These require students to complete thesis proposal, mid-term assessment, and pre-defense within specified timelines in strict accordance with document requirements. Only postgraduates who pass these assessments and meet academic graduation requirements may apply for final defense. Doctoral students who fail to meet thesis requirements within the stipulated period will be transferred to master's programs or subject to withdrawal.

Upon enrollment, postgraduates should, under the guidance of their supervisors, review literature, conduct in-depth research, determine research topics, and complete literature review reports. For doctoral students, literature review reports are evaluated centrally and publicly within the discipline by an assessment panel led by the supervisor. Relevant faculty and postgraduates should be invited to attend the review meeting, and for interdisciplinary topics, teachers from related disciplines must be included. Master's students' literature review reports are directly assessed by their supervisors. Those who pass receive 1 compulsory credit; students who fail to complete the requirements or receive failing grades may be granted extended study time and delayed defense.

Thesis proposal is a critical phase in thesis work. To ensure thesis quality, postgraduates must, under supervisor guidance, determine research topics through literature review and academic research, and prepare proposal reports in accordance with the *Thesis Proposal Assessment Form for Postgraduates.* A public proposal defense meeting must be held in the third semester; those who pass receive 1 compulsory credit recorded in their transcripts.

Mid-term assessment of thesis work is a key monitoring link in whole-process training, helping identify issues promptly and ensuring thesis quality. Mid-term assessments are organized by the department to inspect students' progress, primarily through defense-style evaluations. Expert panels provide assessment opinions and complete the *Mid-term Assessment Form for Postgraduate Thesis Work.* Students who fail the assessment must rectify issues based on expert feedback and re-take the assessment after one semester. Results are reported to the college for filing.

Doctoral students may apply for pre-defense six months after passing the mid-term assessment. Pre-defense committees consist of 5 peer experts, with at least 2 experts from related disciplines for interdisciplinary theses. Master's pre-defense committees generally include 3 peer experts. Pre-defenses must be conducted publicly (except for classified theses), with advance publication of thesis titles, presenters, supervisors, committee members, time, and venue. For failed reviews or defenses, re-applications must focus on addressing prior feedback. Students who pass pre-defense must revise their theses under supervisor guidance, complete revisions before blind review, and undergo college review before entering the blind review stage. Those who fail pre-defense cannot proceed to blind review and must re-apply for pre-defense after a six-month interval (typically). Doctoral students unable to meet thesis requirements within the deadline will be transferred to master's programs or withdrawn.

3.4 Standardization of Defense Requirements and Thesis Review System

The college has established management measures such as the *Doctoral Defense Application Criteria* and *Master's Graduation Requirements* to strictly control thesis quality and comprehensively enhance degree awarding standards. In 2021, the college promulgated the *Innovation Achievement Requirements for Doctoral Applicants*, actively responding to the Ministry of Education's philosophy of "breaking the five唯" (breaking the sole emphasis on papers, theses, academic titles, degrees, and awards). It established a diversified degree awarding standard referencing papers, projects, and patents. Accordingly, before applying for doctoral thesis defense, students must pass an innovation level assessment by meeting the required achievement points. Doctoral applicants with unmet or no academic achievements may also apply through the procedures specified in the documents. Meanwhile, master's students must fulfill the following requirements.

- complete curriculum study and obtain 32 credits;
- complete literature review to achieve the ability to understand disciplinary frontiers and grasp disciplinary development trends;

- complete assessments for thesis proposal, mid-term evaluation, and thesis writing.

To further improve the quality of doctoral dissertations and the standardization of degree awarding, the university has successively issued a series of management documents, including the *Implementation Measures for Postgraduate Thesis Review*, *Scoring Measures for Doctoral Thesis Review*, and *Measures for Sampling and Handling Doctoral and Master's Theses**. After the pre-defense, the college added an additional doctoral thesis submission review link, which has significantly improved academic quality. Data shows that the pass rate of double-blind reviews for doctoral theses has increased annually, reaching nearly 96% in 2024. This institutional arrangement of multi-layered quality control and whole-process management not only ensures the standardization and fairness of degree awarding but also effectively promotes the continuous improvement of postgraduate training quality.

3.5 Construction of Academic Training Matrix

The training program sets clear requirements for postgraduates' participation in academic activities. Doctoral students should actively engage in academic activities such as specialized lectures, academic seminars, annual conferences, invention competitions, and thesis peer review. During their thesis work, they must attend **at least 8 academic activities, including at least 1 individual academic report**. Master's students in academic programs are also required to participate in various academic activities, attending **at least 5 specialized academic events** such as lectures, seminars, annual conferences, invention competitions, or thesis review sessions during their thesis period, and must achieve certain academic outcomes.

The college and supervisors provide a diversified academic training system to promote postgraduates' comprehensive development, specifically including the following aspects: First, regularly held academic workshops; second, scientific research supported by research projects; third, a training model integrating practical teaching with academic training; additionally, 3–5 high-level academic lectures are scheduled weekly, along with corporate internship opportunities to enhance practical capabilities. Notably, the college has invited 9 national-level talents and 2 industry experts to teach the *Academic Writing Guidance* course, while 16 outstanding faculty members jointly instruct the *Frontiers of Computer Science* course. Since 2021, the college has annually organized the ***Yanxue Lundao*** Academic Salon for postgraduate students, which has successfully held 5 academic years and over 50 activities to date. The salon aims to **deepen academic exchange and interaction, broaden cognitive boundaries, keep pace with disciplinary frontiers, and catalyze scientific and technological innovation vitality**, establishing a high-quality platform for postgraduates to exchange ideas. Through international cooperation programs such as the CSC Joint Training Program for Doctoral Students and the Publicly Funded Postgraduate Program for Building High-Level Universities, the college has supported 11 postgraduates to pursue overseas studies. Meanwhile, it actively encourages and subsidizes students to attend high-level academic conferences, providing rewards and supporting a total of 148 participants.

These systematic academic training measures have significantly enhanced students' research capabilities and innovation levels. Data shows that during the 13th Five-Year

Table 2. Publication Burst of Top Academic Papers

	2016~2020	2021	2022	2023	2024	2025(till May)
CCF-A Journal/Conference Paper Acceptance	24	13	20	55	77	54

Plan period (2016–2020), postgraduates published 24 CCF-A category papers (as shown in Table 2), with a sustained growth trend. By 2024, the number exceeded 70, including 20 journal articles and 50 conference papers.

3.6 Integration Model of Ideological and Political Education

The college has always adhered to party building as the core guidance, comprehensively and deeply integrating party building work into all aspects of its operations. At present, it has successfully achieved full coverage of "double leaders" (party branch secretaries who are also academic leaders) for all branch secretaries. The college organically integrates education in patriotism, professionalism, and integrity throughout the entire process of teaching and research, creating a favorable atmosphere for mutual learning between teachers and students. It deeply explores the party spirit and scholarly spirit of senior computer scientists, inherits disciplinary culture, and strengthens the college's core values. Documents such as the *Implementation Plan for Ideological and Political Tutoring of Postgraduates in Teaching and Research Sections* and the *Interim Provisions on Combating Academic Misconduct in Theses* have been formulated. The college offers a 20-h compulsory course on *Scientific Ethics and Academic Norms* for new master's and doctoral students, and each postgraduate must participate in a university-wide examination on scientific ethics and academic norms. Candidates must complete the examination through the *Postgraduate Education Management Information System.* Those who pass the exam earn 1 compulsory credit, and the results are recorded in their academic files.

In addition to various national and university-provided scholarships and grants, the university also offers many research assistant, teaching assistant, and administrative assistant positions, which not only provide practical opportunities for postgraduates but also increase their financial resources. Rules and regulations such as student internship agreements have been established to clarify the responsibilities of the college, students, and internship units, ensuring postgraduates' normal scientific research practices and personal safety while maintaining the college's teaching management order.

4 Conclusion

Based on the college's practices, this paper deeply explores the construction and implementation of a whole-process postgraduate training mechanism, focusing on standardized management and quality control in each link from curriculum study to degree application. By establishing strict academic requirements, a sound review system, and diversified achievement evaluation standards, the college has effectively improved the quality of postgraduate training. In the future, it is necessary to continuously optimize the training system, further enhance postgraduates' innovative capabilities and academic standards, and provide a strong guarantee for cultivating high-quality talent for society.

Acknowledgment. This paper is supported by the funding of 'Jilin University English Postgraduate Course Construction Project'-2023YJSYW15.

References

1. Wang, C., Yair, G.: Basic Characteristics, content system, and practice path of israeli graduate education. Res. Graduate Educ. **2024**(2), 111–117. https://doi.org/10.19834/j.cnki.yjsjy2011.2024.02.16. (2025)
2. Zhang, D., Li, Y., Huang, H.: Preliminary analysis of the postgraduate education quality assessment for first-class talent cultivation: a study on the indicator system based on the AHP and FCE. J. Graduate Educ. **2020**(02), 60–67 (2020)
3. Chai, T., Gao, J., Zhao, M., et al.: Thoughts on the construction of graduate education quality evaluation system based on value added evaluation. Comput. Educ. (01), 56–60 (2024). https://doi.org/10.16512/j.cnki.jsjjy.2024.01.038
4. Chen, L., Huang, Z., Li, W.: Construction of a world-class university talent cultivation index guided by educational evaluation reform. J. Shanghai Jiao Tong Univ. (Philosophy Soc. Sci. Edn.) **32**(08), 82–92+132 (2024). https://doi.org/10.13806/j.cnki.issn1008-7095.2024.08.006
5. Yang, Q., Yang, Q.: Generative AI empowering postgraduate education:theoretical logic,legal risks,and governance approaches. Res. Graduate Educ. **2**, 26–33 (2025). https://doi.org/10.19834/j.cnki.yjsjy2011.2025.02.03(2025)
6. Wang, Y., Wang, F.: A data-driven data-based model for assessing the quality of graduate quality education. Appl. Math. Nonlinear Sci. **10**(1) (2025). https://doi.org/10.2478/amns-2025-0801.(2025)
7. Liu, L., You, X., Ban, X., et al.: Research on the model and method of postgraduate education evaluation based on BP neural network. In: 2023 Cross Strait Radio Science and Wireless Technology Conference: Cross Strait Radio Science and Wireless Technology Conference (CSRSWTC 2023), pp. 1–3. 10–13 Nov 2023. Guilin, China (2023)
8. Lu, C., Chan, K., Martin, L., et al.: "We need all hands on deck": characterizing addiction medicine training in canada—a mixed methods study of fellowship program directors. Add. Sci. Clin. Pract. **20**(1) (2025). https://doi.org/10.1186/s13722-025-00543-4
9. Chen, P., Liu, H., Ma, Y., et al. Executives' postgraduate education and corporate ambidextrous innovation: evidence from china's listed companies. Hum. Soc. Sci. Commun. **12**(1) (2028). https://doi.org/10.1057/s41599-025-04426-6
10. Razak, F.Z.A., Abdullah, M.A., Ahmad, B.E., et al.: The acceptance of artificial intelligence in education among postgraduate students in Malaysia. Educ. Inform. Technol. **30**(3), 2977–2997 (2025). https://doi.org/10.1007/s10639-024-12916-4

Exploring an Intelligent and Innovative Programming Teaching Model Based on Agent Programming Paradigm

Xin Xie, Yuantao Chen, Lixia Luo, and Yonghui Cui(✉)

School of Computer Science and Engineering, Hunan University of Information Technology, Changsha 410008, Hunan, China
{xiexin1,chenyt,luolixia1,cuiyonghui}@hnuit.edu.cn

Abstract. This paper addresses key limitations in traditional programming education, particularly the lack of support for student autonomy and innovation. We propose an intelligent and innovative programming teaching model based on the agent-oriented paradigm. The model integrates instructional content, evaluation, and feedback mechanisms around three core components: self-directed learning, intelligent tutoring, and practical innovation. It is implemented through a collaborative "student–agent–teacher" framework. Empirical evidence from case studies demonstrates the model's effectiveness in enhancing students' autonomy, programming proficiency, and innovative capacity. The approach provides a promising pathway for the intelligent transformation of programming education in application-oriented undergraduate contexts.

Keywords: Application-oriented undergraduate education · Programming teaching · Agent programming · Self-directed learning

1 First Section

With the vigorous development of the digital economy, digital technologies are profoundly reshaping industrial structures and social life. The 14th Five-Year Plan for the Development of the Digital Economy explicitly states that by 2025, the added value of China's core digital economy industries will account for 10% of GDP. The advent of the digital economy has led to a significant increase in demand for high-quality, interdisciplinary digital talent, particularly technical professionals with programming skills and innovative thinking. Simultaneously, the emergence of new-generation artificial intelligence (AI) technologies has further underscored the importance of programming competencies, placing higher demands on learners' computational thinking, self-directed learning abilities, and innovative practical skills [1]. Since 2015, the Ministry of Education and other governmental departments have advocated for the transformation of local undergraduate institutions toward an application-oriented model, emphasizing industry-education integration and collaborative education to cultivate innovative professionals aligned with industrial upgrading needs [2]. In recent years, the construction of Emerging Engineering Education (3E) has further driven curriculum reform in universities,

W. Hong et al. (Eds.): ICCSE 2025, CCIS 2761, pp. 390–403, 2026.
https://doi.org/10.1007/978-981-95-7731-6_30

encouraging the cultivation of interdisciplinary and compound talent profiles [3]. However, many application-oriented undergraduate institutions continue to face challenges, including a misalignment between talent development and industrial demand, as well as homogenization of teaching models. There is an urgent need to reform the programming education model to enhance students' practical abilities and innovative awareness in the AI era, thereby improving the programming proficiency and creative capabilities of graduates to better serve the development of China's digital economy [4].

In international higher education, developed countries such as the United States, European nations, and Japan have established relatively mature systems for programming education. These systems generally advocate student-centered teaching philosophies and adopt project-based and problem-oriented learning models that focus on cultivating students' problem-solving abilities, innovative thinking, and engineering practice skills [5]. In parallel, intelligent tutoring systems and agent technologies have been actively integrated into teaching processes to support personalized learning and autonomous exploration [6]. International trends emphasize the value of real-world project practice, interdisciplinary learning, and the integration of intelligent technologies to enable students to apply programming knowledge to complex problems, thereby promoting the transition of programming education toward higher-order cognitive and application capabilities. Domestically, some application-oriented universities have begun experimenting with teaching models that integrate theory and practice. These include "teaching-while-practicing" approaches and the use of real-world cases or projects to cultivate students' engineering development and teamwork skills. Additionally, information technology (IT) has been increasingly adopted in instruction [7]. For example, online practical training platforms such as Educoder enhance classroom engagement and enable personalized instruction through interactive coding environments and AI agent assistants.

Nevertheless, programming education at the application-oriented undergraduate level in China continues to face several pressing issues. First, many classrooms still rely heavily on didactic instruction, resulting in passive knowledge reception and limited student engagement or innovation awareness. Second, teaching pathways are often rigid, offering few opportunities for autonomous exploration and practice, which hampers the development of critical thinking and problem-solving skills. Third, instructional content is updated slowly, lacking integration of cutting-edge technologies and real-world application cases, leading to a disconnect between academic learning and industry needs. Fourth, project-based teaching rarely incorporates agent-oriented design thinking, leaving students underprepared for the technological paradigm shifts introduced by AI.

In response, exploring a new instructional model grounded in agent programming presents a promising solution to these challenges. It not only provides an effective path for addressing deficiencies in current programming education and enhancing classroom quality, but also holds significant implications for cultivating high-quality, application-oriented talent capable of meeting the demands of the digital economy and the AI era. To this end, this paper proposes an intelligent and innovative programming teaching model that integrates self-directed learning, intelligent tutoring, and practical innovation as core teaching components. The instructional process is reconstructed through a tripartite collaboration among students, agents, and teachers, aiming to foster autonomous learning, enhance programming proficiency, and stimulate innovative capacity. This model offers a new educational pathway for application-oriented talent cultivation under the framework of Emerging Engineering Education (3E).

2 AI Agent Programming Paradigm

Prior to the advent of AI-assisted programming, code completion primarily relied on static analysis and template-based tools integrated within IDEs (e.g., IntelliSense in Visual Studio), which could only provide basic syntactic suggestions. In 2018, deep learning-based code completion tools such as TabNine emerged, but their capabilities remained limited to completing single lines or small code fragments. In 2021, OpenAI released Codex and integrated it into GitHub Copilot, thereby expanding the functionality of AI programming assistants from simple code completion to the generation of complex functions. In 2022, the release of ChatGPT significantly broadened the application scope of natural language-driven code generation. The subsequent launches of GPT-3.5 and GPT-4 in 2023 elevated AI-assisted programming to a new level, enabling a hybrid paradigm that combines conversational and task-oriented programming approaches. Following this evolution, tools such as GitHub Copilot X and Amazon Q CLI were introduced, allowing developers to write and modify code through natural language commands, effectively completing the programming loop. By 2024, AI programming had begun to evolve toward greater autonomy and intelligence, demonstrating the initial capability of automatically transforming requirement descriptions into functional code prototypes.

Through this progression, AI-assisted programming has gradually formed four distinct paradigms: 1) IDE-based automatic completion [8], which provides real-time code suggestions through intelligent plug-ins; 2) Conversational programming, which supports natural language-based code generation, explanation, and debugging [9]; 3) Task-driven programming, which generates complete code modules from structured task descriptions [10]; 4) Agent-based programming [11], in which intelligent agents autonomously plan and execute tasks to generate code.

The term "agent" originates from the Latin word "agere", meaning "to act." In the context of computer science and artificial intelligence, an agent is defined as a system capable of autonomously perceiving its environment, making decisions, and executing actions [12]. With the advent of large language models (LLMs), agents now possess advanced capabilities in natural language understanding, complex reasoning, and autonomous task planning. They can independently complete tasks based on human instructions, exhibiting characteristics of general intelligence [13].

The core of agent-based autonomous programming lies in enabling the agent to act as the primary programming entity, thereby minimizing human intervention through a process of "requirement understanding → autonomous planning → tool invocation → code generation." Compared with traditional programming paradigms, agent-based approaches offer three key advantages: first, autonomy, the ability to independently explore and derive solutions, reducing reliance on explicit programmer instructions; second, interactivity, the capacity to perceive and adapt to environmental changes in real time; and third, intelligent decision-making and learning ability, the capability to optimize performance through continuous self-improvement.

3 Design of the Intelligent and Innovative Programming Teaching Model

The Intelligent and Innovative Programming Teaching Model is structured around clearly defined teaching objectives and comprises three core modules: theoretical knowledge, skills training, and comprehensive practice. It builds an interactive learning environment supported by a digital platform. The model adopts a student-centered approach, encouraging learners to actively acquire knowledge, solve problems, and complete complex engineering projects through interaction with intelligent agents. In this model, the agent provides real-time guidance, coding support, and automated evaluation, while the teacher is responsible for designing cases and projects, supervising the instructional process, and ensuring overall teaching quality. The platform records learning behavior data and generates feedback reports, supporting both formative and summative assessments, as well as continuous instructional improvement, as illustrated in Fig. 1. The remainder of this paper elaborates on the teaching model from four perspectives: teaching objectives, content, methods and implementation, and evaluation and feedback.

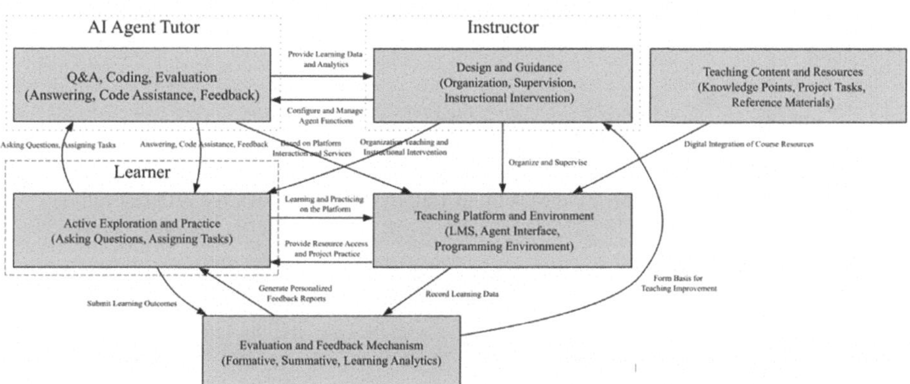

Fig. 1. The Intelligent and Innovative Programming Teaching Model.

3.1 Teaching Objectives

The Intelligent and Innovative Programming Teaching Model aims to cultivate high-quality, application-oriented programming professionals capable of adapting to the evolving demands of the AI era. The teaching objectives, as shown in Fig. 2, include the following:

Objective 1: Students are able to clearly articulate fundamental concepts and the paradigm evolution of program design, and demonstrate a certain level of computational thinking in problem-solving processes.

Objective 2: Students can autonomously acquire knowledge using digital resources and AI agent tutors, and formulate viable strategies to adapt to rapidly changing technological environments and engage in continuous learning.

Objective 3: Students can proficiently utilize at least one AI-based coding tool and its corresponding agent platform, achieve measurable improvements in programming efficiency, and deliver code that meets established quality standards.

Objective 4: Students are able to apply programming skills to solve practical engineering problems and design and implement software prototypes with innovative features.

Objective 5: Students possess critical thinking abilities, can evaluate the strengths and weaknesses of agent-generated code, and optimize relevant solutions accordingly.

Objective 6: Students demonstrate comprehensive competencies and transferable skills aligned with real-world industrial scenarios, preparing them for sustainable professional development.

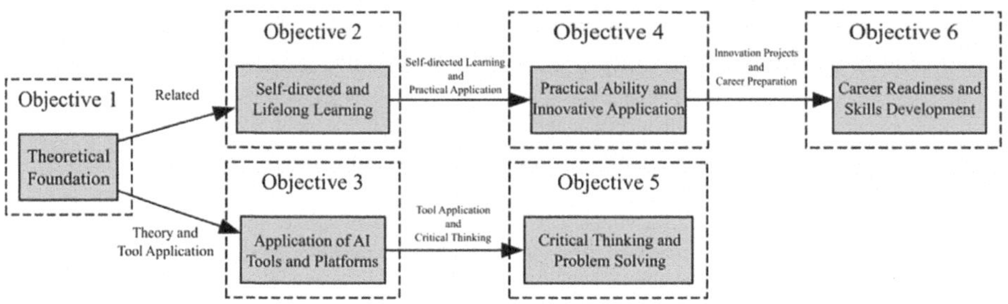

Fig. 2. The Teaching Objective System of Intelligent and Innovative Programming.

3.2 Teaching Content

Aligned with the characteristics of agent-based programming, the teaching content of the Intelligent and Innovative Programming Model comprises three components: theoretical knowledge, skills training, and comprehensive practice, as illustrated in Fig. 3.

The theoretical knowledge module systematically introduces the fundamental concepts of both traditional and agent-based programming. It first outlines the developmental trajectory of conventional programming paradigms such as procedural, object-oriented, and functional programming, and then focuses on the principles of agent systems. Key topics include agent architecture, operational mechanisms (e.g., the "perception–decision–execution" cycle), tool invocation, and memory module management. This module is designed to help students build a solid foundation for intelligent agent programming.

The skills training module emphasizes the development of core programming competencies, including syntax, data structures, and algorithms, in conjunction with AI agent-assisted programming. By incorporating intelligent code completion tools,

the module enhances students' programming efficiency and accuracy. Furthermore, this module places particular focus on prompt engineering, cultivating students' ability to use natural language effectively to guide AI in generating accurate and functional code, which is an essential skill for unlocking the full potential of intelligent agents.

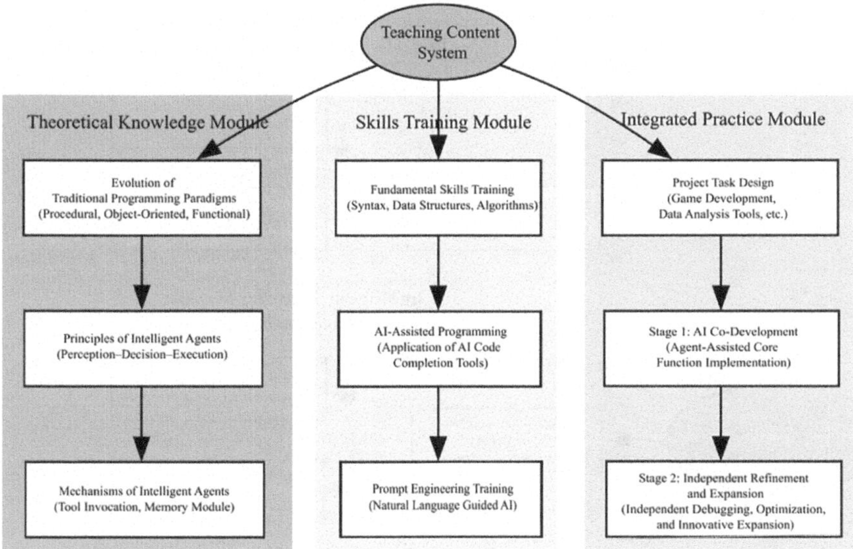

Fig. 3. The Framework of Teaching Content for Intelligent and Innovative Programming.

The comprehensive practice module adopts a project-based learning approach that fully integrates the "self-directed learning – intelligent guidance – practical innovation" process. A series of progressive project tasks, such as interactive game development and data analysis tool design, are carefully designed to guide students through two phases of practice. In the first phase, students collaborate with agents to implement the main functional components of their projects, enabling rapid prototyping. In the second phase, students independently debug, refine, and expand the prototype, incorporating innovative features and reflecting on their design choices. This approach not only leverages the strengths of AI agents as collaborative assistants, but also ensures active student participation, fostering the dual enhancement of comprehensive abilities and innovative competence.

3.3 Teaching Strategies and Implementation

Through flipped classroom and blended learning methods, the teaching strategies and implementation of the intelligent and innovative programming model emphasize the integration of self-directed learning, intelligent tutoring, and practical innovation, as illustrated in Fig. 4.

Self-directed Learning. The course adopts a flipped classroom approach, where students engage in pre-class self-study using microlecture videos, textbooks, and supplementary materials on the learning management system. When encountering difficulties, students can consult AI agents for real-time guidance. To enhance learning effectiveness, students are required to take notes or complete formative quizzes. In addition to flipped classroom instruction and agent support, the following strategies are employed to strengthen students' self-directed learning abilities: First, at the beginning of the course,

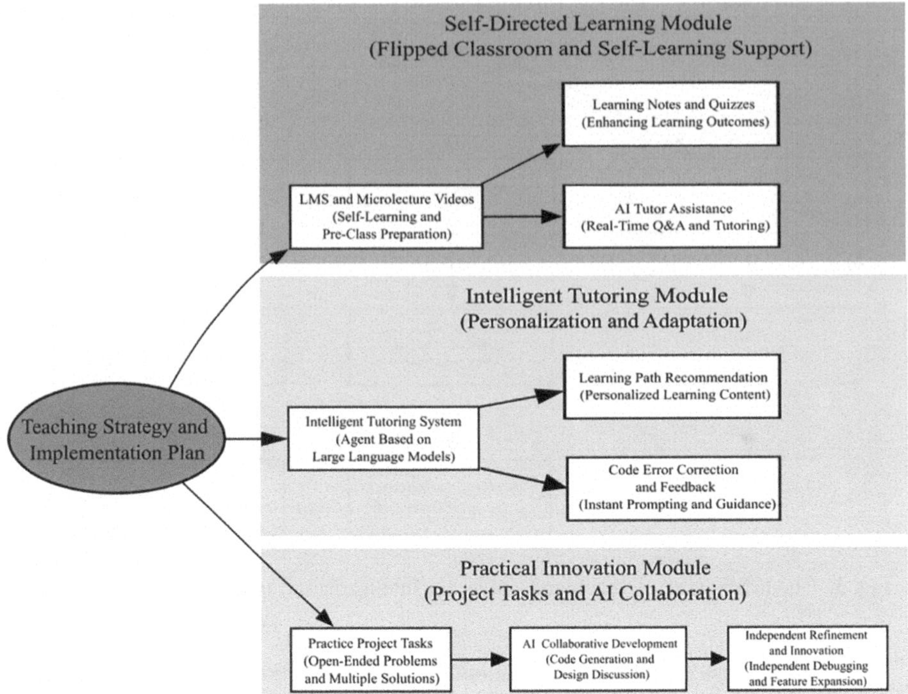

Fig. 4. The Framework of Teaching Strategies and Implementation for Intelligent and Innovative Programming.

the teacher introduces the agent's role and usage methods in facilitating autonomous learning and clarifies its limitations, encouraging students to maintain critical thinking and avoid blindly accepting agent-generated outputs. Second, students are encouraged to maintain interaction logs with agents and share challenges, solutions, and suggestions for agent improvement with peers, thereby fostering metacognitive awareness and self-regulation. Third, teachers assign extension tasks or challenge problems to inspire creativity and promote exploratory learning.

Intelligent Tutoring. Powered by large language models, the agent supports all aspects of the instructional process, including intelligent Q&A, personalized learning path generation, and dynamic evaluation. Based on students' performance, the agent can adjust the difficulty of exercises, recommend tailored learning materials, and provide real-time feedback and guidance. To ensure effective agent utilization, suitable tools and platforms must be adopted, for example, cloud-based development environments or online IDEs (e.g., Tencent Cloud Development, ByteDance Trae) that support agent-assistant plugins. These tools should be tested in advance to ensure reliability. In the later stages of the course, students are introduced to open-source agent frameworks (e.g., OpenDeAI, PaddlePaddle) and guided to develop simple agent applications, transitioning from users to developers. Teachers also require students to record programming interaction logs with agents to assess their quality of usage and promote responsible engagement.

Practical Innovation. Course knowledge is integrated into real-world project tasks, where students apply what they have learned with the assistance of AI agents. Project design follows a tiered approach: initial tasks focus on fundamental skills, intermediate tasks incorporate innovative requirements, and advanced tasks involve coordinating multiple agent tools to solve complex, open-ended problems. During project development, students are encouraged to design alternative technical solutions, evaluate trade-offs, and make informed decisions, thereby cultivating creativity and critical thinking. It is important to clearly identify which components of the project are agent-generated and which result from independent student input—for example, using the agent to generate an initial codebase, with students refining and annotating subsequent modifications. Collaborative elements such as team-based challenges and peer competition are also introduced to enhance engagement, teamwork, and human-AI co-creation capabilities.

Transformation of Teacher Roles. In agent-augmented classrooms, teachers are repositioned as "co-learners" and adopt the following strategies: On one hand, teachers must gain hands-on experience with agent tools by completing course assignments themselves, improving their AI literacy to better support student collaboration with agents. During instruction, they should employ heuristic and inquiry-based teaching to explore new technologies together with students, fostering a shared learning community. On the other hand, teachers are responsible for incorporating clear guidelines into the syllabus, specifying when and how agents may be used, emphasizing academic integrity, and outlining consequences for misuse, such as passing off agent-generated content as original work. Additionally, teachers can utilize agent tools to improve lesson planning efficiency and focus on creative instructional design. Teaching materials should be redesigned to include agent-assisted learning packages that help students efficiently leverage AI tools. Finally, teachers must attend to students' higher-order thinking and emotional needs. By analyzing interaction data, teachers can identify struggling students and intervene as needed, preventing over-reliance on or fear of agents. Emphasis should always be placed on the fact that agents are assistive tools—core creativity and critical thinking must remain with the students themselves. Through these strategies, the model aims to shift students from "I have to learn" to "I want to learn," fostering intrinsic motivation and sustainable learning habits.

3.4 Evaluation and Feedback Mechanisms

The evaluation and feedback mechanism focuses on the comprehensive assessment of students' learning progress and final outcomes. By integrating formative and summative assessments, real-time feedback, and reflection mechanisms, the model ensures the achievement of teaching objectives and supports the development of students' self-directed learning, innovation capabilities, and critical thinking skills, as illustrated in Fig. 5.

Teaching Evaluation. Formative evaluation emphasizes students' engagement in self-directed learning, intelligent tutoring, and practical innovation. Students are required to regularly document their interactions with agents, including the problems addressed, challenges encountered, and feedback received. Teachers analyze these logs to understand students' thought processes, assess the depth of learning and autonomy, and

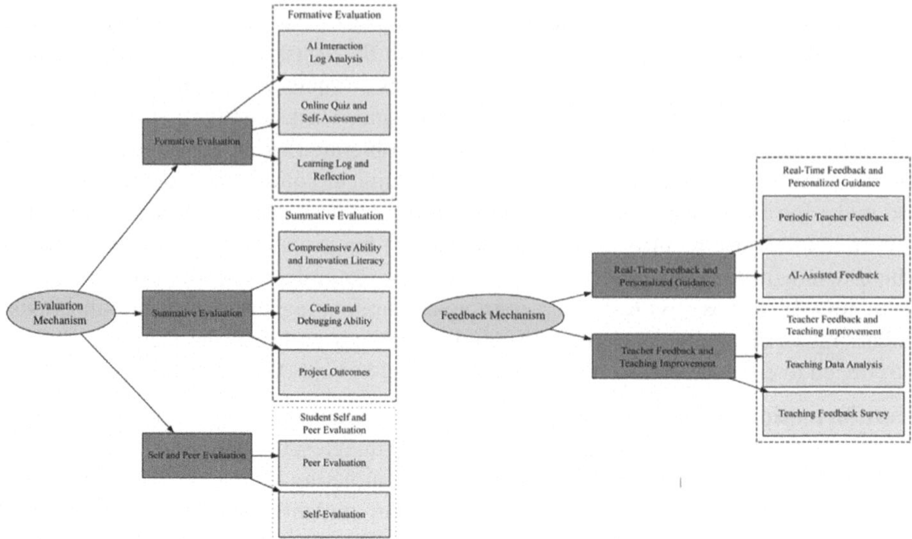

Fig. 5. The Framework of Teaching Evaluation and Feedback Mechanisms for Intelligent and Innovative Programming.

provide targeted instructional guidance. In addition, platform-generated data is used to monitor learning progress, ensure comprehensive understanding of course content, improve human–agent collaboration, and prevent over-reliance on agents. Summative evaluation assesses students' overall performance and learning outcomes. Key indicators include: completion and quality of project tasks; technical complexity and innovation in agent-assisted project implementation; comprehensive competencies such as self-directed learning, teamwork, innovative thinking, and problem-solving abilities. Students complete self-assessment questionnaires to reflect on their mastery of core knowledge, confidence in independent problem-solving, and proficiency in using agent tools. By engaging in self-assessment and evaluating team collaboration performance, students are encouraged to develop critical thinking and teamwork capabilities.

Teaching Feedback and Improvement. The Intelligent and Innovative Programming Model emphasizes feedback and continuous improvement, enabling students to receive timely support throughout the learning process. On one hand, agents provide instant feedback by identifying code issues and suggesting improvements. Teachers synthesize agent feedback with their own observations to deliver personalized guidance, organize regular group discussions or one-on-one tutorials, monitor students' progress, identify technical challenges and innovation highlights, and propose improvement plans and resource support accordingly. On the other hand, teachers gather feedback from students on the effectiveness of the teaching model, agent usage, and course content via questionnaires or in-class discussions. Based on this feedback, teaching strategies are adjusted in a timely manner. The achievement of instructional objectives is assessed through platform data, including learning logs, test scores, and project progress, to ensure that each student receives effective and personalized support.

4 Case Analysis

This case selects the intelligent question answering system development unit from the intelligent application development course, targeting junior software engineering students. It aims to cultivate students' comprehensive ability to develop intelligent applications using front-end, back-end, database, and AI technologies. Over the course of four weeks of classroom instruction and project-based practice, students will master the design and implementation of intelligent question answering systems through collaborative teamwork and experience a human-AI co-development workflow. This project enhances students' technical implementation and innovative thinking skills through real-world development tasks, as outlined in Table 1.

Table 1. Project Implementation Steps and Objectives.

Step	Content	Goal
Requirement Analysis (Week 1)	① Introduce the task context through case studies ② Explain QA system principles and key challenges ③ Discuss how to use AI agents to enhance the system ④ Use agents for brainstorming and drafting a preliminary project plan	① Stimulate students' interest ② Understand system architecture and key concepts ③ Develop an initial project plan
Solution Design (Week 2)	① Refine the solution based on peer and instructor feedback ② Begin system and knowledge base design ③ Use AI agents to assist with coding, database schema design, and front-end development ④ Review and test the generated code collaboratively	① Improve system design ② Develop coding and architecture skills ③ Strengthen teamwork and ensure code quality
Integration & Development (Week 3)	① Integrate the agent with the QA system ② Implement API calls and backend logic ③ Use agents to generate code templates and test queries ④ Instructor reviews and optimizes agent prompts	① Achieve system integration ② Master API interaction and data handling ③ Optimize agent-generated output

(continued)

Table 1. (*continued*)

Step	Content	Goal
Testing & Enhancement (Week 4)	① Conduct system optimization and peer evaluation ② Address issues such as "agent hallucination." ③ Design innovative features (e.g., context memory, adaptive feedback) ④ Generate advanced code ⑤ Compile and organize project documentation	① Improve system performance and accuracy ② Implement creative functionalities ③ Prepare for final presentation
Presentation & Evaluation	① Present the final QA system, explaining agent integration and encountered challenges ② Instructors assess technical implementation and innovation ③ Peer evaluation and submission of personal reflection reports	① Summarize outcomes; demonstrate collaboration and innovation ② Encourage self-reflection on learning achievements and areas for improvement

By implementing this project, the goal is to enhance students' self-directed learning ability, practical innovation skills, programming efficiency, and comprehensive competencies such as AI literacy. Evaluation indicators are employed to track student performance throughout the project and provide a foundation for the iterative improvement of the teaching model, as summarized in Table 2.

Table 2. Expected Results and Evaluation Methods.

Expected Outcome	Description	Evaluation Method
Significant Improvement in Student Autonomy	Students take the lead throughout the project, make independent decisions, and proactively solve problems, demonstrating strong self-directed learning and problem awareness	Use questionnaires or interviews to assess whether students proactively utilized agent tools to solve problems, and track changes in the quantity and quality of student-initiated questions
Improvement in Practical Innovation Ability	Through task-driven activities, students implement innovative features and validate the feasibility of their solutions, thereby enhancing technical creativity and practical skills	Evaluate via project assessment and teacher feedback, focusing on students' ability to implement and deploy agent-assisted innovations

(*continued*)

Table 2. *(continued)*

Expected Outcome	Description	Evaluation Method
Improved Programming Efficiency and Code Quality	Students increase programming efficiency with agent-assisted code generation, allowing more time for system optimization and code refinement	Compare programming efficiency, code quality, and time savings attributable to agent assistance. Assess the use of agents to automatically generate test cases and identify bugs
Personalized Growth Trajectory	Students follow individualized learning paths based on team role assignments; agents support learning in areas of strength and enhance self-awareness	Analyze self-assessments and reflective reports. Evaluate the impact of team role division on outcomes, as well as students' understanding of and suggestions for reducing agent dependence
Enhanced AI Literacy	Students understand both the capabilities and limitations of agents, learn to design and refine prompts, validate output correctness, and improve their overall ability to apply agents effectively	Assess students' grasp of agent functionality and limitations, their ability to design and adjust prompts, validate agent outputs, and demonstrate AI literacy

5 Discussion

The traditional teaching model primarily relies on teacher-centered lectures and after-class computer exercises. In such settings, students are often in a passive learning state, and it is difficult for instructors to address individual learning differences. In contrast, the proposed teaching model introduces intelligent agents to highlight student agency and support personalized learning. With this model, students can access knowledge and feedback on demand and flexibly adjust their learning trajectory. In particular, the traditional model lacks innovation in the practical component. With agent support, however, students are able to take on more complex projects, significantly expanding both the depth and breadth of their practical learning experience.

Although traditional flipped classrooms and project-based learning approaches also emphasize self-directed learning and hands-on practice, students frequently lack sufficient guidance during self-study phases, which can lead to fragmented learning and reduced motivation. This model addresses such shortcomings by introducing agents that provide continuous, real-time assistance and idea generation throughout the learning process.

Conventional intelligent tutoring systems are typically rule-based and cannot flexibly respond to complex, dynamic learning scenarios. In contrast, the agents used in this model are powered by large language models (LLMs), enabling human-like dialogue, reasoning, and deep problem analysis. By integrating multiple agents—such as those for Q&A, code generation, and evaluation—the model constructs a "team of agent teaching assistants" that goes beyond traditional agent-assisted tools, offering comprehensive support to students in solving complex learning problems.

While existing explorations of AI agent-assisted instruction treat agents primarily as accelerators, they often do not fundamentally alter students' learning goals or break away from the traditional instructional process. In contrast, this model elevates the agent to an active participant in the teaching process. Through autonomous task planning and execution, students are guided to engage with emerging AI programming paradigms—such as prompt engineering and human–AI collaborative development—while also being supported by structured strategies involving specifications, log documentation, and reflection tasks. Through ongoing process management and outcome monitoring, the model ensures that the integration of agents enhances rather than disrupts the learning process.

In the field of educational informatization, research on agent-empowered instruction is rapidly expanding. Some studies explore the development, applications, and future potential of educational agents. However, much of the existing literature remains at the theoretical or technical level, with limited focus on classroom-level implementation. Our approach begins from the perspective of instructional design, integrating intelligent technology into the entire teaching–learning process, offering strong practical and pedagogical relevance.

6 Conclusion

The Intelligent and Innovative Programming Teaching Model overcomes the limitations of traditional programming instruction by organically integrating self-directed learning, intelligent tutoring, and practical innovation. It reconstructs both the teaching process and the roles of teachers and students. In this model, teachers shift from knowledge transmitters to mentors of human-AI collaboration; students evolve from passive recipients to active partners of intelligent agents; and agents serve not only as tools but also as active participants in instructional interactions. The model places particular emphasis on cultivating students' AI literacy. Through embedded evaluation and feedback mechanisms, it encourages students to maintain critical thinking and self-motivation while collaborating with agents. Although full-scale implementation of this model may face certain practical challenges, it aligns with the transformative needs of education in the AI era and offers a promising pathway for cultivating application-oriented talent.

Acknowledgments. This work was supported by the Key Teaching Reform Research Project of Hunan Province for Regular Higher Education Institutions, titled "Research on the Digital Transformation of Applied Undergraduate Courses in the Context of Large Language Models—A Case Study of Discrete Mathematics" (Project No. HNJG-2023-1520), and "Research and Practice on the Reform of Application-Oriented Talent Cultivation Mechanism for Blockchain Engineering under the Background of Emerging Engineering Education" (Project No. HNJG-2023-1521). We sincerely appreciate the support from the Department of Education of Hunan Province and the valuable guidance provided by experts throughout the research process. Their insights and encouragement have been instrumental in shaping our exploration of digital pedagogy and AI-driven instructional innovation in applied undergraduate education.

References

1. Tian, S.: The integration of computational thinking and artificial intelligence serves to enhance the cognitive processes and skill acquisition of students. In: Proceedings of the ISAIE 2024, pp. 564–567. ACM, New York (2024). https://doi.org/10.1145/3700297.3700394
2. Shah, R., Gillen, A.L.: A systematic literature review of university–industry partnerships in engineering education. Eur. J. Eng. Educ. (2023). https://doi.org/10.1080/03043797.2023.2253741
3. Zuo, D., Samuel, M., Tan, S.Y.: Emerging engineering education in china: a systematic literature review. Int. J. Eng. Pedagogy **15**(2), 153–164 (2025). https://doi.org/10.3991/ijep.v15i2.53627
4. Yilmaz, R., Karaoglan Yilmaz, F.G.: The effect of generative artificial intelligence (AI)-based tool use on students' computational thinking skills, programming self-efficacy and motivation. Comput. Educ.: Artific. Intell. **4**, 100147 (2023). https://doi.org/10.1016/j.caeai.2023.100147
5. Zhang, L., Ma, Y.: A study of the impact of project-based learning on student learning effects: a meta-analysis study. Front. Psychol. **14**, 1202728 (2023). https://doi.org/10.3389/fpsyg.2023.1202728
6. Lin, C.C., Huang, A.Y.Q., Lu, O.H.T.: Artificial intelligence in intelligent tutoring systems toward sustainable education: a systematic review. Smart Learn. Environ. **10**, 41 (2023). https://doi.org/10.1186/s40561-023-00260-y
7. Zhang, S., Yang, J., Sang, X.: Exploring the applications of EduCoder platform in blended teaching for computer major. J. Educ. Educ. Res. **4**(2), 100–103 (2023). https://doi.org/10.54097/jeer.v4i2.10819
8. Svyatkovskiy, A., Lee, S., Hadjitofi, A., Riechert, M., Franco, J.V., Allamanis, M.: Fast and memory-efficient neural code completion. In: 18th IEEE/ACM International Conference on Mining Software Repositories (MSR 2021), pp. 329–340. IEEE, New York (2021). https://doi.org/10.1109/MSR52588.2021.00045
9. Wang, J., Fan, W.: The effect of ChatGPT on students' learning performance, learning perception, and higher-order thinking: insights from a meta-analysis. Hum. Soc. Sci. Commun. **12**, 621 (2025). https://doi.org/10.1057/s41599-025-04787-y
10. Liu, J., Xia, C.S., Wang, Y., Zhang, L.: Is your code generated by ChatGPT really correct? Rigorous evaluation of large language models for code generation. Adv. Neural Inform. Process. Syst. **36**, 21558–21572 (2023). https://doi.org/10.48550/arXiv.2305.01210
11. Yang, H., Yue, S., He, Y.: Auto-GPT for online decision making: benchmarks and additional opinions. arXiv:2306.02224 (2023). https://doi.org/10.48550/arXiv.2306.02224
12. Wang, L., Ma, C., Feng, X., et al.: A survey on large language model-based autonomous agents. Front. Comp. Sci. **18**, 186345 (2024). https://doi.org/10.1007/s11704-024-40231-1
13. Bubeck, S., Chandrasekaran, V., Eldan, R., et al.: Sparks of artificial general intelligence: early experiments with GPT-4. arXiv:2303.12712 (2023). https://doi.org/10.48550/arXiv.2303.12712

A Knowledge Graph-Based Study on the "Four-Step" Model for Practice-Oriented Teaching

Rui Wen(✉), Yuefeng Cen, Jingjing Liang, Gangyi Zhang, Shuai Jiang, and Gang Cen

School of Information and Electronic Engineering, Zhejiang University of Science and Technology, No. 318 Liuhe Road, Hangzhou 310023, Zhejiang, China
zustwen@foxmail.com, cyf@zust.edu.cn

Abstract. Practical teaching is essential for talent development in higher education. However, the absence of an effective mentoring mechanism between senior and junior students, coupled with the underutilization of existing learning resources, results in low teaching efficiency and limited teacher engagement. To address these issues, a knowledge graph construction method based on the "Four-Step" Model for Practice-Oriented Teaching is proposed. By extracting key elements—such as practical projects, courses, and knowledge points—from diverse educational sources, a heterogeneous graph is constructed that represents multiple entity types and semantic relationships. HGNN is then used for node representation learning. The HGNN integrates relation-aware message passing and attention mechanisms, improving its ability to model complex teaching relationships. Experimental results show that the proposed method outperforms traditional graph neural networks in accuracy, F1 score, and AUC, demonstrating strong representation ability and practical value. HGNN provides a new technical approach for digitally modeling practical teaching in higher education.

Keywords: Practical Teaching · Knowledge Graph · Heterogeneous Graph Neural Network

1 Introduction

Practical teaching plays a vital role in talent development at higher education institutions, especially in improving students' innovation and hands-on skills, which are essential and irreplaceable [1]. However, two key challenges remain. First, the absence of an effective mentoring system between senior and junior students hinders experience sharing. Second, the limited use of existing learning resources leads to weak knowledge continuity and support, reducing teaching effectiveness.

W. Hong et al. (Eds.): ICCSE 2025, CCIS 2761, pp. 404–415, 2026.
https://doi.org/10.1007/978-981-95-7731-6_31

As a powerful tool for knowledge organization and representation, knowledge graphs can integrate complex relationships among practical projects, competency elements, and teaching resources, offering structured support for practical teaching [2]. By constructing a knowledge graph aligned with the "Four-Step" model for practice-oriented teaching, it becomes possible to systematically present teaching content, support personalized student learning, and assist teachers in designing targeted practical tasks [3].

This study proposes a knowledge graph construction plan tailored to "Four-Step" model for practice-oriented teaching [4]. It incorporates graph neural network modeling for entity relationships and includes functions for visualization and recommendation. The goal is to support the organization, inheritance, and intelligent development of practical teaching.

2 Related Work

2.1 Practice-Oriented Teaching

Practice-Oriented Teaching has become a key approach in higher education for developing student competencies. It has gained particular attention in engineering education and the training of applied talents in recent years. Studies show that task-driven practical teaching improves students' problem-solving and collaboration skills. Based on professional learning theories and prior research, our team has proposed a "Four-Step" model for practice-oriented teaching designed to support the cultivation of applied talents in software engineering.

The "Four-Step" model is developed under the guidance of the CDIO (Conceive, Design, Implement, Operate) framework [5]and constructivist learning theory [6]. It was formulated after an in-depth analysis of practical teaching methods in software engineering programs at higher education institutions. The model includes four stages: foundational innovation practice, technology project practice, discipline competition practice, and results refinement and promotion practice [7]. However, its implementation still faces challenges. These include low efficiency in using educational resources and weak transfer of knowledge outcomes. The experiences of senior students are often not transformed into structured knowledge, which limits their usefulness for junior students and prevents the formation of an effective mentoring system.

2.2 Educational Knowledge Graphs

Knowledge graph technology has been widely applied in the organization of educational resources and intelligent service systems. Existing studies have achieved notable progress in areas such as curriculum modeling, learning path recommendation, and student profiling. For example, Wang [8] et al. constructed a knowledge graph that integrates courses, knowledge points, and teaching resources to support personalized teaching recommendations. Chen [9] et al. developed educational knowledge graphs using syllabi and learning behavior data to provide decision support for teaching management. However, most of these works focus primarily on modeling theoretical course content and lack comprehensive representations of practical projects, competency indicators, and teaching processes. As a result, they do not fully meet the needs of practical teaching, which demands high operational relevance and complex task structures.

2.3 Knowledge Graph Construction Based on the "Four-Step" Model

To address the above limitations, recent research has explored the integration of knowledge graphs into practical teaching. For instance, Zhang et al. proposed a method that maps students' practical activities and competency assessments into a graph structure to support dynamic capability tracking and learning path planning. However, existing approaches often lack specialized designs aligned with the "Four-Step" model for practice-oriented teaching, resulting in weak representation of semantic relationships between projects. This limitation hinders task-related reasoning and resource allocation optimization. Therefore, there is a pressing need to develop knowledge graph construction methods specifically tailored to the "Four-Step" model. Such methods would improve the organization of knowledge across projects and enable visualized recommendations and accurate teaching support.

In addition to theoretical exploration, several universities have begun to apply knowledge graph technology in practice-oriented teaching scenarios. For example, Zhejiang University of Science and Technology has integrated students' course projects, competition records, and practical task reflections into a structured knowledge graph. This enables the automatic recommendation of follow-up practice activities for junior students based on the experience of seniors. In another case, a software engineering program developed a system to track students' skill growth using a graph of project participation and learning outcomes, supporting personalized training plans and bridging gaps in competency development. These real-world applications demonstrate the feasibility and effectiveness of educational knowledge graphs in enhancing the "Four-Step" teaching model.

Beyond specific applications, the use of knowledge graphs in education presents a unique opportunity to bridge the gap between fragmented educational resources and structured, competency-driven learning models. However, challenges remain. One key issue is the quality and standardization of input data. Many institutions store project records, course materials, and student feedback in inconsistent formats, which hinders graph construction and reduces semantic accuracy. Another difficulty lies in maintaining the graph's currency over time. As courses evolve and competencies shift, an outdated graph may mislead students or educators. Therefore, establishing scalable update mechanisms and incorporating real-time feedback loops are crucial for sustaining the graph's instructional value. Furthermore, the need for faculty training and interdisciplinary collaboration must not be overlooked, as effective graph implementation relies on coordinated efforts across departments, including teaching, IT, and academic affairs.

In the context of modern higher education, particularly in engineering and applied disciplines, the strategic integration of knowledge graphs extends beyond technical innovation—it reflects a shift toward competency-based and evidence-driven talent development. By capturing and modeling the evolving relationships among knowledge, skills, projects, and learning outcomes, a knowledge graph acts as a digital infrastructure that supports transparent, adaptive, and personalized education. This aligns with global education trends that emphasize learning traceability, real-time feedback, and data-informed decision-making. Institutions that adopt such systems are better positioned to align teaching with industrial demands, monitor skill progression at scale, and generate actionable insights for continuous curriculum improvement.

3 Methods

To effectively capture the complex entity relationships and semantic structures within the "Four-Step" model for practice-oriented teaching framework, this paper proposes a knowledge graph construction and representation learning method based on Heterogeneous Graph Neural Networks (HGNN). The approach includes four main stages: data preprocessing, entity and relation extraction, graph construction, and the design and training of the HGNN model.

3.1 Data Processing

To begin with, based on the key components of the "Four-Step" practice-oriented teaching model, a knowledge graph ontology is constructed that includes three core entity types: Project, Course, and Knowledge Point. Four primary relation types are defined: Project–Knowledge Point, Knowledge Point–Course, Course–Course, and Knowledge Point–Knowledge Point. The data sources include teaching task documents, project manuals, instructor profiles, and equipment management systems.

Entity recognition and relation extraction are carried out using a combination of rule-based pattern matching and deep learning techniques, resulting in a set of triples. These triples are used to construct a heterogeneous graph:

$$G = (V, E, \phi, \psi)$$

where ϕ and ψ denote the type mapping functions for nodes and edges, respectively.

3.2 Entity and Relationship Modeling

To support heterogeneous structure modeling, each type of entity and relation in the graph is processed using separate embedding and propagation strategies. The initial node features are obtained from their textual descriptions, such as project summaries and competency statements, and encoded using BERT [10].

These embeddings are then mapped to a unified vector space through a fully connected layer. Relation types are represented as relation-specific embeddings and are integrated into the neighbor aggregation process to enable relation-aware feature propagation.

3.3 HGNN Model Design

HGNN is used to learn multi-level semantic embeddings of nodes in the constructed heterogeneous graph. The model includes two core mechanisms: a relation-aware message passing mechanism and an attention-based neighbor aggregation module.

The overall architecture of the HGNN model is illustrated in Fig. 1, where the key components and their interactions are systematically presented. This diagram summarizes how input features are processed layer by layer through relation-specific transformations and combined using attention mechanisms.

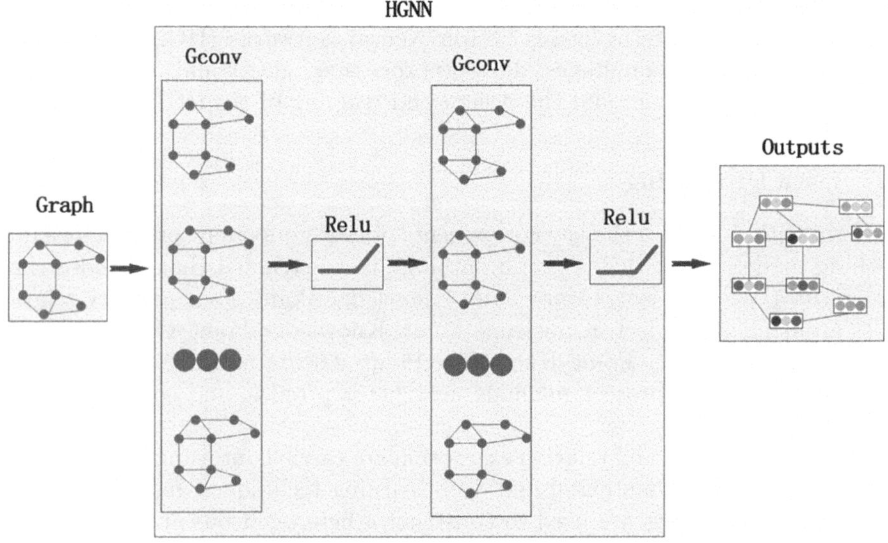

Fig. 1. Overall architecture of the HGNN model

Message Passing Mechanism. HGNN addresses semantic heterogeneity by assigning separate linear transformation matrices to different edge types. At the l-th layer, the representation of node i is updated as follows:

$$h_i^{(l+1)} = \sigma\left(\sum_{r\in R}\sum_{j\in\mathcal{N}_r(i)}\frac{1}{|\mathcal{N}_r(i)|}W_r^{(l)}h_j^{(l)} + W_0^{(l)}h_i^{(l)}\right) \tag{1}$$

where, $h_i^{(l)}$ denotes the representation of node i at layer l; $\mathcal{N}_r(i)$ is the set of neighbors of node i connected via relation type r; $W_r^{(l)}$ is the transformation matrix for neighbors linked through relation r; $W_0^{(l)}$ is the residual weight matrix for the self-connection of node i; σ is the activation function, and Leaky ReLU is used in this study.

To further explain how the HGNN handles diverse relation types during message propagation, Fig. 2 visualizes the relation-specific aggregation process. Each relation type is associated with a distinct transformation and attention path, enabling fine-grained feature learning.

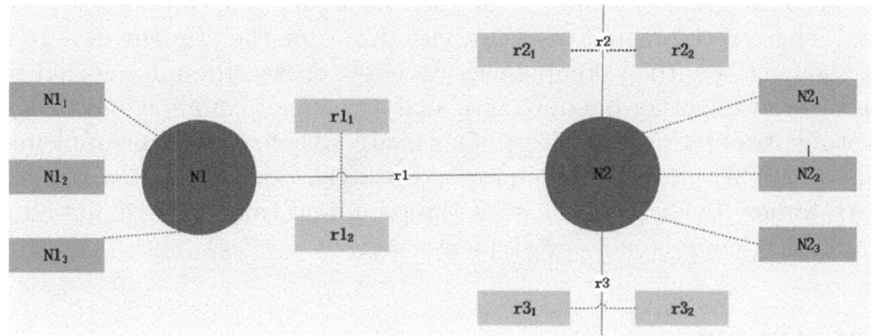

Fig. 2. Relation-aware message passing and attention in HGNN

This architecture uses type-aware neighbor aggregation and residual connections to enhance the model's ability to learn deep semantic representations and to improve training stability.

Attention Mechanism Enhancement. To improve the model's ability to capture important relational semantics, an attention mechanism is introduced during neighbor aggregation. This mechanism assigns different weights to neighbors based on their relation types. The attention score for node i attending to neighbor j under relation r is computed as:

$$\alpha_{i,j}^{(r)} = \frac{\exp\left(\text{LeakyReLU}\left(a^\top [W_r h_i \parallel W_r h_j]\right)\right)}{\sum_{k \in \mathcal{N}_r(i)} \exp\left(\text{LeakyReLU}\left(a^\top [W_r h_i \parallel W_r h_k]\right)\right)} \tag{2}$$

where, a is the attention weight vector for relation r; $\parallel$ denotes the vector concatenation operator; $\alpha_{i,j}^{(r)}$ is the attention coefficient assigned by node i to neighbor j under relation r.

This mechanism helps the model focus on more informative neighbors and reduces semantic loss caused by infrequent relation types, thereby improving the robustness of representation learning in heterogeneous graphs.

3.4 Application Scenario Simulation in Teaching

To illustrate the application potential of the proposed HGNN-based knowledge graph in practical teaching, a simulated teaching scenario was constructed. Suppose a junior software engineering student has completed two foundational innovation practice projects and is now entering the "technology project practice" phase. Based on the graph, the system identifies that the student has partially covered concepts related to software testing and frontend development but lacks exposure to containerization technologies like Docker.

Using this insight, the system recommends a mid-level project titled "Microservice Deployment Practice," which involves using Docker and Kubernetes. It also suggests enrolling in an elective course on "Cloud Native Development." These recommendations are visualized for the student in a roadmap format, showing how their competency coverage grows through selected paths.

Teachers, on the other hand, receive analytics about common knowledge gaps among students entering this phase. This enables them to design supplementary tutorials or modify project guidelines accordingly. Such simulated applications demonstrate how the system can shift the paradigm from one-size-fits-all teaching to adaptive, competency-aware mentoring.

4 Experiments

4.1 Dataset

The dataset used in this study consists of two parts. The first includes reflective writings and experience reports from students who participated in the "Four-Step" practice-oriented teaching program at Zhejiang University of Science and Technology. These documents were collected over a ten-year instructional initiative led by a faculty member and are primarily in textual form. The second part comprises publicly available course data related to information science majors, obtained from a MOOC platform.

The dataset contains three main files: the node feature file, the initial edge table, and the edge attribute and relation label file. The node feature file stores attribute vectors for both course and knowledge point nodes, totaling approximately 2,720 nodes—104 representing courses and the remainder representing knowledge points. Each node is encoded as a 128-dimensional feature vector. These features include course-specific attributes such as credit hours, total instructional hours, and update timestamps, as well as textual embeddings extracted from the names and definitions of corresponding knowledge points.

The initial edge table aligns with the node feature file and includes about 6,000 edges. These edges capture various types of relationships between courses and knowledge points, including prerequisites, knowledge coverage, and other derived associations. These relational links form the topological structure of the heterogeneous graph and provide the basis for learning graph-based representations.

4.2 Experimental Environment

The model was implemented using Python 3.6 and the PyTorch 1.12.1 deep learning framework. All experiments were conducted on a Tesla K80 GPU with 128 GB of RAM. To prevent overfitting, the dropout rate was set between 0.2 and 0.3. Neighbor sampling followed a batch-wise strategy, selecting 2–3 layers of neighbors per batch, with 15 and 10 neighbors per layer, respectively. The learning rate was set to 0.001. The neural network included two hidden layers with 128 and 64 neurons, respectively. Each experimental setting was trained for 200 to 300 iterations.

In addition, a manually annotated edge feature file was created to enrich the graph with textual segments, confidence scores, and relation-type labels. A total of 200 edges were manually labeled with semantics such as "responsible for" or "participates in." The dataset was divided into training, validation, and test sets using a 70%–15%–15% split.

4.3 Experimental Results and Analysis

To evaluate the effectiveness of the Heterogeneous Graph Neural Network (HGNN) for knowledge graph tasks, we compared it with three representative graph-based models: a traditional homogeneous Graph Convolutional Network (GCN) [11], a relation-aware model (R-GCN) [12], and the proposed HGNN.

First, as one of the classical models in graph neural networks, GCN has been widely applied in various fields such as social network analysis and recommendation systems. It is well known for its effective capability of aggregating information from local neighbors. When quantifying the dependency between courses and knowledge points, GCN provides a solid baseline for learning path recommendation. Therefore, its inclusion offers a reliable point of reference for evaluating the effectiveness of the proposed method.

Second, R-GCN extends GCN by incorporating support for multiple relation types, making it more suitable for handling heterogeneous graph data. In the construction of educational knowledge graphs, relationships between courses and knowledge points are often diverse and complex. R-GCN is capable of modeling such intricate relations, thus serving as a more representative model for processing course-related information.

Three evaluation metrics were used in this study: Accuracy, F1 score, and Area Under the ROC Curve (AUC). The performance results on the test set are summarized in Table 1.

As shown in Table 1, HGNN outperforms all baseline models across all evaluation metrics, demonstrating consistent and significant performance gains. Specifically, HGNN achieves an accuracy of 0.738, representing an improvement of approximately 4.2% over GCN. Similarly, the F1 score and AUC are improved by 2.7% and 3.6%, respectively.

These improvements result from two key architectural features of the HGNN model. First, in the message passing mechanism, HGNN assigns separate linear transformation matrices to each edge type. This allows the model to preserve

Table 1. Experimental Results of Different Graph Models

Model	Accuracy	F1	AUC
GCN	0.708	0.683	0.751
R-GCN	0.721	0.692	0.764
HGNN	**0.738**	**0.710**	**0.778**

semantic distinctions among heterogeneous entities. At each layer, node representations are updated by aggregating multi-relation neighbor information while incorporating residual connections to retain the original node signals. This design helps prevent gradient vanishing and information loss in deeper networks.

Second, HGNN introduces a relation-aware attention mechanism that enhances its ability to focus on important neighbors. By assigning different weights to neighbors based on relation types, the model emphasizes edges with higher semantic relevance—such as `design_knowledge_point` and `involving_course`. This is particularly beneficial in practice-oriented teaching contexts, where many relations are infrequent or weakly connected. The attention mechanism ensures that these meaningful yet sparse connections are not overshadowed, thus improving prediction quality.

Moreover, HGNN demonstrates strong adaptability to complex educational data. The constructed practice-oriented knowledge graph combines MOOC course data with university-level project-based texts, resulting in diverse node types, complex semantic relations, and noise in textual attributes. HGNN addresses these challenges by using BERT-based embeddings for initial node representation, providing a robust foundation for graph-based learning. Overall, HGNN's superior performance confirms its effectiveness and potential for broader application in modeling practice-oriented educational knowledge graphs.

4.4 User Feedback from Educators and Students

To evaluate the practical usability and acceptance of the knowledge graph system in real teaching settings, a pilot feedback survey was conducted among 12 instructors and 38 undergraduate students who used the system in a 6-week project practice course. Instructors highlighted that the system offered clear visualizations of student progression and competency gaps, which improved their task design and guidance strategies. Over 83% of teachers agreed that the system helped reduce redundancy in project topic selection and improved alignment between practice tasks and course objectives.

From the student perspective, the recommendation interface and personal knowledge dashboards were especially well received. Students reported feeling "more in control" of their learning plans and noted that the graph interface helped them understand how different courses and projects connected logically. Some students also suggested integrating peer learning opportunities based on graph similarity, which is a direction for future enhancement. These results indicate that beyond algorithmic performance, the system offers practical benefits and strong user acceptance in actual educational scenarios.

4.5 Practical Teaching Applications of HGNN

Beyond improved classification metrics, the HGNN-based knowledge graph offers practical benefits for enhancing teaching in real-world scenarios. Firstly, it can generate personalized learning recommendations by analyzing a student's current knowledge graph position and proposing the most relevant practice tasks or courses. Secondly, it enables dynamic student profiling by integrating learning behaviors and project participation, thereby supporting tailored mentoring strategies. Thirdly, teachers can use the knowledge graph to identify frequently missing competencies across students and design targeted interventions or workshops. These applications demonstrate that HGNN is not only technically effective but also educationally impactful in realizing the goals of the Four-Step practice-oriented model.

5 Conclusion

This study presents a knowledge graph construction method based on HGNN, designed for the "Four-Step" practice-oriented teaching model. The approach addresses key challenges, including the lack of effective mentorship between senior and junior students and the gap between theoretical instruction and practical application. By extracting core elements—practice projects, courses, and knowledge points—a heterogeneous graph was constructed with multiple entity and relation types. The HGNN model was developed to capture both structural and semantic information within the graph.

Experimental results show that the proposed HGNN outperforms baseline models such as GCN and R-GCN in Accuracy, F1 score, and AUC, confirming its expressive capacity and potential for modeling complex educational graph structures. The combination of type-specific message passing and relation-aware attention mechanisms significantly improves the model's ability to represent important entities and relations.

From a strategic perspective, the adoption of knowledge graph-driven teaching infrastructures also aligns with national initiatives promoting smart education and digital transformation in higher education. By embedding semantic-level intelligence into teaching systems, universities can not only enhance individual learning outcomes but also improve institutional teaching quality evaluation, accreditation readiness, and interdisciplinary collaboration. Furthermore, such systems can play a pivotal role in integrating industry feedback loops into curriculum development, aligning educational outputs with real-world skill demands more dynamically. However, realizing this vision requires policy-level support, standard-setting in educational data structuring, and sustained investments in digital infrastructure and faculty upskilling.

Future work may incorporate dynamic graph evolution and student behavior features to enhance the model's adaptability to teaching processes and its capability for intelligent recommendation. One promising direction involves the integration of large language models (LLMs), enabling natural language queries such as "Which projects are suitable after completing Course A and B?" or "What knowledge is required for a specific competition?" This functionality would make the system more accessible and interactive for non-technical users, including students and educators unfamiliar with graph structures.

Additionally, reinforcement learning mechanisms could be explored to allow the recommendation engine to self-optimize based on student outcomes and feedback. For example, if a project recommended by the system consistently leads to improved student engagement or assessment results, the system could adaptively reinforce similar recommendations. By combining the structured reasoning of knowledge graphs with the adaptive capabilities of modern AI models, the platform can evolve into a more intelligent and responsive educational assistant, supporting practice-oriented learning with greater precision and personalization.

Acknowledgements. This work was supported by Zhejiang University of Science and Technology Teaching Research and Reform Project (Major Project) (2023-jg02).

References

1. Wang, J.-Y., Peng, H., Gao, J.: Practical teaching system based on innovation and entrepreneurship education. In: DEStech Transactions on Social Science, Education and Human Science (2017)
2. Li, X., Liu, Y., Chen, J.: Knowledge graph-based teaching resource recommendation system. In: Lecture Notes in Computer Science, vol. 12842, pp. 45–56. Springer, Cham (2021)
3. Lin, X., Cen, G., Zhou, X.: Some key technologies of scientific research management system. Mechatronic Syst. Control **42**(1), 44–49 (2013)
4. Cen, G., Lin, X.: Research and Exploration of "Four Steps" Open Practical Teaching Activities. China Water & Power Press (2016)
5. Jiang, X., Zhu, R., Cen, G., Song, S., Li, X., Wang, S.: Design of student affairs management system of 'Plam Academy' smart campus. J. Zhejiang Univ. Sci. Technol. **32**(02), 139–144 (2020)
6. Cen, G.: Teaching research and exploration of open-ended 'Four-Step' project practice teaching mode in innovative and application-oriented talents training. J. Zhejiang Univ. Sci. Technol. **32**(05), 413–419 (2020)
7. Cen, G., Wu, S., Jiang, X., Lv, B., Zhu, R., Ding, Z.: Research and exploration on construction management of project practice innovation base based on 'Four Steps'. Res. Explor. Lab. **40**(07), 244–248 (2021)
8. Lang, Y., Wang, G.: Personalized knowledge point recommendation system based on course knowledge graph. J. Phys.: Conf. Ser. **1634**, 012073 (2020)
9. Chen, Y., Chen, W.: Knowledge graph technology helps intelligent reform of innovation and entrepreneurship guidance courses for college students. Appl. Math, Nonlinear Sci (2025)

10. Devlin, J., Chang, M.-W., Lee, K., Toutanova, K.: BERT: pre-training of deep bidirectional transformers for language understanding. In: Proceedings of the 2019 Conference of the North American Chapter of the Association for Computational Linguistics: Human Language Technologies, pp. 4171–4186. ACL, Minneapolis (2019)
11. Kipf, T.N., Welling, M.: Semi-supervised classification with graph convolutional networks. In: 5th International Conference on Learning Representations (ICLR) (2017)
12. Schlichtkrull, M., Kipf, T.N., Bloem, P., van den Berg, R., Titov, I., Welling, M.: Modeling relational data with graph convolutional networks. In: Proceedings of the European Semantic Web Conference (ESWC 2018), LNCS, vol. 10843, pp. 593–607. Springer, Cham (2018)

Computational Thinking Curriculum Design: A Triadic Integration of Listening, Teaching, and Practicing

Juan Zhou[1(✉)], Yonghui Wu[2], Zhiwei Zhang[1], Hui Luo[1], Xiong Li[1], and Nan Xiao[1]

[1] East China Jiaotong University, Nanchang 330013, China
422879727@qq.com
[2] Fudan University, Shanghai 200433, China

Abstract. This paper introduces the new course "Computational Thinking and Programming" created by the author, proposing a three-dimensional course construction model of "enjoy listening, excel at teaching, and master practicing." Through strengthening classroom management, assigning problem-solving exercises, and designing multi-level experimental tasks, the course aims to cultivate students' computational thinking and innovation abilities. Taking the "Touge Practical Teaching Platform" as an example, the paper explains how this platform supports computer education in universities by providing practical teaching cases and courses, thereby facilitating the development of computer science and engineering disciplines. Furthermore, this paper presents the textbook and online course resources specifically authored and developed by the research team for this curriculum." Finally, the article explores the role of extended programming competition training in cultivating scientific and technological talents.

Keywords: Computational thinking · Practical teaching · University Programming Courses and Competitions · Programming Contest

1 Introduction

Computational thinking is one of the basic qualities of college students in the digital era, and it is a necessary thinking ability for integrating into society.Computational thinking, as a universal skill, is a core competency essential for digital talents in the 21st century [1]. Professor Zhou Yizhen from Carnegie Mellon University in the United States first proposed in March 2006 that Computational Thinking is a series of thinking activities that apply fundamental concepts of computer science to solve problems, design systems, and understand human behavior, covering the breadth of computer science [2]. That is to say, computational thinking is when people stand from the perspective of computers, using them as tools and means to analyze and solve problems. Its important characteristics are "abstraction and decomposition" [3].

With the development of the times, computational thinking is no longer a requirement for computer courses, but should rather be integrated into students' comprehensive qualities as a form of "thinking". The "cognitive level" requires students to have a clear understanding of the current status of the computer field; the "thinking level" requires students

W. Hong et al. (Eds.): ICCSE 2025, CCIS 2761, pp. 416–427, 2026.
https://doi.org/10.1007/978-981-95-7731-6_32

to be able to integrate computational thinking into the process of solving natural/social problems; and the "spiritual level" requires students to internalize computational thinking as a kind of literacy, to inherit and carry it forward. Computational thinking is extensively applied in solving real-world problems, encompassing not only various daily life scenarios but also numerous professional challenges likely to be encountered in future careers, such as network communications, path planning, simulation modeling, and tactical decision-making [4]. Therefore, it is imperative to cultivate computational thinking in university-level fundamental computer science courses. The development of computational thinking aims not merely to enhance students' programming proficiency, but more fundamentally, to empower them with systematic problem-solving methodologies applicable to everyday situations [5].

How to effectively integrate computational thinking into teaching practice? The support of practical platforms is essential. Currently, the "Touge Practice Teaching Platform" is a widely used online practical teaching service platform and innovation environment in Chinese universities. Entering a phase of rapid development in 2020, EduCoder Practical Teaching Platform now serves over 2,500 universities and hundreds of enterprises, supporting more than 1 billion on-campus (private cloud solutions) and public cloud experimental training sessions. It has built over 150,000 practical teaching cases covering fields including artificial intelligence, big data, cloud computing, computer programming, computer system competency, software engineering, computer networks, blockchain, and the Internet of Things (IoT). Additionally, it has developed more than 3,500 practical courses, comprehensively supporting the development of computer-related and engineering disciplines while continuously improving the teaching, research, and scientific innovation environment.

The author thoroughly analyzed problems in computer education, identified key focus areas, innovated the computational thinking curriculum, implemented it, and achieved continuous improvements with sustained results.

2 Problems

In traditional computer education, programming courses have always held a significant position, including fundamental programming courses such as "C/C++ Programming," "Java Programming," and the recently popular "Python Programming," as well as core algorithm courses like "Data Structures," "Computer Algorithm Design and Analysis," or "Data Structures and Algorithms." With the rapid advancement of technology, particularly the swift rise of the computer and internet industries, societal demand for talent has far surpassed the supply capacity of higher education. On one hand, students are compelled to extensively study various subjects to achieve outstanding academic performance. On the other hand, many graduates face difficulties securing ideal employment. Meanwhile, award-winning participants in programming competitions have become highly sought-after by companies, with demand outstripping supply. This stark contrast highlights the contradictions in current computer education and underscores the urgent need for deeper reforms to enhance educational quality and better cultivate talent capable of meeting market demands.

2.1 Analyze the Problem

Virtually all academic disciplines now require computer proficiency, particularly for STEM students who must master programming. Programming has become an essential skill for university students, and computational thinking is emerging as a critical component of innovative mindset training. There is an urgent need for such courses, leading the author to pioneer the "Computational Thinking and Programming" course in 2021.

The central challenge in advancing computer education in higher institutions is clear: how to bridge the gap between theoretical knowledge and practical application? While students may acquire knowledge, they often lack the capability to solve real-world problems like software development. The author contends that the solution lies in strengthening computational thinking, particularly by enhancing its integration into traditional programming courses. However, improving these courses requires a systematic process involving textbook development, laboratory construction, and curriculum design - this transformation cannot be achieved overnight.

2.2 Entry Point

The development of computational thinking compensates for the deficiencies of traditional knowledge-application teaching models. Traditional teaching cannot cover all problems and solutions within limited class hours, and remains teacher-centered, with students passively receiving pre-arranged content [4]. After leaving the classroom, students will face various scenarios and problems, at which time they need to actively develop the ability to abstract and analyze problems, and master the skills to solve problems through algorithms or methods. To possess such abilities, teaching must transform from the very beginning, adopting a "student-centered" approach and emphasizing thinking training. These are precisely the capabilities required of participants in the International Collegiate Programming Contest (ICPC). Contestants must independently solve problems during competitions, and regular team members typically develop strong innovative abilities through several years of training, enabling them to solve practical problems using computer programming. In the past, due to limited team quotas in ICPC, the number of school team members was small. However, with the emergence of various programming competitions, such as the Blue Bridge Cup Information Technology and Software Talent Competition included in the regular college discipline competition catalog, the Team Programming Ladder Tournament, the Baidu Star Programming Competition, and the equally mainstream China Collegiate Programming Contest (CCPC), the demand for more students to participate has been met, with approximately 200,000 college students participating annually in recent years. Although the knowledge points tested in some competitions are subsets of ICPC, the syllabus of each type of competition generally exceeds the teaching content of current university courses, and all require solving new problems under pressure, making them effective approaches for cultivating innovative talent. Against the backdrop of rapid technological developments such as artificial intelligence, with 20 years of experience in guiding student competitions and training, the author has thorough knowledge of the entire scientific training system and has mentored over 10,000 students to win thousands of awards at provincial to international levels. Based on these experiences, the author has identified a key solution to address the contradiction between talent demand and current education: introducing the successful educational model of extracurricular competition training into the classroom, thereby creating the new course "Computational Thinking and Programming."

3 "Listen-Explain-Practice" Trilateral Pedagogy Framework

The course "Computational Thinking and Programming" is designed to cultivate innovative talents by focusing on three dimensions: motivating students to "listen" attentively in class, encouraging them to actively "discuss" problem-solving, and designing multi-level experimental exercises for students to "practice" extensively—summarized as the "Listen, Discuss, Practice" approach.

3.1 Joyful Listening

Strengthen classroom discipline, strictly require attentive listening, and create a lively yet focused classroom atmosphere through frequent questioning. For student responses, even if not entirely correct, identify and praise their strengths to help students develop a genuine fondness for listening to lectures.

3.2 Effective Teaching

Assign explanation exercises where students pair up to teach each other after class ("peer teaching"). Classmates provide evaluations, then selected students present in class with teacher feedback. This aligns with the 90% retention rate at the base of the learning pyramid (Fig. 1), transforming passive learning into active engagement. This approach also motivates more attentive listening. Finally, incorporate peer evaluation into the assessment criteria.

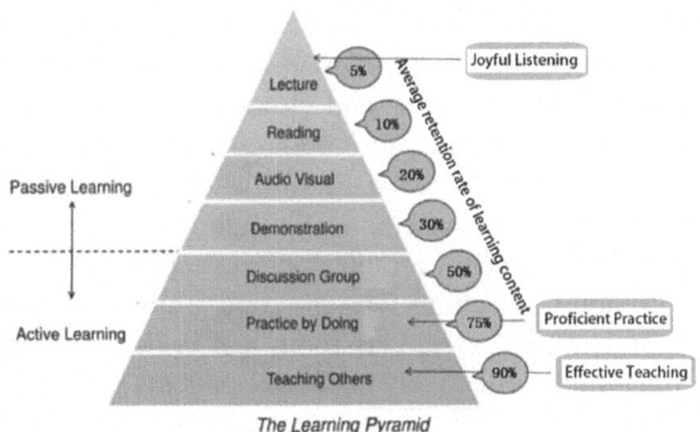

Fig. 1. Teaching methods aligned with the learning pyramid

3.3 Proficient Practice

The teaching videos and synchronous experiments for this course are constructed using the textbook "Introduction to Programming Practice," published by the author at Mechanical Industry Press. The course is built on EduCoder Practical Teaching Platform, which is the most famous professional online platform for computer-related courses in the country. Complete teaching videos have been recorded, and each exercise is published in the form of a practical project within the course on the platform. The book contains 84 exercises, and each video provides a detailed analysis of the problems, demonstrating the computational thinking training involved in solving problems through programming. Particularly in the "Mathematical Calculation" chapter, it shows the process of using mathematical and physical knowledge for derivation and solving problems through programming. This approach enables students to transition from watching videos before practicing exercises to practicing first and then watching videos as needed. It not only cultivates their innovative thinking but also addresses their fear of difficulties.

3.4 Enhanced Cognition

The course enables students to engage in seamless practice exercises. When they encounter difficulties in understanding the problem or lack coding skills they can watch the videos to gain clarity and then proceed with the practice. Each exercise can be attempted multiple times. By repeatedly writing the same code outside of class, students reinforce their memory and gradually master the logical process through continuous practice, ultimately training their minds to achieve a state of "superior cognitive ability."

3.5 Inquiry and Debate

Using the flipped classroom approach, students are organized to discuss both in and out of class, which guides them to identify, filter, deeply investigate, and ultimately solve problems. This process unfolds a research-oriented teaching model, cultivating students' awareness of inquiry and critical spirit.

3.6 Integration of Competition and Education

This course has been successfully implemented in multiple majors at our university, including software engineering, big data, and virtual reality. We innovatively integrate teaching with competition, relying on over 3,000 programming contest problems available on the EduCoder Practical Teaching Platform to significantly expand students' extracurricular practice space. By systematically organizing lectures on real competition problems and guiding students in their contest preparation, we have achieved a virtuous cycle of "promoting teaching through competition and integrating competition with teaching," creating a second classroom that is both content-rich and highly effective. This teaching model effectively enhances students' practical abilities and has cultivated a large number of excellent competitors with solid technical skills and strong competitive capabilities.

In summary, this course is systematically constructed from three dimensions: "listening," "explaining," and "practicing," focusing on cultivating students' three core abilities: "enhanced thinking," "in-depth investigation," and "practical competition." These innovative teaching contents are not only to be implemented in the classroom but also to be effectively realized through large-scale open online practice platforms in the "cloud-based" environment. The course is distinctively characterized by "open practice projects" and has been developed into a demonstrative large-scale online open practice course on the EduCoder Practical Teaching Platform. Based on the cloud-based teaching support system of software, testing, tools, and environment, and leveraging the reconfigurable software architecture proposed by the EduCoder platform, the flexible combination and intelligent connection of teaching methods have been achieved. This system is notable for its divisibility, evaluability, evolvability, and disseminability, providing a general reference model for constructing various training systems and practice components. Through this innovative model, we are able to provide precise personalized teaching services for teachers and students, realizing true differentiated instruction. As a pioneering and exemplary course nationwide, this course will lead the direction of teaching reform in computer-related majors and make significant contributions to the cultivation of high-level talents in artificial intelligence, computer science and technology, software engineering, big data, and other majors!

4 Happy Teaching and Teaching Students According to Their Aptitude

4.1 The Numerical Beauty of Computational Thinking – Embracing Life with Passion

The first example problem in the "Computational Thinking and Programming" course is calculating Fibonacci numbers. This naturally leads to an extended discussion about the origin of Fibonacci numbers and their beautiful manifestations in nature.

The Fibonacci sequence exhibits highly symmetrical and stable structures that represent optimal solutions for natural movements and formations. In the natural world, such symmetry often indicates healthier and more robust life forms. By maintaining balance and harmony between components, it enhances organisms' growth, reproduction, and chances of survival. The Fibonacci sequence is not merely a string of numbers - it resembles nature's source code, governing the patterns of growth, movement, and beauty in all living things.

So who wrote this magnificent code? Through a simple programming exercise, we aim to inspire students' curiosity and appreciation for nature. After taking this course, students may find themselves counting flower petals during nature walks. Conversely, when seeing flowers in bloom, they might recall this course and think: "Perhaps it's time to practice some programming problems?".

4.2 Peer Assistance and Mutual Learning—Q&A Appreciation Points

In each instructional class, several students are permitted to select one topic each and deliver a full lecture session to their peers. These student instructors are required to emulate teaching professionals by carefully designing classroom interactions and questions in advance. Observation shows that most participants prepare diligently and earn enthusiastic applause from their classmates. As recognition for their exceptional performance, these student instructors are rewarded with an exemption from the final computer-based examination while receiving an excellent grade. This practice aligns with the Pyramid of Learning principle, where the most effective knowledge retention (over 90%) occurs at the base level - when learners teach the material to others.

When a student earns admiration by explaining concepts in class, the instructor introduces a new bonus point system to encourage peer-to-peer learning. Here's how it works: (1) After receiving help from a classmate, the assisted student (Student A) should post in the course group chat: "Thank you [Student B] for explaining [specific problem/topic]." Then The class academic committee will document these acknowledgments. (2) Point allocation rules is that each student can accumulate a maximum of 20 Appreciation Points per semester. These points will first be applied to the 'Class Participation' score (10% of final grade).Once the Class Participation score reaches full marks (10/10), any remaining points will be added to the final computer-based exam score. (3) Grading Structure: Assignments: 20%, Lab Work: 20%,Class Participation (including Appreciation Points): 10%, and Final Exam: 50%.

4.3 Teaching Students According to Their Aptitude – Supplementary Assignment

This course is an optional professional assessment course. Initially, all students were required to take a final computer-based exam consisting of 5 programming questions on the Touge practical teaching platform. The exam lasted 2 h, with questions adapted from problems covered in lectures.

During the semester, students were given the previous year's final exam questions for practice. Due to the university's curriculum reform - changing from a 16-week system to two separate 8-week terms - adjustments were made based on student feedback: this year's exam featured reduced question quantity, lower difficulty, and shorter duration.

All students participated in the final computer-based exam, with very few submitting their papers early, indicating the difficulty level was appropriately challenging. Approximately 20% of students failed to achieve a passing score on the written exam. These students were subsequently given the opportunity to submit a major assignment as an alternative means to pass the course.

The major assignment requires students to select one problem from the recently concluded 16th Blue Bridge Cup Provincial Competition (C++ Group B) and write a solution report. The report should include Problem description, Solution approach and complete code implementation. The writing style should follow the format used in this course's textbook Introduction to Programming Practice [7].

While these competition problems are newly released with no existing solutions available for copying, we acknowledge that many students may consult AI tools—an emerging issue worthy of discussion in higher education. Thereby guiding students to properly utilize AI tools as part of forward-looking pedagogy, which can further enhance their in-depth learning and mastery of programming techniques.

Given the condensed 8-week duration of this course and the varying foundational knowledge among students, we have implemented a dual-assessment approach combining computerized exams and major assignments. This methodology serves multiple purposes: it accommodates diverse evaluation needs across the student population, achieves the pedagogical goal of differentiated instruction tailored to individual capabilities, and most importantly, provides positive reinforcement upon course completion.

This positive outcome motivates a greater number of students to pursue advanced studies in programming and computer algorithms, fostering continued engagement with the subject matter beyond the classroom. The structure intentionally creates multiple pathways to success, recognizing that students may demonstrate mastery through different modalities of assessment while maintaining rigorous academic standards.

5 Textbook Resources

After several iterations of improvement, the course adopted the textbook "Introduction to Programming Contests" [6] from our university's ACM-ICPC training base for the introductory programming training in 2021. After using it for two years, it was found that the difficulty level was somewhat high for many students in the entire class. Although every year 300 to 500 students from various colleges across the university enroll in the introductory training, and this textbook is also very popular among students participating in the introductory activities and is highly applicable, surveys revealed that in each class of the "Computational Thinking and Programming" course, generally fewer than five students enroll in the training, and most students are not suitable for such a challenging textbook. Therefore, in 2023, another textbook, "Introduction to Programming Practice" [7], was chosen. This textbook contains 84 problems, with the code for almost every problem being no more than half a page, making it very concise. The problem statements are easy to understand, yet they still involve logical and mathematical thinking, meeting the course's requirements for recursive thinking, structured thinking, and mathematical computation in programming.

This textbook selects real contest problems, sourced from the easy questions of ACM-ICPC competitions across various continents over decades, which are highly interesting and serve as preferred cases for case-based teaching. This textbook is the introductory volume of the "University Programming Course and Contest Training Textbook" series. The series also includes "Data Structure Programming Experiment" [8], "Algorithm Design Programming Experiment" [9], "Data Structure Problem-Solving Strategies" [10], "ACM-ICPC World Finals Problem Analysis" [11], and the forthcoming "Algorithm Design Problem-Solving Strategies," forming a complete system. Most of the textbooks in this series have been reprinted 2 or 3 times and have been published for over a decade. In addition to being issued in simplified Chinese in Mainland China, they have been published in English overseas and in traditional Chinese in Taiwan, and are highly popular among global contest participants. The explanations are thorough, making them convenient for self-study. Moreover, they are accompanied by online courses, such as the 2024 ICPC Training League Winter Camp in Programming (https://www.educoder.net/paths/mf9ewr7h). Students, through studying this course, can also continue to self-study or learn together in their school's training team along the series of textbooks in the future.

6 Outcomes

According to the Outline of the National Action Plan for Scientific Literacy (2021–2035) issued by the State Council [12], China will prioritize enhancing science education during the K-12 phase, promote pedagogical innovation through heuristic, inquiry-based, and open-ended approaches, and safeguard students' curiosity to stimulate intellectual inquiry and imagination. This policy framework establishes strategic guidance for science education reform, necessitating systemic transformations across educational paradigms, curricular content, and instructional methodologies.

An integrated cultivation system bridging K-12 and tertiary education should be established. Through project-based learning (PBL) and interdisciplinary integration, programming education shall be universalized to enhance students' mathematical cognition and logical reasoning capabilities, while fostering curiosity and learning motivation. Particular emphasis must be placed on developing computational thinking literacy during compulsory education to establish a foundation for future professional development.

As highlighted in our 2025 study [13], it is imperative to advance the development of instructional materials, curricula, and cross-institutional experimental teaching systems that integrate programming training with computational thinking and mathematical thinking. These initiatives effectively address the talent cultivation demands of the AI era by demonstrating pedagogical innovation and practical efficacy. Against the backdrop of rapid AI advancement, this perspective gains heightened significance. Consequently, greater emphasis should be placed on context-adaptive approaches starting from universal programming education. Leveraging high-quality resources such as MOOC platforms, virtual simulation labs, and programming competition systems, we propose constructing a multitiered and diversified pedagogical support framework. Through designing practical projects anchored in real-world scenarios—e.g., smart home control systems and data analytics visualization—students may comprehend programming's tangible value, thereby establishing foundations for tertiary education and future careers.

Regarding implementation pathways, collaborative initiatives between universities, local education authorities, and K-12 schools should be strengthened to optimize disciplinary structures while incorporating innovative mechanisms such as academia-research synergy and industry-education integration. Specific measures include establishing structured faculty exchange programs between tertiary and K-12 institutions to co-develop age-appropriate computational thinking curricula; constructing region-wide programming education resource hubs for equitable distribution of high-quality pedagogical materials; deploying technology innovation incubators providing personalized resources for promising students—collectively enabling proactive identification and cultivation of exceptional talents through integrated pipeline development.

Professor Chen Guoliang, Academician of the Chinese Academy of Sciences, emphasizes that computational thinking (CT) demonstrates universal pervasiveness, asserting that when pervasively integrated into the fabric of human activities, CT serves as an instrumental problem-solving framework requiring universal mastery and ubiquitous application [14]. This profound insight reveals CT education's transdisciplinary value, necessitating its seamless embedding in every instructional context [15]—transcending computer science to permeate mathematics, physics, biology, and other disciplines. Concrete implementations include introducing algorithmic reasoning in mathematics instruction, cultivating computational modeling capabilities through scientific experimentation, and applying information processing techniques in humanities/social sciences, thereby establishing CT as students' fundamental cognitive paradigm for understanding the world.

Future educational reforms should advance through dual coordinated dimensions. First, the pedagogical innovations from Computational Thinking and Programming courses—including curriculum architecture, instructional methodologies, and assessment mechanisms—must be systematically disseminated across all higher education institutions. Second, CT cultivation elements should be embedded throughout programming curricula at all levels, establishing a progressive cultivation pathway from foundational to advanced competencies. Concurrently, three critical initiatives require implementation: enhancing teacher development programs to elevate CT pedagogical proficiency; enriching educational resources through discipline-specific case repositories and experimental projects; and innovating evaluation systems by integrating process-oriented assessment with competency-based evaluation. This multi-pronged approach will institutionalize CT education, thereby providing robust support for cultivating digital-era innovators.

7 Closing Thoughts and Future Directions

In accordance with the "Action Plan for Improving Public Scientific Literacy(2021–2035)" issued by the State Council [12],there is a clear emphasis on enhancing the level of science education at the basic education stage. This includes guiding the transformation of teaching methods, advocating inquiry-based, problem-solving, and open-ended teaching, protecting students' curiosity, and stimulating their desire for knowledge and imagination. An integrated training system should be established at the basic education stage to connect with higher education, promote the popularization of programming education to improve students' mathematical thinking and logical abilities, and stimulate curiosity and interest in learning. In 2025,the author's article pointed out that "the construction of textbooks and courses for programming problem-solving training integrated with computational thinking and mathematical thinking, the construction of cross-school and cross-regional teaching experiment systems, and their innovation points and practical effects meet the requirements for training computer talents in the AI era." [13] Therefore, more attention should be paid to adapting measures to local conditions, starting with the popularization of programming education, and using a series of high-quality educational resources to help students lay a foundation for their university studies and future career development. By strengthening cooperation between universities and localities, optimizing the academic disciplines, and introducing mechanisms for coordinated development of science and education, resources and support can be provided for students with potential, and top-notch innovative talents can be cultivated. Academician Chen Guoliang pointed out that computational thinking is ubiquitous. When computational thinking is truly integrated into all human activities, it serves as an effective tool for problem solving, which everyone should master and use everywhere[14]. It should be effectively integrated into every class we teach [15]. Therefore, in the future, on the one hand, the course "Computational Thinking and Programming" needs to be promoted to other universities, and on the other hand, the cultivation of computational thinking should be introduced into all programming courses.

Acknowledgments. This study was funded by Key Projects of Jiangxi Provincial Higher Education Teaching Reform Research (JXJG-23-5-7);Jiangxi Provincial Higher Education Teaching Reform Research Projects (JXJG-21-5-29, JXJG-24-5-25);Ministry of Education Industry-University Cooperative Education Programs (230801311034605, 230901311065830);Computer Foundation Education Research Project of National Higher Education Computer Education Research Association (2024-AFCEC-027);Ministry of Education College Computer Courses Teaching Guidance Committee Project for Empowering Education: First-Class Course Construction and Teaching Reform in University Computer Science (FNJY-2024-19);East China Jiaotong University Innovation and Entrepreneurship Education Reform Projects (1600223042, 1600223049);Fudan University "Double First-Class" Initiative International Cooperation Office Global Development Strategy Promotion Project (IDH6282016).

Disclosure of Interests. The authors have no competing interests to declare that are relevant to the content of this article.

References

1. Wei, W., Zhao, R., Sun, S., et al.: Analysis of research paths and trends in computational thinking education at the international K-12 level. Software Guide **23**(08), 135–144 (2024)
2. Wing, J.M.: Computation thinking. Commun. ACM **49**(3), 33–35 (2006)
3. Peter, J.: Computational thinking. MIT Press, Massachusetts (2019)
4. Wang, M., Li, H., et al.: Exploration of higher-order skill development in college computer fundamentals courses. Comput. Educ. 03-0035-06:35-40 (2024)
5. Meng, H.: "Computational Thinking" for the digital future. China Educ. Technol. **30**(02), 3–12 (2024)
6. Zhou, J., Yang, S., Lu, J.: Introduction to programming competitions. China Water & Power Press, Beijing (2021)
7. Zhou, J., Wu, Y.: Introduction to programming practice: a university programming course and competition training textbook. China Machine Press, Beijing (2021)
8. Wu, Y., Wang, J.: Programming experiments in data structures: a university programming course and competition training textbook, 3rd edn. China Machine Press, Beijing (2021)
9. Wu, Y., Wang, J.: Programming experiments in algorithm design: a university programming course and competition training textbook, 2nd edn. China Machine Press, Beijing (2020)
10. Wu, Y., Wang, J.: Problem-solving strategies in data structures: a university programming course and competition training textbook. China Machine Press, Beijing (2023)
11. Wu, Y., Wang, J.: Analysis of ACM-ICPC world finals problems (2004–2011)*. China Machine Press, Beijing (2012)
12. Outline of the National Action Plan for Scientific Literacy (2021–2035) (State Council Document No. 9 [2021]) (2021). https://www.gov.cn/zhengce/zhengceku/2021-06/25/content_5620813.htm
13. Wu, Y., Zhou, J.: Constructions of teaching materials, curriculums, and the teaching system cross-region for "Solving Problems by Programming". In: Proceedings of The 30th International Computing and Combinatorics Conference, Springer in Lecture Notes in Computer Science (LNCS 15163), 24–29, 2025, COCOON (2024)

14. Chen, G., Dong, R.: Computational thinking and fundamental computer education in universities. China University Teaching (2011)
15. Yu, N., Dai, H., Jifang, A., et al.: Exploration of teaching reform in university computer fundamentals course based on computational thinking cultivation. Comput. Era (09), 72–74+78 (2017). https://doi.org/10.16644/j.cnki.cn33-1094/tp.2017.09.024

Interesting Teaching of Algorithm Courses Supported by Syllabus, Textbooks and Cases

Xiong Li, Kun Rao, Hui Song, and Juan Zhou(✉)

East China Jiaotong University, Nanchang 330013, China
422879727@qq.com

Abstract. This paper writes interesting teaching into the course outline and optimizes the interesting teaching cases of specific courses. Taking the traveling salesman problem, Kruskal algorithm, and the personalized recommendation algorithm that breaks the information cocoon as examples, this paper explains the analysis and presentation of interesting teaching, designs teaching details, and improves the quality of the course. It also introduces the writing of interesting algorithm design teaching materials to stimulate students' enthusiasm for designing more advanced algorithms, in order to provide a reference for the teaching of related courses.

Keywords: Algorithm Design And Analysis · Information Cocoon · Interesting Teaching · Teaching Case · Personalized Education · Learning resources

1 Introduction

The course "Algorithm Design and Analysis" is one of the core basic courses of software engineering. Through systematic study of this course, students can understand and master the core ideas of common classic algorithms, such as recursion, divide and conquer, dynamic programming, etc., and when understanding the ideas of algorithm design, focus on cultivating students' ability to correctly analyze the computational complexity of algorithms, laying a solid theoretical foundation for independent algorithm design and complexity analysis of algorithms.

Algorithm technology has always adhered to the concept of encouraging innovation and giving equal importance to regulation. The "New Generation Artificial Intelligence Development Plan" [1] emphasizes breakthroughs in core algorithm technology and promotes the autonomy, controllability and security of algorithms. It has been implemented in a series of fields such as AI-assisted diagnosis and intelligent traffic dispatching. The "White Paper on the Training of Artificial Intelligence Talents in China" has triggered the rise of an independent "algorithm ethics" section, with the aim of protecting users' right to know and right to choose, and avoiding information cocoons and big data price discrimination [2].

As the core foundation of computer science, algorithm design is not only a "mental gymnastics" to cultivate logical thinking, but also a key bridge connecting theory and practice. However, current algorithm teaching generally faces the dilemma of "abstract

W. Hong et al. (Eds.): ICCSE 2025, CCIS 2761, pp. 428–436, 2026.
https://doi.org/10.1007/978-981-95-7731-6_33

and difficult to understand, lack of interest" - in college C language classes, students are often discouraged by complex algorithms and fall into the vicious circle of "forgetting what they have learned" [3]; in high school VB programming classes, boring code debugging makes it difficult for students to experience a sense of accomplishment [4]; even in elementary school mathematics classes, the understanding of abstract concepts requires interest. As Einstein said: "Interest is the best teacher", how to transform the "rational beauty" of algorithms into the "source of interest" that students can perceive has become a topic that educators urgently need to solve.

From the perspective of educational psychology, the stimulation of interest needs to rely on situational creation and multi-faceted interaction. Some people have found in C language teaching that by analogizing algorithm logic with real-life cases such as "The Farmer Crossing the River", the cognitive threshold can be effectively lowered [3]. The Rosenthal effect shows that teachers' positive feedback can enhance students' confidence and change "fear of difficulty" into "daring to do". Others have practiced the "game introduction + task-driven" model in high school teaching, such as using the suspense of "cracking the password lock" to introduce the loop structure, allowing students to experience the practicality of the algorithm in solving practical problems [4]. This idea of "coming from life and going to practice" coincides with the "contextualized inquiry" advocated in mathematics teaching in the article "Stimulating learning interest and promoting self-learning" - through the formation of multimedia animation demonstration corners and the design of the "guess the snowflake" game to understand the decomposition of numbers, it has confirmed the key role of "concrete experience" in activating interest [5].

We need to build a virtuous cycle of "stimulating interest, deepening thinking, and improving ability" to inject lasting power into algorithm teaching. As Tolstoy said, "Successful teaching requires not coercion, but stimulation." Only by making algorithm design truly "alive" can students transform from "passive recipients" to "active explorers" and discover their own stars and sea in the world of code and logic. This article writes fun teaching into the course outline and optimizes the fun teaching cases of specific courses. Taking the traveling salesman problem, Kruskal algorithm, and the discussion of personalized recommendation algorithms that break the information cocoon as examples, this article introduces the writing of interesting algorithm design teaching materials, explains the analysis and presentation of interesting teaching, designs teaching details, and improves the quality of the course, in order to provide a reference for the teaching of related courses.

2 Course Background and Writing Interesting Teaching Content into the Algorithm Design and Analysis Course Outline

Pay attention to the fun of teaching, stimulate students' interest, and improve the syllabus. Write the following course objectives in the syllabus:

(1) Students know the advanced deeds of relevant computer pioneers, understand the important position of "craftsman spirit" in algorithm design and analysis, and appreciate the "big picture awareness" and "long-term planning" ideas in life decision-making and planning. Through specific examples, they understand the important

role of algorithms in daily life, medical care, national defense and other fields, and stimulate their enthusiasm for learning.

(2) Understand the analysis methods of algorithm complexity. Master the quantitative or qualitative analysis of the time complexity and space complexity of algorithms by solving recursive equations and basic statement statistics; master the design ideas and algorithm implementation methods of classic algorithms. Including common algorithms such as recursion and divide-and-conquer, dynamic programming, tree-based search algorithms, greedy algorithms, and understand the relationship between data structure design and algorithm implementation. The teaching content is combined with professional frontiers and industry development, and infiltrated into disciplines and traditional historical culture. Construct interesting teaching cases to stimulate students' interest in algorithms and enhance students' internal motivation and creativity in learning algorithm design and analysis courses.

(3) Be able to compare the advantages and disadvantages of different algorithms for the problems to be solved. Through algorithm complexity analysis, we evaluate the performance of different algorithms in solving problems, and use experimental methods such as simulation to verify and explain the evaluation conclusions, laying the foundation for algorithm innovation.

(4) Be able to apply algorithm design, analysis and implementation techniques to solve complex software problems. Provide systematic programming training for students to cultivate their programming skills, compile efficient and reliable programs and teamwork spirit.

Through the study of this course, students' abstract thinking ability, logical reasoning ability, ability to analyze and solve problems by comprehensively applying the knowledge they have learned, as well as software design and programming ability will be improved. Students will master the common strategies of algorithm design and analysis, and the skills and methods of algorithm analysis and design. At the same time, they should master the basic concepts and methods of computer algorithms. Through the discussion of some representative algorithms, they can achieve the purpose of understanding or mastering and applying. This can lay a solid foundation for independent work in algorithm design, software design and other work in the future.

Algorithms not only promote technological innovation, but also have a profound impact on social and economic development and ecological environmental protection. However, the coordinated development of key factors such as algorithms, data and computing power has created conditions for the advent of the artificial intelligence era. In the development of artificial intelligence technology, algorithms, data and computing power complement each other and jointly promote technological innovation and breakthroughs. Excellent algorithms require powerful computing power to support the training and reasoning process (including the learning of hundreds of millions of parameters), while data is the basis for the algorithms and computing power to play a role. The synergy of the three has gradually enabled artificial intelligence to move from theory to practical application, bringing many conveniences to human life, production and survival. Among them, algorithms are the core of artificial intelligence. Algorithms determine the learning ability, generalization ability, reasoning ability and decision-making ability of intelligent systems. Excellent algorithms are the foundation of the development of artificial intelligence, which determines the capabilities and effects of technology [6].

3 Write Interesting Algorithm Design Textbooks

In 2024, the author compiled and published a new textbook for this course, Algorithm Design Practice [6]. The exercises in each chapter are given meaningful aliases to increase the interest of the textbook, making the science and engineering textbook more literary and humorous (Table 1).

Table 1. A partial list is listed below

Chapter	Chapter Title
Chapter 3 Dynamic Programming	3.6.1 Packing Problem - A Puzzling Mathematical Journey of Dynamic Programming 3.6.2 The Longest Rising Subsequence - Exploring the Path of Rising 3.6.3 The Best Time to Buy and Sell Stocks Including the Freezing Period - I am not a Stock God 3.6.4 Block Painting - A Wonderful Interweaving with Algorithms 3.6.5 Digital Triangle - Exploration of Mathematical Art under Dynamic Programming 3.6.6 Mo Bai Da Jiu - Drinking with Flowers, Happy God of Wine 3.6.7 Improvement of Calculators - Mathematical Innovation is in You and Me 3.6.8 Array Jump - Who can get to the end 3.6.9 Nuclear Power Plant Problem - Explosion is Prohibited 3.6.10 Skating Game - Everyone has Shoes
Chapter 4 Greedy Algorithm	… 4.6.8 Farmers Racing Against Time - Don't Try to Eat My Flowers 4.6.9 Rectangle Division - Minimum Cost 4.6.10 Best Order - I Want to Be No.1
Chapter 5 Search	5.8.1 Solve Sudoku and unleash your wisdom! 5.8.2 Cut off the sequence! The programmer who saves the world … 5.8.10 Underground Maze - The Little Frog's Adventure

For example, "I want to be No. 1" and "Explore the road to rise" have positive meanings, "Don't try to eat my flowers" and "Little Frog Adventure" are full of joy, "Solve Sudoku problems and release your wisdom!" "Cut off the sequence! Programmers who save the world" humorously make students fall in love with algorithms and their majors.

4 Interesting Case Study Construction in Algorithm Design and Analysis Course

In today's era of rapid development of information technology, algorithms, as the core of computer science, are driving technological innovation. The "Algorithm Design and Analysis" course should not only impart theoretical knowledge and practical skills in algorithm design, but also guide students to establish a global awareness of peace and cooperation, and advocate the values of respecting diversity and embracing differences. On this basis, we can reduce energy consumption by designing more optimized algorithms, and deeply integrate the concept of green development into algorithm design and analysis, so as to promote the harmonious coexistence of technology and ecology.

4.1 Interesting Course on the Traveling Salesman Problem

The traveling salesman problem is a classic combinatorial optimization problem. Given a set of cities and the distance between each pair of cities, the traveling salesman needs to find the shortest path that starts from a certain city, passes through each city exactly once, and finally returns to the starting city.

The goal of the traveling salesman problem is to find the shortest path, which reflects the importance of efficiency and resource optimization. The course combines students' experience in planning travel to cultivate students' awareness of resource optimization and efficiency, so that they can understand how to maximize benefits through reasonable planning under limited resources. Students can also be organized to discuss how to improve efficiency in learning and work, such as arranging time reasonably and optimizing work processes. Let students transform from problem solvers to problem setters, abstract production problems into mathematical problems, and then establish mathematical models, use algorithms to solve problems, and build data verification algorithms.

4.2 Kruskal Algorithm Course Fun

Minimum spanning tree (MST): For the spanning tree of an undirected connected graph, the sum of the weights of each edge is called the weight of the spanning tree, and the spanning tree with the smallest weight is called the minimum spanning tree. Kruskal's algorithm is used to solve the minimum spanning tree.

The basic idea of Kruskal's algorithm is to take the edge as the dominant factor and always select the edge with the smallest weight currently available. Specifically:

Let a connected network with n vertices be G(V, E). Initially, construct a non-connected graph $T = \{V, \Psi\}$ with only n vertices and no edges. Each vertex in the graph is a connected component.

When selecting an edge with the smallest weight in E, if the two vertices of the edge fall on different connected components, add this edge to T; otherwise, that is, the two vertices of this edge fall on the same connected component, discard this edge (never select this edge afterwards. If it is selected, a loop will be formed, and a new edge with the smallest weight will be selected.

Repeat this process until all vertices are on the same connected component.

From the algorithm principle, Kruskal algorithm gradually builds the global optimal solution (minimum spanning tree) by selecting the edge with the smallest weight (local optimum), while avoiding the formation of loops. Loops destroy the properties of the tree, and the integrity of the tree must be considered. From this, several interesting cases can be constructed:

(1) Greedy gourmet: Just like in a buffet restaurant, you only take the most expensive one every time (local optimum), and finally put together a luxurious meal with the highest cost performance (global optimum), but you cannot take the same food repeatedly (avoid loops) - just "eat" out the minimum spanning tree.
(2) WIFI coverage: Use the shortest network cable to connect all routers (minimum spanning tree), but never connect them into a loop, leading students to be a "topological magician".
(3) Class friendship network: In class, students can shake hands (edges) in pairs, and each time choose the combination with the best relationship (minimum weight), but no small circles (loops) will appear, so that students can move and liven up.

4.3 Time-Pressed Farmer: Don't Even Think About My Flowers

Problem Description:The old man is the owner of a farm where he keeps N cows. One day, while he was away chopping firewood, he returned in horror to find the cows devouring the flowers in his garden. To minimize the damage, he immediately started herding the cows back to their respective barns. Each cow takes T_i minutes to return to its barn from its current position. While waiting to be moved, each cow continues to eat $D_i f$lowers per minute. No matter how hard the old man tries, he can only drive one cow at a time.Moving a cow to its barn and returning to the garden takes $2 \times T_i$ minutes (T_i to go, T_i to return). Once back in the garden, the old man can immediately proceed to the next cow without additional delay. Your task is to write a program to determine the optimal order in which the old man should drive the cows back to minimize the total number of flowers eaten.

The input consists of the following:

(1) The first line contains a single integer N, representing the total number of cows.
(2) The next N lines each contain two space-separated integers:

T_i: The time (in minutes) required to drive the i-th cow to its barn.
D_i: The number of flowers the i-th cow eats per minute while waiting.

Output Specification:

Print a single integer representing the minimum total number of flowers eaten.

This problem employs a greedy algorithm strategy, prioritizing cows with higher flower consumption rates (Di) to minimize the total cost of herding operations.

Define a struct 'Node' to represent cow attributes, where '*t*' denotes the time required for the cow to return to its barn, and '*d*' represents the flower consumption cost (flowers eaten per minute).

Iterate through each cow's attributes using a loop, store them in the struct array '*p*', and concurrently compute the total cost '*answer*' as the cumulative sum of all cows' flower consumption rates.

Define a custom comparator function 'cmp' to sort the cow array '*p*' in descending order based on the ratio (d/t) of flower consumption rate to barn return time, prioritizing cows with higher damage potential.

Initialize a variable 'sum' to track the total herding cost.

Enter a loop to iterate through the cow array p, computing the total cost following the greedy strategy. In each iteration: Subtract the current cow's flower consumption rate p[i].d from the global cost accumulator 'answer'; Accumulate p[i].d to the running total 'sum'; Compute the product of the cow's barn-return time (p[i].t) and flower cost (p[i].d), multiplied by twice the remaining global cost (answer); Add this product to the cumulative sum.

Design concrete test cases and have students role-play the cow-herding scenario. One student acts as the farmer, and multiple students play cows holding large signs showing their (T, D) values. Then The 'farmer' determines herding order while classmates calculate costs. Other students can then take the challenge. They may step up to play the farmer and attempt alternative herding sequences on stage, potentially achieving better numerical outcomes through different ordering strategies.

Through this engaging role-play activity, students develop a genuine passion for algorithms by physically experiencing optimization strategies in action.

4.4 Discussing the Algorithm for Breaking the Information Cocoon

Information cocoon refers to the process in which individuals gradually limit themselves to a certain type of information or viewpoints due to algorithm recommendations or personal choices during the process of obtaining information, resulting in a narrow field of vision and difficulty in accessing diverse information and viewpoints. Its formation mechanism mainly includes the following aspects [7, 8]:

The impact of personalized recommendation algorithms: Modern Internet platforms use data mining and machine learning technologies to accurately capture users' browsing history, search history, social behavior and other data, and push content that users may be interested in. Although this personalized recommendation improves the user experience, it may also lead to information homogeneity and trap users in information cocoons.

User psychological factors: Humans generally have a psychology of seeking common ground while reserving differences, tend to seek identity and avoid cognitive conflicts. In the process of obtaining information, users often actively screen and filter information that does not conform to their own views, further consolidating the information cocoon.

Social network effect: The "circle culture" in social networks strengthens the information sharing and resonance of views within the group, forming an "echo chamber effect" and limiting the scope of individual information acquisition.

Media environment changes: In the process of transformation from traditional media to new media, the way of obtaining information has shifted from passive acceptance to active selection. Users have unprecedented control over information, but excessive personalized choices may lead to increasingly narrow sources of information.

On April 26, 2025, Xinhua News Agency reported that Douyin algorithm engineer Liu Chang introduced the algorithm principle. In order to guide the algorithm to break the "information cocoon", the Douyin algorithm set up a special exploration dimension under the multi-objective modeling system. First, we recommend as many diverse contents as possible to users who have shown interests on the platform, and control the frequency of similar contents by methods such as diversity fragmentation, multi-interest recall, and support for niche (long-tail) interests. Second, we help users explore more new interests by using random recommendations, expanding interests based on user social relationships, search and recommendation linkage, and no longer displaying "not interested" content, so that users' active behaviors can influence the recommendation system and make recommendations more personalized and diversified [9].

In class, we invite students to brainstorm on how to build an algorithm to break the information cocoon. In the discussion, we make students aware of the harm of information cocoons, which will cause cognitive bias, social division and limited innovation. Because people are in information cocoons for a long time, they may form a single and one-sided cognition and find it difficult to accept different views and information; information cocoons may lead to the widening of cognitive differences between different groups, exacerbating social division and confrontation; lack of stimulation of multiple information, personal innovation ability and flexibility of thinking may be limited. At the same time, we also let students think deeply, do not fall into the information cocoon, and do not regard games, certain media, etc. as their spiritual opium, manage their extracurricular time well, and prevent dopamine addiction. We must establish correct values and outlook on life, and have firm willpower.

5 Conclusion

By exploring the fun of algorithm courses, we construct vivid course cases of specific algorithms such as divide and conquer, dynamic programming, greedy, search, network flow, etc. By explaining the historical background and process of the classic algorithms, as well as the solutions to real production problems, we encourage students to deepen their understanding and application of theoretical knowledge in practice, and further guide students to actively participate in algorithm-related competitions, such as ICPC (International Collegiate Programming Contest), Blue Bridge Cup Software and Information Talent Competition, College Student Mathematical Modeling Competition, Group Programming Ladder Competition, etc., to stimulate students' interest in algorithms, temper their willpower, strengthen their ability to work in teams, train their ability to analyze and solve practical problems, thereby improving their innovation ability and cultivating their thinking about their careers.

Acknowledgments. This study was funded by Provincial-level research project on teaching reform in higher education institutions in Jiangxi Province (JXJG-24-5-25);Provincial-level key project on teaching reform in higher education institutions in Jiangxi Province (JXJG-23-5-7); Industry-university cooperation and collaborative education project of the Ministry of Education (230801311034605); Innovation and entrepreneurship education and teaching reform project of East China Jiaotong University (1600223042, 1600223049).

Disclosure of Interests. The authors have no competing interests to declare that are relevant to the content of this article.

References

1. The website of the Central People's Government of the People's Republic of China, the State Council issued the "Plan for the Development of New Generation Artificial Intelligence". https://www.gov.cn/xinwen/2017-07/20/content_5212064.htm
2. Zhang, W., Bi, Z., Zhou, P.: Exploration and practice of ideological and political courses in algorithm design and analysis under STT teaching mode. Comput. Educ. (03), 126–129 (2022). https://doi.org/10.16512/j.cnki.jsjjy.2022.03.017
3. Ye, F.: Improving students' learning interest in C language teaching. J. Nanjing Popul. Manag. Cadre Coll. (04), 53–55 (2003)
4. Teng, L.: On how to stimulate students' learning interest in algorithm and programming teaching. J. Yanbian Educ. Coll. **28**(04), 83–84+88 (2014)
5. Xiong, Y.: Stimulate learning interest and promote self-learning. Sci. Consult. (Educ. Res.) (07), 66 (2015)
6. Li, X., Zhou, J.: Algorithm Design and Practice. China Water Resources and Hydropower Press, Beijing, May 2024. ISBN: 9787522624082
7. Flowing wine, breaking out of the cocoon: in-depth analysis and response to the "information cocoon" phenomenon, 09 April 2024. https://zhuanlan.zhihu.com/p/691604222
8. Cao, Y.: The coping strategies of college counselors under the prevalence of "fan circle culture". University (38), 89–91 (2021)
9. Xinhuanet: Revealing how algorithms help users break out of the "information cocoon": Douyin's open day reveals the algorithm principle, 16 April 2025. https://www.xinhuanet.com/tech/20250416/cb30d07cc64f497b938b82f551204e05/c.html.221

Research on AI-Driven Hierarchical Teaching Mode: A Case Study of Database Principles Course

Wei Yan(✉)

School of Cybersecurity, Liaoning Police College, Dalian 116036, Liaoning, China
yanwei1211@163.com

Abstract. To address the issue of unsatisfactory teaching effectiveness caused by the "one-size-fits-all" approach in traditional Database Principles course teaching, this paper proposes an AI-driven hierarchical teaching mode. By constructing a hierarchical teaching resource recommendation system based on student ability models and combining real-time learning situation analysis, complex teaching contents such as SQL practical operations and relational normalization theory are dynamically adjusted in difficulty and explained in a differentiated manner. Relying on the case of an AI teaching assistant in a university, this paper elaborates on the design concept, implementation process, and technical realization methods of this mode. Experimental results indicate that this mode significantly enhances the learning effectiveness and enthusiasm of students at different levels, providing new ideas and practical references for the reform of university curriculum teaching.

Keywords: AI-Driven · Adaptive Learning Path · Hierarchical Teaching · Dynamic Difficulty Adjustment

1 Introduction

In the context of the popularization of higher education, the learning foundations, abilities, and needs of student groups exhibit significant diversity. However, traditional Database Principles course teaching often adopts a "one-size-fits-all" mode, where teachers conduct teaching activities according to a unified schedule and depth, failing to meet the personalized learning needs of students at different levels [1]. This results in students with strong foundations feeling "underfed" and those with weak foundations struggling to "keep up," significantly reducing teaching effectiveness.

Meanwhile, the rapid development of artificial intelligence (AI) technology has brought new opportunities to education. AI applications in education are becoming increasingly widespread, from intelligent tutoring systems to personalized learning recommendations, gradually transforming traditional teaching modes [2]. Integrating AI technology with hierarchical teaching concepts to construct an AI-driven hierarchical teaching mode holds promise in addressing the pain points of traditional teaching and achieving more efficient and personalized instruction. Taking the Database Principles course as an example, this paper delves into the AI-driven hierarchical teaching mode,

W. Hong et al. (Eds.): ICCSE 2025, CCIS 2761, pp. 437–449, 2026.
https://doi.org/10.1007/978-981-95-7731-6_34

aiming to provide beneficial explorations and practical experiences for the reform of university curriculum teaching [3, 4].

2 Literature Review

2.1 Research on Hierarchical Teaching Theory

The theory of hierarchical teaching can be traced back to ancient educational thoughts, such as Confucius' concept of "teaching students in accordance with their aptitude". In the process of modern educational development, hierarchical teaching has gradually built a sound theoretical system. Its core essence lies in breaking through the traditional "one-size-fits-all" teaching mode. Based on multiple dimensions such as students' learning ability, knowledge foundation, and cognitive style, students are divided into different levels [1]. On this basis, for the cognitive characteristics, learning needs, and development potential of students at each level, differentiated teaching objectives are tailored - the basic level focuses on the solid mastery of knowledge, the advanced level emphasizes the training of thinking ability, and the elite level focuses on the cultivation of innovative application ability. At the same time, it matches gradient teaching contents. For example, the basic level mainly includes basic database concepts and simple operation skills, the advanced level adds complex query and data modeling contents, and the elite level introduces cutting-edge knowledge such as big data processing and database optimization. Moreover, diversified teaching methods are adopted, including lecture-based teaching at the basic level, case discussion-based teaching at the advanced level, and project-driven teaching at the elite level, ultimately achieving the maximum development of each student at their original level.

In the teaching exploration of database principle courses, the practical forms of hierarchical teaching are increasingly rich. Some scholars conduct quantitative evaluation on students' database basic knowledge reserve and logical thinking ability through pre-class diagnostic tests, and divide students into basic group, advanced group and innovative group accordingly. Students in the basic group focus on completing basic exercises such as creating database tables and writing simple SQL statements, the advanced group further studies complex contents such as multi-table join queries and view design, and the innovative group carries out database design and optimization work around actual projects. In addition, some studies adjust the hierarchical results periodically by dynamically tracking indicators such as students' classroom performance and homework completion quality [5]. However, the traditional hierarchical teaching mode has obvious limitations: on the one hand, the hierarchical standards mostly rely on teachers' subjective judgment formed through classroom observation and homework correction, which is difficult to fully cover students' implicit learning characteristics; on the other hand, once the hierarchical results are determined, they often remain fixed for a long period and are difficult to respond to the dynamic changes of students' abilities in real time. For example, when students in the basic group have reached the level of the advanced group through a period of study, their hierarchical affiliation cannot be adjusted in time, which restricts the further improvement of teaching effect.

2.2 Research on AI Applications in Education

The application of AI in the field of education has formed a multi-dimensional and in-depth development pattern, and its technical empowerment penetrates into the whole teaching process. Intelligent teaching systems, through technologies such as natural language processing and knowledge graphs, build intelligent models that simulate the teaching logic of human teachers. They can not only provide students with real-time explanation of knowledge points, but also answer personalized questions through dialogue interaction. For example, an intelligent mathematics tutoring system can locate weak knowledge points and generate targeted explanation videos by analyzing the types of errors in students' problem-solving steps [6]. Learning analysis technology, relying on big data mining algorithms, conducts in-depth analysis on multi-dimensional information such as students' classroom interaction data, online learning duration, and exercise error rate to build students' learning portraits [7]. A study successfully predicted the group of students at risk of dropping out by analyzing students' code submission records in online programming courses and provided intervention suggestions for teachers. Personalized learning recommendation systems, based on algorithms such as collaborative filtering and content matching, accurately capture students' learning preferences [8]. For example, they recommend database principle animation tutorials for students who prefer visual learning, and push programming practice projects for students who prefer practical learning.

In the teaching of database principle courses, the application exploration of AI technology has made certain progress. In addition to developing intelligent programming tutoring systems to detect SQL statement errors in real time and provide modification suggestions, some studies have built database knowledge graphs. Through AI algorithms, they identify students' deviations in concept understanding and automatically generate targeted remedial plans. For example, when the system finds that students frequently confuse the concepts of "primary key" and "foreign key", it will push special explanations containing comparative cases. However, current research mostly focuses on the application of AI technology in single teaching links, and the exploration of deep integration with hierarchical teaching is still insufficient [3]. In existing practices, AI mostly participates in certain links of hierarchical teaching as an auxiliary tool, such as data collection or resource recommendation, and has not formed an intelligent hierarchical system that runs through the whole process of "hierarchical diagnosis - dynamic adjustment - precise teaching". Especially in realizing dynamic stratification based on the real-time changes of students' abilities, there is a lack of mature technical frameworks and practical cases [5].

3 Design of AI-Driven Hierarchical Teaching Mode

3.1 System Overall Architecture

The AI-driven hierarchical teaching mode centers on a student ability model, combining real-time learning situation analysis to realize dynamic recommendation of teaching resources and adaptive adjustment of teaching difficulty. The system's overall architecture is shown in Fig. 1.

The system mainly includes the following modules:

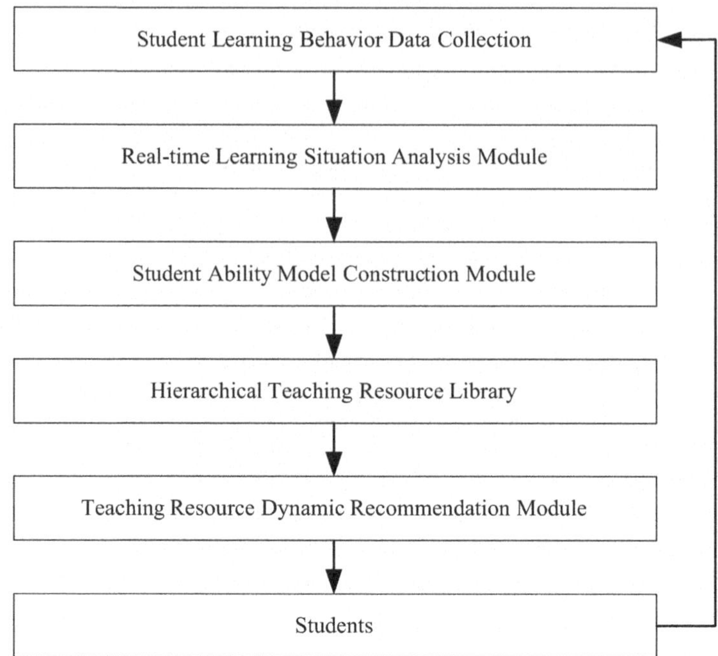

Fig. 1. System Overall Architecture of AI-Driven Hierarchical Teaching Mode

Student Learning Behavior Data Collection Module: Relying on the log system of the online learning platform, the behavior tracker of the programming practice environment, and the classroom interaction feedback terminal, a multi-dimensional data collection network is built. It captures real-time full-scene data of students in the study of database principle courses, including the distribution of error types in classroom answers, the number of modifications in homework submission, the code debugging steps in SQL programming practice (such as whether breakpoint debugging is used, debugging duration), the drag progress and pause nodes of teaching videos, the keyword extraction of forum questions, etc. For example, when students write "multi-table join query" code, the system will record details such as whether they miss join conditions, the number of times they modify conditions, and the execution efficiency of the final code.

Real-Time Learning Situation Analysis Module: It uses distributed data processing frameworks (such as Spark) to clean and extract features from the collected massive data, and combines machine learning algorithms such as decision trees and random forests to deeply analyze students' learning characteristics. Specifically, it includes: identifying weak knowledge chains by analyzing the correlation of answer errors (for example, students who frequently make mistakes in "foreign key constraints" often have an inadequate understanding of "relational models"); judging learning concentration through video viewing behavior (for example, students who frequently fast-forward in the "index principle" chapter may have concept understanding obstacles); evaluating problem-solving styles through debugging strategies in programming practice (for example, students who rely on hints and those who explore independently need differentiated guidance).

Student Ability Model Construction Module: Based on the output results of real-time learning situation analysis, a dynamic Bayesian network is used to build a time-series student ability model. This model decomposes the database principle course into 28 core knowledge points (such as SQL grammar, transaction processing, concurrency control, etc.), and each knowledge point corresponds to four ability levels: "unmastered, initially mastered, proficiently applied, innovatively expanded". The model can update the ability value of each knowledge point in real time. For example, after students successfully complete the "nested query" programming task three times in a row, the ability level of this knowledge point will automatically rise from "initially mastered" to "proficiently applied".

Hierarchical Teaching Resource Library: It divides resource levels according to the dual dimensions of "cognitive rules + disciplinary characteristics", and subdivides the teaching resources of database principle courses into basic level, advanced level and expansion level. The resources at each level cover a complete learning chain of "theoretical explanation, case demonstration, practical training, extended reading": the basic level includes animated tutorials with subtitles (such as demonstrating the "data table creation process" with cartoon characters), exercises with step-by-step hints (such as SQL statement filling exercises); the advanced level is equipped with video explanations of real enterprise cases (such as the table structure design of e-commerce databases), medium-sized projects that need to be completed independently (such as the database construction of student information management systems); the expansion level provides academic paper interpretations (such as "Consistency Algorithms for Distributed Databases"), industry cutting-edge technology white papers (such as application scenarios of NewSQL databases) and other resources.

Teaching Resource Dynamic Recommendation Module: Based on the real-time data of the student ability model, it uses a hybrid recommendation algorithm combining collaborative filtering and content similarity calculation to realize the precise matching and dynamic adjustment of teaching resources. The system generates a personalized learning list every day. For example, for students who are "initially mastering" "relational normalization", it pushes "paradigm transformation example" videos + "abnormal data detection" exercises; when it detects that the student's ability level in the "stored procedure" knowledge point has improved, it automatically transfers them from the advanced level resource pool to the expansion level and pushes practical cases of "stored procedure performance optimization". At the same time, it supports students to manually adjust the resource difficulty, and the system will optimize the recommendation strategy according to the feedback of the learning effect after adjustment.

3.2 Student Ability Model Construction

The student ability model is the core of the AI-driven hierarchical teaching mode. This study adopts a multi-dimensional evaluation method to construct the model, assessing students from three dimensions: knowledge mastery, learning ability, and learning attitude [9].

Knowledge Mastery: Three-dimensional indicators of "correct rate, complexity, stability" are used to evaluate the mastery depth of each knowledge point. The correct rate is the proportion of correct answers to exercises of specific knowledge points; complexity is assigned according to the cognitive difficulty of knowledge points (for example, "single-table query" is level 1, "dynamic SQL" is level 5); stability is measured by the score fluctuation coefficient of five consecutive tests. For example, in the "SQL aggregate function" exercise, a student has a 90% correct rate in simple questions (such as the application of COUNT function) and a 60% correct rate in complex questions (such as the combined use of GROUP BY and HAVING), with a score fluctuation coefficient of 0.15, indicating that they have a solid grasp of the basic usage but are insufficient in comprehensive application ability. The system will generate a mastery heat map for each knowledge point to intuitively present the shortcomings of students' knowledge structure.

Learning Ability: It constructs an ability evaluation matrix from three dimensions of "progress control, knowledge transfer, problem solving". The learning progress is calculated by comparing the deviation rate between the time when students complete phased tasks and the average time of the class (for example, students who complete the study of "transaction ACID properties" in advance have a positive progress coefficient); the knowledge transfer ability is evaluated by the performance in cross-knowledge point test questions (for example, the degree of understanding "SQL stored procedures" by analogy with "functions in programming languages"); the problem-solving ability is subdivided into "error diagnosis speed" (the time from error reporting to locating the cause), "strategy effectiveness" (whether the optimal debugging method is adopted) and "depth of independent exploration" (whether official documents or academic materials are consulted). For example, students who can locate the cause of "slow query" by analyzing the execution plan within 2 min have a significantly higher problem-solving ability rating than those who rely on teachers' hints.

Learning Attitude:
Quantitative evaluation is made through "participation, persistence, concentration". Participation covers the number of hands raised in classroom interaction, the originality of forum posts (such as whether they are copied and pasted), and the speaking time in group discussions; persistence is measured by the number of consecutive study days and the standard deviation of weekly study hours (for example, students who keep studying for 10 consecutive days have a higher persistence score); concentration is calculated by analyzing distraction behaviors during learning (such as the number of times non-teaching related web pages are opened during learning) and the completeness of task completion (such as whether the "extended reading" link is skipped). For example, students who

often watch teaching videos completely and upload notes have an excellent learning attitude rating.

Using machine learning algorithms (e.g., neural networks), a student ability model is constructed, updating in real-time based on learning behavior data to reflect dynamic ability changes.

3.3 Hierarchical Teaching Resource Design

The design of hierarchical teaching resources follows the principle of "targeted supply", closely links the knowledge system of database principle courses with the cognitive needs of students at different levels, and builds a three-stage resource system of "basic consolidation, ability improvement, innovative expansion" [10]. The resources at each level achieve "diversified forms, gradient difficulty, and application scenarios".

Subsequent Basic Level Resources: Facing students with weak knowledge reserves and lagging learning progress, they focus on the understanding of core concepts and the mastery of basic skills. The contents include: graphic tutorials on basic database concepts (such as sorting out the hierarchical relationship of "database, table, record" with mind maps), interactive exercises on basic SQL grammar (such as online editors that highlight grammar errors in real time and prompt modifications), and animation demonstrations of relational models (such as showing the corresponding relationship between "entities and attributes" with dynamic charts). The resource presentation form is mainly "audio-visual combination + step-by-step guidance". For example, SQL introductory tutorials adopt dual-screen videos of "teacher's explanation + real-time running effect of code", and exercises are set with "hint buttons" (click to view relevant grammar rules) to help students build learning confidence.

Advanced Level Resources: For students who have mastered basic knowledge and need to deepen their understanding and application, they focus on the integration of knowledge and the improvement of practical skills. The contents include: case studies on logical decomposition of complex SQL queries (such as equivalent conversion skills for converting "nested queries" into "join queries"), advanced applications of relational normalization theory (such as practical operations of the third normal form in eliminating data redundancy), and methodological guidance for database design (such as the complete process from demand analysis to E-R diagram drawing). The resource form is mainly "case-driven + task challenge". For example, provide a database backup of an enterprise's order management system and require students to optimize query statements to improve execution efficiency; design a "database performance bottleneck diagnosis" task, allowing students to put forward index optimization schemes by analyzing slow query logs.

Extended Level Resources: Facing students with strong learning ability and pursuing in-depth exploration, they focus on disciplinary frontiers and innovative applications. The contents involve: practical guides on advanced SQL technologies (such as using stored procedures to realize complex business logic, advanced usage of triggers in maintaining data consistency), engineering schemes for database performance tuning (such as the application of database and table sharding strategies in high-concurrency scenarios), and architectural analysis of distributed databases (such as the collaborative working mechanism between HBase and MySQL). The resource form is mainly "project research and development + academic exploration". For example, arrange students to participate in the design and optimization project of the "campus smart library" database, requiring them to submit technical schemes including performance test reports; recommend reading top conference papers in the database field and write critical reading reports.

4 Implementation of AI-Driven Hierarchical Teaching Mode

4.1 Teaching Implementation Process

The teaching implementation process of the AI-driven hierarchical teaching mode is shown in Fig. 2.

Course Initiation Stage: At the start of the Database Principles course, comprehensive initial data collection of students is completed using a "multi-dimensional diagnostic tool." The online test covers content of varying difficulty levels, including basic questions examining "fundamental database definitions," introductory questions involving "basic SQL statement structures," and a small number of extended questions on "preliminary understanding of relational models," to fully assess students' knowledge reserves. A questionnaire survey focuses on students' learning backgrounds, such as whether they have been exposed to programming languages, their level of understanding of databases, and their preferred learning methods (e.g., independent reading, video learning, or group discussions). After systematic integration and analysis, these data form an initial student ability model encompassing "knowledge foundation, learning habits, and potential abilities," providing a scientific basis for subsequent hierarchical teaching. For instance, students with programming foundations who can quickly grasp simple SQL logic will be marked as "having potential for advancement" in the model.

Teaching Resource Recommendation Stage: Based on the hierarchical results of the student ability model, the system customizes exclusive learning resource packages for students at different levels. Resources for students at the basic level focus on "consolidating fundamentals," including SQL basic grammar teaching videos with detailed subtitles (each segment lasting 10–15 min), single-table query exercises with immediate prompts (e.g., popping up "Please check the syntax of the WHERE clause" when an error is input), and graphic interpretation manuals of core database concepts. Resources for students at the advanced level emphasize "deepening application," including case analysis videos of complex query statements (e.g., explaining join queries through e-commerce order cases), medium-sized database design tasks (e.g., designing the table structure of a simple library management system), and topic guides for online case discussions (e.g., "How to avoid data redundancy in multi-table queries"). Resources for students at the extended level focus on "expanding innovation," covering practical tutorials on advanced SQL technologies (e.g., design and application of stored procedures), case analysis reports on database performance optimization (e.g., index optimization strategies for large e-commerce platforms), and interpretive articles on cutting-edge industry technologies (e.g., development trends of distributed databases). Students conduct learning activities according to the pushed resource list, and the system records the completion status of resources, such as video viewing progress and exercise accuracy rates.

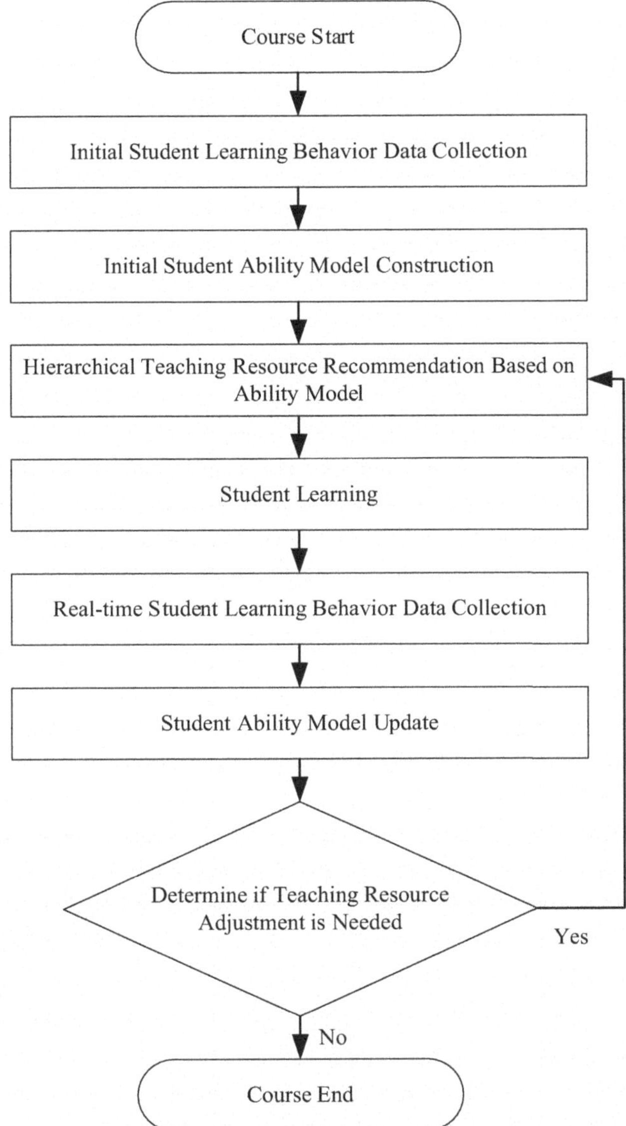

Fig. 2. Teaching Implementation Process of AI-Driven Hierarchical Teaching Mode

Learning Process Monitoring Stage: Throughout the students' learning cycle, the system captures learning behavior data in real-time through multiple channels to construct a comprehensive portrait of the learning process. During classroom interactions, the intelligent answering system records students' answer choices, thinking duration (interval from question display to answer submission), and the number of answer modifications. During online learning, it tracks teaching video viewing behaviors (e.g., replay times and pause durations in the "ACID properties of transactions" chapter), annotation status of e-textbooks (e.g., annotation content for the concept of "data consistency"), and speech content in learning forums (e.g., types of questions asked and activity levels in discussions). During programming practice, it records the SQL code writing process (e.g., whether logic is conceived before writing code, steps of code modification), types of errors encountered (e.g., keyword spelling errors, query logic errors), and ways of resolving errors (e.g., whether to consult help documents provided by the system, seek help from classmates or teachers). These data are transmitted to the background analysis system in real-time, providing a basis for subsequent updates to the ability model.

Teaching Resource Dynamic Adjustment Stage: Based on the real-time updated student ability model, the system regularly evaluates students' learning progress and dynamically adjusts teaching resources. When the system detects that a student performs excellently in learning tasks at a certain level (e.g., the accuracy rate of two consecutive assignments exceeds 85%, or scores high in understanding tests of complex knowledge points), it will automatically adjust them to a higher level, push corresponding advanced resources, and send an adjustment notification (e.g., "Congratulations on your outstanding performance in learning complex SQL queries; your learning resources have been upgraded to the extended level"). If a student encounters significant difficulties in learning at the current level (e.g., the accuracy rate of repeatedly submitted exercises is below 60%, or scores on basic concept tests remain low), the system will temporarily adjust them to a lower level, supplement basic resources for consolidation, and provide targeted tutoring suggestions (e.g., "It is recommended that you first review the join query part in SQL basic grammar; the system has pushed relevant review materials for you"). Teachers can view students' adjustment records through the background and manually intervene in special cases (e.g., delayed learning progress due to leave) to ensure the rationality of adjustments.

Course Completion Stage: After the course concludes, the system conducts a multi-dimensional comprehensive evaluation of students' learning outcomes. The evaluation content includes the final mastery level of each knowledge point (e.g., assessing mastery of knowledge points such as SQL programming and relational normalization through summative tests), performance during the learning process (e.g., resource completion rate, classroom interaction participation, and progress in programming practice), and ability to solve complex problems (e.g., quality of completing comprehensive database design tasks). Meanwhile, it summarizes and analyzes the learning data of the entire class, such as the average progress of students at different levels, the overall mastery of each knowledge point, and the usage effect of teaching resources, forming an analysis report on the course teaching effect to provide a reference for optimizing and improving the model.

4.2 Teaching Case Analysis

Taking a teaching class of the Database Principles course in a university as an example, an AI-driven hierarchical teaching model was implemented. There are 60 students in this class. Before the course started, the students were divided into the Basic Level (20 students), the Advanced Level (30 students) and the Extension Level (10 students) through an online test.

In the teaching session of SQL practical operation, students at the Basic Level first studied the instructional videos on basic SQL syntax and completed simple single-table query exercises. The system recorded students' answer status in real time. When a student's correct rate on single-table query exercises reached more than 80% and the average answer time met the requirements, the system promoted the student to the Advanced Level and delivered teaching resources on complex SQL query statements (such as join queries and nested queries). While learning complex query statements, students at the Advanced Level carried out practical operations through an online programming platform. The system conducted real-time analysis of students' programming codes to assess their grasp of knowledge points. If a student made repeated errors in join query exercises and failed to achieve the expected learning effect after a certain period of study, the system would temporarily adjust the student back to the Basic Level to strengthen the learning and practice of basic syntax. After mastering advanced SQL techniques, students at the Extension Level participated in actual database performance optimization projects. The system provided them with more challenging learning tasks and extended resources based on project progress and their performance.

In the teaching session of relational normalization theory, hierarchical teaching and dynamic adjustments were also implemented according to students' learning conditions. Students at the Basic Level focused on learning the basic concepts and application methods of the First Normal Form and the Second Normal Form, and consolidated their knowledge through simple case analyses and exercises. Students at the Advanced Level delved into the theory of the Third Normal Form and higher normal forms, and conducted exercises on complex relational schema decomposition. Students at the Extension Level studied optimization strategies of relational normalization theory in practical database design, and participated in group discussions and academic research activities.

5 Experimental Design and Result Analysis

5.1 Experimental Design

To verify the effectiveness of the AI-driven hierarchical teaching mode, a comparative experiment was designed. Two classes with similar academic backgrounds were selected, with one adopting the AI-driven mode (experimental group) and the other the traditional "one-size-fits-all" mode (control group). Both classes shared the same curriculum, duration, and instructor.

The experimental period lasts for one semester. Before and after the experiment, students from both classes are subjected to identical theoretical knowledge tests and SQL practical operation assessments, and their scores are recorded. Simultaneously, through questionnaire surveys and interviews, we aim to gauge students' satisfaction with the teaching mode and their learning experience.

5.2 Experimental Result Analysis

The Academic Performance Comparison: Post-experiment, theoretical and SQL practical scores were statistically analyzed, as shown in Table 1.

Table 1. Average Score Comparison Between Experimental and Control Groups

Class	Theoretical Knowledge Test Average Score	SQL Practical Assessment Average Score
Experimental	82.5	84.3
Control	75.2	73.8

The experimental group outperformed the control group in both theoretical and practical assessments, indicating the AI-driven mode's effectiveness in improving academic performance across diverse student levels.

Learning Satisfaction Survey: A satisfaction survey was conducted, with results shown in Table 2.

Table 2. Student Learning Satisfaction Survey Results

Class	Satisfied (%)	Unsatisfied (%)
Experimental	85	15
Control	60	40

The experimental group reported 85% satisfaction compared to 60% in the control group. Students appreciated the personalized resources and adaptive learning paths, which increased their motivation and engagement.

6 Conclusion and Outlook

This paper explored an AI-driven hierarchical teaching mode using the Database Principles course as a case study. By constructing a student ability model-based hierarchical teaching resource recommendation system and combining real-time learning situation analysis, dynamic resource recommendation and adaptive difficulty adjustment were achieved. Experimental results demonstrated improved academic performance and satisfaction, effectively addressing the "one-size-fits-all" issue in traditional classrooms.

However, the study has limitations. The student ability model requires further refinement to more accurately reflect true abilities, and the hierarchical resources' richness and quality need enhancement. Future research will optimize the ability model with more evaluation indicators and advanced algorithms, develop higher-quality resources incorporating technologies like VR/AR, and expand experimental scope to validate the mode's effectiveness and applicability across more courses and scenarios, providing stronger support for university curriculum reforms.

References

1. Tao, L., Mi, Q.: The online teaching reform and practice of database principles under the background of engineering certification. Creat. Educ. Stud. **11**(04), 705–710 (2023)
2. Xiao, T.: New opportunities, new challenges: reflections on higher education teaching models under generative artificial intelligence. Creat. Educ. Stud. **12**(5), 1–7 (2024)
3. Luan, H., Tsai, C.C.: A review of using machine learning approaches for precision education. Educ. Technol. Soc. **24**(1), 250–266 (2021)
4. Abuhassna, H., Awae, F., Adnan, M.A.B.M., Daud, M., Almheiri, A.S.B.: The information age for education via artificial intelligence and machine learning: a bibliometric and systematic literature analysis. Int. J. Inf. Educ. Technol. **14**(5), 700–711 (2024)
5. Molenaar, I., Horvers, A., Baker, R.S.: Dynamic student modeling in adaptive learning environments. IEEE Trans. Learn. Technol. **12**(3), 346–356 (2019)
6. Lee, C.A., Tzeng, J.W., Huang, N.F., Su, Y.S.: Prediction of student performance in massive open online courses using deep learning system based on learning behaviors. Educ. Technol. Soc. **24**(3), 130–146 (2021)
7. Llurba, C., Fretes, G., Palau, R.: Pilot study of real-time emotional recognition technology for secondary school students. Interact. Des. Archit. **52**, 61–80 (2022)
8. Tzeng, J.W., Lee, C.A., Huang, N.F., Huang, H.H., Lai, C.F.: MOOC evaluation system based on deep learning. Int. Rev. Res. Open Dist. Learn. **23**(1), 21–40 (2022)
9. Sathasivam, R.V., Rahim, S.S.A.: I do it better: how social and emotional learning environment enhances assessment for learning strategies in science classrooms. J. Int. Comp. Educ. **10**(2), 117–131 (2021)
10. Haider, U.: Innovative pedagogy: melding interdisciplinary and artificial intelligence in education. J. Environ. Sci. Technol. **2**(1), 176–183 (2023)

An Innovative Models for AI-Oriented Information Security Practical Capabilities Development

Pengcheng Liu, Yongwei Wang(✉), Xiaohu Liu, and Hao Hu

Information Engineering University, Zhengzhou 450001, Henan, China
wywyongwei@163.com

Abstract. Amidst the continuous advancement of artificial intelligence (AI) technologies driving social development, cultivating innovative talents oriented towards the AI era has become an unprecedented challenge for computer technology disciplines. As a multidisciplinary field, the traditional curriculum system and knowledge structure in computer technology education have demonstrated relative lag compared to the rapid evolution of AI technologies. To address this issue, we propose a 'four-dimensional integrated' training model from the perspective of professional development. Focused on enhancing innovation capabilities of computer technology students in the AI era, the model integrates four strategic components: curriculum system reconstruction, advanced pedagogical optimization, practical training innovation, and teaching methodology empowerment. The effectiveness of this training framework is rigorously validated through systematic implementation in contemporary educational practices.

Keywords: AI-Oriented · Information Security · Computer Technology · Integrated Innovation

1 Introduction

The ongoing technological revolution characterized by digitalization, networking, and intellectualization has opened new frontiers for economic and social development. Industrial digitalization continues to drive economic growth, while the advent of the AI era has profoundly transformed higher education paradigms. As a critical component of information security technology, computer science has undergone continuous iteration through the emergence of big data, artificial intelligence (AI), and data integration technologies. Notably, the rise of large language models (LLMs) has accelerated the intelligent transformation of computer science research. Against this backdrop of intelligent evolution in information security, cultivating students' innovation capabilities oriented toward future AI-driven development has become an urgent imperative in computer science education.

Addressing this challenge, we proposes a 'four-dimensional digital-intelligent transformation' model for nurturing innovation capabilities in computer science majors. Synthesizing current disciplinary developments and talent cultivation requirements, the

W. Hong et al. (Eds.): ICCSE 2025, CCIS 2761, pp. 450–461, 2026.
https://doi.org/10.1007/978-981-95-7731-6_35

framework integrates four strategic dimensions: (1) Reconstruction of disciplinary systems, (2) Advancement of high-order curricular content, (3) Innovation in practical training paradigms, and (4) Empowerment through teaching methodologies. The model's efficacy is rigorously validated through systematic implementation in contemporary educational settings, achieving a fundamental transition from knowledge acquisition to capability development.

2 Background

With the rapid development of artificial intelligence technology and the accelerated transformation of the global economy, the information security situation is also facing many challenges and transformation requirements, which need to be adjusted and optimized in the teaching and ability training of computer technology specialty.

2.1 Information Security in AI Era

Thanks to the wide application of artificial intelligence, big data and other technologies, social productivity and people's quality of life have been greatly improved, but it has also brought new risks and challenges to social development, especially the information security situation has become increasingly severe. With the endless emergence of new AI technologies, the object of information security work has gradually changed from paper and optical media to electronic media, and then to large-scale data processing. Security protection technology pays more attention to the protection of network information system on the basis of physical protection, and information management has changed from manual management to technology assisted and even intelligent assisted management.

Orienting the transformation and development of computer technology, relevant researchers also put forward some countermeasures. Under the information risk brought by the new technology in the digital age, we should strengthen scientific and technological innovation in the aspects of automatic and efficient early warning and preliminary processing, improving accuracy, and the combination of civil air defense and technical defense [1]. Improve the construction of computer science and technology regulations in the aspects of information system, mobile Internet and electronic document signs to adapt to the development trend of the era of big data [2]. In terms of data collection, training and application of large language model, the data security risks of generative artificial intelligence are analyzed [3]. To sum up, the new challenges faced by computer technology mainly include three aspects: Open Source Intelligence Association and aggregation brought about by big data analysis, network security risks brought about by the popularity of network information systems, and changes in intelligent auxiliary protection analysis brought about by artificial intelligence technology.

To navigate these tripartite challenges, a neuro-symbolic governance framework must be architected, merging AI's predictive prowess with regulatory logic. For Open Source Intelligence (OSINT) aggregation, deploy federated correlation engines where transformer models trained on cross-jurisdictional legal corpus dynamically redact sensitive entities during data fusion, while zero-knowledge proofs verify intelligence authenticity without exposing raw sources—achieving entropy-reduction in information chaos without compromising privacy. Concurrently, counter network security risks through autonomic cyber-immunity systems: neuromorphic computing hardware accelerates anomaly detection in 5G slicing environments by processing encrypted traffic spikes at nanosecond latency, while blockchain-orchestrated honeynets autonomously mutate decoy configurations via generative adversarial networks (GANs), deceiving advanced persistent threats into revealing novel attack signatures. These signatures then train living digital vaccine libraries that propagate immunization protocols across critical infrastructure through software-defined networking (SDN) arteries. Crucially, transform intelligent protection via sovereign AI alignment protocols—embedding constitutional constraints directly into large language models' latent spaces. For instance, network defense co-pilots generating DDoS mitigation strategies must satisfy formally verified safety predicates: mathematical proofs ensuring no collateral service disruption, with each decision auditable through homomorphically encrypted log trails meeting GDPR Article 30 obligations. Implementation demands triple-helix innovation: 1) Technological - Photonic tensor processors enable real-time vetting of AI-generated security policies at optical speeds; 2) Regulatory - Smart contract-based compliance engines automatically void operations violating Cybersecurity Law Article 26; 3) Sociotechnical - Citizen oversight DAOs (Decentralized Autonomous Organizations) govern vulnerability disclosure equilibriums using quadratic voting. Ultimately, this crystallizes as a continuous cyber-resilience metabolism—an organic defense ecosystem where quantum-resistant homomorphic encryption allows collaborative threat analysis on encrypted operational data, swarm intelligence optimizes firewall rule evolution through federated reinforcement learning, and cyber-physical systems achieve self-regeneration via neuromorphic self-healing fabrics detecting hardware tampering through electromagnetic fingerprinting. The emergent paradigm transcends reactive protection toward proactive civilization-scale immunization, positioning China's digital infrastructure as both technologically sovereign and inherently antifragile—turning adversarial evolution into fuel for collective security intelligence.

2.2 AI-Empowered Computer Technology Education

In the AI era, higher education needs to adapt to the development of new quality productivity, especially the construction of engineering majors needs teaching combined with the development of industrial technology. In terms of specialty construction, Ni [4] proposed a professional talent training path based on "Artificial Intelligence+", "Traditional Specialty+", production and education integration and innovative education in the AI era. Zhao [5] analyzed the 2024 horizon report of the American Association for higher education informatization, and explained that the key technologies affecting the development of higher education in the future include six items, including intelligent learning tools, intelligent learning analysis, hybrid learning mode, and micro certificate authentication. Wang [6] started from the new concept of knowledge in the AI era, put forward the new quality education concept of transforming from school education to lifelong education, and from knowledge transfer as the center to the realization of personalized learning, so as to cultivate talents who can work with intelligent machines and are good at innovation and creation. The adjustment of specialty construction in the AI era has three main characteristics: first, the education mode is transformed to multi-disciplinary integration, and traditional specialties are improved and empowered with the help of emerging technologies such as artificial intelligence or specialties in other fields. Second, the teaching content has changed from Limited traditional high-quality resources to globally shared intelligent resources, and from teacher-student interaction to in-depth teacher-student interaction. Third, the teaching method has realized the transformation from traditional classroom teaching to personalized teaching with the help of intelligent technology, and from knowledge transfer to ability shaping.

2.3 How to Cultivate Students' Innovative Ability?

In the face of the changes brought about by the AI era, the traditional engineering talents training mode still has a large space for optimization and adjustment in the knowledge structure, teaching methods, especially in the cultivation of innovation ability. In terms of the innovation ability training reform of higher education, Guo [7] took the intersection of information technology and nursing as an example and proposed the new engineering talent training path of teaching and research integration, cross hospital cooperation and curriculum intersection. Yan [8] analyzed the impact and challenges of generative AI on higher education, and proposed the transformation strategy of education in the digital age from knowledge learning to comprehensive application, from interpersonal collaboration to human technology collaboration, from knowledge-based to ability-based, from homogeneous development to unique growth. Wu [9] proposed a "five level whole chain" innovative talent training mode based on normal communication, knowledge foundation, system improvement, competition practice and mass entrepreneurship and innovation into the sea, aiming to build talent training elements for the frontier field of artificial intelligence. Combined with the characteristics and teaching practice of the computer technology specialty, the innovation ability model is constructed, which mainly includes the cross-border integration ability of information security computer technology including computer, management, law, artificial intelligence and network security interdisciplinary, the human-computer cooperation ability of AI enabling the comprehensive application of network security, physical security and data security computer technology, and the protection technology innovation ability of artificial intelligence technology combined with engineering practice.

This tripartite innovation model necessitates educational biomimicry frameworks that reconfigure engineering pedagogy as self-evolving cognitive ecosystems. Cross-domain integration is operationalized through neurolaw-embedded curricula where students architect blockchain-based evidence chains meeting both cryptographic integrity standards and Criminal Procedure Law Article 54 chain-of-custody requirements—simultaneously negotiating HIPAA-compliant data flows in simulated telemedicine attacks. Human-AI collaboration transcends tool usage via cognitive federalism: during cyber range exercises, spiking neural networks dynamically adjust threat difficulty levels by monitoring learners' galvanic skin responses, while GPT agents morph from assistants to adversarial trainers that generate polymorphic malware mimicking Lazarus Group TTPs (Tactics, Techniques, Procedures). Protection technology innovation crystallizes in quantum pedagogy laboratories implementing error-corrected knowledge distillation: students optimize homomorphic encryption parameters on photonic processors to secure federated learning workflows, with each engineering decision validated against both

Shannon entropy minima and National Encryption Standard GM/T 0022 compliance. Crucially, assessment shifts from competency verification to cognitive entropy reduction metrics—AI-driven neuroimaging tracks prefrontal cortex activation during zero-trust architecture design, quantifying how effectively learners suppress legacy TCP/IP mind-set interference when innovating post-quantum VPN protocols. Faculty become neuro-symbolic conductors orchestrating three-phase growth cycles: 1) Epigenetic priming through adversarial prompting drills that rewire neural pathways for regulatory-aware innovation; 2) Collective intelligence pollination via DAO-governed research hubs where students' blockchain-published threat models attract industry co-evolution; 3) Cognitive quantum annealing where superconducting qubit arrays simulate 10^18 solution spaces for 6G security dilemmas, compressing decade-long innovation cycles into semester projects. The emergent engineer embodies quantum-superpositioned mastery—fluent in Python and Contract Law Article 124 as complementary syntaxes, architecting self-sovereign digital infrastructures that encode China's cyber sovereignty directly into the topology of space-air-ground integrated networks.

3 Four-Dimensional Integrated Cultivation Model

In view of the demand for innovative ability training of computer technology professionals in the AI era, we propose a "four in one" innovative ability training mode based on the reconstruction of professional curriculum system, the optimization of high-level teaching content, the setting of innovative practice links, and AI enabled teaching methods.

3.1 Adjust the Professional Curriculum System

The traditional computer technology professional courses include four types of basic courses, professional courses, professional elective courses and comprehensive teaching links [10]. The reconstruction of the professional knowledge system based on the existing curriculum system is mainly carried out in three aspects. First, the professional courses are centrally adjusted according to the current situation of computer technology production and research, focusing on the supplement of big data analysis, association and aggregation data analysis, open source intelligence analysis and other contents, so as to cultivate students' cross-border analysis ability. Second, on the basis of updating the content of professional elective courses, we will add high-level AI general courses, including information hiding technology, natural language processing, etc., focusing on intelligent security inspection technology, intelligent auxiliary early warning technology, etc., to cultivate students' human-computer cooperation ability in using intelligent technology. The third is to introduce high-level innovation projects in the comprehensive training link, mainly including subject clubs, subject competitions, high-level completion projects, etc., to cultivate students' application ability and innovation ability in engineering practice.

In terms of specific implementation, the number and total class hours of basic courses and professional courses have been reduced, while the number of advanced courses and AI general courses has been increased. Finally, the total class hours of undergraduate training have been reduced from about 3400 class hours to about 2600 class hours. In the construction of teaching materials, according to the application of the latest artificial intelligence technology, the selection and self compilation of teaching materials are carried out, focusing on elective courses and high-level AI general courses. In terms of teacher construction, we will increase the proportion of young and middle-aged teachers in high-level innovation projects and AI general courses, readjust the content of professional core courses and professional elective courses, and select and increase the content of artificial intelligence technology.

3.2 Optimizing High-Level Teaching Content

The optimization of high-level teaching content focuses on the teaching of AI general courses in the reconstruction of curriculum knowledge system, mainly including updating and optimizing professional elective courses, setting up "AI+" courses and setting up interdisciplinary general courses [11].

First, in the optimization of professional elective courses, according to the development status of information and computer technology, add, delete or update knowledge points. For example, in the network engineering course, the traditional teaching contents include IP protocol, network OSI model, routing and switching technology, etc. on this basis, the courses of cloud computing, big data, SDN and automation are added, focusing on cultivating students' big data analysis and correlation ability for future work scenarios. Secondly, "AI+" courses are offered. For example, data hiding technology, based on the existing data hiding layer and data recovery, increases the technology of data confrontation and intelligent analysis, and cultivates students' application of agent technology in data hiding and data detection. Finally, in the interdisciplinary general education course, the construction of interdisciplinary integrated teaching content is carried out in combination with multidisciplinary knowledge, especially AI cutting-edge technology and change situation. For example, on the basis of existing laws and regulations, the course of artificial intelligence regulations focuses on how to improve the construction of information technology related regulations in the AI era and cultivate students' legal literacy and interdisciplinary application ability in combination with the generative artificial intelligence management regulations and artificial intelligence development initiatives issued by countries around the world, as well as the legislation of artificial intelligence.

3.3 Design and Implementation of Innovative Practice

As an engineering specialty, the practice teaching of computer technology specialty is particularly important. Its practice links include four parts: discipline basic experiment, professional experiment, expansion experiment and high-level experiment. The innovation in the practice link of artificial intelligence technology mainly focuses on professional experiments and high-level experiments, including computer technology, C language programming, python programming and other courses. According to the characteristics of different courses, frontier artificial intelligence technology experiments, interdisciplinary experiments and other subjects are added. Taking the core course of computer technology as an example, the practice of the course includes three modules: database design, system analysis and design, and network attack and defense.

In the database design module, the traditional practical subjects include database analysis, table construction, connection testing, etc. on this basis, combined with the development of information security situation, the information system design experiment of integrated database, front-end interface, LAN management is carried out to cultivate students' system engineering ability. In the information system analysis and design module, traditional subjects are mainly based on process development, but the popularity of big data and artificial intelligence technology makes AI assistance gradually become one of the main means of system design. Based on the update and development of artificial intelligence technology, cloud architecture design experiments are carried out on the basis of website system design. The network attack and defense module is a high-level experiment of computer technology specialty, including CTF (Capture The Flag) event attack and defense, AWD (Attack With Defense) event attack and defense, simulation range, etc. on the basis of this kind of attack and defense scenario, the experiment of Threat Intelligence Analysis and network deception defense is innovated according to the information security situation and course content.

3.4 AI-Enhanced Teaching Methodologies

The application of artificial intelligence technology has brought profound changes in the field of higher education, such as intelligent learning situation analysis, the construction of subject knowledge map, intelligent question and answer and so on [12]. The teaching means of computer technology specialty have been adjusted in three aspects in combination with the actual situation. The first is to realize the practical teaching from teacher-student interaction to Teacher-Student machine interaction, and then carry out AI teaching assistant and AI learning situation analysis. Second, based on the existing online and offline mixed teaching content of the professional courses of the basic courses of the discipline, the knowledge map of the field of computer technology was constructed, mainly including three core courses, including the fundamentals of program design, data structure, and principles of computer composition, and the professional ability map was initially constructed. The third is to build a high-level experimental system platform, which is connected with the setting of innovative practice links, including high-level modules such as situational awareness, network attack and defense, and continuously and dynamically update the experimental content.

This pedagogical triad converges into a cognitive cybernetic ecosystem where human-machine interactions transcend transactional assistance to achieve neural co-evolution. AI teaching assistants now deploy affective computing modules that analyze galvanic skin response and eye-tracking data during programming labs, dynamically adjusting code complexity levels to maintain optimal cognitive load—transforming instructor-student-machine relationships from hierarchical instruction to tripartite synaptic partnership. The domain knowledge graph evolves beyond static mapping into a living epistemic architecture: embedded with temporal graph neural networks, it autonomously restructures connections between foundational courses (e.g., linking pointer arithmetic in C to cache coherence protocols in computer architecture) based on real-time analysis of global research trends and industry vulnerability reports. Crucially, this graph becomes a pedagogical predictive engine, preemptively generating personalized learning paths before conceptual gaps manifest as errors in Python data structure implementations. High-level experimental platforms correspondingly morph into autonomous innovation crucibles—situational awareness modules integrate neuromorphic processors that convert raw packet captures into holographic attack scenarios through real-time ray tracing, while network attack-defense ranges employ generative adversarial networks to synthesize zero-day exploits calibrated to students' evolving skill profiles. These platforms implement continuous adversarial deployment: every student mitigation strategy automatically mutates into new attack vectors via differentiable programming, creating an infinite curriculum co-evolution loop. Underpinning this ecosystem are self-regulating blockchain pedagogic contracts that tokenize learning outcomes: smart contracts release encrypted lab credentials only upon mastering prerequisite concepts, while faculty intervention triggers when AI-detected cognitive dissonance exceeds neuroscience-defined thresholds. Ultimately, this crystallizes as cognitive singularity education—a seamless fusion where machine intelligence amplifies human creativity without ontological subsumption, producing engineers capable of co-designing self-aware network infrastructures that intrinsically balance NIST cybersecurity frameworks with Confucian pedagogical ethics.

4 Teaching Implementation of Innovative Ability Training

4.1 Outcome Based Teaching

As an engineering major, the teaching of computer technology needs to be combined with the actual work field. On the one hand, in computer technology, the outcome based teaching mode is used in the teaching process of professional courses and advanced courses [13], to see the achievement completion degree of middle school students in the process of learning and practice, and promote the implementation of student-centered education concept. On the other hand, in terms of professional ability, professional teaching needs to pay attention to the particularity of information security work, which not only requires students to have good professional and technical ability, but also have excellent ideological and political quality. Teachers should first establish correct teaching ideas and improve teaching ability [14]. By analyzing the role of artificial intelligence technology and information security work, guide students to fully understand the importance and intrinsic value of computer technology in the AI era, and comprehensively realize the cultivation of interdisciplinary and high-quality talents on the basis of teaching students in accordance with their aptitude.

This dual mandate necessitates cortico-pedagogical alignment frameworks where outcome-based education evolves into autonomous competency markets. Neural-symbolic AI agents now continuously recalibrate learning objectives by analyzing real-time industry threat intelligence feeds—transforming static syllabi into dynamic skill matrices. For instance, when NIST releases new post-quantum cryptography standards, blockchain oracles automatically trigger smart contracts that inject lattice-based cryptography modules into network security courses, while student progress is quantified through zk-SNARK-verified mastery tokens demonstrating zero-knowledge proofs of understanding BGP hijacking countermeasures. Simultaneously, ideological-political cultivation transcends abstract discourse through homomorphic ideological auditing:

during SDN controller programming exercises, students' code commits undergo real-time compliance checks against constitutional principles, with AI-driven sentiment analysis detecting deviations from core socialist values at the lexical level—flagging unethical optimization practices like traffic discrimination for remediation. This operationalizes virtue through cryptographic ethics enforcement. Crucially, professional aptitude develops within neuromorphic industrial simulators replicating cyber-physical attack scenarios: holographic ransomware incidents projected via AR glasses require students to negotiate payment dilemmas under Ministry of Public Security Article 285 constraints, with each decision training prefrontal cortex activation patterns for value-based technical judgment. Faculty transformation is catalyzed by pedagogical DAOs (Decentralized Autonomous Organizations) where educators stake reputation tokens to co-govern curriculum evolution, receiving automated royalties when their designed adversarial training scenarios are adopted by critical infrastructure partners. The ultimate manifestation is epistemic sovereignty ecosystems—self-balancing pedagogical architectures that generate AI-native engineers capable of architecting Confucian-encoded network infrastructures: autonomous intrusion detection systems that dynamically adjust alert thresholds based on socialist rule-of-law calculus, and self-healing data centers where hardware fault recovery prioritizes public service continuity per Cybersecurity Law Article 21. Herein lies the ontological shift: from training technicians to cultivating cybernetic philosopher-engineers who perceive TCP/IP stacks as embodiments of digital governance philosophy, transforming routers into sentinels of technological self-reliance.

4.2 Combining AI Knowledge

Computer technology work needs the empowerment of emerging technologies to realize the leap from traditional productivity to new quality productivity. Therefore, in addition to the adjustment and update of knowledge system, professional courses and AI general courses, both course teaching and practice teaching need to be based on the implementation means and teaching content combined with digital intelligent technology. For example, in the programming implementation of big data analysis experiment, students use DeepSeek, Kimi and other large language models to program auxiliary file processing, and automatically generate small programs for data format processing, which not only solves repetitive work, but also exercises students' ability to process data in the whole process and forms teacher-student interaction in practical teaching. Finally, the goal of training students to have a shared vision in the AI era and to be able to use AI technology well is achieved.

This pedagogical symbiosis evolves into cognitive co-programming ecosystems where AI transcends assistive tools to become constitutional collaborators. Students now engineer prompt chaining pipelines that embed domain constraints directly into LLM interactions—for instance, generating GDPR-compliant data anonymization scripts by initializing DeepSeek with Article 4 definitions as immutable system prompts, while Kimi agents autonomously refactor network log parsers under formal verification of Cybersecurity Law Article 21 compliance. Crucially, such collaboration cultivates algorithmic constitutionalism literacy: learners dissect AI-generated code through dual lenses—evaluating computational efficiency via Big-O analysis while auditing ethical alignment using NIST AI RMF frameworks. Practice teaching correspondingly adopts adversarial co-creation models where students prompt-engineer offensive AI agents simulating APT TTPs (Tactics, Techniques, Procedures), then collaboratively develop mitigation strategies with defensive LLMs constrained by Geneva Convention-inspired digital warfare conventions.

Underpinning this is neuromorphic assessment infrastructure: FPGA-accelerated platforms track micro-expressions during human-AI debugging sessions, quantifying cognitive load distribution while blockchain notarizes contribution graphs. Faculty transform into prompt architects designing constitutional guardrails—e.g., embedding "Three Laws of Cybersecurity" into LLM latent spaces via RLHF. The emergent paradigm achieves sovereign AI co-learning: graduates architect neuro-symbolic SOCs (Security Operations Centers) where Chinese-developed LLMs like DeepSeek autonomously correlate threat intelligence under Cryptographic Law Article 24 constraints, while human analysts focus on strategic deception frameworks. Ultimately, this crystallizes dual-code citizenship—engineers fluent in Python and Socialist Core Values as complementary syntaxes, co-evolving with constitutional AI to pioneer new quality cybersecurity productivity grounded in technological self-reliance and digital civilization confidence.

4.3 Innovation Project Implementation

In terms of AI innovation projects, the practical innovation projects represented by discipline competitions and discipline clubs are one of the important links in the application of AI technology, which can enable students to receive training through the practical application of AI technology, obtain opportunities for practical innovation, and realize the cultivation of talents with innovation ability and engineering ability. In terms of on-the-job internship practice, we will carry out internship practice in the computer technology department in combination with the characteristics of the computer technology specialty. The training mode has been implemented for 3 rounds and 6 shifts in total. It has achieved good results in the second classroom, which is dominated by subject clubs, subject competitions and internships. In the past three years, students majoring in computer technology have won about 12 special awards and first prizes in the subject competitions. In addition, it has guided undergraduates to convert 12 original patents and publish 15 academic papers, and has achieved some results in cultivating innovative ability.

These empirical outcomes catalyze the evolution of innovation pipelines into cognitive industrialization ecosystems. Discipline competitions now operate as neuromorphic proving grounds—blockchain-secured challenge platforms deploy adversarial GANs that autonomously escalate problem complexity based on real-time FMRI scans of participants' prefrontal cortex activation, optimizing challenge-response cycles for neural plasticity enhancement. Patents undergo neuro-symbolic maturation: student inventions like homomorphic-encrypted intrusion detection modules are stress-tested in digital twin cities simulating 10^8 attack vectors, while reinforcement learning agents validate novelty against global patent landscapes using quantum annealing accelerators. Crucially, academic publications transform into living knowledge graphs—each paper becomes a dynamic node in federated learning networks, where industry consortiums inject real-world data streams to continuously refine student-proposed algorithms.

The internship architecture correspondingly adopts autonomous apprenticeship markets. AI-orchestrated talent exchanges match students with enterprises via zero-knowledge proof credentials—Smart contracts release genomic data analysis permissions only when interns demonstrate FHE (Fully Homomorphic Encryption) mastery during hospital cybersecurity drills. Faculty now curate neuro-competitive DAOs where competition trophies mint as NFTs governing curriculum voting rights, while corporate sponsors fund brain-computer interface labs that convert competition insights into cortical implants enhancing spatial reasoning. The emergent paradigm achieves cognitive capital conversion: graduates initiate neuro-industrial foundries producing China-certified encryption chips designed via competition-honed intuition, with each silicon die embodying competition-forged cognitive patterns. Ultimately, this manifests as new quality innovation productivity—transforming competition endorphins into algorithmic innovation, patent filings into digital sovereignty infrastructure, and academic citations into national strategic advantage matrices.

5 Conclusion

Facing the application prospect of artificial intelligence technology in the field of computer technology, we put forward the cultivation mode of undergraduate higher education talents' Innovative Ability Based on the reconstruction of professional curriculum system, the optimization of high-level teaching content, the setting of innovative practice links, and AI enabled teaching methods. Based on the adjusted and optimized curriculum system, the teaching combining the field of computer technology and cutting-edge AI knowledge is realized, and through the implementation of AI innovation project, the engineering ability and innovation ability of students are improved, laying a good foundation for students to engage in computer technology related jobs. In the future, the adjustment and optimization of the training mode of innovative ability of computer technology professionals will be continuously promoted according to the application and development of artificial intelligence technology.

References

1. Libin, Z.: Research on college network information security protection in the digital economy era. Proc. Bus. Econ. Stud. **7**(2), 132–137 (2024)
2. Qisheng, D.: Research on the teaching reform of college computer basic courses driven by intelligent technology. Educ. Reform Dev. **7**(4), 189–195 (2025)
3. Wei, G., Zhang, Z., Zhang, S.: The application of generative artificial intelligence in the teaching of machine learning courses in colleges and universities. Front. Educ. Times **6** (7) (2024)
4. Ni, H., Zhang, Z., Cheng, G.: Research on the construction of compound talent training system in local colleges and universities in the digital intelligence era. J. Wuhan Univ. Sci. Technol. (Soc. Sci. Ed.) **23**(06), 645–649 (2021)
5. Zhao, F., Dai, Y.: Key technologies and development scenarios of digital transformation of higher education – interpretation of EDUCAUSE horizon report 2024 (teaching and learning edition). China Educ. Inf. **30**(12), 44–57 (2024)

6. Wang, Z.: Constructing a new pedagogical system and developing new quality education – starting with the new concept of knowledge in the digital age. Open Educ. Res. **30**(3), 15–23, 36 (2024)
7. Xing, G., Zou, Z., Jia, S.: Collaborative driving of teaching and research, multidimensional cross integration – exploration on the training path of new engineering talents with the intersection of information technology and nursing. Res. High. Eng. Educ. (05), 15–20 (2024)
8. Yan, Y., Ding, J., Gao, Y.: Generative AI empowers the transformation of education in the digital age. Open Educ. Res. **30**(02), 42–48 (2024)
9. Wu, Z., Li, D.: Innovative talent training for the frontier of artificial intelligence. Res. High. Eng. Educ. (05), 48–53 (2023)
10. Liu, B.: Smart classroom leads the digital transformation of teaching: trends, characteristics and practical strategies. Res. Audio Vis. Educ. **44**(08), 71–79 (2023)
11. Luo, H., He, L., Liu, B.: Exploration of the flipped classroom educational model for cognitive education of specialized computer majors. J. High. Educ. Teach. **1**(6) (2024)
12. Zhang, R.: Discussion on the application of computer technology in mechatronics. Educ. Discuss. **7**(1) (2025)
13. Yang W.: A three-phase professional development approach to improving robotics pedagogical knowledge and computational thinking attitude of early childhood teachers. Comput. Educ. 231105282–105282 (2025)
14. Lee, H., Bryan, M.L.: Integrating AI in teacher education: exploring the impact on preservice teacher competencies. Prof. Dev. Educ. **51**(3), 478–494 (2025)

Data-Driven I^3 Framework: Modeling and Visualization for Applied Higher Education

Yundi Guo, Xianghua Fu(✉), and Yongsheng Liang

Shenzhen Technology University, Shenzhen, China
fuxianghua@sztu.edu.cn

Abstract. In the context of modern industrial system development and economic transformation, higher education faces three major challenges in cultivating applied talents: limited internationalization, insufficient integration between industry and education, and weak connections between innovation and teaching. Many institutions struggle with decision-making due to a lack of effective feedback mechanisms for tracking educational development. This paper introduces the I^3 (Internationalization, Integration, Innovation) Higher Education Development Assessment Model, which is based on constructivist learning theory, Bloom's taxonomy, and behaviorist learning principles. The model uses data-driven methods and visualization tools to monitor talent development indicators and provide evidence-based support for educational decision-making. Research results show that the model effectively improves the quality of applied talent training and supports sustainable institutional growth.

Keywords: Data-Driven Assessment · Educational Visualization · Applied Talent Cultivation · Higher Education Development

1 Introduction

In the context of modern industrial system construction and economic transformation, higher education institutions face significant challenges in advancing applied talent cultivation, particularly in terms of internationalization lag, insufficient industry-education integration, and inadequate innovation-education convergence. The absence of a robust development feedback mechanism often leads to misjudgments in self-assessment and strategic planning, making it difficult to formulate scientific and efficient decisions.

To address these three major challenges, we propose the "I^3 Integration, Student-Teacher-Enterprise Co-development" concept, which emphasizes the deep integration of internationalization, innovation, and industry to promote collaborative development among students, teachers, and enterprises. This concept provides a comprehensive framework for addressing the core challenges in applied talent cultivation.

W. Hong et al. (Eds.): ICCSE 2025, CCIS 2761, pp. 462–475, 2026.
https://doi.org/10.1007/978-981-95-7731-6_36

However, the implementation of this concept faces additional challenges in data management and analysis. Data management chaos and comprehension bias present significant obstacles. Without systematic digital analysis, data leads to fragmented management, low efficiency, and frequent errors, which not only delays problem resolution but also reduces information transparency and weakens external trust. Additionally, the lack of intuitive visualization tools creates information asymmetry in decision-making, affecting communication and understanding, and diminishing organizational credibility.

To overcome these data management challenges, we develop the I^3 Higher Education Development Assessment Model, which integrates data-driven approaches, modeling, and visualization with the "I^3 Integration, Student-Teacher-Enterprise Co-development" concept. The development of this model is grounded in constructivist learning theory [4] and Bloom's taxonomy of educational objectives [2]. The former emphasizes the active and practical nature of learning, suggesting that learners construct knowledge through personal experience, reflection, and interaction, which guides our approach to data collection and analysis. The latter emphasizes the hierarchical and diverse nature of educational objectives, helping us develop more comprehensive and detailed assessment indicators. Within this theoretical framework, our model can effectively collect and analyze student learning data to demonstrate learning outcomes and progress in practical activities, thereby stimulating students' interest and motivation. The educational objectives are transformed into specific assessment indicators, with visualization tools providing intuitive displays of student achievement, offering precise assessment feedback and personalized learning guidance for teachers and administrators.

The model addresses key challenges in data management and analysis faced by higher education institutions in advancing applied talent cultivation. Through the construction of a scientific quantitative evaluation system and the application of digital analysis and visualization technologies, the model can intuitively present and accurately assess the development status of internationalization, innovation, and industry elements, thereby optimizing talent cultivation quality. Furthermore, the model ensures data standardization and comparability, enhances information transparency, and promotes communication and cooperation among different departments and stakeholders. As a result, this model provides institutions with an effective tool for dynamic monitoring of development status, timely strategy adjustment, and resource optimization, addressing broader challenges including internationalization lag, insufficient industry-education integration, and inadequate innovation-education convergence.

2 Data Architecture and Analysis Framework

In the context of increasing informatization, while achievement management systems have been widely adopted in higher education institutions [5], several areas require improvement. The main limitations are as follows:

(1) **Imbalance in Research and Teaching Achievement Records:** Current systems predominantly focus on research outputs such as publications and research projects, while inadequately documenting teaching-related activities including curriculum development and student activities. This limitation hinders comprehensive and detailed presentation of teaching effectiveness, potentially impeding educational innovation exploration.
(2) **Insufficient Coverage of Applied Content:** Systems often concentrate on internal affairs such as research and competitions, while providing inadequate coverage and organization of key aspects relevant to applied universities, including university-enterprise cooperation, enterprise development, and industry-education integration. This restricts the system's support for applied talent cultivation.
(3) **Limited International Information Organization:** Despite the current research evaluation system having certain reference value domestically, it remains limited in organizing crucial information regarding international exchanges and internationalization levels. This may affect institutions' competitiveness and influence on the global stage.

This paper constructs a comprehensive I^3 information system that tightly integrates internationalization, innovation, and industry, systematically organizing higher education development data related to high-quality applied talent cultivation. The collected data categories are shown in Table 1.

2.1 Data-Driven Analysis and Decision Model

University rankings such as QS World University Rankings, Times Higher Education World University Rankings (THE), and U.S. News Global Best Universities have long provided rich data analysis frameworks for higher education development [1]. However, these ranking systems have limitations in reflecting comprehensive university strength, particularly in their overemphasis on academic research and scientific output quantification, while insufficiently addressing the multi-dimensional characteristics of applied talent cultivation emphasized in China. In computer science education, with the deepening practice of the "New Engineering" education concept [7], this limitation becomes particularly prominent. Traditional ranking systems focus more on academic research and scientific achievements, overlooking the crucial value of computer science in practical applications, social services, industry-academia integration, and innovation capability cultivation. This paper proposes a data-driven analysis and decision model based on the I^3 framework, focusing on evaluating universities' performance in internationalization, industry-education integration, and innovation-education convergence. By collecting and analyzing various data on research outputs, teaching activities, university-enterprise cooperation, and international exchanges, the model employs digital analysis and visualization techniques to intuitively present key indicators and trends in these areas, providing scientific and precise decision support for educational administrators. The core parameters are shown in Table 2.

Table 1. Data Categories and Their Significance

No.	Data Category	Significance
1	Research Papers	Track academic output and support performance evaluation
2	Patent Information	Reflect technology transfer and industry alignment
3	Copyrights	Establish academic rights and asset protection
4	Innovation Competition Awards	Quantify innovation outcomes and teaching feedback
5	Research Projects	Monitor resource effectiveness and decision-making
6	Teaching Research Papers	Document teaching reform and academic development
7	Teaching Research Projects	Validate teaching methods and model evolution
8	Textbooks and Monographs	Standardize quality teaching content
9	Teaching Awards	Set excellence benchmarks and incentives
10	Major Event Organization	Measure service capacity and resource integration
11	Curriculum Development	Ensure plan implementation and quality monitoring
12	University-Enterprise Cooperation	Connect industry-academia chain and talent model
13	Enterprise Exchange	Guide major optimization and cultivation plans
14	Student Internships	Bridge theory-practice and assess capabilities
15	Student Employment	Evaluate market fit and system optimization
16	Faculty-Student Entrepreneurship	Foster innovation ecosystem and knowledge transfer
17	Activity Participation	Assess quality education and second classroom
18	High-quality Profiles	Track talent growth and development paths
19	International Student Exchange	Monitor global cultivation effectiveness
20	International Faculty Exchange	Build academic capital and innovation
21	International Cooperation	Enhance cross-border research collaboration

2.2 Parameter Settings

The key parameters of the model are shown in Table 3.

2.3 Normalization Process

In multi-dimensional university development assessment, normalization is essential to eliminate unit differences and enrollment scale interference. This process establishes comparable benchmarks, prevents assessment sensitivity decay due to data saturation, and ensures weights reflect strategic value rather than numerical magnitude.

Each parameter requires annual normalization for proper comparison and calculation. The normalization formula is:

$$N_{i,t} = \frac{P_{i,t}}{N_{i,max} \cdot Z_t} \tag{1}$$

where:

- $N_{i,t}$ represents the normalized value of parameter i in year t
- $P_{i,t}$ represents the actual value of parameter i in year t

Table 2. Core Parameters and Their Significance

Category	Parameters	Significance
Internationalization	Overseas Study	Reflects student international competitiveness
	Student Exchange	Evaluates cross-cultural practice capabilities
	Faculty Exchange	Measures faculty internationalization level
	Activities	Monitors global campus ecosystem
	Overseas Experience	Ensures international curriculum standards
	Curriculum Standards	Validates transnational education equivalence
	English-taught Courses	Assesses bilingual teaching quality
	International Projects	Measures global research collaboration
	International Classes	Validates international education models
	International Labs	Evaluates cross-border R&D capabilities
Innovation	Research Papers	Measures academic innovation capability
	Patents	Reflects technology transfer potential
	Copyrights	Evaluates knowledge accumulation
	Innovation Awards	Assesses practical innovation ability
	Teaching Research Projects	Monitors teaching reform implementation
	Textbooks	Measures curriculum standardization
	Teaching Awards	Evaluates teaching excellence
	Conference Organization	Assesses academic influence
	Vertical Projects	Reflects basic research strength
	Horizontal Projects	Evaluates social service contribution
Industry	Industry Projects	Measures industry-education integration
	Industry Funding	Evaluates industry collaboration intensity
	Technology Transfer	Validates innovation chain integration
	Student Internships	Assesses practical skill development
	Student Employment	Reflects talent-market alignment
	Faculty-Student Startups	Measures innovation ecosystem vitality
	Industry Awards	Evaluates industry recognition
	Industry Courses	Validates curriculum responsiveness
	Enterprise Exchange	Monitors industry interaction frequency
	Partner Enterprises	Measures service network coverage

- $N_{i,max}$ represents the normalization maximum of parameter i
- Z_t represents the enrollment scale in year t

2.4 I^3 Composite Index

The I^3 composite index consists of three components:

$$I_t^{intl} = \sum_{i=1}^{n_{intl}} (W_i \cdot N_{intl,i,t}) \tag{2}$$

Table 3. Key Parameters and Descriptions

Parameter	Description	Purpose
Z	Enrollment Scale	Controls other parameters based on institutional size and positioning
N_{max}	Normalization Maximum	Normalizes independent indicators proportionally to enrollment
W	Base Weight	Determines importance in I^3 analysis
W_t	Faculty Development Weight	Measures correlation with faculty development
W_s	Student Development Weight	Measures correlation with student development
W_c	Industry Development Weight	Measures correlation with industry development
I^3	I^3 Composite Index	Evaluates internationalization, industry, and innovation performance
G	Development Index	Assesses faculty, student, and industry development

$$I_t^{ind} = \sum_{i=1}^{n_{ind}} (W_i \cdot N_{ind,i,t}) \tag{3}$$

$$I_t^{inno} = \sum_{i=1}^{n_{inno}} (W_i \cdot N_{inno,i,t}) \tag{4}$$

$$I_t^3 = I_t^{intl} + I_t^{ind} + I_t^{inno} \tag{5}$$

where n_{intl}, n_{ind}, and n_{inno} represent the number of parameters for internationalization, industry, and innovation respectively, and W_i is the base weight.

2.5 Development Index

The development index evaluates three key aspects:

$$G_t^{teacher} = \sum_{i=1}^{n} (W_{i,t} \cdot N_{i,t}) \tag{6}$$

$$G_t^{student} = \sum_{i=1}^{n}(W_{i,s} \cdot N_{i,t}) \tag{7}$$

$$G_t^{industry} = \sum_{i=1}^{n}(W_{i,c} \cdot N_{i,t}) \tag{8}$$

where $W_{i,t}$, $W_{i,s}$, and $W_{i,c}$ represent the weights for faculty development, student development, and industry development respectively.

2.6 Time Series Analysis for Trend Prediction

Time series analysis models [6] are employed to analyze and predict university development trends across different time points. These models analyze historical data to forecast future indicator trends. In the I^3 information system, time series analysis helps administrators predict future indicator changes, enabling long-term development strategy formulation, preventing sudden issues, and ensuring sustainable development. By analyzing historical data such as "overseas study" and "research papers," the model predicts these indicators' changes over the coming years.

The k-year prediction formula is:

$$\hat{P}_{i,t+k} = \alpha_t P_{i,t} + \alpha_{t-1} P_{i,t-1} + \alpha_{t-2} P_{i,t-2} + \cdots \tag{9}$$

where α is the annual weight coefficient that decays over time, and $P_{i,t}$ represents the actual value of indicator i in year t.

2.7 Unsupervised Learning-Based Parameter Auto-Update

Initial parameter settings are based on historical experience and domain knowledge, providing baseline rationality for system initialization and anchoring fundamental value orientations for educational assessment during the data-scarce phase. However, as the system guides long-term university development, the educational ecosystem exhibits continuous evolution characteristics. Static parameter systems cannot adapt to policy orientation changes, technological development iterations, and assessment dimension reconstruction brought by university strategic transformations, necessitating the introduction of dynamic update mechanisms [3].

Through dynamic adjustment of extreme values and weights, the system avoids subjective bias from manual presets while capturing implicit correlations between elements from continuously accumulated objective data. This maintains the assessment model's sensitivity to real development trends, ultimately achieving a paradigm shift from "experience-driven" to "data-knowledge dual-driven" assessment.

Parameters such as N_{max}, W, W_s, W_t, and W_c are initially set based on experience. After system deployment, they are dynamically updated through unsupervised learning using annually collected university data, with gradual fine-tuning guided by Chinese higher education development needs.

N_{max} is updated using a sliding window combined with statistical distribution, introducing the enrollment scale factor:

$$F_{scale,t} = \frac{S_t}{\bar{S}} \tag{10}$$

where $\bar{S}$ is the mean enrollment scale within the sliding window T_Y. Using a fixed-length sliding window T_Y referencing recent years' data, we calculate:

$$\mu = \frac{1}{T_Y}\sum_{t=1}^{T_Y} P_t \cdot F_{scale,t} \tag{11}$$

$$\sigma = \sqrt{\frac{1}{T_Y}\sum_{t=1}^{T_Y}(P_t \cdot F_{scale,t} - \mu)^2} \tag{12}$$

The normalization maximum is updated using a 3-sigma threshold (99.7% confidence interval):

$$N_{max}^{new} = \max(\mu + 3\sigma, N_{max}^{old}) \tag{13}$$

W is updated using correlation matrices. Let $N_{i,t}$ be the normalized data for parameter i in year t, we calculate the Pearson correlation coefficient between time series:

$$r_{ij} = \frac{\sum_{t=1}^{T}(N'_{i,t} - \bar{N'_i})(N'_{j,t} - \bar{N'_j})}{\sqrt{\sum_{t=1}^{T}(N'_{i,t} - \bar{N'_i})^2}\sqrt{\sum_{t=1}^{T}(N'_{j,t} - \bar{N'_j})^2}}, \quad i,j = 1,2,\ldots,n \tag{14}$$

Constructing an $n \times n$ correlation matrix R, where r_{ij} represents the correlation coefficient between parameters i and j, we calculate the average correlation for each parameter:

$$ac_i = \frac{\sum_{j=1,j\neq i}^{n} r_{ij}}{n-1} \tag{15}$$

The parameter weights are updated as:

$$W_i^{new} = \alpha \cdot W_i^{old} + (1-\alpha) \cdot ac_i \tag{16}$$

where $0 < \alpha < 1$ is a tuning factor balancing the influence of original and newly calculated weights.

The weights for student, faculty, and industry development (W_s, W_t, W_c) are updated using PCA to identify correlations. First, we arrange all parameter time series into a $T \times n$ data matrix X and standardize it to zero mean and unit variance. We then calculate the covariance matrix $S = \frac{1}{T-1}X^T X$, perform eigenvalue decomposition, and select the top k largest eigenvalues as principal components, forming a new $n \times k$ matrix V_k. The loadings $L = V_k$ are used to update the weights:

$$W_{i,s}^{new} = \alpha W_{i,s}^{old} + (1 - \alpha) \cdot |L_{i,1}| \tag{17}$$

$$W_{i,t}^{new} = \alpha W_{i,t}^{old} + (1 - \alpha) \cdot |L_{i,2}| \tag{18}$$

$$W_{i,c}^{new} = \alpha W_{i,c}^{old} + (1 - \alpha) \cdot |L_{i,3}| \tag{19}$$

Through time series analysis and other digital methods, the I^3 index provides comprehensive insights into institutional development. It enables trend prediction and status evaluation across internationalization, industry, and innovation domains, while identifying key influencing factors. These analytical capabilities support evidence-based decision-making for educational administrators, facilitating high-quality development in applied higher education.

3 Visualization and Analysis Dashboard

The complex I^3 higher education development assessment model is transformed into intuitive and easily comprehensible information visualization through multiple visualization tools. This transformation aims to convert complex data into accessible information displays that support educational administrators' decision-making processes. The visualization system encompasses five key dimensions:

(1) Internationalization level, evaluating overseas study, international exchange, and global collaboration projects
(2) Innovation capability assessment, analyzing research outputs, patents, and innovation competition achievements
(3) Industry-education integration depth, monitoring university-enterprise cooperation, internship participation, and graduate employment
(4) Student and faculty development, tracking academic and professional growth trajectories
(5) Overall development trends, utilizing time series analysis and heat maps for real-time monitoring and early warning of key indicators

This comprehensive visualization approach enables administrators to make data-driven decisions and implement timely interventions for institutional development.

3.1 I^3 Composite Index

Through the annual changes of normalized and weighted internationalization index I_t^{intl}, innovation index I_t^{inno}, and industrialization index I_t^{ind}, the system demonstrates universities' development changes and comprehensive performance in internationalization, innovation, and industrialization. This provides managers with intuitive data support for overall development trends, facilitating comprehensive analysis and decision-making. As shown in Fig. 1:

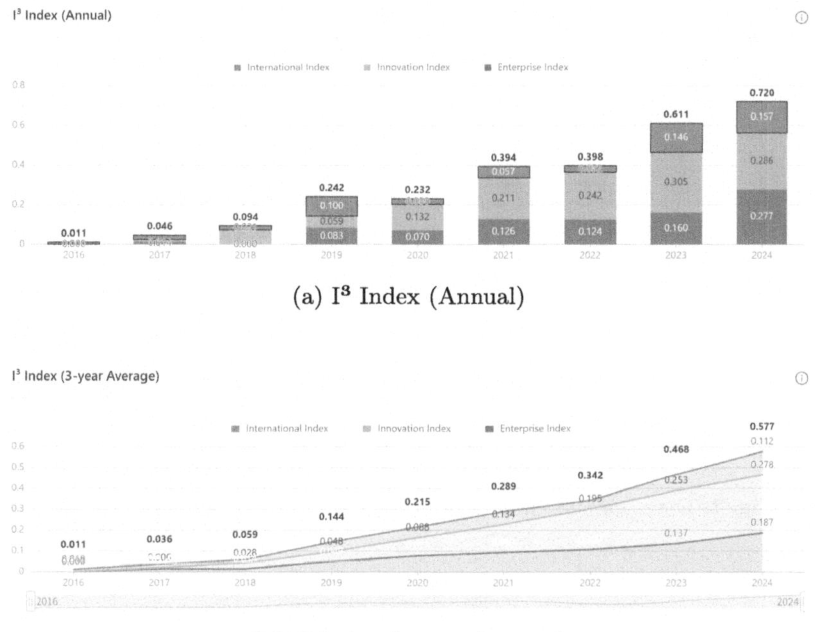

(a) I³ Index (Annual)

(b) I³ Index (3-year Average)

Fig. 1. Example of I^3 Composite Index

3.2 Student-Teacher-Enterprise Development Index

The student development index $G_t^{student}$, teacher development index $G_t^{teacher}$, and enterprise development index $G_t^{industry}$ are calculated based on their respective weight parameters. These indices are presented using grouped bar charts to demonstrate the development status of students, teachers, and enterprises across different years, providing data support for analyzing university development across various dimensions, as shown in Fig. 2.

The Sankey diagram further reveals the detailed I^3 distribution among students, teachers, and enterprises, providing insights into the balance of development across these three dimensions, as illustrated in Fig. 3.

3.3 Radar Analysis of Development Dimensions

The radar chart analysis provides a comprehensive visualization of the development status across different dimensions. By mapping the normalized values of various indicators onto a radar chart, we can intuitively observe the strengths and weaknesses in each dimension, as shown in Fig. 4.

This visualization enables educational administrators to identify areas requiring immediate attention and strategic improvement. The radar chart effectively demonstrates the balance and distribution of development across international-

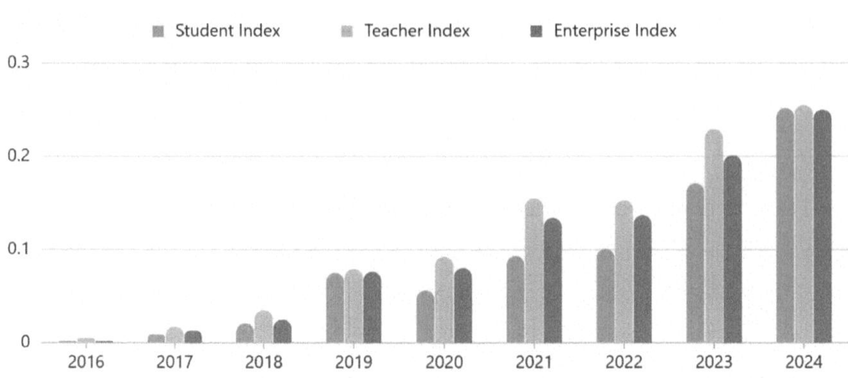

Fig. 2. Development Indices of Students, Teachers, and Enterprises

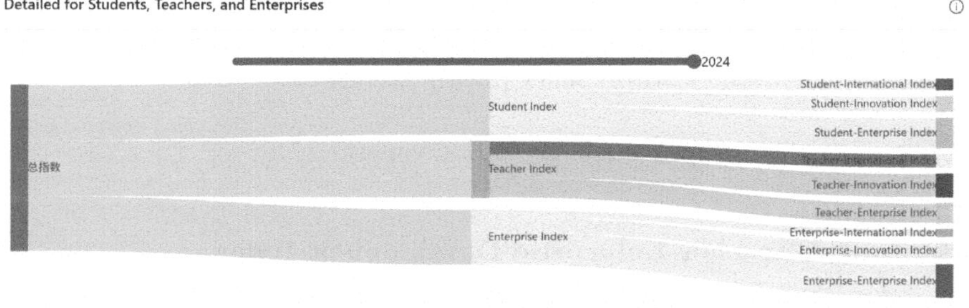

Fig. 3. Example of Detailed I^3 Indices for Students, Teachers, and Enterprises

ization, innovation, and industry integration dimensions, facilitating data-driven decision-making for institutional development.

3.4 Heat Map Analysis and Trend Warning

The comprehensive development level is visualized through a heat map of the composite index, combined with growth rate curves from the past three years to analyze temporal change characteristics. This approach provides educational administrators with a holistic view of development trends and key variable correlation analysis, enabling them to trace the causes of acceleration or deceleration phases and dynamically optimize institutional development strategies, as shown in Fig. 5.

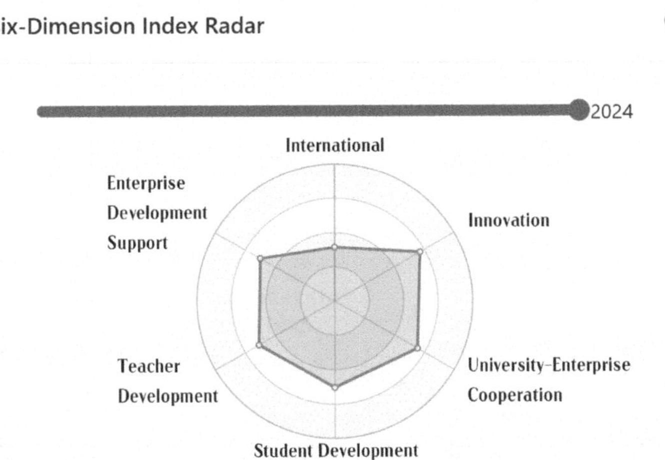

Fig. 4. Radar Analysis of I^3 Development Dimensions

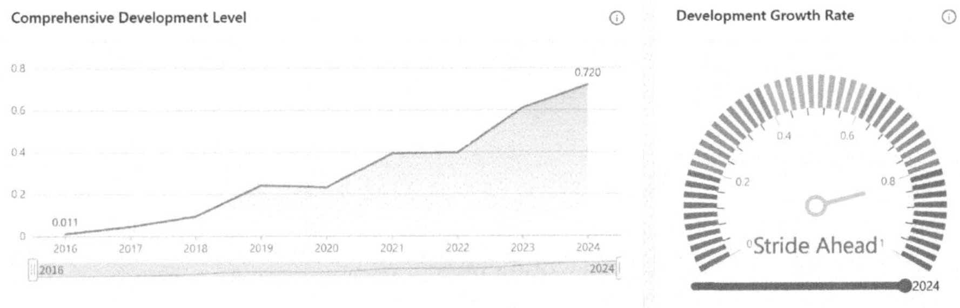

Fig. 5. Heat Map Analysis of I^3 Development Trends

4 Closed-Loop Optimization Mechanism and Practical Outcomes

The I^3 model establishes a comprehensive closed-loop optimization mechanism for higher education, as illustrated in Fig. 6. This mechanism systematically integrates data from enterprises (cooperation, internships, employment), faculty (research, courses, mentoring), and students (research, competitions, practice) into the I^3 core model. Through intelligent analysis, it generates key indices—student, teacher, and enterprise development—which drive targeted strategies such as curriculum optimization, international exchange, faculty development, and university-enterprise collaboration. The outcomes of these strategies are continuously fed back into the model, enabling real-time quality assessment, dynamic adjustment, and sustainable improvement in education, talent cultivation, and industry-education integration. The closed-loop process encompasses three core dimensions:

1. Personalized learning path optimization based on student development indices
2. Dynamic teaching quality improvement through faculty development indices
3. Industry-education integration enhancement via enterprise collaboration indices

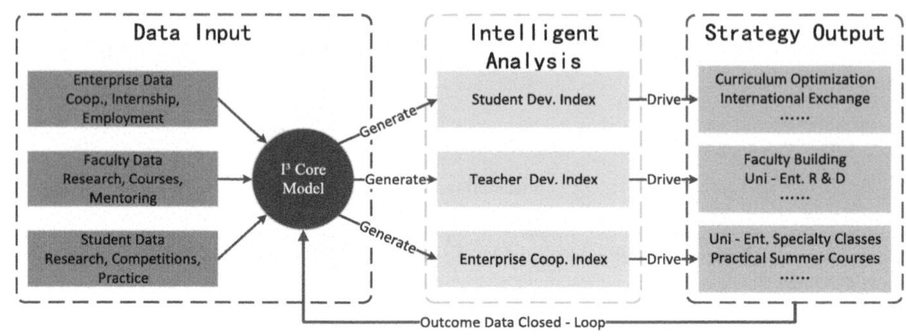

Fig. 6. Closed-Loop Optimization Mechanism of I^3 Data-Driven Higher Education Development

This data-driven feedback loop ensures systematic, adaptive, and iterative advancement of institutional development.

The implementation of the I^3 data-driven assessment and visualization system in our School of Big Data has significantly advanced student, faculty, and university-enterprise collaboration. For students, there have been over ten thousand participations in innovation activities, nearly 500 innovative projects, and more than 150 national competition awards. Nearly 20% of graduates join top companies such as Tencent and Huawei each year. For faculty, achievements include 7 provincial-level teaching projects, over 30 Ministry of Education collaborative projects, 17 textbooks, and more than 200 high-level academic papers. In university-enterprise cooperation, the school has established several provincial-level joint programs with Huawei and Tencent, built over 10 joint labs and internship bases, and students have participated in over a thousand enterprise projects, earning more than 30 enterprise awards. These results demonstrate the effectiveness of the I^3 closed-loop mechanism in enhancing innovation, teaching quality, and industry integration.

5 Conclusion

This paper presents the I^3 Higher Education Development Assessment Model, which integrates quantitative analysis, dynamic modeling, and visualization to build a multidimensional, data-driven evaluation and feedback system. By precisely quantifying key indicators and visualizing trends, the model provides scientific support for educational decision-making and enables continuous, closed-loop optimization of institutional development. Practical application demonstrates significant improvements in student innovation, faculty research and teaching, and university-enterprise collaboration. Most importantly, the I^3 model effectively addresses the three major challenges faced by applied universities—insufficient internationalization, inadequate industry-education integration, and limited innovation-education convergence—thereby supporting the enhancement of higher education quality and the cultivation of innovative talent. The I^3 framework offers a replicable paradigm for sustainable and connotative development in applied higher education.

References

1. Aguillo, I., Bar-Ilan, J., Levene, M., Ortega, J.: Comparing university rankings. Scientometrics **85**(1), 243–256 (2010)
2. Bloom, B.S., Engelhart, M.D., Furst, E.J., Hill, W.H., Krathwohl, D.R., et al.: Taxonomy of educational objectives: the classification of educational goals. Handbook 1: Cognitive domain. Longman New York (1956)
3. Bolsinova, M., Maris, G., Hofman, A.D., van der Maas, H.L., Brinkhuis, M.J.: Urnings: a new method for tracking dynamically changing parameters in paired comparison systems. J. Roy. Stat. Soc.: Ser. C (Appl. Stat.) **71**(1), 91–118 (2022)
4. DeVries, R., Zan, B., Hildebrandt, C., Edmiaston, R., Sales, C.: Developing constructivist early childhood curriculum: practical principles and activities. Early Childhood Education Series, ERIC (2002)
5. Liu, X., Guo, J., Jiang, J.: Retracted article: The design of college student achievement management system based on GA-BP network. Soft. Comput. **28**(Suppl 2), 489–489 (2024)
6. Sapankevych, N.I., Sankar, R.: Time series prediction using support vector machines: a survey. IEEE Comput. Intell. Mag. **4**(2), 24–38 (2009)
7. Shuguang, L., Yunyan, Z., Chengwei, W., Long, Z.: Path of high quality development of application-oriented undergraduate universities in the new era. In: Proceedings of the 2023 8th International Conference on Distance Education and Learning, pp. 327–332 (2023)

Reflections on the Construction of Digital Courses for Older Adults Education

Junjie Cao[1(✉)] and Zhonghua Jiang[2]

[1] Jing'an Branch, Shanghai Open University, Shanghai 200040, China
cjj@sjdc.net.cn

[2] Shanghai Jing'an District College, Shanghai 200040, China

Abstract. This research focuses on the construction of digital courses for older adults education, aiming to address the "digital divide" and promote high-quality development in older adults education. It analyzes the current status, identifying challenges such as homogeneous course design, insufficient specialized resources, and lagging support systems. The study proposes key construction contents, including a multi-dimensional service system, integration of online-offline learning, integration of information technology, and strengthened digital learning guidance. Optimization paths are suggested, such as improving the "content + technology + service" framework, enhancing platform construction, establishing evaluation-driven management, and boosting teachers' digital capabilities. The research highlights the importance of user-centered design and interdisciplinary collaboration to create inclusive, intelligent digital education ecosystems for older adults, facilitating their integration into the digital society and lifelong learning.

Keywords: Older Adults Education · Digital Courses · Digital Divide

1 Introduction

In the past few decades, our society has undergone tremendous changes. The rapid development of information technology has profoundly transformed our way of life and education. Digitalization has become the "dividend" of the era for people's new lifestyle. However, for most older adults, digitalization has become an "insurmountable digital divide" [1]. As an important social cause, older adults education is also keeping pace with the times to adapt to the needs and challenges of the digital era. Digitalization can fully expand the coverage of education, effectively solve the problem of unbalanced distribution of older adults education resources, and realize the diversification of learning paths for older adults. Among them, the construction of digital courses for older adults education is a key measure for the digital transformation.

Against the backdrop of the rapid development of digital technology, digital courses have evolved alongside transformations in original course resource formats (such as digital teaching materials, multimedia audio-visual products, online resources developed by taking network technology as the carrier, etc.) to changes in the form of the courses themselves (such as micro-courses, MOOCs, open courses on cloud, etc.). The

W. Hong et al. (Eds.): ICCSE 2025, CCIS 2761, pp. 476–487, 2026.
https://doi.org/10.1007/978-981-95-7731-6_37

construction of digital courses not only emphasizes the application of technology or the integration of resources but also needs to pay attention to the people in the courses, including the subjectivity of teachers and students, and the ubiquitous support services.

The use of digital courses can break through the limitations of time and space, and provide older adults with learning opportunities that are anytime, anywhere, interconnected, and real-time interactive through learning platforms and mobile applications. Digital technology can also provide older adults with learning resources in a personalized manner, and make adaptive adjustments according to their interests, abilities, and learning progress, so as to improve learning effects and sense of gain. In addition to the application of technology, dimensions such as curriculum resource integration, curriculum implementation forms, and the main body of digital curriculum implementation are also equally important. How to deepen and advance the digital empowerment of older adults education in all aspects, enhance the digital learning ability of older adults, and create a new model featuring inclusiveness and universality for learners—this has become a matter of utmost research and discussion value in the field of older adults education..

2 Current Situation of the Construction of Digital Courses for Older Adults Education

In an aging society, it is evident that the COVID-19 pandemic has exacerbated the "digital divide" among older adults in the AI-driven society. The most intuitive manifestations include difficulties in access, usage barriers, and lack of relevant knowledge. In the construction of digital courses for elderly education, we have found that practical dilemmas such as the learning obstacles of older adults themselves, the lagging construction of teaching staff and support service environments for digital courses, as well as inherent social perceptions and investment scales, affect the long-term and effective promotion of digital course construction for older adults education.

2.1 Analysis of the "Digital Divide"

While the number of internet users has grown rapidly in recent years, a considerable proportion of older adults still fail to access the convenience afforded by the internet. Drawing on the four-dimensional model proposed by the National Telecommunications and Information Administration (NTIA) [2], this study collected and analyzed feedback from the current elderly population regarding the "digital divide" through surveys, interviews, focus groups, and other research methods. The summarized findings are as follows:

Access Gap (Differences in Infrastructure and Support Environment). Elderly individuals exhibit disparities in both subjective capabilities and objective conditions when it comes to utilizing the internet or smart devices, accessing digital resources, and obtaining support services. These differences primarily stem from variations in infrastructure availability and the comprehensiveness of technical support, leading to gaps in internet connectivity and usability across different demographic groups.

Skill Divide (Differences in Digital Literacy). In the face of the rapidly evolving digital landscape, significant heterogeneity exists among the elderly population regarding their methods, extent, and proficiency in using digital devices and associated software. Individuals lacking digital skills struggle to fully leverage internet resources, creating a divide between them and those possessing higher levels of digital literacy. This challenge is commonly manifested as an inability to use digital technologies effectively ("cannot use").

Content Exclusion (Interface Design Inadequate for Age Demographics). Internet content and interface design may fail to adequately account for the specific characteristics and needs of certain user groups. For instance, some websites or applications feature overly complex interfaces or small font sizes, rendering them unsuitable for elderly users. Furthermore, content often targets younger demographics, inadvertently excluding others. Compounding this, the physical decline associated with aging can lead to operational difficulties, such as difficulty reading or hearing, inaccurate clicking, unsmooth finger swiping, and slower reaction times. These physical limitations contribute to the challenge of using digital tools effectively ("cannot use well").

Motivational Differences (Resistance to Technology Adoption). Clear differences in willingness and motivation towards adopting digital technologies are observed across various groups. Some elderly individuals express fear of online fraud or hacking, coupled with concerns about privacy breaches stemming from their perceived lower capacity for self-protection. This manifests as reluctance to engage with digital platforms ("dare not use"). Others avoid online methods unless absolutely necessary, preferring to delegate tasks to others or stick to traditional approaches when feasible. This resistance, often driven by perceived inconvenience, is commonly expressed as unwillingness to use digital technologies and services ("unwilling to use"). Consequently, even when these individuals possess the necessary access and skills, their reluctance contributes to the digital divide relative to more proactive adopters.

Additionally, the research indicates that the lack of effective social support constitutes a critical factor hindering the mitigation of the digital divide. While many elderly individuals express a desire to utilize smart devices and engage with digital technologies, they often face significant barriers: a lack of accessible instruction, uncertainty about where to acquire skills, difficulties in self-learning, and challenges in obtaining timely assistance when problems arise. This reluctance to impose on their children further exacerbates the issue.

2.2 Challenges in Digital Curriculum Construction for Older Adults Education

The quality of curriculum construction directly affects the quality of older adults education. Multi-dimensional and diversified curriculum design needs to be designed, planned, demonstrated, practiced, and replanned on the basis of researching the learning needs of older adult groups. At present, the homogenization phenomenon of online courses for older adults education is relatively obvious [3], and the scientificity and older adult-friendliness are uneven. Some of them are presented in the form of public general courses, and there are few regional and characteristic courses. In addition to the development of the content of the courses themselves, digital teaching materials supporting online courses are also essential. It is a bridge, link, and catalyst to help older adult students learn knowledge, study theories, and master skills. Older adults are also more accustomed to learning "followed by" teaching materials. However, compared with the huge number of older adult learning groups, the number of digital special teaching materials for the characteristics of older adult learners is not large, and many of them are shells [4] or deletions of the content of traditional teaching materials. In addition, some online courses have problems such as low clarity, slow regeneration, insufficient feedback, and disconnection from actual needs, which will affect the learning enthusiasm of older adult learners.

The main constructors of digital courses for older adults education are generally Open Universities, Adult Higher Education Institutions, Community Colleges, and Senior Universities across the country. They adopt approaches such as self-construction, "self-construction + purchase", and purchase according to the characteristics of disciplines and courses. Learners carry out learning through customized learning platforms, WeChat, mobile APPs, and other channels. However, the various sectors have not yet formed a joint force in the construction of older adults education courses, the scope and intensity of cooperation are insufficient, and the radiation effect of high-quality resources is not strong. In the balanced allocation of regional resources, the advantages of certain professions or industries have not radiated to different types of older adult learning groups.

3 Main Contents of the Construction of Digital Courses for Older Adults Education

The construction of digital courses for older adults education should first be based on the characteristics and needs of older adult learners, take the reform of classroom teaching methods as the focus, take the improvement of teachers' intelligent teaching ability as the key, take the integration of digital course resources as the support, and take the improvement of course evaluation as the guarantee. The construction process necessitates comprehensive top-down planning, and the integration mode of online and offline, the combination of teaching and tools, the use path of resources, and the interaction form of learners should be considered as a whole from the initial stage. so as to break the boundaries of the traditional older adult teaching mode in terms of time and space, expand the scope of teaching services, extend the link of support services, and provide older adult learners with a more multi-dimensional, finer-grained, and more intelligent learning experience.

3.1 Constructing a Multi-dimensional Service System to Extend the Coverage of Courses

The construction of digital courses for older adults education should be based on the learning needs of older adult learners, and through the support and innovation of digital technology, provide older adult groups with a comprehensive and ubiquitous learning service from multiple dimensions to help older adults integrate into the digital era. Its essence is to start from the high-frequency application needs or learning pain points of older adult learners, take curriculum resources and intelligent teaching models as the solution path, and build a learning service system in which online and offline are organically integrated and physical and virtual complement each other, so that the learning process is convenient, effective, and diversified. For different course contents, use digital technology, information equipment, or innovative applications to enhance the user perception of learners through strong interactive, experiential, simulated and other learning forms; at the same time, use technology such as learning process data, behavior records, and user portraits to provide learners with personalized services, such as more targeted resource recommendations and learning evaluations. It can include the following five dimensions (see Fig. 1).

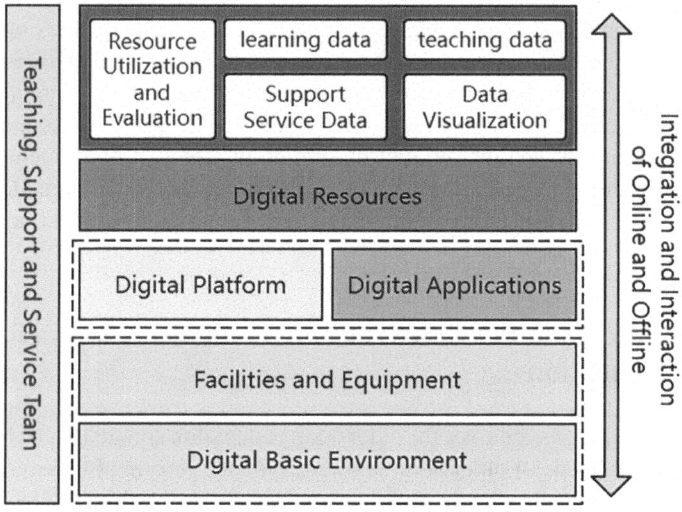

Fig. 1. Multidimensional Service System for Digital Courses

Basic Environment and Facilities. Including teaching places and digital basic environments that meet course requirements, such as network coverage, access via Internet of Things (IoT) devices, live broadcast and recording systems, smart classrooms, etc. In line with the characteristics and requirements of different courses, provide targeted facilities and equipment to support various experiential, practical, and virtual simulation learning.

Digital Platforms and Applications. Provide learners with specific application access and support services through various platforms, systems, and software, including but not limited to client software, adaptive websites, mobile applications, etc., which are the main carriers for constructing online ubiquitous learning.

Digital Resources. Including but not limited to various electronic teaching materials, multimedia resources, interactive courseware, VR/AR resources, artificial intelligence applications, etc., to provide learners with specific learning content. At the same time, it can be effectively integrated into various teaching activities (including regular teaching, forum lectures, theme activities, salons, etc.) to meet the learning needs of older adults. The use of resources supports multi-entry and multi-channel access, and the access method is convenient and efficient, with an aging-appropriate user UI and operation form.

Course Data. Including the utilization and evaluation data of course resources, teaching data, learning data (such as learning process and behavior records, style preferences, learning evaluations, etc.), management data, support service data, and other contents, which can comprehensively reflect the learning situation and teaching effect, as well as the comprehensive situation of digital management, and are presented through data analysis and visualization.

Teaching Staff. Including teaching staff responsible for teaching design and implementation, technical personnel supporting digital venues and facilities, management personnel for daily management and operation and maintenance, explaining personnel or volunteers providing various guidance services during non-routine teaching hours, and logistics support personnel.

3.2 Promoting the Integration of Online and Offline Teaching

With the deepening of the aging society, in order to promote the realization of active aging, older adults education needs to continue to expand its radiation range and highlight its universality. Online courses can break through the bottleneck of offline course implementation conditions, expand the limited classroom capacity through the Internet, effectively solve the problem of insufficient supply of older adults education, make the older adults education courses show openness, break the time and space restrictions of older adult learning, and meet the diversified learning needs of older adults. In the construction of digital courses for older adults education, it is necessary to further deepen the reform of classroom teaching, standardize and normalize the implementation mechanism of "online + offline" integrated older adults education courses [5], promote the construction of intelligent learning scenarios for older adults education, build intelligent classrooms and classrooms, realize the interactive integration of learning means, learning contents, and learning spaces of digital courses for older adults education through the integration of external environments and resources, cultivate the habits of older adults to learn online and use information technology to learn, and promote the formation of a new model of older adults education course implementation.

At the operational level, information platforms, mobile applications, and social media can be leveraged to guide elderly learners in online learning. Promote live-streaming courses, recorded courses, and micro-courses, move offline courses to the cloud, and establish a hybrid course system. Formulate etiquette norms for live-streaming courses, including class check-in, classroom feedback, teacher-student interaction, and course conclusion, to standardize online teaching and make digital classrooms more efficient. In addition, considering the overall low digital literacy of older adults and the strong correlation between digital learning effectiveness and interpersonal interaction between teachers and students, while exploring online courses, we should still focus on further offline communication and interaction between teachers and learners to achieve integrated online-offline development and promote the high-quality sustainable development of curriculum construction.

3.3 Integrating Information Technology Means to Enhance the Course Learning Experience

In the digital era, the demand of older adult learners for mobile learning and fragmented learning is increasing, and the requirements for courses are also getting higher and higher. The construction of digital courses for older adults education should be designed with the purpose of "high-quality, shared, convenient, systematic, and characteristic", combined with the characteristics of older adult learners such as obvious personality, slow information reception, and high forgetting rate. In the presentation form, we should pay attention to diversification and characteristics, and in terms of vision, hearing, interface reading habits, and operation methods, we should attach equal importance to pictures and texts, easy to learn, understand, and operate, and pay attention to digital inclusion for vulnerable older adults. For example, develop electronic teaching material products that are adapted to video resources, intelligent, and interactive; the design of micro-courses or short videos fully considers the characteristics of older adult groups that the information processing speed is slowed down and the working memory capacity is reduced. The amount of information contained in a single video should not be too much, the time should not be too long, the speaking speed should not be too fast, and the subtitle font size should be increased, etc.; enrich the learning scene through AV/VR and other technologies to enhance the learning experience.

Compared with the traditional form, the form of content expression of digital courses has changed, and systematic learning and fragmented learning promote each other. The curriculum can be designed in layers or modules, breaking the content of the course into knowledge units. Each knowledge point can be used as a relatively independent module, which is intuitively explained through courseware, short videos, or micro-courses. At the same time, it can be combined into a systematic whole around the logical thinking of specific learning tasks. Learners can learn in stages according to their actual situation to achieve the local integration and internalization of fragmented knowledge.

3.4 Strengthening Digital Learning Guidance to Bridge the "Digital Divide"

As a new learning paradigm, digital learning has been relatively lagging in popularization for older adult groups. The problem of the digital divide has always existed, restricting the development of older adult smart education [6]. In the process of constructing digital courses for older adults education, it is necessary to strengthen the development and learning guidance of modern information technology, Internet operation, and other contents [7], and increase the popularization education of intelligent terminal applications, and strengthen the education of the digital survival ability of older adult groups. Carry out experiential curriculum construction around social life scenarios, improve the comprehensive digital literacy of older adult learners, and enhance the degree of integration into digital life.

Incorporate network security content into the curriculum system to enhance the understanding of older adult groups on information security. Older adult groups skipped the PC era and entered the mobile Internet era directly, and their network prevention capabilities are generally weak. Therefore, how to guide older adult groups to surf the Internet correctly and safely and avoid network risks is an urgent social and family problem to be solved. Strengthening the publicity of network security awareness, popularizing network security knowledge, and providing basic protection strategies are crucial for older adults to better integrate into the information society.

4 Sustained Optimization Paths for the Construction of Digital Courses for Older Adults Education

At present, the construction of digital courses for older adults education has achieved certain results and taken initial shape, but there are still deficiencies in the construction of the curriculum system and other aspects. During the construction process, we should adhere to the orientation of the learning needs of older adult groups to reconstruct the curriculum system. Curriculum developers need to fully consider the cultivation of digital literacy and value guidance, promote the construction of diversified and comprehensive digital courses for older adults education, and provide all-round services that meet the needs of older adults education in the new era.

4.1 Improving the "Content + Technology + Service" Curriculum Construction System

First of all, we can refer to the requirements of relevant standards, combine the goals and effects of curriculum construction, start from the system, establish construction principles, determine the scope and categories, and plan the construction system. Secondly, it is necessary to be guided by the needs and characteristics of learners, refer to the measurement indicators of various disciplines or fields to mine, select, filter, summarize, analyze, evaluate. And regenerate information resources. And regenerate information resources with reference to the measurement indicators of each discipline or field, and code and integrate them according to specific standards to establish a curriculum digital resource database and a learning platform, integrating self-constructed resources and external resources. Finally, with the rapid development of the times, continuously update and iterate the content, resources, and services of the courses to keep the supply of courses in an effective state.

High-quality digital courses are inseparable from the joint efforts of teaching, management, and technical teams. We should give play to the characteristics and expertise of various universities, departments, and enterprises, do a good job in the overall design in the planning of course content, avoid the fragmentation of teaching content and digital content, uphold the concept of serving lifelong learning, reduce the homogenization phenomenon of digital resources for older adults education, and ensure the production of high-quality digital courses. Through resource integration, use new technologies for innovation, develop serialized, intelligent, and interactive digital products adapted to courses, hold the content standards, and jointly create digital resources that meet the needs of older adult learners. For example, strengthen the research, development, construction, and application of digital teaching materials for older adults education, explore digital course auxiliary derivative products, provide one-stop educational digital services, and build a closed ecological chain of educational digital products.

At the same time, establish a curriculum resource distribution system to provide older adults with online and offline, multi-angle, and diversified learning resource distribution. Let older adults feel the satisfaction of learning needs in the learning process through precise and personalized services.

4.2 Optimizing the Construction of Digital Course Platforms

Relying on technologies such as "big data, cloud computing, the Internet of Things, and artificial intelligence", through in-depth cooperation, build a smart learning platform for older adults education with regional characteristics, and realize a three-dimensional curriculum system that integrates course resources and development and construction, including digital teaching materials, online resources, and offline learning scenarios, and supports multiple terminals. The platform should take the promotion of the self-growth of older adult learners as the goal, integrally support the access of computers and mobile terminals, have a "fault-tolerant" interaction mechanism, alleviate the anxiety and fear of older adult learners in the operation process, and have the functions of openness, compatibility, standardization, security, sharing, and sustainable expansion. The multi-dimensional and multi-level platform can adapt according to the individual situation of older adults. Through big data analysis of students' learning trajectories and behavior data, it can create user portraits for learners, realize accurate push of learning content, make the courses more suitable for the individual characteristics of learners, and can also provide functions such as information release, statistical reports, learning supervision, multi-directional interaction, and fixed-point service in a targeted manner.

Open a cloud community in the platform to meet the needs of older adult groups for social learning, give full play to the enthusiasm and initiative of older adult groups, and enable them to have the opportunity to fully display their own talents, advantages, and wisdom. Give play to the comprehensive teaching efficiency of inside and outside the classroom, online and offline, build a diversified service platform through network platforms and mobile terminals, create an atmosphere of caring for older adults, which can not only reduce the learning barriers of older adults but also imperceptibly change the learning methods of older adults, establish confidence in digital learning and create a better learning atmosphere.

4.3 Constructing a "Feedback + Optimization" Curriculum Management Mode Based on Evaluation

High-quality courses provide strong support for the continuous and good development of older adults education. The construction of digital courses is a process of continuous iteration, which requires an evaluation and feedback mechanism to timely understand the evaluation of older adults on the courses. A good course should keep up with the pace of the times and update and iterate continuously. Compared with the complicated update process of traditional teaching resources, the flexibility of digital resources makes their iteration speed faster. On the basis of following the general laws of education, closely following the learning characteristics of older adult groups, formulate normative standards for the development and quality evaluation of digital resources, analyze and identify the changes in the needs of older adult learners, dig deep into the content value, timely optimize and iterate digital resources, and provide precise resource value-added services to meet the needs of the modern development of the construction of digital courses for older adults education.

Digital technology can provide effective, usable, and narratable support for course production, teaching management, learning management, data statistics, etc., so as to effectively optimize the construction of digital courses for older adults education. Create a teaching management application with digitalization as the core, establish a set of online and offline digital course management systems, standardize the sharing of digital courses, data analysis, and integration of resources, and give feedback in a timely manner. Establish an evaluation mechanism, comprehensively count and analyze the value creation of digital courses in older adults education, carry out phased evaluations, and timely adjust and correct the problems and obstacles existing in the learning process of digital content to promote the efficient and scientific allocation of digital resources for older adults education.

4.4 Strengthening Teachers' Digital Literacy and Enhance the Teaching Proficiency of Digital Courses

Teachers of older adults education are the key factors to achieve the high-quality development of older adults education. Further improving the digital teaching ability and participation awareness, and stimulating them to take the initiative to integrate digital-related contents in the course design and implementation is an important guarantee for the development of digital courses.

Construct a training system for improving teachers' digital capabilities, strengthen the digital teaching training for full-time and part-time teachers of older adults education, and improve teachers' capabilities in information technology application, online teaching, live teaching, and guiding students to learn online. Encourage teachers to actively participate in the construction of hybrid courses, take the initiative to deal with the new challenges brought by digitalization, and continuously improve their professional levels through the application of digital technology.

We can also cooperate with other social organizations or fully tap computer-related professional teachers, cultivate professional digital teaching support teams, build information technology teams and technical backbone teams for older adults education, carry out digital training for other teachers, improve the overall digital literacy of the teaching staff, and make the development of digital courses more professional.

5 Conclusion

5.1 Summary

The construction of digital courses for older adults education is an important measure to address the challenges of the digital era. This research has expounded the connotation and significance of digital courses in older adults education, analyzed the current situation and existing problems in the construction process, and proposed specific construction contents and optimized paths from multiple dimensions. It is found that constructing a multi-dimensional service system, promoting the integration of online and offline, integrating information technology, and strengthening digital learning guidance are crucial to improving the quality of digital courses. In the optimization path, improving the "content + technology + service" system, optimizing platform construction, establishing an evaluation-driven management mode, and enhancing teachers' digital capabilities are effective ways to promote sustainable development.

In the future, with the continuous deepening of digital technology and the changing needs of older adults, the construction of digital courses for older adults education needs to be further promoted in terms of innovation and adaptation. It is necessary to strengthen cross-disciplinary cooperation, deeply integrate technology and education, and continuously improve the scientificity and older adult-friendliness of courses. At the same time, we should pay attention to the dynamic feedback of learners, carry out targeted optimization and innovation, and strive to build a more inclusive, intelligent, and high-quality digital education ecosystem for older adults, so as to help older adults better integrate into the digital society and realize the value of lifelong learning.

5.2 Broader Applications and Future Implications

The core framework of digital course construction for older adults education, characterized by the "content-technology-service" triad and a multi-dimensional service ecosystem, exhibits strong extensibility. This framework can be systematically adapted to community education, serving as a critical driver for modernizing pedagogical practices.

The modular course architecture described in this paper can not only meet the learning characteristics of older adults education but also offer a scalable model for community education. By conducting localized demand assessments—encompassing not only older adults but also adolescents, adults, and other demographic groups within communities—these modules can be reconfigured into community-specific learning units. For instance, basic digital literacy modules (e.g., smart device operation, online security) designed for older adults can be adjusted for children and teenagers to enhance early digital competency, while advanced modules (e.g., data analysis, digital content creation) can cater to working-age adults, forming a vertically integrated learning system within communities.

The adaptive learning platform, featuring multi-terminal accessibility and interactive mechanisms, can be upgraded into a community digital education hub. This hub integrates resources from community centers, educational institutions, and technology enterprises, enabling cross-institutional resource sharing. It supports extended reality (XR)-based training modules—such as virtual simulations of digital payment processes or smart healthcare operations—to enhance experiential learning. Additionally, the dual-mentorship system (combining professional instructors with peer tutors) can be replicated in communities: older adults who have mastered digital skills can act as peer tutors for novices, fostering intergenerational knowledge transfer and mitigating the intergenerational digital divide [8].

In the context of lifelong education, the framework of older adults' digital courses provides a replicable model for building a lifelong learning ecosystem. Its emphasis on personalized learning (via user profiling and big data analytics) can be extended to design age-appropriate learning pathways, covering childhood, adolescence, adulthood, and old age. For example, the same platform can deliver foundational digital skills to children, advanced professional digital tools to adults, and simplified digital life applications to older adults, ensuring continuous skill development across the lifespan. This continuity strengthens societal resilience in adapting to digital transformations.

These extensions yield tangible benefits for the development of the digital economy. First, enhanced digital literacy within communities expands the participant base of the digital economy. Older adults, as a large consumer group, gain the ability to engage in online shopping, digital financial services, and telehealth, thereby increasing market demand for digital products and services. Second, the lifelong education system, supported by the framework, cultivates a workforce with sustained digital competencies, ensuring labor adaptability to evolving digital industries and reducing productivity losses caused by digital skill gaps. Third, the inclusive digital ecosystem minimizes economic exclusion: communities with universal digital literacy attract more digital enterprises and services, stimulating local digital economic growth. Finally, intergenerational digital collaboration—facilitated by community education—drives innovation in digital product design (e.g., age-friendly interfaces), promoting the development of more inclusive digital markets.

Furthermore, pedagogical innovations embedded in digital courses for older adults can accelerate the digital transformation of aging-related industries. User profiling and big data analytics, initially deployed to optimize learning experiences, can be extrapolated to pension systems. This enables the implementation of AI-driven demand forecasting and IoT-supported care solutions. The "online-offline integration" model, proven effective in educational contexts, is adaptable to digital consumption scenarios involving older adults. Such integration not only facilitates the upgrading of aging-related industries but also unleashes the consumption potential of older adults, thereby ensuring their equitable participation in the development of the digital society.

References

1. United Nations Educational, Scientific and Cultural Organization (UNESCO): Digital Literacy for All Ages: Bridging the Gap for Older Adults. UNESCO, Paris (2021)
2. NTIA: Falling Through the Net: A Survey of the 'Have Nots' in Rural and Urban America. [Report]. U.S. Department of Commerce (1995)
3. The Aging AI: Online learning and digital content creation for older adults. Aging AI J. **5**(2), 1–15 (2023)
4. Li, X., Wang, Y.: Digital literacy education for the elderly from a communication theory perspective. J. Broadcast. Knowl. Transf. **45**(3), 67–82 (2021)
5. Beijing Open University: Upgrading digital resources for elderly education: a case study of Beijing senior open university. Chin. J. Distance Educ. **41**(1), 93–102 (2023)
6. FasterCapital: Senior learning goes digital: personalized platforms reshaping elderly education. Glob. EdTech Rev. **12**(1), 45–58 (2024).
7. Chen, L., Wu, S.: Comparative study of foreign models for cultivating digital literacy among the elderly and implications for China. J. Adult Contin. Educ. **34**(2), 111–128 (2023)
8. Wang, Y., Zhang, L.: The tripartite model of elderly digital divide: access, utilization, and knowledge gaps in China. Educ. Gerontol. **51**(4), 102–115 (2025)

Logical Construction and Practical Design of the BOPPPS Teaching Model Based on the "Four Principles and Three Methods" Concept: A Case Study of "Java Framework Technology"

Xianmei Hua and Xinrong Zhan(✉)

School of Artificial Intelligence, Xiamen Institute of Technology, Xiamen, China
15626257844@163.com

Abstract. In response to challenges including outdated teaching content, insufficient cultivation of practical skills, and unitary assessment methods in traditional "Java Framework Technology" courses, this research constructs a teaching framework for applied talent cultivation by integrating the BOPPPS Teaching Model under the guidance of the "Four Principles and Three Methods" Concept (FT Concept). By analyzing the requirements for developing an enterprise-level Contract Management System, we transform industry standards into a BOPPPS closed-loop teaching process. A task-driven mechanism based on specialized role assignment and a multi-dimensional assessment system are designed. Focused on logical construction and practical design, this research deepens technical application understanding via real project scenarios, integrates knowledge transfer paths through systematic workflows, bridges technical theory and engineering practice effectively, enhances students' engineering mindset, and provides replicable structured reform solutions for similar courses.

Keywords: FT Concept · BOPPPS Teaching Model · Java Framework Technology · Application-oriented talent cultivation

1 Introduction

Global education reform trends emphasize industry-academia collaboration and competency-based talent cultivation, with growing demands for practice-oriented education systems and focuses on interdisciplinary integration and innovative practical skills in emerging engineering disciplines [3]. Against this backdrop, the traditional teaching model of "Java Framework Technology" faces significant challenges. Firstly, teaching content fails to keep pace with industry technological advancements, hindering students' grasp of practical application scenarios of mainstream frameworks [9]; Secondly, classroom designs rely on one-way knowledge transmission, lacking real project-driven approaches, resulting in insufficient engineering practice and teamwork skills [5]; Thirdly, evaluation methods

W. Hong et al. (Eds.): ICCSE 2025, CCIS 2761, pp. 488–500, 2026.
https://doi.org/10.1007/978-981-95-7731-6_38

are confined to code submissions and theoretical assessments, neglecting comprehensive assessment of system design capabilities, problem-solving skills, and professional competencies [10].

To address these issues, this research presents an innovative integration of the "Four Principles and Three Methods" Concept (FT Concept) [2] with the BOPPPS Teaching Model [12], reconstructing the teaching logic and practical approaches of "Java Framework Technology". The FT Concept emphasizes "Authentic Environment, Authentic Learning and Practice, Acquiring Authentic Competence", achieving precise alignment between teaching content and industry demands through "Curricularization of Work Tasks, Operationalization of Teaching Tasks, Systematization of the Work Process". The BOPPPS Teaching Model, with its closed-loop structure of Bridge-in, Objective, Pre-assessment, Participatory Learning, Post-assessment, and Summary, strengthens student-centered learning and feedback mechanisms. This collaborative innovation reconstructs teaching content driven by enterprise-level projects, integrates role division and collaborative development throughout the BOPPPS process, and ensures the attainment of students' engineering capabilities via a multi-dimensional assessment system. This approach effectively meets the dual demands of practical ability and innovative thinking in engineering talent cultivation, resolving the deep-seated contradictions inherent in traditional teaching, such as fragmented knowledge, disconnected application, and superficial evaluation, and providing a replicable model for computer-related course reform under industry-academia collaboration.

2 Theoretical Framework

2.1 FT Concept

The FT Concept is an instructional development theory for application-oriented universities, evolved from the long-term teaching reform practices of Qiqihar Institute of Engineering [2]. It integrates advanced educational concepts and forms a distinctive training model for applied talents. This concept has been explored since 2015, continuously improved, and by 2022, has been verified and applied in multiple application-oriented universities. Its core connotation can be intuitively understood through Table 1.

The "Four Principles" originate from the global consensus on high-quality vocational and technical education, which emphasizes "conducting teaching activities in real environments to achieve authentic learning and practice, thereby enabling students to master practical competencies". These principles serve as the fundamental orientation for teaching design:

- Authentic Environment: Construct learning scenarios that highly simulate actual workplace settings, encompassing not only hardware facilities and operational processes but also industry norms and professional ethics, to help students establish a direct connection between learning and future careers;

- Authentic Learning and Practice: Encourage students to engage in learning with a practical orientation, participating in task completion with the same standards as industry practitioners, and integrating theoretical knowledge acquisition with hands-on operation in real contexts;
- Acquiring Authentic Competence: Focus on cultivating competencies that meet industry standards, including professional skills, problem-solving abilities, and teamwork spirit, ensuring that students can quickly adapt to job requirements upon graduation.

Table 1. The Connotation of the FT Concept

Dimension	Specific Items	Connotation
Four Principles	Authentic Environment	Construct teaching scenarios based on enterprise-level project requirements and industry standards
	Authentic Learning and Practice	Students participate in the entire project lifecycle via teamwork and task-driven approaches
	Acquiring Authentic Competence	Focus on engineering capabilities and professional competencies aligned with industry standards
Three Methods	Curricularization of Work Tasks	Transform software development processes into course modules
	Operationalization of Teaching Tasks	Design teaching tasks around real projects, simulating enterprise development team collaboration
	Systematization of the Work Process	Organize teaching according to the workflow: Requirement Analysis, System Design, Development and Integration, Testing and Acceptance

The "Three Methods" are practical strategies derived from the integration of work process systematization theory and curriculum development practices, aiming to bridge the gap between academic education and industry needs:

- Curricularization of Work Tasks: Systematically transform typical workplace tasks into curriculum content by integrating disciplinary theories, enabling students to master professional knowledge while completing practical tasks;

- Operationalization of Teaching Tasks: Design teaching activities around real projects, simulating the collaboration mode of enterprise teams, so that teaching tasks are presented in the form of work assignments, realizing the integration of learning and doing;
- Systematization of the Work Process: Organize teaching content according to the logical sequence of actual work processes (Requirements Analysis, System Design, Development and Integration, Testing and Acceptance), breaking the limitations of traditional disciplinary knowledge structure and facilitating the formation of systematic professional competencies.

In "Java Framework Technology", the FT Concept provides methodological support for teaching reform. By introducing enterprise-level development scenarios, it overcomes the technical isolation of traditional programming courses, facilitating the migration of mainstream framework technologies to real projects. Through the "Three Methods", we transform fragmented knowledge into structured task modules, guiding students to integrate front-end and back-end technology stacks while completing comprehensive projects, thus systematically cultivating engineering capabilities like system design and interface debugging. The innovative diversified evaluation mechanism replaces single code assessment, emphasizing process evaluation and outcome-oriented assessment to highlight the development of engineering standards awareness, teamwork, and innovative thinking.

2.2 BOPPPS Teaching Model

Originating from the Canadian Instructor Skills Workshop (ISW) system, the BOPPPS Teaching Model is an efficient instructional framework centered on student engagement [8]. Based on the natural law that human attention can only last for approximately 15 min, the BOPPPS Teaching Model divides classroom teaching content into a closed-loop teaching process consisting of six interrelated phases [12]. As shown in Fig. 1, the instructional process is structured into six modular components: Bridge-in, Objective, Pre-assessment, Participatory Learning, Post-assessment, and Summary. The specific connotations of the six components are as follows:

- Bridge-in: Serves as the opening of the course. It captures students' attention and stimulates their learning interest by sharing stories, current events related to the core content or connecting previous knowledge, guiding them to focus on the upcoming learning materials;
- Objective: Clarifies the learning goals and expected outcomes of the class, clearly informing students of the knowledge and skills they will master. The goal statement includes elements such as the target audience, content, conditions, and proficiency level, providing direction for teaching activities;
- Pre-assessment: Uses questionnaires, quizzes, or other methods to understand students' mastery of relevant knowledge, interests, and ability foundations. This helps teachers adjust the depth and pace of teaching content to ensure the effective achievement of teaching objectives;

- Participatory Learning: As the core of teaching, this phase encourages students to actively participate in knowledge construction through interactive methods such as group discussions and scenario simulations. Teachers flexibly use teaching resources to create a positive atmosphere, facilitating students to achieve learning goals;
- Post-assessment: Conducts targeted evaluations at the end of the class through tests, practical demonstrations, etc., to assess students' achievement of learning objectives. It provides a basis for teaching improvement and helps students clarify their learning outcomes;
- Summary: Combs through the core knowledge points and skill essentials of the class to consolidate learning results, connects with subsequent course content, assigns after-class tasks, and previews the next class arrangement, playing a linking role.

This model emphasizes instructional practicality and immediate feedback mechanisms, focusing on student engagement and engineering thinking cultivation, addressing issues of one-way transmission and delayed feedback in traditional classrooms [13].

In "Java Framework Technology", the BOPPPS Teaching Model synergizes with the FT Concept, providing a procedural framework for teaching implementation. By introducing real-world problem scenarios, setting competency-oriented objectives, organizing project-based participatory learning, and implementing formative assessments with reflective summaries, it integrates theoretical knowledge and practical skill development organically, offering a replicable approach for constructing efficient computer application course classrooms.

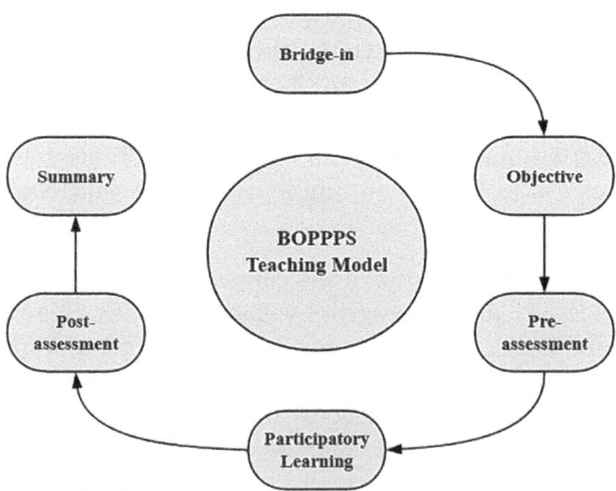

Fig. 1. The six links of the BOPPPS Teaching Model.

3 BOPPPS Teaching Model Empowered by the FT Concept for Classroom Logic Construction

This study deeply integrates the FT Concept with the BOPPPS Teaching Model, reconstructing classroom logic through the "Four Principles" and optimizing instructional pathways with the "Three Methods". It proposes a BOPPPS Teaching Model construction framework based on the FT Concept to resolve traditional classroom issues like theory-practice disconnection and vague professional competency cultivation, achieving a precise alignment between course content and industry needs. Figure 2 demonstrates the universal implementation framework of the BOPPPS Teaching Model integrated with the FT Concept, the classroom logic can be constructed through the following.

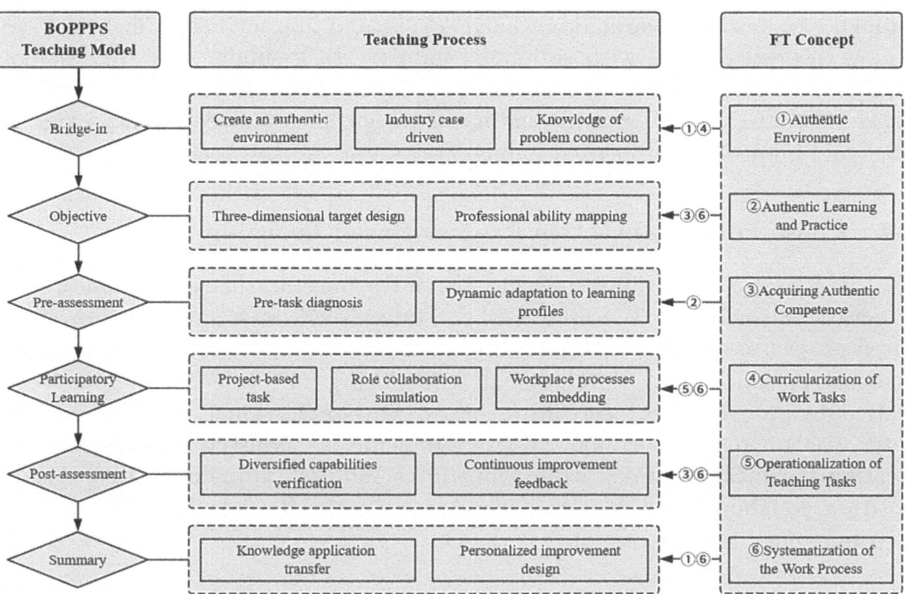

Fig. 2. The classroom framework for the BOPPPS Teaching Model incorporating the FT Concept.

3.1 Phase One: Bridge-In with Authentic Scenarios

Guided by "Authentic Environment", teaching materials are selected from genuine industry scenarios by aligning industry demands with disciplinary issues. Adhering to "Curricularization of Work Tasks", industry standards and professional norms are integrated into instructional design, guiding students to identify connections between real-world problems and theoretical knowledge, stimulating exploration motivation via problem-driven approaches.

3.2 Phase Two: Clarify Career-Oriented Objectives

Based on the "Acquiring Authentic Competence", teaching objectives align precisely with professional core competency requirements. Guided by the "Systematization of the Work Process", measurable goals are set in cognition, skills, and literacy [7]. Knowledge objectives focus on mastering core theories; skill objectives emphasize independent task completion; literacy objectives prioritize professional thinking and teamwork. Goal statements specify audience, behavior, conditions, and degree to ensure alignment with professional competency standards.

3.3 Phase Three: Pre-assessment for Tailored Instruction

Through preparatory tasks embodying the "Authentic Learning and Practice", a diagnostic system covering knowledge, skills, and literacy is established. Combining theoretical tests with simplified industry task simulations, digital tools generate learning analysis reports, and process observations identify weaknesses. Teaching content is dynamically adjusted to optimize knowledge gap explanations and intensify skill-focused hands-on training.

3.4 Phase Four: Interactive Project-Based Learning

As the core stage for implementing the FT Concept, this phase follows the "Operationalization of Teaching Tasks", converting course content into structured project assignments. Organized according to the workflow of requirements analysis, system design, development, and testing [6], project assignments are distributed to students, who are grouped into professional roles to simulate enterprise team collaboration. Instructors serve as industry mentors, demonstrating technical solutions while embedding industry standards. Task decomposition, collaborative development, and real-time feedback facilitate knowledge-to-competency transformation.

3.5 Phase Five: Post-assessment for Competency Verification

A multidimensional evaluation system aligned with professional certification standards is constructed, combining process documentation and outcome validation [11]. The knowledge dimension assesses theoretical application via case reports; the skill dimension evaluates operational standardization through project deliverables; the professionalism dimension examines vocational behaviors via collaborative process tracing. The assessment results integrate quantitative and qualitative analyses to identify competency gaps, thereby generating evidence for continuous improvement.

3.6 Phase Six: Practice-Oriented Experience Summary

The Summary focuses on knowledge's industry application value and vocational ability advancement. By drawing knowledge-to-application mind maps and reviewing project experiences via mentor critiques and self-evaluations, profession-compliant logical thinking is cultivated. Advanced learning plans are developed based on evaluations, recommending industry competitions or internships to achieve closed-loop "learning by doing" iteration.

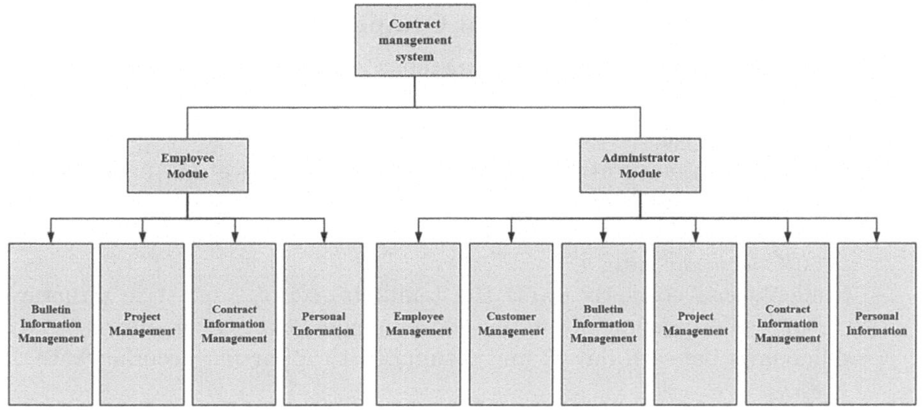

Fig. 3. Functional Module Diagram of Contract Management System.

4 BOPPPS Teaching Model Empowered by the FT Concept for Teaching Practice Design

To facilitate the FT Concept application in the BOPPPS Teaching Model, this study uses the "Java Framework Technology" lab course driven by the authentic "Contract Management System Based on Spring Boot and Vue" project [14] to design an end-to-end instructional classroom.

4.1 Bridge-In: Authentic Business Scenarios

Guided by the "Authentic Environment", manufacturing enterprise contract management scenarios are selected as teaching materials. We construct a cognitive bridge from business challenges to technical requirements using industry research data and pain-point cases:

- Pain point presentation: Highlight traditional contract management issues (e.g., 2-h retrieval for three-year-old contracts, claim disputes from version chaos, 7-day approval cycles) with industry data [1];

- System prototype demonstration: Focus on RESTful API-driven status updates, Shiro permission control, and Redis-optimized query speed. The core system modules are broken down using a functional structure diagram, as shown in Fig. 3;
- Problem-driven questions: "How to use Spring Boot auto-configuration for rapid backend setup?", "How does Vue component-based development optimize the user experience of frontend approval workflows?" Guide students to connect business needs with technical implementation.

4.2 Objective: Three-Dimensional Competency Goals

Based on the "Acquiring Authentic Competence" and industry job requirements, quantifiable objectives are set:

1. Knowledge Objective
   - Students can accurately explain the auto-configuration principles of Spring Boot and Vue in experimental environments, listing $\geq$2 implementation scenarios (e.g., database connection pools, Redis clients) with $\geq$ 90% accuracy rate;
   - Students can correctly parse the template, script, and style structure of single-file components in Vue development, explaining the reactivity differences between data() and setup(), with a parsing accuracy rate of $\geq$ 85%;
   - Students can design role-permission mappings based on Shiro framework for contract system requirements and explain the Realm authentication process, ensuring the design complies with industry standards.
2. Skill Objective
   - Students develop CRUD interfaces for contract data using Spring Boot, achieving $\leq$ 500 ms interface response time and $\leq$ 3% defect rate post-static code analysis (e.g., SonarQube), and $\geq$ 80% unit test coverage;
   - Students implement component-based development for contract approval pages using Vue, achieving a page load speed of 1.5 s, compatibility with 1920 $\times$1080 resolution, and form validation accuracy of 100%;
   - Students complete frontend-backend integration testing in teamwork, achieving 100% Postman API test coverage and $\geq$ 85% Redis cache hit rate.
3. Literacy Objectives
   - Students follow the software development process in simulated projects, clearly identifying enterprise pain points in requirement documents, with documentation adhering to industry templates;
   - During team development, students use Jira daily to track progress, with the backend proactively providing Swagger API documentation and the frontend providing $\geq$ 2 user experience optimization suggestions, achieving a collaboration process compliance rate of $\geq$ 90%;
   - In system security design, students implement Shiro permission control and Redis encryption for sensitive data, resulting in zero security vulnerabilities after code review and meeting data security requirements.

4.3 Pre-assessment: Stereoscopic Diagnostic Conditions

Based on the "Authentic Learning and Practice" requirement of the FT Concept, a three-dimensional diagnostic system for knowledge, skills, and literacy.

1. Theoretical Assessment
   - Conduct time-limited tests on Spring Boot annotations and Vue lifecycle hooks on the cloud platform, generating score rankings and vulnerability reports.
2. Practical Assessment
   - Backend task: Complete the development of a contract status query API within the specified time using Spring Boot. This task evaluates metrics such as API response time and cache hit rate;
   - Frontend task: Implement a contract form page based on Vue within the specified time. This task evaluates indicators such as page loading speed and component standardization.

4.4 Participatory Learning: Project-Driven Practice

As the core component for implementing the FT Concept, the Participatory Learning phase adopts the approach of the "Operationalization of Teaching Tasks", breaking down the Contract Management System into actionable enterprise-level development tasks to simulate real-world development processes.

Real Project-Driven. Taking the "Contract Management System Based on Spring Boot and Vue" as an example, each team must complete four core tasks.

1. Requirements Analysis and System Design
   - Conduct functional requirement analysis based on enterprise pain points, defining core modules such as contract lifecycle management, process engine, and data visualization. Adopt a B/S architecture design, implement data persistence in the backend using Spring Boot, realize visual approval workflows through Vue component-based development in the frontend, and complete entity-relationship modeling for database design in compliance with industry standards.
2. Core Function Development
   - The backend team implements CRUD interfaces for contract information, integrates Shiro for permission control (admin/employee operation tiers) and Redis for caching strategies (high-frequency query data caching). The frontend team develops contract list and detail pages using Vue component-based development, adding JWT tokens validation during Axios API calls to ensure secure data interaction.

3. Backend-Frontend Joint Debugging
   - For potential issues like inconsistent API parameters or cache penetration during joint debugging, students must use Postman for API testing, monitor cache hit rates via Redis visualization tools (Objective $\geq$ 85%), and optimize connection pool parameters based on industry practices.
4. Project acceptance and documentation delivery
   - Submit deliverables such as the "Requirements Analysis Report", "System Design Specification", and "API Documentation" according to enterprise standards. Conduct code reviews and user acceptance testing to ensure the system meets practical needs like contract approval efficiency and data security.

Specialized Role Assignment and Collaboration. Team leader candidates are selected based on comprehensive pre-assessment scores (e.g., theory 30% and practical performance 70%). After a team leader is confirmed for each group, they will form a 3–5 member development team, with the "Team leader responsibility system" running through the entire project management process [4];

- Team leaders oversee project progress and coordinate resource allocation. This role requires proficiency in Spring Boot framework integration;
- Backend developers are responsible for API development, with priority given to those who scored $\geq$ 85 in the Spring Boot practical pre-assessment;
- Frontend developers are responsible for implementing page components, with priority given to those who scored $\geq$ 80 in the Vue practical pre-assessment.

Real-Time Feedback and Industry Standards Integration. Teachers intervene in the teaching process as corporate mentors to ensure students master the technical essentials and engineering standards of enterprise-level project development. They handle common issues by demonstrating optimization methods and providing configuration code, and address individualized problems through one-on-one code reviews to reinforce development norms.

4.5 Post-assessment: Verification of Multidimensional Competency Achievement

Guided by the outcome-oriented "Acquiring Authentic Competence" principle, the post-assessment phase verifies teaching objective attainment through a collaborative evaluation mechanism involving tripartite subjects: instructors, enterprise technical mentors, and student peers. This multidimensional system integrates functional testing, technical competency assessment, and professionalism evaluation, and weight distribution as follows:

- Functional testing accounts for 25%, instructors verify the completion of core workflows against enterprise requirements;

- Technical competency assessment accounts for 35%, with enterprise technical mentors conducting code reviews using tools like SonarQube;
- Professionalism evaluation accounts for 20%, traced through project management tools and collaborative logs to assess teamwork and documentation compliance;
- Self and peer evaluation accounts for 20%, with students reflecting on individual task completion and rating team collaboration effectiveness.

Evaluation results synthesize quantitative data and qualitative feedback, identifying competency gaps for targeted improvement, ensuring comprehensive verification of students' mastery of industry-required capabilities.

4.6 Summary: Systematic Knowledge Construction

In this practice, students completed full-process development of the Contract Management System. The Summary reviewed technical highlights (Spring Boot auto-configuration, Vue componentization, Shiro/Redis practices) and provided quantitative feedback (85% groups achieved Redis hit rate $\geq$ 85%). Extended tasks (e.g., Spring Cloud refactoring) were assigned to plan technological evolution, fostering continuous improvement capability under the FT Concept.

5 Conclusion

This research constructs a real-scene-driven, capability-oriented teaching framework for "Java Framework Technology" by integrating the FT Concept and the BOPPPS Teaching Model. By transforming Contract Management System requirements into structured tasks, it designs a closed-loop teaching process, achieving deep integration of teaching content with industry standards. Relying on task curricularization and process systemization, it addresses traditional classroom issues, providing a replicable paradigm for applied courses. Future research will expand framework adaptability, optimize feedback mechanisms with intelligent technologies, and deepen industry-education integration evaluation innovation.

Acknowledgements. This research was funded by the 2022 Central Government Guided Local Development Science and Technology Special Project (2022L3029).

Disclosure of Interests. The authors declare no conflict of interest.

References

1. Abutabenjeh, S., Rendon, R.G.: Procurement and contract management deficiencies: analysis of state audit reports. Int. J. Public Sect. Perform. Manag. **11**, 81 (2023)
2. Cao, Y.A., Ren, Z.X.: Principles, methods, and evaluation of applied course construction (in Chinese). Vocat. Tech. Educ. Forum **36**, 67–73 (2020)

3. Esangbedo, C.O., Zhang, J., Esangbedo, M.O., Kone, S.D., Xu, L.: The role of industry-academia collaboration in enhancing educational opportunities and outcomes under the digital driven industry 4.0. J. Infrastruct. Policy Dev. **8** (2023)
4. Folsom-Kovarik, J., Sieh, J., Sinatra, A.M.: Reasoning about team roles and responsibilities for team assessment. In: Proceedings of the Ninth Annual GIFT Users Symposium (GIFTsym9), p. 201. US Army DEVCOM–Soldier Center (2021)
5. Hasan, M., Lodge, J.M., Karim, A., Khan, M.S.H.: Exploring students' conceptions of project-based learning: implications for improving engineering pedagogy. IEEE Trans. Educ. **67**, 234–244 (2024)
6. Kasauli, R., Knauss, E., Horkoff, J., Liebel, G., de Oliveira Neto, F.G.: Requirements engineering challenges and practices in large-scale agile system development. J. Syst. Softw. **172**, 110851 (2021)
7. Knoth, N., et al.: Developing a holistic ai literacy assessment matrix – bridging generic, domain-specific, and ethical competencies. Comput. Educ. Open **6**, 100177 (2024)
8. Li, S., et al.: Impacts of blended learning with BOPPPS model on Chinese medical undergraduate students: a comprehensive systematic review and meta-analysis of 44 studies. BMC Med. Educ. **24** (2024)
9. Miranda, J., et al.: The core components of education 4.0 in higher education: three case studies in engineering education. Comput. Electric. Eng. **93**, 107278 (2021)
10. Swan Sein, A., Rashid, H., Meka, J., Amiel, J., Pluta, W.: Twelve tips for embedding assessment for and as learning practices in a programmatic assessment system. Med. Teach. **43**, 300–306 (2020)
11. Welsandt, N.C.J., Fortunati, F., Winther, E., Abs, H.J.: Constructing and validating authentic assessments: the case of a new technology-based assessment of economic literacy. Empirical Res. Vocat. Educ. Training **16** (2024)
12. Xu, Z., et al.: Developing a BOPPPS (bridge-in, objectives, pre-assessment, participatory learning, post-assessment and summary) model combined with the OBE (outcome based education) concept to improve the teaching outcomes of higher education. Hum. Soc. Sci. Commun. **11** (2024)
13. Yan, L., Lu, Z., Yu, Y.: Exploration and practice of BOPPPS model in enhancing effective teaching -taking business communication as an example. In: SHS Web of Conferences, vol. 179, p. 04029 (2023)
14. Zhu, Y.: Contract management system based on SpringBoot and VUE. Adv. Comput. Sig. Syst. **8** (2024)

Analysis and Thinking About the Development Situation of HIS Course in Colleges of Traditional Chinese Medicine in China

Qingyan Wu, Yan Xie, Wenping Deng, and Haifeng Yang(✉)

Hubei University of Chinese Medicine, Wuhan 430061, Hubei, People's Republic of China
yanghaifeng@hbucm.edu.cn

Abstract. Amid significant national initiatives promoting digital health development, advancing New Engineering and New Medical Sciences, and accelerating educational digital transformation, enhancing the educational capacity and teaching quality of Hospital Information System (HIS) courses has become critically urgent. Through a comprehensive questionnaire survey targeting HIS course instructors at Traditional Chinese Medicine (TCM) universities and a systematic literature review of HIS teaching research, this study evaluates the current status of HIS course development in TCM institutions across six key dimensions: course nomenclature and provision, instructional scheduling, content emphasis, faculty composition, digital teaching platforms, textbook resources, and practical teaching implementation. The investigation identifies major challenges and gaps, culminating in proposed construction strategies and quality improvement measures for HIS curriculum enhancement.

Keywords: TCM colleges and universities · HIS · curriculum teaching reform · status analysis

1 Introduction

Hospital Information System (HIS) is a branch of medical informatics that integrates information technology with health services and health management, the most vivid practical results and the hottest research areas. Since the end of 1970s, China's rapid popularization of Health Information Technology (HIT) in various hospitals, clinics and also primary health care institutions, has propelled the vigorous development of the medical informatization industry. In order to meet the demand for medical information technology personnel, a large group of medical schools have opened [1] *Health Information Management, Medical Information Engineering, Intelligent Medical Engineering* and other information specialties, and generally taken HIS courses into their training program. After years of development, the value of HIS courses in professional ideological enlightenment, ability cultivation, value leadership, employment innovation, etc. has been widely recognized by the HIT education community and industry, and a great number of teaching and research results on HIS teaching methods, experimental

W. Hong et al. (Eds.): ICCSE 2025, CCIS 2761, pp. 501–512, 2026.
https://doi.org/10.1007/978-981-95-7731-6_39

teaching and course ideology have emerged. However, the research on how to recognize and solve the common problems of HIS courses in terms of curriculum, teachers, laboratory teaching, teaching materials, etc. is relatively weak, which is not conducive to the role of HIS courses in the development of digital health and the promotion of the construction of "double first-class". In this regard, the authors take HIS courses in TCM colleges and universities as the research object, collect research materials through various channels, analyze the basic situation of HIS course construction, the main difficulties and challenges, and put forward several measures and ideas for peer reference and discussion.

2 Information and Methods

2.1 Sources of Information

Questionnaire survey, literature analysis, and official website review were used to obtain research information. First of all, we designed our own questionnaire and imported it into the Questionnaire Star Platform, and implemented a questionnaire survey for the teachers of HIS courses in higher TCM colleges and universities, through WeChat group of the Information Education Branch of the China TCM Information Society. We recovered 16 valid questionnaires, and then integrated the questionnaires of the same units to get the basic information on the construction of the HIS courses in 14 TCM colleges and universities. Then, the title includes "Hospital Information System", "Hospital Management Information System", "Hospital Clinical Information System", "Hospital Information Management System", "HIS", "HMIS" or "HCIS", and also includes "course", "teaching" or "experiment", and is ranked in the search of the three major periodical databases, such as China Knowledge, Wanfang and Wipo. Subsequently, we obtained 9 HIS teaching and research papers published in the past 20 years with TCM institutions as the first author unit, and extracted the main arguments and data in the papers. Finally, we supplemented and verified the information on the curriculum and experimental teaching of hospital informatization-related courses from the official websites of the above TCM institutions.

2.2 Data Processing Methods and Tools

After using Excel to organize the survey data exported from the Questionnaire Star Platform, we designed the literature review form, and two HIS course instructors were organized to access and extract the curriculum, teaching content, and experimental teaching in the HIS teaching and research papers respectively one by one. Then, we checked the consistency as the supplemental information on the status of HIS course construction in the corresponding TCM colleges and universities, and finally we completed the descriptive statistics. Addtionally, Gephi v0.10 plotting was used.

3 Results

3.1 Course Naming and Setting

The frequency of HIS courses named "Hospital Information System" in TCM colleges and universities is the highest, which is 13. Other HIS courses with similar names and almost the same teaching content include "Hospital Information Management", "Hospital Information System Application and Development", "Hospital Information System Analysis and Design", "Hospital Intelligent Service Information System", "Medical Information System" and so on. These designations may be related to the institutions' attempts to emphasize the goals of professional training and the focus of HIS teaching. There are 11 HIS-related courses with large differences in nomenclature but some overlap in teaching content, of which the top five in terms of frequency are: Medical Informatics, Hospital Informatization Project Management, Health Informatics, Health Information Management, and Case Informatics. The frequency of courses as HIS introductory courses, in descending order, is as follows: basic computer courses (such as Data Structure, Database Principle, Operation System, etc.), Software Engineering, Information System Analysis and Design, Management Information System, and Hospital Management; and the frequency of courses as HIS follow-up courses, in descending order, is as follows: Medical Big Data Analysis Technology, Decision Support System, Hospital Informatization Project Management, and Information system Implementation and Operation and Maintenance Management (Fig. 1).

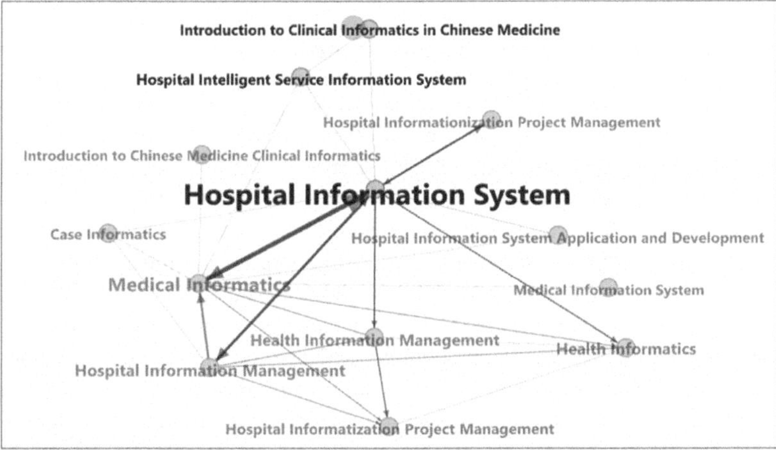

Note: Nodes represent courses, the thicker and darker the connecting line between nodes, the higher the frequency of the corresponding two courses being offered by the same institution.

Fig. 1. Relationship diagram of hospital informatization-related courses in higher TCM colleges and universities.

3.2 Course Audience, Nature, and Instructional Arrangement

In TCM universities, the HIS curriculum primarily targets undergraduate students across three core disciplines: Medical Information Engineering, Health Information Management, and Computer Science and Technology. While less prevalent in Biomedical Engineering and Data Science & Big Data Technology programs, select institutions like Guangxi and Shanghai universities of TCM have extended course offerings to Public Administration majors. At the graduate level, only Hubei and Guangxi universities provide HIS instruction for informatics and management master's programs respectively. Regarding course classification, HIS is designated as a compulsory course for informatics undergraduates in most TCM institutions, with exceptions in Liaoning, Shanxi, and Zhejiang where it serves as an elective for certain informatics tracks. Notably, Shanghai [2] and Gansu [3] universities have implemented institution-wide undergraduate electives. The standard scheduling places HIS in the 6th or 7th semester, following prerequisite coursework in medical sciences, management, and computing - a deliberate sequencing that builds upon foundation courses (1st/2nd semester introductory modules) and intermediate medical informatics training (3rd/4th semesters). Credit hours demonstrate significant variation, ranging from 32 (minimum at Guangxi University of TCM for Public Administration) to 70 (maximum at Shanghai University of TCM for Health Services Management) [2]. Informatics programs universally incorporate laboratory components (12–28 h), reflecting the discipline's applied nature. This structured approach ensures vertical integration with prior coursework while accommodating institution-specific specialization needs through flexible credit allocations.

3.3 Curriculum Objectives and Teaching Priorities

The educational objectives and instructional emphases of HIS courses in TCM universities demonstrate discipline-specific variations aligned with distinct professional competencies. For medical programs, the curriculum prioritizes developing communication proficiency and collaborative capabilities in digital healthcare environments, with concentrated focus on HIT fundamentals, HIS architecture, and operational workflows of clinical systems [4, 5]. Management-oriented programs emphasize cultivating HIT application competencies for administrative problem-solving, particularly examining the interplay between HIS principles, health policy frameworks, and hospital governance [2, 3, 6–8]. Informatics specialties target technical skill development in HIS implementation and maintenance, concentrating on system standards, process modeling, and functional specifications [2, 3, 6–8]. Our institutional survey revealed a consensus hierarchy of teaching priorities: (1) core HIT technologies, (2) medical information standardization, (3) hospital management operations with HMIS applications, (4) clinical workflows with HCIS integration, and (5) foundational HIS concepts including system architecture and historical evolution. Notably, emerging domains such as telemedicine platforms, regional health information exchange systems, and healthcare data governance received comparatively less emphasis in current curricula, suggesting potential areas for future content realignment to address industry advancements.

3.4 Faculty Composition and Professional Development

Historical analyses identified significant limitations in HIS course faculty composition at TCM institutions, characterized by predominant recruitment from information science or computer science backgrounds, resulting in disciplinary homogeneity, inadequate integration of medical-managerial-engineering knowledge domains, and limited practical experience [9, 10]. However, scholarly attention to this critical aspect of HIS education has waned in recent literature. Our institutional survey reveals an evolving faculty profile with these distinctive characteristics: Demographically, the current HIS faculty cohort demonstrates gender imbalance (60% male) and age concentration (85% aged 35–50 years). Academic qualifications show 40% holding doctoral degrees, while professional recognition is evidenced by 86% possessing senior academic titles. Teaching experience reflects substantial institutional memory, with 60% maintaining 15–20 years of dedicated HIS instruction. Disciplinary affiliations present a promising interdisciplinary shift: 46% self-identify as working at the medicine-informatics intersection (particularly TCM informatics), while one-third remain rooted in computer science. Professional backgrounds indicate that one-third possess direct work experience in healthcare IT enterprises or hospital information departments. Notably, among those lacking such experience, one-third have completed intensive (3 + month) industry immersion programs. Continuous professional development appears robust, with over 86% having systematically completed hospital informatization training programs offered by professional associations since assuming HIS teaching responsibilities.

3.5 Development of Instructional Platforms

Our survey reveals significant gaps in platform development for HIS education across TCM institutions. Approximately one-third of participating universities have not pursued any first-class course designation for hospital informatization-related curricula. As of November 2024, institutional achievements in this domain remain limited: Guangxi University of Chinese Medicine's "Hospital Management Information System", and Hubei University of Traditional Chinese Medicine's "Hospital Information System" stand as the provincial-level first-class course, while Nanjing University of Chinese Medicine's "Hospital Information System" holds university-level recognition. Liaoning University of Traditional Chinese Medicine's "Hospital Management Information System" attained college-level status. Notably, three institutions (Jiangxi, Nanjing, and Guangxi Universities of Chinese Medicine) have secured provincial first-class course status for their "Medical Informatics" programs, with Fujian University of Traditional Chinese Medicine achieving similar recognition for "Health Informatics." At the national level, no HIS courses have yet earned prestigious "National Elite Course" designation. The Guangzhou University of Chinese Medicine HIS team represents the sole exception, having developed a "Hospital Information System" SPOC course available through the iCourse (China's MOOC platform) network. Most TCM institutions continue to rely on localized teaching management systems for HIS course delivery, with platforms typically restricted to enrolled students. This insular approach substantially limits both the courses' societal impact and their potential for interdisciplinary knowledge exchange.

The current landscape suggests urgent need for expanded investment in open educational resources and cross-institutional platform development to enhance the visibility and accessibility of HIS education in TCM contexts.

3.6 Course Textbook Development

During China's 11th and 13th Five-Year Plan periods, TCM informatics experts compiled and published two authoritative HIS textbooks that have served as fundamental instructional resources. Despite subsequent proliferation of domestic HIS teaching materials, scholars have identified persistent limitations, including inadequate adaptation for general HIS education and insufficient supplementary teaching resources [7]. Our survey of 14 TCM universities revealed substantial variation in textbook adoption, with five primary options in use. The most frequently selected were Hospital Information System Tutorial (Feng & Shang) and Hospital Information System Analysis and Design (Shi), while six institutions utilized self-compiled or collaboratively edited materials. Faculty evaluations indicated significant dissatisfaction, with only four instructors (7.8% of respondents) considering current textbooks adequate. The predominant criticisms, ranked by frequency, were: (1) absence of supporting experimental environments and practical teaching materials (82.4% of respondents); (2) outdated content failing to reflect contemporary healthcare informatization advancements (76.5%); and (3) excessive abstraction with insufficient case studies, impairing both instructional delivery and student comprehension (68.6%). This disconnect between available resources and pedagogical needs highlights an urgent requirement for comprehensive textbook reform that incorporates practical components, current industry developments, and concrete examples to better support competency-based HIS education in TCM institutions.

3.7 Practical Teaching in HIS Courses

The implementation of practical teaching in HIS courses across TCM universities demonstrates a hierarchical approach, with the following methodologies ordered by prevalence: (1) group-based system design and development projects, (2) hospital process simulation through specialized software, (3) industry expert-led sessions featuring engineers from healthcare institutions or HIT enterprises, (4) field observations at hospital information departments or HIT companies, and (5) instructional video demonstrations. Eight leading TCM institutions - Nanjing, Guangxi, Liaoning, Fujian, and Hubei Universities of Chinese Medicine - have established dedicated HIS laboratories. These facilities are typically equipped with four core teaching software systems, ranked by deployment frequency: outpatient/emergency department management systems, clinical information systems, inpatient management systems, and electronic medical record systems. Notably absent are specialized departmental systems supporting financial operations, medical records management, medical imaging, laboratory workflows, and surgical anesthesia processes. Software acquisition occurs primarily through three channels: commercial procurement (58%), industry donations from HIT providers or partner hospitals (32%), and limited use of freeware or trial versions (10%). While existing literature [2, 6, 11, 12] confirms the pedagogical value of these systems in familiarizing students with hospital workflows and facilitating collaborative learning, instructors report significant implementation challenges. These obstacles, ordered by severity, include: excessive software complexity creating instructional and maintenance burdens (reported by 78% of respondents); scarcity of education-optimized HIS solutions (65%); prohibitive acquisition costs for complete systems (57%); and integration difficulties among heterogeneous software platforms compromising practical training outcomes (42%). This landscape suggests an urgent need for developing tailored teaching solutions that balance functional authenticity with pedagogical accessibility, while fostering stronger industry-academic partnerships to address current resource limitations.

4 Discussion

4.1 Key Challenges in HIS Curriculum Development at TCM Colleges and Universities

While significant progress has been achieved in curriculum design, instructional content, faculty development, teaching platforms, textbook compilation, and practical training, the advancement of HIS courses in TCM institutions continues to encounter substantial obstacles and challenges.

Core Internal Development Challenges. Three primary difficulties hinder the maturation of HIS education in TCM settings. First, the theoretical framework remains underdeveloped, reflecting the evolving nature of healthcare information systems as they increasingly integrate with diverse hospital operations. This disciplinary immaturity manifests through inconsistent course nomenclature, redundant or overlapping chapter content, ambiguous conceptual definitions lacking industry consensus, and insufficiently rigorous logical structures. Second, a pronounced disconnect exists between curricular content and contemporary HIS practice. Current teaching materials fail to keep pace with rapid technological innovations in HIT and evolving healthcare policies and management paradigms. Furthermore, existing university-hospital-industry collaborations have yet to establish effective mechanisms that bridge this theory-practice divide and ensure high-quality instructional delivery. Third, inadequate practical teaching resources significantly constrain curriculum implementation. HIS teaching software frequently proves excessively complex and non-standardized, often misaligned with theoretical course content. These limitations severely impede the execution of comprehensive and innovative laboratory exercises, as well as effective management of experimental teaching activities. The absence of suitable simulation tools and standardized platforms particularly compromises the development of applied competencies essential for healthcare information professionals.

Major Challenges Posed by the External Environment. The evolving landscape presents four primary challenges for HIS curriculum development in TCM institutions. Firstly, adapting to structural transformations in HIT talent demand necessitates cultivating versatile and innovative professionals capable of strategically managing healthcare informatization, tactically driving HIT integration and innovation, and operationally executing complex system development, health big data analytics, data governance, and information security. This imperative concurrently requires enhanced information literacy among healthcare practitioners and demands HIS courses to accommodate discipline-specific knowledge acquisition and competency development requirements. Secondly, professional specialization pressures compel TCM universities to accelerate discipline-focused development. Given that Western medical institutions initiated HIS education earlier, which resulted in more mature pedagogical research and practical training, thus TCM programs must strategically concentrate on TCM informatization. This entails expediting enhancements in core teaching content, experimental instruction, and teaching materials to foster distinctive disciplinary characteristics. Thirdly, alignment with shifting student learning behaviors has become critical. As learning patterns increasingly exhibit self-directed, individualized, and fragmented characteristics [13], HIS courses must urgently undergo digital-intelligent transformation. This requires constructing course knowledge graphs integrated with large language models (LLMs), developing AI-powered teaching assistants, and implementing precision learning path recommendations based on learner profiles. Such advancements enable "on-demand learning" and dynamic assessment to meet personalized educational needs. Finally, supporting China's "Double First-Class" initiative presents a fourth challenge. With HIS widely designated as a signature course underpinning first-class majors and disciplines in medical universities, programs must align with Education Informatization 2.0 standards. This mandates elevating instructional quality and educational outcomes to rapidly establish "First-Class Courses," "Golden Courses," and "Intelligent Courses" that meet national excellence benchmarks.

4.2 Several Suggestions for Strengthening the Construction of HIS Curriculum in TCM Colleges and Universities

As the digital-intelligent transformation of hospitals matures, developing, maintaining, and managing HIS will become increasingly complex. This demands that medical informatics professionals and healthcare practitioners possess a deeper understanding of HIS. To achieve sustainable and healthy development, TCM universities must proactively pursue transformations in the following areas for their first-class HIS course development:

Strengthening HIS Course Instruction Through Enhanced Top-Level Design of the Medical Informatics Curriculum System. HIS courses will inevitably face increasingly diversified and multi-tiered teaching demands stemming from the widespread integration of medical informatics education. Therefore, instructional guidance for HIS courses must be reinforced through comprehensive analysis of the medical informatics curriculum architecture. For instance, medical informatics knowledge should be segmented into discrete modules featuring self-contained logical structures and focused teaching functions. These modules should be organized along key dimensions including: object type (e.g., genes, cells, tissues, organs, human body, populations), institution type, professional field, information lifecycle, and knowledge abstraction level. Subsequently, relevant knowledge modules should be systematically combined to construct a HIS course content framework tailored to meet digital health competency requirements for graduates across diverse specialties (TCM, clinical practice, medical technology, public health, management, and informatics). This framework must reflect the distinctive needs of varying professional categories and educational levels while establishing explicit relationships with other medical informatics courses. Professional accreditation standards should further formalize this structure by mandating specific guidance on HIS course nomenclature, credit hour requirements, core teaching content, assessment foci, and experimental teaching components. Concurrently, while continuously integrating frontier domains such as healthcare big data governance, medical information standardization, and medical artificial intelligence, the fundamental HIS knowledge framework must maintain relative stability. This requires careful articulation of conceptual linkages with foundational and sequential courses (e.g., Health Services Management, Hospital Management, Information Systems Analysis & Design, Healthcare IT Project Management), alongside deliberate mapping of content overlaps with related disciplines including Medical Informatics, Clinical Informatics, Health Information Management, and AI-driven Medical Engineering. Such a structured approach ultimately supports the development of high-quality teaching resources anchored in the HIS course knowledge graph, enables precision learning path recommendations, facilitates dynamic learning assessment mechanisms, and mitigates potential conflicts during knowledge graph integration across the broader medical informatics curriculum cluster.

Promote the Construction of Dual-Teacher HIS Course Teaching Team Oriented to Output High-Quality Course Teaching Service. The combination of medical-industry-medical-credit and school-medicine-school-enterprise to jointly cultivate composite and applied talents has become a common feature of the reform of the new engineering professional training mode in TCM colleges and universities. This should be used as an opportunity to accelerate the exploration of breaking the institutional mechanism that hinders the integration of HIT industry, teaching and research resources, to solve the problem of disconnecting the theory and practice of HIS teaching, and to build a tightly coupled dual-teacher HIS course teaching team. For example: HIS full-time teachers can be required to go to medical enterprises regularly for further training, to understand the new progress of HIS, collect and organize teaching cases and comprehensive experimental needs; HIT engineers can be hired as HIS lecturers, participate in syllabus compilation, teaching design, textbook editing and review, teaching research, etc., and guide them to participate in the practice of teaching in depth; optimize the teaching and management mechanism, and provide HIT engineers with humanized teaching environment and appropriate inclination in the allocation of class time. Optimize the teaching management mechanism, provide HIT engineers with a humanized teaching environment and appropriately tilt the allocation of class hours.

Promoting Open-Access HIS Teaching Platform Development Centered on Cultivating Versatile and Innovative HIT Talent. The establishment of experimental teaching platforms constitutes an essential vehicle for advancing curricular reform and enhancing pedagogical effectiveness within the Education Informatization 2.0 framework. TCM universities should intensify inter-institutional collaboration while strategically leveraging opportunities afforded by the National Digital Educational Resources Public Service System [17]. This necessitates a decisive shift away from fragmented development approaches—characterized by independent construction of virtual hospital simulations [14–16] or institution-specific procurement of proprietary HIS teaching software—toward establishing an HIT Talent Development Public Service Platform Alliance through partnerships with healthcare IT enterprises and medical institutions. Collectively, stakeholders should co-construct an open-access HIS experimental teaching platform integrating core functionalities including online system demonstration, certification testing, experimental teaching management, secondary development capabilities, innovative solution design environments, and sandbox simulation. This multifunctional platform serves tripartite objectives: it provides medical students with authentic system operation practice; enables informatics students to execute design-oriented innovation experiments; and functions as a crowdsourcing ecosystem where entrepreneurial teams rapidly integrate business components (microservices) to prototype novel hospital management models, simultaneously allowing HIT enterprises to harvest solution concepts. Empirical validation emerges from our institution's "Wisdom TCM Hospital Laboratory"—developed collaboratively with industry leaders including Winning Health Technology Group and Nanjing Hitec. Through controlled access to application programming interfaces (APIs), modifiable configuration files, and shared database instances, this platform has become foundational for New Engineering Education initiatives in HIS. It facilitates a pedagogical progression from simulating core healthcare workflows to conducting innovation experiments involving algorithmic implementations of critical modules, thereby bridging theoretical instruction and practical healthcare informatics execution.

Promote the Development of Digital HIS Teaching Materials with the Core of Deepening Research and Practice of Teaching Methods. Digital HIS teaching materials are easy to update and have a large amount of resources and various ways of presenting knowledge [18], which can better support the teaching of flipped classroom, micro-courses, MOOC, etc. and reduce the difficulty of implementation of teaching research and reform. Relying on the mainstream digital course development tools in the market, we can build a digital HIS teaching material resource platform that integrates development, utilization, release and evaluation. Arrange the HIS knowledge system with the main line of "concept-principle-application-method", collect and produce text, pictures, videos, cases, system operation entrances, references and other teaching materials around the knowledge points, and mark and manage the conditions of applicability, access privileges, audience groups, applicable pedagogical methods, and practical teaching projects of each teaching material resource, The digitalized HIS teaching material resource library is formed by marking and managing the applicable conditions, access rights, audience groups, applicable teaching methods, practical teaching projects, assessment methods and other attributes of each teaching material. Support teachers to quickly integrate teaching resources to generate digital teaching materials according to chapter contents and teaching design needs for different majors and learning conditions, and guide students to participate in learning and experiments by inquiry, inspiration and collaborative strategies. It supports students to interact with textbook resource developers, participate in editing and organizing textbook resources, and realize closed-loop management of textbook editing, reviewing, using and evaluating.

5 Conclusion

This study comprehensively synthesizes questionnaire data, pedagogical literature, and institutional documentation to delineate the current state of HIS course development within TCM universities. It identifies critical challenges confronting HIS curriculum construction, and then proposes evidence-based enhancement strategies informed by our institution's implementation experience, including knowledge system standardization, dual-qualified faculty team development, open experimental platform establishment, and digital textbook innovation. These insights provide medical informatics educators, administrators, healthcare organizations, and health IT enterprises with valuable understanding of HIS education in Chinese TCM institutions, thereby fostering multi-stakeholder engagement in synergistic talent cultivation.

Nevertheless, constrained by data limitations and research scope, this work does not fully address three pivotal dimensions of intelligent HIS course advancement: the restructuring of content and resource architectures, pedagogical transformation through blended learning methodologies, and innovation in assessment paradigms. Future research should prioritize four interconnected avenues: First, developing dynamic curriculum adjustment mechanisms using knowledge graphs as scaffolds to synchronize course content with evolving clinical/administrative demands and technological iterations. Second, constructing modular digital resource systems that support responsive content delivery. Third, creating large language model(LLM)-powered teaching assistants that generate personalized learning pathways from student activity analytics. Fourth, implementing multi-agent evaluation frameworks incorporating feedback from HIT enterprises, healthcare institutions, and learners to establish participatory optimization ecosystems. Such initiatives will ensure the digital intelligent transformation of HIS education, so as to tangibly advance medical informatics talent development.

Acknowledgments. The authors express sincere gratitude to the Information Education Branch of the Chinese Association of Traditional Chinese Medicine Information (CATCMI) for its continuous guidance and to all member institutions for their generous support of this study. Financial support was provided by the 2023 Research Project on Computer-Based Education of the National Association for Computer-Based Education in Higher Education Institutions under Grant No. 2023-AFCEC-262, titled "Information-Literacy Needs and Implementation Strategies for TCM Undergraduates Based on the Digital Health Competency Framework," and by the 2024 New Engineering Course Construction Program of the Hubei Provincial Department of Education under Grant No. XGK01069 for the course "Hospital Information Systems."

Disclosure of Interests. The authors have no competing interests to declare that are relevant to the content of this article.

References

1. Wang, Z.Q., He, M.: Study on teaching model of the course of hospital information system in the era of medical big data. China Med. Equip. **16**(12), 90–92 (2019)
2. Yu, J., Hou, Y., Che, L.: Teaching reform of hospital information system for health administration-oriented specialty: taking shanghai university of traditional Chinese medicine as an example. J. Tradit. Chin. Med. Educ. **39**(5), 73–77 (2020)

3. Tao, W.T., Zhang, X.H., Li, Y., Wu, X.D.: Teaching results of medical information system course in Gansu college of traditional Chinese medicine. Chin. J. Med. Libr. Inf. Sci. **22**(11), 54–56 (2013)
4. Gu, L.Y., Cai, X.F., Zhu, X.H.: Discussion and practice on the teaching reform of hospital information system course. Sci. Educ. Lit. (Mon.) **7**(7), 76(2008)
5. Yu, J.: Research on multiform discussion teaching method of hospital information system course. Med. Inf. **33**(2), 8–10 (2020)
6. Qin, X.J., Shi, C.: Education of hospital information system course in TCM universities and the informatization construction of TCM hospitals. Chin. J. Manag. Chin. Med. **10**, 766–768 (2007)
7. Deng, W.P., Wang, S.Q.: Discussion on modular teaching of hospital information system. J. Med. Inform. **36**(11), 82–85 (2015)
8. Zuo, Y.J., Wu, L., Zhao, Q.: On the popularization of hospital information system course in higher medical universities. China High. Med. Educ. **4**, 82–83 (2011)
9. Feng, T.L., Shang, W.G.: Reflections on hospital information system education development. J. Med. Inform. **31**(11), 91–94 (2010)
10. Ye, M.Q.: Research on teaching system for HIS curriculum. J. Med. Inform. **2**, 63–66 (2008)
11. Ouyang, T., Zhang, L., Wang, D.: The exploration of teaching reform for hospital information system courses under the task–driven mode. J. Heze Univ. **40**(5), 102–104 (2018)
12. Gao, C.L., Li, Y.Q., Yang, L.: Design of experimental teaching platform for hospital information system. Commun. World **15**, 25–26 (2013)
13. Wang, Z.L., Guan, X.D., Luo, L.: Digital-intelligent integrated courses: a new direction of curriculum reform in "artificial intelligence + curriculum". Open Educ. Res. **31**(1), 34–41 (2025)
14. Zhu, H., Wang, A.M., Geng, W., et al.: On the course reform of hospital information system based on virtual simulation panoramic hospital. Educ. Teach. Forum (23), 45–48 (2021)
15. Shi, Y.F., Bi, X.H., Du, S.H., Zhao, X.L.: Construction of a network-based digital hospital simulation laboratory. J. Xinjiang Med. Univ. **37**(10), 1409–1413 (2014)
16. Zhao, H.: Practice and analysis of HIS on demand teaching in virtual environment. China High. Med. Educ. (11), 30–31(2018)
17. Ministry of Education of the People's Republic of China. Education Informatization 2.0 Action Plan. http://www.moe.gov.cn/srcsite/A16/s3342/201804/t20180425_334188.html. Accessed 18 Apr 2023
18. Wang, J.H.: Studies on the development strategies of college digitalization textbooks. Educ. Teach. Forum (2), 21–24 (2023

Experimental Platform for Structural Health Monitoring in IoT Engineering

Jin Qian[1], Chengfei Cai[1], Yan Xu[1], Hui Li[1], Xiaoshuang Xing[2], and Shuai Liu[1](✉)

[1] School of Information Engineering, Taizhou University, Taizhou, Jiangsu, China
{qianjin,chengfeicai,xuyan,huili_tzxy,liushuai}@tzu.edu.cn
[2] School of Computer Science and Engineering, Changshu Institute of Technology, Changshu, Suzhou, Jiangsu, China
xing@cslg.edu.cn

Abstract. This article presents the design and implementation of an experimental learning environment for structural health monitoring (SHM) of large-scale buildings within the Internet of Things (IoT) engineering curriculum. In response to the Chinese National Strategy for Educational Digitalization, this research addresses key challenges in traditional IoT experimental teaching, including limited equipment availability, complex real-world scenarios, and high operational risks. The article proposes a hybrid virtual-physical simulation platform modeled after the Taizhou Bridge. The platform aligns with national digital education initiatives and overcomes the constraints of physical experimentation regarding equipment scale and environmental complexity. It adopts a student-centered, problem-oriented approach that addresses instructional challenges related to interdisciplinary knowledge integration, engineering practice transformation, and repeatable experimental validation. Simulation results demonstrate that the environment enhances students' understanding of large-scale IoT systems and cultivates system-level design thinking through scenario-based, task-driven learning. This platform provides an innovative pathway for cultivating application-oriented talent in IoT engineering.

Keywords: Engineering education · Hybrid learning environment · IoT-based experimental environment · Structural health monitoring · Taizhou Bridge case study

1 Introduction

The rapid development of the Internet of Things (IoT) has revolutionized engineering education, particularly in large-scale system integration and real-world application scenarios [14,15]. Traditional physical IoT laboratory experiments are constrained by limited experimental environments and conditions [1,2]. These setups are typically isolated, hardware-dependent, and lack immersion in

W. Hong et al. (Eds.): ICCSE 2025, CCIS 2761, pp. 513–524, 2026.
https://doi.org/10.1007/978-981-95-7731-6_40

real-world industrial scenarios, resulting in low student engagement and insufficient exposure to practical applications [16,17]. However, constructing large-scale IoT systems is crucial for equipping students to address complex, integrated engineering challenges [18]. Among these, structural health monitoring (SHM) of large buildings represents a comprehensive task, involving real-time acquisition of parameters such as stress, wind speed and direction, displacement, settlement, and tilt using various sensors [19,20]. Analytical and early-warning models are developed based on the structure's characteristics, functional requirements, environmental context, and lifecycle, integrating knowledge from sensing technology, communication networks, system design, and data analytics [21,22].

This project uses the Taizhou Bridge as a prototype to construct an experimental environment platform for large-scale SHM. The experiment involves diverse equipment, abstract concepts, and technical integration. This article adopt a "virtual-physical integration" approach guided by the principle of "virtual where necessary, physical where possible." A high-fidelity experimental environment platform has been developed using modern information technologies.

As a practical course in the IoT engineering curriculum, this SHM simulation emphasizes student-centered, problem-oriented, virtual-physical integration, and application-driven innovation. Its practical significance is reflected in four major aspects: **Addressing Challenges in Large-Scale IoT System Construction:** The platform recreates real-world monitoring scenarios for large structures, enabling students to gain a macro-level understanding of IoT systems. The experimental environment supports scenario-based design of monitoring systems, helping students develop and assess comprehensive SHM design capabilities while fostering systems thinking. **Enabling Interdisciplinary Integration in Practice-Based Learning:** The course bridges multiple curriculum modules, such as Computer Networks, Wireless Sensor Networks, IoT Planning and Design, and Comprehensive Practice in IoT Applications. Students apply integrated knowledge from these areas to design and implement hardware-software modules for large-scale SHM systems. **Overcoming Limitations of High-Risk and Repetitive Experiments:** Real-world SHM experiments for large structures often involve extensive setups and safety hazards, preventing students from engaging directly in field operations. This platform simulates the Taizhou Bridge environment, allowing students to virtually deploy hardware, configure sensor parameters, and monitor real-time data transmission in a risk-free, repeatable setting. **Bridging Theory with Real-World Engineering Practice:** By simulating near-authentic engineering scenarios, the platform transforms theoretical modules into hands-on tasks, boosting student engagement, initiative, and problem-solving abilities. It also supports iterative testing, optimization, and evaluation of system designs.

The system leverages a hybrid architecture combining experimental environments with real engineering constraints. The SHM scenario of the Taizhou Bridge is reconstructed with high fidelity using 3D modeling, providing an immersive experience that enhances student participation. Features such as novice guidance, step-by-step instructions, and knowledge prompts help students quickly grasp experimental objectives and procedures. The system is developed in C# using the Unity engine, deployed via WebGL, and communicates with the server using the WebSocket protocol. 3D modeling and visualization are implemented through 3ds Max and Maya. The experimental environment platform runs on Windows 8 or Windows 10 systems and supports modern browsers such as Firefox and Chrome (64-bit), requiring no installation—students can access the environment directly via web browsers.

2 Related Work

The development of experimental learning environments in engineering education has gained momentum, driven by the Chinese National Strategy for Educational Digitalization and the limitations of traditional laboratory settings [20]. Studies have demonstrated the effectiveness of virtual laboratories in overcoming challenges such as limited equipment, high operational costs and risks, and the difficulty of replicating complex real-world scenarios (e.g., [1–4]). These environments provide students with accessible, repeatable, and safe experiential learning opportunities [5,6].

In IoT engineering education, researchers have explored various virtual and remote laboratory solutions [7,8]. Traditional IoT teaching struggles with the isolated nature of hardware-dependent experiments and a lack of immersion in industrial contexts, making it difficult to convey the systemic nature of large-scale IoT deployments [9]. Virtual simulations address these issues by allowing students to design, configure, and test comprehensive IoT systems without the constraints of physical hardware [10,11]. These platforms focus on network configuration, sensor data acquisition, and basic data processing, providing a foundational understanding of IoT principles [12].

The application of simulation for SHM is established in professional engineering for design, analysis, and training [13,14]. However, its integration into educational curricula, especially within IoT programs, is a more recent development [15]. SHM systems involve diverse sensor technologies, data communication networks, and sophisticated analytical models, making them ideal for showcasing interdisciplinary knowledge integration [16,17]. While some educational tools cover individual SHM components, few provide an integrated platform for students to develop a holistic understanding of large-scale IoT systems [18].

Pedagogical approaches underpinning experimental learning environments are crucial. The shift towards student-centered, problem-oriented learning enhances engagement and practical skill development [19,20]. The concept of hybrid virtual-physical integration balances the benefits of simulation with real-world constraints [21]. The construction of a high-fidelity experimental environment modeled on the Taizhou Bridge, specifically to foster system-level design thinking and bridge theory with practice in IoT, distinguishes this work [22,23].

3 System Design and Architecture

3.1 Platform Overview

This experimental teaching platform is built on a B/S architecture, utilizing lightweight programming languages and modular design for easy deployment and scalability. It supports distributed containerized deployment with auto-scaling and includes key modules such as Experimental Training, Lab Reports, Data Analytics, and an Examination System. The platform enables interactive learning through structured course materials, video uploads, and real-time experimental environments, while tracking student progress and offering flexible grading options (automated, instructor-led, or peer-reviewed).

The system accommodates both instructors and students. Instructors can upload resources, manage courses, and grade assignments, while students access learning materials, monitor progress, and engage in discussions. In terms of performance, the platform handles $\leq$500 concurrent users with sub-0.2 s response times, scaling up to 1,000 users (<0.6 s) and 3,000 users (>1 s, with >80% server load). For optimal operation, client devices require a bandwidth of at least $\geq$100 Mbps to avoid latency or packet loss, and a minimum hardware configuration of an Intel® Core™ i5 CPU, 8 GB RAM, and an NVIDIA GTX 1060 GPU.

3.2 Experimental Principle and Framework

The experiment follows a student-centered learning approach with problem orientation, virtual-physical integration, and application-driven innovation. It is structured into multiple stages: foundational learning of wireless sensors, switching, and routing; offline system architecture design; device selection, deployment, connection, and configuration; algorithm design and programming for data sensing, transmission, processing, and application; and analysis of experimental results and simulation of real-world scenarios.

Through three core modules—perception layer, network layer, and platform layer—and 17 interactive experimental operations across seven levels, students gain hands-on experience and consolidate their mastery of 12 key knowledge areas from the following courses: Computer Networks, Wireless Sensor Networks, IoT Engineering Planning and Design, and Comprehensive Practice in IoT Application Development (Fig. 1).

The experimental framework uses the IoT system for health monitoring of the Taizhou Bridge as a prototype, incorporating data acquisition, transmission, and health management systems. Computer modeling and simulation techniques emulate a practical IoT application for large-scale SHM. Students select, install, and configure devices for the sensing, network, and platform layers in the experimental environment, and design management and control software interfaces to meet application requirements.

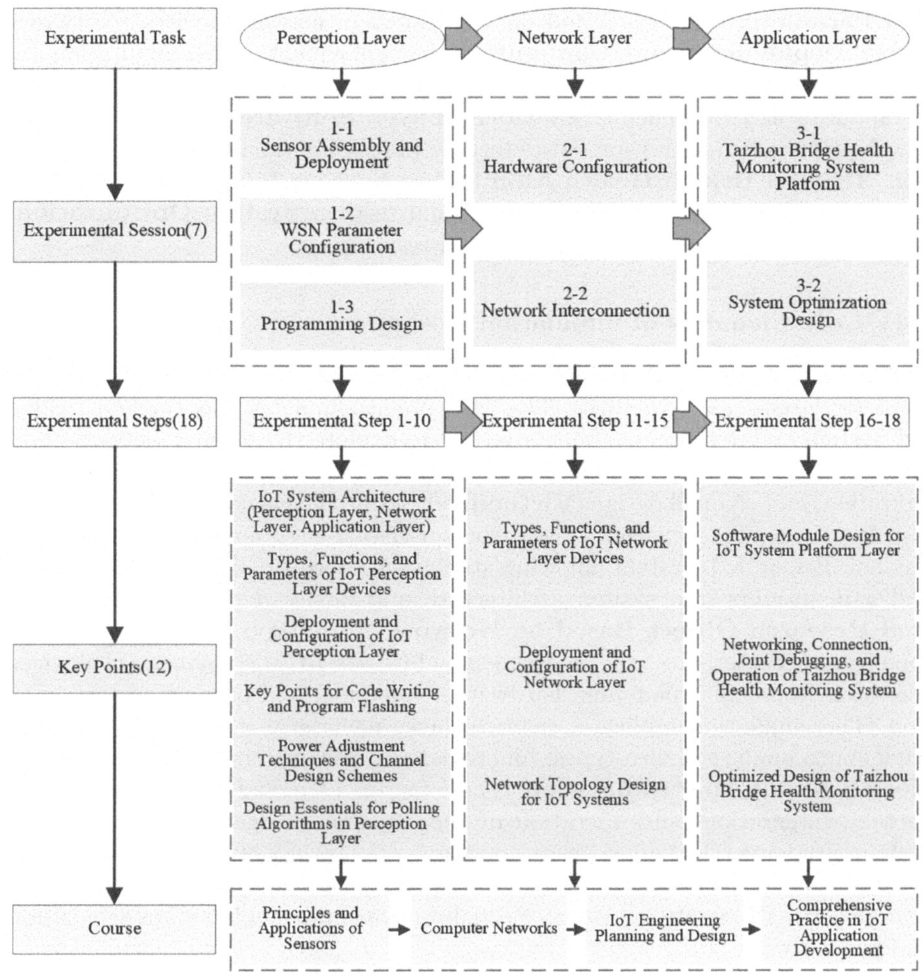

Fig. 1. Structural Framework.

3.3 Key Knowledge Points

The experiment covers 12 critical knowledge points: **IoT System Architecture**: Structure and operational principles of sensing, network, and platform layers. **Sensing Layer Device Types, Functions, and Parameters**: Selection and understanding of device functionality and performance. **Sensing Layer Deployment and Configuration**: Deployment, connection, and configuration of sensing devices. **Code Writing and Firmware Programming**: Firmware development for data acquisition and communication. **Power Adjustment and Channel Design**: Signal transmission analysis and channel selection. **Sensing Layer Polling Algorithm Design**: Polling cycles, data filtering, processing, and anomaly detection. **Network Layer Device Types, Functions,**

and Parameters: Selection and understanding of network devices. **Network Layer Deployment and Configuration**: Deployment and configuration for interconnectivity. **Network Topology Design**: System topology design based on application requirements. **Platform Layer Software Module Design**: Development of modules for data storage, processing, analysis, and visualization. **Taizhou Bridge Health Monitoring System Integration**: Networking, connection, integration, and operational testing. **System Optimization**: Analysis and optimization of experimental results.

3.4 Core Elements of Simulation Design

The simulation design creates virtualized scenarios that replicate IoT deployment for large-scale structures. The experiment simulates the Taizhou Bridge IoT system architecture, enabling students to explore the sensing, network, and platform layers through virtual operations such as sensor installation, node configuration, and channel design. **Virtualized Scenario Based on Engineering Applications**: The experiment constructs a virtual environment replicating the Taizhou Bridge IoT system, allowing students to perform simulated operations and gain insights into system architecture and device deployment. **Virtualized Research Object Based on Network Topology**: Guided by network topology characteristics, the experiment addresses IoT deployment challenges across environmental planning, hardware connection, and parameter configuration. The simulation replicates network layer devices at a 1:1 scale, enabling students to analyze device types, functions, and parameters. **Taizhou Bridge Health Monitoring Simulation**: The experiment includes networking, connection, integration, and operation of the Taizhou Bridge health monitoring system. Students select appropriate communication protocols and network architectures to ensure stable and real-time data transmission, perform system integration testing to verify inter-device collaboration, and simulate data acquisition and processing.

4 Experimental Teaching Process and Methods

This project implements problem-based, guided, scenario-driven, interactive, and inquiry-based teaching methods. Through diverse media such as text, images, and videos, the experiment supports preparation, pre-study, and online instruction, fostering students' practical skills, comprehensive analysis, and innovation capabilities. The teaching methods are integrated into each core experimental step.

4.1 Teaching Process

The teaching process integrates model construction, comparative analysis, pattern exploration, and a blend of virtual and real environments to provide students with an intuitive understanding of experimental system principles. As shown in

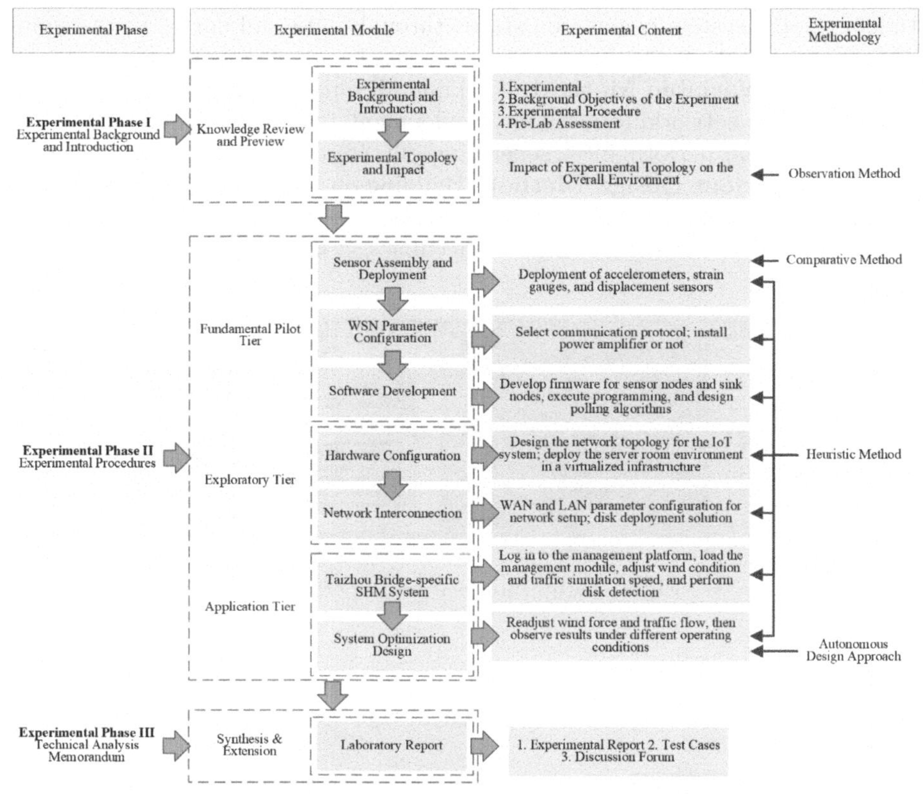

Fig. 2. Virtual Simulation Experiment Teaching Procedures and Methods.

Fig. 2. **Model Construction**: Establishes operational models for scenarios and environmental deployments in large-scale structural IoT systems, organizing the experimental workflow by module. **Comparative Analysis**: Students compare different hardware connection methods and network configurations across various IoT scenarios, mastering configuration patterns and understanding comprehensive IoT deployment principles. **Pattern Exploration**: Investigates the impact of different environmental deployments, hardware connections, and network configurations on IoT network service quality. **Evaluation and Optimization**: Students assess experiment effectiveness using sound, light, data, and charts based on each model's principles and parameters.

4.2 Experimental Methods

Following the principle of "real when possible, virtual-real integration," the project conducts a three-session experimental environment for large-scale structural IoT deployment. Students select hardware, configure parameters, and analyze system performance. The specific methods include: **Observation Method**:

Students assess system connection status through data and curves in the simulation environment, summarizing parameter variation patterns to inform system design. **Fixed Variable Method**: By fixing all but one parameter (e.g., channel parameters, networking methods, deployment types), students explore the impact on system performance, generating curves to summarize variation patterns. **Independent Design Method**: Building on insights from the fixed variable method, students select parameters to optimize system performance based on a scoring table, receiving immediate feedback (Figs. 3 and 4).

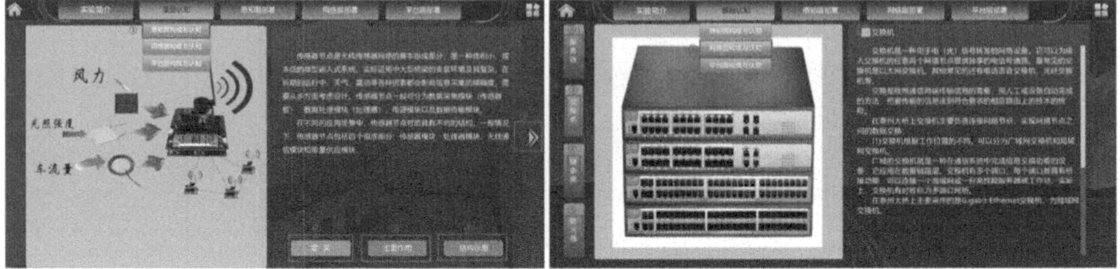

Fig. 3. Setup Interface for Experiment.

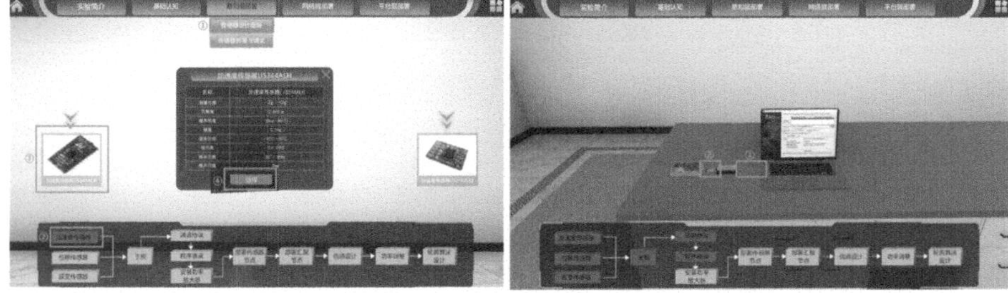

Fig. 4. Hands-on Sensor Manufacturing Experiment.

4.3 Experimental Report and Results

Student operations in the simulation platform—including sensor selection, device configuration, firmware programming, network parameter settings, and sensor parameter adjustments—lead to varied experimental outcomes. The data analysis module visualizes collected data using line graphs, reflecting the impact of different configurations. The experiment is structured in five stages: **Stage 1: Preparation**: Students review IoT knowledge, understand experimental background, objectives, and procedures, and clarify operational conditions and assessment requirements. **Stage 2: Sensor Fabrication**: Students deploy acceleration, strain, and displacement sensors, select communication protocols, program and burn firmware for sensing and aggregation nodes, and install power amplifiers (Figs. 5, 6 and 7).

Fig. 5. Sensor Deployment Experiment Operation.

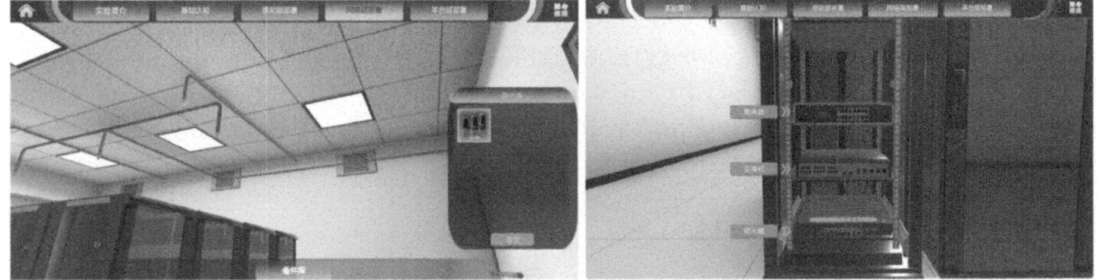

Fig. 6. Network Configuration Experiment Operation.

Stage 3: Sensor Deployment: Students deploy and configure sensor and aggregation nodes, design channels, adjust power, control coverage, and develop polling algorithms. **Stage 4: Network Configuration**: Students design the IoT network topology, deploy the machine room environment, connect firewalls, switches, and routers, configure WAN/LAN parameters, and select disk deployment schemes. **Stage 5: Command Center Operations**: Students log into the management platform, load modules, adjust wind and traffic simulation speeds, test disks, and analyze results under varying conditions.

Fig. 7. Command Center Experiment Operation.

5 Conclusion

This paper presents a comprehensive experimental environment for SHM in IoT engineering, launched in December 2022 and serving over 1,700 students and social learners. The platform adheres to the Outcome-Based Education (OBE) philosophy, emphasizing student-centered and outcome-oriented principles. Students configure parameters such as sensor types, networking methods, and deployment types for a bridge health monitoring system, and only upon correct setup can they obtain the health monitoring data line chart.

Future work will focus on continuously updating the experimental content in line with IoT technological advances and evolving SHM requirements. The platform will explore the integration of artificial intelligence (AI), augmented reality/virtual reality (AR/VR), and other emerging technologies to enhance interactivity and educational value. Faculty development will be prioritized through training, academic exchanges, and research engagement.

Acknowledgment. This work was supported by the National Natural Science Foundation of China (Grant No. 62302332), and the Natural Science Foundation of Jiangsu Higher Education Institutions of China (Grant No. 23KJB510033). This project also received support from the "Qinglan Project" for Outstanding Young and Middle-aged Academic Leaders of Jiangsu Province.

References

1. Huang, J., Broekman, A., Markou, G., Chen, H.: Framework for a practical and cost-effective IoT-enhanced structural health monitoring and damage diagnostics system with digital twinning. J. Civil Struct. Health Monit. **15**(3) (2025). https://doi.org/10.1007/s13349-025-00927-9
2. Bhatta, S., Dang, J.: Use of IoT for structural health monitoring of civil engineering structures: a state-of-the-art review. Urban Lifeline **2**(1), 17 (2024). https://doi.org/10.1007/s44285-024-00031-2
3. Saravanan, T.J., Mishra, M., Aherwar, A.D., Loureno, P.B.: Internet of things (IoT)-based structural health monitoring of laboratory-scale civil engineering structures. Innov. Infrastruct. Solutions **9**(4), 110 (2024). https://doi.org/10.1007/s41062-024-01413-9

4. Zivelonghi, A., Giuseppi, A.: Smart healthy schools: an IoT-enabled concept for multi-room dynamic air quality control. Internet Things Cyber-Phys. Syst. **4**, 24–31 (2024). https://doi.org/10.1016/j.iotcps.2023.05.005
5. Haque, M.E., Asikuzzaman, M., Khan, I.U., Ra, I., Hossain, M.S., Shah, S.B.: Comparative study of IoT-based topology maintenance protocol in a wireless sensor network for structural health monitoring. Remote Sens. **12**(15), 2358 (2020). https://doi.org/10.3390/rs12152358
6. Chu, Y., et al.: Hybrid-learning-based operational visual quality inspection for edge-computing-enabled IoT system. IEEE Internet Things J. **9**(7), 4958–4972 (2022). https://doi.org/10.1109/JIOT.2021.3107902
7. Souri, A., Ghafour, M.Y., Ahmed, A.M., Safara, F., Yamini, A., Hoseyninezhad, M.: A new machine learning-based healthcare monitoring model for student's condition diagnosis in Internet of Things environment. Soft Comput. **24**(22), 17111–17121 (2020). https://doi.org/10.1007/s00500-020-05003-6
8. Khan, A., et al.: A critical review of IoT-based structural health monitoring for dams. IEEE Internet Things J. **12**(2), 1368–1379 (2025). https://doi.org/10.1109/JIOT.2024.3488290
9. Hassan, M., Hussein, A., Nassr, A.A., Karoumi, R., Sayed, U.M., Abdelraheem, M.: Optimizing structural health monitoring systems through integrated fog and cloud computing within IoT framework. IEEE Access **12**, 89628–89646 (2024). https://doi.org/10.1109/ACCESS.2024.3419028
10. Cao, Y., et al.: Economic application of structural health monitoring and internet of things in efficiency of building information modeling. Smart Struct. Syst. **26**(5), 559–573 (2020). https://doi.org/10.12989/SSS.2020.26.5.559
11. Du, B., Lin, C., Sun, L., Zhao, Y., Li, L.: Response prediction based on temporal and spatial deep learning model for intelligent structural health monitoring. IEEE Internet Things J. **9**(15), 13364–13375 (2022). https://doi.org/10.1109/JIOT.2022.3141417
12. Deng, Z., Huang, M., Wan, N., Zhang, J.: The current development of structural health monitoring for bridges: a review. Buildings **13**(6), 1360 (2023). https://doi.org/10.3390/buildings13061360
13. Wang, J., Fu, Y., Yang, X.: An integrated system for building structural health monitoring and early warning based on an Internet of things approach. Int. J. Distrib. Sens. Netw. **13**(1) (2017). https://doi.org/10.1177/1550147716689101
14. Malekloo, A., Ozer, E., AlHamaydeh, M., Girolami, M.: Machine learning and structural health monitoring overview with emerging technology and high-dimensional data source highlights. Struct. Health Monit. **21**(4), 1906–1955 (2022). https://doi.org/10.1177/14759217211036880
15. Yi, L., Deng, X., Yang, L.T., Wu, H., Wang, M., Situ, Y.: Reinforcement-learning-enabled partial confident information coverage for IoT-based bridge structural health monitoring. IEEE Internet Things J. **8**(5), 3108–3119 (2021). https://doi.org/10.1109/JIOT.2020.3028325
16. Ahmad, M.M., Khan, N.M., Khan, F.U.: Bridge vibration energy harvesting for wireless IoT-based structural health monitoring systems: a review. J. Intell. Mater. Syste. Struct. **34**(19), 2209–2239 (2023). https://doi.org/10.1177/1045389X231180040
17. Sadhu, A., Peplinski, J.E., Mohammadkhorasani, A., Moreu, F.: A review of data management and visualization techniques for structural health monitoring using BIM and virtual or augmented reality. J. Struct. Eng. **149**(1) (2023). https://doi.org/10.1061/(ASCE)ST.1943-541X.0003498

18. Lee, M.J., Zhang, R.: Human-centric artificial intelligence of things-based indoor environment quality modeling framework for supporting student well-being in educational facilities. J. Comput. Civil Eng. **38**(2), 04024002 (2024). https://doi.org/10.1061/JCCEE5.CPENG-5632
19. Institute of Visual Informatics, Universiti Kebangsaan Malaysia: Incorporating the Internet of Things (IoT) learning module into the smart building course. Jurnal Kejuruteraan **36**(2), 625–640 (2024). https://doi.org/10.17576/jkukm-2024-36(2)-22
20. Ghashim, I.A., Arshad, M.: Internet of things (IoT)-based teaching and learning: modern trends and open challenges. Sustainability **15**(21), 15656 (2023). https://doi.org/10.3390/su152115656
21. Cawley, P.: Structural health monitoring: closing the gap between research and industrial deployment. Struct. Health Monit. **17**(5), 1225–1244 (2018). https://doi.org/10.1177/1475921717750047
22. Vallabhuni, S., Debasis, K.: Hybrid deep learning for IoT-based health monitoring with physiological event extraction. Digit. Health **11** (2025). https://doi.org/10.1177/20552076251337848
23. Akhtar, M.M., Shatat, A.S., Al-Hashimi, M., Zamani, A.S., Rizwanullah, M., Ayub, R.: MapReduce with deep learning framework for student health monitoring system using IoT technology for big data. J. Grid Comput. **21**(4), 67 (2023). https://doi.org/10.1007/s10723-023-09690-x

The Implementation of Teaching Supervision Work in a Secondary College—Taking the School of Computer and Information Science of Anhui Polytechnic University as an Example

Ping Zhang[1,2,3](✉), Lili Fan[1,2,3], Jiashu Dai[1,2,3], and Tao Liu[1,2,3]

[1] Princeton University, Princeton, NJ 08544, USA
{pingzhang,liutao}@ahpu.edu.cn
[2] Springer Heidelberg, Tiergartenstr. 17, 69121 Heidelberg, Germany
[3] School of Computer and Information Science, Anhui Polytechnic University, Wuhu, China

Abstract. The teaching supervision system has functions like diagnosis, feedback, supervision, evaluation, and promoting improvement. But there are difficulties in implementing it. Focusing on secondary college supervision, the School of Computer and Information Science of Anhui University of Technology and Science has applied student - centered, output - oriented, and continuous - improvement concepts. It has comprehensively supervised educational and teaching work. The school aims to improve teaching quality by following teaching laws. It requires students to be more engaged, teachers to enhance their abilities, management to be stricter, and teaching outcomes to be more practical.

Keywords: Teaching Supervision · Student-Centered · Outcome-Based · Continuous Improvement · Teaching Evaluation

1 Introduction

The teaching supervision system is a crucial component of the educational quality assurance framework. Although the teaching supervision system in primary and secondary schools in China was established in the 1980s, the introduction of teaching supervision in higher education institutions (HEIs) occurred only at the end of the 20th century. By monitoring, guiding, and evaluating the teaching process, the teaching supervision system has effectively enhanced the teaching quality of teachers and ensured the steady improvement of educational standards. This development aligns with the growing scale of higher education and the increasing emphasis on educational quality [1]. Currently, the teaching supervision system has become an indispensable part of teaching management in universities.

In China, there are mainly two types of undergraduate teaching supervision organizational structures in universities: single university-level supervision and a dual-level supervision system involving both the university and colleges. University-level supervision refers to the establishment of a teaching supervision group or committee at the university level, affiliated with the Undergraduate School and operating under the guidance

W. Hong et al. (Eds.): ICCSE 2025, CCIS 2761, pp. 525–533, 2026.
https://doi.org/10.1007/978-981-95-7731-6_41

of the university leader in charge of undergraduate teaching. Smaller-scale universities generally adopt the single university-level supervision model. In contrast, the majority of universities implement a dual-level teaching supervision model. Based on the actual conditions of each college, a college-level teaching supervision group is formed, following the selection criteria and main responsibilities of the university-level teaching supervision group. The college supervision group operates under the leadership of the university-level supervision group to conduct specific supervision of teaching activities across the university [3].

Despite the achievements of the current teaching supervision system in Chinese universities, several challenges remain in its implementation. Zhang Jianmei proposed a people-oriented teaching supervision evaluation method to build a teaching supervision team that adapts to the new era [4]. Wang Fangliang et al. analyzed from an ethical perspective the phenomena of tool rationality overriding value rationality, prioritizing efficiency over fairness, the absence of teachers' legitimate rights and interests, the evaluation authority restricting teaching autonomy, and the antagonistic relationship between evaluators and the evaluated in university supervision systems. They argued that ethics is the foundation for the goodness of university teaching supervision practices, the premise for reasonable systems, and the guarantee for harmonious culture [5]. Ouyang Peng pointed out that university teaching supervision work is constrained by external environmental factors and proposed innovative approaches to the operation of supervision work to effectively promote the "Hóngdào" (upholding the way), "Héfǎ" (legality), "Yùshù" (skillful governance), and "Chéngqì" (achieving excellence) of supervision work [6].

The School of Computer and Information at Anhui Polytechnic University has actively explored and developed a unique teaching supervision model in line with its disciplinary characteristics and teaching realities. The school places high importance on supervision work, actively implementing supervision in teaching, learning, and management. It has adopted advanced concepts such as student-centeredness, outcome-oriented approach, and continuous improvement. Focusing on the goals of "engaging students, strengthening teachers, strict management, and effective outcomes," the school serves the overall teaching situation, follows teaching principles, and aims to improve teaching quality through comprehensive supervision of educational activities. The school has established detailed annual work plans and quality monitoring systems to ensure that supervision work is well-founded. In the cultivation of new teachers, a "seven-step method" is used to develop the teaching abilities of newly recruited teachers. In terms of process monitoring, detailed regulations have been set for course tracking and continuous improvement, the entire process quality monitoring of undergraduate thesis (dissertation), and course construction tracking. In learning supervision, teachers are required to conduct student attendance according to relevant regulations, and activities such as student seminars and assistance for students with academic difficulties are carried out. In teaching supervision, leadership and supervision group listening, as well as teacher teaching support and guidance, are conducted. In management supervision, checks are performed on the construction of basic teaching organizations and the standardization of teaching materials. Additionally, the school emphasizes the application of evaluation results, with clear regulations on the assessment of undergraduate mentors, selection of teaching backbone, and teacher teaching quality evaluation to ensure the effective implementation of supervision work. These measures have achieved significant results in teaching supervision, laying a solid foundation for improving teaching quality.

This paper takes the School of Computer and Information Science at Anhui Polytechnic University as an example to explore the implementation of teaching supervision in a secondary college. It analyzes the specific practices and experiences in system construction, supervision work, and teacher training and guidance. The aim is to provide useful references for teaching supervision in other universities. Unless otherwise specified, "supervision" and "supervision group" in the following text refer to "secondary college supervision" and "secondary college supervision group," respectively.

2 System Construction

Under the guidance of the university leadership and university-level supervision group, the college supervision group actively engages in supervision work in teaching, learning, and management. Compared with the university-level supervision that focuses on the supervisory function, the college-level supervision needs to be deeply integrated into the entire teaching and management process, participate in the formulation of feasible regulations, and monitor the implementation of these regulations. The specific work includes:

1. **New Teacher Training System:** The supervision group is responsible for the training of newly recruited teachers and has developed a new teacher training system. The "seven-step method" is used to cultivate the teaching abilities of new teachers, which includes the following steps:

   - Conducting heart-to-heart talks with newly hired teachers, assigning teaching mentors, and suggesting research teams;
   - Organizing online work reports and exchanges for new teachers during holidays;
   - Conducting new teacher trial lectures at the beginning of the semester;
   - Providing training for undergraduate and innovation and entrepreneurship (I&E) mentors;
   - Holding mid-term work exchanges between new and experienced teachers;
   - Organizing end-of-term growth salon activities for new teachers;
   - Conducting assessments and reporting on assistant teaching.

2. **Laboratory Safety Management System:** The supervision group participates in the formulation of the "Laboratory Safety Management System for the School of Computer and Information Science." Special personnel are organized to conduct regular inspections, with no less than one inspection per month, and records are archived. Problems and hidden dangers identified during inspections are rectified, with rectification reports submitted to the university management department within the specified time and archived. If major hidden dangers are found, laboratory activities are immediately suspended, and corresponding preventive measures are taken or laboratory activities are resumed only after the completion of rectification.

3. **Quality Monitoring System:** At the beginning of each year, an annual work plan is formulated, and a detailed work schedule is developed at the start of each semester. The previous plan is reviewed to identify areas for improvement, and the next plan is formulated accordingly. The supervision group participates in the formulation of multiple quality monitoring systems to ensure that work supervision is well-founded.

Some of the systems and regulations led or participated in by the supervision group in recent years are shown in Table 1.

Table 1.

No	Formulation Time	Name of Regulation	Role of Supervision Group
1	March 2018	Interim Implementation Rules for the Selection of Teaching Backbone in the School of Computer and Information Science	Led the formulation
2	September 2018	Laboratory Safety Management System for the School of Computer and Information Science	Participated in the formulation
3	July 2020	Notice on Strengthening Teacher Teaching Support and Guidance Work	Led the formulation
4	Winter Vacation 2021	Course Tracking and Continuous Improvement Form for the School of Computer and Information Science	Led the formulation
5	May 2021	Interim Implementation Rules for Classroom Attendance Management for Undergraduates in the Computer College	Participated in the formulation
6	July 2021	Revised Implementation Rules for Teacher Teaching Quality Assessment in the School of Computer and Information Science	Participated in the formulation
7	November 2021	Interim Management Rules for Innovation and Entrepreneurship Mentors in the School of Computer and Information Science	Participated in the formulation

(*continued*)

(*continued*)

No	Formulation Time	Name of Regulation	Role of Supervision Group
8	April 2022	Interim Implementation Rules for Course Group and Leader System in the School of Computer and Information Science	Participated in the formulation
9	February 2023	Interim Implementation Rules for Undergraduate Mentor Assistance for Students with Academic Difficulties in the School of Computer and Information Science	Participated in the formulation
10	September 2024	Revised Implementation Rules for Undergraduate Mentor System in the School of Computer and Information Science	Participated in the formulation

3 Process Monitoring

The School of Computer and Information Science divides the teaching process into three parts: student learning, teacher teaching, and departmental management. It fully exerts the process monitoring role of the supervision group, carrying out work from three aspects: supervising student learning, teacher teaching, and departmental management.

3.1 Supervising Student Learning

1. **Regulating Attendance:** In line with the requirements of the "Interim Detailed Rules for the Management of Classroom Attendance of Students in the School of Computer and Information Science (Trial)", it urges teachers to take attendance seriously and report classroom attendance data before the 4th of each month, and then issue a summary and announcement before the 8th. In response to the attendance situation of the school, it organizes a briefing and exchange meeting every month for counselors and undergraduate tutors of classes with relatively high absenteeism, so as to achieve targeted assistance and collaborative education. The supervision group is responsible for feeding back the attendance data of other schools to the relevant schools and accompanying the school leaders in focusing on and inspecting classes with zero absenteeism in the monthly attendance.
2. **Student Seminars**: The supervision group holds four student seminars each semester to learn about students' learning situations and answer their questions, and communicates and provides feedback to the teachers concerned on the opinions put forward by the students.

3. **Supervision of Undergraduate Tutors:** Undergraduate tutors are involved in student management and are required to meet with students monthly, collect and properly solve the problems raised by students, and form records. The supervision group supervises the completion of undergraduate tutors' work on a monthly basis.
4. **Assistance for Students in Difficulty:** In accordance with the provisions of the "Interim Measures for the Work of Undergraduate Tutors in Assisting Students with Learning Difficulties in the School of Computer and Information Science (Trial)", it organizes and carries out the identification and assistance of students with learning difficulties. In addition, for the assistance of freshmen, after the monthly mathematics test, it organizes students who scored below 70 points, especially those below 60 points, to continue studying in the open laboratories of various majors until 10:30–11:00 after the regular evening self-study; after the mid-term examination of the basic course of programming, it provides basic guidance for students who scored below 60 points.
5. **Rectifying Low Classroom Engagement and Front-Row Seating Rates:** The supervision group takes the lead in organizing the reform of teaching methods and content, integrating research into teaching, carrying out case-based teaching, project-based teaching, etc., increasing practical content, and enhancing students' interest in learning.
6. **Monitoring the Learning Process:** The supervision group conducts process monitoring on the school-wide general courses and practical training sessions. It requires teachers of key courses for postgraduate entrance examinations to carry out mid-term tests, analyzes students' learning situations based on the test results, and proposes improvement suggestions. In the process of undergraduate graduation design (thesis), the supervision group is responsible for the full-process quality monitoring, covering every stage from topic selection to thesis submission, including topic proposal defense, mid-term check, system (work) acceptance, graduation defense, and graduation design thesis. It assists school leaders, department heads, and thesis supervisors in carrying out high-quality work.

3.2 Supervising Teacher Teaching

1. **Various Types of Classroom Observation:** There are leader-led classroom observations, supervision-organized observations, department-head-led observations, and peer-to-peer observations. The observations and evaluations are targeted, focusing on courses with high failure rates, student evaluation rankings in the top or bottom 10%, newly-hired teachers, and teachers who apply for teaching ability assessment. After the observations, exchanges on teaching-related issues are carried out with the teachers, which plays a role in promoting and improving their teaching levels. Comprehensive classroom observations are conducted for teachers in the computer science and technology major to support the certification work.
2. **Teacher Teaching Support and Guidance:** In line with the spirit of the "Notice on Strengthening Teacher Teaching Support and Guidance Work", it carries out support and guidance work for the "bottom 10% of teachers".

3. **Urging Teachers to Attend Teaching Meetings:** In 2024, the school held or conducted a total of 21 seminars, including professional development seminars, teaching experience sharing sessions, course-related seminars, and industry-university-institute-collaborative course exchange meetings. It urged teachers to attend 239 teaching-related meetings or training sessions both within and outside the school.
4. **Organizing Teachers to Participate in Teaching Competitions:** For each competition, specific teachers are designated to track, prepare for, and participate in it. In line with the school's development plan, the supervision group thoroughly evaluates the course construction of each course group and, based on the teaching strengths of each teacher, recommends more than twenty teachers to participate in various teaching competitions at different levels.
5. **Course Tracking and Continuous Improvement:** For courses with relatively high failure rates, it is required to fill in the "Course Tracking and Continuous Improvement Form of the School of Computer and Information Science". The form mainly includes course basic information; a summary and analysis of problems in this exam (if there is a make-up exam, the pass rate of the make-up exam should be listed in the analysis); improvement measures (rectification measures for the course's future teaching); support measures (specific measures to improve the make-up exam pass rate); a summary and analysis of the make-up exam results after this make-up exam (to be filled in when submitting the make-up exam results); evaluation of the support effect (to be filled in by the person in charge of the major or course group); analysis of the teaching effect when the major or teacher offers the course again (to be filled in after submitting the next-round course results); overall evaluation of the improvement effect (to be filled in by the person in charge of the major or course group); the major's opinion on whether continued tracking and improvement are needed; and finally, the school's review.
6. **Course Construction Tracking:** In line with the "Interim Detailed Rules for the Course Group and Person-in-Charge System of the School of Computer and Information Science", it checks the work status and course construction of the person in charge based on the rules.

3.3 Supervising Departmental Management

1. **Inspection of Grass-Roots Teaching Organization Development:** It conducts regular supervision of the teaching and research activities of the four departments, participates in the teacher-student seminars organized by each department to learn about typical problems in teaching, and puts forward reasonable suggestions.
2. **Spot-Check of Teaching Materials at the Beginning of the Term:** It compares the school's teaching material standards and points out some problems existing in the spot-check of teaching materials, feeds back these problems to the teachers in the form of a summary table, and the teachers make improvements and corrections within a short time.
3. **Holding Four Department-Level Teacher Seminars:** It holds four department-level teacher seminars to understand teachers' needs and problems in the teaching process. It completes the invigilation of each course's exams (except for exams specially organized by the Academic Affairs Office). For the conducted course exams,

the school-level supervision team is arranged to patrol the exam rooms according to the exam schedule, achieving comprehensive coverage of exam-room patrol and supervision, thereby strengthening and ensuring good exam conduct and discipline.

4. **Completing Inter-School Teaching Material and "Double-Basic" Construction Mutual Inspection Tasks Arranged by the School:** It closely integrates with the review-and-evaluation work. (1) In the early stage of the review and evaluation, it carries out material-inspection work, etc. (2) In the later stage of the review and evaluation, each supervisor is responsible for one chapter of the self-assessment report.

3.4 Effectiveness Evaluation

1. **Undergraduate Tutor Assessment:** In line with the "Detailed Rules for the Implementation of the Undergraduate Tutor System in the School of Computer and Information Science (Revised)", the assessment of the tutoring process records (30%) is conducted. The school's supervision group reviews the tutoring content, time, location, and number of students recorded by the tutors. Tutors with fewer than six tutoring records or falsified records in an academic year receive zero points for this item. (20% assessment is conducted by the Undergraduate Tutor System Work Leadership Group)
2. **Teaching Backbone Evaluation:** In line with the "Interim Detailed Rules for the Selection of Teaching Backbones in the School of Computer and Information Science", the school supervision group is the responsible body for evaluating teaching effectiveness, accounting for 15% of the weighting coefficient.
3. Teacher Teaching Quality Assessment: Based on the "Detailed Rules for the Assessment of Teacher Teaching Quality in the School of Computer and Information Science (Revised)", the team leader of the supervisors scores all teachers except themselves in the "basic points for teaching effectiveness" section.
4. **Double-Innovation Tutor Selection:** In line with the "Interim Management Details for Innovation and Entrepreneurship Tutors in the School of Computer and Information Science", it supervises the duties and employment conditions of the double-innovation tutors.
5. **Implementation of Rectification:** Focusing on teaching style, learning style, and management work mentioned in teaching supervision notifications, the school carefully reviews each notification. The deputy dean of teaching informs the faculty of the issues in the school's work group. The supervisor secretary or the deputy dean communicates with the relevant staff, proposes suggestions and rectification ideas, and urges them to complete the rectification. Common issues are reported and requirements put forward at the Wednesday meeting.

3.5 Conclusion

The School of Computer and Information of Anhui University of Technology and Science has explored and developed a unique model for teaching supervision. Through comprehensive system construction, full-process monitoring and scientific effectiveness evaluation, it has effectively enhanced teaching quality and management.

1. In system construction, it has led or participated in formulating many teaching supervision-related systems, such as those for cultivating new teachers, laboratory safety management, and quality monitoring, providing clear bases and standards for supervision work.
2. In process monitoring, it strictly controls the entire teaching process from three aspects: supervising student learning, teacher teaching, and departmental management. Specific measures include regulating attendance, holding student seminars, supervising undergraduate tutors, assisting students in difficulty, reforming teaching methods, tracking courses and continuously improving, checking course construction, inspecting grassroots teaching organization development, spot-checking teaching materials, holding department-level teacher seminars, invigilating course exams, and conducting mutual checks on teaching materials and "double-basic" construction.
3. In effectiveness evaluation, through assessing undergraduate tutors, evaluating teaching backbones, assessing teacher teaching quality, selecting and appointing double-innovation tutors, etc., it has scientifically and objectively evaluated teaching effectiveness. It has also promptly implemented rectifications for issues raised in supervision notifications, ensuring the practical effectiveness of supervision work.

References

1. Yu, X., Dong, Y.: Practice and exploration of establishing a teaching supervision mechanism in universities. China High. Educ. Res. (01), 89–90 (2004)
2. Ye, X., Xia, L., Cai, J.: Present situation, problems and improvement strategies of undergraduate teaching supervision in universities. China Exam. (03), 37–45 (2024)
3. Sun, H.: Education Supervision and Evaluation Indicators. China Social Sciences Press (2017)
4. Zhang, J.: Innovation in teaching supervision of higher vocational education in the reform of education evaluation. China High. Educ. (17), 56–58 (2021)
5. Wang, F., Zhu, P.: Ethical review of the teaching supervision system in universities: value, loss and return. Educ. Theory Pract. **45**(09), 50–55 (2025)
6. Peng, O.: The trend, problems and countermeasures of university teaching supervision work — from the perspective of "trend, way, method and equipment". Univ. Educ. Sci. (03), 63–72 (2024)

Construction and Practice of Digital Literacy Teaching Quality Improvement Model with Double Helix Structure

Ning Wang[1], Mingming Chen[2(✉)], and Liqing Guo[2]

[1] Ningde Normal University, Ningde 352100, Fujian, China
[2] Xiamen Huaxia University, No. 288 Tianma Road, Jimei District, Xiamen 361024, Fujian, China
xmumingming@163.com

Abstract. This paper explores the needs to enhance digital literacy and skills among university students in the digital age. It centers on the concept of quality control in process management and designs a Double Helix Structure model for improving the quality of digital literacy education. On the teaching content side, it enriches and enhances the quality through selection, supervision, and evaluation. On the student learning side, it encourages students to enhance their self-awareness, independent planning, and personalized learning by holding annual digital literacy competitions, thereby addressing personal shortcomings and achieving continuous improvement. The model has been piloted at multiple universities, yielding significant results in areas such as teaching awards, online courses, teaching materials, question banks, and certifications.

Keywords: Double Helix Structure · Digital Literacy · Undergraduate Teaching · Quality Improvement Mode

1 Introduction

Digital literacy and skills refer to a comprehensive set of qualities and abilities that citizens should possess in a digital society, including the acquisition, creation, utilization, evaluation, interaction, sharing, innovation, security, and ethical considerations of digital technologies [1]. In November 2021, the Cyberspace Administration of China (CAC) released the Action Plan for Enhancing the Digital Literacy and Skills of All Citizens, aimed at improving the digital literacy and skills of all citizens [2]. In April 2024, the Ministry of Human Resources and Social Security, along with seven other departments, jointly issued the Action Plan for Accelerating the Cultivation of Digital Talent to Support the Development of the Digital Economy (2024–2026). This plan aims to meet the demands of the digital industry and industrial digitalization by implementing special measures for cultivating digital talent and increasing the effective supply of digital professionals. In April 2025, the Cyberspace Administration of China and three other ministries jointly issued the *Key Points for Enhancing National Digital Literacy and Skills in 2025*, requiring further improvement of the digital Homo sapiens talent

W. Hong et al. (Eds.): ICCSE 2025, CCIS 2761, pp. 534–544, 2026.
https://doi.org/10.1007/978-981-95-7731-6_42

education system to support the high-quality development of China's Homo sapiens population.

University students are an important source of digital talents, and the quality of their digital literacy training is of strategic significance to the country. This paper is based on the concept of quality control of process management and combines the course teaching mode of smart education [3], under the framework of Double Helix Structure, this paper discusses the construction and practice of the model of improving the quality of digital literacy cultivation for university students.

2 A Double Helix Structure Teaching and Learning Quality Improvement Model Based on Process Management

Process management is a core concept in modern organizational management, defined as the use of practical methods, techniques, and tools to plan, control, and enhance the effectiveness, efficiency, and adaptability of processes. This includes four key stages: process planning, process implementation, process monitoring (inspection), and process improvement (action), known as the PDCA cycle [4]. This concept was introduced by Deming, leading to the PDCA (Plan-Do-Check-Act) cycle being also referred to as the Deming cycle. The goal is to achieve a spiral improvement in quality within management projects.

The Double Helix Structure teaching model (see Fig. 1) aims to enhance the quality of teaching and learning in a spiral manner over time, fostering students innovative thinking and practical skills. In the digital literacy education for university students, the curriculum is divided into core courses and extension courses. The Core Courses cover foundational and key content, such as *Digital Literacy Education for University Students*, while the Extension Courses explore various aspects related to the core content, including general elective courses and general extension activities. In practice, the course team integrates core knowledge with extended knowledge, guiding students through annual competitions to achieve self-awareness, dynamic positioning, autonomous planning, and collaborative learning. This approach encourages students to develop personalized learning plans that meet their individual needs and to feed back their learning outcomes into the next round of systematic planning and restructuring. The model emphasizes the central role of students, enhancing their learning initiative through data analysis and scientific guidance, thereby improving overall student performance. By actively participating in classroom activities and various practical experiences, students can improve their learning efficiency. Additionally, from the teachers perspective, the focus is on aligning teaching content with social needs, strengthening multidimensional thinking and application skills training, and integrating these principles into the construction of the curriculum system, course selection, and practical measures, which are then fed back into the process. Therefore, in the Double Helix Structure of digital literacy education for university students, by integrating the needs of social digital transformation, students are guided to learn the basic knowledge and skills of digital literacy through problem solving and project practice [5, 6].

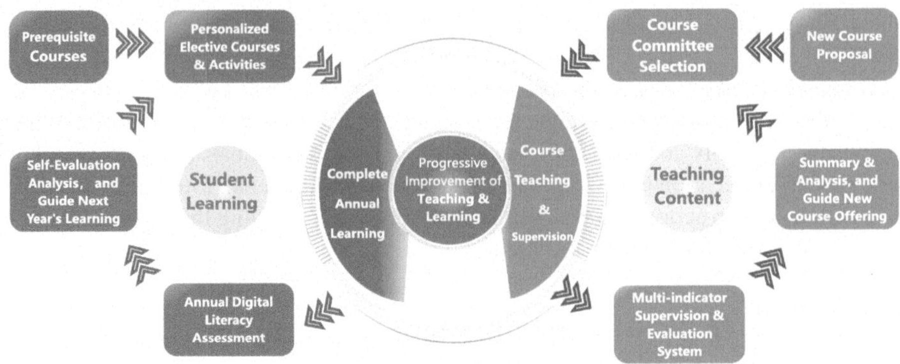

Fig. 1. Teaching and learning Double Helix Structure teaching quality improvement model.

3 Construction of Teaching Quality Improvement Model of the Double Helix Structure

3.1 Construction Principles

Focusing on the improvement of teaching quality and in accordance with national guidelines and the talent cultivation objectives of higher education institutions, a work plan for enhancing university students' digital literacy has been formulated based on the actual implementation conditions of universities. Supported by digital platforms and technologies, a diversified and interconnected applied higher education system for cultivating university students' digital literacy and skills has been established across four dimensions: cultivation objectives, curriculum system development, student activities, and learning environment. The aim is to equip students with digital consciousness, computational thinking, critical thinking, security consciousness, and lifelong learning capabilities, while helping them develop their own unique knowledge system of digital literacy. This will expand students' digital life, digital learning, and digital innovation. Through the differential cultivation and training, unique abilities are developed in life, learning, and professional fields, which are then extended to various social activities, thereby enhancing the digital literacy and skills of the entire population.

On one hand, the principle of student-centered is given top priority. The focus on teaching quality should be on students thinking and ideas, while also considering their needs and future development plans, in line with current social realities. By adjusting the teaching content and methods to meet specific needs, we can enhance students self-awareness, initiative, and critical thinking skills, continuously improving their cognitive abilities and understanding levels. This approach maximizes the effectiveness and applicability of the Double Helix Structure in ensuring undergraduate teaching quality.

On the other hand, there is a growing emphasis on integrating industry with education, combining science with education, and fostering collaborative talent development through diverse collaborations. In the digital age, new-generation information technologies, particularly large models and data elements, have become central to new productive forces and production relations, altering the goals and demands of higher education in talent cultivation. Fragmented learning, lifelong learning, and self-directed learning require collaboration among the government, schools, industries, and enterprises to develop an instructional framework that can rapidly adapt and update to meet the demands of the new era.

3.2 Construction Process

Determine the Differentiated Training Objectives for University Students
The construction process is crucial for the quality of the Double Helix Structure course. Therefore, it is essential to establish teaching quality standards and evaluation criteria that align with the digital literacy of university students at the early stage of this process. Based on the Digital Literacy and Skills Certification group standard (T/CERACU205-2022) led by the National Higher Education Computer Education Research Association, a study was conducted to understand the educational needs of high-quality talent groups among university students. The study set goals for knowledge acquisition, skill development, and personal growth, which can be summarized as: Personal Mastery, Empowering Others, and Serving Society (see Fig. 2).

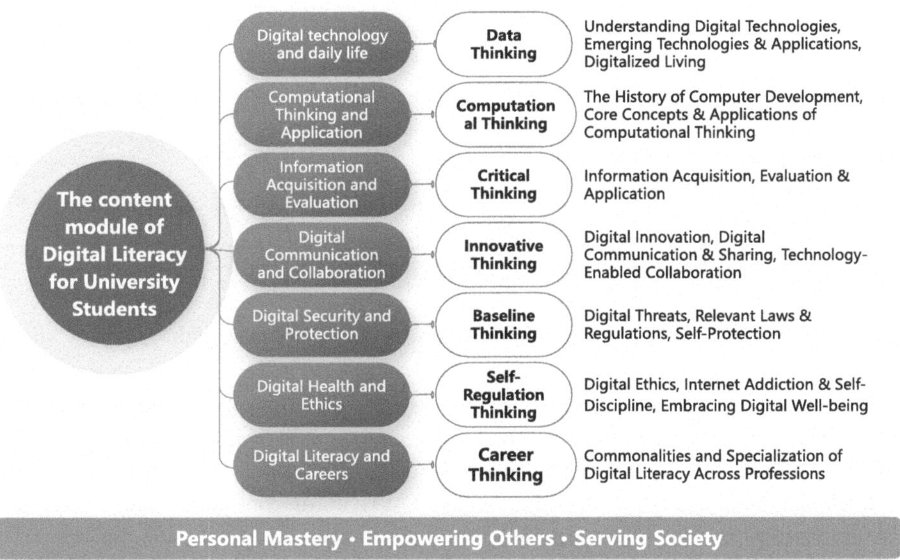

Fig. 2. The content module of *Digital Literacy for University Students.*

Establish an Educational Content System that Integrates General and Specialized Knowledge with Iterative Updates on the Teaching Content Side
Through in-depth research and analysis of the concepts, connotations, and frameworks of digital literacy and skills, we have identified seven dimensions of content modules: digital technology and daily life, computational thinking and application, information acquisition and evaluation, digital communication and collaboration, digital security

and protection, digital health and ethics, and digital literacy and careers. These modules form a comprehensive digital literacy curriculum that integrates general and specialized knowledge, required and elective courses, and activities both inside and outside the classroom (see Fig. 3). The framework includes core general required courses such as *Digital Literacy Education for University Students* and *Basic Computer Skills for University Students*, and extends to a series of general elective courses on digital literacy and professional electives closely related to digital literacy. Additionally, through various practical activities, such as digital literacy lectures, competitions, and programming contests for all students, a "1+1+X" Digital Literacy instructional framework has been established. Specifically, this framework consists of "1" credit of foundational general courses + "1" credit of elective courses + "X" sessions of digital literacy activities. Building on the basics, more elective content is provided at different levels to meet the personalized and diverse needs of students.

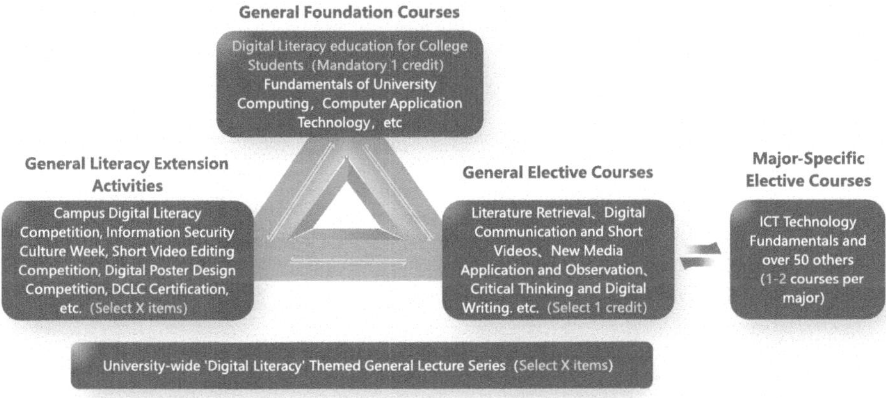

Fig. 3. "1+1+X" Digital Literacy Instructional Framework.

In terms of implementation, elective courses and activities are selected, supervised and evaluated every year to establish a closed loop of quality improvement in teaching content and realize the spiral improvement of teaching content.

Each academic year, the General Education Curriculum Committee receives applications for course offerings. Based on these applications, the committee selects courses for the new semester, arranges and supervises them. The committee evaluates and rewards courses based on multiple criteria, summarizes, analyzes, and guides the selection of new courses to enhance the quality and completeness of the digital literacy curriculum framework.

Establish Student Profiles Through Competition Data Analysis to Achieve a Data-Driven Personalized Study Model on the Student Learning Side

Every year, the school hosts a school-wide digital literacy competition, which all students participate in. By analyzing each students foundational skills and knowledge, a comprehensive data profile is created for each student. This not only helps students enhance their self-awareness but also provides precise guidance for setting learning goals and developing study plans. Annual competition data can be utilized to assist in dynamically updating student profiles, guiding course selection and personalized study plans, thereby establishing a closed-loop system for improving learning quality and achieving spiral enhancement of students' competencies and skills.

The research and development of a question bank based on digital literacy and skills certification standards, the school holds a digital literacy competition for all students from September to November each year. This competition not only enhances students digital literacy and skills but also helps them understand the importance of these skills in their studies, lives, and careers. Additionally, the annual competition provides an annual digital profile of students digital literacy and skills, displayed through radar charts that show changes over the year, guiding students in setting learning directions and plans for the new academic year. Specifically, freshmen immediately participate in the competition after enrollment, collecting initial data to create their first personal digital literacy and skills profiles. In their first year, freshmen will take foundational required courses such as *Digital Literacy Education for University Students*, *Basic Computer Skills for University Students*, *Computer Application Technology*, and *Advanced Language Programming.* At the beginning of their second year, they will participate in the competition again to assess their progress and provide insights into changes in various aspects of their annual personal profiles, which guides the formulation of learning plans. Following this, they continue to study mathematics and computer science courses, elective courses, and at least one general elective course in digital literacy. This evaluation cycle is repeated at the start of each academic year, aiming to enhance overall skills until graduation.

Through diversified activities such as course training, competition participation, and certification assessments, students achieve self-profiling of their foundational literacy and skill competencies. This enables precise guidance in setting learning objectives and study plans for the next stage, with annual dynamic iterations and updates. Through teacher-student interactions, a closed-loop system for enhancing teaching and learning quality is built, facilitating the spiral progression of student literacy.

Joint Social Resources to Organize Diverse Activities and Create a Positive Learning Atmosphere and Environment
Cooperating with the government, industries, enterprises, and other stakeholders, integrating the resources of the school's digital platform and the strengths of partner enterprises, we adhere to the simultaneous advancement of learning, research, and application, tapping into resources and building platforms. Through multi-group, multi-perspective, and multi-channel activity integration, we foster a strong digital literacy learning atmosphere.

On campus, the first initiative is to carry out school-enterprise curriculum design and development, online-offline blended classroom teaching and active learning, as well as the organization and evaluation of competency competitions and certification activities. The second initiative involves regularly releasing digital literacy-related activities through campus networks, WeChat public accounts, bulletin boards, and other channels, as well as designing and printing promotional brochures titled *A Guide to Digital Literacy for University Students.* This fosters a Digital campus culture and enhances the awareness and recognition of digital literacy among faculty and students. The third initiative is to encourage students to participate in practical activities such as a series of general education lectures and professional experimental practices. The fourth initiative involves collaborating with platforms and enterprises to regularly organize university-wide thematic activities aimed at enhancing digital literacy and skills. These include events such as the University Digital Literacy Competition, Digital Poster Contest, Digital Short Video Competition, Digital Literacy Training Camp, and Campus Cyber Culture Week. Additionally, peer institutions are invited to participate, gradually expanding the regional influence of these events.

Outside the campus, we adhere to the integration of learning, research, and application. The first initiative is to carry out standard development and competency certification, fully considering factors such as industry development trends, technological update speeds, and education and training needs to ensure the scientific and practical nature of the *Digital Literacy and Skills Certification* group standard we participate in developing. Meanwhile, the information from the standard development process is used to update teaching content to adapt to the development and changes of the digital era. The second initiative involves the construction of a social training base platform, encouraging faculty and students to conduct horizontal and vertical teaching and research projects related to digital literacy. The third initiative is the integration of industry and education, which encourages teachers to participate in social service and practical activities, providing services to enterprises, youth, teacher training, and other higher education institutions. While improving teaching quality, it also leverages technical expertise to serve society, promotes the dissemination and popularization of digital literacy education, enhances the digital literacy and skills of various social groups, and collects social demands from practical engagements to promptly supplement and update teaching content. This establishes a closed-loop system for the convergence of teaching, research, and teaching quality enhancement, achieving resource sharing and continuous updates.

4 Practice Exploration of Teaching Quality Improvement Mode Under the Double Helix Structure

In order to test the effectiveness of teaching quality improvement under the Double Helix Structure, the author has carried out a series of measures and practical exploration in Xiamen Huaxia University and Ningde Normal University. The results show that this model is effective.

4.1 Overall Planning

Xiamen Huaxia University is a newly established applied undergraduate institution. In line with the 14th Five-Year Plan, the 2035 Long-Range Objectives, the Digital China General Layout Plan, and the Action Plan for Enhancing the Digital Literacy and Skills of All Citizens, the university has developed the Action Plan for Enhancing Digital Literacy. By leveraging the National Digital Resource Sub-center, the Ministry of Educations Demonstration Base for the Integration of Information and Communication Technology Industry and Education, the Provincial Smart Education Engineering Research Center, the digital resource construction base co-built with enterprises, and Xiamen Vocational

Teacher Training Base, among other technical support resources, the university has established a comprehensive system for digital literacy education for university students, covering teaching, practice, research, and social services.

Ningde Normal University, also is a newly established applied undergraduate institution, is guided by the principles of being local, teacher-focused, and application-oriented. By leveraging resources from the Ministry of Educations 100 Schools Project for industry-education integration innovation and the Digital Fujian Elderly Rehabilitation and Nursing Big Data Research Institute, the university has developed a comprehensive educational system that integrates teaching, practice, research, and social services.

4.2 Teaching Content Side

In line with the characteristics of application-oriented universities, through university-wide mobilization, we have leveraged the faculty and resource strengths across various disciplines and collaborated with partner enterprises to establish a digital literacy curriculum system that integrates general and specialized education, combines compulsory and elective courses, and blends in-class and extracurricular activities.

This system takes the twenty compulsory general education courses on digital literacy, such as *Digital Literacy Education for University Students*, as its core, supplemented by the addition of no fewer than two specialized elective courses closely related to digital literacy in each major. Furthermore, dozens of general education lectures and practical activities on digital literacy are regularly organized by inviting experts from other universities or enterprises, keeping pace with the latest societal development needs. Broussonetia papyrifera establishes a "1+1+X" teaching content framework.

Establish "1" Compulsory Foundational Course. A team of experienced teachers, comprising senior faculty from research universities, applied universities, and corporate executives, is responsible for teaching this course. Additionally, seven university teaching assistants have joined the team. The university has collaborated with enterprises to develop and launch a required general education course for freshmen titled - *Digital Literacy Education for University Students*. The course team has not only established an online course website but also created a question bank for assessment and training, and compiled a self-authored textbook titled *Digital Literacy for University Students*. This textbook has been recognized by the National Higher Education Computer Education Research Association as part of the 14th Five-Year Plan textbooks and by the Fujian Provincial Department of Education as part of the 14th Five-Year Plan undergraduate textbooks, thereby facilitating the sharing and dissemination of high-quality educational resources. This course embodies digital teaching methods such as school-enterprise cooperation, integration of teaching and research, and combination of online and offline approaches. It incorporates discussions and policies related to the digital economy, as well as social contexts like Digital Fujian, Digital China, and industrial digital transformation. The course introduces students to the seven dimensions of digital literacy, comprehensively guiding their understanding and cultivation of digital literacy competencies. The course is officially open to all freshmen, providing them with high-quality foundational education.

Expand and Add at Least "1" Elective Course with Differentiation and Personalization. Offering nearly 20 general elective courses such as *Literature Retrieval, Digital Communication and Etiquette, Practical Applications of GPT*, and *Information Security and Protection*, which integrate with various disciplinary fields, as well as a series of specialized elective courses including *Big Data Digital Literacy and Innovation & Entrepreneurship, Frontier Technologies in Information and Communication, Business Decision Support & AI Tool Applications*, and *Data Visualization.* These courses incorporate cutting-edge developments in digital literacy to serve students' diverse and personalized learning needs.

Offering a Diverse Range of "X" Educational and Practical Extension Activities and Courses. Beyond lecture series on digital literacy trends and digital skills competitions, further develop training content tailored to actual industry and professional demands. This includes courses open to the broader society, such as:

- The practical course *Big Data Analysis and Visualization* developed for enterprises in Software Park industry-education collaboration base;
- The training course *Digital Literacy & Office Application Enhancement* for the financial and banking sector;
- The *DCLC Digital Capability Level Enhancement Training* jointly developed with other universities for the tobacco industry;
- The course series From *Digital Literacy & Technology to Digital Leadership* for the financial and banking sector.

These initiatives serve the digital literacy and skills enhancement needs of vocational university students and personnel from enterprises undergoing digital transformation.

4.3 Student Learning Side

Since 2021, the university has annually organized a digital literacy competition for university students, with a participation rate of 98.19%. The approach of integrating competitions with courses enhances the targeted and effective learning of students, scientifically and rationally planning the career development, and organically combining personalized cultivation with comprehensive development.

Over the past four years, students have actively engaged in various innovative projects related to digital technology, such as the China International College Students Innovation Competition, the Challenge Cup, and the E-commerce Innovation Competition. Additionally, they have participated in other innovation competitions, including the National College Students Digital Literacy Skills Competition and the National Software Information Technology Professional Talent Competition, winning a total of 106 national and provincial awards, including a national grand prize.

In the past four years, students' digital-related projects have secured approval for 14 national-level and 54 provincial-level projects under the College Students' Innovation and Entrepreneurship Training Program.

5 Conclusions and Outcomes

After 4 years of exploration, the course *Digital Literacy Education for University Students* has continuously improved in quality. In 2022, it was selected as a university-level high-quality core course and became a recommended training cooperation course for DCLC certification. The final assessment results are recognized and accepted. Those who pass the assessment may apply for the DCLC certificate without examination. We have tutored or collaborated with specialized faculty to offer nearly 20 general elective courses such as *Literature Retrieval (New Edition)* and *Digital Communication and Short Videos*, which integrate with various disciplinary fields, along with over 50 specialized elective courses, helping students establish a professional digital literacy knowledge system. In addition, our team has been invited on multiple occasions to undertake various national digital literacy training activities, share and promote best practices and experiences, as well as self-developed course materials. Based on the actual digital literacy needs of different industries and professions, the team has developed two vocational training content courses to meet the digital literacy and skills enhancement training demands of enterprises undergoing digital transformation. These courses have been procured by enterprises and applied in internal training programs.

The faculty team has also secured 6 provincial and ministerial-level research projects on digital literacy, 1 national first-level society's *14th Five-Year Plan* textbook, and 1 Fujian Province *14th Five-Year Plan* undergraduate higher education textbook. Related research papers have won 4 national first and second prizes at the *China Conference on Computer Education in Colleges* (CCEC). This educational research project was awarded the first prize of university-level teaching achievements and selected as a typical case by *Xiamen Municipal Committee* for *Enhancing Public Digital Literacy and Skills*. The research findings were invited for presentation at 4 international and national conferences, and received coverage or reposts by 8 national and regional party-government media outlets or leading media platforms. The school has become one of the first batch of partners for the *National Digital Competency Level Certification* (DCLC) and an outstanding partner for the year 2023. This model exploration has achieved a promising start.

Acknowledgments. This study was funded by Fujian Provincial Education Science Collaborative Innovation Project (No. Fjxczx23-302), Natural Science Foundation of Fujian Province (No. 2024J011416), Research Projects of Ningde Normal University (No. 2024Y17).

Disclosure of Interests. The authors have no competing interests to declare that are relevant to the content of this article.

References

1. Yan, Y., Wang, N., Chen, T.: Research on the concept, framework, and improvement path of digital literacy. Softw. J. **23**(08), 145–150 (2024)
2. Cyberspace Administration of China. Action Outline for Enhancing the Digital Literacy and Skills of the Entire Population (2021). https://www.cac.gov.cn/2021-11/05/c_1637708867754305.htm. 05 Nov 2021

3. Ying, B.: Exploring the path to enhance teaching quality in smart classrooms —— review of "smart classrooms: new concepts, new models, and new practices" J. China Educ. Soc. **2022**(07), 121 (2022)
4. Wang, N.: Research and implementation of a course scheduling assistance system for vocational colleges based on process management. J. Ningde Norm. Univ. (Nat. Sci. Ed.) **25**(02), 169–173 (2013)
5. Chen, M., Tang, H., Cai, Z., et al.: A study on the integration of industry and education in regional undergraduate universities from the perspective of the triple helix. Educ. Mod. **5**(11), 11–12+20 (2018)
6. Zhu, Z., Kuang, F., Feng, Y., et al.: Construction and application of an undergraduate teaching quality monitoring system based on engineering education professional accreditation. Comput. Educ. (12), 208–213 (2022)

Practical Teaching Reform in Digital Circuit and Logic Design Course Guided by Hardware Thinking

Chunqing Ling(✉), Huan Zhao, Hongping Hu, and Yan Liu

College of Computer Science and Electronic Engineering, Hunan University, Changsha 410082, Hunan, China
jt_lingcq@hnu.edu.cn

Abstract. In view of the current issues in the Digital Circuit and Logic Design course, such as students' weak practical abilities and lack of hardware thinking, this study proposes a practice teaching reform scheme guided by hardware thinking. By constructing a three-dimensional training framework for visualization ability of circuit behaviors, system design ability, and circuit implementation ability, combined with the hierarchical ability training system of FPGA bare board (including assembly, testing, and development), the students' fundamental understanding and engineering practice capabilities of hardware systems are strengthened. The teaching practice shows that the reform has significantly improved students' abilities to solve complex engineering problems and provides a reusable path for the training of digital system talents under the new engineering context.

Keywords: Hardware Thinking · Systematic Ability · Digital Circuit

1 Introduction

The comprehensive and precise cultivation of systematic ability is crucial for the core courses teaching in computer science majors [1]. Currently, many domestic universities pay increasing attention to the shaping of students' systematic abilities. They have conducted numerous innovative explorations in the core professional curriculum system and practical teaching links, introducing new concepts, perspectives, and methods [2]. Taking Hunan University as an example, it aims to systematically cultivate students' overall conception of computer system through the formation of a hierarchical and progressive computing core curriculum group [3]. As the key hardware precursor lesson in this curriculum group, the enhancement of practical abilities in the Digital Circuit and Logic Design course fundamentally lies in the cultivation of hardware thinking.

The primary connotation of hardware thinking is to deeply understand the underlying working principle and inherent limitations of the hardware, and to comprehend the physical realization essence under abstract logic. Its training goal can be summarized as follows: anchored on the physical realization, the ultimate goal is to build a stable and reliable hardware system through systematic design methods and resource-constrained

W. Hong et al. (Eds.): ICCSE 2025, CCIS 2761, pp. 545–557, 2026.
https://doi.org/10.1007/978-981-95-7731-6_43

optimization processes. Without the understanding of the working mechanism of the hardware, hardware design is like "a floating duckweed". Therefore, it is very important to develop students' ability to visualize circuit behavior—students need to clearly grasp the device principles and be able to internally conceive the flow of current, transmission of signals, and driving paths of clocks in circuits. Generally speaking, digital systems adopt top-down design which decomposes complex system into sub-modules layer by layer; then realizes bottom-up implementation starting from basic sub-circuits and gradually constructing complete systems through hierarchical integration. During this whole process of design and implementation, students must have a deep understanding of the performance boundaries and realization details of the system including potential system bottlenecks, ultimate performance indicators, cost constraints, power consumption goals, and manufacturing process impacts etc.

2 Cultivating Visualization Ability of Circuit Behavior

The construction of hardware thinking is based on solid theoretical knowledge. This course implements the "student-centered" concept and carries out five-in-one teaching around the five dimensions of "teach-act-train-test-evaluate", systematically helping students establish a complete knowledge framework [4].

On the basis of solidifying theoretical knowledge, this course secondarily developed more than 70 demonstration circuits based on Logisim virtual simulation software covering core content such as encoders, CMOS gate implementations, functions and applications of combinational logic devices, functionalities and applications of sequential logic devices, register transfers and so on. These demonstration circuits accurately cover course focuses and difficulties guiding students to deeply understand the working mechanism of devices, the flow of current in circuits, the transmission of signals, and clock driving logic, thus systematically cultivating their visualization ability of circuit behavior.

Logisim has significant advantages in teaching adaptability: as an open-source digital circuit simulation platform, it provides a parametrized configurable library of logic gates, triggers, counters and other components supporting graphical drag-and-drop modeling and multi-level sub-circuit packaging significantly simplifying complex system design process. During the simulation debugging process, the real-time visualization mechanism enables students to dynamically observe the changes in port states and storage element values. The color coding of data lines intuitively maps the signal states (bright green = logical "1", dark green = logical "0", red = signal error, yellow = value conflict), significantly enhancing the interpretability of the signal transmission process.

Figure 1 shows a serial adder demonstration circuit (left: D-flip-flop constructed 4-bit shift register; right: integrated 4-bit shift register). By observing the numerical changes of the D flip-flop/register and the color timing of the data line, students can clearly analyze the step-by-step execution mechanism of the 4-bit addition operation and deeply understand the working principle of the shift register. More importantly this demonstration reveals core trade-off logic in hardware design: Serial adders can be extended to operate on arbitrary word lengths with only one full adder, but their operation is constrained by sequential bit-by-bit processing (completing only one addition per clock cycle). In contrast, parallel adders implemented with combinational logic require multiple full adders but enable synchronous multi-bit computation. This comparison vividly illustrates the engineering philosophy of "performance versus cost trade-offs," highlighting the need for hardware designers to optimize solutions under multiple constraints, such as speed, area, and power consumption.

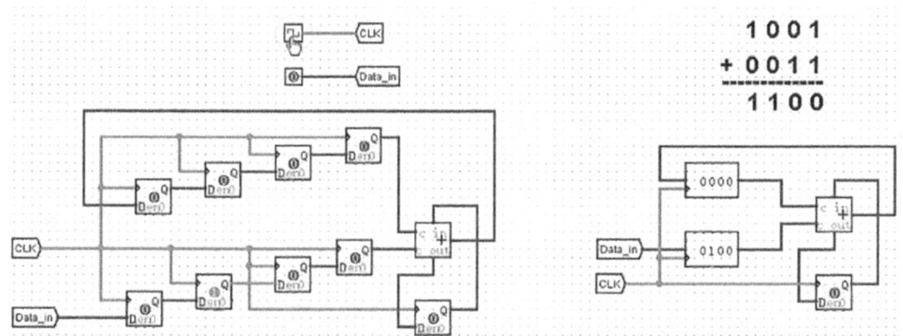

Fig. 1. Serial Adder Demonstration Circuit

3 Cultivation of System Design Capability

Digital system design generally adopts top-down methodology decomposing complex system into independently implementable sub-circuits layer by layer. This course focuses on the register-transfer level (RTL) design paradigm, with its core lying in deconstructing digital systems into two collaborative subsystems: the control unit and the data path. The two achieve timing coordination through the precise interaction of control signal flow and state feedback signals, ensuring a strictly ordered workflow of the system. To materialize the RTL design process, the course utilizes the design of a multifunction counter as a typical case study, teaching the key steps in structural design. In the practical part, students are required to complete the entire RTL design process based on a 12-instruction set model machine (Table 1). The specific steps include:

1. Analyzing functional requirements for instruction sets: Parsing operational semantics and data flows for each instruction.
2. Defining interfaces & register configuration: Determine the data input/output ports and the configuration of registers in the data path (such as PC, IR, the general-purpose register set, etc.).
3. State machine modeling: Drawing a state transition diagram containing operations of register transferring.
4. System decoupling: Separating control unit logic from data path structure according to the state transition diagram.
5. Architecture designing: Building complete framework structure for model machine (Fig. 2).

Through such training, students will gain an in-depth mastery of structured design skills at the RTL (Register Transfer Level) and understand the core role of control-data separation architecture in the implementation of complex digital systems.

Table 1. Model Machine Instruction Set

Mnemonic	Function	Machine Code	Note
MOVA Rd, Rs	Rd ← (Rs)	0100 Rd Rs	
MOVB M, Rs	M(R0) ← Rs	0101 00 Rs	
MOVC Rd, M	Rd ← M((R0))	0110 Rd 00	
MOVD R3, PC	R3 ← PC	0111 11 XX	
ADD Rd, Rs	Rd ← (Rd) + (Rs)	1000 Rd Rs	
SUB Rd, Rs	Rd ← (Rd) − (Rs) IF (Rd) > (Rs), THEN G = 1, ELSE G = 0	1001 Rd Rs	
JMP	PC ← (R3)	1010 XX 11	
JG	IF G = 1, THEN PC ← (R3)	1011 XX 11	
IN Rd	Rd ← Input Device	1100 Rd XX	
OUT Rs	Output Device ← (Rs)	1101 XX Rs	
MOVI #imm	R0 ← #imm	1110 00 XX imm	Double Byte
HALT	halt	1111 00 00	

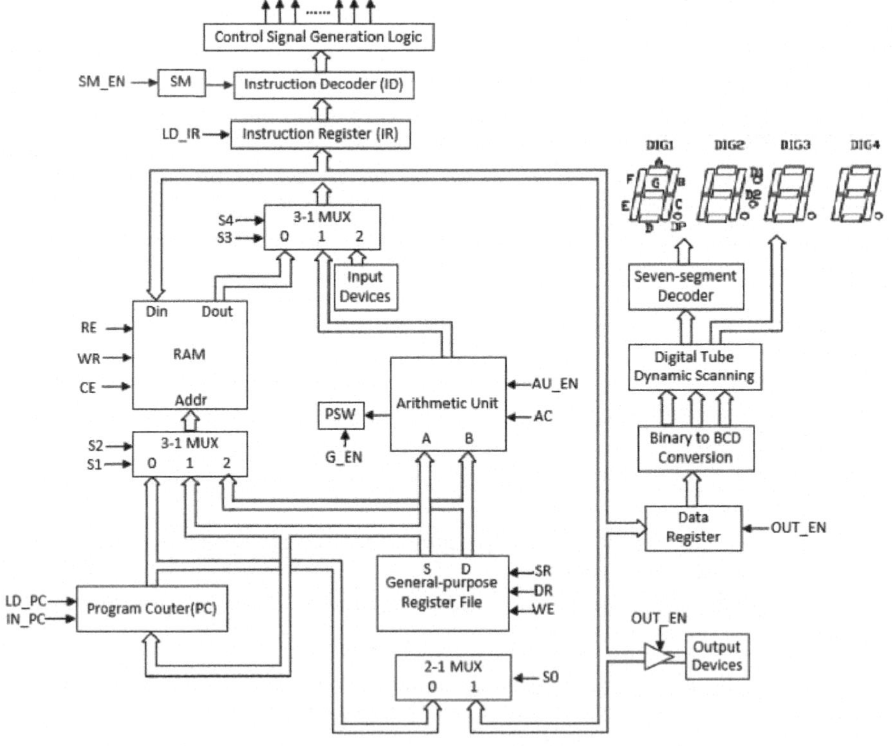

Fig. 2. Structural Framework of the Model Machine

4 Cultivation of Circuit Implementation Ability

Currently, colleges and universities generally adopt multi-mode integration paths in practical teaching reform [5]. For example, they carry out basic experiments with the help of experimental boxes or virtual simulation platforms, while comprehensive projects rely on hardware description languages to be implemented on FPGA. However, such a periodic division of "basic - comprehensive" and the segmented use of experimental platforms are difficult to guarantee the quality of the implementation of comprehensive projects. The core contradiction lies in: The coding logic of hardware description languages (such as Verilog) needs to be based on the circuit structure as the precondition. Even in the face of complex circuit systems, designers also need to plan the circuit framework in advance (that is, "there is a circuit diagram before there are lines of code"), and this planning ability needs to be supported by the hardware design intuition cultivated through a large number of basic experiments.

To address the above-mentioned issues, this course innovatively adopts a dual-track practical mode that combines virtual simulation with hardware description language. For complex circuit modules in the model machine (such as the general-purpose register file), the process begins by constructing a circuit prototype using Logisim, followed by verifying its functional correctness through automated evaluation circuits. Subsequently, the equivalent circuit structure is described using Verilog HDL, and the logical consistency between the code and the circuit is verified by comparing the RTL views. Through multiple circuit modules, students engage in a closed-loop training cycle of "design → evaluation → coding → verification," which progressively cultivates their intuitive understanding of hardware structures. This model not only significantly improves the quality of Verilog code and ensures that the performance of the model machine meets the standards, but also precisely identifies circuit defects through an automated fault localization mechanism. While relieving the pressure on teachers' guidance, it also enhances students' abilities to analyze and solve problems. The following sections will detail the implementation path of this scheme with a general-purpose register file as an example.

4.1 General-Purpose Register File

The general-purpose register file in the model machine includes four 8-bit registers: R0, R1, R2, and R3. The numbering of each register is shown in Table 2. Read and write operations can be performed on these four registers. The ports and functions of the general-purpose register file are as shown in Tables 3 and 4.

Table 2. General Registers Assignment

Register	Number
R0	00
R1	01
R2	10
R3	11

Table 3. Port Descriptions

Port	Direction	Function Description
CLK	Input	Clock Signal
WE	Input	Write Control Signal
SR[1:0]	Input	Source Register Select
DR[1:0]	Input	Destination Register Select
I[7:0]	Input	External Data Input
S[7:0]	Output	Source Register Output
D[7:0]	Output	Destination Register Output

Table 4. Functional Table

CLK	WE	Function
X	X	Output the content of one register selected by SR from R0–R3 through Port S SR=00, S=R0; SR=01, S=R1; SR=10, S=R2; SR=11, S=R3; Output the content of one register selected by DR from R0–R3 through Port D DR=00, D=R0; DR=01, D=R1; DR=10, D=R2; DR=11, D=R3;
falling edge	1	When the control signal WE is asserted (logic high), the external input I is transferred to the register addressed by DR at the falling edge of CLK DR=00, R0=I; DR=01, R1=I; DR=10, R2=I; DR=11, R3=I;

4.2 Implementation of a General-Purpose Register File Based on Logisim

From Tables 2 and 3, it can be seen that the read operation of the general-purpose register file is not controlled by the clock. The control signals SR and DR are used to select one of the registers R0, R1, R2, and R3 to output from the S port and D port, respectively. The write operation occurs at the falling edge of the clock, and when the control signal WE is active, the data from the external input I is written into the register specified by DR. From the above analysis, it can be concluded that the read operation of the general-purpose register can be implemented using two 4-to-1 multiplexers. The control signals for the two multiplexers are SR and DR, respectively, with the data inputs being the registers R0, R1, R2, and R3. The write operation is a sequential circuit, where the control signals WE and DR together control the enable signal of the register. The implementation circuit of the general-purpose register is shown in Fig. 3.

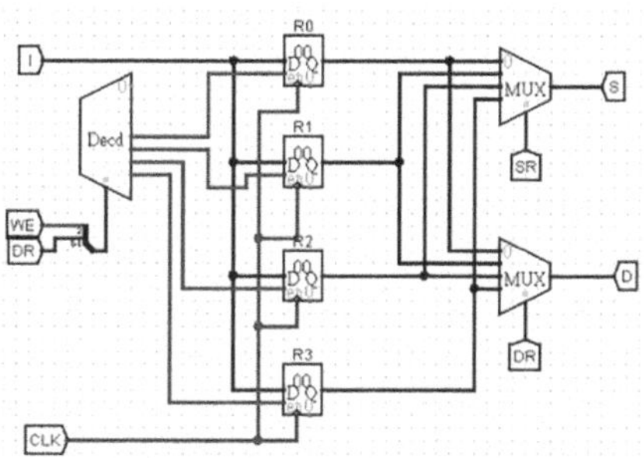

Fig. 3. Circuit of the General-Purpose Register File

4.3 Automatic Evaluation Circuit for General-Purpose Register File

After the circuit is designed, in the traditional approach, the instructor verifies the circuit's correctness—a task that entails significant workload. Since students do not participate throughout the process, they often fail to fully understand the instructor's feedback, making it difficult to enhance their circuit design skills. To enable student participation in the inspection process and enhance their analytical and problem-solving skills, an automated evaluation circuit is designed for each complex module. Using the general-purpose register circuit in Fig. 3 as an example, we introduce how automated evaluation is conducted for such circuits.

First, the design circuit shown in Fig. 3 needs to be modularly encapsulated (Fig. 4), forming a standardized Device Under Test (DUT) module. The encapsulation must meet the following interface specifications:

- Physical Dimension Matching: The packaging dimensions must strictly fit the layout space reserved by the evaluation circuit.
- Interface Compatibility: The physical locations, bit widths, and quantities of the input/output interfaces must exactly match those of the reserved interfaces in the evaluation circuit.

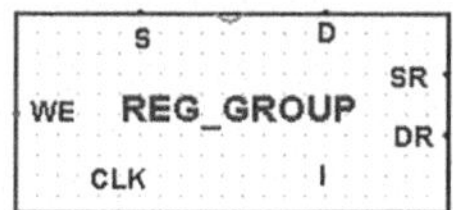

Fig. 4. Packaging of the General-Purpose Register File

Based on the concept of "hardware testing hardware" [5], an automatic evaluation circuit was constructed on the Logisim platform. This system adopts a black-box testing paradigm to achieve automated functional verification of the Device Under Test (DUT), precise fault location, and quantitative scoring. The core idea of its general framework (Fig. 5) is to preset test vectors (including input stimuli and expected outputs) in a storage module; load the input stimuli into the DUT; compare the DUT's output with the expected output in real-time; differences in output trigger the error record and fault location module, which identifies failed test cases and locates faults; a scoring module assigns performance scores to submodules of the DUT based on predefined weights.

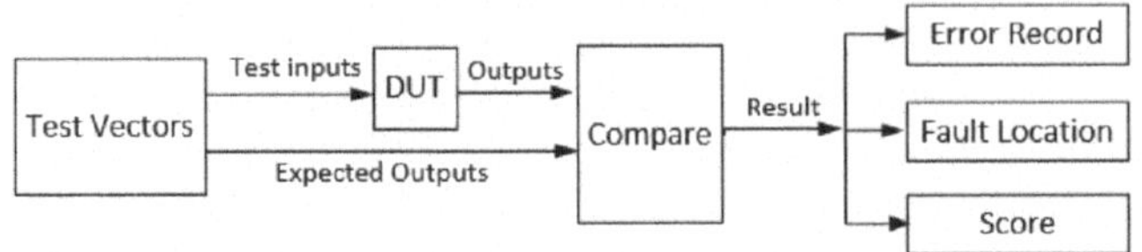

Fig. 5. The General Framework of the Automatic Testing Circuit

Based on the above framework, automatic evaluation trigger mechanism for universal register file (Fig. 6) is constructed. The input vectors (WE, SR, DR, data input I) and the expected outputs (EX_S, EX_D) are pre-stored in the ROM array. The test vectors design covers all functional boundaries (such as critical states and conflict conditions). A clock-driven counter automatically generates the ROM address sequence to achieve test vectors traversal. The DUT output is compared with the expected value in real time, and the difference signal synchronously triggers the scoring logic, fault location and error record module (Fig. 7 and Fig. 8). The stop logic detects the preset termination mark (such as 1Fh), and generates a stop signal to freeze the counter and subsequent modules.

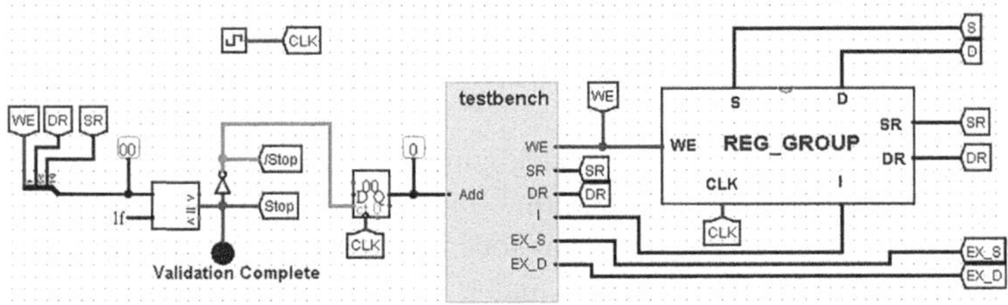

Fig. 6. Automatic Evaluation Trigger Mechanism for General-Purpose Register File

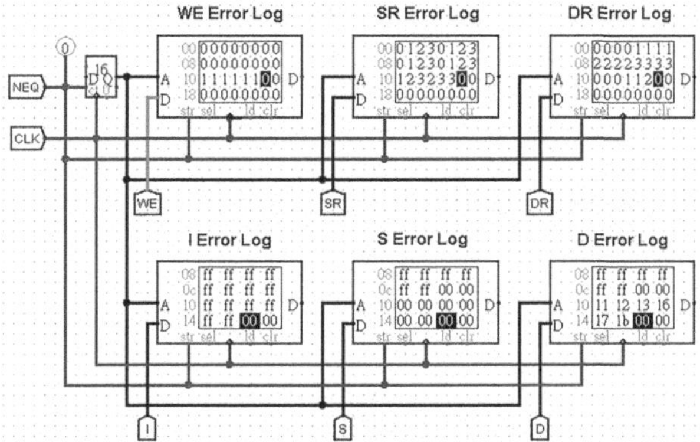

Fig. 7. Error Record of the General-Purpose Register File

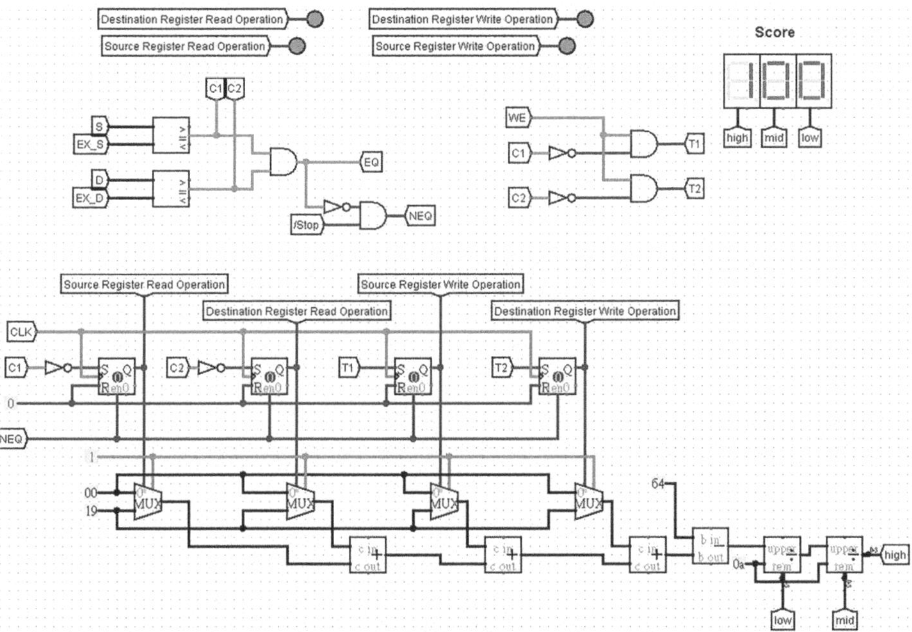

Fig. 8. Fault Location and Score of the General-Purpose Register File

4.4 Verilog Implementation of the General-Purpose Register File

Verilog HDL has become the industry-standard language for digital circuit design due to its three core features: parallel execution model, multi-level abstraction capability, and process independence. To achieve high-quality, synthesizable code, it is essential to follow the core design principle of "circuit first, code later" and strictly adhere to coding standards and design principles. For example, non-blocking assignments (<=) should be uniformly used in sequential circuits to avoid signal hazards; blocking assignments (=) should be employed in combinational logic, and ensuring that the always statement's sensitivity list is complete. Additionally, if/case statements must assign values to all branches to prevent the synthesis of unintended latches.

Having implemented the internal circuit of a general-purpose register file in Logisim and verified its functional correctness through the automatic evaluation circuit, we can proceed with a targeted description of the register file using Verilog HDL. The read operation of the general-purpose register is combinatorial, while the write operation is sequential. According to coding standards, two always blocks are used to describe the read and write operations separately. The sensitivity list for the read operation is comprehensive (always @ (*)), and a case statement is employed to model a 4-to-1 multiplexer, ensuring that the output responds to input changes in real time. The write operation is triggered by the falling edge of the clock (negedge clk), and a case statement is used to synchronously write data on the falling edge of the clock, satisfying setup/hold time constraints. Each line of code corresponds to implementable hardware structures, forming a traceable link from the RTL level to the gate level, which endows the code with engineering attributes such as readability, testability, and scalability.

```
module reg_group (
  input we,rst,clk,
  input [1:0] sr,dr,
  input [7:0] i,
  output reg [7:0] s,d );
reg [7:0] R0, R1, R2, R3;
always @ (*)
 begin
  case(sr)
     2'b00: s=R0;
        ......
     default:;
  endcase
  case(dr)
        ......
  endcase
 end
always @ (negedge clk or posedge rst)
 begin
  if (rst)
  begin
     R3<=8'h07;
      ......
   end
  else
  case ({we, dr})
     3'b100: R0<=i;
        ......
   endcase
  end
endmodule
```

5 Construction of a Hierarchical Competency Training System Oriented Towards Hardware Thinking

The core of hardware thinking lies in the construction of system-level design thinking, which requires designers to deeply understand the performance boundaries of the system (such as timing bottlenecks, resource utilization limits), to coordinate local optimization with global efficiency, and to achieve a dynamic balance among function implementation, power consumption constraints, and cost control. At the same time, it is necessary to precisely control the implementation details—including key factors such as circuit parameter calibration, component selection and matching, and manufacturing process adaptation—thereby sublimating theoretical cognition into engineering intuition and ultimately forming the core capability to solve complex system problems.

This course employs full-process development with bare FPGA boards to construct a hierarchical competency training system:

Hardware Layer Construction: Students observe the SMD chip placement process via an automated SMT line demonstration to comprehend high-density integration technology. For through-hole components, students manually solder and master basic assembly skills alongside troubleshooting logic.

Functional Layer Verification: Post-board assembly, students develop diagnostic programs to conduct comprehensive hardware testing (including I/O electrical characteristics and clock stability validation).

System Layer Development: Students independently select topics to complete end-to-end system development, from architecture design to code implementation.

Engineering Acceptance Criteria: Projects are evaluated across multiple dimensions, including design rationality, functional completeness, and performance benchmark achievement.

The course enables students to advance from physical layer operations (such as soldering and assembling) to system-level development through a full closed-loop training process of "hardware construction → software driving → function implementation → performance optimization." It fosters quality awareness driven by product-level delivery standards (including power consumption, cost, and reliability). Through iterative design under multi-dimensional constraints, it reinforces systematic engineering thinking.

FPGA experimental boards are low in cost, allowing each student to own one, and their compact size makes them easy to carry, breaking the limitations of experiment time and space. Figure 9 shows a portable FPGA experimental platform.

Fig. 9. A Self-made Portable FPGA Experimental Platform

6 Effects of Practical Teaching Reform

With the core orientation of cultivating hardware thinking, this course has constructed a four-stage capability development chain of "laying a theoretical foundation - systematic design - engineering implementation - innovative application" through the deep integration of classroom teaching and practical sessions. The teaching effects demonstrate a systematic improvement across four major dimensions: academic performance, comprehensive practice, engineering training, and competition results. The specific manifestations are as follows:

Academic performance continues to be optimized. In the past three years, students' theoretical scores have shown a stable upward trend. The average score of the final assessment in 2024 reached 72 points, and the score distribution conformed to an approximate normal distribution, indicating that the adaptability of teaching stratification has been significantly enhanced.

Comprehensive practical ability has significantly improved. In the comprehensive training project carried out with the design of the 12-instruction set model machine as the carrier: The pass rate was 98%, reflecting the universal achievement of teaching objectives. The advantage of resource efficiency is prominent: Based on the Altera Cyclone II EP2C5T144C8 FPGA platform, the model machine consistently occupies $\leq$ 5% of logical resources, with the main frequency stably operating at 50 MHz (a 25% improvement over the course baseline requirements).Expanded innovation capabilities are prominently demonstrated: 20% of students independently implemented advanced features such as instruction set expansion (e.g., adding stack operation instructions) and data path optimization, demonstrating the deep internalization of hardware system design capabilities.

The FPGA full-chain training achieved a 100% completion rate, with students successfully constructing multi-cycle/pipelined processor architectures based on the RISC-V instruction set.

Significant breakthroughs in innovative application achievements: Students supervised by the author won first place in the East China Region in both the 4th and 5th National University Internet Application Innovation Competitions, validating the effective transformation of hardware thinking into innovative capabilities.

These reforms have yielded tangible outcomes, benefiting over 5,000 students and training nearly 200 external educators. The experimental platform has been adopted by multiple universities, including Sichuan University, North Minzu University, and Hunan University of Science and Technology. Leveraging this platform, students have secured prestigious awards—including National First Prizes—in major competitions such as the Intel Cup University Student Electronic Design Contest, National College Students' Internet of Things Design Contest, and China Robotics & Artificial Intelligence Competition.

7 Conclusion

This course is guided by hardware thinking and carries out practical teaching reform from three aspects: cultivating the ability to concretely understand circuit behavior, systematic design ability, and circuit implementation ability. The hierarchical ability training in FPGA bare board assembly, testing, and development is emphasized to strengthen the cultivation of hardware thinking. In the future, we will enhance the connection with subsequent courses. We will cooperate with Huawei to build a computer system capability demonstration course, integrate the real development cases of Kunpeng domestic chips into the course, develop complex microsystems, and focus on cultivating system-level engineering thinking.

Acknowledgments. This study was funded by Regular Higher Educational Institutions Teaching Reform Project of Hunan Province "Practical Teaching Reform for Holistic Development of Computer System Capabilities Based on Kunpeng Architecture", 202502000226.

References

1. Wang, Z.Y., Zhou, X.S., Yuan, C.F., et al.: Research on system capability cultivation and curriculum design for computer majors. Comput. Educ. **9**, 1–6 (2013)
2. Yan, S.: Review and prospects of computer system capability training. Comput. Educ. **4**, 1–6 (2024)
3. Zhao, H., Yang, K.H., She, J.K., et al.: "From details to whole": building integrated curriculum around Prototype+PocketCat. Comput. Educ. (12), 221–226 (2024)
4. Ling, C.Q., Kuang, J.S., Xu, C., et al.: Teaching reform in digital circuit courses based on problem-oriented learning. J. Comput. Tech. Educ. **11**(2), 34–38 (2023)
5. Lai, X.Z., Bi, S., Li, Y.P.s., et al.: Practical teaching reform in computer hardware courses for system capability cultivation. Comput. Educ. (2), 161–165 (2018)
6. Hu, D.Q., Tan, Z.H., Qin, L.H.: Design and implementation of an automated hardware lab evaluation system. Electr. Electron. Teach. J. **42**(4), 115–118 (2020)

Teaching Reform of Computer Curriculum System for Cultivating Students' Computer System Ability

Xing Liu, Xing Liu, Jianjun Chen, Qinglan Zhan, and Mengling Chen(✉)

School of Computer Science and Artificial Intelligence, Wuhan University of Technology, Wuhan 430070, Hubei, China
{liu.xing,296489,chen.jianjun,311575,chenmenglin428}@whut.edu.cn

Abstract. Computer system ability (CSA) can enable students to design and analyze a computer problem from a system perspective, understand the integrity, hierarchy and relevance of different modules within a computer system, and master the correlation between computer hardware and software. Since 2015, the CSA training proposal has been widely promoted in many Chinese universities, and has effectively improved the quality of college computer education. However, with the development of computer technologies such as artificial intelligence (AI) and big data, the traditional CSA training proposal cannot fully meet the needs of future computer education. To address this challenge, this paper improves and extends the currently widely used CSA training program. On the one hand, the traditional CSA proposal is improved by integrating the knowledge of more computer science (CS) courses and requiring students to build a more complex computer system. On the other hand, the traditional CSA proposal is extended by proposing a new additional CSA training program dedicated to AI professionals. The above improved and extended CSA training proposals have been implemented in the School of Computer Science and Artificial Intelligence of Wuhan University of Technology for more than five years, and the teaching quality evaluation results show that these proposals have effectively improved the quality of talent training in CS specialty.

Keywords: Computer education · Computer curriculum system · Computer system ability

1 Introduction

Modern computer engineering has shown characteristics such as increasingly large system scale, increasing number of subsystems, and increasingly complex interactions. These features not only require computer technicians to research computer engineering problems from multi-dimensional perspective of computer systems, but also require them to comprehensively use a variety of knowledge to engage in engineering development.

W. Hong et al. (Eds.): ICCSE 2025, CCIS 2761, pp. 558–572, 2026.
https://doi.org/10.1007/978-981-95-7731-6_44

Although most universities in China currently have a complete computer curriculum system and mature teaching content, there are still some common problems in cultivating the above-mentioned high-quality computer professionals: First, most courses are designed independently, and the knowledge system lacks systematicity, making it difficult for students to establish computer system thinking; Second, the scale and complexity of engineering training in the practice process are insufficient, making it difficult to cultivate system capabilities. The above problems have reduced the quality of computer education in China to a considerable extent.

To meet the above challenges, many universities in China have initiated teaching reforms to cultivate students' computer system abilities (CSA). CSA aims to train students to establish a computer system thinking way, understand the integrity, hierarchy and relevance of different computer systems, master the correlation between computer hardware and software, and comprehensively apply different computer knowledge and technologies to complete the development of complex engineering systems.

Currently, a widely used CSA teaching reform program is to build a computer science (CS) curriculum system which integrates four CS courses: Digital Logic, Computer Organization, Operating System (OS) Principle and Compiling Principle. Through the above course integration, students can independently develop one CPU, one OS kernel and one compiler. Not only that, they can also integrate the CPU, OS and compiler into one computer system, as is depicted in Fig. 1. Specifically, the students learn Digital Logic courses firstly, and then use the knowledge of this course to develop various computer components such as adders, decoders, multiplexers and clocks based on the reprogrammable FPGA. Then, they take the Computer Organization course and use the knowledge of this course to combine the different computer components developed in the Digital Logic course to build a multi-cycle or pipelined CPU. Next, they take the OS Principle course and use the knowledge of this course to design an OS kernel dedicated to the previously built CPU. Finally, they learn the Compiling Principle course and develop a compiler to compile the pre-developed OS to make it run on the pre-built CPU. Through the above teaching mechanism, students can integrate knowledge from different courses to develop a complex computer system. More significantly, they can understand the correlation between software and hardware systems.

Since 2015, the above CSA proposal has been widely promoted in many universities in China, and has significantly improved the quality of computer education in Chinese universities. However, with the development of computer technologies such as AI and big data, the above CSA training program needs to be improved to adapt to the development trend of new computer technology. On the one hand, in addition to CPU, OS, and compiler, more technologies such as interface, bus, cache and interrupt need to be integrated to the CS system to enable students to build a more complex computer system. On the other hand, it is essential to design a new CSA training proposal dedicated to the emerging AI technologies.

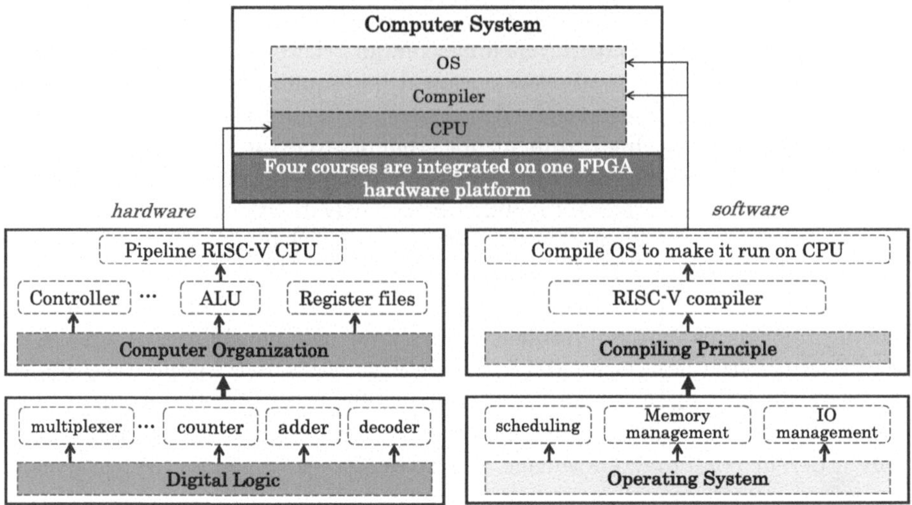

Fig. 1. The basic CSA training proposal.

Regarding the above concerns, the work of this paper aims to make the following contributions: (1) Improve the currently widely used CSA proposal presented in Fig. 1 to enable students to integrate the knowledge from more hardware and software courses so as to build a more complex computer system. (2) Design a specific CSA program dedicated to the AI specialty.

The organization of this paper is as follows: In Sect. 2, the relevant teaching research work on cultivating college students' CSA is presented. In Sect. 3, the basic CSA training proposal which aims to enable the students to independently develop a CPU, an OS and a compiler is introduced, and the improvement to this CSA proposal is discussed. In Sect. 4, a new CSA program dedicated to AI is designed based on Huawei's AI technology stack, for the purpose of cultivating talents who can master Huawei's full-stack AI technology such as the AI chips, AI frameworks, AI algorithms and AI application development. In Sect. 5, the teaching effects of CSA training in Wuhan University of Technology is surveyed and introduced. Finally in Sect. 6, the conclusion is given.

2 Related Work

In the past years, the CSA training proposal has been widely promoted in many universities in China, and has effectively improved the quality of CS teaching.

Mao et al. proposed a new CSA scheme by establishing core courses and optimizing experimental teaching system. With this CSA training, most undergraduate students could independently develop a CPU, an OS and a compiler [1]. Zhang et al. presented a step-by-step practical curriculum system to enhance the students' CSA, and this curriculum system integrated the knowledge of four core courses: Digital Logic, Principles of Computer Organization, Principles and

Implementations of Operating System, and Principles of Compilers [2]. Shi et al. also integrated the knowledge of the four courses as above to train students' CSA, and they conducted the experiments on the FPGA experimental platform [3]. Chen et al. explored the CSA training model for computer majors in the applied undergraduate colleges and universities, and the teaching effect demonstrated that this training way had improved the engineering education level, and could enable students to better adapt to the development needs of society [4]. Zuo et al. presented a practical approach combining simulation software and FPGA platform to effectively help students understand the knowledge of the Computer Organization and Interface course, and their work also had a positive effect on improving students' CSA [5]. Liu et al. opened a new course named Computer System Fundamentals for the purpose of helping students integrate the knowledge of programming, assembly, machine code, instruction set, digital logic and circuits. The teaching effect showed that this course had enabled the students to establish a computer system thinking way, understand the hardware and software co-optimization, and improve the ability to solve the complex engineering problems [6]. Zhang et al. proposed a multi-subject and multi-dimensional hierarchical teaching evaluation system to evaluate the teaching content, implementation, learning experience and teaching effect of CSA training [7]. Zheng presented the teaching work on using technical ways to independently develop a computer system including CPU, OS and compiler [8]. Their work aimed to helping the students deeply understand the overall computer system as well as the correlation and logical level of various software and hardware parts in the computing system. Li et al. proposed a new experimental teaching proposal collaborating the software and hardware design for developing students' system view, structure view and engineering view of computers. In experiment, they developed an FPGA-based CNN accelerator and used it to integrate the knowledge from software to compilation and then to hardware [9]. Liu et al. offered a new course named "Computer System Fundamentals (RISC-V version)". This course designed a representative C program example, and then used it to investigate how a program run inside the computer from the high-level application layer to the low-level hardware layer. The teaching objective of this course was to integrate knowledge from different courses and integrate computer software and computer hardware [10].

3 Improvements to the Basic CSA Training Proposal

The currently widely used CSA training proposal, which is also named the basic CSA proposal, is to guide students to independently design a CPU, an OS and a compiler, as shown in Fig. 1. This program was implemented in Wuhan University of Technology from 2015 to 2018. However, since 2019, this training proposal has been improved in Wuhan University of Technology for the purpose of further enhancing the teaching effect of CSA training. In this section, the curriculum system and experimental teaching work for the improved CSA training program are presented.

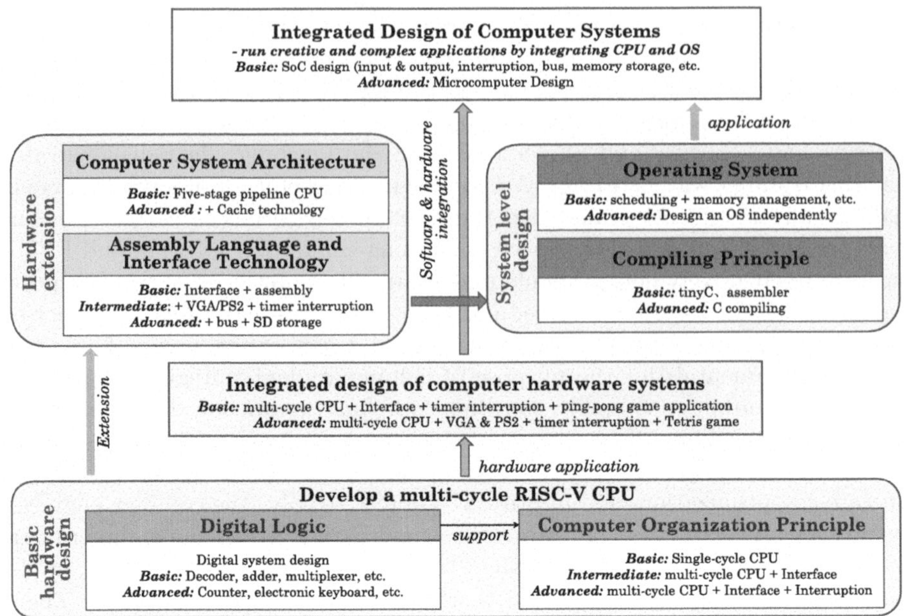

Fig. 2. The improved CSA training proposal.

3.1 Curriculum System for Improved CSA Training Program

The curriculum system for the improved CSA training proposal is depicted in Fig. 2. Compared with the basic CSA proposal, this improved CSA proposal has made the following improvements:

(1) Integrates the knowledge from more CS software and hardware courses. The basic CSA program mainly integrates four courses: Digital Logic, Computer Organization principle, OS and Compiling Principle. The improved CSA program expands the curriculum system from the following two aspects: First, in terms of hardware, two new courses have been added, namely Computer System Architecture, and Assembly Language and Interface Technology. Through the integration of the knowledge from these two courses, students can implement a computer system with more complex hardware functionalities. Secondly, in terms of application, two new courses have been added, namely Integrated Design of Computer Hardware System and Integrated Design of Computer Systems. By offering these two courses, students can train the ability to develop a series of upper-level applications based on the low-level CPU and OS.

(2) To meet the requirements of different students, three difficulty levels are designed for the training program of these course, and they are respectively *basic*, *intermediate* and *advanced*. Different levels have different development difficulties, and can be customized for students of different specialities or meet the needs of students at different learning levels.

(3) A more complex computer system is required to be developed in the new CSA training proposal. In the previous basic CSA proposal, students mainly developed a CPU and an OS and integrated the CPU and OS into one system. However, in the improved CSA training proposal, a more complex computer system which consists of pipelined CPU, multi-threading OS, bus, cache, interruption, SD storage, VGA, PS2, counter, electronic keyboard, as well as a variety of computer system applications such as ping-pong game, Tetris game and snake game should be developed independently by the students. This improved proposal is more systematic, comprehensive and complex.

3.2 Experimental Teaching for Improved CSA Training Program

The experimental tasks for the improved CSA program are organized as follows:

In the third semester, students take the Digital Logic course and then develop logic components such as decoder, adder, multiplexer, counters and electronic keyboard on FPGA.

In the fourth semester, students first take the Computer Organization Principle course and design a multi-cycle CPU with interrupt capabilities. Then, they take the Integrated Design of Computer Hardware Systems course, and develop a computer hardware system with multi-cycle CPU, VGA, PS2, timer interruption, Tetris game and ping-pong game.

In the fifth semester, students first take Computer System Architecture course and develop a pipeline CPU with cache functionality. Then, they take Assembly Language and Interface Technology course to further add bus, SD storage to the hardware system. Next, they take Operating System course and develop an OS dedicated to the above hardware system.

In the sixth semester, students first take Compiler Principle course and develop a compiler to compile the pre-built OS to run on the pre-built CPU. Then, they take Integrated Design of Computer Systems course and develop a comprehensive computer system that integrates software and hardware systems. Finally, they develop various applications based on the above computer systems.

The experimental schemes of the above 8 courses are deeply integrated. This integration is mainly reflected in two aspects: First, all 8 courses use the same hardware experimental platform; Second, the experimental content of the latter courses depends on the experimental content of the former courses.

Through the deep integration of the knowledge of the above 8 courses, students can build a complex computer system and understand the boundaries and relevance of different courses. More importantly, this teaching way can cultivate students' computer system capabilities.

4 CSA Training Proposal for Artificial Intelligence

In recent years, AI technology has developed rapidly and plays an important role in many research fields. To cultivate AI technical talents, Wuhan University of Technology has established AI speciality since 2018.

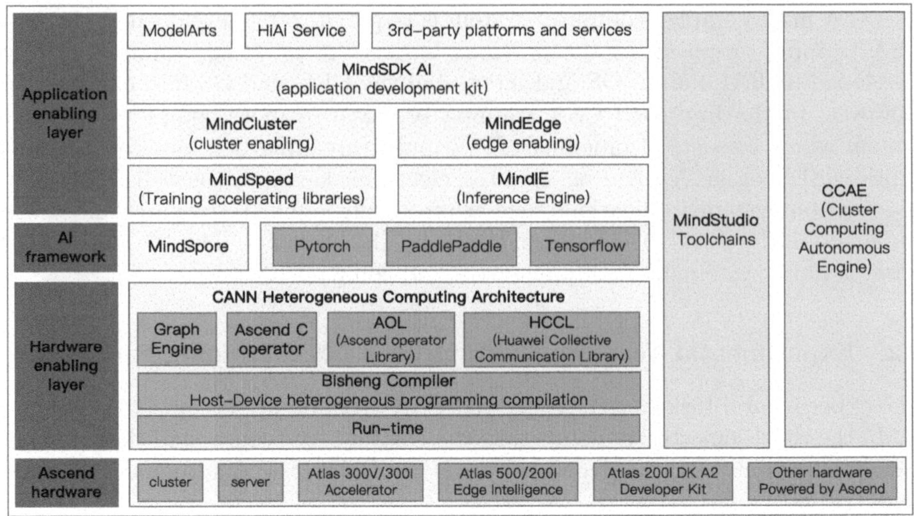

Fig. 3. Huawei's Ascend AI technology stack.

Students majoring in AI also need to cultivate CSA. However, the traditional CSA training proposal presented in Sect. 3 is not suitable for the students of AI speciality. Therefore, Wuhan University of Technology has designed a new CSA program dedicated to AI since 2019. The program is designed based on Huawei's AI technology stack, and its objective is to cultivate talents who can master AI chips, AI frameworks, AI algorithms and AI application development.

4.1 Huawei's Artificial Intelligence Technology Stack

The Huawei's Ascend AI software and hardware platform is shown in Fig. 3.

At the Ascend hardware layer, a series of Ascend hardware products are provided to meet the needs of different application scenarios, including the AI cluster hardware (Atlas 900 A2 PoD, Atlas 900 AI cluster, etc.), AI severs hardware (Atlas 800 inference server, Atlas 800T A2 training server, Atlas 800I A2 inference server, Atlas 500 Pro edge intelligence server, etc.), AI standard cards (Atlas 300V Video resolution card, Atlas 300I Pro/Duo inference card), AI accelerator module (Atlas 200I A2), and AI developer kit (Atlas 200I DK A2).

At the hardware enabling layer, there is the CANN (Compute Architecture for Neural Networks) heterogeneous computing architecture. CANN supports heterogeneous computing programming by using Ascend C language, and provides host-device heterogeneous programming compilation capabilities. It also provides a series of optimized Ascend operator libraries.

At the AI framework layer, many AI development frameworks are provided. In addition to Huawei's mindSpore, the mainstream frameworks such as PyTorch, PaddlePaddle and Tensorflow are also supported.

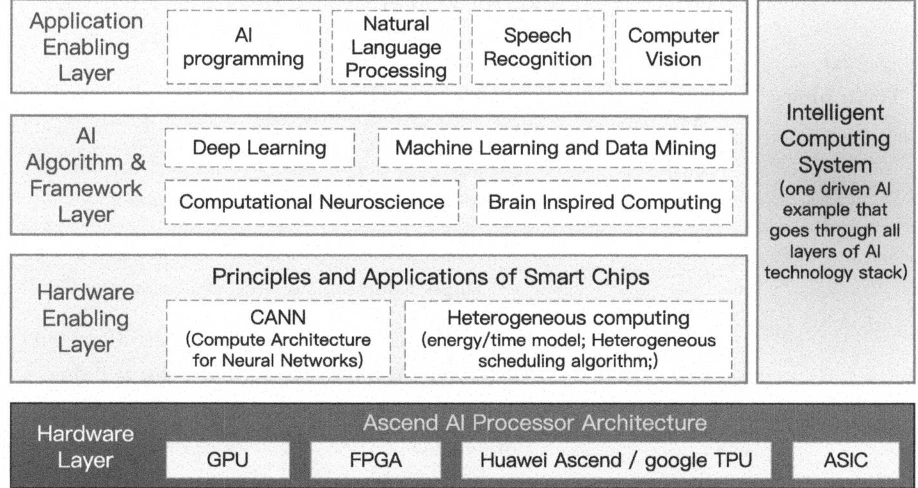

Fig. 4. AI curriculum system for training students' AI system capabilities.

At the application enabling layer, many application development tools and application management suites are provided. ModelArts is an AI development platform for developers. It can quickly create and deploy models and manage full-cycle AI workflows. HiAI is an open AI platform for smart terminals. MindSDK enables simplified development but ultimate performance of industry applications, which includes vision SDK, feature index SDK, search and recommendation SDK, and knowledge enhancement SDK. MindCluster enables full-process operation of cluster construction, supporting cluster job scheduling, fault recovery, operation and maintenance. MindEdge enables the construction of edge-cloud collaborative platforms, manages edge AI services, and provides a secure, reliable, and complete lightweight edge-cloud framework. MindSpeed is a training acceleration library that provides a variety of acceleration algorithms and models to accelerate the entire training process. MindIE is designed for inference execution deployment, enabling efficient application implementation.

4.2 CSA Curriculum System Dedicated to AI

To enhance students' AI system capabilities, 11 courses are offered in AI speciality around the AI technology stack, and the teaching contents of these 11 courses are deeply integrated by using Huawei's AI hardware and software. These 11 courses are respectively "Ascend AI Processor Architecture", "Principles and Applications of Smart Chips", "Computational Neuroscience", "Brain Inspired Computing", "Deep Learning", "Machine Learning and Data Mining", "Natural Language Processing"', "Speech Recognition", "Computer Vision", "AI programming" and "Intelligent Computing System", as shown in Fig. 4.

Table 1. AI Experiment Design for Huawei CANN and MindSpore Framework

AI Technology Stack	Experiment Title	Experiment Contents
CANN	Ascend CANN inference	Use AscendCL to perform ResNet50 network model inference on Atlas 200I DK A2 board
	Ascend C operator development	Use Ascend C programming to complete the development of Add operator
	Ascend CANN model migration	Migrate handwritten digit recognition script trained on GPU by PyTorch to Ascend NPU for training
AI framework	Convolutional Neural Network	Perform Mnist handwritten image recognition through Lenet CNN, Mindspore framework and ModelArts platform.
		Using Mindspore framework and ModelArts platform to achieve flower image classification and recognition
		Using Mindspore framework, Deeplabv3 network model and PASCAL VOC 2012 dataset to achieve image semantic segmentation
		Using MindSpore to train the Yolov3 model to achieve target detection of people, faces, and masks
	Recurrent Neural Networks	Using Mindspore framework and ModelArts platform to train recurrent networks RNN, LSTM, and GRU to implement IMDB sentiment analysis
	MindStudio Practice	Use Mindstudio development tools and Mindspore framework to train the Lenet network

The course "Ascend AI Processor Architecture" describes the acceleration principles of GPU, TPU [11] and Ascend AI processors. It presents the Da Vinci architecture of Ascend AI processor, and explains the principle of convolution computing acceleration.

The course "Principles and Applications of Smart Chips" introduces the CANN heterogeneous computing architecture of Ascend processor, and the teaching content covers the operator development, Ascend C operator programming language, heterogeneous communication, graph engine, model migration and training, and open ecology.

The course "Machine Learning and Data Mining" mainly explains the relevant knowledge of machine learning and data mining, including supervised learning, clustering, dimensionality reduction, structured prediction, anomaly detection, reinforcement learning, etc.

The course "Deep Learning" mainly introduces the principle of deep learning algorithms, including linear regression, multi-layer perceptron, model training and inference, convolutional neural network, recurrent neural network, Ascend tensor boost engine (TBE), TBE operator development, MindSpore framework and MindStudio development tools.

The course "AI programming" mainly involves Python programming and Python common tool libraries.

The course "Natural Language Processing" mainly presents the knowledge such as text classification, text generation, machine translation, automatic question answering, and graph neural network, etc.

The course "Computer Vision" mainly teaches the basic knowledge such as object recognition, image segmentation, image generation, target detection, as well as multi-scenario practice of end-to-end training and deployment of computer vision industry applications.

The course "Speech Recognition" covers the knowledge such as speech signal processing, and traditional speech recognition based on GMM-HMM and DNN-HMM, etc.

The course "Intelligent Computing System" is a systematic course that goes through the entire AI software and hardware technology stack. This course adopts the idea of "application-driven, full-stack integration" and is driven by an example of image style transfer. This course focuses on the design theory, methods, and key technologies of intelligent computing systems, and aims to help students establish a knowledge system for the intelligent computing systems.

4.3 Experiments for CSA Curriculum System Dedicated to AI

In order to cultivate students' AI system capabilities, the full AI technology stack experiments ranging from AI hardware to AI framework and to AI application are conducted, and the experimental contents are shown in Table 1, Table 2 and Table 3. All these experiments are implemented on the same AI hardware platform and use the same AI software technology, so as to integrate the knowledge of different hardware and software courses.

In terms of AI hardware, two experimental platforms are provided: one is Huawei's Atlas 200I DK, and the other is OrangePi AIpro (8T), as is depicted in Fig. 5. Atlas 200I DK A2 is a developer kit product for AI algorithm verification and AI application development. It has 8 TOPS INT8 and 4 TFLOPS FP16 AI computing power, and can meet the needs of multiple AI fields such as video image analysis, natural language processing, and robotics. OrangePi AIpro also uses Huawei Ascend AI technology. It includes a 4-core 64-bit processor and an AI processor, and integrates a graphics processor and supports 8 TOPS AI computing power. It can be used in many AIoT application scenarios including AI edge computing, deep visual learning and video stream AI analysis, video image analysis, natural language processing, smart cars, robotic arms, drones, AR/VR and other fields. It supports openEuler operating systems and meet the needs of most AI algorithm prototype verification.

Table 2. Experiment design for the course "Natural Language Processing"

Courses	Experiment Title	Experiment Contents
Natural Language Processing	Text classification	Implementing the TextCNN model based on Mindspore and using it for text sentiment analysis
		Using MindStudio, using the SentimentNet network built on LSTM for sentiment analysis
	Text generation	Implementing the BERT model based on MindSpore and creating poems with it
	Machine translation	Implementing the seq2seq model with attention mechanism based on MindSpore for Chinese-English translation
		Implementing the Transformer model based on Mindspore for Chinese-English translation
	Automatic question answering	Implementing the BERT model based on MindSpore for automatic question-answering tasks
	Graph neural network	Implementing the GCN model based on Mindspore for scientific publication classification

(a) Huawei Atlas 200I DK A2 (b) OrangePi AIpro (8T).

Fig. 5. AI hardware platforms for experiment teaching of CSA curriculum system.

In terms of AI software, the MindSpore framework, MindStudio tools, ModelArts development platform, and MindX SDK are used for the AI experiments of all the above 11 courses.

5 Evaluation to CSA Teaching Reform

The objective of the teaching reform of CSA training is designed as follows:

(1) Students can independently develop a complex computer system that consists of CPU, OS, bus, cache, interrupt, I/O based on FPGA platform.

(2) Students can use Huawei's full-stack AI technology, including Huawei's AI hardware platform and Huawei's AI software technology (MindSpore framework,

Table 3. Experiment design for the course "Computer Vision" and "Speech Recognition"

Courses	Experiment Title	Experiment Contents
Computer Vision	Object recognition	Use MindSpore, Ascend chip and Cifar10 dataset to achieve image classification
		Use MindSpore to build U-Net training, use MindX SDK MxVision for inference, and achieve image segmentation tasks.
	Image segmentation	Use MindSpore and Ascend chip to implement medical image segmentation experiment based on U-Net model
		Use MindSpore and Ascend chip to achieve image semantic segmentation based on DeepLabv3 model
		Use MindSpore framework, MindStudio tool, Deeplabv4 network model and PASCAL VOC 12012 dataset to achieve image semantic segmentation
	Target detection	Develop target detection application with MindX SDK
		Build SSD target detection model based on MindSpore framework and MindStuido tool, and use COCO2017 dataset for training and evaluation
Speech Recognition	Speech signal processing	Use ModelArts platform and Mindspore framework to load, frame, pre-emphasize the voice data
		Analyze voice signals in time and frequency domains on ModelArts platform
	Speech classification	Achieve voice classification based on ModelArts automatic learning
	Traditional speech recognition	Use EM algorithm to solve the parameters of Gaussian mixture model based on Mindspore, scipy and numpy
		Solve part-of-speech taggingof hidden Markov chain in Mindspore environment
		Achieve simple single word recognition through GMM-HMM system in MindSpore environment
		Achieve continuous word recognition through GMM-HMM system in MindSpore environment

MindArts platform, MindStudio tools, MindX SDK, etc.) to develop various AI applications including NLP, computer vision, speech recognition, and image style transfer.

(3) Students have built the computer system thinking way.

(4) Students are more satisfied with the teaching effect after the teaching reform is implemented.

To evaluate whether the teaching reform has achieved the above goals, we conduct the following statistics and surveys.

5.1 Evaluation to the Ability of Building Complex Computer System

Statistical results showed that 92% of students could complete basic CSA experimental proposal (one CPU plus one OS), and 83% of students could complete intermediate-level CSA experimental proposal (multi-cycle CPU + interface + VGA/PS2 + interruption + basic hardware application), while 72% of students could complete advanced-level CSA experimental proposal (pipelined CPU + interface + VGA/PS2 + interruption + bus + Cache + SD storage + multithreading OS + diverse hardware/software applications). This result demonstrated that most students had built the ability to independently develop a complex computer system based on FPGA.

5.2 Evaluation to Full-Stack AI Technology Training

In order to understand students' mastery of AI full-stack technology, statistics were collected on students' completion of the AI experiments, and the results are depicted in Fig. 6.

It can be seen from the experimental results that most students have mastered the AI development technologies well after the CSA training program is implemented. Relatively speaking, students' mastery of CANN experiment is slightly poor. This is because CANN requires understanding the hardware architecture of Ascend AI processor, and this has high requirements for the cooperative optimization between software and hardware.

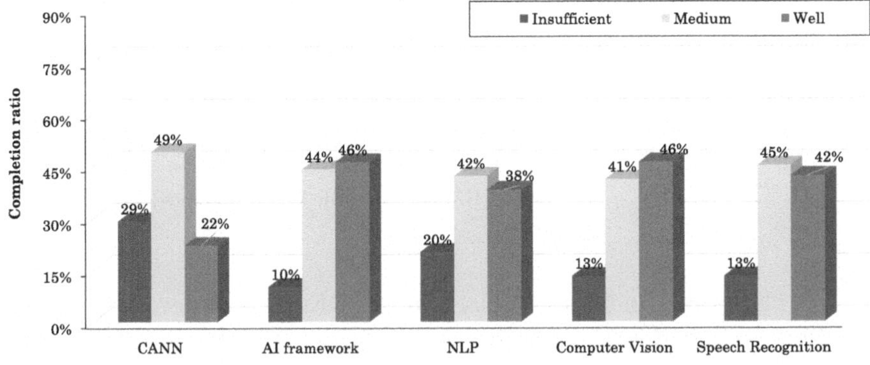

Fig. 6. Completion ratio of conducting full-stack AI experiments.

5.3 Assessment to Computer System Thinking

The survey result shows that students' computer system thinking ability has been significantly enhanced. On the one hand, their ability to integrate software and hardware has been improved significantly. On the other hand, they start to realize that they need to have a deep understanding of how the software operates on the underlying hardware if they want to improve the operating efficiency of software.

5.4 Teaching Satisfaction Feedback

The survey results show that the students' satisfaction for the teaching work has reached 87%, while it was only 72% before the CSA training program is implemented. This shows that students are more accepting of the CSA training program, although most of them think this program is more difficult to learn.

6 Conclusion

This paper not only improves the CSA program currently widely used in Chinese universities, but also proposes a new CSA training program for AI speciality. The work of this paper have been implemented in the School of Computer Science and Artificial Intelligence of Wuhan University of Technology for more than five years, and the teaching evaluation results show that the work in this paper has enhanced students' ability to develop complex computer systems, enabled students to use full-stack AI technology to develop various AI applications, cultivated students' computer system thinking, and improved students' satisfaction with teaching quality.

References

1. Mao, Y., Feng, Y., Cheng, D., Xie, Q.: Computer curriculum system reform based on system ability training. In: 2016 11th International Conference on Computer Science and Education (ICCSE), pp. 907–910. IEEE (2016)
2. Zhang, Y., Chen, X., An, X., Lu, J., Li, X., Zhou, X.: Building step-by-step practical curriculum system for computer systemic ability training. In: Proceedings of the ACM Turing 50th Celebration Conference-China, pp. 1–6 (2017)
3. Shi, Q., Chen, W., Hu, W.: Innovative teaching practice of integrated computer courses with focus on students' system ability. In: 2018 9th International Conference on Information Technology in Medicine and Education (ITME), pp. 521–525. IEEE (2018)
4. Chen, S., Chen, L.: Reform and research of computer professional curriculum system based on systematic capability training under the background of emerging engineering education. In: 2018 13th International Conference on Computer Science and Education (ICCSE), pp. 1–5. IEEE (2018)
5. Zuo, D., Cheng, W., Luo, J.: A practice approach to teach computer organization and interface technology. In: 2021 2nd Information Communication Technologies Conference (ICTC), pp. 338–342. IEEE (2021)

6. Liu, X., Tian, J., Li, Y., Xiong, S., Rao, W., Yuan, J.: Instructional design of computer system fundamentals for cultivating students' computer system ability. In: 2021 16th International Conference on Computer Science and Education (ICCSE), pp. 311–316. IEEE (2021)
7. Zhang, W., Wang, R., Tang, Y., Yuan, E., Wu, Y., Wang, Z.: Research on teaching evaluation of courses based on computer system ability training. In: Zeng, J., Qin, P., Jing, W., Song, X., Lu, Z. (eds.) ICPCSEE 2021, Part II 7. CCIS, vol. 1452, pp. 434–442. Springer, Singapore (2021). https://doi.org/10.1007/978-981-16-5943-0_35
8. Zheng, P.: Research on the cultivation of professional system ability in Computer Education. In: 2021 2nd International Conference on Information Science and Education (ICISE-IE), pp. 1281–1284. IEEE (2021)
9. Li, Y., Niu, J., Matutu, S., Qi, Q.: Teaching practice reforms towards software-hardware collaboration in computer system ability training-Taking FPGA Design course as an example. In: 2021 IEEE Frontiers in Education Conference (FIE), pp. 1–5. IEEE (2021)
10. Liu, X., Wang, Q., Zhu, W., Zhang, X., Chen, M.: Teaching reform to computer system fundamentals (RISC-V version) for developing students' computer system capabilities. In: Hong, W., Kanaparan, G. (eds.) ICCSE 2023. CCIS, vol. 2024, pp. 261–277. Springer, Singapore (2023). https://doi.org/10.1007/978-981-97-0791-1_23
11. Jouppi, N.P., et al.: In-datacenter performance analysis of a tensor processing unit. In: Proceedings of the 44th Annual International Symposium on Computer Architecture, pp. 1–12 (2017)

Hybrid Online-Offline Course Construction on "Compiler Principles"

Wenbi Rao(✉), Yunhua Wang, and Fuyang Li

School of Computer Science and Artificial Intelligence, Wuhan University of Technology, Wuhan, China
{wbrao,yhwang,fyli}@whut.edu.cn

Abstract. The course "Compiler Principles" is designed to enhance students' system-level thinking in computer science and strengthen their ability to solve complex engineering problems. To achieve these objectives, we have structured the "Compiler Principles" course using a hybrid online-offline teaching model. In this paper, we first outline the construction of the hybrid online-offline course. Then, we present a teaching case that demonstrates the effectiveness of this model. Finally, we conclude this paper by sharing valuable experiences gained from implementing hybrid online-offline teaching.

Keywords: Hybrid Online-offline Course · Course Construction · Compiler Principles

1 Introduction

The course "Compiler Principles" [1] is designed for third-year undergraduate students in the School of Computer Science and Artificial Intelligence. By this stage, students have already acquired a solid foundation in computer science and possessed basic programming skills. In line with the program's educational objectives, this course is designed to further cultivate students' system-level thinking in computer science and strengthen their ability to tackle complex engineering problems.

Feedback from in-class discussions and post-class surveys reveals that students generally perceive "Compiler Principles" as more challenging than their previous courses, due to its strong theoretical rigor and significant practical requirements. As a result, some students feel apprehensive about the difficulty of the course. Furthermore, survey data shows that students are already familiar with hybrid online-offline learning models [2]. This familiarity enables instructors to employ a variety of teaching methods and tools to enhance instructional effectiveness and continuously improve the quality of teaching. Previous research has demonstrated the effectiveness of utilizing a hybrid online-offline learning model to enhance the quality of teaching [3]. However, the research primarily focused on the "Introduction to Computer Science." In contrast, "Compiler Principles"

W. Hong et al. (Eds.): ICCSE 2025, CCIS 2761, pp. 573–584, 2026.
https://doi.org/10.1007/978-981-95-7731-6_45

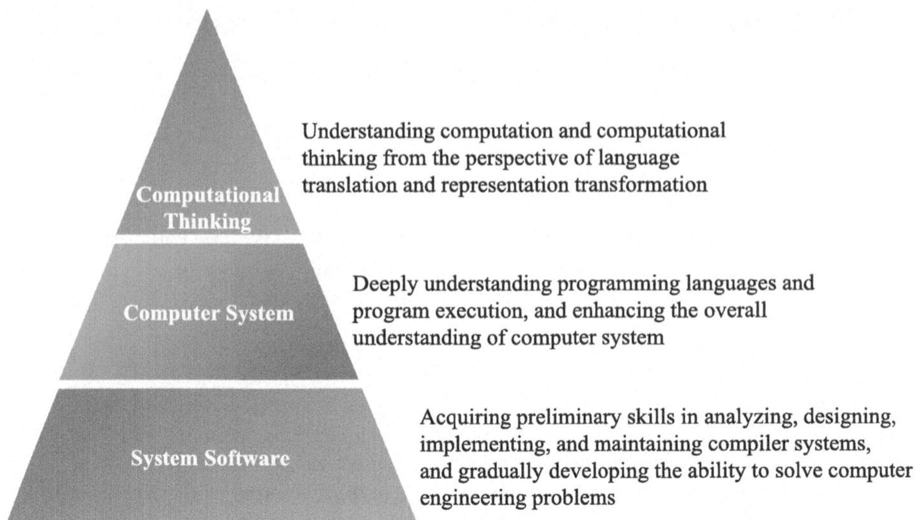

Fig. 1. The instructional objectives of "Compiler Principles".

is a core course in computer science, and the objectives of the two courses differ significantly.

The objectives of this course are designed to help students grasp the fundamental principles of compiler design and enhance their abilities in solving computer engineering problems. The framework consists of three layers of course objectives as shown in Fig. 1.

First Layer: Students will understand computation and computational thinking through the language translation and representation transformation.

Second Layer: Students will gain a deep understanding of programming languages and program execution, thereby enhancing their overall comprehension of computer systems.

Third Layer: Students will acquire foundational skills in analyzing, designing, implementing, and maintaining compiler systems, and gradually developing their capacity to address complex computer engineering challenges.

To achieve these objectives, we have structured the course "Compiler Principles" using a hybrid online-offline teaching model. In this paper, we first propose a variety of strategies for developing the hybrid online-offline course "Compiler Principles". Then, we illustrate a teaching case that demonstrates how we implement the hybrid online-offline teaching model to instruct students effectively. Finally, we conclude with valuable teaching experiences gained throughout the course teaching.

2 Related Work

Previous researchers have explored and studied online teaching, offline teaching, and hybrid online-offline teaching models, as well as the use of new technologies to support hybrid online-offline teaching. Bhardwaj et al. [4] studied three teaching modes: online, hybrid online-offline, and offline. Using descriptive and inferential statistical methods, it was found that students' performance in the online mode differs significantly from that in the hybrid online-offline and offline modes. The results indicated that a hybrid online-offline teaching mode should be adopted in the future to achieve better teaching outcomes. Thelma and Phiri [5] investigated online learning and traditional face-to-face learning modes using a combination of qualitative and quantitative methods. The results showed that although online learning offered flexibility and accessibility, it lacked face-to-face interaction. Offline learning, which provided immediate feedback, remained highly valued. The findings suggested that higher education institutions should strengthen the integration of online and face-to-face learning modes in the future to achieve better teaching outcomes. Qi [6] proposed a method for sharing hybrid online-offline teaching resource based on cloud computing to address issues such as low resource request success rate and weak data sharing capability.

In the field of computer science, researchers have examined and investigated the implementation of hybrid online-offline teaching modes for courses. Zhang [7] conducted research in the field of computer programming language teaching and designed a hybrid online-offline teaching strategy. The strategy included face-to-face teaching and online self-directed learning, guided by project-based approaches. During the learning process, immediate feedback on the learning status was provided and Bayesian models were used to evaluate the indicators of students' learning behaviors. Yuan et al. [8] studied the hybrid online-offline teaching approach for the course "Operating System". First, the teaching resources were reconstructed on the Treenity online teaching platform. Then, a student-centered hybrid online-offline teaching model was designed. The course contents were optimized following the direction of "value leadership - theoretical learning - practical improvement"and the course evaluation system was continuously improved. Mao et al. [9] studied the teaching of practical training courses for "Embedded Systems" and proposed a hybrid teaching mode combining online and offline methods. Before class, teachers published teaching resources on the teaching platform. During the teaching process, teachers provided one-on-one guidance to students through the platform. After class, teaching was further extended through online simulation, overcoming the limitations of time and space in teaching. Cao et al. [10] explored the hybrid online-offline teaching method for "Micro-controller" course. It enhanced students' engagement in both theoretical and practical learning through the project-based learning (PBL) approach. Deng et al. [11] proposed teaching reform measures for the "Digital Circuit" course. It emphasized strengthening the integration of theory and practice learning, and performed a hybrid online-offline teaching model to reconstruct the course's instructional design, practical sessions, and assessment system.

For graduate-level course instruction, some researchers have designed and explored hybrid online-offline teaching approaches for courses. Zhang [12] took the postgraduate course "Digital Image Processing" as an example and proposed a hybrid online-offline teaching method centered on students. Students can independently choose the learning contents and learning methods for the course. The principles for case design in postgraduate courses were presented, and a teaching evaluation method based on the revised Bloom's taxonomy was introduced in the work [12]. Wei and Zhao [13] conducted a study on hybrid online-offline course teaching for the graduate-level course "Software Architecture." The BOPPPS teaching theory was introduced into the construction of the hybrid online-offline course and integrated with the three stages of pre-class, in-class, and post-class to design a BOPPPS-based hybrid teaching model.

Compared with other courses in the field of computer science, the theoretical contents of the "Compiler Principles" course are relatively challenging. Learning "Compiler Principles" also requires integrating theory with practice. This paper explores and investigates the hybrid online-offline teaching approach for the fundamental core course "Compiler Principles" in the fields of Computer Science. While emphasizing theoretical instruction, it also connects theory with practice to enhance students' ability to acquire theoretical knowledge and practical skills.

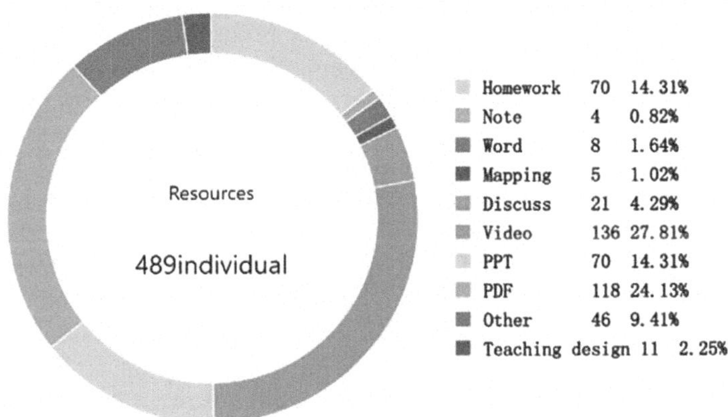

Fig. 2. The digital learning resources of "Compiler Principles" on the WHUT Smart Learning Platform.

3 Construction Measures

The course "Compiler Principles" has long been recognized as one of the most challenging subjects in computer science. To address this challenge, we focus on stimulating students' participation, enhancing teaching effectiveness, and achieving the course objectives. In line with our goal of developing a high-quality hybrid online-offline course, we implemented the following key measures during last semester's instruction:

(1) Outcome-Based Education [14] for Curriculum Design. We established a unified teaching framework that uses the compilation process as the central

organizational thread, seamlessly connecting hardware and software systems. Students are required to master the fundamental concepts, principles, and methods of "Compiler Principles," re-evaluate programs and algorithms at the system level, develop the ability to analyze and design solutions for complex problems, and enhance their foundational skills in computer science.

(2) Digital Course Resource Development. Since 2019, the Compiler Principles teaching team has systematically developed digital learning resources as shown in Fig. 2. The course was successfully certified as a university-level online open course in 2019. Following this, we completed comprehensive upgrades to our digital resources by migrating to the WHUT Smart Learning Platform[1] in September 2024, thereby supporting hybrid online-offline learning.

(3) Hybrid Online-Offline Teaching Design. In last semester, the teaching team developed a hybrid teaching model for the course, structuring each class into several distinct phases: pre-class (introduction, objectives, and preparation), in-class (student-centered participatory learning), post-class (assessment), and summary (evaluation). This design emphasizes active learning and deep students' engagement, complemented by collaborative feedback and reflection from both teachers and students throughout the teaching process. The goal is to establish a closed-loop teaching system that significantly enhances the overall effectiveness of classroom teaching.

(4) Teaching Organization Integrating Multiple Teaching Methods. Case Study Teaching Method: We used compilers as case studies to design and develop online teaching resources, including detailed explanations of typical algorithmic principles, algorithm implementations, and practical application cases of compiler systems. Our teaching approach centered on a case-driven model, structured around three key components: core knowledge points, algorithm implementation cases, and compilation module experiments.
Heuristic Teaching Method: Many abstract concepts and algorithmic processes in the "Compiler Principles" course—such as the LR(0) analysis method and register allocation algorithms—are well-suited to heuristic teaching.
Flipped Classroom [15]: In this model, students prepare for class by engaging with course materials or watching online videos in advance. During class sessions, teachers pose thought-provoking questions to stimulate in-depth discussions and encourage diverse viewpoints. This approach promotes critical thinking and enables students to communicate from multiple perspectives, thereby fostering collaborative problem-solving and enhancing teamwork skills.

(5) Cultivating Humanistic Spirit, Scientific Spirit, and Academic Ambition. We employ a hybrid online-offline teaching model to nurture students' spirit of scientific exploration and their dedication to continuous improvement. This approach also encourages students to set high academic aspirations.

[1] The course "Compiler Principles" website in the WHUT Smart Learning Platform. https://whut.ai-augmented.com/app/jx-web/mycourse/6519251470498449200.

4 A Teaching Case

In this section, we use the course unit "DFA Lexical Analysis and Application" as a teaching case to illustrate the complete process of hybrid online-offline teaching.

4.1 Teaching Objectives

After studying the overview of compiler principles, the fundamentals of formal grammar and languages, the theoretical foundations of lexical analysis, and the method for constructing DFAs, students will have developed an understanding of the basic logical structure of compilers, acquired essential techniques for language representation, and mastered the core theories and methods of lexical analysis and DFA construction.

This course unit is designed to provide students with a comprehensive understanding of the application of Deterministic Finite Automata (DFA) in the design of lexical analyzers, integrating theoretical instruction with hands-on practice. Furthermore, it aims to inspire students to explore real-world applications of DFA in solving scientific research problems, thereby deepening their appreciation of the importance of this approach in software design. The specific objectives are as follows:

(1) Knowledge Objectives: Students will master the construction methods of lexical analysis and Deterministic Finite Automata (DFA), and understand how to apply DFA techniques effectively.
(2) Skill Objectives: Students will acquire foundational skills in system software design and develop the ability to utilize DFA techniques for analyzing and solving software design problems.
(3) Emotional Objectives: Throughout the learning process, students will watch the "Lexical Analysis Program Construction" video prior to class to foster the spirit of craftsmanship and pursuit of excellence.

Students will engage in classroom interactions by sharing their homework, collaborating in groups, and participating in peer evaluations. This collaborative approach will help them cultivate a team spirit characterized by unity, cooperation, and mutual assistance.

4.2 Teaching Process

In this section, we illustrate the process of hybrid online-offline teaching with the course unit "DFA Lexical Analysis and Application" study.

Preparation. The teaching team carefully prepared pre-class guidance, lexical analysis program construction, and DFA lexical analysis demonstration video materials. These materials were pushed to students through the online smart platform. The teacher's preparation for the course unit "DFA Lexical Analysis and Application" teaching is shown in Fig. 3.

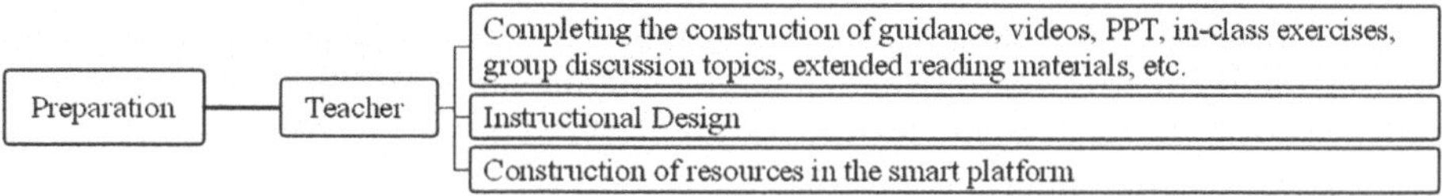

Fig. 3. The preparation for the course unit "DFA Lexical Analysis and Application" teaching.

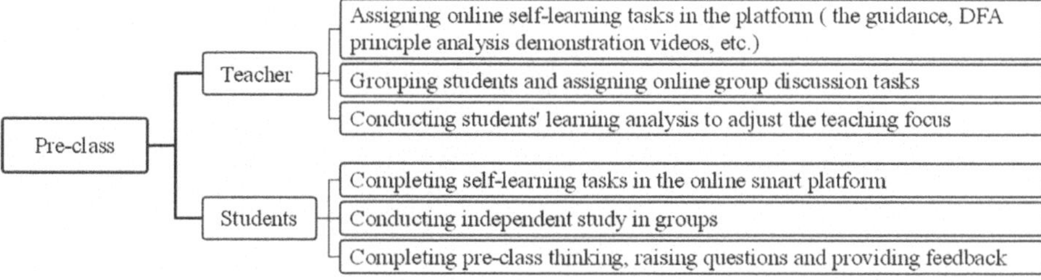

Fig. 4. The pre-class for the course unit "DFA Lexical Analysis and Application" study.

Pre-class. The pre-classs roles for both teacher and students are shown in Fig. 4. Students were organized into groups using the online smart platform and assigned self-learning tasks prior to class. Figure 5 shows that the students were discussing the group tasks in the pre-class stage.

These tasks included reading pre-class guidance materials and watching videos on the construction of lexical analysis program and DFA demonstrations. After completing the self-learning tasks, the teacher collected feedback from the students to adjust the key points and challenges for the class instruction and to design effective flipped classroom implementation strategies. The feedback provided by students highlighted two main areas of confusion:

1. There are still uncertainties regarding the two algorithms: NFA determinization and DFA simplification in the context of DFA construction.
2. The teacher needs to clarify the application of DFA techniques to solve practical problems by integrating relevant case studies.

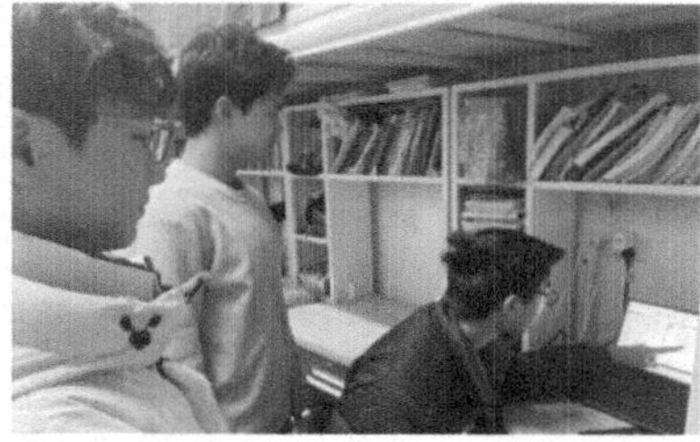 

Fig. 5. The students were discussing the group tasks before class.

In formulating classroom teaching strategies, we will build upon previous conventional designs while also incorporating the following considerations based on student feedback: reviewing the key points and challenges of NFA determinization and DFA simplification, conducting classroom tests and interactions, analyzing scientific research cases of DFA applications, and sharing and discussing exemplary cases from previous students.

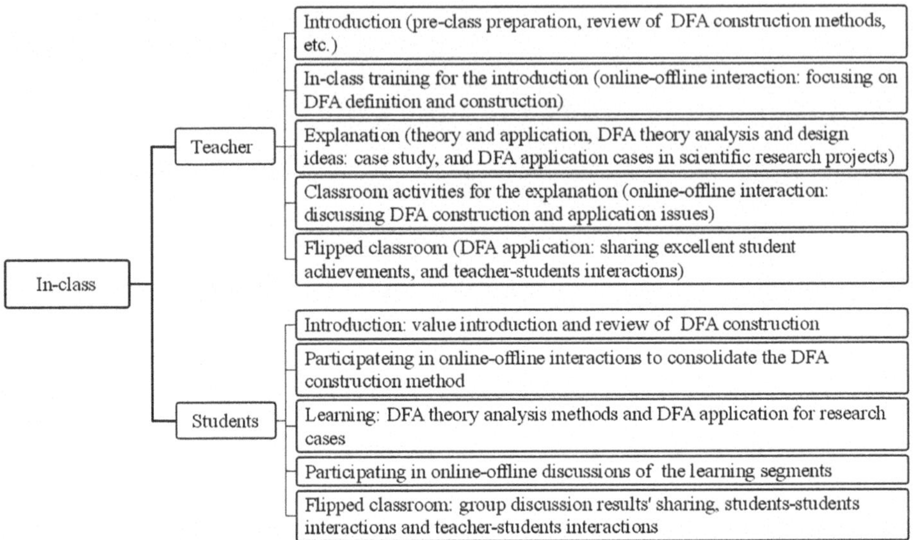

Fig. 6. The in-class for the course unit "DFA Lexical Analysis and Application" study.

In-class. The in-classs roles for both teacher and students are shown in Fig. 6. The teacher reviewed the key points and challenges of the DFA construction method, including the conversion of NFA to an equivalent DFA and DFA simplification. Following this, case-based and heuristic approaches were employed to teach the application of DFA.

For the heuristic teaching and interaction on DFA lexical analysis, the instructional strategy followed the sequence of "retracing the lexical analysis task", "analyzing the DFA recognition method", and "inspiring the development of design thinking for DFA lexical analysis". This approach enabled students to gain a deep understanding of how to use DFA to recognize each word (token) in an input string.

Subsequently, we conducted both online and offline interactive discussions to guide students in internalizing and understanding the class contents. For challenging topics such as NFA determinization and DFA simplification, which students found particularly confusing, we designed in-class tests on the platform to promptly assess their learning outcomes. Additionally, students were randomly

Fig. 7. The scenes of the flipped classroom.

selected via the platform to answer questions on the lectern, while the rest of the students participated in answering as well. This teaching design placed students at the center of the learning process and significantly enhanced their sense of achievement.

The case-based teaching and interactions on DFA applications illustrated the role of DFA in the design of transaction management software systems. Specifically, to address the lack of formal descriptions for state transitions in the transaction life cycle in such software design, we introduced a formal method for describing these transitions using DFA technology and provided a practical case demonstrating its application in such design modeling.

After the in-class teaching, students had mastered the definition, construction methods, and lexical analysis of DFA, and gained an understanding of the fundamental concepts behind DFA applications. Based on the group topics selected by students before class, we will propose specific discussion topics, organize students to think and communicate from multiple perspectives, encourage the exchange of ideas, and foster teamwork and collaboration skills. Figure 7 shows that the student was presenting the group discussion results in the flipped classroom.

Post-class. The post-classs roles for both teacher and students are shown in Fig. 8. The teacher utilized the platform to publish homework assignments, assign tasks for group discussions, and provide additional learning resources. Students reinforced their knowledge through homework and practice questions, assessed their learning outcomes, and expanded their thinking based on their individual circumstances. Through the implementation of this teaching design, students not only systematically mastered the knowledge and skills related to lexical analysis and DFA application but also effectively enhanced their indepen-

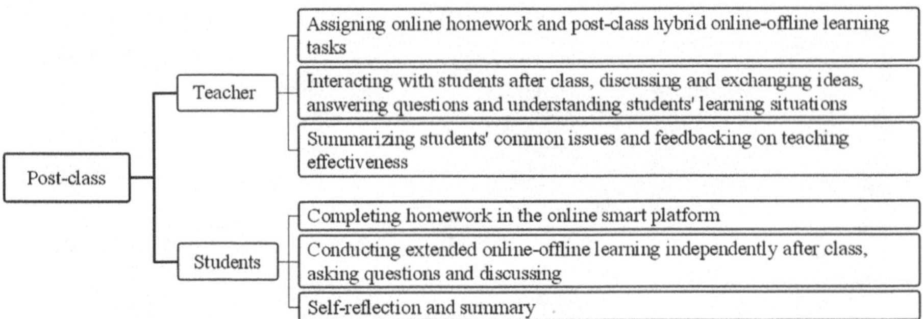

Fig. 8. The post-class for the course unit "DFA Lexical Analysis and Application" study.

dent learning abilities and teamwork spirit. This approach laid a solid foundation for the subsequent compiler course design.

4.3 Evaluation

The evaluation encompassed process evaluation, project evaluation, peer evaluation, and self-reflection. For process evaluation, we assessed students' learning progress through online in-class tests, participation in group discussion discussions, homework submissions, and independent study. Project evaluation involved a comprehensive assessment of each group project, considering its innovation, practicality, and the quality of the research report. Peer evaluation was facilitated through the platform, enabling both inter-group and intra-group assessments based on the outcomes of group discussion projects, thereby encouraging students to learn from one another and provide constructive feedback. For self-reflection, students were encouraged to write learning logs to reflect on their achievements and areas for improvement throughout the learning process.

4.4 Teaching Summary

According to the homework completion records, 73 students were expected to submit their assignments. Among them, 1 student was absent and 72 students actually completed the homework, achieving an average score close to 90 points. This indicated that students had a solid grasp of the knowledge points covered in this section.

For the group discussion project, students demonstrated great enthusiasm, engaging in thorough discussions and learning both inside and outside the class, and ultimately submitting outstanding final results. These group discussion outcomes were showcased in the answer sheet demonstration section of the course platform, allowing students to further communicate and learn from each other.

In terms of extended learning, students also participated actively, especially in utilizing the supplementary resources provided by the course platform for extracurricular study. Some students even expressed their interest in participating in the "Compiler Principles" competition.

As we move forward in adjusting our teaching strategies, we plan to further expand the range of DFA application cases and tailor instruction according to students' majors. For example, students majoring in computer science and software engineering will explore DFA applications in software design, while those in big data and artificial intelligence will examine comparative cases between DFA lexical analysis techniques and natural language word segmentation methods.

We also intend to leverage the course platform to preset knowledge and skill "thresholds." If a student's learning outcome falls below this threshold, the platform will trigger targeted teaching interventions focusing on key difficulties during online sessions.

Furthermore, we will continue to optimize the hybrid teaching design, taking into account students' individual needs through pre-tests, post-class questionnaires, and other feedback mechanisms, in order to refine learning tasks before, during, and after class.

5 Conclusion

Through the implementation of hybrid online and offline teaching for the "Compiler Principles" course last semester, the following results have been achieved:

(1) A sustainable and continuously improved multi-dimensional hybrid online-offline teaching model has been initially established. Additionally, a fully evaluable hybrid online classroom has been created based on the smart platform. According to the 2024 annual report of the platform, "Compiler Principles" emerged as the "most popular course," with 59,270 visits, ranking fifth in the university.

(2) Comprehensive digital resources for hybrid online-offline teaching have been developed, including instructional videos, experimental manuals, study cases, supplementary resources, and extracurricular reading materials.

(3) The formative evaluation mechanism has effectively encouraged students to fully engage in the course. The "process assessment" covered all aspects of the hybrid online-offline teaching process, significantly enhancing student participation. During implementation, the course team continuously optimized measurable online teaching activities to ensure the effectiveness of course challenges. The teaching outcomes were positive, with 51.39% of students achieving an excellent overall evaluation at the end of the semester. Additionally, this approach stimulated students' enthusiasm for learning, and most students expressed their willingness to participate in the national "Compiler Principles" competitions in the future.

Acknowledgments. This study was partially funded by the grant "Compiler Principles" - Hybrid Online-Offline Gold Course of Wuhan University of Technology (2024-2025-1 (44)) and the grant Competency-Oriented Hybrid Teaching Reform of "Compiler Principles" (Undergraduate Teaching Reform Research Project, School of Computer and Artificial Intelligence, Wuhan University of Technology, 2025).

Disclosure of Interests. The authors have no competing interests to declare that are relevant to the content of this article.

References

1. Louden, K.C.: Compiler Construction: Principles and Practice. PWS Publishing Co. (1997)
2. Sharma, D., Sood, A.K., Darius, P.S.H., et al.: A study on the online-offline and blended learning methods. J. Inst. Eng. (India): Ser. B **103**(4), 1373–1382 (2022)
3. Xiong, Y., Ji, C., Wang, H., et al.: Research on online and offline mixed teaching mode-taking "introduction to computer science" as an example. Int. Core J. Eng. **8**(7), 454–457 (2022)
4. Bhardwaj, A., Vashisth, M., Arora, S.: Analyzing students performance in online, hybrid and offline mode–a cross-sectional study. Grenze Int. J. Eng. Technol. (GIJET) **10** (2024)
5. Thelma, C.C., Phiri, E.V.: The efficacy and acceptance of online learning vs. offline learning in higher learning institutions: a systematic review. Int. J. Res. (IJR) (2024)
6. Qi, H.: An online and offline hybrid teaching resource sharing method based on cloud computing. Int. J. Reason.-Based Intell. Syst. **16**(3), 195–205 (2024)
7. Zhang, L.: Blended pedagogy for computer programming language. Pedagogical Res. **9**(3), em0218 (2024)
8. Yuan, W., Wang, M., Liu, G., et al.: Reform and research on online and offline hybrid teaching of operating system focusing on cultivating students' innovative and practical abilities. In: 2023 13th International Conference on Information Technology in Medicine and Education (ITME), pp. 755-759. IEEE (2023)
9. Mao, F., Hou, L., Yang, X., et al.: Online and offline hybrid embedded system practical training teaching reform. In: 2023 4th International Conference on Big Data and Informatization Education (ICBDIE 2023), pp. 440–448. Atlantis Press (2023)
10. Cao, D., Xu, G., Wu, Y., et al.: Hybrid online-offline teaching mode in microcontroller project-based learning. In: 2025 IEEE Conference on Education and Training in Optics and Photonics (ETOP), pp. 1–4. IEEE (2025)
11. Deng, X., Cheng, W., Zuo, Y., et al.: Teaching reform and practice of digital circuit course based on hybrid teaching model. Int. Educ. Res. **8**(1), 74-p74 (2025)
12. Zhang, X., Zhang, B., Zhang, F.: Student-centered case-based teaching and online–offline case discussion in postgraduate courses of computer science. Int. J. Educ. Technol. High. Educ. **20**(1), 6 (2023)
13. Wei, L., Zhao, Q.: Application of blended teaching in software architecture for graduate students. In: 2023 2nd International Conference on Social Sciences and Humanities and Arts (SSHA 2023), pp. 588–596. Atlantis Press (2023)
14. Rao, N.J.: Outcome-based education: an outline. High. Educ. Future **7**(1), 5–21 (2020)
15. Bishop, J., Verleger, M.A.: The flipped classroom: a survey of the research. In: 2013 ASEE Annual Conference and Exposition, pp. 23.1200. 1–23.1200. 18 (2013)

Collaborative Construction of Computational Thinking and Digital Thinking Empowered by Programming Agents from the Perspective of "Integrating Morality and Skills"—A Case Study of Judicial Police Colleges

Zongmei Liu[1] and Jianxin Tan[2](✉)

[1] Department of Information Management, Guangdong Justice Police Vocational College, Guangzhou 510520, Guangdong, China

[2] Network Information and Educational Technology Center, Guangdong University of Finance and Economics, Guangzhou 510320, Guangdong, China

tjx@gdufe.edu.cn

Abstract. In the context of vocational education reform featuring "integration of morality and skills, and combination of work and study", programming courses in judicial police colleges are facing dual challenges of integrating technical capability cultivation with legal professional literacy. Aiming at the current problem of "emphasizing skills over ethics" in programming education, this study constructs a three-dimensional cultivation model of "ideological and political guidance-technical capability foundation-professional ethics development", and develops scenario-based programming agents with functions such as code logic verification and professional ethics guidance. By deeply exploring the collaborative construction path of computational thinking and digital thinking in judicial professional scenarios, it systematically explores the integration mechanism of technical training and moral education infiltration. The research shows that the agent significantly improves students' problem decomposition ability and data security awareness, providing a reproducible and promotable innovative paradigm for the high-quality cultivation of judicial professionals in the era of "digital rule of law".

Keywords: Integration of Morality and Skills · Programming Agents · Computational Thinking · Digital Thinking · Judicial Police Colleges

In April 2025, the Ministry of Education and other nine departments issued the Opinions on Accelerating Educational Digitalization, designating artificial intelligence as the core engine for educational digital transformation and requiring the enhancement of digital literacy and skills for all citizens with teachers and students as the focus. Under the guidance of this policy, driven by the dual forces of national vocational education strategic transformation and digital upgrading in the judicial field, programming education has become increasingly prominent as the core foundation for cultivating computer professionals in judicial police colleges, urgently needing further strengthening and improvement. As the cradle for cultivating judicial professionals, institutions of

W. Hong et al. (Eds.): ICCSE 2025, CCIS 2761, pp. 585–598, 2026.
https://doi.org/10.1007/978-981-95-7731-6_46

the judicial administrative system shoulder the mission of safeguarding people's security and defending fairness and justice. The unique spiritual core of "blue uniform responsibility" continuously shapes students' integrity, perseverance, and professional ethics of loyalty and dedication through daily details such as interior organization and queue training. Aiming at the current pain point of programming education focusing on codes while neglecting ethics, the study finds a deep-value resonance between "blue uniform responsibility" and programming education—the pursuit of rigor in programming echoes the judicial commitment to justice, and the perseverance of programmers in debugging programs is akin to the dedication of prison police in performing their duties. Based on this, this study is committed to expanding the connotation of "integrating morality and skills" in programming education, clarifying the functional positioning and action path of programming agents in promoting the integration of morality and skills, constructing a two-dimensional training theoretical framework of "technology-ethics", so as to promote the collaborative development of computational thinking and digital thinking, achieve the organic integration of technical training and police moral cultivation, and inject new momentum into the cultivation of modern talents for the judicial cause.

1 Core Disciplinary Competencies of Programming Courses

1.1 Deep Integration of Ideological and Political Guidance with Professional Training

Programming practice not only focuses on cultivating students' technical capabilities but also places great emphasis on shaping their sense of social responsibility and professional ethics. Throughout the teaching process, ideological and political education is integrated into professional instruction to achieve the synchronous development of value shaping and knowledge and skill transmission. In line with the educational characteristics of judicial police colleges, the ethos of "blue uniform responsibility" and other ideological and political elements are taken as the guiding principles. With the technical empowerment of programming agents, the professional ethical norms in the judicial field are deeply integrated into teaching practices. For example, legal compliance checks are embedded in code reviews, and ethical dilemmas in judicial scenarios are incorporated into task design. This approach enables the infiltration of moral education during technical training, ensuring that while students master programming techniques, they also establish a sense of police professional ethics. During the team collaboration phase, students are required to complete judicial project development through division of labor and cooperation. In this process, their communication and coordination abilities are enhanced, they learn to respect intellectual property rights, and a sound cooperation mechanism is established. Through practical projects, students are guided to understand the role of programming technology in promoting judicial justice and social governance, thus inspiring a sense of mission to serve the judiciary and give back to society through technology.

1.2 Synergizing Computational and Digital Thinking

Computational thinking emphasizes the logical ability to decompose complex problems into computable steps, whereas digital thinking focuses on the comprehensive literacy of data-driven decision-making, technological tool application, and ethical judgment. Programming agents, as AI-integrated teaching tools, break the isolation between these two thinking modes through intelligent interaction, personalized feedback, and scenario-based tasks, promoting students' synchronous improvement in logical analysis and data ethics awareness during programming practice. For example, programming courses train students to deconstruct complex problems with computational thinking, requiring algorithm design and code implementation for real-world scenarios. In debugging, students use tools to locate errors and optimize algorithms for performance. Facing judicial scenarios, they are encouraged to break conventions and explore innovations, strengthening problem-solving and creative thinking in practice.

2 An Analysis of the Current Situation of Programming Courses

2.1 In Terms of Teaching Content

Programming course teaching focuses on basic syntax and traditional algorithms, favoring one-way transmission of programming knowledge, ignoring the active construction of students' computational thinking and digital thinking, resulting in students only mastering mechanical coding skills, and it is difficult to cope with the demand for technological transformation of complex problems in the judicial scenario; the implementation of the course ideology and politics fails to systematically tap the intrinsic correlation between programming knowledge and judicial ethics, and ideology and politics education flows superficially, resulting in the formation of "two-skin" phenomenon between ideology and politics education and professional teaching. Civic and political education is superficial, resulting in the phenomenon of "two skins", making it difficult to realize the goal of educating people with "moral and technical training".

2.2 In Terms of Teaching Methods

Programming courses have the problems of outdated teaching methods and rigid mode. The teaching process relies on the one-way instillation mode of "teacher demonstration-student imitation", which inhibits the active construction of students' computational and numerical thinking and leads to insufficient learning motivation. In addition, the teaching mode lacks personalized design, which is unable to match students' differentiated learning bases and abilities, making it difficult to meet diversified learning needs.

2.3 In Terms of Course Evaluation

Programming practice courses are evaluated in a single way, mainly relying on theoretical exams and lab reports, but ignoring the comprehensive consideration of students' programming practice ability, problem solving ability and innovative thinking ability. It is not possible to comprehensively and objectively show the students' learning results and actual level, and it is also difficult to stimulate students' learning interest and innovation motivation, which may lead to students' rote memorization to cope with the examination instead of truly understanding and mastering programming skills.

2.4 In Terms of Learning Status

Programming course involves abstract logical thinking and algorithm design, which leads to some students' fear of difficulty and even inertia of "fetishism", and their learning attitude is not serious enough; in the face of complex problems such as grammatical errors and logical loopholes in program debugging, students rely excessively on teachers or network search, and lack of independent analysis and trial-and-error ability. In addition, in programming practice, most students are only satisfied with completing basic project tasks according to textbook examples or teachers' instructions, mechanically applying fixed templates, seldom exploring innovative solutions on their own initiative, and finding it difficult to make breakthroughs and innovations.

3 Curriculum Design of "Forging Programming Proficiency Through Analogous Police Academy Experiences"

3.1 Integration of Warm-Hearted Cases

Judicial police colleges and universities adhere to the school motto, relying on the political nature of the "police academy surnamed party", to build the "Civic and political navigation + professional enlightenment" two one sportsman system, through the infiltration of the Civic and political and project practice to stimulate professional learning interest, establish a correct attitude to learning, and integrate the loyalty gene into all aspects of professional education, to cultivate "moral and technical" talents. We integrate the loyalty gene into all aspects of professional education to cultivate talents with "both moral and technical talents". Actively organize social practice activities, and at the same time, based on the intersection of programming practice courses and police management in terms of disciplinary norms, teamwork, etc., explore the path of ideological and political reform of computer language practice courses [1].

In the programming practice course, many teaching links contain rich ideological and political connotations. For example, in the algorithm design session, the clever construction and optimization of algorithms can not only exercise students' logical thinking in depth, but also effectively cultivate their rigorous and meticulous work attitude, which coincides with the requirements of the judicial administration work for precision and rigor. When promoting team projects, students can effectively improve their teamwork spirit and enhance their sense of responsibility towards the collective and their work by collaborating with each other and solving problems together, thus laying a foundation for teamwork in judicial practice in the future [2]. The design of the course is analogous to the program design stage of the growth process of police cadets, and the "Tibetan Blue Spirit" is carried throughout the whole course, combining the principles of algorithms with the police academy life scenarios, so as to enhance the affinity and sense of immersion of professional knowledge, as shown in Table 1.

Table 1. Comparison of Integration Points in the "Virtue and Skills" Curriculum.

Technology Module	Civic and political integration point	Implementation Cases
Basic grammar	Data security awareness, disciplinary and normative thinking	In the teaching of variable definition and data types, combined with the Personal Information Protection Law, students are guided to understand the storage requirements of personal privacy and establish the concept of the rule of law on data security; in the teaching of conditional/loop statements, the screening work is realized through programming using the evaluation of excellence as a prototype, so as to cultivate the students' sense of discipline in rigorous execution
Algorithm design and analysis	Logical thinking, innovative spirit, craftsmanship spirit	In the process of algorithm design, students are trained to think logically, guiding them to abstract mathematical models from complex problems and design efficient algorithms. Encourage students to try different algorithmic ideas and optimization methods to cultivate the spirit of innovation. At the same time, through the continuous polishing and optimization of algorithmic details, students can experience the connotation of craftsmanship and the pursuit of excellence in programming quality

(*continued*)

Table 1. (*continued*)

Technology Module	Civic and political integration point	Implementation Cases
Object-oriented programming	Abstract thinking, standardization awareness	Abstract the actual processing flow of work, participants, related documents, etc. into classes and objects, and realize the functions of the system through the features of encapsulation, inheritance and polymorphism of classes. In this process, students develop their abstract thinking ability, so that they learn to extract key features from the complexities of the real world and build appropriate programming models
Exception handling	Adaptability, problem-solving ability	Introduce a variety of exceptions in the programming project, requiring students to design a reasonable exception handling mechanism. Analogous to the various emergencies encountered in the actual work, to develop students' resilience and problem solving ability
Graphical user interface (GUI) design	Aesthetic awareness, user-oriented philosophy	Cultivate students' aesthetic sense, optimize the interface design from the user's needs and experience, and improve the user satisfaction of the system. As in the work, we should focus on the service users and emphasize the concept of user first

3.2 Innovative Teaching Methods

3.2.1 Intelligent Agent Interaction Empowerment Mode

Aiming at the real pain points of programming teaching in judicial police colleges and universities, such as "the separation of technology and moral education" and "the disconnection of practice scenarios", we have developed the Programming Intelligent Body, which integrates the three core functions of intelligent code review, ethical risk warning, and task generation in judicial scenarios. The intelligent body can not only verify the correctness of code logic in real time, but also provide intelligent warning of ethical risks such as data security loopholes and privilege abuse in the process of students' programming; at the same time, it generates programming tasks through real judicial scenarios such as encrypted transmission of data related to the case, and provides teachers with a teaching resource library that is "compatible with morality and technology" by means of text-to-diagram and text-to-video. "At the same time, the programming tasks are generated through real judicial scenarios such as encrypted transmission of case-related data. Empirical analysis shows that the programming intelligence effectively promotes the synergistic development of students' computational and digital thinking, and significantly improves their technical application ability and judicial professional ethics.

3.2.2 Project-Driven Teaching Method

Design the "Work Assistant" practical project around daily office needs. Students need to use basic syntax, file reading and writing and function encapsulation techniques to complete the development of three core functional modules. The first is an attendance management module, which realizes daily attendance data entry, absence statistics and visual chart generation; the second is an intelligent duty reminder module, which automatically generates reminder information by reading the preset schedule; and the third is a work logging system, which supports fast log entry, keyword retrieval and archiving of historical records [3].

3.2.3 Error Scenario Simulation Strategy

In the process of programming teaching, targeted implantation of security vulnerabilities such as buffer overflow, so that students can personally experience the damage that may be caused by security vulnerabilities, prompting students to deeply understand the seriousness and importance of programming work, and strengthening their sense of responsibility for the quality of the code and system security. So that students in the future programming work, always maintain a rigorous attitude, pay attention to the security and stability of the code, from the source to prevent the generation of security vulnerabilities [4].

3.3 Measurable Teaching Evaluation

Formulate diversified evaluation indexes, paying attention to students' programming skills while emphasizing their growth in comprehensive literacy. At the same time, improve the feedback mechanism of learning effect, through timely collection of students' feedback information, in-depth analysis of problems and deficiencies in the teaching process, and then flexibly adjust the teaching strategy to ensure that the teaching activities can accurately meet the learning needs of students. In addition, the construction of "technology - ideology" two-dimensional evaluation matrix, to realize the all-round and multi-angle evaluation of students [5], as shown in Table 2.

Table 2. Course Teaching Evaluation Comparison.

dimension	traditional evaluation criteria	transformed evaluation criteria
Evaluation subject	Dominated by teacher-only evaluation	A multi-evaluation system involving "teachers + intelligent agents + students' self-evaluation + industry mentors" is constructed, where teachers control the evaluation direction and conduct comprehensive analysis; intelligent agents monitor students' programming works in real time and generate diagnostic reports; students carry out self-evaluation through project summaries; and industry mentors conduct evaluation from the perspective of industry norms
Evaluation content	Focusing on the correctness of code syntax and the completeness of algorithm implementation functions	On the basis of conventional evaluation of code syntax and functionality, the evaluation dimensions are expanded. Newly added considerations include compliance with regulations in data processing and other links; professional ethics indicators are incorporated to assess awareness of privacy protection and the like
Evaluation method	Mainly based on final project assessment and written examinations, with a high proportion of summative evaluation	A combination of formative evaluation (with intelligent agents recording code iteration logs) and summative evaluation is adopted, with the addition of scenario-based task summaries
Evaluation cycle	Conducted centrally on a semester basis	Real-time feedback from intelligent agents is introduced to realize full-cycle dynamic evaluation covering "pre-class preview - in-class practice - after-class extension", so as to timely adjust learning and teaching strategies

(*continued*)

Table 2. (*continued*)

dimension	traditional evaluation criteria	transformed evaluation criteria
Evaluation tool	Using paper-based test papers and manual grading	With the help of an intelligent evaluation system, code vulnerabilities, legal risk points, etc., are automatically detected, and dual-dimensional analysis reports (technical and ideological-political) are generated

4 "Multi-dimensional Integration, Learning, Thinking, Practicing and Understanding Integration" Programming Intelligence Body Model Construction

4.1 Design Objectives

4.1.1 Responsibility Mapping

Police officers in the administration of justice system have the sacred mission of "guarding security". In the hands-on programming course, this mission is skillfully translated into strict requirements for code robustness. For example, in the actual programming process, the emergence of anomalies is just like a crisis in reality, and the exception handling mechanism is like a carefully formulated crisis response plan, which can effectively capture and deal with exceptions to ensure the stable operation of the program. Through this analogy, students deeply understand that every line of code they write carries a responsibility, just like police officers guarding security, the code also needs to guard the stability and security of the system, so as to cultivate a high sense of responsibility and mission among students [6].

4.1.2 Rigorous Training

The police academy housekeeping standards are known for their strictness, meticulousness and standardization, reflecting a rigorous work attitude and style. In the programming practice course, this standard is fully drawn upon and the code normality scoring rule is carefully designed. The rules cover a number of aspects, such as the naming of variables should follow the principles of clarity and significance, and be able to accurately reflect the function and use of variables; the completeness of comments requires students to make detailed comments on key code segments so that others can understand the logic and function of the code. Through such rigorous training, students can develop meticulous habits in the programming process, just as police officers strictly observe the housekeeping standards, strictly follow the code specifications, improve the quality of the code, and cultivate students' rigorous attitude and professionalism.

4.1.3 Collaboration Enhancement

The teamwork model in police work emphasizes close cooperation, collaborative work and clear division of labor among members. In the project development of the programming practice course, different roles are reasonably divided into "requirement analysis, module development, and coordination and testing". Each student has a clear role in the project, just like a member of a police team. In the process of the project, students need to collaborate, communicate and support each other to accomplish the project goals. In this way, the students not only developed their programming skills, but more importantly, strengthened their sense of collective responsibility and teamwork ability, so that the students deeply realized the importance of individual's work to the whole team, as well as the key role of teamwork in achieving the goals, and laid a solid foundation for them to better integrate into the team and collaborate in the future work of judicial administration [7].

4.2 Functional Modules

4.2.1 Functional Profile

As an intelligent entity with the ability of environment perception, autonomous decision-making and action execution, the architecture of the intelligent body covers the core modules of user interaction, information perception, knowledge base and workflow. The programmed intelligent body can be customized for course-specific requirements to achieve tasks that are difficult to accomplish with large models [8]; it can also provide a data source through the answer traceability mechanism to support users in verifying the authenticity of the answers; it can also dynamically optimize the response content based on students' feedback, and intelligently deploy resources in conjunction with real-time operation and monitoring to guarantee the timeliness of the information and the effectiveness of the teaching and management, as shown in Fig. 1.

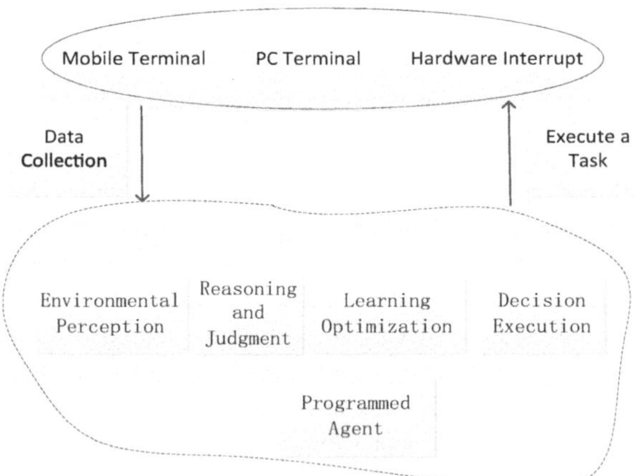

Fig. 1. Programming Intelligentsia Architecture.

4.2.2 Intelligent Q&A

Programming Intelligence relies on the document understanding and Q&A capabilities of the Big Language Model to build a domain-specific knowledge base through semantic parsing and knowledge extraction of course materials uploaded in the background. At the same time, it carries out continuous self-training based on historical Q&A data, and adopts reinforcement learning and knowledge graph technology to dynamically optimize the knowledge representation and reasoning logic, so as to achieve iterative expansion of the knowledge base and improvement of Q&A efficiency. During the interaction process, the intelligent body accurately labels the source of course documents and specific chapters corresponding to the answer through traceability marking technology, and the user can directly access the original documents through hyperlinks, thus constructing a credible Q&A closed loop of "Question Generation - Intelligent Response - Source Tracing", effectively improving the accuracy of the answer. The closed loop of "question generation-intelligent response-source tracing" effectively improves the accuracy and verifiability of the answers [9].

4.2.3 Basic Management

Programming Intelligence has highly flexible interaction configuration and multi-end adaptation capabilities. Through the cue word engineering module, it supports teachers to customize semantic parsing rules to guide the big model to accurately identify the user's intention in teaching scenarios; relying on the model interface adaptation framework, it can seamlessly switch between multiple mainstream general big models to meet the demand for differentiated performance and cost. At the same time, the built-in sensitive word management system and standardized response templates are preset for questions triggered by sensitive words to achieve real-time control and audit trails of risky conversations. At the interactive terminal level, Smart Body is compatible with multi-platform access such as PC and mobile through responsive design, and combined with personalized recommendation algorithms, it provides students with 7×24-hour full-scene, one-on-one intelligent learning support services.

4.2.4 Knowledge Base Management

Programming Intelligence realizes the structured management of common learning problems by building domain-specific knowledge maps. In the knowledge base module, it supports the four-dimensional structure of "question-answer-similar questioning method-micro-application correlation" to pre-record teaching resources. When the user asks a question, the intelligent body extracts the key features through semantic parsing and vector retrieval technology, performs multi-dimensional matching in the knowledge base and dynamically correlates the answer with the corresponding programming training micro-applications and law query tools. The answers are dynamically associated with corresponding programming training micro-applications, legal query tools, etc., which significantly improves the response efficiency of high-frequency questions. In addition, the application library module provides a low-code task flow development environment, allowing users to customize the business logic chain, combining the interface management system with the parameter dictionary to achieve data interaction and configuration, and the enabled customized applications can be directly embedded into the foreground Q&A process, forming the intelligent service of "question identification - rule matching - application invocation - result feedback". Closed loop.

4.2.5 Task Flow Management

The backend of the Programming Intelligence Body supports customized function nodes and big models, from which school-based task flows can be constructed. Visualized orchestration supports multi-node combinations of big models, knowledge base, application library, code blocks, selectors, etc., to achieve specific and intelligent questions in accordance with a certain workflow when conversing with the Programming Intelligence Body. Once set, the built-in big model will stand parsed and automatically provide precise and efficient guidance for each task, ensuring smooth execution and continuous optimization of the teaching management process.

4.3 Collaborative Construction

4.3.1 Agent-Student Interaction Dimension

Programming Intelligent Body, as a dual carrier of technology and moral education, guides students' technical thinking compliance through real-time interaction. During the code writing process, the intelligent body not only provides technical support such as syntax error correction and algorithm optimization, but also actively pushes moral education tips such as data security and legal compliance based on the judicial business rule base.

4.3.2 Task-Scene Mapping Dimension

The programming tasks are deeply connected to the ethical dilemmas in judicial practice, so as to build a "learning and using" educational scenario. The programming tasks generated by the smart body are all derived from real judicial scenarios. These tasks imply ethical requirements such as data privacy protection and law enforcement procedural compliance, and in the process of solving technical problems, students need to think about how to balance the technical feasibility and judicial ethical norms, so as to realize the moral education penetration of "learning by doing and understanding by learning" [10].

4.3.3 Thinking-Ability Transformation Dimension

Promote two-way empowerment of computational thinking and digital thinking through programming practices. Computational thinking focuses on technical skills such as algorithm design and problem decomposition, while digital thinking emphasizes ethical judgment of data and technical application compliance. In the three-dimensional model, when students complete programming tasks in judicial scenarios, they need to use computational thinking to optimize the code logic as well as digital thinking to assess whether the program complies with judicial business rules.

4.4 Effectiveness Evaluation

Design the experimental group (applying educational intelligences) and the control group (adopting traditional teaching methods) to ensure that the two groups are comparable in terms of students' foundation and teachers' teaching level. For the innovative practice of multi-scenario application of Educational Intelligence Body, different experimental variables are set up in the scenarios of classroom teaching, after-school counseling and vocational training. For one, questionnaires, interviews, classroom observation and other methods are used to collect experimental data; for another, data on students' learning behaviors (e.g., learning time, correct answer rate, interaction frequency, etc.) are collected through the Programming Intelligent Body to assess the effect of the Programming Intelligent Body's application and performance of the safety protection system. Students' programming ability is assessed through the functional realization of the project results and code quality; third, the development of students' disciplinary core literacy such as computational thinking, problem solving ability, innovative thinking, etc. is assessed; and fourth, the cultivation of students' civic and political literacy such as confidentiality awareness, legal awareness, teamwork, and responsibility is assessed through the students' performance and self-reflection in the project. The results showed that the experimental group had relatively less code debugging time, relatively higher code specification scores, and many of the codes contained compliant comments, while the students showed significant positive migration in the dimensions of computational thinking, procedural justice practices, and legal awareness.

5 Conclusion

Incorporating the spirit of "Tibetan Blue Responsibility" into programming education is not only a useful attempt to integrate technical training and value leadership, but also an innovative response to and practice of the fundamental educational issue of "what kind of people should be cultivated". Through the construction of "responsibility-driven code, rigorous casting system, collaboration to create value" human ecology, and ultimately achieve the cultivation goal of "code has a temperature, technology has a soul, engineers have a responsibility", realize the organic combination of the elements of ideology and politics and programming teaching, and effectively It realizes the organic combination of ideological elements and programming teaching, and effectively cultivates students' disciplinary core qualities, as well as values and professional qualities that fit the requirements of judicial police officers' occupation. However, there are some limitations in this study, such as the selection of practice cases is relatively single, and the long-term tracking mechanism of the reform effect is not yet perfect. In the future, it is planned to further broaden the scope of the selection of practice cases, strengthen the long-term tracking and evaluation of the effect of the reform of curriculum Civics, and continuously improve the teaching mode and method of curriculum Civics, so as to cultivate more high-quality professionals for the judicial police colleges and universities.

Funding Projects. Guangdong Provincial Education Science Planning Project (Higher Education Special) "Research on the Optimal Path of Digital Intelligence Empowering the Cultivation of School Prison Police Talents from the Perspective of 'Integrating Morality and

Skills'" (2024GXJK986); Special Project on Information Technology and Digital Literacy Curriculum Construction in Higher Vocational Colleges in Guangdong Province "Research on Digital Construction of Computer Public Basic Courses Guided by Information Literacy" (2023-GHITDL-026).

References

1. Yan, X.: Exploration on the synergistic cultivation of college students' ideological education and national defense practice. China High. Educ. (24), 28–30 (2020)
2. Li, X., Li, Z., Ge, W.: Analogizing military training experience, casting programming hard skills - a study on the ideological reform of geographic information system practice class courses. Surv. Mapp. Bull. (S2), 105–110 (2023)
3. Su, X., Miao, Q., Chen, W.: A personalized teaching model to improve programming ability based on AI empowerment and industry-teaching integration. China Univ. Teach. (06), 4–9 (2023). Author, F.: Contribution title. In: 9th International Proceedings on Proceedings, pp. 1–2. Publisher, Location (2010)
4. Sun, T., Wang, C., Du,. W.: Exploration of civics-driven practical course teaching based on Civics–Python programming practical teaching reform. Lab. Res. Explor. **43**(07), 187–191+233 (2024).https://doi.org/10.19927/j.cnki.syyt.2024.07.037
5. Zhang, Y.: Teaching reform of "database and program design" course based on learning community. Educ. Career (05), 144–145 (2014)
6. Liu, J., Han, L., Liu, X., et al.: Exploration on the reform of intelligent experimental teaching of program design courses by "individualized synergization". Lab. Res. Explor. **42**(12), 179–183 (2023)
7. Liu, X. Liu, X., Xue, L., et al.: Research and practice of interactive teaching cases in modern pedagogy. Exp. Technol. Manag. **35**(05), 10–12+16 (2018)
8. Zhang, S., Meng, L., Liu, J., et al.: DeepSeek into the classroom - exploration and reflection on the application of AI intelligences in the teaching of organ system integration course. China Med. Educ. Art, 1–6 (2025). http://kns.cnki.net/kcms/detail/61.1317.G4.20250604.1309.004.html
9. Gordon, M., Daniel, M., Ajiboye, A., et al.: A scoping review of artificial intelligence in medical education: BEME guide no.84. Med. Teach. **46**(4), 446–470 (2024)
10. Tang, Y., Chen, Q., Xiao, H., et al.: Construction and application of an intelligent body for teaching ideology and politics of "microcomputer principle" course based on AI big model. China Med. Educ. Technol., 1–8 (2025). http://kns.cnki.net/kcms/detail/61.1317.G4.20250602.1509.002.html

Toward System- and Theory-Oriented Talent Cultivation in Computing

Yu Zhang(✉), Hu Ding, Ye Tian, Defu Lian, Hongli Xu, and Xiangyang Li

University of Science and Technology of China, Hefei 230027, China
yuzhang@ustc.edu.cn

Abstract. Driven by rapid advances in computing technologies and increasing interdisciplinary demands, there is a growing need for flexible and forward-looking models of computing talent cultivation. This paper presents an ongoing exploration within the Huaxia Computer Science and Technology Talent Program at USTC, which has focused on system-oriented training for more than a decade. Since 2022, the program has been developing a dual pathway model that incorporates both system-oriented and theory-oriented approaches to better address evolving academic and industry needs. Putting emphasis on research-driven learning, open source practice, and academic competitions, the program encourages interdisciplinary thinking and early-stage innovation. The theory-oriented path is currently under active development to address curricular gaps in algorithms and computational theory. This work reflects efforts to build a flexible student-centered model under the "System/Theory + X" paradigm.

Keywords: computing talent cultivation · curriculum structure · research-driven Learning · System/Theory + X paradigm

1 Introduction

"Those who govern the world rely on talent; those who cultivate talent rely on education; and the foundation of education lies in schools." This ancient wisdom from *Zizhi Tongjian* continues to resonate in the modern era, where talent remains the cornerstone of national development and innovation. As China advances toward modernization and scientific self-reliance, top research universities bear the critical responsibility of nurturing original, high-caliber talent, particularly in foundational scientific fields.

In recent years, the global rise of the digital economy, characterized by intelligent computing, quantum advances, and multidisciplinary integration, has intensified the demand for computing talent. Centered on data, algorithms, and computing platforms, and driven by modern information and communication technologies, the digital economy has become a national strategic priority in China.

W. Hong et al. (Eds.): ICCSE 2025, CCIS 2761, pp. 599–611, 2026.
https://doi.org/10.1007/978-981-95-7731-6_47

Key initiatives, such as the *14th Five-Year Plan for Digital Economy Development* and the "Eastern Data, Western Computing" project, aim to build an integrated digital infrastructure across cloud, network, sensing, and artificial intelligence (AI). These efforts bring new challenges in computer systems and theoretical computer science, highlighting the urgent need for interdisciplinary talent capable of driving both foundational and applied innovation.

Guided by its motto *Hong Zhuan Bing Jin* (advancing both ideological commitment and professional excellence) and *Li Shi Jiao Rong* (integrating theory with practice), the University of Science and Technology of China (USTC) is a research-oriented university with a strong national reputation. Known for its "small but elite" educational model, USTC holds leading positions in fields such as physics, chemistry, biology, quantum information, and earth and space sciences. The university emphasizes cultivating students with solid fundamentals and creative thinking. Over the years, it has embraced a student-centered educational spirit of "I innovate, therefore I am", integrating scientific research and interdisciplinary exploration into all stages of talent development.

Fig. 1. HUA Luogeng and XIA Peisu, pioneers of USTC's computer discipline. Left: Mr. Hua teaching mathematics. Right: Mr. Xia guiding 1958 computer science students in a laboratory session.

Within USTC, the *Huaxia Computer Science and Technology Talent Program* (abbreviated as the *HuaXia Class*) has served as a flagship initiative to cultivate world-class undergraduate talent in computing since 2009. The program is named in honor of mathematician HUA Luogeng and electrical engineer XIA Peisu, pioneers of USTC's computer discipline (see Fig. 1). It emphasizes a system-oriented training model focused on computer systems, operating systems, and compilers, complemented by immersive research-driven learning. Through laboratory courses and competitive programming, the program has consistently fostered early innovation and deep engagement in system-level thinking.

Since 2022, responding to both internal reflections and external trends, the program has evolved into a flexible dual-pathway model with system-oriented and theory-oriented tracks. The goal is to better serve diverse student interests and strengths, including those attracted to mathematical theory.

This paper presents the motivation, design, and early outcomes of this shift. We outline the curriculum, implementation strategies, and the pedagogy that support a student-centered, interdisciplinary "System/Theory + X" paradigm.

2 Background and Related Work

In an era of rapid innovation, cultivating top-tier scientific talent is key for countries to lead rather than follow. Such talent combines *broad academic vision* and *creative thinking*, qualities rooted in deep disciplinary knowledge and shaped by interdisciplinary inquiry and research practice. Many countries have launched initiatives to strengthen science and engineering education. This section outlines the multilevel honors education, from global initiatives and national strategies to USTC's exemplary HuaXia Class.

2.1 Global Initiatives in Honors Education

Top universities around the world have established honors programs to cultivate scientific talent through interdisciplinary education and research immersion. Honors education, developed since the 1920 s in the United Kingdom (UK) and the United States (US), has evolved into institutionally supported models that balance academic rigor with flexibility [1]. Selection mechanisms vary across countries, from GPA-based systems to national exams, yet often overlook creative potential. To better support such students, honors models adopt enriched curricula, close faculty mentorship, and research-driven learning environments to foster elite innovative talent.

Established in 1988, the Barrett Honors College at Arizona State University is recognized as one of the top honors colleges in the US, known for its customized curricula, multi-mentor guidance system, and integrated opportunities for research and global engagement aimed at fostering holistic student development[1] MIT and Stanford embed research into undergraduate education. MIT emphasizes science-industry integration[2], while Stanford advances interdisciplinary clusters[3] such as chemical biology and electronics, leading to innovation ecosystems like Silicon Valley. The University of Tsukuba in Japan focuses on interdisciplinary education and research collaboration [2], offering early access to complex and cross-disciplinary challenges.

These programs share structural characteristics such as early research participation, flexible curricula, and layered mentorship, all aimed at cultivating top-tier talent in science and engineering.

---

[1] https://barretthonors.asu.edu/heru/know-barrett.
[2] https://urop.mit.edu/.
[3] https://www.stanford.edu/list/interdisc/.

2.2 China's Top Talent Training Initiative

China has elevated honors education and top talent training, which began in the 1970 s, into a national strategic priority. This effort has been driven by government policy, university-led innovation, and strong student engagement. In 2015, the State Council issued *Overall Plan for Promoting World-Class Universities and First-Class Disciplines*, emphasizing the cultivation of outstanding innovative students as a core mission of higher education reform and national competitiveness. In 2018, the Ministry of Education (MOE) and five other agencies released *Top Talent Training Program 2.0* to strengthen foundational disciplines and position China as a global hub of science and ideas. In 2020, the MOE launched the *Strengthening Foundation Plan* aimed at recruiting students with both academic excellence and national service aspirations. That same year, the *Guidelines for Future Technology Colleges (Trial)* encouraged the creation of interdisciplinary platforms to nurture talent in emerging domains.

Over four decades, China's honors education has gradually blended elements of international small-class and mentorship-based models with localized systems. Universities have been key actors in this transformation, experimenting with diverse approaches. From USTC's Gifted Young Class in 1978 to the Everest Plan in 2009 and the nationwide rollout of Top Talent 2.0, universities have developed distinctive strategies tailored to disciplinary strengths. A growing focus on interdisciplinary innovation has shaped recent initiatives. Tsinghua University's Institute for Interdisciplinary Information Sciences (Yao Class), Peking University's Academy for Advanced Interdisciplinary Studies, and Shanghai Jiao Tong University's Zhiyuan College have established integrative programs across mathematics, computer science, physics, chemistry, biology, and medicine to foster next-generation STEM leaders.

Despite decades of institutional practice, research on honors education in China remains limited and primarily descriptive. Most programs emphasize academic excellence, international exposure, flexible curricula, and small-class, personalized instruction, with doctoral pursuit rates serving as a key metric. Existing studies adopt localized approaches to explore features such as classroom waiting time and student well-being [3], highlighting the need for more systematic and empirical research.

2.3 USTC's Top Talent Training Initiative

Since its founding in 1958, USTC has upheld a tradition of integrating scientific rigor with practical relevance, following the principle of institute-department collaboration with the Chinese Academy of Sciences (CAS). To strengthen the integration of science and education, USTC proposed the creation of Talent Classes in 2008, aiming to nurture top-tier talent in science and engineering.

The first class, HUA Luogeng Mathematics Talent Class, was launched in 2009. Since then, USTC, in collaboration with CAS institutes, has established 19 university-level Talent Classes across key disciplines, grounded in a core model of science-education and institute-department integration. Among these initiatives, the Huaxia Class was jointly founded by the former School of Information Science and Technology, which later split to form the School of Computer Science and Technology, and the Institute of Computing Technology of CAS. Designed to explore new modes of training talent in advanced computer systems. In 2011, it was designated as one of the five key talent programs supported by the university, along with mathematics, physics, chemistry, and biology, which were included in MOE's Everest Program. In 2021, it was incorporated into the National Top Talent Program 2.0. The program combines honors courses with extensive research exposure, cultivating a new generation of rising academic talent.

HuaXia Class Curriculum and Talent Development: Since its inception, the Huaxia Class has offered three honors courses: Introduction to Computer Systems (H), Operating Systems: Principles and Design (H), and Compiler Principles and Techniques (H). Starting with the 2020 cohort, Introduction to Computer Systems (H) became a required course for all students, and an additional honors course, Computer Organization Principles (H), was introduced to the Huaxia curriculum. The program places strong emphasis on developing students' ability to apply knowledge in real-world contexts. Students are encouraged to engage in academic exchange, disciplinary competitions, and lab-based research activities. These efforts have produced some emerging talents who are beginning to shine in both domestic and international academic communities.

3 Emerging Opportunities and Evolving Needs

The deepening integration of computer science with other scientific domains is giving rise to a new generation of interdisciplinary research frontiers. Once confined to algorithmic problem solving and system design, computational thinking [4–6] is now embedded at the core of scientific workflows across physics, chemistry, biology, materials science, and quantum information [7–9]. This convergence is fueling vibrant areas like computational chemistry [9], first-principles materials modeling [10,11], quantum-classical hybrid computing [12], and intelligent robotics [13].

In parallel, national initiatives such as the *14th Five-Year Plan* and the "East Data, West Computing" strategy are driving the expansion and upgrading of digital infrastructure. These developments require not only domain expertise but also a new class of computing innovators who are fluent in either system-level design or theoretical foundations, and capable of advancing scientific discovery and technological applications through a "Computer Science + X" paradigm.

In response to these evolving needs, the Huaxia Class has built a strong foundation in advanced computer systems education. Its curriculum and practice in areas such as system architecture, operating systems, and compiler optimization have matured, producing students with strong engineering capabilities and translational insight. However, to fully realize the potential of interdisciplinary innovation, especially in theory-intensive areas, the program must strengthen its coverage of theoretical computer science. Key topics such as algorithmic complexity, logical reasoning remain underdeveloped, yet they are crucial for enabling breakthroughs in both computing and the sciences they empower.

USTC offers a fertile ground for bridging this gap. For example, in computational chemistry, students can explore quantum mechanical models and density functional theory (DFT) to simulate molecular interactions and guide drug design. In materials science, large-scale first-principles simulations, which are powered by parallel computing and numerical solvers, enable the discovery of new functional materials. In quantum science and technology, classical control and simulation techniques are indispensable for managing hybrid quantum-classical systems. Similarly, bioinformatics, robotics, and computational neuroscience integrate systems-level thinking to model life, motion, and intelligence.

These emerging intersections underscore the strategic importance of cultivating talent with both computational depth and an interdisciplinary perspective. To meet this goal, we advocate a flexible and interest-driven training model that supports differentiated pathways. Students may choose to build a strong foundation in theoretical computer science, such as logic, algorithms, and formal methods, or focus on system-level expertise, including architectures, operating systems, and compilers. By aligning curriculum tracks with students' academic strengths and domain interests, the program aims to foster a diverse cohort of computing innovators capable of engaging deeply with scientific challenges and driving interdisciplinary breakthroughs.

4 Training Design for "System/Theory + X" Paradigm

To cultivate talent that is both grounded in computer science and prepared for interdisciplinary innovation, we propose a structured yet flexible program design. This section introduces its overall objectives and distinctive features, followed by the selection mechanism, four-year academic plan, honors curriculum, and hands-on research and innovation platforms.

4.1 Goals and Distinctive Features

The HuaXia Class is committed to cultivating future leaders in computer science with a strong foundation in *computing systems* and/or *theoretical computer science*. It aims to develop high-level talent with a global perspective, capable of making original contributions in theory and technology across disciplines.

To achieve this goal, the HuaXia Class emphasizes a balanced educational philosophy that integrates: theory and practice, research and education, as well as institutes and departments. The program is closely aligned with national strategic priorities and the frontiers of scientific research, emphasizing mathematical rigor, theoretical depth, and system-level design capabilities.

As shown in Fig. 2, the HuaXia Class explores a new talent development model through six key components:

1. *Strengthen Theory and Systems* - ensuring solid academic foundation.

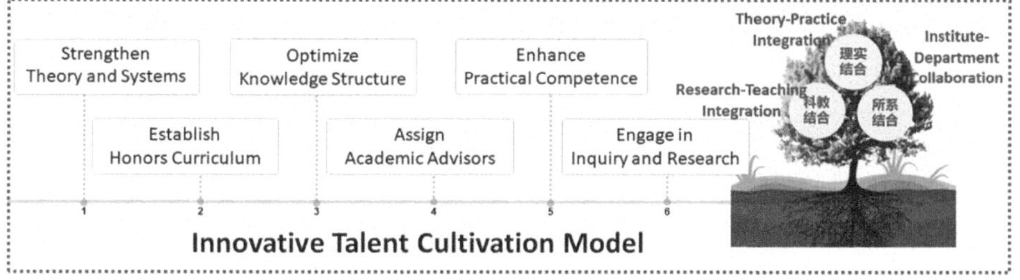

Fig. 2. Innovative Talent Cultivation Model.

2. *Optimize Knowledge Structure* - promoting interdisciplinary integration.
3. *Enhance Practical Competence* - through hands-on learning.
4. *Establish Honors Curriculum* - offering theoretical and system coursework.
5. *Assign Academic Advisors* - offering academic and career support.
6. *Engage in Inquiry and Research* - fostering innovation early.

Together, these efforts form a comprehensive framework for cultivating research-driven, practice-capable, and innovation-oriented computing talent.

4.2 Management and Selective Advancement

The HuaXia Talent Program is managed by a team of dedicated professors and teaching secretaries in the School of Computer Science and Technology. This team is responsible for designing the curriculum, managing domestic and international exchange initiatives, and overseeing all aspects of the program operations. Course teaching is organized by the school and taught by either internal faculty or outstanding instructors invited from leading universities worldwide. Starting with students entering in 2023, each class of students will be equipped with a dedicated faculty advisor from the second year to enhance student participation and promote the implementation of program-specific activities.

The program adopts a dynamic enrollment model. Students apply during their first year and are selected based on national entrance exam results and internal assessments. Additional outstanding students from computer science-related majors may be admitted at the start of the second or third year, based on availability and performance. Newly admitted students are not required to make up prior Talent Program courses or activities. Annual academic reviews ensure high standards; students who do not meet expectations in performance or conduct may be transitioned to other academic tracks.

4.3 Huaxia Honors Program Training System

The Huaxia Honors Program adopts a two-stage, all-around, long-term, personalized, and internationalized training framework that seamlessly integrates foundational education with advanced academic development. Emphasizing personalized and internationalized cultivation, the program features a full-cycle model covering undergraduate through graduate study.

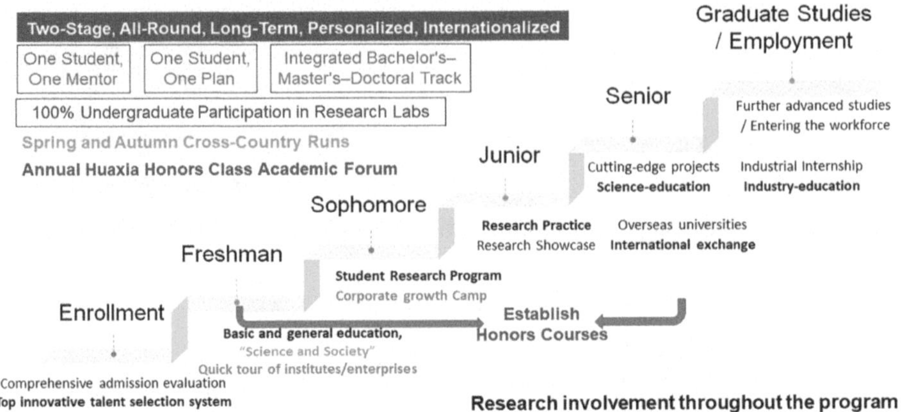

Fig. 3. Huaxia Honors Program Training System.

Each student is paired with a dedicated faculty mentor ("one student, one mentor") and follows an individualized academic plan ("one student, one plan"). Research practice is embedded throughout the entire training process, with all undergraduates participating in laboratory work from an early stage. Students are actively encouraged to engage in undergraduate research projects, corporate innovation camps, and international academic exchanges.

Figure 3 illustrates the main structure of the four-year undergraduate training system. Since 2021, the Annual Huaxia Honors Class Academic Forum has been held every May, featuring student research presentations, invited talks by alumni or external experts, faculty-student networking events, and institutional visits. Additionally, each spring and autumn, the university organizes cross-country running events for students across all honors programs, promoting physical health and opportunities to enjoy fresh air.

The following outlines the year-by-year training plan for Huaxia students:

- **First Year**: Huaxia students take the university-wide small-group seminar "Science and Society" and focus on foundational and general education. In summer, they participate in a brief exploratory tour to research institutes and industries, such as the Laoshan Laboratory and Qingdao Port, to broaden their horizons.
- **Second Year**: Students initiate independent research topics and engage in undergraduate research projects. In summer, they participate in a one-week or longer Corporate Growth Camp, gaining practical industry insight.
- **Third Year**: Students continue their research and present their findings. They are encouraged to participate in international exchange programs or pursue summer research abroad.
- **Fourth Year**: students undertake their graduation project, which may involve frontier research, corporate internships, or other innovation-oriented practical work.

4.4 Honors Courses: Overview, Challenges, and Strategies

Starting from the second year, the Huaxia Talent Program offers a series of honors courses (shown in Table 1) designed to deepen students' theoretical knowledge and system understanding.

Table 1. Honors Course Arrangements Across Different Plans

Semester	Previous Plan	Current Plan	Theory/Systems Track Plan
3rd Sem	ICS-H	Same as previous	Theory: Graph Theory Systems: ICS-H
4th Sem	OS-H	Added Corg-H	Theory: ICT-H Systems: COrg-H or OS-H
5th Sem	Compiler-H	Same as previous	Theory: Algo-H Systems: Compiler-H
6th Sem	None	Added CArch-H	Systems: CArch (standard required course, honors version canceled)

ICS-H: Introduction to Computer Systems (H) **OS-H**: perating System Principles and Design (H)
Compiler-H: Principles and Techniques of Compilers (H) **COrg-H**: Computer Organization Principles (H)
CArch-H: Computer Architecture(H) **ICT-H**: Introduction to Computation Theory (H)
Graph-H: Graph Theory(H) **Algo-H**: Fundamentals of Algorithms(H)

Traditionally, the honors curriculum included ICS-H in the second year, followed by OS-H in the second semester of sophomore year, and Compiler-H in the first semester of junior year. Later, Corg-H was added in the second semester of sophomore year, and CArch-H in the second semester of junior year.

Currently, the honors courses are divided into two streams: theory and systems. The theory track comprises three core courses: Graph-H (second year, first semester), ICT-H (second year, second semester), and Algo-H (third year, first semester). Regarding the systems track, a restructuring plan has been proposed to discontinue the honors version of Computer Architecture (CArch-H), replacing it with the standard required architecture course. Students will choose between Corg-H and OS-H in the second semester of their sophomore year.

In addition to the core honors curriculum, students are encouraged to explore a range of elective courses offered by the university in mathematics, physics, and emerging areas of science and technology. These electives complement the honors training by deepening interdisciplinary knowledge and broadening academic perspectives. Students are expected to meet a minimum elective credit requirement to ensure a well-rounded and rigorous academic experience.

Challenges and Strategies. Implementing a training model that integrates system-level and theoretical computer science with interdisciplinary domains presents several key challenges:
Balancing Depth and Breadth: Students must develop deep expertise in core areas of computing while also gaining exposure to cross-disciplinary knowledge.

This dual requirement risks overloading the curriculum and diluting academic focus.
Strategy: Adopt a modular curriculum with layered specialization tracks. Early-stage training emphasizes foundational theory and systems, while upper-level modules enable targeted exploration in areas such as quantum computing, computational chemistry, robotics, and scientific computing.
Sustaining Student Motivation and Individual Development: With diverse academic backgrounds and career goals, students may struggle to maintain long-term motivation or to identify personalized growth trajectories.
Strategy: Establish a robust mentorship framework, involving both faculty advisors and dedicated academic coordinators. Provide personalized guidance through regular progress assessments and encourage exploratory research from early stages.
Integrating Research and Teaching Resources: High-level research opportunities in emerging interdisciplinary areas may not be readily accessible or aligned with undergraduate curricula.
Strategy: Build long-term partnerships with leading research labs within and beyond USTC. Promote research-led teaching and facilitate early access to projects through summer research programs, innovation labs, and supervised thesis work.
Ensuring Program Sustainability and Visibility: Developing and maintaining a high-impact honors program requires sustained institutional support and external recognition.
Strategy: Create a coordinated management structure with a committed teaching team, dedicated coordinators, and engagement from university leadership. Enhance the program's visibility through outreach, national competitions, and collaborations with industry and international partners.

4.5 Practice Platforms and Research Innovation

Practical engagement is a cornerstone of the HuaXia Class. The program integrates hands-on training with frontier research to cultivate students' system-building capabilities and scientific creativity. Key initiatives include:
Tiered Practice Platforms. A multi-level practice ecosystem is established, ranging from foundational engineering labs to advanced systems innovation platforms. Students participate in structured project-based courses covering compiler construction, operating system design, and algorithm engineering, progressing toward open-ended system projects and real-world applications.
Integrated Research Pathways. From their second year, students are encouraged to engage with cutting-edge research through lab rotations, supervised projects, and faculty-guided reading seminars. These activities help them identify research interests early and build competency in original inquiry, particularly in computing-augmented domains such as quantum simulation, computational materials, or AI-driven scientific discovery.
Innovation and Competition Programs. The program supports participation in national and international competitions, such as the ICPC, CCF Elite Cup, and

open-source contributions. Cross-disciplinary contests like mathematical modeling, synthetic biology design, or robotics programming further broaden students' exposure and integration skills.

Summer Schools and Exchange Programs. To extend learning beyond the classroom, students take part in summer research camps, industry internships, and international exchanges. These experiences deepen their understanding of real-world challenges and build a foundation for global collaboration.

5 Practice and Reflection

This section first provides an overview of the program's practical achievements, then focuses on rethinking theoretical computer science education.

5.1 Practice Overview

Since its inception in 2009, the HuaXia Talent Program has graduated 332 students by 2025. Over 98% pursued further studies immediately after graduation, with 53% enrolling in top-tier institutions within mainland China and 45% continuing their education at leading universities and research institutes overseas (including Hong Kong, Macao, and Taiwan). The remaining 2% entered the workforce directly, securing positions with competitive salaries on par with graduate-level hires.

HuaXia students have collectively won over 200 major awards in prestigious competitions such as the ASC Student Supercomputer Challenge, ICPC, the National System Capability Contest, and Synthetic Biology contests. They have undertaken more than 100 faculty-led or independent research training projects, contributing to over 30 peer-reviewed publications. Notable examples include DENG Haowei(Class of 2016), who presented quantum compilation work at DAC 2020, and XU Hangyu (Class of 2021), whose research on differentially private synthetic graphs was accepted by COLT 2025. In 2024, YE Shengyu (Class of 2020) was awarded funding through the inaugural National Natural Science Foundation of China's Undergraduate Basic Research Program.

Despite the program's achievements, recent years have shown a slight decline in student motivation, partly due to the heavy workload of system-oriented honors courses and the rise of alternative programs like the AI honors track. Balancing academic rigor with evolving student interests and institutional innovations remains a key challenge. Meanwhile, the theory-oriented honors track is still developing and requires ongoing refinement. The next subsection reflects on our initial experiences in teaching theory courses.

5.2 Rethinking Theoretical Education

Traditional algorithm courses often focus on asymptotic complexity, emphasizing time and space analysis. Although this approach is fundamental, it no longer meets the needs of the big data era. As data scales grow, exact algorithms become infeasible, and new paradigms such as approximation, randomization, and distributed computation become essential.

Modern theoretical tools like coresets, randomized reduction, and locality-sensitive hashing combine mathematical rigor with practical impact. Teaching should move beyond listing algorithms to developing students' skills in problem modeling, constraint management, and theory-practice integration. Rethinking theoretical education requires reinforcing core foundations, incorporating frontier topics, and fostering students' capacity for applied innovation.

Timeless Foundations in a Changing Landscape. As AI and data scale rapidly, theoretical education must stay rooted in enduring principles. Concepts like the Johnson-Lindenstrauss lemma reveal how randomness enables dimensionality reduction with provable guarantees, while Optimal Transport bridges 18th-century formulations with modern ML tasks like generative modeling. Teaching coresets and LSH in connection with ϵ-nets and probabilistic thinking similarly builds lasting insight. By anchoring instruction in such timeless ideas, we cultivate clarity, curiosity, and readiness for future innovation.

Bridging Frontiers and Foundations. To keep pace with rapid advances, theory courses must go beyond traditional topics like Kd-trees to include modern nearest neighbor methods such as LSH and PQ, widely used in search and recommendation systems. LSH illustrates how probability guides algorithm design, while PQ ties large-scale vector retrieval to quantization theory. Additional topics like Count-Min Sketch and distributed algorithms expose students to real-world tools. By anchoring these advances in classical principles, we train students to think rigorously and adapt confidently to emerging technologies.

Fostering Student-Centered Innovation. Traditional theory teaching often overemphasizes exhaustive proofs and knowledge coverage, limiting engagement and creativity. We promote active, research-driven learning that encourages problem-solving and independent thinking. Students explore core concepts through guided challenges and open questions, boosting interest and innovation. Examples include XU Xiaoyang (Class of 2020)'s novel data structure for dynamic optimal transport (AAAI 2024) and HUANG Zhen (Class of 2019)'s application of coresets in chemical yield prediction (Communications Chemistry), illustrating how theory combined with practice drives breakthroughs and nurtures top talent.

6 Conclusion

In response to the evolving landscape of computing and the diverse aspirations of students, we have progressively enriched our honors curriculum through the dual axes of "Systems and Theory + X". This structure balances foundational rigor with interdisciplinary breadth, offering both depth for academic pursuit and flexibility for innovation.

Yet, true education lies not just in structure but in philosophy. Like great teachers of the past, we uphold rigorous instruction while embracing individualized guidance, helping each student uncover strengths, spark curiosity, and find their path—whether in theory, systems, or new frontiers. Such an approach may not yield immediate results, but like spring rain nurturing roots, it lays the foundation for lasting growth and empowers a new generation to not only master the present but shape the future.

Acknowledgments. This work was funded by the 2022 Key Research Project under the Ministry of Education's Top Talent Training Program for Basic Disciplines 2.0 (Grant No. 20221023).

References

1. Marca Wolfensberger, D.V.: Talent development in European higher education: Honors programs in the Benelux, Nordic and German-speaking Countries. Springer Nature (2015)
2. Maeno, T., et al.: Interprofessional Education Program of the University of Tsukuba: A Program to Develop Interprofessional Competence, pp. 23–38. Springer Japan, Tokyo (2010)
3. Hinterplattner, S., Wolfensberger, M., Lavicza, Z.: Honors students' experiences and coping strategies for waiting time in secondary school and at university. J. Educ. Gifted **45**(1), 84–107 (2022)
4. Wing, J.M.: Computational thinking. Commun. ACM **49**(3), 33–35 (2006)
5. Hambrusch, S., Hoffmann, C., Korb, J.T., Haugan, M., Hosking, A.L.: A multidisciplinary approach towards computational thinking for science majors. In: [40th] SIGCSE, SIGCSE 2009, pp. 183–187, New York, NY, USA, ACM (2009)
6. Aho, A.V.: Computation and computational thinking. Comput. J. **55**(7), 832–835 (2012)
7. Tariq, R., Babines, B.M.A., Ramirez, J., Alvarez-Icaza, I., Naseer, F.: Computational thinking in stem education: current state-of-the-art and future research directions. Front. Comput. Sci. **6**, 1480404 (2025)
8. Maqsood, A., Chen, C., Jacobsson, T.J.: The future of material scientists in an age of artificial intelligence. Adv. Sci. **11**(19), 2401401 (2024)
9. Song, T., Luo, M., et al.: A multiagent-driven robotic AI chemist enabling autonomous chemical research on demand. J. Am. Chem. Soc. **147**(15), 12534–12545 (2025)
10. Hu, W., et al.: 2.5 million-atom ab initio electronic-structure simulation of complex metallic heterostructures with dgdft. In: SC, pp. 1–13 (2022)
11. Lu, M., Marghetis, T., Yang, V.C.: A first-principles mathematical model integrates the disparate timescales of human learning. npj Complexity **2**(1), 15 (2025)
12. Whitlow, L.: A comprehensive survey of quantum computing: principles, progress, and prospects for classical-quantum integration. J. Comput. Sci. Softw. Appl. **5**(6), (2025)
13. Sadeghi, S., Canty, R.B., Mukhin, N., Xu, J., Delgado-Licona, F., Abolhasani, M.: Engineering a sustainable future: Harnessing automation, robotics, and artificial intelligence with self-driving laboratories. ACS Sustain. Chem. Eng. **12**(34), 12695–12707 (2024)

Exploration of Data Science Course Teaching Based on the RAP Model

Wenxing Hong[1], Fan Xiao[2], Binyue Cui[3], and Huan Wang[1](✉)

[1] School of Aerospace Engineering, Xiamen University, Xiamen 361100, China
{hwx,wanghuan}@xmu.edu.cn

[2] Institute of Artificial Intelligence, Xiamen University, Xiamen 361100, China
xiaofan@stu.xmu.edu.cn

[3] The Belt and Road Research Institute, Xiamen University, Xiamen 361000, China
binyuecui@gmail.com

Abstract. To meet the urgent demand for data-science talent in the big-data era and to remedy the deficiencies of traditional teaching models, this paper analyzes key instructional pain points and proposes a triadic RAP instructional model integrating Resources (R), an AI assistant (A), and a practical Platform (P), respectively. By systematically unifying these components, the model effectively addresses existing instructional challenges and enhances both the quality and the efficiency of data-science courses.

Keywords: Data Science · Teaching Reform · RAP Framework · Large Language Model

1 Introduction

With the rapid advancement of big data and artificial intelligence technologies, data science has emerged as a vital and indispensable discipline in modern society. To meet this growing demand, there is an urgent societal need to efficiently produce a large number of well-trained data science professionals [1]. In response, universities have increasingly introduced data science courses aimed at cultivating talent equipped to meet contemporary challenges. Given the central role of artificial intelligence in data-intensive applications, existing data science curricula must be fundamentally restructured to systematically develop high-level professionals who can build feedback-driven data systems, process massive real-world datasets, and integrate diverse technologies to tackle complex engineering problems [2]. To this end, course content should integrate both foundational and cutting-edge case studies in data technologies, effectively bridging theoretical knowledge and practical application, thereby aligning more closely with the demands of technological progress and industrial transformation.

W. Hong et al. (Eds.): ICCSE 2025, CCIS 2761, pp. 612–623, 2026.
https://doi.org/10.1007/978-981-95-7731-6_48

2 Teaching System Based on the RAP Model

2.1 Limitations of Traditional Instructional Models

Amid the comprehensive digital transformation of education, information technology has permeated every aspect of higher education, raising the bar for students' digital literacy. Data-science courses—characterized by rapid knowledge iteration and tight integration of theory and practice—must not only provide foundational theoretical instruction but also develop students' core competencies in real-world contexts, including problem identification, data analysis and insight communication.

However, many traditional data science curricula remain centered on knowledge transmission, lacking a structured approach to cultivating digital literacy. As illustrated on the left side of Fig. 1, this lecture-centered model suffers from three persistent issues that critically hinder the systematic development of digital literacy:

1. **Fragmented and insufficient teaching resources** In traditional settings, students often encounter a disjointed collection of textbooks with varying editions and recommended materials. Without clear guidance, it becomes difficult to select appropriate resources. Compounding this issue is the widespread absence of standardized teaching aids—such as structured slide decks and mind maps—which limits instructional coherence and support. Consequently, students struggle to build an integrated knowledge framework and frequently encounter difficulties when tackling abstract concepts or complex principles.
2. **Ineffective and delayed instructional support.** Traditional classrooms often cannot accommodate students' intensive demands for timely feedback. With limited instructional staff and multiple competing responsibilities such as research and administration, teachers are constrained in their capacity to provide individualized guidance [3]. This leads to slow response times and limited interaction, which not only hampers students' ability to resolve problems but may also erode their motivation and active engagement.
3. **Inflexible and fragmented practical environments.** Hands-on learning in data science is particularly challenged by students' diverse disciplinary backgrounds and inconsistent local computing environments. For example, the "Introduction to Data Science" course often serves students from non-computing majors [4], many of whom lack the technical foundation needed for basic configuration tasks. Moreover, fragmented and non-standardized practical platforms complicate deployment and prevent unified instructional support. Unlike traditional algorithmic tasks, data science projects emphasize real-world context and flexibility. Rigidly mapping them onto Online Judge (OJ) systems may misalign with learning objectives. Such inflexible platforms often divert students toward irrelevant technical hurdles, detracting from meaningful learning outcomes.

2.2 Overview of the RAP Instructional Model

To address the limitations of traditional teaching models outlined above, this study proposes a novel RAP (Resource–Assistant–Platform) instructional model, systematically developed based on the DL-S framework from the Digitalization Capability Level Certification (DCLC) system [5]. As illustrated on the right side of Fig. 1, the RAP model integrates high-quality instructional resources (R), AI-powered assistants (A) and a unified hands-on platform (P) to form a triadic structure. While maintaining a strong emphasis on knowledge delivery, the model shifts the focus toward holistic cultivation of students' digital literacy, aiming to enhance both their comprehensive capabilities and practical competencies.

1. **Resource: Comprehensive and well-integrated instructional content.** The RAP model establishes a cohesive and complete resource ecosystem, addressing the issues of fragmentation and inconsistency in traditional approaches. This system is anchored around a curated suite of core textbooks and is supplemented by standardized slide decks, mind maps and a rich set of diverse, high-quality case materials. These resources reduce students' cognitive load associated with locating and filtering information, thereby supporting their structured internalization of knowledge and fostering systematic understanding. By clarifying the disciplinary knowledge framework, this approach improves both learning efficiency and digital literacy.
2. **Assistant: Instant and effective learning support.** To overcome the inefficiencies of conventional Q&A systems, the RAP model incorporates an AI-based teaching assistant powered by large language models. This intelligent assistant offers instant responses and context-aware explanations, empowering students to solve problems efficiently during independent study. In addition, the AI assistant supports instructors by automating routine tasks such as lecture preparation and grading, alleviating workload and enhancing the overall effectiveness and sustainability of the instructional support system.
3. **Platform: Unified and user-friendly practice environment.** The RAP model integrates a dedicated data science platform that provides a streamlined and cohesive environment for practical learning, resolving the disjointed and rigid nature of traditional platforms. This one-stop platform supports core functions such as case-based learning, programming exercises and project-based competitions, along with personalized case recommendations. It combines the necessary data resources, analytical tools and computing capabilities, offering students a smooth, efficient and accessible hands-on experience.

As shown in Fig. 1, the RAP instructional model establishes a triadic support system centered on instructional resources, AI-based assistants, and an integrated practice platform. These components are interconnected and work in synergy to enhance the teaching process.

Instructional resources serve as the knowledge base for the AI assistant and provide case materials and analytical tools for the practice platform. In turn,

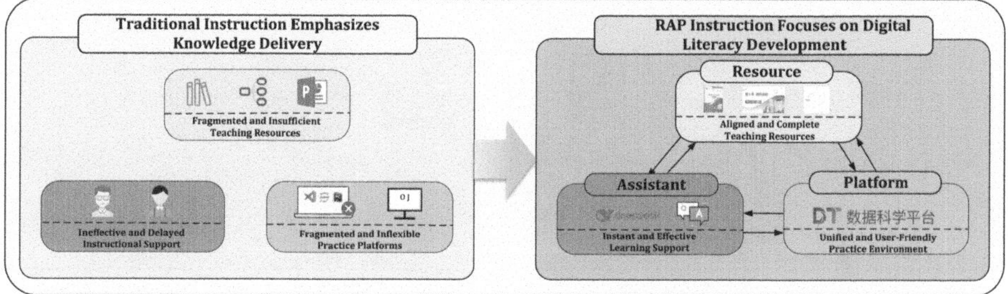

Fig. 1. Traditional Instructional Model vs. RAP Instructional Model.

the AI assistant continuously refines resource content based on student learning data and delivers real-time guidance during hands-on activities. Meanwhile, the practice platform collects feedback on students' operational behavior, which further drives the iterative improvement of both the resources and the assistant.

Together, these three elements form a closed-loop instructional ecosystem that collaboratively improves instructional efficiency, optimizes resource utilization, and fosters students' digital literacy.

3 Instructional Resources for Data Science Courses

In the RAP instructional model, teaching resources serve as the foundation, playing a pivotal role in both the construction of conceptual knowledge and the support of practical learning. These resources primarily comprise a series of core textbooks and a range of supplementary materials. This chapter provides a detailed overview of the design philosophy and structural composition of the comprehensive resource system that has been developed.

3.1 Design Philosophy

The core philosophy behind the development of instructional resources for data science courses emphasizes student-centered learning, integrating both theoretical and practical dimensions to support a comprehensive learning paradigm.

This requires not only a well-structured and complete resource system to ensure knowledge integration but also continuous content updates to keep pace with rapid disciplinary advancements.

Equally important is the digitalization and accessibility of the resources. Instructional design should be problem-oriented and application-driven, enhancing students' ability to solve real-world data science challenges. Ultimately, the goal is to construct a highly efficient and collaborative ecosystem of instructional resources, as illustrated in Fig. 2.

Guided by these principles, the RAP instructional model has established a dual-structured resource system composed of a core textbook series and a suite of supplementary materials, laying the foundation for comprehensive instructional support.

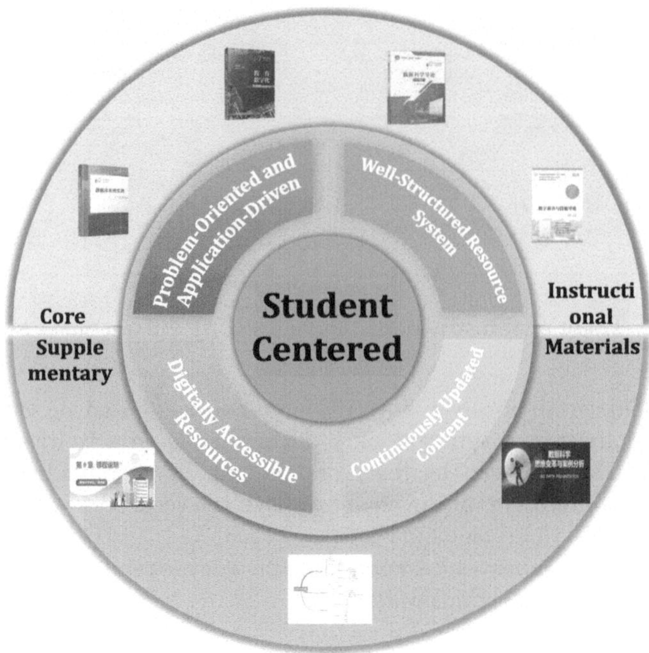

Fig. 2. Design Philosophy for Instructional Resources in Data Science Courses.

3.2 Core Textbook Series

The core textbook series consists of carefully authored and officially published professional textbooks. These materials are designed to systematically cover foundational theories in data science while deeply integrating practical case studies and hands-on guidance. The content aims to address the diverse learning needs of students from various academic backgrounds. The main titles include:

1. *Practice of Database Systems* (2020, Xiamen University Press): Focuses on the practical and applied aspects of database systems, equipping students with key skills in data storage, management, and operations.
2. *Digitalization in Education* (2021, Xiamen University Press): Explores the digital transformation of the education sector and cultivates students' ability to apply innovative thinking to promote educational development in the digital era.
3. *Introduction to Data Science: Case-Based Edition* (2024, Beijing University of Posts and Telecommunications Press): Combines foundational theories with real-world case studies to strengthen students' capacity to solve practical problems through data science.
4. *Introduction to Digital Literacy and Skills* (2024, Tsinghua University Press): Systematically explains key concepts, technologies, and societal impacts of the digital age, aiming to enhance students' digital literacy and core competencies for navigating a digital society.

3.3 Supplementary Materials

The supplementary materials in the RAP instructional model form a high-quality, multidimensional resource collection that supports both student learning and teaching delivery. These materials are designed to facilitate deeper knowledge comprehension, reduce cognitive load, and foster a diversified and immersive learning environment. The key components include:

- **Lecture Slide Decks**: Standardized instructional slides based on the core textbooks, offering clear structure to assist instructors in effective teaching and to serve as review and preview outlines for students.
- **Mind Maps**: Visual representations aligned with textbook content, designed to help students organize complex concepts and develop a systematic understanding.
- **Case and Exercise Bank**: A curated collection of real-world case studies and accompanying exercises derived from industry-academia integration projects. These provide students with abundant practice opportunities and supply instructors with diversified materials for teaching and assessment.

4 AI Teaching Assistant Based on Large Language Models

The AI teaching assistant powered by large language models plays a dual role in data science instruction: it provides intelligent support for teachers and effective learning assistance for students. The assistant functions across all three key stages of instruction—pre-class, in-class, and post-class. This chapter details the design philosophy and functional implementation of the AI assistant in six specific instructional scenarios, as illustrated in Fig. 3, which clearly depicts how it supports both instruction and learning at different stages.

4.1 Teacher Perspective

Pre-Class Support. Prior to classroom instruction, the AI teaching assistant s students' assignments or post-lesson exercises to automatically assess their grasp of the key concepts covered in the previous session. This enables instructors to quickly identify both common areas of weakness and individual learning gaps. Based on this feedback, instructors can flexibly adjust the focus of the current lesson, reinforce difficult content, or provide additional explanations—thereby optimizing course structure and aligning instructional content with students' actual learning needs. In parallel, the AI assistant also examines the logical progression and cross-chapter conceptual links to generate structured instructional suggestions, helping instructors organize content more effectively and enhance the overall coherence of the curriculum.

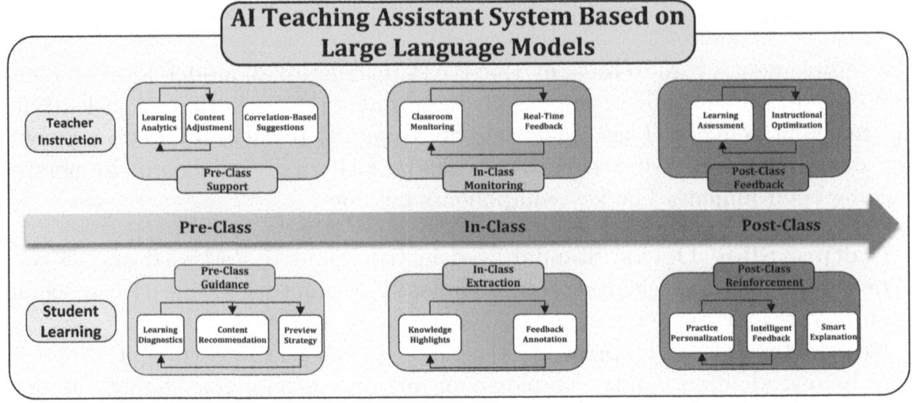

Fig. 3. AI Teaching Assistant System Based on Large Language Models.

In-Class Monitoring. During classroom instruction, the AI teaching assistant captures and analyzes the instructor's delivery in real time. By transcribing spoken content, it extracts and summarizes key lecture information to enable intelligent monitoring and feedback. The system identifies the distribution of key concepts, coverage depth, and instructional pacing based on the transcript and integrates this with real-time student feedback to evaluate comprehension. If the system detects potential misunderstandings or insufficient grasp of critical topics, it promptly notifies the instructor and suggests adjustments in pacing or additional clarification. This process enhances the immediacy of classroom interaction and the precision of instructional responses, supporting a more efficient teaching flow and deeper student understanding.

Post-Class Feedback. After classroom instruction, the AI teaching assistant automatically grades and analyzes student assignments, systematically identifying common mistakes and highlighting key concepts students found difficult. It assesses each student's mastery level, detects both widespread misconceptions and individual learning gaps, and generates individualized diagnostic feedback. Simultaneously, it enables instructors to gain a comprehensive view of student progress and conceptual weaknesses, allowing for targeted adjustments to subsequent instructional content and pacing—ultimately enhancing teaching quality and learning effectiveness.

4.2 Student Perspective

Pre-Class Guidance. Prior to instruction, the AI teaching assistant delivers personalized study recommendations based on students' learning history, assignment performance, and mastery of key concepts. By analyzing prior data, it identifies weak areas and recurring misconceptions to generate targeted strategies for review and preview, helping students prepare effectively and engage more actively in class. Additionally, the assistant dynamically matches each learner with tailored explanations and practice tasks, enabling differentiated instruction and resource allocation to foster personalized learning.

In-Class Extraction. During class, the AI assistant transcribes spoken content in real time and extracts key concepts and challenging points, presenting them in a structured format to enhance information processing. It also integrates live feedback to dynamically annotate unclear or poorly understood concepts, helping students focus on individual learning gaps and improving both engagement and comprehension.

Post-Class Reinforcement. After each lesson, the LLM-powered course assistant generates personalized practice tasks for every student, drawing on both course content and individual performance to support post-class consolidation of learning. Automated grading and adaptive feedback boost learning efficiency and outcomes. The assistant also adjusts task difficulty in real time and enriches instruction by retrieving and presenting clear, in-depth explanations of concepts that need further clarification. These measures ensure that students close any remaining knowledge gaps and achieve a deeper, more comprehensive understanding of the material.

5 Data Science Course Practice Platform

In the context of data science education, the Data Science Course Practice Platform is an innovative and intelligent instructional system designed to provide integrated support throughout the entire learning process. This chapter outlines its system architecture and key functional modules.

5.1 System Architecture

The platform adopts a modular, multi-layered architecture that emphasizes high availability and scalability, ensuring stable and efficient operation. As illustrated in Fig. 4, it consists of the frontend, gateway, backend, and data layers. Built upon this structure is a suite of integrated functional modules covering learning resource management (e.g., cases, news), practical training (e.g., competitions, online coding), intelligent recommendation, and user and access control. Together, these modules provide a comprehensive and intelligent environment for teaching and practicing data science.

5.2 Functional Modules

The platform's key modules work in coordination to provide comprehensive, personalized support:

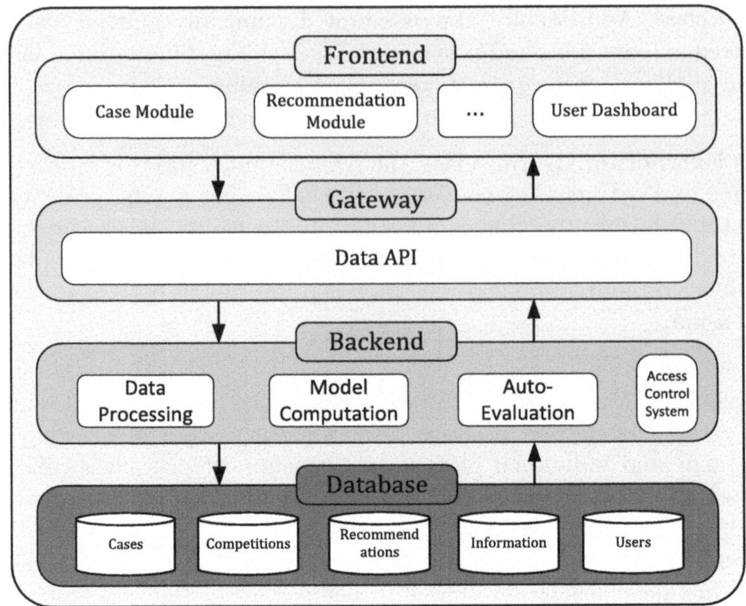

Fig. 4. System Architecture of the Data Science Course Practice Platform.

- **Case Management Module**: Facilitates CRUD operations and multi-dimensional access to curated case resources, enabling structured exploration of exemplary data science scenarios.
- **Competition Module**: Supports competition setup, team management, code submission, and immediate result feedback, fostering hands-on skills in programming and data problem-solving.
- **Recommendation Module**: Leverages user profiles and behavioral analytics to push personalized case studies and resource suggestions, enhancing the relevance of learning materials.
- **Information Aggregation Module**: Consolidates authoritative data science news and industry reports to keep learning materials synchronized with emerging trends.
- **Interactive Coding Module**: Embeds browser-based environments supporting real-time coding, debugging, and auto-evaluation, lowering the barrier to practice setup.
- **User Dashboard Module**: Manages individual profiles, learning preferences, and interaction history, ensuring continuity and traceability of learning paths.
- **Access Management Module**: Enforces fine-grained role-based access control policies to ensure secure, role-appropriate platform operations.

6 Development and Achievements of the RAP Instructional Model in Data Science

Over the course of several years, our team has systematically developed a robust and comprehensive instructional model. Table 1 outlines the key milestones in its evolution.

In the initiation phase, efforts centered on aligning curriculum content with industry demands through multiple teaching reform initiatives. These projects laid the groundwork for curriculum optimization and the introduction of industrial platforms, fostering academia-industry collaboration.

In the establishment phase, we introduced the pedagogical vision of *The Beauty of Data*, which emphasized the fusion of general education and data literacy. This vision led to the formation of a talent development framework grounded in real-world applications, gradually shaping the foundational structure of the RAP model.

In the application phase, we focused on refining and publishing core instructional materials while exploring the integration of AI technologies into data science teaching practices.

Internationally, similar initiatives have emerged, such as the Research-Practice Partnership (RPP), which embeds data science modules into curricula through multi-institution collaboration [6]. However, such approaches often depend on individual instructor expertise and lack standardized resources and platform infrastructure, making them difficult to scale or adapt across disciplines. By contrast, the RAP model was designed from the outset with structural coherence and systemic integration, enabling high levels of standardization, reusability, and transferability. The model's closed-loop architecture—centered around **Resource**, **Assistant**, and **Platform**—enhances its scalability and sustainability.

Through years of progressive exploration, our team has made significant achievements in textbook development, instructional platform construction, and

Table 1. Exploration Timeline of the RAP Instructional Model in Data Science

Phase	Key Projects	RAP
Initiation (2019–2020)	**2019** Teaching Reform Project: Curriculum Construction for Database Courses Oriented Toward Industry–Academia Integration (JG20190136)	R
	2019 First-Class Course Project: *Principles and Techniques of Databases*	R
	2020 Collaborative Project: *Data Science* Curriculum with Jiudou Platform	R/P
Establishment (2022)	**2022** General Education Pilot: *The Beauty of Data*	R
	2022 Provincial Research Project: RAP-Based Talent Training System	A, P
Application (2024–2025)	**2024** Textbook Project: *Database Systems in Practice*	R
	2024 AI-Empowered Reform Project: *Case-Based Introduction to Data Science*	A

Table 2. Key Outcomes of the RAP Instructional Model in Data Science

Outcome	Year	R/A/P
Database Systems in Practice textbook published	2020	R
Digitalization in Education textbook published	2021	R
Digital Literacy and Skills Certification standard released	2022	P
Data Science Practice Platform launched	2023	P
Introduction to Data Science: Case-Based Edition textbook published	2024	R
Introduction to Digital Literacy and Skills textbook published	2024	R
AI Teaching Assistant System launched	2025	A

AI assistant system deployment, as summarized in Table 2. Specifically, we have consistently developed a series of core textbooks to support theoretical learning. In parallel, we promoted industry-academia integration by releasing the *Digital Literacy and Skills Certification* standard and launching the Data Science Practice Platform. In the domain of AI-enhanced instruction, we developed and deployed an AI assistant system powered by large language models. Collectively, these multifaceted efforts have laid a solid foundation for implementing the RAP-based instructional model in data science education.

7 Conclusion

This study proposes a triadic RAP instructional model that integrates instructional resources, an AI assistant, and a practice platform. It effectively addresses persistent issues in traditional teaching models, such as fragmented resources, delayed feedback, and disjointed practice tools. The model contributes to the systematic development of students' digital literacy and practical competencies.

In future work, we will conduct controlled instructional experiments to quantitatively assess the effectiveness of the RAP model. Furthermore, in response to the Ministry of Education's initiative to build international strategic alliances under the *Belt and Road* framework, we plan to pilot the RAP model in universities along the route [7]. Local adaptation based on regional culture and educational ecosystems will be explored to assess its cross-cultural transferability and scalability.

Acknowledgments. This work was supported by the Major Project of the Key Research Institute of Humanities and Social Sciences at Universities, Ministry of Education (Grant No. 22JJD880033).

References

1. Qin, X., Chen, Y., Fan, J.: Construction and reflection on the course "Introduction to data science". Comput. Educ. **2023**(2), 64–73 (2023)
2. CCF Xiuhu Meeting Experts: In the era of artificial intelligence, how should computer curricula be reformed?

3. Xiao, L., Shan, X., Deng, M.: Curriculum system of computer programming based on AI-assisted teaching. Comput. Educ. **2024**(7), 134–146 (2024)
4. Shi, Y., Liu, X.: Teaching exploration of the "Introduction to Data Science" course under the New Engineering initiative. J. Lanzhou Inst. Technol. **31**(4), 131–135 (2024)
5. Cui, B., Hong, W.: Research on an Evaluation System of Individual Digitalization Capability. In: Hong, W., Weng, Y. (eds.) Computer Science and Education, CCIS, vol. 1811, pp. 315–323. Springer, Singapore (2023)
6. Naseri, M.Y., Snyder, C., Pérez-Rivera, K.X., et al.: Integrating data science into undergraduate science and engineering courses: lessons learned by instructors in a multi-university research-practice partnership. IEEE Trans. Educ. **68**(1), 1–12 (2025)
7. Ministry of Education, Ministry of Industry and Information Technology, Chinese Academy of Engineering: Opinion on accelerating the development of New Engineering disciplines to implement the Excellent Engineer Training Program 2.0. http://www.moe.gov.cn/srcsite/A08/moe_742/s3860/201810/t20181017_351890.html (accessed 08 Oct 2018)

Author Index

W. Hong et al. (Eds.): ICCSE 2025, CCIS 2761, pp. 625–627, 2026.
https://doi.org/10.1007/978-981-95-7731-6

The manufacturer's authorised representative in the EU is Springer Nature Customer Service Centre GmbH, Europaplatz 3, 69115 Heidelberg, Germany. If you have any concerns regarding our products, please contact ProductSafety@springernature.com

Printed and bound by CPI Group (UK) Ltd, Croydon, CR0 4YY
07/07/2026
02160906-0019